# THE RIGHTS OF INDIGENOUS PEOPLES IN MARINE AREAS

The question of what rights might be afforded to Indigenous peoples has preoccupied the municipal legal systems of settler states since the earliest colonial encounters. As a result of sustained institutional initiatives, many national legal regimes and the international legal order accept that Indigenous peoples possess an extensive array of legal rights. However, despite this development, claims advanced by Indigenous peoples relating to rights to marine spaces have been largely opposed. This book offers the first sustained study of these rights and their reception within modern legal systems. Taking a three-part approach, it looks firstly at the international aspects of Indigenous entitlements in marine spaces. It then goes on to explore specific country examples, before looking at some interdisciplinary themes of crucial importance to the question of the recognition of the rights of Indigenous peoples in marine settings. Drawing on the expertise of leading scholars, this is a rigorous and long-overdue exploration of a significant gap in the literature.

# The Rights of Indigenous Peoples in Marine Areas

Edited by
Stephen Allen
Nigel Bankes
and
Øyvind Ravna

•HART•
OXFORD • LONDON • NEW YORK • NEW DELHI • SYDNEY

HART PUBLISHING

Bloomsbury Publishing Plc

Kemp House, Chawley Park, Cumnor Hill, Oxford, OX2 9PH, UK



First published in Great Britain 2019



A catalogue record for this book is available from the British Library.

Library of Congress Cataloging-in-Publication data

Names: Allen, Stephen, 1968-, editor. | Bankes, Nigel, 1956-, editor. | Ravna, Øyvind, editor.

Title: The rights of indigenous peoples in marine areas / edited by Stephen Allen, Nigel Bankes, Øyvind Ravna.

Description: Chicago : Hart Publishing, 2019. | Includes bibliographical references and index.

Identifiers: LCCN 2019021091 (print) | LCCN 2019021906 (ebook) | ISBN 9781509928651 (EPub) | ISBN 9781509928644 (hardback)

Subjects: LCSH: Indigenous people—Legal status, laws, etc. | Indigenous people—Fishing—Law and legislation. | Water rights. | Right to food.

Classification: LCC K3260 (ebook) | LCC K3260 .R55 2019 (print) | DDC 342.08/72—dc23

LC record available at https://lccn.loc.gov/2019021091

ISBN: HB: 978-1-50992-864-4
ePDF: 978-1-50992-866-8
ePub: 978-1-50992-865-1

Typeset by Compuscript Ltd, Shannon
Printed and bound in Great Britain by CPI Group (UK) Ltd, Croydon CR0 4YY

MIX
Paper from responsible sources
FSC® C013604

To find out more about our authors and books visit www.hartpublishing.co.uk. Here you will find extracts, author information, details of forthcoming events and the option to sign up for our newsletters.

# *Acknowledgements*

THIS VOLUME OF essays on Indigenous rights in marine areas draws on papers presented at a workshop in Tromsø, Norway in June 2018. The workshop was convened by the editors with the support of the KG Jebsen Centre for the Law of the Sea at UiT, the Arctic University of Norway (Tromsø, Norway), the research group on Sami and Indigenous law of the Faculty of Law at UiT, and the Centre for Sami Studies at UiT. Funding for the workshop was provided by the Jebsen Centre.

Christin Skjervold, Senior Advisor at the Jebsen Centre, handled the administrative arrangements for the workshop and Margherita Poto, a postdoctoral research fellow at the Jebsen Centre, provided additional on the ground assistance. Logan Turner, a visiting student from McMaster University, ably summarised the discussion during the workshop. We are grateful to all of them for their assistance.

Finally, we wish to thank Sinead Moloney, Editorial Director at Hart Publishing, and her team for all their help in producing this book. Their encouragement and support has been instrumental to the success of this project.

Stephen Allen, Nigel Bankes and Øyvind Ravna
*February 2019*
*London, Calgary and Tromsø*

# *Contents*

# *List of Contributors*

**Stephen Allen**, Senior Lecturer in Law, Queen Mary, University of London and Barrister (Door Tenant, 5 Essex Court Chambers, Temple, London).

**Nigel Bankes**, Professor and Chair in Natural Resources Law, Faculty of Law, University of Calgary, and Adjunct Professor, KG Jebsen Centre, UiT – the Arctic University of Norway.

**Jay L Batongbacal**, Associate Professor at the University of the Philippines College of Law and Director of the UP Institute for Maritime Affairs & Law of the Sea.

**Michael C Blumm**, Jeffrey Bain Faculty Scholar and Professor of Law, Lewis and Clark Law School, Portland, Oregon.

**Camilla Brattland**, Associate Professor, Department for Social Sciences, Faculty of Humanities, Social Sciences and Education, UiT – the Arctic University of Norway.

**Else Grete Broderstad**, Professor (Dr Polit) of Indigenous Studies, coordinator for the Master's Programme in Indigneous Studies, Faculty of Humanities, Social Sciences and Education, UiT – the Arctic University of Norway.

**Dorothée Cambou**, Postdoctoral Researcher, Faculty of Arts, University of Helsinki and member of the Helsinki Institute of Sustainability Science (HELSUS).

**Marlène Dégremont**, PhD student in Anthropology, Ecole des Hautes Etudes en Sciences Sociales, Paris and Institut de Recherche pour le Développement, Montpellier.

**Endalew Lijalem Enyew**, PhD research fellow, KG Jebsen Center for the Law of the Sea, Faculty of Law, UiT – the Arctic University of Norway.

**Andrew Erueti**, Nga Ruahinerangi, Ngati Ruanui, Associate Professor, Faculty of Law, University of Auckland.

**Einar Eythórsson**, Senior Researcher (Dr Polit) in Social Science, High North Department of Norwegian Institute for Cultural Heritage Research, Tromsø.

**Sue Farran**, Professor of Laws, Faculty of Business and Law, Northumbria University, Newcastle upon Tyne and Associate Centre for Pacific Studies, University of St Andrews.

**Isabela Figueroa** Professor of Law, Faculty of Humanities, Universidad del Magdalena.

**Malgosia Fitzmaurice**, Professor of International Law, Queen Mary University of London, Co-Director of the Centre of International and European Law Affairs, Editor-in-Chief of *International Community Law Review*, General Editor of Queen Mary Studies in International Law series.

**Ruslan Garipov**, Associate Professor at International and European Law Department, Kazan Federal University and Adjunct Professor at American University School of International Service, Woodrow Wilson Center Fellow, Arctic Institute.

**Jérémie Gilbert**, Professor of Human Rights Law, University of Roehampton.

**Lee Godden**, Professor and Director, Centre for Resources, Energy and Environmental Law, Melbourne Law School, University of Melbourne, and member of the Academy of Law and the Academy of Social Sciences in Australia.

**Robert Hamilton**, Assistant Professor, Faculty of Law, University of Calgary.

**Olivier Jamin**, Environmental Associate Attorney at Davis Wright Tremaine LLP; JD & LLM Lewis and Clark Law School.

**Line Kalak**, Sámi University of Applied Sciences.

**Steve J Langdon**, Professor Emeritus, Department of Anthropology, University of Alaska, Anchorage.

**Evelyn Pinkerton**, Professor, School of Resource and Environmental Management, Simon Fraser University, British Columbia.

**Øyvind Ravna**, Professor (Dr Juris) of Law, head of the Research Group of Sámi and Indigenous Law, Faculty of Law, UiT – the Arctic University of Norway and Editor-in-Chief of *Arctic Review on Law and Politics*.

**Caskey Russell**, Associate Professor in Literature and Indigenous Studies, Department of English, University of Wyoming.

**Dorothee Schreiber**, Visiting Researcher, Center for Sámi Studies, University of Tromsø.

**X̱'unei Lance Twitchell**, Associate Professor of Alaskan Native Languages, College of Arts and Sciences, University of Alaska Southeast.

**Ekaterina Zmyvalova**, PhD student in Sámi studies, Umeå University.

# Introduction

STEPHEN ALLEN, NIGEL BANKES, ENDALEW LIJALEM ENYEW AND ØYVIND RAVNA

THE QUESTION OF what rights should be afforded to Indigenous peoples has preoccupied the municipal legal systems of settler states since the earliest colonial encounters. More recently, the United Nations (UN) and other international institutions have grappled with the content and scope of Indigenous rights through a number of sustained initiatives. As a result, many national legal regimes and the international legal order now accept that Indigenous peoples possess an extensive array of legal rights and that those states which have enveloped them are subject to corresponding legal obligations. In particular, states have increasingly been willing to acknowledge that Indigenous peoples possess a meaningful set of rights over those traditional lands and terrestrial territories which they continue to occupy or use. These rights have further evolved through litigation conducted in national courts, regional human rights courts, the adjudicative processes of treaty-monitoring bodies and through a substantial body of enlightened scholarship.

In contrast, individual states and the inter-state system have remained remarkably unreceptive to the claims advanced by Indigenous advocates concerning Indigenous rights to marine spaces (including access and associated resources rights) beyond a few isolated thematic cases (eg, whaling). In the rare situations where governments and national courts have been prepared to acknowledge the existence of Indigenous marine entitlements in specific contexts, they have typically been read down and narrowly interpreted. Further, Indigenous peoples barely feature in the key multilateral treaties concerning the law of the sea and there is scant treaty practice addressing the Indigenous/state relationship in the marine environment.[1] Even the most ambitious global instrument on the rights of Indigenous peoples – the UN Declaration on the Rights of Indigenous

[1] The most important examples include the Treaty between Australia and the Independent State of Papua New Guinea concerning sovereignty and maritime boundaries in the area between the two countries, including the area known as Torres Strait, and related matters, signed at Sydney on 18 December 1978 (entered into force on 15 February 1985) and the Agreement between the Government of the Republic of Indonesia and the Government of Papua New Guinea Concerning Maritime Boundaries between the Republic of Indonesia and Papua New Guinea and Cooperation on Related Matters, signed at Jakarta on 13 December 1980 (entered into force 10 July 1982).

Peoples (UNDRIP) – only references Indigenous marine entitlements in passing, whereas a number of its key provisions are dedicated to elaborating the rights of Indigenous peoples to their traditional lands and continental territories.[2] And although there is recent scholarly literature on the issue of Indigenous rights in respect of marine spaces, this topic has received scarce attention when compared with the question of Indigenous terrestrial entitlements – an observation that is supported by a cursory glance at virtually all of the *general* works concerning Indigenous rights in international law.[3]

This recognition gap continues to be a grave problem for Indigenous communities around the world. Many Indigenous peoples occupy coastal territories; they have been termed 'salt water' peoples, coastal or sea peoples (Sámi), or peoples with a 'sea country' or 'sea estates'.[4] They invariably maintain an intimate association with the sea and its vital resources, which may be crucial for their 'subsistence, economic livelihood, spirituality and cultural identity'.[5] The relative willingness of individual states and the international community of states to accept Indigenous land and continental territorial rights (albeit in moderated and contingent form) while largely rejecting indigenous claims in relation to marine spaces stems, in part, from the predominant Western (or Eurocentric) view which has long drawn a clear distinction between territorial and marine areas. By contrast, Indigenous peoples generally do not distinguish between such geographical features and instead see continuity between them, with the concomitant rights and responsibilities also being viewed holistically. For marine-oriented Indigenous peoples, 'land and sea space are integrated within systems of customary tenure, local knowledge, and resource use and management'.[6] In marked contrast, modern states tend to view continental lands and territories as capable of giving rise to

[2] United Nations Declaration on the Rights of Indigenous Peoples, UNGA Res 61/295 (13 September 2007). Article 25 provides: 'Indigenous peoples have the right to maintain and strengthen their distinctive spiritual relationship with their traditionally owned or otherwise occupied and used lands, territories, waters and *coastal seas* and other resources and to uphold their responsibilities to future generations in this regard' (emphasis added).

[3] Consider, eg, James Anaya, *Indigenous Peoples in International Law*, 2nd edn (Oxford University Press, 2004); Patrick Thornberry, *Indigenous Peoples and Human Rights* (Manchester University Press, 2002); M Åhrén, *Indigenous Peoples' Status in the International Legal System* (Oxford University Press, 2016).

[4] Nonie Sharp, *Saltwater People: The Waves of Memory* (University of Toronto Press, 2002); Nonie Sharp, 'Following in the Seamarks? The Salt Water Peoples of Tropical Australia (2000) 4 *Indigenous Law Bulletin* 4. For 'sea estates' and more general ideas of customary marine tenure (CMT), see Nicolas Peterson and Bruce Rigsby, 'Introduction' in Nicolas Peterson and Bruce Rigsby (eds), *Customary Marine Tenure in Australia* (University of Sydney Press, 1998) 2.

[5] Carsten Smith and Michael Dodson (special rapporteurs), Report on indigenous fishing rights in the seas with case studies from Australia and Norway, Report to the Permanent Forum on Indigenous Issues (2010) E/C.19/2010/2 [28].

[6] Colin Scott and Monica Mulrennan, 'Land and Sea Tenure at Erub, Torres Strait: Property, Sovereignty and the Adjudication of Cultural Continuity' (1990) 70 *Oceania* 146. See also V Toki, 'Study on the Relationship between Indigenous Peoples and the Pacific Ocean', *Permanent Forum on Indigenous Issues*, UN Doc E/C.19/2016/3 (New York, 2016).

private/individualised property rights, including ownership and possession, while the seas (coastal and otherwise) and the associated resources are considered to be public commons.[7] As Jackson puts it: 'while the land has been seen … as layered with proprietary rights, use rights and cultural symbols, the [sea] has been seen empty' – empty because of the Western cultural construction of the sea as being not subject to any such rights.[8] Meanwhile, the damage wrought by the statist conceptual position is already considerable – especially when backed up by the advantages in technology and access to capital enjoyed by non-Indigenous communities in exploiting the natural resources found in marine spaces.[9]

There are additional reasons for the modern preoccupation with land territory. The use of marine resources is invariably less visible than the use of land-based resources. In addition, popular culture may associate particular Indigenous communities with specific resources. For example, the Sámi peoples of Fennoscandinavia are associated in popular culture with reindeer, although 'fishing has always been the main livelihood for the many Saami living permanently in seaside areas'[10] and 'there is a perception of Australian aboriginal groups as essentially land-based',[11] notwithstanding the fact that the Miriam Islanders who began the groundbreaking Aboriginal title case in Australia – *Mabo v Queensland (No 2)* – were and are the quintessential example of a marine-oriented people.[12] In other cases, the lack of current attention to marine claims may be related to the geography of colonial settlement, which forced Indigenous incumbents to retreat from valuable and desirable coastal areas early on in the colonial encounter.[13] But overall, if it was possible for settlers to ignore the existence of Aboriginal customs and laws in relation to land in the name of *terra nullius* or the doctrine of discovery, it must have been even easier for those settlers to ignore the possibility of ownership-like rights in relation to the sea and marine areas.[14] Anthropologists have also noticed

[7] Peterson and Rigsby (n 4) 3.

[8] SE Jackson, 'The Water is Not Empty: Cross-cultural Issues in Conceptualizing Sea Space' (1995) 26 *Australian Geographer* 87, 93. See also Nonie Sharp, 'Reimagining Sea Space: From Grotius to Mabo' in Peterson and Rigsby (eds) (n 4) 79; and Richard Barnes, *Property Rights and Natural Resources* (Hart Publishing, 2009) 2.

[9] Preferential access to technology and capital has often allowed settler interests to capture a disproportionate share of resources historically harvested by Indigenous communities. For the west coast of Canada, for example, see Dianne Newell, *Tangled Webs of History: Indians and the Law in Canada's Pacific Coast Fisheries* (University of Toronto Press, 1993); for Norway, see Ravna and Kalak (ch 9 in this volume); and for Alaska, see Pinkerton and Langdon (ch 17 in this volume).

[10] Smith and Dodson (n 5) [48]; see also Ravna and Kalak (ch 9 in this volume).

[11] Bryce Barker, 'Use and Continuity in the Customary Marine Tenure of the Whitsunday Islands' in Peterson and Rigsby (eds) (n 4) 91.

[12] Barker (n 11) 90; *Mabo v Queensland (No 2)* (1992) 175 CLR 1 (HCA).

[13] Andrew Lipman, *Saltwater Frontier: Indians and the Contest for the American Coast* (Yale University Press, 2015).

[14] R Dillon, 'Seeing the Sea: Science, Change and Indigenous Sea Rights' (2002) 123 *Maritime Studies* 12.

a similar gap in the literature in relation to marine resource management by Indigenous communities. In this context, resource management refers to choices by individuals or the community 'that could influence the resource' or resource availability.[15] Land-based management activities (such as the use of fire) have long been studied, but comparatively less attention has been paid to marine resource management practices.[16] While Indigenous management activities were repressed or curtailed through colonisation, it has been suggested that traditional management practices are re-emerging. One study offers examples from both New Zealand and Canada. In New Zealand, the authors point to forms of marine reserves known as *taiāpura* and *mātaitai* within which local Māori may be involved in fisheries management.[17] On the west coast of Canada, the authors reference the important co-management arrangements between the Haida Nation and the federal and provincial governments. Beginning first with the Gwaii Haanas National Park Reserve (principally on land), these co-management arrangements have been extended to include the Gwaii Haanas National Marine Conservation Area as well as a marine protected area (MPA) known as SG̲aan K̲inghlas-Bowie Seamount MPA.[18] These arrangements, based on mutual recognition and cross-designation, are characterised by multi-level governance approaches that value 'locally-specific feedbacks and management techniques developed and used by people who have a long term commitment to place' rather than 'top-down, one-size-fits-all policy solutions'.[19]

Continued access to marine resources (physical as well as economic) is essential for the identity, autonomy, sovereignty and culture of Indigenous peoples, as well as for local monitoring and stewardship capacity.[20] While the last few decades have seen improvements in some settler states in terms of the legal access of Indigenous communities with respect to harvesting and profiting from traditional resources, the more systemic forces of neoliberalism may make it difficult for these communities to exploit this access.[21] A recent review of the

[15] D Lepofsky and M Caldwell, 'Indigenous Marine Resource Management on the Northwest Coast of North America' (2013) 2 *Ecological Processes* 12, 13.

[16] For instance, Lepofsky and Caldwell (ibid) note that these practices might include harvesting methods (eg, nets and weirs), enhancement strategies (eg, building clam gardens, transferring fish eggs to different habitats or removing beaver dams), tenure systems (which might be confined to harvesting locations or fish trap locations or be more extensive), and worldviews and social relations (eg, protocols and rituals recognising 'connection to ocean-bound kin' such as first fish or first salmon ceremonies).

[17] J Stephenson, F Berkes, N Turner and J Dick, 'Biocultural Conservation of Marine Ecosystems: Examples from New Zealand and Canada' (2014) 13 *Indian Journal of Traditional Knowledge* 257, 259. See also Erueti (ch 10 in this volume).

[18] ibid 261–62.

[19] ibid 264.

[20] Nathan Bennett et al, 'Coastal and Indigenous Community Access to Marine Resources and the Ocean: A Policy Imperative for Canada' (2018) 87 *Marine Policy* 186, 187.

[21] Neoliberalism emphasises the importance of private property rights, free markets and free trade. Within the context of marine space and fisheries, the implications include an emphasis on

challenges faced by coastal and Indigenous communities in maintaining access to marine resources suggested that in order to counter the forces of neoliberalism and globalisation, actors should engage with both policy development and legal reform. Legal reforms might include explicit language addressing concepts such as adjacency, access, equity and benefits 'to guarantee consideration and protection of access of adjacent [and Indigenous] communities'.[22] Fisheries legislation needs to be reviewed to allow for active participation by Indigenous communities and harvesters.[23] Other scholars have argued that fishery policies that make room for Indigenous world views need to be focused less narrowly on objectives such as optimal utilisation and instead incorporate ideas such as 'optimal benefits' which might embrace 'political, economic, social and cultural dimensions'.[24] In such circumstances, according to Scott and Mulrennan, what is needed is a 'relaxation of the state's hegemonic ambition, permitting a sharing of 'property' *and* 'sovereign' jurisdictional rights as between distinctive social and cultural orders'.[25]

Against this background, this volume draws attention to the under-explored theme of Indigenous entitlements in marine spaces with the ultimate aim of providing an evaluation of the shape and content of the rights of Indigenous peoples and the concomitant obligations owed by states in this setting, as well as assessing the basis and scope for future developments in this area.

The volume is divided into four parts. Part I sets the stage with a single chapter reflecting on the historical aspects and contemporary relevance of the colonial encounter in marine spaces. Robert Hamilton reminds us that many of the early encounters between would-be colonisers and Indigenous communities occurred in marine spaces and on the coasts. He emphasises that these encounters were not only physical encounters between peoples, but also normative encounters between the laws and customs that the settlers brought with them, and the legal systems of Indigenous communities which extended to marine spaces and marine resources. These encounters led, at least initially, to a body of inter-societal law governing the use of marine resources sometimes embodied, as on the east coast of North America, in peace and friendship treaties between European states and their Indigenous allies. But as colonial power expanded, the more hegemonic ideas of the settlers undermined both Indigenous norms as well

individual transferable quotas (ITQs) as a way of apportioning a total allowable harvest as well as the privatisation of ocean space to facilitate 'exclusive' activities such as mariculture and alternative energy facilities. See generally Evelyn Pinkerton and Reade Davis, 'Neoliberalism and the Politics of Enclosure in North American Small-Scale Fisheries' (2015) 61 *Marine Policy* 303; and Christine Knott and Barbara Neis, 'Privatization, Financialization and Ocean Grabbing in New Brunswick Herring Fisheries and Salmon Aquaculture' (2017) 80 *Marine Policy* 10.

[22] Bennett et al (n 20) 191.

[23] Dillon (n 14).

[24] Annie Lalancette, 'Creeping in? Neoliberalism, Indigenous Realities and Tropical Rock Lobster (Kair) Management in Torres Strait, Australia' (2017) 80 *Marine Policy* 47, 56.

[25] Scott and Mulrennan (n 6) 171.

as inter-societal norms, replacing them with ideas of marine spaces as unownable commons, the resources of which could be appropriated by the newcomers. This appropriation was endorsed by settler legal systems and facilitated by access to technology and capital. While modern ideas of Indigenous rights have imposed some limits on these appropriations, Hamilton argues that the rights paradigm tends to confine Indigenous communities to the right to engage in discrete activities and fails to recognise Indigenous understandings of territory, jurisdiction and sovereignty. Accordingly, Hamilton calls for a revival of a more pluralist and inter-societal understanding of relations between Indigenous and settler communities with respect to marine spaces.

Part II of this volume comprises a set of three chapters all concerned with the international law dimensions of the relationship between Indigenous communities and marine space and resources. To this end, Endalew Lijalem Enyew's chapter examines this connection through the lens of international human rights law, looking, in turn, at the right to self-determination, the right to culture, the right to property and the right not to be discriminated against, as well as procedural rights based on the right to be consulted and the right of free prior and informed consent. In each case, Enyew examines both general human rights instruments (universal and regional) as well as the more specific instruments that speak to the rights of Indigenous peoples, the UNDRIP,[26] ILO Convention 169[27] and the American Declaration on the Rights of Indigenous Peoples.[28] Enyew shows that these instruments are equally applicable to marine spaces as well as terrestrial areas.

Malgosia Fitzmaurice's chapter deals with a particular body of treaty law that has long engaged with, and recognised, the rights of Indigenous peoples in relation to marine resources, namely the law pertaining to marine mammals and, specifically, whales. Indigenous harvesting rights first obtained international legal recognition in the Behring Fur Seals Arbitration of 1893,[29] and the subsequent fur seal treaties;[30] however, Indigenous harvesting rights also continue to be recognised in the International Convention for the Regulation of Whaling (ICRW).[31] This regime and the work of the International Whaling Commission (IWC) and its Aboriginal Subsistence Whaling Sub-committee is the focus of Fitzmaurice's chapter. While most whaling is prohibited under the terms of the controversial 'moratorium' first adopted by the IWC in 1982 and

[26] See n 2.

[27] ILO Convention 169 on Indigenous and Tribal Peoples in Independent Countries, concluded Geneva 27 June 1989, in force 5 September 1991, 1650 UNTS 383.

[28] American Declaration on the Rights of Indigenous Peoples, AG/Res 2888 (XLVI-0/16), 15 June 2016.

[29] Behring Fur Seal Arbitration Award, 15 August 1893, 28 UNRIAA 263, art 8 of the regulations proposed by the tribunal.

[30] Convention for the Preservation and Protection of Fur Seals, 7 July 1911. 37 Stat 1342, art IV; and Interim Convention on the Conservation of North Pacific Fur Seals, 9 January 1957, 314 UNTS 106, art VII.

[31] 161 UNTS 72.

effective for the 1985/86 season, Indigenous whaling continues to be authorised for specific communities and stocks of whales by amendments to the ICRW's schedule adopted by IWC at its regular meetings (including its most recent meeting in Brazil in 2018).[32] There are signs within the IWC that the discourse with respect to Indigenous whaling has changed with the adoption of the UNDRIP and has become much more rights-focused, but there remains a tension between the right to harvest traditional species as part of the right to subsistence and the need to acquire the votes necessary to secure an amendment to the Schedule.[33] One other chapter in this volume also touches on whaling issues, which is the chapter by Michael Blumm and Olivier Jamin dealing with Indigenous harvesting rights on the Pacific Northwest Coast of the US. While Blumm and Jamin's chapter is principally concerned with Indigenous rights to harvest fish and to protect fish habitat under the terms of the so-called Stevens Treaties of the 1850s between the tribes and the US government, the authors also examine as part of their analysis the treaty right of the Makah people to resume whaling.

Stephen Allen's chapter explores the juridical foundations of artisanal fishing rights within the broader context of the law pertaining to vested rights. While artisanal fishing rights may be distinct from Indigenous rights in relation to marine spaces, it is clear that there is often a degree of overlap between the two in concrete circumstances, much as there is frequently an overlap between the rights that Indigenous peoples may claim by virtue of their Indigeneity and the rights they may claim as a minority within a dominant settler society. Moreover, as Allen's chapter shows, artisanal fishing communities and Indigenous peoples often share experiences as marginalised sub-state groups seeking to secure recognition of their traditional rights in marine settings and maintain ancient marine entitlements. Allen's analysis assumes particular salience in light of a series of recent arbitral awards that have examined artisanal fishing rights – including the *Eritrea/Yemen Awards*,[34] the *Chagos Marine Protection Area Award*[35] and the *South China Sea Award* – decisions which

[32] 67th Meeting of the International Whaling Commission, Florianopolis, Brazil, 10–14 September 2018. The Meeting adopted an amendment to the Schedule that authorised quotas or strike for the next seven years and also established a procedure for extending these quotas every seven years, subject to some conditions. There were also updated carryover provisions to allow unused quota to be carried over to later years. Indigenous spokespersons at the Meeting noted the importance of the renewal provisions as ensuring that 'the end of each quota block would not bring the threat of hunger'. See Chair's Report of the 67th Meeting, 16, and additional discussion at 7–9 and 15–18. The amendment is Annex P to the chair's report. See https://archive.iwc.int/pages/view.php?ref=7592&k=.

[33] Chris Wold, 'Integrating Indigenous Rights into Multilateral Environmental Agreements: The International Whaling Commission and Aboriginal Subsistence Whaling' (2017) 40 *Boston College International and Comparative Law Review* 63.

[34] First Award in the Eritrea/Yemen Case (Territorial Sovereignty), PCA, 9 October 1998; and its Second Award (Maritime Delimitation) PCA, 17 December 1999.

[35] *Chagos Marine Protected Area Award (Mauritius/UK)*, Annex VII LOSC Tribunal, PCA (18 March 2015).

have recognised the scope for accommodating traditional fishing rights within a coastal state's territorial sea and, to a lesser extent, its Exclusive Economic Zone at the level of international law.[36]

Part III offers a series of chapters that examine the rights of Indigenous peoples with respect to marine space within particular countries. While it was obviously not possible to canvass all jurisdictions, we did strive to include examples of countries that do not often find a place in English-language collections. Thus, we are particularly pleased to have chapters discussing Indigenous rights in marine areas from such different jurisdictions as Colombia (Isabela Figueroa), New Caledonia (Dorothée Cambou, Jérémie Gilbert and Marlène Dégremont), Norway (Øyvind Ravna and Line Kalak), the Philippines (Jay L Batongbacal) and Russia (Ekaterina Zmyvalova and Ruslan Garipov). These contributions stand alongside contributions from common law jurisdictions that are more frequently canvassed in the literature: Australia (Lee Godden), Canada (Nigel Bankes), New Zealand (Andrew Erueti) and the US (Michael Blumm and Olivier Jamin).

In addition to examining how Indigenous rights in marine areas have been addressed within their jurisdiction (both by the courts and by the legislatures), the authors were invited to comment on the constitutional framework for their particular jurisdiction as well as the relationship between international law and domestic law. The coverage across these chapters is not uniform. Some chapters emphasise particular parts of the jurisdiction. For example, Blumm and Jamin's chapter focuses on the Pacific Northwest area of the US, while Bankes' chapter focuses on the treatment of Indigenous rights to marine areas in the context of northern land claims agreements in Canada. Similarly, the chapter by Ravna and Kalak necessarily focuses on the northern part of Norway. In some of the country studies, international law and standards play a much larger role than in others. For example, in Norway and New Zealand, commentators routinely use international law as a basis to argue for the enhanced recognition of Indigenous rights or, perhaps, to critique legislative or other measures that limit such rights. In other jurisdictions, such as Canada, the US or Russia, international law plays a more limited role, even though in the case of the latter, the Russian Constitution affords international law an important role within the legal system. Figueroa's comments on this issue in her chapter on Colombia are of particular interest. She notes that whereas the Colombian Constitutional Court is typically open to the jurisprudence of the Inter-American Court of Human Rights and its decisions relating to Indigenous peoples, this has not been the case with respect to marine areas. This perhaps reflects what we observed earlier with respect to the divide between terrestrial and marine areas and the perception of marine areas as an open commons.

[36] *South China Sea (Merits) Award (Philippines/People's Republic of China)*, Annex VII LOSC Tribunal, PCA (12 July 2016); United Nations Convention on the Law of the Sea (adopted 10 December 1982, entered into force 16 November 1994) 1833 UNTS 396.

A common theme in these chapters is that of the reluctance of the state (and its courts) to recognise and respect the importance of Indigenous laws, norms and customs, thus continuing a theme introduced by Hamilton in Chapter 1. One of the implications of this is that the scope of Indigenous rights in marine areas come to be defined and categorised by the state rather than through a more pluralist interaction between Indigenous and state norms. Thus, harvesting rights are frequently characterised as subsistence or non-commercial rights or traditional rights rather than in terms of commercial rights or the right to secure well-being. Similarly, state systems either reject or are very reluctant to accommodate ideas of title with respect to marine space because title with respect to marine space is largely unknown to the norms of the dominant legal system. Instead, ideas of property are framed in terms of a Eurocentric 'bundle of rights'[37] rather than inquiring into Indigenous normative orders which might include, for example, the right to speak for sea country or the right to perform rituals with respect to particular bodies of water.[38] The dominant legal system may find it equally difficult to contemplate or recognise exclusive use rights (eg, to particular species or to particular marine areas such as bays or harvesting sites) because such rights might conflict with historical ideas of the right of all to engage in the fishery in common with others.[39]

The implications and scope of the conception of Indigeneity are explored – either directly or indirectly – in several chapters of this book. Readers will be familiar with Martinez-Cobo's well-known attempt at defining the concept of Indigeneity.[40] However, in the light of the immense social diversity, and particular histories of Indigenous communities, the problematic quest for definitional clarity has been set aside in favour of an approach which identifies a broad set of criteria which can be used to guide contextual assessments of a given societal group's status.[41] To this end, the indicia

[37] AM Honoré, 'Ownership' in AG Guest (ed), *Oxford Essays in Jurisprudence* (Oxford University Press, 1961) 113: 'Ownership comprises the right to possess, the right to use, the right to manage, the right to the income of the thing, the right to the capital, the right to security, the rights or incidents of transmissibility and absence of term, the duty to prevent harm, liability to execution, and the incident of residuarity.'

[38] Bruce Rigsby, 'A Survey of Property Theory and Tenure Types' in Peterson and Rigsby (n 4) 29–30; Geoffrey Bagshaw, 'Gapu Dhulway, Gapu Maramba: Conceptualization and Ownership of Saltwater among the Burarr and Yan-nhangu Peoples of Northeast Arnhem Land' in Peterson and Rigsby (n 4) 162–63 (references omitted); and *Commonwealth v Yarmirr* (2001) 208 CLR 1 (HCA) [85].

[39] In addition to Hamilton's chapter, see the chapters by Bankes (Canada), Figueroa (Colombia), Godden (Australia), Erueti (New Zealand), and Ravna and Kalak (Norway).

[40] J Martinez-Cobo, *Study of the Problem of Discrimination against Indigenous Populations*, E/CN4/Sub2/1986/7/Add 4, [379]. See Åhrén (n 3) 143–45.

[41] See, eg, B Kingsbury, 'Indigenous Peoples in International Law: A Constructivist Approach to the Asian Controversy' (1998) 92 *American Journal of International Law* 414, 453–55; EI Daes, as reproduced in Working Paper on the relationship and distinction between the rights of persons belonging to minorities and those of indigenous peoples, 19 July 2000, E/CN 4/Sub 2/2000/10; and Thornberry (n 3) 37–40.

of Indigeneity include: (i) communal attachments to 'place'; (ii) historical precedence over dominant societies; (iii) experience of severe disruption, dislocation and exploitation; (iv) 'historical continuity'; (v) ongoing oppression/exclusion by dominant societal groups; (vi) distinct ethnic/cultural groups; and (vii) self-identification as an Indigenous community. In keeping with such a sliding scale approach, a given societal group may be categorised as an Indigenous people even though it may not be able to satisfy all of the above criteria. Notwithstanding the obvious appeal of this multi-faceted approach, the element of historical priority has assumed decisive importance in understandings of Indigeneity and, linguistically, it appears to be innate, as is apparent from the terms 'Aboriginal' and 'First Nations'.

In line with current thinking, the UNDRIP does not seek to define the notion of Indigeneity, but, in contrast, ILO Convention 169 on Indigenous and Tribal Peoples does offer definitions of both Indigenous peoples and tribal peoples.[42] In this respect, it is notable that the element of historical priority plays a pivotal role in distinguishing these two societal categories.[43] But while historical priority is undoubtedly a social fact in many situations involving Indigenous peoples and the concept of Indigeneity clearly derives much of its contemporary resonance from the idea of societal precedence, whether this component is a precondition for Indigenous status in all cases is less certain. In her contribution, Figueroa analyses the situation of two distinct traditional communities whose ancestors were brought to Colombia from Africa as slaves by European colonisers in the sixteenth century. However, subsequently, these communities established themselves in particular territories and maintained their traditional cultural practices across the generations. Such communities claim to possess ancestral lands and marine resource rights, but they did not occupy these lands before the advent of European colonisation.[44] It could be argued that such marginalised communities cannot be classified as Indigenous, but, instead, they might qualify as 'tribal' peoples. Nonetheless, it is notable that ILO Convention 169 does not distinguish between these categories as far as the ensuing entitlements and responsibilities are concerned. At a broader level, it is unclear why challenged minorities who can satisfy the criteria of Indigeneity, save for the criterion of historical precedence, should be denied access to the canon of Indigenous

[42] ILO Convention 169 (n 25) art 1.

[43] Article 1(1) provides that: 'This Convention applies to: (a) tribal peoples in independent countries whose social, cultural and economic conditions distinguish them from other sections of the national community, and whose status is regulated wholly or partially by their own customs or traditions or by special laws or regulations; (b) peoples in independent countries who are regarded as indigenous on account of their descent from the populations which inhabited the country, or a geographical region to which the country belongs, at the time of conquest or colonisation or the establishment of present state boundaries and who, irrespective of their legal status, retain some or all of their own social, economic, cultural and political institutions.'

[44] These cases are not unique – eg, the Chagos Islanders have had similar experiences and they have been accepted as an indigenous people. See Allen (ch 4 in this volume).

rights in principle.[45] Against this background, a number of other chapters in this volume attest to the existence of a degree of flexibility in the concept of Indigeneity. For instance, in his chapter on the Philippines, Batongbacal points out that the statutory definition of Indigeneity contained in the Indigenous Peoples' Rights Act 1997 is necessarily open-ended, with section 3(h) acknowledging that Indigenous communities may have been displaced from their ancestral lands, resulting in their resettlement elsewhere. In his view, such an approach is justified in order to protect the 110 Indigenous communities found in that the Philippines. In the context of her chapter on MPAs and Indigenous rights, located in Part IV of the book, Sue Farran uses the combined notion of 'Indigenous peoples and local communities' to indicate the relevant stakeholders in the creation and management of MPAs. At first glance, this approach might appear to be too broad; however, at the level of effects, the participation of vulnerable communities in decision-making processes that directly and significantly affect them makes sense. Moreover, it is striking to note that the contentious reforms of marine resource entitlements in coastal regions of the Sámi areas of Norway have not been restricted to the Sámi alone. Instead, as Ravna and Kalak's chapter shows, in a spirit of inclusivity and for practical reasons, recent changes and outstanding reform proposals have been formulated on a geographical basis rather than by reference to ethnic and cultural characteristics, despite the fact that the Sámi have been in the vanguard of these initiatives. Similarly, the chapter by Evelyn Pinkerton and Steve Langdon in Part IV demonstrates that marginalised communities that may not be entirely Indigenous may be able to exploit highly contingent statutory provisions designed to benefit adjacent coastal communities as well as building upon laws specifically designed to benefit Indigenous peoples. Finally, as noted above, Enyew's chapter on international human rights law and Allen's contribution concerning artisanal fishing rights show that Indigenous peoples have benefited, and may make further gains from accessing standards which serve the interests of minorities and local communities more generally. The concept of Indigeneity is clearly strong enough to withstand the recognition of penumbral cases. Accordingly, in principle, there seems to be little value in limiting access to Indigenous standards so long as claimant groups are able to establish a clear preponderance of the criteria of Indigeneity and there is much to be gained from working closely with other vulnerable communities where such strategies are mutually advantageous.

As noted above, Hamilton's chapter highlights the inter-societal laws which arose during the early encounters between Indigenous peoples and European explorers/traders. In particular, he recounts the ways in which hybrid norms

[45] See, eg, Will Kymlicka, 'Beyond the Indigenous/Minority Dichotomy' in Stephen Allen and Alexandra Xanthaki (eds), *Reflections on the UN Declaration on the Rights of Indigenous Peoples* (Hart Publishing, 2011) 183.

evolved through the normative inter-mingling that occurred during this period and he draws attention to the fact that coastal and marine areas typically provided the initial settings for the development of thicker versions of legal pluralism than those which existed at the height of European imperialism (and those which have endured in the postcolonial era). Nevertheless, Hamilton points out that, in the Indigenous context, legal plurality has persisted, notwithstanding the extent to which the norms and sovereignty of Indigenous peoples have been compromised by dominant national legal systems on such grounds as 'incommensurability'. In this vein, Godden shows how the common law – this narrow legal heritage as Hamilton calls it – has been used to accommodate Indigenous laws in Australia by reference to thin forms of legal pluralism which do not challenge the dominant legal system or its sovereignty. In this context, pluralism has been imposed rather than shared or negotiated. As Godden shows us, anomalous variants of hybridity are well illustrated through the doctrine of Aboriginal title, which, while providing a degree of recognition for native title claims, originates neither in the common law nor in Indigenous law. The phenomenon of hybridity is not one restricted to national legal systems. For example, Allen discusses how international law has embraced the vested rights doctrine – originally a common law device used, inter alia, to accommodate the rights of Indigenous peoples in Anglo-American jurisdictions – to account for traditional fishing regimes that are not necessarily explicable by recourse to (modern) municipal legal systems or to the international legal order itself. Nonetheless, as Allen's chapter demonstrates, the recognition and enforcement of these hybrid normative orders invariably depends on a state's willingness to exercise its discretionary right of diplomatic protection at the inter-state level, thereby creating a different kind of vulnerability for marginalised sub-state groups.[46]

Part IV comprises four chapters. Three of these chapters draw upon the insights of other disciplines, while Farran's chapter considers a single issue: that of Indigenous rights and MPAs across a range of jurisdictions. Clearly, as Farran shows, MPAs have become attractive mechanisms by which states can prove their 'blue planet' credentials by reference to a host of evolving international standards on biodiversity and sustainable development. These initiatives are regulated, or overseen, by international institutions (such as the International Union for Conservation of Nature) and are often pushed by powerful private global actors. However, in pursuing such strategies, states are adopting policies over coastal and marine areas that have been traditionally used by Indigenous peoples (and other vulnerable communities). Farran catalogues the drawbacks and uncertainties associated with a range of MPAs for these groups (which often include the introduction of 'no-take' zones). She pays particular attention to the lack of Indigenous participation in decision-making processes

[46] See Figueroa (ch 7 in this volume) for a concrete example of this kind of vulnerability.

concerning the creation and management of MPAs, rights to access, harvest and use of marine resources, and ways of improving marine conservation in affected areas, in keeping with Indigenous cultures. The issue of governance (and especially of co-management) in relation to MPAs is further considered by Godden in relation to MPA initiatives in Australia and by Cambou, Gilbert and Dégremont with regard to the MPA created in New Caledonia.

Alaska provides the geographical frame of reference for two very different contributions in Part IV: one by Caskey Russell and X'unei Lance Twitchell and the other by Pinkerton and Langdon. Russell and Twitchell describe the central cultural significance of salmon and the work (and indeed celebration) of 'putting up fish' for the Tlingit people, a cultural practice of traditional and contemporary significance. Their chapter also emphasises the importance of the practice of 'putting up fish' as a means of transmitting both language and culture across generations. But the authors also tell a story of resistance and resilience; a story of the devastating consequences of contact with Europeans, yet also a story of survival; a story of surviving the acquisition of sovereignty by Russia and then the cession of Alaska by Russia to the US. More recently, Tlingit and other Indigenous nations in Alaska have had to grapple with both the benefits and the burdens of Congressional recognition and reaction through the Alaska Native Claims Settlement Act and its corporate, neoliberal model for 'settling' Indigenous claims. Through all of this, 'putting up fish' is not simply catching and preserving fish, but active participation in a living tradition, the custom and practice of participating in one's ancestral heritage.

Pinkerton and Langdon also explore ideas of resistance (and agency) amongst Alaska's Indigenous communities, but from a very different perspective, a perspective that demonstrates how Indigenous communities may be able to 'Indigenise modernity' within the context of access to marine resources. They relate how Indigenous communities in the Norton Sound Region of Alaska have been able to prioritise traditional subsistence activities and small-scale commercial fisheries by leveraging statutory entitlements to participate in more highly capitalised (and potentially destructive) larger-scale fisheries. As a result, communities have been able to exercise what the authors characterise as a series of collective choice rights (and powers), including: exclusion rights, allocation rights, harvesting rights, monitoring, habitat protection, conservation and fisheries enhancement, as well as (and crucially) the right to secure optimum benefit from the sale of fish and the right to community benefits to enhance well-being. An important point here is that the community opportunity to participate emerged through the concept of adjacency rather than on the basis of an Indigenous entitlement.

Resistance is also a theme that is common to the comparative chapter authored by Einar Eythórsson, Dorothee Schreiber, Camilla Brattland and Else Grete Broderstad. This chapter looks at the rights and governance seascape in two areas where Indigenous peoples have claimed rights to marine space – in British Columbia, Canada and northern Norway – and where these claims conflict with the demands of the growing salmon aquaculture industry for additional marine space. This chapter demonstrates that Indigenous communities may achieve a measure of success in resisting the expansion of the aquaculture industry by using a number of different tools. In Norway, the Sámi have been able to achieve a measure of influence both through the planning process and through the consultation protocol between the government and the Sámi parliament. In British Columbia, First Nations have secured influence through litigation based on Aboriginal rights and title, the duty to consult and accommodate, and through impact and benefit agreements with the industry.

In conclusion, the chapters in this volume aim to fill a gap in the literature pertaining to Indigenous rights by focusing on the rights of Indigenous peoples in relation to marine spaces and resources. While the chapters demonstrate that both national law and international law are increasingly engaging with Indigenous rights in a marine context, they also demonstrate that it is not a respectful engagement between equals. Instead, the terms of the debate are still largely statist, whether within the meeting rooms of the IWC or within domestic courts and legislatures. However, the chapters also show that the interaction between domestic law and international law, and indeed the interaction between different streams of international law (eg, human rights law and international environmental law), may in some cases afford enhanced recognition of Indigenous rights. Finally, while the forces of globalisation threaten traditional economies and ways of being, and create increased competition for resources, several of the contributions here point to opportunities to resist and to exploit openings in both domestic law and international law in order to regain control over resources, territory and livelihood, and create a more pluralist understanding of the relationship between Indigenous peoples and the states within which they live their lives and practise their culture, language, spirituality and deep connection with ocean space.

# Part I

# The Colonial Encounter in Marine Space

# 1

# *Indigenous Legal Traditions, Inter-societal Law and the Colonisation of Marine Spaces*

ROBERT HAMILTON

## I. INTRODUCTION

IN 1604, A French vessel approached the shores of Mi'kma'ki, later also known as Acadie, and later still as the British colony and then Canadian province of Nova Scotia. As the vessel entered the calm waters of the Annapolis basin, a birch bark canoe came out to meet it. Membertou, Sagamaw of the Mi'kmaq peoples of the region, pulled the canoe aside the French ship and boarded. Membertou addressed those aboard in broken French.[1] The Mi'kmaq that these early French colonists encountered were familiar not only with French, but traded with Europeans in a pidgin-Basque language developed through a century of trade with Basque fishermen.[2] In addition to several types of canoes designed for a variety of purposes, the Mi'kmaq sailed single-mast European shallops that they controlled with a proficiency that impressed European observers. The Mi'kmaq were a coastal people.[3] Their interactions with Europeans over the first two centuries of contact took place on the shores and on the water.

As a coastal people, the Mi'kmaq had law regulating the use of marine spaces and resources. Over the centuries of contact with European colonists and fishermen, a body of inter-societal law, first customary and later positive

[1] John Mack Faragher, *A Great and Noble Scheme: The Tragic Story of the Expulsion of the French Acadians from Their American Homeland* (WW Norton & Company, 2006) 11.

[2] Harald EL Prins, *The Mi'kmaq: Resistance, Accommodation, and Cultural Survival* (Harcourt Brace, 1996) 117.

[3] As Jeffers Lennox writes: 'As much as the British or the French, the Mi'kmaq were a maritime people.' Jeffers Lennox, *Homelands and Empires: Indigenous Spaces, Imperial Fictions, and Competition for Territory in Northeastern North America, 1690–1763* (University of Toronto Press, 2017) 5.

in nature, developed to regulate the relations between peoples and their use of marine spaces and resources. This pattern is observable in many colonial spheres. However, most of the analysis of the impact of European imperial projects on Indigenous peoples has focused on land. This is not without reason. The voracious European appetite for land and land-based resources drove an acquisitive form of colonialism that dispossessed Indigenous peoples of their lands the world over. Particularly in settler-colonial states, much of the contemporary opposition to colonial power has therefore focused on gaining recognition of rights to land.

However, legal disputes between Indigenous peoples and colonial states over rights and jurisdiction in marine areas have also played a prominent role in contemporary rights disputes. The long histories of Indigenous and inter-societal law in marine areas should inform how legal doctrine in common law countries treats these disputes. From a common law perspective, the long-standing doctrine of continuity recognises that Indigenous legal traditions could survive the assertion of colonial sovereignty.[4] Their historical and ongoing importance shapes contemporary doctrines. As Lamer CJ stated in *Delgamuukw*: 'The common law should develop to recognize aboriginal rights as they were recognised by either *de facto* practice or by aboriginal systems of governance.'[5] Contemporary attempts to facilitate this development in the common law have not been as successful as higher-minded statements from common law courts suggest they could have been. One of the reasons for this is that courts have failed to fully acknowledge and conceptualise the nature and role of Indigenous and inter-societal law in the early colonial period. If the common law is to develop in a manner that reflects 'aboriginal systems of governance' and the customary forms of inter-societal law that shaped de facto practice, it must strive to understand those systems of law.

With that in mind, the following two sections of this chapter describe the ways in which two types of law – Indigenous law and Indigenous-European inter-societal law – each historically regulated the use of marine areas and resources. This overview illustrates how de facto practice and 'aboriginal systems of governance' understood the rights and jurisdiction of Indigenous peoples in colonial spheres in the common law world and brings to the fore the legal pluralism that characterised Indigenous spaces in the imperial age. Section IV argues that the theoretical discourses and legal categories that shaped the 'doctrine of discovery' applied equally to marine spaces. In doing so, it juxtaposes European theorising which justified imperial expansion with the legal pluralism and negotiated forms of law and authority described in the two prior sections. The section concludes by illustrating how these European

[4] On the doctrine of continuity, see Mark D Walters 'The "Golden Thread" of Continuity: Aboriginal Customs at Common Law and under the Constitution Act, 1982' (1999) 44 *McGill Law Journal* 711.

[5] *Delgamuukw v British Columbia* [1997] 3 SCR 1010, 153 DLR (4th) 193 [159].

theories supported an extension of jurisdiction which dispossessed Indigenous peoples in marine areas through the development of colonial legal and regulatory regimes.

Section V briefly connects the contemporary rights paradigms of settler-colonial states to this longer history. In doing so, it seeks to chart a path for the development of common law doctrine which could be informed by a reading of Indigenous law and governance free from preconceptions that have historically worked to minimise those traditions.[6] This provides the foundation for a re-assessment of Indigenous marine rights in the contemporary context.

## II. INDIGENOUS LAWS IN MARINE SPACES

The image of Indigenous peoples as lawless and uncivilised prior to European contact has been conclusively undermined.[7] However, this framing has had pernicious political and legal consequences, as Indigenous law, sovereignty and jurisdiction were eliminated by a way of seeing the world that could not admit of their existence.[8] Several damaging legacies of these early beliefs are still present today. This is despite the fact that these views were contrary to the lived reality recorded by European observers, who consistently noted the well-developed legal and social structures of the Indigenous nations they encountered.[9] Indigenous peoples had laws that governed their relationships within their communities, with other peoples and with the world around them. Their laws touched on matters such as trespass, property, marriage, adoption, crime, hunting, trade and so on.[10] Indigenous rights in marine areas today must be considered in light of the history of Indigenous law in those spaces and the jurisdiction that such law illustrates. As Eddie Mabo Jr has written: 'We have always operated out of an understanding of our own ... jurisdictions to land and water.'[11]

[6] In the Supreme Court of Canada's decision in *R v Van der Peet* [1996] 2 SCR 507, for example, constitutionalised Aboriginal rights were construed as emanating from 'pre-contact' practices that were 'integral to the distinctive culture' of the people in question. This has had the effect of limiting the recognition of jurisdiction and governance as constitutional rights.

[7] See, eg, John Borrows, *Canada's Indigenous Constitution* (University of Toronto Press, 2010); Ani Mikaere, 'Tikanga as the First Law of Aotearoa' (2007) 10 *Yearbook of New Zealand Jurisprudence* 24 (2007); Linda Te Aho, 'Tikanga Māori, Historical Context and the Interface with Pakeha Law in Aotearoa/New Zealand' (2007) 10 *Yearbook of New Zealand Jurisprudence* 10; Robert Williams Jr, *Linking Arms Together: American Indian Treaty Visions of Law and Peace, 1600–1800* (Oxford University Press, 1997).

[8] Robert Williams Jr, *The American Indian in Western Legal Thought: The Discourses on Conquest* (Oxford University Press, 1990).

[9] Stuart Banner, *How the Indians Lost Their Land: Law and Power on the Frontier* (Harvard University Press, 2005) 22–28.

[10] Borrows (n 7).

[11] Eddie Mabo Jr, 'A Treaty for Whom? Indigenous Jurisdictions and the Treaty Sideshow' in Peter Read, Gary Meyers and Bob Reece (eds) *What Good Condition? Reflections on an Australian Aboriginal Treaty 1986–2006* (ANU Press, 2006) 99.

Indigenous notions of territoriality and conceptions of distinctions between marine and dry land areas shaped the ways in which Indigenous jurisdiction in marine spaces was conceived.[12] Indigenous legal systems often conceptualised distinctions between marine, foreshore and dry land areas of territory differently than common, civil or international law systems. As the Waitangi Tribunal wrote in its *Report on the Crown's Foreshore and Seabed Policy*: 'The need to distinguish the foreshore from the adjacent dry land and seabed arises from the English common law, which developed distinct rules for that zone. In Maori customary terms, no such distinction exists.'[13]

Before turning to Indigenous legal principles in marine areas, two notes of caution are warranted. First, it is important to recognise the heterogeneity of Indigenous peoples in order to avoid essentialist or reductionist approaches to Indigenous cultures and identity.[14] Though I draw on several Indigenous legal traditions in the following analysis, the aim is to draw out similarities between distinct peoples with vastly divergent legal traditions. Second, Indigenous law must not be tethered to the past. Law is continually re-shaped to meet the demands of the present, and its present legitimacy cannot be assessed in terms of its adherence to an idealised past. The legitimacy of Indigenous peoples' contemporary laws concerning marine areas is not tied to their fidelity to historical laws. Further, Indigenous law is shaped and created in the present. As John Borrows writes: 'Indigenous people's laws hold contemporary relevance for themselves and others, and can be developed through contemporary practices.'[15] That is not to say that historic laws do not provide guidance: the historical role of Indigenous legal traditions clarifies how Indigenous laws came to sit in relation to state laws in the manner they do today and informs the articulation of contemporary Indigenous legal principles.

[12] Jonathan K Patton, 'Considering the Wet Homelands of Indigenous Massachusetts' (2014) 14 *Journal of Social Archaeology* 87, 90.

[13] New Zealand, Waitangi Tribunal, Report on the Crown's Foreshore and Seabed Policy, Wai 1071 (Wellington, NZ, Legislation Direct, 2004) xi. Here I take 'customary terms' to refer to Indigenous *law*. On customary law *as law*, see Lon Fuller, *Anatomy of Law* (Greenwood Press, 1977); Borrows (n 7) 5–55. David V Williams addresses the use of the term 'customary law' in the following way: 'I use the term "indigenous customary rights" in an attempt to ensure that the rights and obligations established by the legal practices of indigenous societies in this part of the globe are not equated with the rather static notion of local custom – established since "time immemorial" – that once was important but now remains as only a very limited source of law in English law. I am also happy to apply the term "custom law" to tikanga Maori, as used by Durie and the New Zealand Law Commission. I am not happy, however, to diminish and demean the significance of tikanga Maori by describing it as "lore" rather than "law" – with the implication that it is an inevitably inferior source of obligations that can always be trumped by "real" law. I have long advocated the importance of legal pluralism to understand the role of law in society and I prefer the more far reaching and open-ended version of legal pluralism which holds that the concept of law "does not necessarily depend on state recognition for its validity".' David V Williams, 'Indigenous Customary Rights and the Constitution of Aotearoa New Zealand' (2006) 14 *Waikato Law Review* 120, 120.

[14] John Borrows, *Freedom and Indigenous Constitutionalism* (University of Toronto Press, 2016) 19.

[15] Borrows (n 7) 10.

How, then, can Indigenous legal principles in relation to marine spaces and resources be identified? John Borrows identifies five sources of Indigenous law that are a useful starting point when analysing Indigenous legal traditions. These sources are not exhaustive, but they offer a way to begin *seeing* Indigenous law. Those sources are 'sacred teachings, naturalistic observations, positivistic proclamations, deliberative practices, and local and national customs'.[16] The particular, contingent circumstances of each people shape how the distinct sources inform law.[17] There are many ways in which the law derived from these sources can be recorded and communicated. Stories and oral histories can record aspects of Indigenous law. Stories express community norms, standards of judgement, and modes of reasoning and present examples of proper and improper behaviour. As such, stories can be analogous to 'cases' in the common law.[18] The stories of coastal Indigenous peoples may articulate legal principles concerning marine spaces and resources.

The Mi'kmaq were 'hunters for marine animals such as walrus, seal, and small whales, and before the arrival of Europeans they had depended primarily on marine resources, including cod and bass, as well as the deep-sea swordfish'.[19] They travelled in sea-going canoes that took them across open waters as far as Newfoundland and by the beginning of the seventeenth century sailed European shallops.[20] The norms associated with this intensive use of, and existence with, the sea and sea life were developed and shared partly through stories and songs, and the Mi'kmaq have many stories that are set in marine spaces. A story called 'Gluskape, the Giant Killer, and the Whales' recounts that Gluskape (who is the 'first man' in Mi'kmaw creation stories, often playing the role of creator himself) was a fisherman. The story tells of a whale hunt and the sharing of the harvest.[21] When heard or read in concert with similar stories, a story such as this can provide legal principles about fishing locations, protocols for fishing different species and the distribution of the harvest.

[16] ibid 23–24.

[17] ibid. As Borrows writes, these sources are 'entwined with the social, historical, political, biological, economic, and spiritual circumstances of each group'. Aaron Mills elaborates on this point, arguing that there is a fundamental connection between law and the 'life-world' from which law emerges. In his view, legal analysis that cuts across legal traditions must be attentive to the difficulty of translating law 'across distinct constitutional contexts'. Aaron Mills, 'The Lifeworlds of Law: On Revitalizing Indigenous Legal Orders Today' (2016) 61(4) *McGill Law Journal* 847, 854–55.

[18] John Borrows, *Recovering Canada: The Resurgence of Indigenous Legal Traditions* (University of Toronto Press, 2002). For a description of the 'story method' of researching and articulating Indigenous law, see Hadley Friedland and Val Napoleon, 'Gathering The Threads: Developing a Methodology for Researching and Rebuilding Indigenous Legal Traditions' (2015–16) 1 *Lakehead Law Journal* 16.

[19] Olive Patricia Dickason, *Canada's First Nations: A History of Founding Peoples from Earliest Times* (McClelland & Stewart, 1992) 107.

[20] ibid.

[21] Alice Mead and Arnold Neptune (eds), *Giants of the Dawnland: Ancient Wabanaki Tales* (Loose Canon Press, 2015) 10–14. See also 'The Magic Giants' (at 34–42); and 'Partridge's Canoe' (at 56–57).

On the west coast of Canada, the reef net was an important salmon fishing technique that was central to W̱SÁNEĆ society. The reef net fishery required a system for allocating resources and distributing property-like entitlements; that is, it required law. This fishing technique, which was held to be sacred, was intertwined with the law and governance of the marine territory and its resources. Reef net fishing served an important organising function in W̱SÁNEĆ life and was tied to W̱SÁNEĆ identity, governance and law.[22] To see reef net fishing only as a fishing practice is to under-state its importance. W̱SÁNEĆ law, for example, detailed the rights and obligations associated with a given fishing location, or SWÁLET. As Earl Claxton Sr and John Elliot Sr write, 'a SWÁLET or fishing location of the reef net was not owned. Rather, the families belonged to the location. The location of such a fishery within Saanich [W̱SÁNEĆ] territory was a birthright of the Saanich [W̱SÁNEĆ] people. SWÁLET was passed down in a traditional way along with the ancient family names. All close relatives belonged to the SWÁLET'.[23] The technique and, implicitly, its associated legal and social functions, featured in W̱SÁNEĆ stories. For example, the origin story of the reef net technique taught that the technique was a gift from the Salmon People, given in exchange for a W̱SÁNEĆ princess.[24] In stories such as this, agency and kinship ties were extended beyond the human world. Modes of tenure in marine spaces, distribution of the harvest of the sea, and the extension of kinship relations and reciprocity to sea life were all tied to the reef net fishery and were articulated in stories.

In parts of Northern Australia, the connections between creation stories, law and marine spaces are explicit. The law of the Meriam people, known as Malo's Law, is named 'after their sea god Malo'. Malo's Law 'forbids them to trespass on each other's land, and Malo's law is also the law of the sea'.[25] The Meriam stories of creation describe a supernatural sea-being from whom law is derived. Again, these stories describe legal principles from which concrete legal practices, dividing fishing territories, managing the harvest, and shaping group and individual responsibilities were articulated. As Nonie Sharp observes: 'If you follow good custom, or *debe tonar*, in the Meriam language, you take only what you need from the sea and the land, you respect other people's property rights and above all, you share.'[26] For the Meriam, the stories

[22] Earl Claxton Sr and John Elliot Sr, *Reef Net Technology of the Saltwater People* (Saanich Indian School Board, 1994). On the explicit connection between the reef net fishery and W̱SÁNEĆ law and governance, see Nicholas Xumthoult Claxton, 'ISTÁ SĆIÁNEW, ISTÁ S̱XOLE "To Fish as Formerly": The Douglas Treaties and the W̱SÁNEĆ Reef-Net Fisheries' in Leanne Simpson (ed), *Lighting the Eighth Fire: The Liberation, Resurgence, and Protection of Indigenous Nations* (Arbeiter Ring, 2008); Nicholas Xumthoult Claxton, 'To Fish as Formerly: A Resurgent Journey back to the Saanich Reef Net Fishery', PhD dissertation, Victoria University, 2015.

[23] ibid.

[24] ibid.

[25] Nonie Sharp, *Saltwater People: The Waves of Memory* (University of Toronto Press, 2002) 6.

[26] ibid 5.

of creation associated with the sea god Malo ground a legal order in relation to both marine and dry-land spaces.

Stories speak not only to legal norms, but also to the territorial aspects of law. For example, stories often contain oral maps that track travel routes and describe sites of resource abundance. This is prominent in the naming of geological features in stories.[27] For Indigenous peoples in present-day New England, stories account for the creation of geological features, with the islands, inlets and bays being shaped by the footsteps of giants.[28] The routes that characters followed in stories such as these would contain important information about the nature of the region and resources. In Mi'kma'ki, easily identifiable geological features 'acted as guide posts for Mi'kmaq travelling along the waterways of Eastern Canada much like latter-day lighthouses. These rock formations were honorifically referred to as Kukumijinu ("our Grandmother") or Kniskamijinu ("our Grandfather") and commonly have legends associated with them, such as Kluscap turning his Grandmother or Grandfather to stone'.[29] Similarly, the Yolnu people of Northern Australia believe that 'their entitlement to this saltwater world finds expression in a profound and detailed knowledge of its geography: the reefs, the channels, the currents'.[30]

Place names also expressed views about how people should live in relation to the territory they inhabited. In addition to recording knowledge about geography and resources, place names 'act as a mnemonic device to remind people how to "live right"'.[31] Place names in Mi'kmaq, for example, could identify 'that place's special significance for specific families. Certain families had responsibilities to use certain animals, plants, materials and access sites, eg, hunting and fishing traps, because of their particular relationships'.[32] In W̱SÁNEĆ stories, the islands of the territory were created when XALS, the creator, threw some W̱SÁNEĆ people into the ocean.[33] The islands, whose name translates as 'relatives of the deep', were brought into webs of kinship, establishing legal obligations for W̱SÁNEĆ people in relation to those places.[34] The non-human world is understood as having agency and is brought into reciprocal systems of rights and obligations in this way. W̱SÁNEĆ people in the present day invoke

[27] Trudy Sable and Bernie Francis, *The Language of This Land, Mi'kma'ki* (CBU Press, 2012) 19.

[28] Andrew Lipman, *The Saltwater Frontier* (Yale University Press, 2015) 19: 'Once there was a moody giant who roamed the waters from the Hudson River to Cape Cod and ate roasted whales for breakfast. When he enjoyed a pipe, the smoke became fogbanks that shrouded the coast for miles. With taps of ash from his pipe's bowl, he created the two sandy lumps we now call Martha's Vineyard and Nantucket.'

[29] Sable and Francis (n 27) 43.

[30] Sharp (n 25) 11.

[31] Sable and Francis (n 27) 50.

[32] James [Sakéj] Youngblood Henderson, 'First Nations' Legal Inheritances in Canada: The Mikmaq Model' (1996) 23 *Manitoba Law Journal* 1, 21.

[33] Robert Clifford, 'W̱SÁNEĆ Legal Theory and the Fuel Spill at SELEK-TEL- (Goldstream River)' (2016) 61(4) *McGill Law Journal* 755, 758, 773.

[34] ibid.

this kinship-based conception of place in discussing disputes over the use of islands in their traditional territory.[35] Animals, too were described in kinship terms. The 'Mi'kmaq believed that animals allowed themselves to be killed so that humans could live. However, the continuance of this relationship depended upon respecting the laws which governed the relationship, such as properly disposing of fish and animals bones and not over-hunting'.[36] In this way, stories encode customary law while articulating normative frameworks to guide future behaviour. The obligations that people and communities have in relation to each other and the management of resources are detailed in origin stories and place names.

Law is also expressed through rituals, procedures and practices. For the Torres Strait peoples in Australia: 'Use of the sea (and land) is mediated by long-term patterns of customary tenure and reinforced through rituals to maintain and negotiate boundaries and interfaces, and through these interactions, maintain individual and group identities.'[37] The sacred and supernatural can become intertwined with the legal through the use of rituals. The importance of marine areas in many Indigenous cosmologies brings this connection between the territory, the sacred and the law to the fore. For Polynesians, for example, navigational knowledge 'was sacred and the arts of the navigator were closely linked with those of the priest'.[38] Codes of conduct concerning the use of marine spaces and resources develop through these stories, rituals, protocols and practices.

In the application of these legal principles to specific places, modes of tenure, ownership and jurisdiction were created.[39] Jurisdiction extended in relation to foreshore, reefs and other marine areas. For the Meriam, for example, 'the entire perimeter of the island was divided into eight clan territories',[40] the boundaries of which extended over the shores, foreshore and reefs.[41] Saltwater, for Meriam and Croker Islanders, is owned on a clan or patrilineal basis in the same way that they divide ownership of land.[42] Recalling the importance of creation stories to law, the 'Yolnu people of northeast Arnhem Land continue to believe today that their sea rights come from creator beings who shaped the seas'.[43] This includes 'rights and responsibilities for the beaches,

[35] ibid 772–75.

[36] William Wicken, 'Treaty of Peace and Friendship 1760', *Indigenous and Northern Affairs Canada*, https://www.aadnc-aandc.gc.ca/eng/1100100028599/1100100028600.

[37] Sharp (n 25) 11.

[38] John Gascoigne, 'Cross-cultural Knowledge Exchange in the Age of the Enlightenment' in Shino Konishi, Maria Nugent and Tiffany Shellam (eds), *Indigenous Intermediaries: New Perspectives on Exploration Archives* (ANU Press, 2015) 137.

[39] See Allan Greer, *Property and Dispossession: Natives, Empire and Land in Early Modern North America* (Cambridge University Press, 2018).

[40] Sharp (n 25) 6.

[41] ibid.

[42] ibid 10.

[43] ibid 11.

reefs, seabed, sea life and waters adjoining their lands'.[44] It was a violation of these marine ownership rights that led to the *Croker Island Seas* case.[45] The Croker Islanders believed that non-Indigenous fishers 'required their permission to fish there'.[46] Similarly, W̱SÁNEĆ fishing locations, or SWÁLET, were distributed by assigned decision makers and established protocols and could not be violated without causing conflict. In this way, places were brought within the territorial jurisdiction of Indigenous legal regimes and property entitlements were distributed among families. Indigenous legal regimes determined access to marine areas and resources, outlining who could fish what species, at what times and where. These laws and usage patterns created notions of tenure which guided behaviour both within Indigenous nations and between them; that is, they had both domestic and inter-societal elements. Upon engagement with Europeans, these domestic and inter-societal elements would contribute to shaping the law between Indigenous peoples and those entering their territories.

## III. INTER-SOCIETAL LAW IN MARINE AREAS

Inter-societal law refers to law that developed between distinct societies or nations. The focus here is on law that formed between Indigenous and European peoples rather than law as between Indigenous nations. Early European travellers observed the existence of Indigenous laws pertaining to their external relations. Jesuit Paul Le Jeune, for example, wrote in the seventeenth century of the Indigenous peoples in the St Lawrence Valley: 'Besides having some kind of Laws maintained among themselves, there is also a certain order established as regards foreign nations.'[47] Indigenous-European inter-societal law existed in both customary and positive forms. In marine and foreshore areas, customary law developed through repeated interactions and governed the relations between the nations and each nation's use of space and resources.[48] Positive forms developed later and were explicitly negotiated.

As Europeans arrived on Indigenous lands by sea, initial encounters between Indigenous peoples and Europeans happened on the water and the coasts.

[44] ibid 12. As Sharp writes: 'In owning sea territory saltwater peoples are radically different to the modern west. Their ways of owning marine areas are unfamiliar to the European mind: the sea property includes foreshore, reefs and sandbanks, sites of spiritual potency and seabed. It also includes the saltwater itself.'

[45] *Commonwealth v Yarmirr; Yarmirr v Northern Territory* [2001] HCA 56.

[46] Sharp (n 25) 9.

[47] Dickason (n 19) 79.

[48] For an account of this process in southern New Zealand, see Kate Stevens and Angela Wanhalla, 'Intimate Relations: Kinship and the Economics of Shore Whaling in Southern New Zealand, 1820–1860' (2017) 52 *Journal of Pacific History* 135. James Cook articulated five 'rules' governing the conduct of his charges with the Indigenous peoples they encountered in Tahiti: Bruce Buchan, *The Empire of Political Thought: Indigenous Australians and the Language of Colonial Government* (Pickering & Chatto, 2008) 47–50.

Frequently, European ships were met on the water by great numbers of boats and people. Richard Hakluyt reported in his account of the circumnavigation of the globe by Thomas Candish between 1568 and 1588 that the group was approaching the isles of Ladrones when 'we were coming up within 2 leagues of the island, where we were met with 60 or 70 canoes full of savages, who came off to sea unto us, and brought with them in their boats plantains, cocos' etc for trade.[49] Similar accounts are repeated in a harbour near Manhattan in 1534, where European boats were met by 'a flotilla of boats "carrying innumerable people"',[50] and in Nootka Sound on the west coast of Vancouver Island, where Captain Cook was 'immediately surrounded by canoes full of Natives eager to trade'.[51] Dutch arrivals to New Zealand and French arrivals in North America follow similar patterns.[52] In many cases, interactions centred in those coastal and marine areas for a century or more before European populations began to move inland and attempted to establish territorial control in a concerted manner.[53] Despite exploring North American shores from the sixteenth century onwards and developing significant fishing interests off the coasts, the British Empire did not conceive of itself as a territorial empire until after the end of the Seven Years' War in 1763.[54] Early British imperial activity was focused on trade and on the seas. Territorial sovereignty was not an aim or a reality, as control was only achieved in relation to particular sites and routes, and conceptions of bounded territorial sovereignty were only beginning to emerge.[55] Imperial sovereignty was, to use Lauren Benton's term, 'patchwork'.[56]

By the end of the sixteenth century, significant economic ties bound Europe and North America. European fishermen fished near the North American coasts and dried their fish on the shores before returning to Europe. Hundreds of European boats arrived annually.[57] Similarly, after the initial voyages of 'discovery', whaling and sealing ships were a main cause of European travel to New Zealand

[49] Richard Hakluyt, *The Voyage of Sir Francis Drake Around the Whole Globe* (Penguin, 2015) 40.
[50] Lipman (n 28) 54.
[51] Noel Elizabeth Currie, *Constructing Colonial Discourse: Captain Cook at Nootka Sound* (McGill-Queen's University Press, 2015) 83.
[52] On the French arrival in North America, see Marc Lescarbot, *History of New France*, vol 1 (Champlain Society, 1907 [1607]).
[53] Brian W Richardson, *Longitude and Empire: How Captain Cook's Voyages Changed the World* (UBC Press, 2005) 75–77.
[54] PJ Marshall, *The Making and Unmaking of Empires: Britain, India, and America c.1750–1783* (Oxford University Press, 2005) 6.
[55] On early conceptions of sovereignty and the relatively recent emergence of the nation-state, see Quentin Skinner, 'The Sovereign State: A Genealogy' in Hent Kalmo and Quentin Skinner (eds), *Sovereignty in Fragments: The Past, Present and Future of a Contested Concept* (Cambridge University Press, 2010).
[56] Lauren Benton, *A Search for Sovereignty: Law and Geography in European Empires, 1400–1900* (Cambridge University Press, 2010).
[57] NES Griffiths, '1600–1650: Fish, Fur, and Folk' in Phillip A Buckner and John G Reid (eds), *The Atlantic Region to Confederation: A History* (University of Toronto Press, 1994) 40.

prior to European settlement.[58] Yet, owing to the seasonal nature of the fisheries and the types of technologies deployed, the establishment of fisheries did not require permanent European settlements.[59] These seasonal visits represented the first sustained contact and interaction, and a body of customary inter-societal law developed to mediate relations. Marriage was particularly important in this regard, as inter-societal marriages formed the basis of trade alliances while bringing non-Indigenous men into Indigenous kinship systems.[60] With intermarriage and increasing year-round settlement, more robust practices of law developed to mediate relations.

However, the need for inter-societal legal norms arose at the earliest points of contact. Dutch explorer Abel Tasman brought a ship to New Zealand in December 1642, resulting in the first known meeting of Maori and European peoples. In the result: 'Cross-cultural misunderstandings resulted in the killing of four of his crew, with an unknown number of local Māori killed in retaliation.'[61] Abel recorded the first encounter in his journal:

> Early in the morning a boat manned with thirteen Natives approached our ships; they called out several times, but we did not understand them ... We repeatedly made signs for them to come on board us, showing them white line and some knives that formed part of our cargo. They did not come nearer, however, but at last paddled back to shore.[62]

An inability to find grounds for communication ultimately led to several deaths. This illustrates the need to develop shared sets of norms governing interactions, a need which was further illustrated in two later events in Aotearoa. In the first, French explorer Marion du Fresne breached Tapu by using a sacred beach. Tapu denotes, roughly, a place or thing designated as sacred or as 'under religious restriction' in Maori law.[63] O'Malley explains:

> Marion's entire ignorance of the customs of the New Zealanders occasioned that distressing event: as ... strangers, not acquainted with their religious prejudices,

[58] Anne Salmond, *Between Worlds: Early Exchanges between Maori and Europeans, 1773–1815* (Viking 1997) 282–320.

[59] Griffiths (n 57) 50.

[60] See Stevens and Wanhalla (n 48) for discussion of the role of marriage in shaping inter-societal law in the context of shore-based whale fishing in Southern New Zealand. For the same in the Canadian context, see Sylvia Van Kirk, 'From "Marrying-in" to "Marrying-out": Changing Patterns of Aboriginal/Non-Aboriginal Marriage in Colonial Canada' (2002) 23(3) *Frontiers: A Journal of Women Studies* 170; Jennifer SH Brown, *Strangers in Blood: Fur Trade Company Families in Indian Country* (UBC Press, 1980).

[61] Vincent O'Malley et al (eds), *Treaty of Waitangi Companion: Maori and Pakeha from Tasman to Today* (Auckland University Press, 2011) 9.

[62] Abel Tasman, Journal, 19 December 1642, in Robert McNab (ed), *Historical Records of New Zealand*, vol 2 (Government Printer, Wellington, 1914) 21–22, cited in Vincent O'Malley, *Meeting Place: Maori and Pakeha Encounters, 1642–1840* (Auckland University Press, 2012) 9.

[63] See Herbert W Williams, *Dictionary of the Maori Language*, 7th edn (Legislation Direct, 1971) 222–23, 385, quoted in Adele Fletcher, 'Sanctity, Power, and the "Impure Sacred": Analyzing Maori Concepts of Tapu and Noa in Early Documentary Sources' (2007) 47(1) *History of Religions* 51.

> are likely to commit some fatal error; and no action is more likely to lead a party into danger than an incautious use of the seine, for most of the beaches … are taboo'd. This led to the dreadful fate of Marion and his party. I understood from George, that when Marion's men assembled to trail their net on the sacred beach, the natives used every kind of entreaty and remonstrance to induce them to forbear, but either from ignorance or obstinacy, they persisted in their intentions, and drew their net to the land.[64]

Du Fresne and his party were later killed. While this could be construed as 'cultural misunderstanding', a more appropriate framing is that Maori law prevailed in relation to that place and the trespassers were punished, albeit harshly, for their transgression of the laws which governed in that space. A second event occurred in December 1809, when most of the crew of the *Boyd* were killed due to their mistreatment of a Maori leader while he was a passenger aboard this ship.[65] In these examples, the Maori exercised jurisdiction over the beaches and extended their law to non-Maori activity in marine areas.

However, the exercise of Maori jurisdiction came increasingly into conflict with asserted Pākehā jurisdiction. Richard White's well-known 'middle ground' is an apt descriptive tool for understanding these jurisdictional clashes.[66] As O'Malley writes, 'encounters occurred in many coastal locations … Distinctive patterns of interaction developed in both Tai Tokerau and Murihiku – Northland and Southland – with southern relationships centred mainly on sealing and later whaling'.[67] Notably: 'What took place on the "middle ground" of cross-cultural interaction often would not be replicated in solely Māori or Pākehā situations.'[68] In other words, the products of the meeting of cultures were unique to that relationship and the protocols and norms that guided inter-societal interaction were not carried into strictly domestic situations.

Marine and foreshore spaces were the scene of the mingling of normative systems and the development of negotiated inter-societal norms. Where no party could impose unilateral authority and power over others, the need for negotiated solutions was foregrounded. Indeed, in many cases, the imposition of unilateral authority may not have been the goal. Where cultural exchange and economic trade were desired, parties were motivated to find shared norms which could govern their interaction.[69] Much of the associated body of inter-societal law was customary in nature and developed through frequent interaction.[70] For example,

[64] Augustus Earle, *A Narrative of a Nine Months' Residence in New Zealand* (Green & Longman, 1832) 122.

[65] O'Malley (n 62) 12–13.

[66] Richard White, *The Middle Ground: Indians, Empires, and Republics in the Great Lakes Region, 1650–1815* (Cambridge University Press, 1991).

[67] O'Malley (n 62) 70.

[68] ibid 6.

[69] Gascoigne (n 38).

[70] Common law Aboriginal rights, especially in Canada, have developed in explicit recognition of this: *Van der Peet* (n 6) paras 31–43; *Delgamuukw* (n 5) para 148.

owing to their facility in the dangerous coastal waters, their knowledge of local geography and their abundance of vessels suited to the task, Narragansett mariners helped colonists with transportation needs in coastal New England, acting as couriers and ferries for early colonists.[71] These forms of trade and service provision required shared norms, and customary law developed to govern this co-existence.[72]

There were also positive iterations of this law, most clearly captured in Indigenous–European treaty relationships. Indeed, to the eyes of a legal positivist, no inter-societal law existed until treaty relationships were developed. The Treaty of Waitangi, for example, states: 'So the Queen desires to establish a government so that no evil will come to Maori and European living in a state of lawlessness.'[73] While this problematically assumes either that the Maori had no law or that Maori law could not apply to settlers, it explicitly notes the need for inter-societal law. Across areas of British colonisation, inter-societal law was negotiated through treaties to guide future relations. Treaties are constitutional in nature in the sense that they articulate mutually recognised norms for interaction between political communities; they establish constitutional relationships and structures, and shape the relations between settler and Indigenous peoples. Treaties were also a means of expanding empire, as treaty making was seen by Europeans as 'a more legitimate means of acquiring land than were conquest or occupation, and therefore as a way to reconcile expansion with moral and juridical legitimacy'.[74] While the acquisition of land was undoubtedly an important consideration for European powers, many Indigenous–European treaties did not focus on acquiring land, but rather on negotiating jurisdiction and co-existence, including in marine areas. Expanding empire was a central goal, but this could be achieved not only through treaty relationships designed to acquire land, but also through treaty relationships that defined areas of shared and exclusive jurisdiction, and established structures of trade and alliance.

Historical treaties had, and continue to have, important implications for jurisdiction in marine areas. In Canada's present-day Maritime Provinces, 'peace and friendship' treaties were signed throughout the eighteenth century. The treaty of 1726, renewed in several later treaties, was a treaty of peace, ending a conflict between the British and the Mi'kmaq and their Wolastoqiyik and Abenaki allies. The war which preceded the treaty was caused to a large extent by the expansion of New England colonies. While the Abenaki were concerned with the presence of settlers along the rivers in their territories in violation of

[71] Lipman (n 28).

[72] See, eg, Janna Promislow, '"I Smooth'd Him up with Fair Words": Intersocietal Law, from Fur Trade to Treaty', PhD dissertation, Osgoode Hall, 2013.

[73] https://tiritiowaitangi.govt.nz/treaty/translation.pdf.

[74] Saliha Belmessous, 'The Paradox of an Empire by Treaty' in Saliha Belmessous (ed), *Empire by Treaty: Negotiating European Expansion, 1600–1900* (Oxford University Press, 2014) 1.

their seventeenth-century treaties with the British, the Mi'kmaq were concerned that: 'New England fishermen had pushed more aggressively into Nova Scotia's coastal waters than had been true before 1713. For the Mi'kmaq, the fishermen's aggressive actions sparked concerns about possible interference in the fishery.'[75] The year 1713 is of note, as that is the year that, from the British perspective, they acquired sovereignty over the area and rights to the offshore fishery under the Treaty of Utrecht.[76] In the 1726 treaty, the British explicitly sought to have the Treaty of Utrecht recognised by the Indigenous peoples of the region.[77] In doing so, the British agreed that Indigenous 'fishing, hunting, planting and "other lawful activities"' would carry on as before. Nothing was included in the written documents about the nature or scope of these activities. In the 1752 treaty, the British agreed 'that the said Tribe of Indians shall not be hindered from, but have free liberty of Hunting & Fishing as usual'.[78] In the 1760–61 treaty, the Mi'kmaq agreed that 'we will not traffick, barter or Exchange any Commodities in any manner but with such persons or the managers of such Truck houses as shall be appointed or Established by His Majesty's Governor at Lunenbourg or Elsewhere in Nova Scotia or Accadia', a clause interpreted by the Supreme Court as protecting a right to small-scale commercial fisheries.[79] The treaties of peace and friendship clearly contemplate ongoing Indigenous use of marine resources. Though the treaties are silent on foreshore and marine spaces, the Supreme Court has held on several occasions that they do not cede land.[80] Given this, there is a strong case to be made that the Indigenous peoples of the region continue to hold an unextinguished title interest in foreshore areas and, if Canadian law moves to recognise title in marine areas or submerged lands, in those spaces as well.[81]

The Vancouver Island Treaties on Canada's west coast state that the Coast Salish signatories would 'carry on our fisheries as formerly'.[82] Today, many Coast Salish peoples argue that this phrase protects a right to fish in the manner and in the locations used when the treaty was signed. The W̱SÁNEĆ won recognition of these rights at the British Columbia Court of Appeal in 1989. This court held that the treaty right of the W̱SÁNEĆ would be unjustifiably

[75] Wicken (n 36).

[76] William C Wicken, *Mi'kmaq Treaties on Trial: History, Land, and Donald Marshall Jr.* (University of Toronto Press, 2002) 99–118.

[77] ibid.

[78] 'Treaty or Articles of Peace and Friendship Renewed 1752', *Indigenous and Northern Affairs Canada*, https://www.aadnc-aandc.gc.ca/eng/1100100028593/1100100028594.

[79] *R v Marshall* [1999] 3 SCR 456, 1999 CanLII 665 (SCC)

[80] *Simon v The Queen* [1985] 2 SCR 387 [112]; *Marshall* (n 79) 21.

[81] On the strength of a potential title claim in the Maritime provinces, see Robert Hamilton, 'After Tsilhqot'in Nation: The Aboriginal Title Question in Canada's Maritime Provinces' (2016) 67 *University of New Brunswick Law Journal* 58. On title to marine areas in the region, see Douglas JR Moodie, 'Aboriginal Maritime Title in Nova Scotia: An Extravagant and Absurd Idea' (2004) 37 *University of British Columbia Law Review* 495. See also Bankes (ch 6 in this volume).

[82] *Saanichton Marina Ltd v Claxton* (1989) 36 BCLR (2d) 79, 57 DLR (4th) 161 (BCCA) 3.

interfered with should a proposed marina development in the Saanichton Bay go ahead.[83] In doing so, it recognised a property-like interest that preserved the area for W̱SÁNEĆ fishing purposes. In other words, the right to fish was found to have a proprietary element insofar as it protected a right to fish in a particular place. As discussed elsewhere in this volume, a similar fishery was at issue in the US in the Stevens Treaties.[84] A decade before the Vancouver Island treaties were signed, the Treaty of Waitangi was negotiated in Aotearoa/New Zealand.[85] Article 2 of the English version of the Treaty of Waitangi guarantees the Maori 'full exclusive and undisturbed possession of their Lands and Estates Forests Fisheries and other properties'.[86] Interpretation of this clause has led to considerable Maori participation in commercial fisheries in Aotearoa/New Zealand.[87]

In considering the nature of the interests protected in these treaties, phrases such as 'carry on our fisheries as formerly' and 'shall not be hindered from, but have free liberty of Hunting & Fishing as usual' need to be considered in light of the histories of Indigenous and inter-societal law that formed an important part of the context in which the treaties were negotiated. The Indigenous peoples discussed in this chapter were maritime peoples. They had law and modes of tenure regulating the use of resources. In short, they exercised jurisdiction in marine areas. Indigenous parties who were assured that they would not be disturbed in fishing in the same manner and in the same places as they had done before would naturally assume that the broader social structures in which those activities took place would also remain. In other words, is it conceivable that in agreeing that they would continue to fish 'as formerly', Indigenous peoples intended that they should be renouncing all authority to determine the scope of their activities in relation to fisheries, as they had undoubtedly done before, thereby subjecting themselves to overarching Crown authority? None of the varied contexts in which the treaties discussed here were signed suggest such an intention.

What is common in these treaty relationships is the attempt to craft a negotiated structure of inter-societal law to govern the use of territory

[83] ibid.

[84] See Blumm and Jamin (ch 13 in this volume).

[85] The written versions of the Vancouver Island Treaties were in fact templates based on a deed used by the New Zealand Company: Neil Vallance, 'Sharing the Land: The Formation of the Vancouver Island (or "Douglas") Treaties of 1850–1854 in Historical, Legal and Comparative Context', PhD dissertation, Victoria University, 2015, 183–87.

[86] Treaty of Waitangi, art 2, available at https://nzhistory.govt.nz/politics/treaty/read-the-treaty/english-text. There does not appear to be a conflict between the English and Maori versions of the Treaty in respect of this article. See: Report of the Waitangi Tribunal on a Claim by J.P. Hawke and Others of Ngati Whatua Concerning the Fisheries Regulations, Wai 1, 1978, at para 5.

[87] As of 2016, Maori owned approximately 50 per cent of the fishing quota set under New Zealand's Individual Transferable Quota system. Though this is significant, the quota is often leased to non-Maori fishers, with processing and distribution rarely undertaken by Maori companies: Hekia Bodwitch 'Challenges for New Zealand's Individual Transferable Quota System: Processor Consolidation, Fisher Exclusion, & Māori Quota Rights' (2017) 80 *Marine Policy* 88, 88–89.

and resources. The treaty relationship represented a positive negotiated body of inter-societal law, binding as between distinct nations, which dealt with marine spaces and resources. This existed alongside an older body of customary inter-societal law governing these issues. From the time of contact until at least the mid-nineteenth century, the regions examined in this chapter can best be described as legally pluralistic spheres where distinct bodies and systems of law existed in relationships of tension and accommodation while practices of inter-societal law developed and shaped the relations between diverse parties. Only once colonial power sufficiently expanded was it possible for colonies and states to regulate the use of marine spaces and resources, and treat the Indigenous legal traditions and systems of inter-societal law, including treaties, as subject to colonial law. The extension of the specific legal mechanisms used to bring about this regulation relied on European legal traditions and theories for their legitimacy.

## IV. THE LAW OF NATIONS AND THE DOCTRINE OF DISCOVERY IN MARINE AREAS

Despite the multiple legal systems and contested and negotiated forms of authority that prevailed in spheres of imperial activity, European theorists expounded theories of politics and law that ignored this pluralism. Christopher Tomlins reminds us that the development of empire required ways of knowing and understanding the world that could facilitate its expansion; that is, 'empires had an epistemology of their own'.[88] The pernicious myth of Indigenous peoples as lawless and uncivilised was central to this understanding.[89] There were also more nuanced expressions of imperial epistemology. The presumption of European superiority at sea is one telling example. Coastal Algonquians who Europeans encountered in the waters around present-day New York rode in dugout canoes which could average 30 feet in length. Their larger craft were upwards of 60 feet in length and were reported by one European observer to hold as many as 80 men. As Andrew Lipman notes: 'Even if that account was an exaggeration, it is clear that the grandest Native boats had a longer waterline and could hold more people than the smallest European ships that crossed the Atlantic.'[90] The Narragansetts also used sails to power their boats – a practice which early colonists acknowledged pre-dated their arrival.[91] However, these sailing boats have been largely absent from the historical record.

[88] Christopher Tomlins, 'Law's Empire: Chartering English Colonies on the American Mainland in the Seventeenth Century' in Diane Kirkby and Catherine Coleborne (eds), *Law, History, Colonialism: The Reach of Empire* (Manchester University Press, 2001) 27.

[89] See Peter Fitzpatrick, *The Mythology of Modern Law* (Routledge, 1992).

[90] Lipman (n 28) 54.

[91] ibid.

A similar pattern can be seen in cartography, where the historical record often reads as though map making and navigation were the exclusive purview of 'literate' European societies. In fact, the early explorers often relied extensively on Indigenous geographical knowledge, frequently having Indigenous peoples draw maps for them.[92] Lipman notes the role of artistic representations in minimising the extent of Indigenous technologies: 'Artists often use a lazy iconography of dynamic, seaborne Europeans and static, landbound Indians: indigenes stand awestruck on beaches or paddle ahead in tiny craft overwhelmed by looming ships.'[93] Historians have contributed to this misunderstanding by casting Indigenous peoples as primitive, weak and passive.[94] The impact of these representations is not trivial. As Lipman argues: 'If we include confident Native mariners and their hefty boats in our imaginings of early contact, we remember that coastal encounters were formed by two maritime cultures, never just one.'[95] The image of confident mariners from maritime cultures also serves as a reminder of the existence and importance of Indigenous legal traditions in marine areas. The historical imagination which misconstrues the relationship of Indigenous peoples to marine areas and minimises the extent of their technologies serves a present purpose: it reinforces stereotypes of 'backwards' groups of 'scattered' people receding in the face of oncoming European settlement. This image then leads to the circumscription of Indigenous rights in the present day when courts tie contemporary rights to the exercise of specific historical activities.[96]

An imaginative impulse also impacted the way in which prominent European thinkers such as Grotius, Locke, Vattel and Gentili thought about the colonial world and the legal parameters of empire. The theories they developed, collectively now referred to as the 'doctrine of discovery',[97] were central to the imperial epistemology that supported colonisation.[98] First brought into common law courts by Chief Justice John Marshall of the US Supreme Court in 1823, the doctrine of discovery holds that a European nation gained sovereign rights over territory by discovering it. The 'discovering' nation then had the exclusive right

[92] Gascoigne (n 38).

[93] Lipman (n 28) 55. On how artistic representations shaped imperial attitudes towards Indigenous peoples, see Edward Said, *Culture and Imperialism* (Vintage, 1994); Leonard Bell, *Colonial Constructs: European Images of Maori, 1840–1914* (Auckland University Press, 1992).

[94] ibid.

[95] ibid.

[96] See Bradford Morse, 'Permafrost Rights: Aboriginal Self-Government and the Supreme Court in *R v Pamajewon*' (1997) 42 *McGill Law Journal* 1011; Russel L Barsh and James Y Henderson, 'The Supreme Court's *Van der Peet* Trilogy: Naive Imperialism and Ropes of Sand' (1997) 42 *McGill Law Journal* 993.

[97] For an early use of the phrase 'doctrine of discovery', see US Supreme Court Chief Justice John Marshall's decision in *Johnson & Graham's Lessee v McIntosh* (1823) 21 US 543.

[98] See Robert J Miller, Jacinta Ruru, Larissa Behrendt and Tracey Lindberg (eds), *Discovering Indigenous Lands: The Doctrine of Discovery in the English Colonies* (Oxford University Press, 2010).

to acquire the discovered lands from Indigenous inhabitants and those inhabitants retained only a limited form of internal sovereignty.[99] Limiting the political autonomy of Indigenous nations by discovery and asserted sovereignty required the deployment of legal doctrines and categories. Roman law categories such as *res nullius*, for example, described land as *legally* vacant and were deployed in relation to both the land and sea.[100] Where such categories could not be put to use – in Vitoria's view, for example, Indigenous peoples' factual occupation of their territories meant that their property rights had to be respected[101] – theories had to be developed which could render the inhabitants as being without legal rights. The Iberian powers relied on variants of Aquinian just war theory to justify the enslavement and dispossession of Indigenous peoples. The English relied instead on the agriculturalist thesis, which held that property rights could only be held to land under agricultural production, and the civilisational development thesis, which posited that Indigenous peoples were so low on the scale of civilisations that they could not possess or own land.[102] Indigenous peoples were thereby construed as mere 'occupants' and any subsequent right to the land was a mere right of occupancy 'dependent on the goodwill of the sovereign'.[103] While there is an extensive literature dedicated to the doctrines of discovery and *terra nullius* and their impact on Indigenous peoples, it is rarely noted that these same arguments were drawn on to conceptualise the sovereignty, property and jurisdiction in relation to marine areas and resources.

In the seventeenth and eighteenth centuries, debates about marine spaces among European legal thinkers focused specifically on what type of jurisdiction could exist in relation to two distinct areas: the open seas and coastal areas.[104] In his famous early treatment of the law of the sea, *Mare Liberum*, first published in 1609, Hugo Grotius 'refutes the claim of any country to dominion over the seas'.[105] Grotius rejected the notion that a sovereign could hold either *imperium* or *dominium* in the sea. He grounded this partly in a right to free trade under the law of nations and partly by denying that the

[99] *Johnson* (n 97).

[100] It is important to note that the term *terra nullius*, while a highly charged contemporary term, was not explicitly deployed in the service of dispossessing Indigenous peoples until the late nineteenth century: Andrew Fitzmaurice, 'The Genealogy of *Terra Nullius*' [2007] *Australian Historical Studies* 1. Yet, the idea that colonial lands could be categorised as legally vacant – that is, without proprietor – has a much longer history.

[101] Fransiscus de Vitoria, *De Indis et de Ivre Belli Reflectiones*, Ernest Nys (ed), John Pawley (trans) (Carnegie Institution, 1917 [1534]) 120. As Vitoria writes, 'the people in question were in peaceable possession of their goods, both publicly and privately. Therefore, unless the contrary is shown, they must be treated as owners and not be disturbed in their possession unless cause be shown'.

[102] Ken MacMillan, *Sovereignty and Possession in the English New World: The Legal Foundations of Empire 1576–1640* (Cambridge University Press, 2006) 9.

[103] *St Catherine's Milling and Lumber Co v The Queen* (1888) 14 AC 46 (JCPC) 54.

[104] Ivan Shearer, 'Grotius and the Law of the Sea' [1983] *Bulletin of the Australian Society of Legal Philosophy* 46, 50–55.

[105] ibid 49.

conventional justifications for *imperium* and *dominium* could apply to the seas.[106] His reasoning was nuanced in *The Rights of War and Peace*, where he elaborated on the creation of property, arguing that the seas are not 'susceptible of property' because they are boundless and, he supposed, their resources are unlimited. The need for moving from communal to private property, occasioned by the advent of scarcity and the coming together of people in political communities, did not apply in the sea.[107] Regarding lands themselves, including foreshore areas, Grotius anticipated later agriculturalist arguments, contending that 'whatever remains uncultivated, is not to be esteemed Property'.[108] The relation between the reasoning applied to the land and the sea is made explicit. Speaking of the sea, Grotius reiterates scarcity as a governing factor: because marine resources were inexhaustible, conventional justifications for the development of property rights did not apply.[109] Further, Grotius followed Horace in arguing that 'unbounded' lands are defined not as unoccupied per se, but as commonly held lands where there is 'a harvest free for all'.[110] The application of notions of property tied to cultivation, scarcity and determinable bounds to the sea would have a significant impact on Indigenous peoples.

However, Grotius' emphasis on freedom of the seas in *Mare Liberum*, and his somewhat less absolute approach in *The Rights and War and Peace*, did not represent a consensus in the thought of the day. In *Mare Liberum*, he was working to build a legal case for the activities of the Dutch East India Company. Many of the positions he put forward were intensely contested when he acted as a negotiator on the company's behalf.[111] As he himself noted in *Rights of War and Peace,* jurisdiction over seas was recognised at Roman law. Bodin, in his seminal 1582 text expounding on the nature of territorial sovereignty, 'proclaimed that a State might exercise power over shipping within 60 miles of its coast, citing as authority the writings of the Italian jurist Baldus de Urbaldis (1327–1404)'.[112] While in *Mare Liberum* Grotius rejected this, in *The Rights of War and Peace*, he concluded that 'as the several Parts of the Sea came to be known, People sooner or later possessed themselves of some of them to a certain extent'.[113] Grotius seems to have reconciled this divergence by grounding his absolute freedom of the seas in the law of nature, and his more conventional reading, which would seem to admit the possibility of

[106] Hugo Grotius, *The Free Sea*, David Armitage (ed) (Liberty Fund, 2004) 10. See also David Armitage, *The Foundations of Modern International Thought* (Cambridge University Press, 2013) 52–53.

[107] Hugo Grotius, *Rights of War and Peace: in Three Volumes*, Richard Tuck (ed) (Liberty Fund, 2005) 420–30.

[108] ibid 448.

[109] Grotius (n 107) 430 fn 5.

[110] George B Wheeler (ed), *The Works of Horace: The Odes on the Basis of Anthon, The Satires and Epistles by McCaul* (Cumming and Ferguson, 1846) 241.

[111] Shearer (n 104) 50.

[112] ibid.

[113] Grotius (n 107) 432 fn 12.

*imperium* in coastal regions, in the law of *nations*. Further, his most strident critiques in *Mare Liberum* speak not to sovereignty or jurisdiction, but to rights of property.

In 1758, Vattel discussed the issue in his seminal work *The Law of Nations*. Vattel followed Grotius in arguing that whether or not a 'thing' is susceptible of becoming property is determined by its relative scarcity and whether allowing common access does any injury.[114] Vattel writes:

> It is manifest that the use of the open sea, which consists in navigation and fishing, is innocent and inexhaustible; that is to say – he who navigates or fishes in the open sea, does no injury to any one, and the sea, in these two respects, is sufficient for all mankind. Now nature does not give to man a right of appropriating to himself things that may be innocently used, and that are inexhaustible, and sufficient for all.[115]

Again following Grotius, Vattel grounds this in a 'state of nature' analysis, arguing that property needed to be introduced to manage the use of finite resources as people came together in societies.

Important justifications for war follow from this. Because the sea is open to all, preventing one nation from entering waters is justification for the use of force.[116] This recalls Vitoria's just war theory, which held that the use of force could be justified against Indigenous peoples if those peoples violated the freedom of movement and trade of another nation.[117] While every nation has the right to travel and extract resources from the sea, and limitations on that right can justify war, those rights can be renounced. By treaty, Vattel argues, nations can renounce the 'the rights they derive from nature'.[118] This can be seen in practice in the Treaties of Breda and Utrecht, which saw the British and French negotiating exclusive rights to fisheries off the coasts of Nova Scotia and Newfoundland.[119] While they had rights to the resource under the laws of nature, they could, and did, voluntarily renounce those rights.

Regarding the high seas, then, Vattel changed little from Grotius. However, he provides more clarity in respect of the coastal areas. For Vattel: 'The various uses of the sea near the coasts render it very susceptible of property.'[120] The reasoning for this draws heavily on the availability of resources. Many of the resources in coastal areas, which for Vattel include 'fish, shells, pearls, amber, &c', are 'not inexhaustible'.[121] Because these resources are limited, they may come under the *dominium* of the nation whose territory they abut. Thus, where

[114] Emer de Vattel, *The Law of Nations*, Béla Kapossy (ed) (Liberty Fund, 2008) 249 §281.
[115] ibid.
[116] ibid.
[117] Vitoria (n 101).
[118] Vattel (n 114) 251 §284.
[119] Dale Miquelon, 'Envisioning the French Empire: Utrecht, 1711–1713' (2001) 24 *French Historical Studies* 653, 654.
[120] Vattel (n 114) 252 §287.
[121] ibid.

a nation appropriates those resources, it may hold them 'in the same manner as they possessed themselves of the dominion of the land they inhabit'.[122] In setting out a clear limit on the basis of these principles, Vattel concluded that 'the dominion of the state over the neighbouring sea extends as far as her safety renders it necessary and her power is able to assert it'.[123] Further: 'The shores of the sea incontestably belong to the nation that possesses the country of which they are a part.'[124]

The acquisition of territorial sovereignty on land thus became a precondition for the acquisition of sovereign rights over the coastal areas up to the distance recognised at a given time under the law of nations. The impact on Indigenous rights in marine areas is clear. Where European law espouses a strict freedom of the seas approach such as that articulated in *Mare Liberum*, which would prohibit *imperium* or *dominium* in both the high seas and coastal waters, Indigenous legal traditions that regulate marine areas and resources are ignored. However, the more prominent position from at least the mid-eighteenth century onwards was that coastal areas and the resources they provided could be under the control or ownership of the adjacent sovereign or state. While not subject to individual property rights, foreshore and coastal areas could be under the *dominium* of the sovereign or the *imperium* of the sovereign and state. This later articulation would seem on its surface to provide room for Indigenous laws in relation to marine spaces. Applying the same standards used by European nations to Indigenous nations would, after all, result in Indigenous control of coastal areas and 'not inexhaustible' resources. In other words, even without asking what Indigenous peoples' own laws might say, the equal application of European law would recognise Indigenous rights of ownership where Indigenous peoples held adjacent territories. Yet, as we know, European law was not applied equally. Indigenous peoples were excluded from Eurocentric forms of 'international' law which denied their sovereignty. Racist legal fictions such as the doctrine of discovery and *terra nullius* extended the 'sovereignty' of nascent nation-states over vast territories populated primarily by Indigenous peoples. Territorial sovereignty being a condition precedent to sovereign rights in coastal areas, denying Indigenous territorial sovereignty had the effect of excising Indigenous jurisdiction from marine spaces as well.

Indigenous peoples were thus deprived of both jurisdiction and property in marine areas. 'Discovery' obviated their jurisdiction, and the European view that the sea could not be the subject of proprietary interests undermined their traditional forms of tenure. As Nonie Sharp writes, 'in the eye of the colonizer, the marine domain was, unlike land, unownable space. The freedom to fish, enshrined in English common law, brought saltwater industries to the

[122] ibid.
[123] ibid 254 §289.
[124] ibid 255 §290.

tropical coasts. And it did so in the belief that the territorial seas are open to everyone'.[125] Allan Greer, writing of land, but equally applicable to marine spaces, notes that 'natives were dispossessed as much by the settler commons as by any sort of colonial version of the Enclosure movement'.[126] Once sovereignty was asserted, the imposition of European law followed. Communal free use rather than individual ownership became the rule among settlers. However, much as with land, control over the seas in imperial theatres was often only theoretical. As Guy Chet notes in his history of piracy in the Atlantic, it was not until well into the nineteenth century that piracy was effectively curtailed.[127] Imperial and colonial law and authority did not extend evenly through those spaces until then. As on land, jurisdiction was extended not by the assertion of sovereignty, but gradually by the extension of specific legal mechanisms.[128]

An early example presaged what was to come in later decades and centuries. The Innu are an Algonquian people whose historical territory included the eastern reaches of the vast St Lawrence River, particularly along its northern shores and watershed. They moved seasonally, following fish and game to different locations in their territory. In the spring and summer months, they tended towards large congregations in important fishing locations. One such location was an eel fishing location at Kâ Mihkwâwahkâšič. Beginning in the late 1620s, the Company of New France began to grant seigneurial title to colonists along the St Lawrence, with the company itself acting as chief seigneur and claiming feudal title to much of North America.[129] Meanwhile, Jesuit missionaries were working to exert control over the Innu. They received a grant at Kâ Mihkwâwahkâšič, which they named Sillery. While the Innu continued to use the location seasonally and some accepted baptism, French settlers also began to settle in the location by the 1640s. While the settlers' use of land did not in itself disrupt the Innu, their interest in the eel fishery did.[130] The eel fishery proved highly profitable, and in 1646 the Jesuits recorded that the settlers pulled 40,000 eels from the river that year. Though the stock of eels remained plentiful, the fishing locations became scarce. The Innu had developed a weir fishing system that worked according to the flows and tides of the river at Kâ Mihkwâwahkâšič. Other locations were simply not suitable to the weir fishery. The colonists adopted this fishing technology and the locations where it worked.

[125] Sharp (n 25) 46.
[126] Greer (n 39) 4.
[127] Guy Chet, *The Ocean is a Wilderness: Atlantic Piracy and the Limits of State Authority, 1688–1856* (University of Massachusetts Press, 2014) 14, 33.
[128] For an analysis of this process in relation to land, see Lisa Ford, *Settler Sovereignty: Jurisdiction and Indigenous People in America and Australia 1788–1836* (Harvard University Press, 2011).
[129] Greer (n 39) 75.
[130] ibid 76.

The Company of New France was anxious to capitalise on the profitability of the fishery. To this end, 'the company therefore began charging rent for the use of the foreshore, invoking feudal law that accorded control over the shore between high tide and low tide marks to the superior seigneur, regardless of any grants to adjoining land'.[131] Annual rents were charged in barrels of eels. Though the Innu were exempt from the seigneurial rents, the physical dislocation caused by the settler fishery was severe. By 1650, when the Innu arrived to set traps, the 'tenants threw rocks at them and chased them away'.[132] Though the Jesuits would secure royal intervention on behalf of the Innu, their ongoing fishing now took place under the supervision of zealous missionaries. This proved intolerable for the Innu, who moved on, completing the dispossession of important fishing grounds that provided winter sustenance in the form of smoked eels.[133] This example illustrates the way in which the presumption of sovereignty led to the imposition of specific legal mechanisms that dispossessed Indigenous peoples. The authority of the French to create seigneurial tenures and demand rent for the use of foreshore required first the assertion of sovereign authority. Similarly, French law also allowed for unfettered communal access to the fishery itself. To the extent that the imposition of specific French laws to the Innu was questioned, the authority to make law to control activity in that space was not. While the French were willing to recognise special Innu rights to the fishery, the authority to determine the scope and ambit of those rights through French law was never questioned. The tension between regulation and the recognition of special rights in the eel fishery at Kâ Mihkwâwahkâšič in the mid-seventeenth century anticipates both later regulatory regimes, which limited Indigenous access to marine resources, and contemporary rights regimes that emerged in common law countries in response to these limitations.

## V. THE RIGHTS PARADIGM

Indigenous control over seabed, foreshore and marine resources in common law states has come to be assessed on the basis of domestic rights paradigms. Indigenous claims regarding the use of marine spaces and resources in the jurisdictions discussed in this chapter are of two types: (1) claims to Indigenous or treaty rights to fish or use marine resources; and (2) claims for the application of common law Aboriginal title to seabed and foreshore areas. The latter seems to hold the most promise for Indigenous peoples insofar as Aboriginal title provides for the 'exclusive use and occupation' of title areas,[134] which would result in a fuller 'basket' of rights than site and/or species-specific harvesting rights.

131 ibid 77.

132 ibid.

133 ibid 78–81.

134 See, eg, *Tsilhqot'in Nation v British Columbia* [2014] SCC 44.

However, both of these approaches face the fundamental problem that they ultimately rely on the doctrine of discovery and the unilateral imposition of Crown sovereignty. The result has played out differently across common law jurisdictions. These are covered in detail in other chapters in this volume.[135] Importantly for the purposes of this chapter, across jurisdictions the rights at issue are subject to considerable limitations, including the possibility of unilateral state infringement. In all cases, title rights are property rights that sit atop 'radical' Crown title, minimising the jurisdictional aspect of the Indigenous interest.[136] Commercial rights tend to be quite constrained.[137] Rights are assessed by colonial courts and tend to aim at sustenance and cultural purposes.[138] The exercise of rights is always subject to ongoing regulation.[139]

These limitations are perhaps most clear in a series of decisions regarding title to the seabed in the American context. In 1998 and 2002, five Alaska Native villages claimed that government fishing regulations which imposed fish quotas and closed halibut and sablefish fisheries for part of the year 'violated their fishing rights based on aboriginal title to areas of the Gulf of Alaska'.[140] In those cases, the Ninth Circuit Court of Appeals and the District Court for the District of Alaska 'held that the paramountcy doctrine had extinguished the villages' rights'[141] – in other words, Aboriginal title to the seabed was considered 'incompatible with federal sovereignty over those areas'.[142] This reasoning concerning the incommensurability of sovereignty and Aboriginal title is clearly at odds with Aboriginal title jurisprudence in the common law world. As David Bloch writes:

> *Native Village of Eyak v. Trawler Diane Marie, Inc. (Eyak)* repudiates the underlying principle of federal Indian law – that the federal government's sovereignty is subject to a tribe's right of occupancy of land to which it holds aboriginal title and that such title survives unless Congress extinguishes it clearly – in favor of a view of aboriginal title never before countenanced in the United States and long discredited in common law jurisdictions which once entertained it – that pre-existing rights will be deemed extinguished by the mere assertion of sovereignty over the area to which they pertain until their formal recognition by an act of state.[143]

[135] See the Introduction as well as the chapters by Bankes (ch 6), Erueti (ch 10), Godden (ch 5) and Blumm and Jamin (ch 13) in this volume.

[136] Jacinta Ruru, 'Lenses of Comparison across Continents: Understanding Modern Aboriginal Title in *Tsilhqot'in Nation* and *Ngati Apa*' (2015) 34 *University of British Columbia Law Review* 903, 905; Williams Jr (n 8) 126.

[137] *R v Marshall* (n 79).

[138] See, eg, *R v Sparrow* [1990] 1 SC R 1075, 1099.

[139] *R v Marshall* (n 79).

[140] Andrew P Richards, 'Aboriginal Title or the Paramountcy Doctrine: *Johnson v. Mcintosh* Flounders in Federal Waters off Alaska in *Native Village of Eyak v. Trawler Diane Marie, Inc.*' (2003) 78 *Washington Law Review* 939, 940–41.

[141] ibid.

[142] ibid.

[143] David J Bloch, 'Colonizing the Last Frontier' (2003) 29 *American Indian Law Review* 1, 3.

This is the clearest example of the power that assertions of sovereignty continue to have on the rights of Indigenous peoples. While in most instances sovereignty fades into the background as the unquestioned basis for 'underlying title and legislative power',[144] in this instance sovereignty was held to have extinguished title to the seabed.

Even where rights regimes are more amenable to Indigenous claims, they often fail to adequately address Indigenous concerns about their use of marine spaces and resources. This is due in large part to the fact that common law countries have tried to wedge claims for Indigenous jurisdiction into a rights paradigm.[145] Indigenous peoples use litigation as a means of asserting control of spaces and resources according to their own legal regimes; that is, they assert jurisdiction and contest the nature of their constitutional relationship with the state. Contemporary rights regimes obscure the bodies of Indigenous and inter-societal law outlined above by framing Indigenous claims as claims to engage in discrete activities. In doing so, contested constitutional relationships are treated as discrete rights claims from a cultural minority. The question of Indigenous *peoples'* place in the constitutional framework is bypassed. But, as Kiera Ladner argues, 'Indigenous people are now engaging in jurisdictional debates (often perceived as "rights" debates) in an attempt to challenge the Canadian constitutional order and Crown sovereignty and, most importantly, to re-affirm their own constitutional order and autonomy'.[146] As Eddie Mabo Jr writes, 'the legal system of this country remains blind to a concept of a sovereignty enjoyed by Aboriginal and Torres Strait Islander groups prior to European invasion'. Further:

> The Australian High Court recognised native title as arising from a prior Aboriginal title to land and waters, but its decision stopped well short of recognising our sovereignty. In fact it stopped well short of recognising the kind of land and sea tenure that is consistent with the concepts of property that we know all too well.[147]

Insofar as contemporary rights regimes consider Indigenous law, they do so not to establish or recognise Indigenous jurisdiction; instead, they tend to emphasise rights to engage in specific activities (eg, hunting or fishing). Though common law Aboriginal title has a 'public law' dimension, it is, in the rare cases that it can be established, construed more frequently as a proprietary interest. To support this vision of aboriginal rights within structures of state jurisdiction and authority, common law courts' historical gaze requires that the complex and contested jurisdictional aspects of marine spaces in the imperial period be re-arranged to reflect stories associated with sovereignty put forward by European thinkers

[144] *Sparrow* (n 138) 1103.

[145] Kiera L Ladner, 'Up the Creek: Fishing for a New Constitutional Order' (2005) 38(4) *Canadian Journal of Political Science* 923, 924.

[146] ibid.

[147] Mabo Jr (n 11) 99.

such as Vattel. In other words, the rejection of Indigenous jurisdiction and the limitation of Indigenous rights to discrete activities require the application of a theoretical understanding of sovereignty which is at odds with historical practice in colonial theatres, but aligns with a body of European theory now widely understood as deeply discriminatory. Re-assessing the earlier colonial period in a way that reflects earlier understandings of Indigenous and inter-societal law thus becomes an important tool in critiquing contemporary doctrine.

## VI. CONCLUSION: ON JURISDICTION AND PLURALISM

There is an important distinction to be drawn between descriptive accounts of legal pluralism and normative accounts.[148] What has been said to this point is the former. This chapter has illustrated in an abbreviated way the historical *fact* of legal pluralism in relation to marine spaces and resources. From this, it has attempted to show how Eurocentric theories and law laid the foundations for the erasure of that pluralism. However, as Indigenous peoples have been consistently arguing for centuries, that erasure, though severe, was never complete. Indigenous legal traditions and traditions of inter-societal law have survived attempts to impose a unilateral constitutional vision. Thus, quite apart from normative justifications for the contemporary recognition of pluralism, we remain faced with the fact of pluralism. Quoting Eddie Mabo Jr again, as the common law loosens its grip on Indigenous peoples: 'A diverse range of Indigenous jurisdictions will emerge, a united yet diverse range of jurisdictions which cannot be washed away by any tide of history.'[149] This chapter has argued that contemporary state law and common law will struggle to make this transition if they remain tied to a narrow legal heritage which obscures the historical relationship between the parties and the rich legal pluralism that characterised those relationships.

[148] See Paul Schiff Berman, *Global Legal Pluralism: A Jurisprudence of Law Beyond Borders* (Cambridge University Press, 2014)

[149] Mabo Jr (n 11) 100.

# Part II

# International Dimensions

# 2

# *International Human Rights Law and the Rights of Indigenous Peoples in Relation to Marine Space and Resources*

ENDALEW LIJALEM ENYEW

## I. INTRODUCTION

As THE INTRODUCTION to this volume demonstrates, Indigenous peoples have developed a strong relationship with their traditional lands, territories and natural resources, including marine areas and marine living resources (MLRs). The seas and the oceans not only provide a vital source of food and economic security for Indigenous peoples living along coastlines, but also shape their cultural identity and spiritual values.[1] To put it simply, the use of ocean space and MLRs are indispensable for the continued existence of coastal Indigenous peoples as culturally distinct peoples.[2] This chapter explores the extent to which international human rights law recognises Indigenous peoples' customary rights to the marine space and associated resources through an assessment of the general and Indigenous-specific human rights instruments, relevant case law and practices of treaty-monitoring bodies. Section II establishes that human rights law applies equally to marine areas as well as land territory. Section III examines some specific human rights norms relating to traditional 'lands' and 'natural resources', and considers how they might apply to the recognition and protection of the customary rights

[1] C Smith and M Dodson, 'Report on Indigenous Fishing Rights in the Seas with Case Studies from Australia and Norway', *Permanent Forum on Indigenous Issues*, UN Doc E/C 19/2010/2 (New York, 2010) 3.

[2] V Toki, 'Study on the Relationship between Indigenous peoples and the Pacific Ocean', *Permanent Forum on Indigenous Issues*, UN Doc E/C 19/2016/3 (New York, 2016) [4].

of Indigenous peoples to marine areas and the associated MLRs. Section IV provides concluding remarks.

## II. APPLICABILITY OF HUMAN RIGHTS LAW TO MARINE SPACE

The territorial scope of a treaty is determined by the parties to the treaty. Some human rights treaties contain a separate provision dealing with their spatial scope of application. Article 2(1) of the International Covenant on Civil and Political Rights (ICCPR) stipulates that: 'Each State party … undertakes to respect and to ensure [the rights contained in the convention] to all individuals *within its territory and subject to its jurisdiction*'.[3] The European Convention on Human Rights (ECHR) and the American Convention on Human Rights (ACHR) similarly apply to all persons '*"within" or "subject" to the [states parties'] jurisdiction*'.[4] The ordinary meaning of the italicised terms unequivocally confirm that these treaties apply within the parties' national territorial limits.[5] With respect to 'freestanding' treaties – treaties that do not contain a territorial scope clause[6] – Article 29 of the Vienna Convention on the Law of Treaties (VCLT) provides a general rule regarding their spatial scope of application. It provides that '*unless a different intention appears from the treaty or is otherwise established*, a treaty is binding upon each party in respect of *its entire territory*' (emphasis added).[7] The territorial limits of a coastal/archipelagic state include its internal waters, the territorial sea and

[3] International Covenant on Civil and Political Rights, concluded at New York on 16 December 1966, 999 UNTS 171 (entered into force 23 March 1976), art 2(1).

[4] European Convention on Human Rights, signed at Rome, on 4 November 1950, 213 UNTS 2 (entered into force 3 September 1953), art 1; and American Convention on Human Rights, signed at San Jose on 22 November 1969, 1144 UNTS 143 (entered into force 18 July 1978), art 1(1).

[5] See HRC, *General Comment No 31, 'The Nature of the General Legal Obligation Imposed on States Parties to the Covenant'*, CCPR/C/21/Rev 1/Add 13 (2004); *Issa and Others v Turkey*, ECtHR (Judgment) [2004]; *Case Concerning Armed Activities on the Territory of the Congo (Democratic Republic of the Congo v Uganda)* Judgment [2005] ICJ Rep 168.

[6] For example, the following human rights instruments do not contain any specific provision dealing with their territorial scope of application: International Covenant on Economic, Social, and Cultural Rights, concluded at New York on 16 December 1966, 993 UNTS 3 (entered into force 3 January 1976); International Convention on the Elimination of All Forms of Racial Discrimination (CERD Convention), concluded at New York on 21 December 1965, 660 UNTS 195 (entered into force 4 January 1969); African (Banjul) Charter on Human and Peoples' Rights, concluded at Nairobi on 27 June 1981, 1520 UNTS 217 (entered into force 21 October 1986); ILO Convention on Indigenous and Tribal Peoples in Independent Countries, concluded at Geneva on 27 June 1989, 1650 UNTS 383 (entered into force 5 September 1991); and United Nations Declaration on the Rights of Indigenous Peoples, UNGA Res 61/295 (13 September 2007).

[7] Vienna Convention on the Law of Treaties, concluded at Vienna on 23 May 1969, 1155 UNTS 331 (entered into force 27 January 1980) art 29. For a detailed commentary on art 29 VCLT, see ME Villiger, *Commentary on the 1969 Vienna Convention on the Law of Treaties* (Martinus Nijhoff Publishers, 2009) 392–93.

archipelagic waters.[8] This means that human rights law applies within these maritime zones in the same manner as land territories.

However, the term 'jurisdiction' has a broader meaning. It includes the exercise of authority or effective control over an area or persons.[9] Thus, human rights law also applies within maritime zones beyond a state's territorial limit within which a state exercises jurisdiction, ie, within the exclusive economic zone (EEZ) and on the high seas, based on the principle of 'extraterritorial application of human rights law'.[10]

Sufficient judicial authority also exists to support the application of human rights law to marine space. For example, in *Women on Waves and Others v Portugal*, the European Court of Human Rights (ECtHR) found Portugal to be in violation of the freedom of expression recognised under Article 10 ECHR by banning the applicants (employees of a Dutch non-governmental organisation (NGO)) from conducting an awareness campaign on family planning and sexual health issues aboard their own vessel (*Borndiep*) in Portugal's territorial sea.[11] Similarly, in *Medvedyev and Others v France*[12] (where French authorities, with the consent of Cambodia, interdicted and boarded a Cambodian vessel (*the Winner*) suspected of drug smuggling off the coast of Cap Verde) and *Hirsi Jamaa and Others v Italy*[13] (where Italy intercepted migrants traveling from Libya on the high seas), the ECtHR found France and Italy to be in violation of their human rights obligations under the ECHR.

In conclusion, human rights law applies both on the land and marine territories where a state has sovereignty or exercises 'jurisdiction'. This is consistent with the universal character of human rights, whereby all states are bound 'to promote universal respect for, and observance of, human rights and freedoms'[14]

[8] United Nations Convention on the Law of the Sea, concluded at Montego Bay, on 10 December 1982, 1833 UNTS 3 (entered into force 16 November 1994), arts 2(1) and 49.

[9] See HRC (n 5) [10]; *Al-Skeini and Others v United Kingdom*, ECtHR (Judgment) [2011] [130]–[150]; and *Legal Consequences of the Constraction of a Wall in the Occupied Palestinian Territory* (Advisory Opinion) [2004] ICJ Rep 136.

[10] See D Guilfoyle, 'Human Rights Issues and Non-flag State Boarding of Suspect Ships in International Waters' in CR Symmons (ed), *Selected Contemporary Issues in the Law of the Sea* (Martinus Nijhoff Publishers, 2011). For a general discussion of the extraterritorial application of human rights law, see R Wilde, 'Human Rights beyond Borders at the World Court: The Significance of the International Court of Justice's Jurisprudence on the Extraterritorial Application of International Human Rights Law Treaties' (2013) 12 *Chinese Journal of International Law* 639; and T Meron, 'Extraterritoriality of Human Rights Treaties' (1995) 89 *American Journal of International Law* 78.

[11] *Women on Waves and Others v Portugal*, ECtHR (Judgment) [2009] (in French language only). For a discussion of the case, see T Treves, 'Human Rights and the Law of the Sea' (2010) 28 *Berkeley Journal of International Law* 1, 10–11.

[12] *Medvedyev and Others v France*, ECtHR (Judgment) [2010] (see in particular [64] and [67]).

[13] *Hirsi Jamaa and Others v Italy*, ECtHR (Judgment) [2012] (see in particular [74], [77], [81]–[84], [219(3)]).

[14] UN Charter, art 1(3); ICCPR, preamble, recital 4; ICESCR, preamble, recital 4; ECHR, preamble, recital 2.

without being 'parceled off by territory on the checkerboard of geography'.[15] This general proposition of applicability applies to all peoples, including Indigenous peoples. Thus, a coastal state is duty bound to respect the human rights of Indigenous peoples falling under its territory or jurisdiction.

## III. HUMAN RIGHTS NORMS RELEVANT TO INDIGENOUS PEOPLES' RIGHTS TO MARINE SPACE AND MARINE RESOURCES

This section examines specific norms of international human rights law relevant to the rights of Indigenous peoples to marine space and marine resources. These norms include the right to self-determination, the right to culture, the right to property, the right to non-discrimination and the right to consultation.

### A. The Right to Self-Determination: An Overarching Right to the Governance of Marine Space and Resources

The right to self-determination is a collective right of peoples. It is recognised in various general global and regional human rights instruments, including Article 1(2) of the UN Charter, common Article 1 of the ICCPR and the International Covenant on Economic, Social, and Cultural Rights (ICESCR) (the twin human rights conventions),[16] and Articles 20–21 of the African Charter on Human and Peoples' Rights (ACHPR).[17] Though initially conceptualised to apply only to peoples under colonial domination or to the 'aggregate populations' of a state,[18] the right to self-determination has evolved over time to accommodate the contemporary needs of Indigenous peoples.[19] In recent decades, treaty-monitoring bodies and human rights courts have accepted Indigenous peoples as 'peoples' entitled to the right to self-determination,[20] and this is confirmed by the recently adopted Indigenous-specific human rights instruments, such as the United Nations Declaration on the Rights of Indigenous Peoples (UNDRIP)[21] and the American Declaration on the Rights

[15] Concurring opinion of Judge Bonello in *Al-Skeini and Others* (n 9) [9].

[16] Common Article 1(1) of the ICCPR and the ICESCR provides that: 'All peoples have the right of self-determination. By virtue of that right they freely determine their political status and freely pursue their economic, social and cultural development.'

[17] The ECHR and the ACHR do not contain a provision dealing with the right to self-determination.

[18] K Knop, *Diversity and Self-Determination in International Law* (Cambridge University Press, 2002) 58.

[19] A Farmer, 'Towards a Meaningful Rebirth of Economic Self-Determination: Human Rights Realization in Resource-Rich Countries' (2006) 39 *Journal of International Law and Politics* 417, 440.

[20] The details of the treaty bodies' practices are discussed below in connection with the right to economic self-determination in order to avoid repetition.

[21] UNDRIP (n 6).

of Indigenous Peoples (ADRIP).[22] Both instruments recognise that self-determination may have an internal aspect in the context of Indigenous peoples, ie, the exercise of autonomy or self-government in matters relating to internal and local affairs, including political, social, cultural and economic aspects.[23]

The economic dimension of the right to self-determination is of paramount importance in the present context. Common Article 1(2) of the ICCPR and the ICESCR provides that: 'All peoples may, for their own ends, freely dispose of their natural wealth and resources … In no case may a people be deprived of its own means of subsistence.'[24] Article 25 of the ICESCR and Article 47 of the ICCPR in identical wording re-affirm this right, stating that: 'Nothing in the present Covenant[s] shall be interpreted as impairing the inherent right of all peoples to enjoy and utilize fully and freely their natural wealth and resources.'[25] The ACHPR similarly provides that 'all peoples shall freely dispose of their wealth and natural resources. This right shall be exercised in the exclusive interest of the people. In no case shall a people be deprived of it'.[26] These general human rights instruments recognise the right to dispose of natural resources as an inalienable and absolute right of all peoples. They affirm that peoples are the sole beneficiaries of exploitation of natural resources and have decision-making powers as to how such resources should be utilised.[27]

Treaty-monitoring bodies have applied the right to dispose freely of natural resources in the specific contexts of Indigenous peoples. Even though the Human Rights Committee (HRC) does not have jurisdiction to consider the right to economic self-determination under its complaint procedure, it has endorsed this right in its concluding observations in a number of cases.[28] Likewise, the Committee on Economic Social and Cultural Rights (CESCR)

[22] American Declaration on the Rights of Indigenous Peoples, AG/Res 2888 (XLVI-O/16), (15 June 2016). While ILO Convention 169 does not contain express provision on the right to self-determination, the UNDRIP and the ADRIP expressly recognise the right to self-determination of Indigenous peoples under common art 3.

[23] UNDRIP, arts 4 and 46; ADRIP, arts 4 and 21(1). For a general discussion of the scope of internal self-determination of Indigenous peoples, see J Anaya, 'The Right of Indigenous Peoples to Self-Determination in the Post-Declaration Era' in C Charters and R Stavenhagen (eds), *Making the Declaration Work: The UN Declaration on the Rights of Indigenous Peoples* (Copenhagen, IWGIA, 2009); M Åhrén, *Indigenous Peoples' Status in the International Legal System* (Oxford University Press, 2016).

[24] ICCPR and ICESCR, art 1(2).

[25] ICCPR, art 47; ICESCR, art 25.

[26] ACHPR, art 21.

[27] NJ Schrijver, *Sovereignty over Natural Resources: Balancing Rights and Duties* (Cambridge University Press, 1997) 36.

[28] See, eg, HRC, *Concluding Observation: Norway*, UN Doc CCPR/C/79/Add 112 (1999) [17]; HRC, *Concluding Observation: Sweden*, UN Doc CCPR/CO/74/SWE (2002) [15]; HRC, *Concluding Observation: Canada*, UN Doc CCPR/C/79/Add.105 (1999) [8]; HRC, *Concluding Observation: United States of America*, UN Doc CCPR/C/USA/CO/3/Rev.1 (2006) [37]; HRC, *Concluding Observation: Mexico*, UN Doc CCPR/C/MEX/CO/5 (2010) [22]; HRC, *Concluding Observation: Chile*, UN Doc CCPR/C/CHL/CO/5 (2007) [19]; and HRC, *Concluding Observation: Australia*, UN Doc A/55/40, vol I (2000) [506] and [507].

has evolutively interpreted[29] Article 1(2) of the ICESCR to embrace Indigenous peoples' right to own their lands and to freely dispose of their natural resources.[30] The African Commission on Human and Peoples Rights (AfComHPR) in *Endorois v Kenya*[31] and the African Court of Human and Peoples' Rights (ACtHPR) in *African Commission on Human and Peoples' Rights v Kenya*[32] have applied Article 21 of the African Charter to the Endorois and Ogiek Indigenous peoples respectively. These bodies clearly recognise the right of Indigenous peoples to freely dispose of their natural resources 'for their own ends', including to fulfil their means of subsistence, as their inherent right. They have adapted the general right of economic self-determination to the specific situations of Indigenous peoples' relationship to traditional lands and natural resources.[33]

This right applies equally to Indigenous peoples' rights to marine areas and MLRs. While none of these human rights instruments defines the term 'natural resources', the term is broad and its ordinary meaning must extend to marine natural resources. Thus, the right to economic self-determination entitles Indigenous peoples to own or possess certain marine areas, which they occupy or use as part of their traditional territories, or to harvest the associated MLRs including marine mammals, on a non-exclusive basis to satisfy their subsistence needs.[34] The right also entitles Indigenous peoples to actively participate in the conservation and management of marine resources.

### B. Access to Marine Areas and Harvesting of MLRs as a Cultural Right

The right to culture is a widely recognised human right incorporated in various instruments. Article 15(1) of the ICESCR recognises the right of 'everyone to take part in the cultural life of [the community]'.[35] Article 27 of the ICCPR

[29] The principle of 'evolutive' or 'dynamic' interpretation of a treaty requires a treaty to be interpreted not only in the light of the circumstances prevailing at the time of its conclusion, but also in the light of subsequent factual and legal developments. For a detailed discussion of the concept of evolutive interpretation, see J Arato, 'Subsequent Practice and Evolutive Interpretation: Techniques of Treaty Interpretation over Time and Their Diverse Consequences' (2010) 9 *The Law and Practice of International Courts and Tribunals* 443.

[30] See, eg, CESCR, *Concluding Observation: Finland*, UN Doc E/C 12/FIN/CO/6 (2014) [9(a)]; CESCR, *Concluding Observation: Paraguay*, UN Doc E/C.12/PRY/CO/4 (2015) [6]; CESCR, *Concluding Observation: Chile*, UN Doc E/C.12/CHL/CO/4 (2015) [8].

[31] *Endorois Welfare Council v Republic of Kenya*, AfComHPR [2009] [268].

[32] *African Commission on Human and Peoples' Rights v Republic of Kenya* (Judgment) ACtHPR [2017] [201] and [227].

[33] For a detailed discussion, see EL Enyew, 'Application of the Right to Permanent Sovereignty over Natural Resources for Indigenous Peoples: Assessment of Current Legal Developments' (2017) 8 *Arctic Review on Law and Politics* 222.

[34] For a discussion of the rights of Indigenous peoples to harvest marine mammals, particularly of whales and seals, see Fitzmaurice (ch 3 in this volume).

[35] ICESCR, art 15(1)(a). Article 27(1) of the Universal Declaration of Human Rights (UDHR) stipulates similar provision.

provides that persons belonging to minorities 'shall not be denied the right, in community with the other members of their group, to enjoy their own culture'.[36] The International Convention on the Elimination of All Forms of Racial Discrimination (hereinafter the CERD Convention) similarly recognises the right of everyone 'to equal participation in cultural activities', affirming that all cultures deserve equal recognition and protection as they have equal value and no culture is superior to another.[37] Of the general regional human rights instruments,[38] the ACHPR recognises the right of every individual to freely take part in the cultural life of his community.[39] These provisions have all been evolutively interpreted and applied by their respective treaty-monitoring bodies and human rights courts to recognise and protect the cultures of Indigenous peoples.[40] These bodies have also recognised that the individual right to culture also has a collective dimension in the context of minorities and Indigenous peoples.

The human rights instruments specific to Indigenous peoples also reference the protection of the cultures, traditions and worldviews of Indigenous peoples. For example, the ILO Convention on Indigenous and Tribal Peoples in Independent Countries (hereinafter ILO Convention 169) imposes an obligation on states to take measures for 'promoting the full realization of the social, economic and cultural rights of [Indigenous] peoples with respect for their social and cultural identity, their customs and traditions and their institutions'.[41] The UNDRIP similarly recognises the right to culture of Indigenous peoples in all its manifestations, including the 'right to maintain, control, protect and develop their cultural heritage, traditional knowledge and traditional cultural expressions'.[42]

Of the many manifestation of Indigenous peoples' culture, the material basis of culture is the most important here. The HRC has offered a broad interpretation of culture as used in Article 27 of the ICCPR in its General Comment No 23:

> [C]*ulture manifests itself in many forms*, including a particular way of life associated with *the use of land resources, especially in the case of Indigenous peoples.*

[36] ICCPR, art 27.

[37] CERD Convention, art 5(e)(vi).

[38] The ACHR and the ECHR do not expressly recognise the right to culture. In relation to Indigenous peoples, the Inter-American Commission and Court of Human Rights have protected the right to culture implicitly in connection with other rights, most importantly the right to property over their traditional lands. The European Court of Human Rights (ECtHR) has not been as proactive. For detailed discussion of this, see B Saul, *Indigenous Peoples and Human Rights: International and Regional Jurisprudence* (Hart Publishing, 2016).

[39] ACHPR, arts 17 and 22.

[40] See, eg, HRC, *General Comment No 23(50)*, UN Doc CCPR/C/21/Rev.1/Add.5 (1994); CESCR, *General Comment 21: Right of Everyone to Take Part in Cultural Life* (art 15, para 1(a) of the International Covenant on Economic, Social and Cultural Rights), UN Doc E/C.12/GC/21 (21 December 2009); *Endorois* (n 31); and *African Commission on Human and Peoples' Rights v Republic of Kenya* (n 32).

[41] ILO Convention 169, art 2(2)(b). See also arts 4(2), 5, 7, 13 and 23.

[42] UNDRIP, arts 15 and 31.

> That right may include such *traditional activities as fishing or hunting* and the right to live in reserves protected by law. (Emphasis added)[43]

The HRC has applied this understanding of culture in a number of cases dealing with Indigenous communities under Article 27.[44] The CESCR has taken a similar approach in its interpretation of Article 15(1)(a) of the ICESCR. The Committee has affirmed that 'the strong communal dimension of Indigenous peoples' cultural life ... includes the right to the lands, territories and resources which they have traditionally owned, occupied or otherwise used or acquired'.[45] At the regional level, the African human rights system has affirmed the critical importance of ancestral lands and traditionally used natural resources for the cultural survival of Indigenous communities. In *Endorois*, the AfComHPR interpreted culture under Article 17(2) and (3) broadly to include 'a spiritual and physical association with one's ancestral land, knowledge, belief ... customs, and any other capabilities and habits acquired ... as a member of a distinct society'.[46] The Commission, then, found Kenya to be in violation of the cultural rights of the Endorois because its measures 'denied the community access to an integrated system of beliefs, values, norms, mores, traditions and artifacts closely linked to access to the Lake [Bogoria]'.[47] Building on the Commission's finding in *Endorois*, the African Court on Human and Peoples' Rights has recently joined this consensus in affirming the material foundation of culture in *Ogiek*,[48] the Court's first and only case relating to Indigenous peoples.

The human rights instruments specific to Indigenous peoples are explicit in their recognition of the material content of the right to culture. ILO Convention 169 expressly recognises the special connection of Indigenous peoples with their lands, territories and natural resources, and its importance for the survival and development of their culture. Article 13 obligates states to 'respect the *special importance for the cultures and spiritual values* of the peoples concerned of *their relationship with the lands or territories*, or both

[43] HRC (n 40) [7].

[44] HRC, *Ivan Kitok v Sweden*, Communcation No 197/1985, UN Doc CCPR/C/33/D/197/1985 (27 July 1988) [9.2]; HRC, *Ominayak v Canada*, Communication No 167/1984, UN Doc CCPR/C/38/D/167/1984 (26 March 1990) [32.2] and [33]; HRC, *Ilmari Länsman et al v Finland*, Communication No 511/1992, UN Doc CCPR/C/52/D/511/1992 (26 October 1994) [9.2]; HRC, *Jouni E Länsman et al v Finland*, Communication No. 671/1995, UN Doc CCPR/C/58/D/671/1995 (30 October 1996) [10.2]; HRC, *Apirana Mahuika et al v New Zealand*, Communication No 547/1993, UN Doc CCPR/C/70/D/547/1993 (27 October 2000) [9.3]; HRC, *Jouni Länsman et al v Finland*, Communication No 1023/2001, UN Doc CCPR/C/83/D/1023/2001 (17 March 2005) [10.1]; and HRC, *Ángela Poma Poma v Peru*, Communication No 1457/ 2006, UN Doc CCPR/C/95/D/1457/2006 (27 March 2009) [7.2] and [7.3].

[45] CESCR (n 40) [36].

[46] *Endorois* (n 31) [241].

[47] ibid [250].

[48] *African Commission on Human and Peoples' Rights v Republic of Kenya* (n 32) [190].

as applicable, which they occupy or otherwise use, and in particular *the collective aspects* of this relationship' (emphasis added).[49] Moreover, Article 23(1) specifically provides that:

> Handicrafts, rural and community-based industries, and *subsistence economy and traditional activities* of the [Indigenous] peoples concerned, such as *hunting, fishing, trapping and gathering, shall be recognized as important factors in the maintenance of their cultures* and their economic self-reliance and development. Governments shall, with the participation of these peoples and whenever appropriate, ensure that these activities are strengthened and promoted. (Emphasis added)[50]

The provision affirms not only that hunting and fishing practices of Indigenous peoples are traditional activities that form the basis for their subsistence economy, but also that these activities are indispensable for the maintenance and continued development of their cultures. ILO Convention 169 thus obligates states parties to recognise such activities as part of Indigenous peoples' cultural rights and to take positive measures to strengthen and promote them.[51] The UNDRIP provides similar recognition and protection to Indigenous peoples' right to natural resources as an integral part of their culture in a number of articles, including Articles 11, 12, 15, 25 and 31.

There is no reason to confine the cultural rights provisions of general and Indigenous-specific human rights instruments as well as the observations of the relevant human rights treaty-monitoring bodies on the material basis of culture to land territory, and it follows that the above conclusions are equally applicable to marine space and resources.[52] This is confirmed by the HRC's views in *Apirana Mahuika*, which deals specifically with Maori rights in relation to marine fisheries. As the HRC noted:

> It is undisputed that the authors are members of a minority within the meaning of article 27 of the Covenant; it is further undisputed that *the use and control of fisheries is an essential element of their culture*. In this context, the Committee recalls that *economic activities* may come within the ambit of article 27, *if they are an essential element of the culture of a community*. The recognition of Maori rights in respect of fisheries by the Treaty of Waitangi confirms that *the exercise of these rights is a significant part of Maori culture*. (Emphasis added)[53]

The HRC makes it clear that it is the importance of the fishing activity to the cultural identity of Indigenous peoples rather than the location of harvest

[49] ILO Convention 169, art 13(1).

[50] ibid art 23(1).

[51] ibid art 23(1)(2).

[52] Smith and Dodson (n 1) and Skogvang share this view. See SF Skogvang, 'Local Community Right to Fish: A Sami Perspective' in C Allard and SF Skogvang (eds), *Indigenous Rights in Scandinavia: Autonomous Sami Law* (Ashgate, 2015) 136.

[53] HRC, *Apirana Mahuika* (n 44) [9.3]. For a discussion of national developments relating to Maori rights to marine resources in New Zealand, see also Erueti (ch 10 in this volume).

(whether fresh waters or the seas) that must be assessed in connection with the application of Article 27.[54]

The protection of the right to culture under Article 27 extends not only to fishing practices by traditional means, but also to practices that have been adapted to modern fishing technologies. In *Apirana Mahuika*, the HRC observed that: 'The right to enjoy one's culture cannot be determined in *abstracto* but has to be placed in context. In particular, Article 27 does not only protect traditional means of livelihood of minorities, but *allows also for adaptation of those means to the modern way of life and ensuing technology*' (emphasis added)[55] This progressive understanding of culture is particularly relevant for Indigenous peoples, because many states restrict the rights of Indigenous peoples to harvest MLRs by prohibiting the use of modern means of harvesting.

In conclusion, international human rights law recognises the right to culture of Indigenous peoples, including its material content. This entails that Indigenous peoples should be able to continue to harvest MLRs, including marine mammals, insofar as such harvesting practices are integral to their culture.

### *i. The Threshold of Illegitimate Interference to the Right to Culture*

Not every state interference with the right to culture of a minority can be regarded as a denial of the right within the meaning of Article 27.[56] Thus, a coastal state may legitimately take measures that place restrictions on the right to culture of Indigenous communities. Yet, the scope of a state's freedom to adopt such measures '*is not to be assessed by reference to a margin of appreciation*, but by reference to the obligations it has undertaken in article 27' (emphasis added)[57] – obligations not to deny the right to culture.

In a number of cases, the HRC has adopted different tests to determine when state measures will amount to a denial of the right to culture. The Committee has held that restrictions on the right to culture based on 'both a reasonable and objective justification' may be consistent with obligations under Article 27.[58] The HRC has further held that 'measures that have a certain limited impact on the way of life of persons belonging to a minority will not necessarily amount

[54] The HRC has re-affirmed this understanding in its 2018 concluding observation on Norway regarding the Sami people's fishing rights in the sea (see HRC, *Concluding Observations on the Seventh Periodic Report of Norway*, UN Doc CCPR/C/NOR/CO/7 (25 April 2018) [36] and [37(d)(e)]). For a discussion of the legal protection of coastal Sami culture and livelihood in Norway, see Ravna and Kalak (ch 9 in this volume).

[55] HRC, *Apirana Mahuika* (n 44) [9.4].

[56] HRC, *Sandra Lovelace v Canada*, Communication No R 6/24, UN Doc Supp No 40 (A/36/40) at 166 (30 July 1981) [15]; HRC, *Ilmari Länsman* (n 44) [9.4]; HRC, *Apirana Mahuika* (n 44) [9.4]; HRC, *Poma Poma* (n 44) [7.4].

[57] HRC, *Apirana Mahuika* (n 44) [9.4]. See also HRC, *Ilmari Länsman* (n 44) [9.4]; HRC, *Poma Poma* (n 44) [7.4].

[58] HRC, *Sandra Lovelace* (n 56) [16]; HRC, *Ivan Kitok* (n 44) [9.8]. The CESCR also provides a similar test (see CESCR (n 40) [19]).

to a denial of the right under article 27'.[59] The Committee makes it clear that measures taken on unjustifiable grounds or that have 'adverse impacts'[60] on the way of life of the Indigenous community concerned amount to a denial of the right to culture. The reasonableness, objectivity and gravity of the impact of state measures should be assessed in light of the context and the facts of individual cases.

The HRC has also introduced additional stand-alone procedural protections. In *Apirana Mahuika* and *Poma Poma*, the Committee concluded that 'the acceptability of measures that affect or interfere with the culturally significant economic activities of [Indigenous community] depends on whether the members of the [community] in question *have had the opportunity to participate in the decision-making process in relation to these measures and whether they will continue to benefit from their traditional economy*' (emphasis added).[61] Thus, in order for state measures to be compatible with the obligations under Article 27, the coastal state should demonstrate that it has consulted or obtained the free, prior and informed consent (FPIC) of the affected Indigenous communities beforehand, and has devised appropriate mechanisms to enable the communities concerned to continue to harvest traditionally used MLRs, perhaps on a more limited scale than before. The possible approaches of ensuring the continued exercise of traditional activities may take different forms, including providing open or quota-based exemptions from strict fisheries conservation measures.

In sum, a coastal state may interfere with the right of Indigenous communities to access culturally important marine sites or harvest traditionally used MLRs up to a certain point insofar as the interference is justifiable and proportionate with the interests of the community, and that the community concerned participated in the decision-making process. The substantive tests and procedural protections are cumulative. Thus, if state measures fail to meet the substantive tests, the state infringes Article 27 regardless of whether it consulted the affected community. Similarly, even if state measures are within the threshold of the substantive tests, the state still violates the right to culture if it fails to involve the community in the decision-making process. These stringent tests clearly demonstrate that international law provides special safeguards against illegitimate interference with the right to culture of Indigenous peoples.

[59] HRC, *Ilmari Länsman* (n 44) [9.4]; HRC, *Jouni E Länsman* (n 44) [10.3]; HRC, *Apirana Mahuika* (n 44) [9.4]; HRC, *Jouni Länsman* (n 44) [10.1]; HRC, *Poma Poma* (n 44) [7.4].

[60] For example, the HRC in *Ilmari Länsman* ((n 44) [9.6]) held that the quarrying 'does not appear to have … *adversely affected*' reindeer herding; and in *Jouni Länsman* ((n 44) [10.3]), the HRC concluded that 'the effect of logging carried out in … areas have not been *shown to be serious enough* as to amount to a denial of the authors' right to enjoy their own culture … under article 27'. On the other hand, in *Poma Poma* ((n 44) [7.7]), the HRC found that the water divertion '*has substantively compromised* the way of life and culture of the … community'.

[61] HRC, *Apirana Mahuika* (n 44) [9.5]; HRC, *Poma Poma* (n 44) [7.6].

## C. The Right to Marine Space and Resources as a Property Right

The Indigenous-specific human rights instruments expressly recognise the right of Indigenous communities[62] with respect to their traditional lands and natural resources as a protected property right.[63] Similarly, even though the property right provisions of the general global and regional human rights instruments[64] do not expressly reference Indigenous peoples, treaty-monitoring bodies and human rights courts have concluded that these provisions protect the rights of Indigenous communities with respect to their traditional lands and natural resources.[65] Indeed, commentators suggest that the right of Indigenous peoples to traditional lands, territories and natural resources as a property right is now a right under customary international law.[66] This right extends to freshwater fisheries in lakes and rivers.[67] However, the application of exclusive property rights to marine areas and MLRs remains controversial.

The practices of treaty-monitoring bodies and regional human rights courts in adapting the property rights provisions of the general human rights instruments to the specific context of Indigenous peoples' rights to marine areas and MLRs is scarce.[68] The issue of whether the principal provision of the ILO Convention 169 concerning property rights to traditional lands (Article 14) should apply to sea territories was discussed during the negotiation of the Convention. Indigenous peoples' organisations expressed their strong concern that the right of ownership and possession of Indigenous peoples to lands 'should be broadened to a territorial one which would encompass flora, fauna,

[62] The proper legal subjects of property rights over marine areas and MLRs are Indigenous communities rather than Indigenous peoples as a whole. Hence, the use of the term 'Indigenous peoples' in connection with the right to property should be understood to mean 'Indigenous communities'.

[63] See ILO Convention 169, arts 14–16; UNDRIP, arts 25 and 26; ADRIP, art 25.

[64] The following general human rights instruments provide specific property right provisions: UDHR, art 17; CERD Convention, art 5(d)(v); ECHR, Optional Protocol 1, art 1; ACHR, art 21; ACHPR, art 14. The twin human rights conventions (the ICCPR and the ICESCR) do not provide a separate provision recognising the right to property.

[65] See, eg, *Mayagna (Sumo) Awas Tingni Community v Nicaragua*, Case No 79 (IACtHR, 31 August 2001) [148]; *Yakye Axa Indigenous Community v Paraguay*, Case No 125 (IACtHR, 17 June 2005) [137] and [143]; *Saramaka People v Suriname*, Case No 172 (IACtHR, 28 November 2007) [95]; *African Commission on Human and Peoples' Rights v Republic of Kenya* (n 32) [128]. See also the jurisprudences of human rights commissions: *Maya Indigenous Communities of the Toledo District v Belize*, Report No 40/2004 (IAComHR, 12 October 2004); *Endorois* (n 31) [196].

[66] International Law Association, *Rights of Indigenous Peoples: Final Report* (Sofia Conference, 2012) 27; Åhrén (n 23) 165; J Anaya and RA Williams, 'The Protection of Indigenous Peoples' Rights over Lands and Natural Resources under the Inter-American Human Rights System' (2001) 14 *Harvard Human Rights Journal* 33, 55.

[67] Skogvang (n 52) 131; A Scott, 'Introducing Property in Fishery Management' in R Shotton (ed), *Use of Property Rights in Fisheries Management*, FAO Fisheries Technical Paper No 404/1 (Rome, 2000) 4.

[68] The practices of the CERD Committee and the HRC in the context of the right to non-discrimination is the exception in this regard; this is discussed in section III.D below.

resources … as well as *sea ice, sea and coastal fishing rights*' (emphasis added).[69] Nonetheless, this effort to extend the provisions of the Convention dealing with the rights of ownership and possession of Indigenous peoples over their traditional lands to saltwater areas failed.[70] However, the Convention does include other provisions, which indirectly capture the application of its property right provisions to marine areas and marine resources. The following sub-section uncovers these provisions.

### *i. Unpacking the Meaning of Article 13(2) of the ILO Convention: Indigenous 'Land' Includes Marine Space*

ILO Convention 169 defines 'land' broadly. Article 13(2) provides that:

> The use of the term lands in Articles 15 and 16 *shall include the concept of territories, which covers the total environment of the areas* which the [Indigenous] peoples concerned occupy or otherwise use. (Emphasis added)[71]

The italicised text is broad and includes marine space, and the ILO Secretariat emphasises that: 'The concept of land usually embraces *the whole territory* [Indigenous peoples] use, including forests, rivers, mountains and *sea*, the surface as well as the sub-surface' (emphasis added).[72] The Secretariat further states that 'the concept of land encompasses the land which a community or people uses and cares for as a whole'.[73] This interpretation apparently embraces marine areas as part of Indigenous peoples' traditional lands insofar as they have been traditionally occupied or used by the Indigenous peoples concerned. Xanthaki concurs arguing that Article 13(2) of ILO Convention 169 'widens the concept of [land] considerably, and consequently widens the protection of Indigenous peoples' rights to lands to include water resources and other elements',[74] including the marine space.

The UNDRIP reinforces this broader understanding by explicitly recognising the rights of Indigenous peoples to 'maintain and strengthen their distinctive spiritual relationship with their traditionally owned or otherwise occupied and used *lands, territories, waters and coastal seas and other*

[69] ILO, *Partial Revision of the Indigenous and Tribal Populations Convention*, 1957 (No 107), Report IV(1), International Labour Conference, 76th Session (Geneva, 1989) 4.

[70] ILO, *Partial Revision of the Indigenous and Tribal Populations Convention*, 1957 (No 107), Report VI(1) (Geneva, 1987), International Labour Conference, 75th Session (Geneva, 1988) 44; Smith and Dodson (n 1) 8.

[71] ILO Convention 169, art 13(2).

[72] International Labour Office, *ILO Convention on Indigenous and Tribal Peoples, 1989 (No 169): A Manual* (Geneva, 2003) 29.

[73] ibid 30.

[74] A Xanthaki, *Indigenous Rights and United Nations Standards: Self-Determination, Culture and Land* (Cambridge University Press, 2007) 81.

*resources*' (emphasis added).[75] A recent UN study on the relationships between Indigenous peoples and the Pacific Ocean embraces the broader meaning incorporated under Article 25 of the UNDRIP. The study found that 'the scope of [Indigenous peoples'] rights to their lands, territories and oceans is not limited to the orthodox perception of a sea boundary but extends to [the sea areas including] the seabed'.[76]

Thus, Article 13(2) of ILO Convention 169 and subsequent developments affirm that the meaning of 'land' when applied to Indigenous peoples covers the marine space, where Indigenous peoples occupy or use as part of their traditional territories, or traditionally had access to satisfy their subsistence needs or to conduct their spiritual, customary and traditional activities. These marine areas may include internal waters (such as foreshores and fjords), archipelagic waters, the territorial sea and the EEZ to the extent that Indigenous peoples have traditionally used them. The actual extent of Indigenous peoples' occupation or traditional use determines the areal extent of 'land' or territory out in the sea.[77]

The broader understanding of 'land' indicates the nature and extent of Indigenous peoples' rights over marine areas and marine resources. Article 13(2) clearly provides that the broader meaning of 'land' applies to Article 16 – a provision that prohibits the removal of Indigenous peoples from their traditional lands. This, by implication, means that Article 16 of ILO Convention 169 provides protection against the eviction of Indigenous peoples from their traditionally used coastal areas or traditional fishing grounds. Such protection against removal from traditionally used coastal areas necessarily presupposes a recognition and protection of Indigenous peoples' ownership or possession rights over those marine areas. Therefore, even though states parties declined to include express provision regarding ownership or possession rights over marine areas under Article 14, a cumulative reading and a proactive interpretation of Articles 13(2) and 16 of ILO Convention 169 reveals that such rights fall within the ambit of the Convention. Thus, states parties have a duty to recognise Indigenous communities' exclusive area-based rights over traditional fishing grounds or sacred sites in certain parts of the marine space, particularly in waters close to the shore.[78] This in turn entails the right of Indigenous communities not to be relocated from those areas unless such relocation is exceptionally necessary, in which case the relocation 'shall take place only with their free and informed consent'.[79]

[75] UNDRIP, art 25.

[76] Toki (n 2) [7].

[77] V Prescott and S Davis, 'Aboriginal Claims to Seas in Australia' (2002) 17 *International Journal of Marine and Coastal Law* 1, 15.

[78] For example, the Norwegian Sami fishing rights' claim in Finnmark follows this area-based approach. See Norges Nasjonale Institusjon for Menneskerettigheter, 'Sjøsamenes rett til sjøfisk', *Temarapport* 2016; Skogvang (n 52) 127–28.

[79] ILO Convention 169, art 16 (1); UNDRIP, art 10. See section III.E below for the details.

Article 13(2) of ILO Convention also references Article 15, which provides that:

> The rights of the [Indigenous] peoples concerned to the *natural resources pertaining to their lands* shall be specially safeguarded. These rights include the right of these peoples to participate in *the use, management and conservation of these resources*. (Emphasis added)[80]

A reading of this provision together with Article 13(2) suggests that the phrase 'natural resources pertaining to their lands' covers not only terrestrial natural resources but also marine natural resources located within the marine areas traditionally occupied or used by coastal Indigenous communities.[81] The rights protected under Article 15(1) 'include the right to participate in the use, management and conservation of the [marine] resources'.[82] However, the bundles of property rights mentioned in the provision are not exhaustive, as the term 'include' indicates; hence, it may include exclusive ownership and possession rights over a certain fishing area. Article 15(2) also provides other sets of rights that Indigenous communities have in connection with the exploitation of sub-surface resources within, or close to, traditionally occupied or used marine areas. This includes the right to consultation, including the right to FPIC, before the government undertakes or grants permits for sub-surface resource exploration and exploitation projects (see section III.E below for details). If the government permits the project, Indigenous communities still have the right to participate in the benefits resulting from the exploitation of natural resources and a right to receive fair compensation for any damages caused as a result of the extraction activities. In this way, the Convention tries to balance the interests of states over sub-surface resources and Indigenous peoples' rights to traditionally used marine space and resources.

In conclusion, it is permissible to interpret the property rights provisions of general human rights instruments as protecting the property rights of Indigenous communities to marine areas and marine resources. Moreover, ILO Convention 169 offers a broad definition of 'land' and this can be interpreted to include marine space. The UNDRIP reinforces this approach with its express reference to the sea as part of Indigenous peoples' traditional territory. This expansive understanding of 'land' has two important effects: first, it reflects Indigenous peoples' worldviews of land and sea territories as a single integrated unit as opposed to the binary conception which many states adopt; and, second, it justifies the application of property rights norms relating to Indigenous peoples'

[80] ILO Convention 169, art 15(1).

[81] For a similar viewpoint, see Smith and Dodson (n 1) 8; RL Johnstone, *Offshore Oil and Gas Development in the Arctic under International Law: Risk and Responsibility* (Martinus Nijhoff Publishers, 2014) 61, 63.

[82] ILO Convention 169, art 15(1).

traditional lands and 'natural resources' *mutatis mutandis* to marine areas and MLRs.

### *ii. Limits to the Right to Property over MLRs*

The right to property, like the right to culture, is not absolute. However, restrictions on the property rights of Indigenous communities over traditionally used marine space and resources must be 'established by law',[83] necessary to achieve a legitimate objective in the general public interest,[84] and proportional.[85] The fulfilment of these tests should be assessed on a case-by-case basis depending on the type of interference. For example, the introduction of marine resources conservation measures or the approval of a resource extraction project may be considered necessary to protect endangered species or to encourage economic development respectively; thus, they may fulfil a legitimate aim in the public interest. Yet, such measures should be proportional, and a fair balance must be established between such public interest and the essential rights of Indigenous communities. This balance may require the state to exempt Indigenous harvesters from the proposed conservation measure or may require the state to reduce the size and scope of a proposed resources extraction project so that Indigenous communities will be able to continue with their traditional activities. The acceptability of the interference may also depend on whether the Indigenous communities concerned have had the chance to participate in the decision-making process.[86] Thus, international law provides guarantees against arbitrary restrictions on the property rights of Indigenous communities in relation to marine resources.

## D. Non-discrimination in Property Rights over Marine Resources

The right to non-discrimination requires the absence of any form of discrimination against Indigenous peoples as a precondition for the full enjoyment of their human rights.[87] In this regard, ILO Convention 169 stipulates that: 'Indigenous … peoples shall enjoy the full measure of human rights and fundamental freedoms without hindrance and discrimination.'[88] The UNDRIP similarly provides that: '[I]ndigenous peoples and individuals are free and equal to all other peoples and individuals and have the right to be free from any kind

[83] ACHR, art 21; ACHPR, art 14.

[84] ACHPR, art 14.

[85] *African Commission on Human and Peoples' Rights v Republic of Kenya* (n 32) [129]; *Saramaka* (n 65) [127]; *Yakye Axa* (n 65) [145].

[86] *Saramaka* (n 65) [130].

[87] J Anaya, *Indigenous Peoples in International Law*, 2nd edn (Oxford University Press, 2004) 129.

[88] ILO Convention 169, art 3(1).

of discrimination, in the exercise of their rights, *in particular that based on their Indigenous origin or identity*' (emphasis added).[89] These Indigenous-specific human rights instruments provide general protection to Indigenous peoples against discrimination in the enjoyment of all types of their human rights.

The right to equality and non-discrimination is also widely recognised in general global and regional[90] human right instruments, including the ICCPR (Articles 2(1) and 26), the ICESCR (Article 2(2)) and the CERD Convention in its entirety.[91] While none of these general human rights instruments makes specific reference to Indigenous peoples, the respective treaty-monitoring bodies have addressed this issue. The Committee on the Elimination of Racial Discrimination (hereinafter CERD Committee), for example, has issued a general recommendation specifically devoted to Indigenous peoples where it recognises that 'discrimination against Indigenous peoples falls under the scope of the [CERD] Convention'.[92] Accordingly, it calls upon states parties to take all appropriate measures to combat and eliminate all forms of discrimination against Indigenous peoples in their application of the Convention.[93] The HRC and the CESCR adopt similar interpretations.[94]

The right to equality and non-discrimination is not a stand-alone right exercisable independently, but rather in conjunction with other human rights, including the right to property.[95] Article 5 (d)(v) of the CERD Convention, for example, obliges states parties to prohibit discrimination in all its manifestations in the enjoyment of 'the right to property alone or in association with others'. For the CERD Committee, this includes the duty to recognise and protect Indigenous peoples' property rights to their communal lands and natural resources. A failure to do so is discrimination against Indigenous peoples.[96]

The right to non-discrimination has two main dimensions when applied to Indigenous peoples' property rights over marine resources. First, Indigenous peoples must be treated in the same manner as non-Indigenous peoples in the enjoyment of the right to property.[97] Thus, if domestic law acknowledges property rights to marine areas and MLRs for non-Indigenous peoples, it should also recognise the property rights of Indigenous communities over their traditionally

[89] UNDRIP, art 2.

[90] The regional human rights instruments which recognise the right to equality and non-discrimination include the ECHR (art 14), the ACHR (arts 1(1) and 24), and the ACHPR (arts 2 and 3).

[91] See, in particular, CERD Convention, arts 1(1), 2(1)(a) and 5.

[92] CERD Committee, *General Recommendation No 23: Indigenous Peoples* (fifty-first session, 1997) [1].

[93] ibid [1] and [2].

[94] See HRC, *General Comment No 18: Non-discrimination* (thirty-seventh session, 1989); CESCR, *General Comment No 20: Non-discrimination in Economic, Social and Cultural Rights* (art 2, para 2 of the International Covenant on Economic, Social and Cultural Rights), UN Doc E/C.12/GC/20 (2 July 2009).

[95] CESCR (n 94) [7].

[96] CERD Committee (n 92) [5].

[97] Åhrén (n 23) 150–51.

used marine areas and marine resources.[98] Many coastal states have established different forms of quota-based or territorial-based property rights systems over commercial fisheries, including different forms of individual transferable quotas (ITQs)[99] and territorial use rights for fisheries (TURFs).[100] Hence, the right to equality and non-discrimination requires coastal states to recognise Indigenous communities' customary property rights over traditional fishing grounds and marine resources in the same manner.

The CERD Committee applied this dimension of the right to non-discrimination in the foreshore[101] and the seabed-related dispute between the Maori and New Zealand. Following the New Zealand Court of Appeal's decision in the *Ngati Apa* case that affirmed customary Maori property rights to the foreshore and seabed areas of the Marlborough Sound,[102] the New Zealand government enacted the Foreshore and Seabed Act of 2004. The Act declared the foreshore and seabed to be owned by the Crown in order to preserve them as 'the common heritage of all New Zealanders'.[103] The Maori claimants argued that the Act was discriminatory as it unjustifiably extinguished their customary property rights over the foreshore and the seabed (which is protected under the Treaty of Waitangi), while vesting those areas in the Crown. The CERD Committee held that the legislation 'contains discriminatory aspects against the Maori, in particular in its extinguishment of the possibility of establishing Maori customary titles over the foreshore and seabed and its failure to provide a guaranteed right of redress, notwithstanding the State party's obligations under articles 5 and 6 of the Convention'.[104] The Committee further recommended two possible ways to eliminate, or mitigate, the discriminatory effects of the Foreshore and Seabed Act. First, it urged New Zealand to resume dialogue with the Maori community in order to amend the legislation.[105] Secondly, and

[98] Skogvang (n 52) 137.

[99] Various types of ITQs exist with different names and forms, such as Individual Fishing Quotas (IFQs) and Individual Vessel Quotas (IVQs). Generally on this issue, see D Symes and K Crean, 'Privatization of the Commons: The Introduction of Individual Transferable Quotas in Developed Fisheries' (1995) 26 *Geoforum* 175.

[100] CNT Quynh et al, 'Territorial Use Rights for Fisheries (TURFs): State of the Art and the Road Ahead' (2017) 75 *Marine Policy* 41; JC Afflerbach et al, 'A Global Survey of "TURF-reserves", Territorial Use Rights for Fisheries Coupled with Marine Reserves' (2014) 2 *Global Ecology and Conservation* 97.

[101] The foreshore is the area of land between the low and high tide marks. For further discussion, see Erueti (ch 10 in this volume).

[102] *Ngati Apa v Attorney-General* [2003] 3 NZLR 643 (CA). See also S Fiorletta-Leroy, 'The Attorney-General v Ngati Apa ("Ngati Apa" or "Marlborough Sounds") Case' (2006) 3 *New Zealand Postgraduate Law E-Journal* 1, 9.

[103] R Stavenhagen, *Report of the Special Rapporteur on the Situation of Human Rights and Fundamental Freedoms of Indigenous Peoples*, Mission to New Zealand, UN Doc E/CN.4/2006/78/Add.3 (March 2006) [48].

[104] CERD Committee, *New Zealand Foreshore and Seabed Act 2004: Decision 1(66)*, UN Doc CERD/C/DEC/NZL/1 (27 April 2005) [6].

[105] ibid [7]. The Special Rapporteur on the Situation of Human Rights and Fundamental Freedoms of Indigenous Peoples, on his Mission to New Zealand, also issued a similar recommendation (see Stavenhagen (n 103) [55]).

alternatively, it requested New Zealand to closely monitor the implementation of the Act and its impact on the Maori peoples, and 'to take steps to minimize any negative effects [of the Act], especially *by way of a flexible application of the legislation and by broadening the scope of redress available to the Maori*' (emphasis added).[106] Yet, the Committee did not provide any guidance as to what constitutes flexible application and broader redress, and thereby left wide discretion to the state. The HRC also criticised the Act in its 2010 concluding observation on New Zealand's periodic report. Emphasising the cultural and religious significance of access to the foreshore and seabed for the Maori, the Committee recommended that New Zealand increase its efforts for 'effective consultation' of representatives of all Maori groups with a view to amending or repealing the Act.[107]

New Zealand did replace the Act in 2011 with the Marine and Coastal Area Act, but the new Act is still the subject of criticism. In its 2016 concluding observation, the HRC noted that the new Act 'has not adequately addressed the discriminatory effects on Maori claims to their customary land and their right to cultural development' and recommended New Zealand to revise the Act.[108] The CERD Committee issued similar recommendations in its 2017 concluding observation requesting New Zealand to review the Act with a view to respecting and protecting the full enjoyment by Maori communities of their rights to marine resources and their access to places of cultural and traditional significance.[109]

The second dimension of the right to non-discrimination requires not only that all cases be treated equally, but also that groups with different cultural backgrounds and ways of life be treated differently.[110] Eide argues that the core of Indigenous peoples' claim is not only to be given equal opportunities in the mainstream culture, but also 'a right to maintain a different culture' – a way of life of their own.[111] The relevant human rights treaty-monitoring bodies have clearly affirmed this notion of the right to non-discrimination in their jurisprudence. For example, the HRC observes that the right to equality 'does not mean identical treatment in every instance'.[112] The CERD Committee

[106] CERD Committee, *New Zealand Foreshore and Seabed Act 2004: Decision 1(66)* (n 104) [8].

[107] HRC, *Concluding Observation: New Zealand*, UN Doc CCPR/C/NZL/CO/5 (7 April 2010) [19].

[108] HRC, *Concluding Observation: New Zealand*, UN Doc CCPR/C/NZL/CO/6 (28 April 2016) [43] and [44].

[109] CERD Committee, *Concluding Observations on the Combined Twenty-First and Twenty-Second Periodic Reports of New Zealand*, UN Doc CERD/C/NZL/CO/21-22 (22 September 2017) [20] and [21].

[110] For an excellent discussion of this evolved understanding of the right to equality and non-discrimination, see Åhrén (n 23) 152; and W Jonas and M Donaldson, 'Legitimacy of Special Measures' in S Garkawe, L Kelly and W Fisher (eds), *Indigenous Human Rights* (Sydney Institute of Criminology Monograph Series No 14, 2001) 12.

[111] A Eide, 'Indigenous Self-Government in the Arctic, and Their Right to Land and Natural Resources' (2009) 1 *Yearbook of Polar Law* 245, 250.

[112] HRC, *General Comment No 18* (n 94) [8].

similarly observes that the uniform treatment of individuals or groups whose situations are objectively different will constitute 'discrimination in effect'.[113] The CERD Committee underlined that 'differentiation of treatment will not constitute discrimination if the criteria for such differentiation, judged against the objectives and purposes of the Convention, are legitimate'.[114] Likewise, the CESCR notes that eliminating discrimination requires 'paying sufficient attention to groups of individuals which suffer historical or persistent prejudice'.[115] It specifically emphasised the need to recognise the rights of Indigenous peoples through 'appropriate' modalities, meaning that 'the realization of [their] specific human rights in a way that is pertinent and suitable to [their] cultural modality or context, that is, respectful of the culture and cultural rights of … Indigenous peoples'.[116] In light of this, Åhrèn argues that since 'international legal sources sing the same hymn' in affirming the new notion of the right to non-discrimination and because there is little evidence of non-acceptance by states, this second dimension of the right to non-discrimination 'has crystalized into customary international norm'.[117]

This second dimension is relevant to the rights of Indigenous peoples to marine areas and marine resources. First, the norm requires states to recognise the property rights of Indigenous communities over MLRs in a manner that respects their customary or traditional resource use and management systems, consistent with their distinct way of life and cultural identity. In particular, this requires recognition of the use of traditional fishing and hunting methods, which also embraces the freedom to adapt those methods to modern technologies. Second, the norm requires states to take special measures to enable Indigenous communities to use marine areas and to harvest marine resources.[118] Such special measures or preferential rights may take different forms, including the reservation of traditional fishing grounds for the exclusive use of Indigenous peoples or by providing exemptions (open or quota-based exemptions) to Indigenous communities to harvest certain MLRs of special significance even if these are included in a marine protected area (MPA).[119]

[113] CERD Committee, *General Recommendation No 32: The Meaning and Scope of Special Measures in the International Convention on the Elimination of All Forms of Racial Discrimination*, CERD/C/GC/32 (24 September 2009) [8].

[114] CERD Committee, *General Recommendation No 14 on Article 1, Paragraph 1, of the Convention* (forty-second session, 1993) [2].

[115] CESCR, *General Comment No 20* (n 94) [8 (b)].

[116] CESCR (n 40) [16(e)].

[117] Åhrén (n 23) 155.

[118] CERD Convention, arts 1(4) and 2(2); ILO 169, art 4; UNDRIP, art 21(2). For a detailed discussion of special measures, see P Thornberry, *The International Convention on the Elimination of All Forms of Racial Discrimination: A Commentary* (Oxford University Press, 2016) ch 9.

[119] See NC Ban and A Frid, 'Indigenous Peoples' Rights and Marine Protected Areas' (2018) 87 *Marine Policy* 180; K Davis et al, 'The Evolution of Marine Protected Area Planning in Aotearoa New Zealand: Reflections on Participation and Process' (2018) 93 *Marine Policy* 113. See also Farran (ch 14 in this volume) and Cambou, Gilbert and Dégremont (ch 8 in this volume).

In conclusion, the right to equality and non-discrimination serves as an additional legal basis for the recognition of property rights of coastal Indigenous communities over their traditionally used marine areas and MLRs. The norm obliges states to make sure that they do not implement any policy, law or practice that discriminates against Indigenous peoples in the enjoyment of their property rights over marine space and resources, and it also requires states to provide differential treatment and special measures geared towards strengthening Indigenous peoples' unique way of life and marine tenure systems.

## E. Procedural Safeguards: The Right to Consultation and FPIC

The right to consultation is an essential procedural right, which makes the substantive rights of Indigenous peoples relating to traditionally used marine areas and marine resources effective and applicable.[120] It entitles Indigenous peoples to participate either directly or through their chosen representatives in all matters, which may negatively affect their rights and interests. Article 6(1)(a) of ILO Convention 169 stipulates that states parties 'shall consult the [Indigenous] peoples concerned, through appropriate procedures and in particular through their representative institutions, whenever consideration is being given to legislative or administrative measures which may affect them directly'.[121] The consultations 'shall be undertaken *in good faith* and in a form appropriate to the circumstances, with *the objective of achieving agreement or consent to the proposed measures*' (emphasis added).[122] Similarly, Article 19 of the UNDRIP obliges states parties to consult and cooperate in good faith with coastal Indigenous peoples in order to obtain their FPIC before adopting measures that may affect them.[123] These two provisions are general and apply to a wide range of matters. In the present context, this might require consultation before the adoption of any fishery conservation and management measures having a negative impact on Indigenous communities, such as prohibition of fishing and hunting, processes to determine quotas, restrictions on fishing and hunting methods, or the establishment of MPAs within traditional fishing grounds.

Article 15(2) of ILO Convention 169 and Article 32(2) of the UNDRIP require consultation in the specific context of resource exploitation projects in Indigenous peoples' traditional lands and territories. This would require a coastal state to consult Indigenous communities in good faith before 'the approval of any project' affecting their traditionally used marine areas and

[120] V Tauli-Corpuz, 'Consultation and Consent: Principles, Experiences and Challenges', *International Colloquium on the Free, Prior, and Informed Consultation: International and Regional Standards and Experiences* (Mexico City, 8 Novmber 2016) 4.

[121] ILO Convention 169, art 6(1)(a). See also arts 7, 15 and 16.

[122] ibid art 6(2).

[123] UNDRIP, art 19.

traditional fishing grounds, particularly with respect to projects involving 'the development, utilization or exploitation of … resources',[124] and to involve them in impact assessment studies.[125] This might include commercial fishing operations, fish farming (acquaculture or mariculture), various forms of extractive industrial development activities (including oil and gas, and mineral extraction) and marine renewable energy development within or close to marine areas traditionally used by Indigenous communities – collectively discussed in the literature as 'ocean grabs' or 'coastal grabs'.[126] *Good faith* requires that coastal states must be open to hear, and be influenced by, the views of the coastal Indigenous communities concerned, and be prepared to abandon or modify the proposed measure or marine-related project in a manner that minimises its potential impacts. Consultation undertaken solely as a symbolic gesture or to provide information without follow-up action does not constitute good faith consultation.[127]

Procedural rights may also go beyond good faith consultation and require the state to obtain the FPIC of the affected community. There are two clear and unambiguous cases where FPIC should be required: where the implementation of the proposed project requires the removal of Indigenous communities from their traditionally used marine areas and traditional fishing grounds;[128] and where the project involves the storage or disposal of hazardous waste in those areas.[129] In other cases, the issue of whether FPIC is required depends on the nature of the proposed measure and the extent of its impact. This must be determined on a case-by-case basis. The Expert Mechanism on the Rights of Indigenous Peoples (EMRIP) concluded that the consent of Indigenous peoples is mandatory with respect to 'matters of fundamental importance for their rights, survival, dignity and well-being'.[130] Similarly, the Inter-American Court of Human Rights (IACtHR) in *Saramaka v Suriname*[131] and the HRC in *Poma Poma*[132] adopted 'a major impact' and 'substantial interference'

[124] ibid art 32(2); ILO Convention 169, art 15(2). See also J Anaya, 'Indigenous Peoples' Participatory Rights in Relation to Decisions about Natural Resource Extraction: The More Fundamental Issue of What Rights Indigenous Peoples Have in Land and Resources' (2005) 22 *Arizona Journal of International and Comparative Law* 7.

[125] ILO Convention 169, art 7.

[126] See M Bavinck et al, 'The Impact of Coastal Grabbing on Community Conservation: A Global Reconnaissance' (2017) 16 *Maritime Studies* 1; NJ Bennett, H Govan, and T Satterfield, 'Ocean Grabbing' (2015) 57 *Marine Policy* 61.

[127] ILO Committee of Experts on the Application of Conventions and Recommendations (CEACR), General Observation on the Right of Indigenous and Tribal Peoples to Consultation (Observation 2010/81) 8–9.

[128] ILO Convention 169, art 16; and UNDRIP, art 10.

[129] UNDRIP, art 29(2).

[130] Expert Mechanism Advice No 2(2011): Indigenous Peoples and the Right to Participate in Decision-Making, UN Doc A/HRC/18/42 [22].

[131] *Saramaka* (n 65) [134] and [137].

[132] HRC, *Poma Poma* (n 44) [7.6].

test respectively to assess whether a state has a duty to obtain the FPIC of the Indigenous peoples concerned.[133] Relevant factors in such an assessment might include the location and areal coverage of the project, the extraction and disposal method, and the extent of disturbance to sea habitats, fish stocks and marine mammals of special significance to Indigenous communities.[134]

In sum, the rights to consultation and FPIC serve as important procedural safeguards against all measures, including resource development projects, which involve the re-allocation of rights to access, control or use of the marine space and the associated resources away from the traditional user coastal Indigenous communities. The norm promotes an inclusive approach requiring coastal states to involve Indigenous peoples in the governance and management of marine areas and resources, including in impact assessment studies of proposed in/offshore resource development project.

## IV. CONCLUSION

Marine space and MLRs are the economic and cultural centres for coastal Indigenous peoples. Despite this significance, international human rights law does not expressly protect the rights of Indigenous peoples with respect to these marine areas and resources. Yet, this chapter has shown that it is possible to derive such rights protections from the general rules and principles of law applicable to traditional 'lands' and 'natural resources'. It has demonstrated this application at two levels: first, at the general level, it concluded that human rights instruments bind contracting states throughout their national territorial limits and within areas under their 'jurisdiction' including maritime space; and, second, it concludes that specific human rights norms applicable to traditional lands and natural resources, such as the right to self-determination, the right to cultural integrity, the right to property, the right to non-discrimination and the right to consultation and participation including FPIC also implicitly, if not expressly, recognise and provide protection to Indigenous peoples' right to traditionally used marine areas and to harvest MLRs. The chapter has also demonstrated that the HRC and the CERD Committee have played a significant role in proactively interpreting and adapting the general human rights norms, particularly the right to culture and the right to non-discrimination, to the specific contexts of Indigenous peoples' rights to marine areas and MLRs. Yet, this practice is still limited with respect to marine resources and is certainly not as extensive as the practice relating land-based territories and resources.

[133] For a general discussion on this matter, see L Heinämäki, 'Global Context – Arctic Importance: Free, Prior and Informed Consent, a New Paradigm in International Law Related to Indigenous Peoples' in TM Herrmann and T Martin (eds), *Indigenous Peoples' Governance of Land and Protected Territories in the Arctic* (Springer, 2016).

[134] Toki (n 2) [35].

To sum up, a combination of the various international human rights law instruments pertaining to Indigenous peoples, and the practices of judicial and treaty bodies adapting the general human rights norms to the specific contexts of Indigenous peoples' traditional lands and natural resources together constitute the basis for recognition and protection of the long-standing customary rights of Indigenous peoples relating to marine areas and MLRs. The chapter has shown that the tendency of states to treat the marine space and MLRs differently from traditional lands and natural resources has no legal basis and serves no purpose other than perpetuating the 'customary international law of Indigenous exclusion'.[135]

[135] B Clavero, 'The Indigenous Rights of Participation and International Development Policies' (2005) 22 *Arizona Journal of International and Comparative Law* 41, 43.

# 3

# *Indigenous Peoples in Marine Areas* Whaling and Sealing

MALGOSIA FITZMAURICE

## I. INTRODUCTION

WHALING AND SEALING by Indigenous peoples are not without controversy. Indigenous or Aboriginal whaling, as with all whaling activities, under the Whaling Convention (including commercial and scientific whaling) are complex and contentious.[1] There are several examples of Aboriginal whaling that illustrate these problems: the best known is that of the Makah peoples and of the Inuit peoples in Greenland. The compatibility and harmonisation issues which arise in relation to this type of whaling indicate the difficulties resulting from specific attempts to reconcile conflicting policy objectives. In recent times, whales have acquired a totemic symbolism; this is one of the reasons that have prompted often emotional approaches concerning the regulation of whaling activities. There are several legal questions that connect Indigenous whaling to human rights in the areas of the law of the sea, international environmental law and philosophy (ethics), thereby demonstrating its significance beyond narrow considerations involving hunting.[2] The focus of this chapter will be mostly on Indigenous whaling within the Whaling Convention. Sealing is less complex than whaling, but it has also given rise to legal and moral controversies, which were exemplified by recent European Union (EU)

[1] International Convention for the Regulation of Whaling (adopted 2 December 1946, entered into force 10 November 1948) 161 UNTS 72, amended by the Protocol to the International Convention for the Regulation of Whaling (hereinafter 'Whaling Convention').

[2] For a broader approach to whaling (including from a philosophical perspective), see Malgosia Fitzmaurice, *Whaling and International Law* (Cambridge University Press, 2015); see also the excellent analysis of indigenous whaling within the context of human rights, the law of the sea and the International Whaling Commission (IWC) by Hilde Woker, 'The Rights of Indigenous Peoples to Harvest Marine Mammals in the Arctic', 2015, https://munin.uit.no/bitstream/handle/10037/8468/thesis.pdf?sequence=2.

and World Trade Organization (WTO) cases (see below). These clearly illustrate that sealing also polarises states and is far from clear, but, unlike whaling, it is regulated largely by national legislation.

This chapter will not engage in the debate regarding the definition of Indigenous peoples, as this issue has been addressed in the Introduction to the present volume.[3] However, the definition provided by the International Whaling Commission (IWC) within the context of subsistence whaling for the purposes of the International Convention on the Regulation of Whaling (ICRW) is worth referring to at this point: 'aboriginal, indigenous or native peoples who share strong community, familial, social and cultural ties related to a continuing traditional dependence on whaling and on the use of whales'.[4]

## II. INDIGENOUS WHALING

### A. Regulating Whaling in International Law: The International Convention on the Regulation of Whaling and the International Whaling Commission

Over-exploitation of whales during the period between the two World Wars led to the conclusion of two international conventions on the protection of whales: the 1931 Geneva Convention for Regulation of Whaling[5] and the 1937 Agreement for the Regulation of Whaling.[6] The 1931 and 1937 Conventions did not prove to be particularly effective,[7] but they provided a legal framework for the future regulation of whaling, which while not perfect continues to the present day and is regulated by the 1946 ICRW. Issues such as the complete protection of certain species via the ban on commercial whaling or moratorium, the establishment of whale sanctuaries and the organisation of Aboriginal whaling are inherited from these earlier Conventions. These legal approaches correspond to the whale as a sacred object and the whale as a utilitarian animal. Therefore, the inter-war period saw the beginning of international law's approach to a whale, on the one hand, as an object of economic exploitation and legal regulation, and, on the other, as a totemic object.

[3] On this topic, see Mattias Åhrén, *Indigenous Peoples' Status in the International Legal System* (Oxford University Press, 2016) and Woker (n 2) 4–9.

[4] GP Donovan, 'The International Whaling Commission and Aboriginal/Subsistence Whaling: April 1979 to July 1981' in GP Donovan (ed), *Aboriginal/Subsistence Whaling (with Special Reference to the Alaska and Greenland Fisheries* (Reports of the International Whaling Commission Special Issue 4, Cambridge, 1982) 79, 83.

[5] Convention for Regulation of Whaling (adopted 4 September 1931, entered into force 16 January 1935), 155 LNTS 349.

[6] International Agreement for the Regulation of Whaling (adopted 8 June 1937, provisionally entered into force 1 July 1937) 190 LNTS 79. The initial Contracting Parties to the Convention were: the Union of South Africa; the US; Australia, Germany; the UK; Ireland; New Zealand and Norway. Canada and Mexico acceded afterwards.

[7] Larry L Leonard, 'Recent Negotiations toward the International Regulation of Whaling' (1941) 35 *American Journal of International Law* 90, 100.

The ICRW consists of the Convention itself, as well as a Schedule that is an integral part of the Convention text. The Convention sets out the general regulatory scheme for the management of whale stocks. The Schedule, according to Article V(1), introduces standards to be followed regarding the 'conservation and utilization' of whale species. It deals with the specific issues relating to conservation, such as: open and closed seasons; whaling methods; size limits for each whale; and inspection of whaling ships. Article III(2) sets out the procedure for the amendment of the Schedule, which must be effected by a three-quarters majority of voting members. There have been several subsequent amendments to the Schedule, including the imposition of the Moratorium, the establishment of the Indian Ocean Sanctuary and the Southern Ocean Sanctuary.[8]

The ICRW does not actually include a generic definition of a 'whale'; instead, it lists species under its protection in the Schedule to the Convention. The Schedule only lists so-called great whales. Such totemic whales as the narwhal whale are probably outside of the remit of the ICRW as a medium-sized whale. However, in order to preserve such objects of beauty as the narwhal, many states claim that the IWC has a remit to deal with all whales.[9] In practice, the Convention's object of regulation remains vague and difficult to determine.

The whaling regime under the Convention provides for three types of whaling: commercial (at present zero 'quotas'); Aboriginal (Indigenous whaling); and scientific whaling. The Preamble to the ICRW includes amongst its aims 'the proper conservation of whale stocks and … the orderly development of the whaling industry'. Thus, it preserves the historical binary objectives of conserving whale stocks and preserving the industry. However, even in terms of this fairly contained objective, the IWC has never really successfully 'delivered'. Stocks, especially in the past, were inadequately monitored, and depletion has continued.[10] As a result (but against the backdrop of a very much changed membership and a fundamentally different concept as to what the purpose of control should be), in 1982, the IWC introduced a complete ban on commercial whaling (known generally as the Moratorium or 'zero quotas'), which came into effect in the 1985/1986 season. However, the Moratorium was only intended to be temporary. It was anticipated that stocks would recover and that, in due course, safe and sustainable levels of stocks of at least some species would have recovered sufficiently to allow for the resumption of whaling. However, all

[8] 'Two Sanctuaries are currently designated by the International Whaling Commission, both of which prohibit commercial whaling. The first of these, the Indian Ocean Sanctuary, was established in 1979 and covers the whole of the Indian Ocean south to 55°S. The second was adopted in 1994 and covers the waters of the Southern Ocean around Antarctica. The precise coordinates are recorded in the Schedule at paras 7(a) and 7(b). An additional proposal for a Sanctuary in the South Atlantic Ocean has been repeatedly submitted to the Commission in recent years. To date, it has not achieved the three-quarters majority of votes needed to amend the Schedule and thus become designated by the IWC. See International Whaling Commission, Whale Sanctuaries', https://iwc.int/sanctuaries.

[9] Fitzmaurice (n 2) 50–54 and 276–306.

[10] ibid 66.

attempts at finding an acceptable basis for a properly controlled resumption of whaling have so far failed and the Moratorium is still in effect.[11]

Conflicting attitudes to the Moratorium exemplify the meaning of a 'whale' for different societies. They show the dividing line between two diametrically opposed camps: conservationist (conservation of whales for ultimate exploitation) and preservationist (the whale as a beautiful object which should not be exploited).[12] The ambiguous and indecisive wording of the Convention clearly indicates that most of the issues in relation to the ICRW are contentious, starting with its binary object and purpose: on the one hand, the conservation and management of whale stocks in order to provide for the 'orderly development of the whaling industry' and, on the other, recognition that whales constitute a 'general trust' to be safeguarded for 'future generations'.

Norway and Iceland have opted out of the Moratorium on whaling and are conducting legal commercial whaling operations. Scientific whaling is based on Article VIII of the ICRW and is outside of the regulatory scope of the IWC as the permits for scientific whaling are issued by national authorities.[13] Nonetheless, substantial levels of whaling continue, on the alleged basis of other provisions of the ICRW, and to a considerable extent outside the direct purview of the IWC.[14] While there are also other points of contention, including the validity of sanctuaries introduced, or proposed, by the IWC and the IWC's interpretation of such terms as 'Aboriginal whaling',[15] it is the meaning of 'scientific whaling' and the issue of a resumption of commercial whaling that underlies the state of conflict that currently exists within the international whaling regime.[16]

The IWC is riddled with irreconcilable differences and it has become a somewhat divisive body. There are still a few states that passionately uphold what they see as an inalienable right to continue commercial whaling. Accordingly, a fundamental difference of attitude has developed among the ICRW Member States towards whaling and, indeed, towards the Convention's underlying objectives. For the remaining 'whaling nations', whaling remains a legitimate activity, along with other sustainable forms of exploitation of marine resources, if it is undertaken in a properly controlled and sustainable manner. However, for non-whaling nations, vociferously backed by the powerful lobby of environmental and preservationist non-governmental organisations (NGOs)[17] – as well as by the majority of the general public opinion – whaling in any form is seen as an unnecessary and, indeed, immoral activity which should, at least as an eventual objective, be permanently banned.

[11] ibid 66–71.

[12] Michael Heazle, *Scientific Uncertainty and the Politics of Whaling* (University of Washington Press, 2006) 170.

[13] ICRW, art VIII.

[14] Fitzmaurice (n 2) 261–64.

[15] ibid 273.

[16] ibid.

[17] Charlotte Epstein, *The Power of Words in International Relations* (MIT Press, 2006).

Underlying the protectionist stance are theories that accord inherent value, even rights, to the whale. There are numerous theories relating to the place of animals in our universe and the relationship between animals and humans.[18] The direct anthropocentric approaches that characterised early environmental treaties were replaced by approaches that recognise an intrinsic value of the environment and the fauna and flora it contains and animal rights.[19] The animal rights debate has undergone a significant change since the advent of modern international law and there is now a range of controversial but important rights-based theories which also underpin the idea of the protectionist stance.[20]

One of the factors that has been suggested as being detrimental to the effectiveness of the Whaling Convention is its advanced age. The ICRW was negotiated and structured over 70 years ago and its main provisions were based on two pre-war treaties from 1931 and 1937. The basic structure of the Convention reflects the approaches to environmental matters of the period when it was negotiated and, as a result, it was not based on principles that characterise contemporary approaches to environmental protection. It may be argued that the imposition of the Moratorium on whaling and its continuation is an expression of the application of the precautionary principle within the IWC. One of the ICRW's major weaknesses is its very rudimentary international enforcement mechanism. The main responsibility for the enforcement of the provisions of the Convention remains with the parties to the Convention. According to Article IX(1), a state party to the ICRW is in charge of its enforcement in relation to actions of 'persons under its jurisdiction', as for the prosecution of its violations, in the absence of an international enforcement mechanism.

The IWC now has to attempt to operate as a *forum* within which apparently irreconcilable conflicts of interest may be resolved. The aspirations of the whaling nations, as they stand at present, simply cannot be met without some level, however contained, of resumption of commercial whaling. On the other hand, the aspirations of the preservationists, who now form a majority within

[18] See, eg, Claude Levi-Strauss, *The Savage Mind* (Chicago University Press, 1968); Rene Descartes, *Discourse on Method and Meditation on First Philosophy*, John Cottingham, Robert Stoothoff, and Dugald Murdoch (trans) (Cambridge University Press, 1991); Immanuel Kant, *Lectures on Ethics*, Peter Heath (trans) (Cambridge University Press, 1997); Jeremy Bentham, *The Principles of Morals and Legislation* (Prometheus Books, 1988) 310–11; Michael Bowman, 'The Philosophical Foundations of International Wildlife' in Peter Davies and Catherine Redgwell (eds), *Lyster's International Wildlife*, 2nd edn (Cambridge University Press, 2010) 62–63.

[19] Bowman (n 18) 62–63.

[20] Peter Singer, *Animal Liberation* (Harper Perennial, 2001); Roderick Frazier Nash, *The Rights of Nature: A History of Environmental Ethics* (Wisconsin University Press, 1989).

See, eg, Cass R Sunstein, 'The Rights of Animals: A Very Short Primer', The Law School, University of Chicago, John M Olin Law and Economics Working Paper No 157 (2D Series), Public Law and Legal Theory Working Paper No 20; Sue Donaldson and Will Kymlicka, *Zoopolis: A Political Theory of Animal Rights* (Oxford University Press, 2013); Anthony D'Amato and Sudhir K Chopra, 'Whales: Their Emerging Right to Life' (1991) 85 *American Journal of International Law* 21. See also Hope M Babcock, 'Putting a Price on Whales to Save Them: What Do Morals Have to Do with it?' (2013) 43 *Environmental Law* 1.

the IWC, cannot be entirely fulfilled unless the possibility of any resumption of commercial whaling is abandoned. Therefore, the most important question is whether the ICRW is still a relevant international instrument or whether it would have to be revised (or even abandoned) given that it is falling short of meeting the current set of needs of the parties to it. The lack of common understanding, and the acrimonious atmosphere between the members of the Whaling Commission, has had a paralysing effect on the functioning of the Commission and has led to international litigation, as will be discussed in the next section.

The Review of the International Whaling Commission published in 2018 identified several areas of possible improvement in the functioning and governance of the Commission.[21] First, the report recommended the preparation of work programmes with strategic and prioritised directions, both for the Commission itself and for its subsidiary bodies. To this effect, the IWC should develop and adopt a Strategic Plan and multi-year programmes of work setting strategic directions and clear priorities for the work of the IWC.[22] One of the most important areas of the functioning of the IWC concerns the participation of NGOs (civil society). It was noted that the IWC has already made efforts to increase the involvement of NGOs and other observers in Commission meetings and in the work of the IWC in general. However, there is still room for improvement and it was suggested that, inter alia, the IWC Secretariat should consult with NGOs to ensure that other relevant measures are taken to ensure the more effective involvement of NGOs in future IWC meetings.[23]

One of the most the incendiary questions under the ICRW has become Japanese scientific whaling, which led to the *Whaling in Antarctic (Australia v Japan, New Zealand Intervening)* judgment of the International Court of Justice (ICJ) in 2014.[24] Both Australia and New Zealand alleged that Japanese scientific whaling (so-called JARPA II) was in fact not 'in purpose of scientific whaling'. The Court agreed and ordered Japan to withdraw all pending scientific permits. The judgment is only applied to this particular instance of scientific whaling by Japan and will not affect any future whaling.

As has been correctly observed, the ICJ's decision revealed the weaknesses of the review process within the IWC and its Scientific Committee, where science

[21] Christian Prip, David Sheppard and Fabio Hazin, 'Report Submitted by the IWC Review Team' (Final Report), https://archive.iwc.int/pages/view.php?ref=6890&k.

[22] ibid 18, Recommendation 6: 'The IWC should develop and adopt a Strategic Plan and a multi-year work programme setting strategic directions and clear priorities for the work of IWC and its subsidiary bodies in line with best practice of other treaty bodies. Ideally, "what", "why", by "whom" and by "when" should be clearly defined for each task agreed in the strategic plan.'

[23] See ibid 19, Recommendation 9: '[The] IWC should continue to support and increase the involvement of NGOs in IWC Meetings and should consider ways to improve the effectiveness of their involvement, such as: (i) providing better facilities for NGOs at Commission meetings, including tables and microphones; (ii) allowing adequate time for NGO interventions; (iii) updating the existing Code of Conduct for NGO involvement; and (iv) enabling NGOs to have documents tabled. In this regard, the Secretariat should communicate with NGOs to assess what more could be done.'

[24] *Whaling in Antarctic (Australia v. Japan, New Zealand Intervening) (Merits)* [2014] ICJ Rep 226.

mixed with politics is not an uncommon phenomenon in inter-governmental fora where political considerations habitually determine outcomes.[25] This observation is equally applicable to all types of whaling.

## B. Aboriginal Whaling within the Jurisdiction of the IWC

### *i. Aboriginal Subsistence Whaling: Historical Background and General Outline*

In the 1960s and 1970s, Aboriginal whaling was not a significant issue on the agenda of the IWC.[26] While the 1946 ICRW does not itself include any special provisions regulating Aboriginal subsistence whaling, the ICRW's Schedule recognises its special position by excluding it from the definition of, and the provisions relating to, commercial whaling. When the ICRW was originally concluded, the second paragraph of the Schedule prohibited the taking and killing of gray whales and right whales due to their fragile status. This prohibition did not apply where the whaling of such species was conducted for local consumption of meat and other products by Indigenous peoples. The second paragraph of the Schedule stated that: 'It is forbidden to take or kill gray whales or right whales, except when the meat and products of such whales are to be used exclusively for local consumption by the aborigines.'[27] Thus, it appears to be clear that even when conducted by Indigenous whalers, the whaling of gray whales or right whales for either commercial purposes or when the meat or products are to be distributed extensively outside the communities of those Indigenous peoples was prohibited.[28] The definition of 'subsistence whaling' has since evolved. In brief, there are two fundamental requirements for the allocation of quotas for Aboriginal whaling: ensuring that hunts do not seriously increase the risks of extinction and that hunted whale populations are then maintained at healthy, relatively high levels, enabling native people to hunt whales at levels appropriate to cultural and nutritional requirements (known as 'cultural and nutritional needs'). National governments provide the IWC with evidence of the needs of their Indigenous peoples. This is presented in the form of a 'Needs Statement' that details the cultural, subsistence and nutritional aspects of the hunt, products and distribution. The Scientific Committee provides advice on the sustainability of proposed hunts and safe catch limits.[29]

[25] William de la Mare, Nick Gales and Marc Mangel 'Applying Scientific Principles in International Law on Whaling' (2014) 345 *Science and Law* 1124, 1126.

[26] Alexander Gillespie, 'Aboriginal Subsistence Whaling: A Critique of the Inter-relationship between International Law and International Whaling Commission' (2001) 12 *Colorado Journal of International Law and Policy* 77, 81.

[27] Hisashi Hamaguchi, 'Aboriginal Subsistence Whaling Revisited' in Nobuhiro Kishigami, Hisashi Hamaguchi and James M Savelle (eds), *Anthropological Studies of Whaling* (Senri Ethnological Studies, 2013) 81, 82.

[28] ibid.

[29] International Whaling Commission, Aboriginal Subsistence Whaling, http://iwc.int/aboriginal.

In 1979, the IWC Anthropology Panel adopted an unofficial definition of 'subsistence whaling' as comprising:

(1) the personal consumption of whale products for food fuel, shelter, clothing, tools or transportation by participants in the whale harvest;
(2) the barter, trade or sharing of whale products in their harvested form with relatives of the participants in the harvest, with others in the local community or with persons in locations other than the local community with whom local residents share familial, social, cultural or economic ties – a generalised currency is involved in this barter and trade, but the predominant portion of the products from each whale is ordinarily directly consumed or utilised in their harvested form within the local community; and
(3) the making and selling of handicraft articles from whale products, when the whale is harvested for the purposes (1) and (2) above.

Aboriginal subsistence whaling was again defined in 1981, this time by the IWC's Technical Committee Working Group on Development of Management Principles and Guidelines for Subsistence Catches of Whales by Indigenous (Aboriginal) Peoples as comprising whaling conducted for the 'purposes of local aboriginal consumption, carried out by or on behalf of aboriginal, Indigenous or native people who share strong community, familial, social and cultural ties related to a continuing traditional dependence on whaling and on the use of whales'.[30] These definitions appear to raise more questions than answers. For instance, the interchangeable use of terms 'Aboriginal', 'native' and 'Indigenous' is confusing, as in many Indigenous communities, this leads to different meanings.[31] For example, there has been discussion as to whether whaling in Greenland can qualify as Aboriginal. The 1979 definition of 'subsistence use of whale products', coined by cultural anthropologists, is more restrictive as to the area in which the distribution of whale products is permitted, and it does not recognise the distribution of whale products that involve monetary exchanges, as in Aboriginal subsistence whaling.[32]

It may also be noted that the report proposing the definitions was perhaps inconsistent as it states that, in some cases, products are distributed to, and used by, communities away from the coastal areas where whaling is actually conducted, and in some areas, the practice of trading to meet subsistence needs has emerged. Further, the IWC ad hoc Working Group stated that it was arguable whether there is a difference in principle between the sale of whale products in order to buy essential goods and the direct exchange of whale products for such goods. According to Hamaguchi, this is indicative of the fact that even

[30] Report of the Cultural Anthropology Panel, reprinted in Donovan (ed) (n 4) 35.

[31] Randall Reeves, 'The Origins and Character of "Aboriginal Subsistence" Whaling: A Global Review' (2002) 32 *Mammal Review* 71.

[32] Hamaguchi (n 27) 86.

the ad hoc Working Group's definition did not completely deny in all cases the extensive distribution of whale products or their distribution involving monetary exchanges for whale-related goods.[33]

At the outset, therefore, it appears that confusion arose due to the lack of any conclusive definition of what constitutes 'commercial' whaling, which, at times, makes the distinction between 'Aboriginal' and 'commercial' whaling challenging, despite the efforts of the ad hoc Working Group to distinguish between them. These two forms are considered to be different due to their different objectives. The main objective of the management of Aboriginal subsistence whaling was to maintain individual stocks at the highest possible level, and the main purpose of catching whales was to fulfil the nutritional and cultural needs of the Indigenous peoples contemplated by the relevant agreements. In contrast, the main objective of commercial whaling was to maximise yields from individual stocks and to ensure the longevity of the respective whaling industries of the states parties to ICRW, while the main purpose of catching whales was to sell their products. Hamaguchi observes that 'these differences indicate that Aboriginal subsistence whaling prioritizes quality (the cultural aspect) and commercial whaling prioritizes quantity (the economic aspect)'.[34] However, as Reeves postulates, the distinction between commercial and subsistence whaling still remains crude and ambiguous.[35]

The Aboriginal Subsistence Whaling Sub-Committee (hereinafter ASW) was established in order to consider documentation on needs relating to Aboriginal whaling and to advise the IWC Technical Committee on the setting-up of proper management measures. The field of Aboriginal subsistence whaling was, consequently, sub-divided into the following fields:

(i) subsistence whaling;
(ii) nutritional whaling;
(iii) cultural whaling.

In 1982, the ASW adopted basic principles concerning Aboriginal whaling which were formalised by a Resolution:

> The Commission also recognizes the importance and desirability of accommodating, consistent with effective conservation of whale stocks, the needs of aboriginal people who are dependent upon whales for nutritional, subsistence and cultural purposes … the Commission believes it appropriate and desirable to establish principles and guidelines for the management of aboriginal subsistence whaling which recognize and seek to accommodate conservation, nutritional, subsistence and cultural needs.[36]

[33] ibid 86.
[34] ibid.
[35] Reeves (n 31) 77.
[36] See 'Report of the Thirty-First Meeting of the International Commission on Whaling', cited in Gillespie (n 26) 82.

Doubleday argues that the Commission's assessment of 'need' has proved to be difficult and controversial. There are several reasons for this state of affairs, such as what constitutes the concepts of 'Aboriginal', 'subsistence' and the 'need' itself.[37] Doubleday is of the view that Aboriginal whaling requires reconsideration, such as the at times troublesome proving of needs, as well as the prohibition against trade of edible products.[38]

Thus, as Gillespie has noted, the definitions of Aboriginal whaling set out above indicate that Aboriginal whaling should be local and non-commercial in nature. However, this conflicts to some extent with the definition of 'consumption', which allows the sale of by-products.[39] Heinämäki correctly criticises this sub-division, observing that 'in practice … the "subsistence requirement" seems to be a kind of main category, including "food" by definition, whereas nutritional and cultural needs are subcategories to "Aboriginal Subsistence Whaling," which are closely connected to each other'.[40] However, apart from this, there are a number of problems relating to the definition of the three categories themselves and to their inter-relationship. Indeed, the practice of states indicates that the submission of the required evidence proving 'nutritional and cultural need', which is a fundamental requirement for allocation of quotas for Aboriginal peoples, has frequently been very difficult to achieve.[41] But, crucially, Heinämäki points out that the distinction that the IWC sought to make between subsistence and nutritional needs conflicts with the interpretation of the Human Rights Committee (HRC), which construed traditional livelihoods and means of subsistence (including traditional diet) as an integral part of Indigenous culture under Article 27 of the International Covenant on Civil and Political Rights (ICCPR). In addition, the HRC allows for the inclusion of some commercial elements within the definition of 'Aboriginal subsistence' and, indeed, stresses the economic viability of a livelihood as a material criterion of the fulfilment of the provisions of Article 27.[42]

Hamaguchi is of the view that the imposition of the Moratorium on commercial whaling has impacted on aspects of Aboriginal subsistence whaling due to extensive revision to paragraph 13 of the Schedule, which followed the setting-up of the Moratorium.[43] As it now stands, paragraph 13 of the Schedule establishes an ample set of conditions for setting quotas for Aboriginal

[37] Nancy Doubleday, 'Arctic Whales: Sustaining Indigenous Peoples and Conserving Arctic Resources' in Milton MR Freeman and Urs Kreuter (eds), *Elephants and Whales: Resources for Whom?* (Gordon and Breach Science Publishers, 1994) 254.

[38] ibid.

[39] Gillespie (n 26) 77.

[40] Leena Heinämäki, 'Protecting the Rights of Indigenous Peoples: Promoting the Sustainability of the Global Environment?' (2009) 11 *International Community Law Review* 3, 45.

[41] ibid 44.

[42] ibid 45.

[43] Hamaguchi (n 27) 87.

subsistence whaling.[44] For example, changes were made to whaling in Greenland. Due to the revision of paragraph 13b of the Schedule, catch limits were only granted for Aboriginal subsistence whaling, which meant that only the indigenous people in Greenland were allowed to be involved in whaling,'[45] whereas before the Moratorium all inhabitants of Greenland were permitted to hunt whales. Although Indigenous peoples are heard at the forum of the IWC through their states, significant changes have taken place in relation to their position therein. It was recommended at the workshop held in 2015 that the IWC:

> [C]onsider exploring options regarding how the IWC could stay better informed of current developments regarding indigenous peoples' rights; look at mechanisms to improve the status of indigenous delegates to IWC meetings to establish a more timely, distinct and steady approach to ASW issues; discuss the appointment of an IWC representative to attend a session of the UN Permanent Forum on Indigenous Issues; and explore the potential benefits of joining the UN Inter-Agency Support Group on Indigenous Issues, through its Secretariat.

The workshop also recommended that the term 'need statement' be replaced by the term 'Description on the [insert name] hunt relevant to catch/strike limit requests' and that a draft outline be developed, taking into account the need for flexibility, to avoid any indication of prescription or compulsion, and to minimise the effort involved and avoid duplication.[46] The recently established Aboriginal Subsistence Whaling Fund may also mentioned, which will assist Aboriginal hunters who do not otherwise have the means to participate in the IWC's work.[47]

### *ii. Commercial and Aboriginal Whaling*

Greenland's Aboriginal whaling is a good example of the great difficulties in drawing a clear division between commercial and Aboriginal whaling. As stated in the previous sub-section, the ad hoc Working Group also considered the difference between Aboriginal subsistence whaling and commercial whaling.

[44] Paragraph 13 of the Schedule establishes two sets of conditions for ASW. Paragraph 13(a) establishes first set of conditions which generally apply to ASW quotas for any stock, which are permitted, according to para 13(b), notwithstanding para 10 (which imposes the moratorium on commercial whaling). Paragraph 13(a) introduces the three conditions of allocating aboriginal quotas: (1) the satisfying aboriginal subsistence 'need'; (2) for each whaling season; and (3) in accordance with principles. These five principles regard the conservation of the stock; the prohibition against striking or killing calves or suckling calves; and the need for national legislation to be in accordance with para 13. Paragraph 13(b) provides a specific set of conditions relating to specific stocks as well as establishing specific quotas for each and every stock.

[45] Hamaguchi (n 27) 87

[46] IWC Report Details Recommendations on Aboriginal Subsistence Whaling, 20 October 2015, http://sdg.iisd.org/news/iwc-report-details-recommendations-on-aboriginal-subsistence-whaling.

[47] IWC (n 29).

These two forms were different in relation to two aspects: management and catching.[48] Several writers argued that the approximation of hunting and fishing activities with waged employment has contributed to a blurring of the distinction between commercial and non-commercial activities. The confusion is compounded by the unclear and inconsistent drafting of paragraph 13.[49] A substantial part of the *mattak* (the skin and adhering blubber) from beluga whales and narwhals is sold by hunters and marketed in shops in Greenland. The same applies to narwhal tusks that are sold either to visitors or in shops in Greenland (with a view to exporting them). It has been suggested that 'whaling had become more commodity-based and commercialised as a result of the high monetary value of *mattak* in particular, and that as a result policy makers in Greenland have become engaged in "redefining" of subsistence hunting'.[50] However, others are of the view that sharing, gift-giving and household consumption of whale products in Greenland still predominate, and that cash transactions have more of an incidental than a central character.[51] According to Hamaguchi:

> [T]he establishment of aboriginal whaling as aboriginal subsistence whaling would result in this being treated as a practice devoid of commercial elements, at least in ideological terms. However, it is difficult for an outsider to comprehend the concept of the distribution of whale products involving cash that is not meant for profit-making purposes; it was here that the misfortunes of aboriginal subsistence whaling began.[52]

This quotation clearly indicates the unresolved Gordian knot of Aboriginal whaling in which ideology is often contradicted by practice. The blurred notions of commercial whaling and non-commercial but still involving cash transactions result in a very difficult to comprehend legal and ethical issues, which defy definitions and a strict legal framework.

### *iii. Aboriginal Subsistence Whaling under the IWC at Present*

According to the IWC, the objectives of Aboriginal subsistence whaling are as follows:

(i) to ensure that the risk of extinction is not seriously increased (the objective with the highest priority);
(ii) to enable harvests in perpetuity appropriate to cultural and nutritional requirements; and

[48] Hamaguchi (n 27) 86.
[49] See in detail Chris Wold and Michael S. Kearney, 'The Legal Effects of Greenland's Unilateral Aboriginal Subsistence Whale Hunt' (2015) 3 *American University International Law Review*, 561, 580–81.
[50] Reeves (n 31) 79.
[51] ibid 79.
[52] Hamaguchi (n 27) 88.

(iii) to maintain stocks at the highest net recruitment level, and, if they fall below that, to ensure they move towards it.[53]

In general, the IWC has identified four specific whaling operations as qualifying for the status of Aboriginal subsistence whaling:

(i) minke and fin whales (formerly also humpback whales) in Greenland;
(ii) humpback whales in the Lesser Antilles (specifically the island of Bequia, St Vincent and the Grenadines);
(iii) bowhead whales (and formerly also gray whales) in the US (Alaska), and gray whales in Russia (Chukotka); and
(iv) bowhead and gray whales in the US (Alaska).[54]

On the basis of the above objectives and criteria, Aboriginal subsistence whaling is allowed at present for the following countries:

(i) Denmark (in relation to the Inuit peoples of Greenland) – fin and minke whales;
(ii) Russian Federation (Siberia) – gray and bowhead whales;
(iii) St Vincent and the Grenadines (Bequia) – humpback whales; and
(iv) the US (Alaska and Makah Indigenous peoples) – bowhead and gray whales.

It should be recalled it is the responsibility of national governments to provide the IWC with evidence of the cultural and subsistence 'needs' of their Aboriginal peoples, while the Scientific Committee provides scientific advice on safe catch limits for such stocks as two necessary requirements for the allocation of quotas.[55] The IWC has for many years been developing the Aboriginal Whaling Management Scheme (AWMS), which aims to include two elements:

(i) a quota-setting mechanism (which is already in place); and
(ii) a supervision and control scheme in order to establish the future management of aboriginal subsistence whaling.

At present, Aboriginal subsistence quotas under the quota-setting mechanism are adopted for a period of five years. Under the IWC, there is a marked limitation in the number of species of whales that have been singled out as eligible for Aboriginal hunting, as indicated by the inclusion of bowhead whales in the Moratorium. Eventually, the AWMS (including the Aboriginal Whaling Management Procedure (AWMP) once it becomes fully operational) will provide guidelines and will set requirements for surveys and data as well as case-specific elements. It is also likely to cover certain scientific, logistical and regulatory aspects of aboriginal whaling, including the inspection/observation of catches. The IWC Plan for 2012 was a system of block quotas with internal

[53] See IWC (n 29).
[54] ibid.
[55] ibid.

allocations. Provisions include a quota of 289 bowhead whales landed (by agreement, the Alaska Inupiat may take up to 255 whales, with 125 allocated to Russian Aboriginal bowhead whalers). In each of these years, the number of bowhead struck may not exceed 67 whales and up to 15 unused strikes may be carried forward to the next year.[56] The Inupiat people have about 200 years of history of whaling. In contemporary Inupiat society, whaling is very important culturally, socially spiritually, politically and nutritionally. Whaling is one of the factors defining their community identity. It appears that whaling is absolutely fundamental for Inupiat cultural and social continuation of them as a people, given that members of this society regard it as a defining aspect of their cultural identity.[57]

At the 2002 meeting, the IWC Scientific Committee completed its work with respect to Bering-Chukchi-Beaufort Seas stock of bowhead whales.[58] It agreed a Strike Limit Algorithm (SLA) for this stock of whales and the scientific aspects of the scheme (ie, how many bowheads can be taken in a sustainable manner). The SLA system was adopted by the IWC in 2004. However, the situation of Greenland's whaling for fin and minke whales has proved to be more complicated and requires more scientific research to be conducted in cooperation with Greenland's scientists.

Discussions regarding Aboriginal whaling quotas can be highly divisive in the IWC. An example of this is the 2009 meeting, where the primary issue was a discussion regarding a request for a catch of 10 humpback whales for Greenland. The debate focused on the statement from the IWC Scientific Committee as to whether such a catch would not harm the stock of these whales and whether Denmark (on behalf of Greenland) had adequately made the case for the 'needs' of Inuit peoples for humpback whales, both of which are necessary conditions for the allocation of quotas for Aboriginal subsistence whaling. In the event, Denmark's request was unsuccessful. It may be added that there are also voices that support the view that there are insufficient quotas assigned to Russia's Chukchi people. It appears to be a general trend in relation to Indigenous peoples that they will try to argue for higher allocations than those awarded to them.

St Vincent and the Grenadines has whaling quotas allocated for Bequia, a small island which is a part of its territory (whose population does not appear to be more than 5,000).[59] The total catch of whales from 1991 to 2010 was 22 whales, that is to say, on average one whale per year. There have been

[56] See NOAA, Protecting Marine Life in Alaska, alaskafisheries.noaa.gov/protectedresources/whales/bowhead/bowheadbrochure1208.pdf.

[57] See Nobuhiro Kishigami, 'Aboriginal Subsistence Whaling in Barrow, Alaska' in Kishigami, Hamaguchi and Savelle (eds) (n 27) 101, 116.

[58] The Chukchi are an indigenous people living in the circumpolar Arctic of northeastern Russia. There are two types of these peoples: 'the Reindeer Chukchi' (who tend reindeer herds) and the 'coastal dwellers' whose subsistence is based primarily on sea mammals. They hunt with a rifle, a harpoon with a whale line and a harpoon with a drogue, as well as a boat with an outboard motor.

[59] See the Bequia's Tourism Association's website: www.bequiatourism.com/facts.htm.

two whaling boats in operation since 2002.[60] In Bequia, the principal whaling method is rather rudimentary: whales are weakened by thrusting harpoons into their bodies and are dispatched with lances.[61]

At present, there are chiefly four contentious issues that arise with regard to Aboriginal (subsistence) whaling, namely:

(i) ongoing hunts that were traditionally considered to be 'Aboriginal subsistence', but are at present undergoing an evaluation;
(ii) small-scale shore-based hunts (which had previously avoided international scrutiny, but have been recently discovered and analysed);
(iii) defunct or suspended whaling operations by Aboriginal peoples that have resumed (or are expected to resume in the near future);[62] and
(iv) the question of so-called small cetaceans (such as the narwhal, which many states contest as being outside the jurisdiction of the IWC).

There is a significant difference between the regulation of Aboriginal rights in connection to the use of natural resources within domestic legal systems,[63] and the system of Aboriginal whaling under the ICRW and the IWC regimes. In principle, commercial use of natural resources is permitted in marine areas in Australia (although in practice it is still more confined to subsistence use). Indigenous peoples are also included in some common governance arrangements concerning natural resources. Under the international regime, commercialisation of subsistence whaling is impossible and also undesirable, as it would change without amendment the object and purpose of the Whaling Convention and its fundamental provisions. It is suggested that a certain modification may be introduced, ie, participation (along with states) of Indigenous peoples in a discussion of the allocation of Indigenous quotas at the meetings of the IWC. As it stands at present, only states have a decisive vote regarding the management of Aboriginal subsistence whaling.

### *iv. Outstanding Issues*

As Woker correctly observes, there are many limitations concerning Indigenous (Aboriginal) whaling. They relate to the species that can be hunted, the method of hunting and an overall duty of ecological approach in general environmental law of preservation of endangered species, which is based on the premise that the taking of animals by Indigenous peoples can only be done if the practice is sustainable.[64] This is consistent with a Resolution adopted by the 1983 IWC on Indigenous whaling, which states that Indigenous subsistence whaling should

[60] Hamaguchi (n 26) 141.
[61] ibid.
[62] Reeves (n 31).
[63] See Godden (ch 5 in this volume).
[64] Woker (n 2) 36–40.

be 'consistent with effective conservation of whale stocks'.[65] Woker rightly notes that the term 'effective conservation' is very vague and it is unclear to which aspect of conservation it refers.[66] In addition, Indigenous peoples have little say in the matters of Aboriginal whaling; it is up to respective governments to represent them in the IWC.[67] This lack of legal clarity and consistency in the drafting of paragraph 13 and in state practice makes the politicisation of Aboriginal whaling inevitable. By gaining a three-quarters majority in the IWC, any form of whaling that possesses some elements of Aboriginal subsistence whaling could potentially be considered and thus endorsed by the IWC (via this institutional mechanism) as Aboriginal subsistence whaling. Consequently, such whaling, which seems to have all the hallmarks of Aboriginal subsistence whaling, would not be endorsed by the IWC if, say, marginally more than a quarter of IWC members vote against it. Hamaguchi concludes that Aboriginal subsistence whaling should be approved only on condition that there is a cultural, nutritional and economic need for it, and that the whales being harvested are not threatened with extinction. Presumably, if the IWC members feel strongly about this lack of legal certainty and can form some majority to push for this, they could adopt some statement or declaration to shed more light on what constitutes ICRW-compliant Aboriginal subsistence whaling. Such a development could address the seeming inconsistency in the IWC and thus enhance the integrity of the regime in the minds of all its members. It is reasonable to assume that Aboriginal whaling, whilst not without its controversies, seems more acceptable for many than commercial whaling, given that the former involves strong arguments in relation to the cultural rights of marginalised social groups. However, as we have seen, the fact that Aboriginal whaling may be less opposed than commercial whaling does not mean that it is not contentious. A detailed analysis of Aboriginal whaling leads to the conclusion that it is equally problematic and involves its fair share of contentious issues that are questions of law and issues of ethics. The lack of agreement as to the definitive content of the term 'Aboriginal whaling' and the ongoing disputes regarding the number of whale stocks open to Aboriginal whaling result in the inability of the IWC to manage and regulate Aboriginal whaling effectively and consistently. This is further compounded by the fact that Aboriginal whaling also takes place outside the remit of the IWC and, with regard to such whaling, the real dearth, in many cases, of statistical data, along with the unilateral regulation on the part of other states, significantly undermines the chances for the effective multilateral regulation of this type of whaling.

[65] IWC, Report of the Thirty-Fourth Meeting, Chair's Report (1983), 38 Appendix 3, cited in Woker (n 2) 37.

[66] Woker (n 2) 37.

[67] ibid 38.

### C. Case Studies (under and outside the IWC)

Some Aboriginal whaling takes place outside the purview of the IWC in states that are not party to the ICRW, such as Equatorial Guinea, Indonesia, Canada and the Philippines, in which there are no quotas allocated by the IWC for Aboriginal whaling. These examples illustrate the difficulties in assessing the impact of Aboriginal whaling on the whale population, due to the lack of accurate data.

#### *i. Canada*

Canada is not a party to the ICRW, having withdrawn from it in 1982.[68] However, Canada has continued Aboriginal whaling since its departure and has shown reluctance to provide any statistics regarding whaling.[69] It is argued that the departure of Canada from the IWC had some beneficial effects, in particular as it regarded the IWC as a body only in fact in charge of commercial whaling, an assertion that may be disputed.[70]

Since Canada's withdrawal, whaling in Canada is regulated by national law. Aboriginal whale hunting is only permitted for the Inuit peoples (in the eastern Arctic) and by the Inuvialuit (in the western Arctic). In the eastern Arctic, whale hunting (for bowheads) occurs in the Nunavut Settlement Area, which is a self-governing Inuit territory within Canada. Quotas are set by the Nunavut Wildlife Management Board (NWMB) under the 1993 Nunavut Land Claims Agreement The NWMB has a mandate to adopt all decisions about the management of wildlife in Nunavat. It consists of four representatives of the Inuit peoples and four government representatives, plus a chairperson. Canada's Department of Fisheries and Oceans (DFO), the Hunters and Trappers Organizations and the Regional Wildlife organisations are co-management partners. The DFO acts only in an advisory capacity to the NWMB and to the hunting communities, advising on sustainable hunting levels.

The quotas for hunting whales used to be set on the basis of Marine Mammals Regulations by the DFO. However, a new decentralised system was put in place, taking the form of 'community-based management'. Under the new system, the quota system has been lifted and the local Hunters and Trappers Organizations (HTOs) manage the hunt. They have placed harvest limits on communities using a set of rules or by-laws which are developed by the local HTO. This set of rules or by-laws addresses the conservation and

[68] On Canada, see Milton MR Freeman et al, *Inuit, Whaling, and Sustainability (Contemporary Native American Communities)* (AltaMira Press, 1998) 62.

[69] Reeves (n 31) 90.

[70] Niall Alexander Rand, 'Reforming the International Whaling Commission: Indigenous Peoples, the Canadian Problem and the Road Ahead' (2017) 19 *International Community Law Review* 324, 353.

management of the whale population, the reduction of waste, hunter education and safety. The HTOs are commissioned to collect information on the number of whales wounded, killed and not landed. Inuit whaling relied on heavier bore rifles to kill the whales after a number of floats had been attached by harpoons. However, animal welfare, governed in Canada by section 446 of the Criminal Code, does not provide for routine inspections of animal care or enforcement of maintenance standards. To fill these gaps, an addition has been proposed to the Marine Mammal Regulations.[71] As Reeves notes:

> The legal status of whaling by Inuit in Canada was ambiguous. It was implicitly understood, at least by some Inuits and some bureaucrats, that a licence to hunt from the federal government was required, yet the documented killing and wounding of Bowheads in eastern Canada through the 1970s … and 1980s … remained outside any formal management context.[72]

In the western Arctic, the Inuvialuit have an ancient tradition of hunting bowheads. The management strategy was created by the 1984 Inuvialuit land claims agreement and developed jointly by the Canadian DFO, the Fisheries Joint Management Committee and the Aklavik Hunters and Trappers Committee relies on the IWC data. Reeves described the Aboriginal whaling of bowhead situation as follows:

> In effect, Canada was intent upon unilateral management of the Bowhead hunt while at the same time depending upon data, analysis and management advice generated within the IWC (primarily owing to the research programme of the North Slope Borough in Alaska).[73]

It is stated that Canada successfully created a limited Indigenous exception while banning any commercial whaling within its waters, which is attempting to reconcile the interests of whales and communities, accommodating their cultural diversity. Therefore: 'Ultimately Canada's experiment outside of the IWC should be regarded as a unique example of domestic regulatory success trying to achieve a specific domestic results.'[74] However, it may also set a precedent that successful whaling operations can be conducted outside the IWC.[75]

### *ii. Makah Indians*[76]

The case studies concerning the Makah peoples in the US and Inuit peoples in Canada have been included here to illustrate the complex issues that arise

[71] Reeves (n 31) 79.
[72] ibid 90.
[73] ibid 90.
[74] Rand (n 70) 359.
[75] ibid.
[76] For an in-depth discussion, see Jeremy Firestone and Jonathan Lilley, 'Aboriginal Subsistence Whaling and the Right to Practice and Revitalize Cultural Traditions and Customs' (2005) 8 *Journal of International Wildlife Law and Policy* 177.

with regard to Aboriginal whaling (internationally within the IWC and nationally within the US) and to illustrate how the definition of Aboriginal cultural needs can be very divisive. Whaling by the Makah peoples is one of the most controversial cases of Aboriginal whaling. It has been the subject of much discussion at the IWC and was also the subject of much legislative regulation and legal debate within the US, and it still remains controversial in various ways, including the following:

(i) it is an instance of a claim (there are others) to resume Aboriginal whaling after a period during which, for different reasons, whaling had been abandoned, in this case, a claim by the Makah people to resume whaling after a hiatus of several decades;
(ii) there were also doubts as to whether their whaling was purely Aboriginal subsistence whaling or whether a commercial dimension was also present;
(iii) the claim raised ethical concerns regarding the resumption of Aboriginal whaling; and
(iv) it also raised the issue as to whether Aboriginal whaling constitutes a cultural exemption.[77]

These outstanding questions in relation to the Makah peoples can be said to reflect general confusion surrounding Aboriginal whale hunting. Most importantly, the commercial aspect of whaling is very much at the centre of the debate on the nature of Aboriginal whaling.

## D. Concluding Remarks

The studying of whaling indicates that modern international law acknowledges a well-established status to the traditional livelihood of Indigenous peoples.[78] Heinämäki suggests that, from a legal point of view, Indigenous whaling should be treated as lawful if it complies with IWC measures and guidelines. However, she observes that growing environmental pressures (such as climate change) may eventually force Aboriginal peoples to abandon their whale hunting altogether.[79] The controversial approach to Aboriginal whaling was very visible during the 65th meeting of the IWC in 2014.[80] The meeting started with a vote (of 46 votes for, 11 against and three abstentions) regarding Denmark's proposal to raise Greenland's quotas per year from 2015 to 2018 (which was supported by the EU and the US) for: 19 fin whales, two bowhead whales, 10 humpback whales and 176 minke whales (12 from the common minke whale stock and

[77] Heinämäki (n 40) 46–52.
[78] ibid 45.
[79] ibid 57.
[80] http://iwc.int/iwc65docs.

164 from the West Greenland stock).[81] This proposal, which was defeated in 2012, gained approval in 2014, notwithstanding strong opposition within the IWC. Many states such as Monaco questioned the methods used to calculate 'need'. The Latin American group of countries known as the Buenos Aires Group, including Argentina, Chile and Uruguay, questioned Denmark over not reporting Greenland's catches taken since the last meeting as infractions. Counter-arguments were voiced by Guinea, Japan, Antigua and Barbuda, Norway and Iceland.[82] The Whale and Dolphin Conservation Society (WDCS), an NGO, which also spoke on behalf of the Animal Welfare Institute, has challenged the tonnage of whale meat that Greenland seeks because it is significantly more than all the marine protein currently being consumed by Greenlandic people from whales, seals and small cetaceans combined. Iceland and Norway were strongly criticised at the same meeting for their continuation of commercial whaling. Thus, the divisive approaches within the IWC relate to all types of whaling, also including Aboriginal whaling. It may be noted that that in relation to this type of whaling, there is a persistent question of discontent regarding the lack of any uniform approach to what constitutes 'needs'. There are also continuing discussions regarding the dividing line between commercial and Aboriginal whaling. In this respect, there are views expressed that the IWC has a 'money fetish', which results in an approach that all whaling that brings in money must be by nature unsustainable.[83] As Freeman aptly notes, Aboriginal whalers can be tolerated because they are poor, they do not have opportunities and they are isolated from the mainstream. On the other hand, non-Aboriginal whalers and their customers are intolerable, as they hold a privileged position in the mainstream.[84] Therefore, we can say that the whaling debate (involving Aboriginal whaling) has also 'been clouded with fuzzy indictments of money and capitalism, wrapped up in capricious notions about noble savages'.[85] According to Stone, the main problems with Aboriginal whaling are the special

[81] 'More than 800 whales were condemned today just in the Greenland vote', Wendy Higgins of the Humane Society International (HSI) told Agence France Press (AFP) on the first day of the controversy-laden gathering in Slovenia. 'We are concerned that the new IWC quota will give Greenland more whale meat than its native people need for nutritional subsistence and that the surplus will continue to be sold commercially, including to tourists', said the Animal Welfare Institute (AWI). See Celine Serrat, 'Whaling: Greenland Hunt Gets Okay, Iceland Blasted', *Yahoo News*, 15 September 2014, http://news.yahoo.com/whale-huddle-braces-clash-over-japanese-hunting-004713474.html.

[82] According to the AWI: 'When the non-governmental organizations were allowed to speak, the chair called on Whale and Dolphin Conservation, which spoke on behalf of itself and AWI and challenged the tonnage of whale meat that Greenland seeks because it is significantly more than all the marine protein currently being consumed by Greenlandic people, from whales, seals and small cetaceans put together' (AWI, Reports from the 65th Annual Meeting of the International Whaling Commission, https://awionline.org/content/2014-iwc-65-meeting-slovenia).

[83] Milton R Freeman, 'Is Money the Root of the Problem? Cultural Conflicts in the IWC' in Robert L Freidheim (ed), *Towards a Sustainable Whaling Regime* (University of Washington Press, 2001) 129.

[84] ibid 130.

[85] Christopher D Stone, 'Summing Up: Whaling and its Critics' in Friedheim (n 83) 180.

rules dealing with it, as the application of the Aboriginal exception to the Moratorium has been very uneven and inconsistent.[86] Stone asks whether in light of Aboriginal questionable quotas, it is just to deprive non-Aboriginal groups such as the Faroese and the Norwegians of whale meat in such an arbitrary fashion.[87]

Different views on this type of whaling vary from rather averse to Aboriginal whaling (or at least its current regulation by the IWC) to overly enthusiastic (professing that Aboriginal whaling trumps whale welfare). Therefore, without doubt, the question of Aboriginal whaling also contributes to misunderstandings, and the tense atmosphere and at times unproductive work at the IWC. Hossain suggested that that the full decision-making power should be vested in Indigenous peoples and not in states regarding the questions of Aboriginal hunting (whales and polar bears).[88] Such a solution appears to be unrealistic in the present circumstances. However, some participation of Indigenous peoples in the allocation of Aboriginal quotas would appear to be of merit and perhaps even helpful in terms of breaking the impasse in the IWC. It would also provide Indigenous peoples with the opportunity to voice their points of view which might contribute to achieving more understanding and coherence in the regulation of Aboriginal whaling.

## III. INDIGENOUS SEALING[89]

### A. Introduction

The question of Indigenous sealing is less complicated than that of whaling, but is not without its own controversies. The 1911 Fur Seal Treaty (Japan, Russia, Great Britain for Canada, and the US) was one of the first international instruments granting an Aboriginal exception to the Aleut and Aino (Ainu) peoples, who hunted seals using traditional methods and for non-commercial purposes, including food and shelter.[90] The hunting for seals was exempted for Aboriginal peoples hunting in canoes, not transported by or used in connection with other vessels and propelled wholly by paddles, oars and sails, and manned by no more

[86] ibid. Stone argues that the system of allocation of whale quotas for Aboriginal whaling leads to unexpected results, such as the Chukchi people feeding farmed foxes with allocated gray whale meat. He also presents a very interesting analysis of the Makah people's resumption of whaling, asking if this is really good to step backwards (ibid 283).

[87] ibid 281.

[88] Kamrul Hossain, 'Status of Indigenous Peoples in International Law' (2008) 5 *Miskolc Journal of International Law* 10.

[89] On sealing in general, see Nikolas Sellheim, *The Sea Hunt: Cultures, Economies and Legal Regimes* (Brill, 2018).

[90] Convention between the United States and Other Powers Providing for the Preservation and Protection of Fur Seals (adopted 7 July 1911) 37 Stat 1542, T S No 56.

than five persons each, in a way practised by Aboriginal peoples. The use of firearms was not permitted, nor were such peoples allowed to be employed or under the contract of delivery of the skins to other persons (Article I). As a result of the conclusion of the Treaty, the seal population increased significantly in the area of the Pribiloff Islands.[91]

The contemporary regime of Indigenous seal hunting is regulated at the international, regional and national levels, with the national level taking precedence in such a regulation. Unlike the regulation of Indigenous whaling, there is no international Convention to regulate sealing. This section will not deal with national regulation and will only analyse Indigenous sealing at the international level. It will briefly mention the North Atlantic Marine Mammal Commission (NAMMCO) regulation and the recent WTO case concerning sealing, which are a result of the sealing regulation by the EU.

### B. Sealing in European and International Law

This sub-section of the chapter will focus on sealing in EU law and international law. Both these areas are interlinked; as a result of the European regulation, a case was brought before the dispute settlement body of the WTO. The European regulation of sealing will be introduced with a view to providing some background to the WTO case. For the sake of completeness, the NAMMCO will be included, although its regulatory powers are weak and it has little influence on the quotas regarding Indigenous sealing, given that its powers are confined to the undertaking of research into stock conservation.

#### *i. The NAMMCO and the Joint Norwegian–Russian Fisheries Commission*

The NAMMCO has only recommendatory jurisdiction. Therefore, similar to whaling, it recommends rather than allocates quotas to Indigenous peoples (and local communities, including non-Indigenous peoples). In the inclusion of local peoples, the NAMMCO regime goes beyond the regulation in some other regimes, which only include the Indigenous exclusion, unlike, however, the Convention on Biological Diversity (CBD) (Article 8(j)), which also includes both Indigenous peoples and local communities.[92]

[91] US Fish and Wildlife Service, https://www.fws.gov/news/Historic/NewsReleases/1961/19610702.pdf.

[92] According to art 8(j) of the 1992 Convention on Biological Diversity (entered into force 29 December 1993, 1760 UNTS 79): 'Subject to its national legislation, respect, preserve and maintain knowledge, innovations and practices of indigenous and local communities embodying traditional lifestyles relevant for the conservation and sustainable use of biological diversity and promote their wider application with the approval and involvement of the holders of such knowledge, innovations and practices and encourage the equitable sharing of the benefits arising from the utilization of such knowledge, innovations and practices.'

The main goal of management is usually to ensure that human impacts on marine mammal populations are sustainable, meaning that they do not cause the populations to decrease below a predefined threshold. To do this, estimates of abundance are combined with past, present and projected future catch levels in a population model, a mathematical model that mimics the response of the population to catch. This enables managers to set allowable direct and/or indirect catch levels that will not endanger the population of seals.[93] The bilateral Norwegian–Russian Fisheries Commission also includes an Indigenous exemption. Its primary objective is the management of fisheries but nevertheless it allocates quotas for harp seals. Although in 2012 a ban on import seal products came into force in the Customs Union of Russia, Belarus and Kazakhstan, Indigenous sealing was exempted.[94]

### *ii. A Short Introduction to Sealing under EU Law*

The legislative history of sealing within the EU has a long and rather turbulent history.[95] It resulted in the adoption of Regulation No 1007/2009.[96] On 10 August 2010, the ban on trade in seal products came fully into effect, according to Commission Regulation 737/2010.9.[97] It was amended in October 2015 by Commission Regulation 737/2010. The ban was amended in 2015 in order to reflect the outcomes of WTO rulings in the *EC-Seal Products* case.[98] The ban applies to seal products produced in the EU and to imported seal products. Article 3(1) of Regulation (EC) No 1007/2009 as amended introduced an Inuit exception (the so-called 'IC' exception'). As Hennig explained:

> One of the most problematic aspects of the Seal Regime is the exclusionary effect the ban has had on Canadian Inuit sealers. Since the ban came into force, and up until 2015, the Canadian Inuit have not been able to benefit from the exception.[99]

[93] Cameron SG Jefferies, *Marine Mammal Conservation and the Law of the Sea* (Oxford University Press, 2016) 5.

[94] Nikolas Sellheim, 'A Legal Framework for Seals and Sealing in the Arctic' in Natalia Loukacheva (ed), *Polar Law and Resources* (Norden, 2015) 113; see also www.jointfish.com/eng/THE-FISHERIES-COMMISSION/HISTORY.html.

[95] On this, see ibid 140–67.

[96] Regulation No 1007/2009 of the European Parliament and Council on Trade in Seal Products (Basic Regulation) by the Council of the European Union on 27 July 2009, signed on 16 September and published in the Official Journal of the European Union on 31 October 2009.

[97] Commission Regulation (EU) No 737/2010 of 10 August 2010 laying down detailed rules for the implementation of Regulation (EC) No 1007/2009 of the European Parliament and of the Council on trade in seal products; Commission Implementing Regulation (EU) 2015/1850 of 13 October 2015 laying down detailed rules for the implementation of Regulation (EC) No 1007/2009 of the European Parliament and of the Council on trade in seal products [2015] OJ L271, 16 October, 1–11.

[98] Commission Implementing Regulation (EU) 2015/1850 of 13 October 2015 (n 96) 1–11. See Dorothée Cambou, 'The Impact of the Ban on Seal Products on the Rights of Indigenous Peoples: A European Issue' (2013) 5 *Yearbook of Polar Law* 389.

[99] Martin Hennig, 'The Untouchable Nature of the "EU Seal Regime": Is the European Union Liable for the Damages Suffered by the Canadian Inuit Due to the Violation of WTO Law in EC–Seal Products?' (2018) 33 *International Journal of Maritime & Costal Law* 403, 404.

The seal hunt is part of the socio-economics, culture and identity of the Inuit and other Indigenous communities, and it contributes greatly to their subsistence and development. This is the reason that the Regulation provides for an Inuit exception. It allows the placing on the EU market of seal products that result from hunts traditionally conducted by Inuit and other Indigenous communities if the conditions under Article 3(1) of Regulation (EC) No 1007/2009, as amended, have been met. Before being introduced into the EU market, seal products that qualify under the Inuit exception must first be attested by bodies recognised in accordance with Article 3 of the Commission Implementing Regulation (EU) 2015/1850.[100]

Some authors are very critical towards the EU regulation of sealing and are of the view that:

> The European Union's stance towards seal hunting follows narratives of preservation and thus does not show support of any trade in products stemming from hunts with high animal welfare standards… the welfare of seals only played a passing role in the adoption process of the regime. While the Proposal still aimed to improve the welfare of individual seals by providing economic incentives for sealers, this was fully replaced by the narrative of non-utilisation, manifested in a total ban on trade in seal products for the European Union. While inevitably the number of seals that was killed went down after the adoption of the regime, this does not mean that the welfare of those seals which are still hunted has improved.[101]

The regulation of sealing and whaling is a mixture of law and ethics, without clearly defined borders. This results in misunderstandings and conflicts. The commercial and cultural aspects of whaling and sealing and the welfare of animals appear to constitute a problem which may never be solved.

### *iii. WTO and Sealing*

The regulation of Indigenous sealing was the subject of a well-known case before the WTO,[102] which resulted from complaints by Canada and Norway

[100] http://ec.europa.eu/environment/biodiversity/animal_welfare/seals/seal_hunting.htm.

[101] Sellheim (n 89) 171.

[102] WTO, *European Communities – Measures Prohibiting the Importation and Marketing of Sea Products* (25 November 2013) WT/DS400/R, WT/DS04IR; AB, *European Communities – Measures Prohibiting the Importation and Marketing of Sea Products* (22 May 2014) WTDS400/AB/R. See also Elisabeth Whitsitt, 'A Comment on the Public Morals Exception in International Trade and the *EC-Seal Products* Case: Moral Imperialism and Other Concerns' (2014) 4 *Cambridge Journal of International and Comparative Law* 1376; Martin Hennig, 'The EU Seal Products Ban: Why Ineffective Animal Welfare Protection Cannot Justify Reade Restrictions under European and International Trade Law' (2015) 6 *Arctic Review on Law and Politics* 74; Rob Howse, Joanna Langille and Katie Sykes, 'Sealing the Deal: The WTO's Appellate Body Report in EC–Sea Products' (2014) 18(12) *ASIL Insights*, www.asil.org/insights/volume/18/issue/12/sealing-deal-wto%E2%80%99s-appellate-body-report-ec-%E2%80%93-seal-products; Ludwig Kramer, 'Case Note: Sea Killing, The Inuit and European Union Law' (2012) 21 *Review of European, Comparative & International Environmental*

against legislation adopted by the EU in 2009 to prohibit the importation and marketing of seal products (the EU Seal Regime),[103] with an IC exception.[104] The issue of the ban proved to be very emotive, as in the context of Indigenous culture in Canada, subsistence seal hunting plays an important role, but such hunting was fiercely opposed by animal welfare organisations.[105] On 24 January 2014, Canada and Norway filed an appeal against the earlier panel's decision, which resulted in the report of the WTO Appellate Body (AB). Under the EU Seal Regime, there was one exception to the overall import ban, namely, for products of traditional Indigenous hunting ('the Indigenous communities' or the 'IC exception'). Canada and Norway challenged the EU Seal Regime at the WTO. According to these states, this regime was discriminatory against their sealing industries, as Indigenous sealers comprise a very small proportion of the seal industry in Canada. The hunting of seals is carried out mainly by non-Indigenous fishermen on Canada's East Coast and in Newfoundland, whereas in Greenland, the sealing industry is almost entirely conducted by the Inuit peoples. According to Canada and Norway, the EU Seal Regime entailed de facto discrimination, 'as the seal products made by hunters in Greenland can more easily enter the EU's market, given the higher percentage of Indigenous hunters as compared to that of Canada or Norway vis-à-vis their seal industries'.[106]

The EU Seal Regime breached the 'most-favoured-nation' clause in Article I:1 of the General Agreement on Tariffs and Trade (GATT) 1994. The Regime distinguished between 'commercial' seal products (prohibited) and seal products the import of which was allowed into the EU under the IC exception. Furthermore, the AB stated that the EU had not done enough to facilitate access of Canadian Inuit seal products to the exception.[107] It was said that some steps

*Law* 291 (according to whom the Canadian government's quota of seals has been increased beyond 250,000 each year; the protests against these quotas also concerned the allegedly inhumane methods of killing and suffering caused for seals). See also Dorothée Cambou, 'The Impact of the Ban on Seal Products on the Rights of Indigenous Peoples: A European Issue' (2013) 4 *Yearbook of Polar Law* 389; Nikolas Selheim, 'The Neglected Tradition? The Genesis of the EU Seal Products Trade Ban and Commercial Sealing' (2013) 5 *Yearbook of Polar Law* 417; Rob Howse, Joanna Langille and Katie Sykes, 'Animal Welfare, Public Morals and Trade: The WTO Panel Report in EC–Seal Products' (2014) 18(2) *ASIL Insights*, www.asil.org/insights/volume/18/issue/2/animal-welfare-public-morals-and-trade-wto-panel-report-ec-%E2%80%93-seal?; Nikolas Sellheim, 'Policies and Influence. Tracing and Locating the EU Seal Products Trade Regulation' (2015) 17 *International Community Law Review* 3.

[103] Regulation (EC) No 1007/2009 of the European Parliament and of the Council of 16 September 2009 on Trade in Seal Products [2009] OJ L286, 36; Regulation (EC) No 737/2010 of the European Parliament and of the Council [2010] OJ L216, 1.

[104] Regulation (EC) No 1007/2009 (n 103) art 3: 'The placing on the market of seal products shall be allowed only where the seal products result from hunts traditionally conducted by Inuit and other indigenous communities and contribute to their subsistence. These conditions shall apply at the time or point of import for imported products.'

[105] Sellheim (n 102) 9.

[106] Howse, Langille and Sykes (n 102).

[107] WTO (n 102) para 5.319; AB (n 102) para 5.337; Howse, Langille and Sykes (n 102).

could be taken to encourage improved welfare standards in IC hunts and to facilitate Canadian Inuit hunters' access to the EU market under:

(i) the quota-setting mechanism (which is already in place); and
(ii) a supervision and control scheme in order to establish the future management of Aboriginal subsistence whaling.

In fact, all almost Greenlandic seal products qualified under the IC exception, but Canadian seal products were unable to meet the requirements of the IC exception; therefore, Canadian seal products were treated in a disadvantageous way.[108]

The AB upheld the Panel's conclusion that the EU Seal Regime may be justified under the general exceptions to WTO rules (as per Article XX of GATT, given that the offending measure (the EU Seal Regime) may be necessary to protect public morals regarding seal welfare, as per Article XX (a) of GATT.[109] However, the AB decided that the EU Seal Regime did not meet the requirements of the chapeau to Article XX of GATT because the IC exception operates in a way that amounts to 'arbitrary or unjustifiable discrimination'[110] due to the lack of a sufficient explanation from the EU as to how the IC exception was related to the objectives of the EU Seal Regime.[111]

The EU has not sought to explain how seal products hunted by Inuit or other Indigenous peoples could be reconciled with, or related to, the policy objective of addressing public moral concerns regarding animal welfare, as seal hunting for commercial or Indigenous purposes causes the same suffering. Another issue which was raised by the AB was the establishment of the 'recognized body', which is a burdensome task, especially in the view of the EU assistance in the establishment of a 'recognized body' in Greenland, but not in Canada.[112] Despite the amended Directive, the Seal Regime has led to an almost complete collapse of the sealing industry in Canada.[113] In this context, two cases before the CJEU have to be mentioned: the 2013 case of *Inuit Tapiriit Kanatami and Others v Parliament and Council*[114] and the 2015 case of *Inuit Tapiriit Kanatami and Others v Commission*.[115] Both of these cases were unsuccessful. The first was considered to be inadmissible and the second was rejected on its merits. The Court has rejected the Inuit pleadings, inter alia, that the EU Seal Regime breached the fundamental economic and social rights of the seal hunting communities. Despite the five-year ban on the trade on seal products,

[108] Hennig (n 102) 405.
[109] AB (n 102) para 5.167.
[110] ibid para 5.328.
[111] ibid para 5.319.
[112] ibid paras 5.337–5.338.
[113] Hennig (n 102) 408.
[114] Case C-583/11 *Inuit Tapiriit Kanatami and Others v Parliament and Council* [2013] ECLI:EU:C:2013:625.
[115] Case C-398/13 *Inuit Tapiriit Kanatami and Others v Commission* [2015], ECLI:EU:C:2015:535.

'under current EU law, the prospects of bringing an action for damages before the CJEU seeking damages for the five-year exclusion from the EU market of Canadian Inuit seal products are grim'.[116]

## IV. CONCLUSIONS

This chapter has dealt with Indigenous whaling and sealing in marine areas. The analysis of both activities has clearly shown that there are some common issues. However, there are also significant differences. Aboriginal whaling is governed by an international and global convention and sealing is not regulated by such a treaty, but instead is subject to very divergent national regulations. The Indigenous whaling under the ICRW is a contentious issue from the point of view of quotas allocated and the lack of precise definitions of what constitutes Aboriginal whaling, and at times the lack of a clear division between commercial and Aboriginal whaling activities. Another problem is the lack of the direct participation of Indigenous peoples in the decision-making process in the IWC, but, as noted above, certain changes are under consideration. It may also be that the governing body, the IWC, is an outdated institution, which is not capable of dealing with contemporary questions. This situation is exacerbated by a notorious lack of cooperation between the Member States. Some evidence of this state of affairs is the withdrawal of Japan from the Whaling Convention, effective on 30 June 2019.

Sealing is no less contentious, as evidenced by the WTO cases. The lack of an international regulation of sealing and relying on national regulation is not conducive to the development of sustainable sealing. Killing methods used by Indigenous peoples at times raise animal welfare and human safety issues. It has also been suggested that training, education, technology transfer and monetary contributions can be employed to standardise Indigenous killing methods.[117] However, as things stand, both Indigenous whaling and sealing should be subject to far-reaching reforms, as the current state of affairs in both areas is far from satisfactory.

[116] Hennig (n 102) 414.
[117] Jefferies (n 93) 106–07.

# 4

# *The Jurisprudence of Artisanal Fishing Rights Revisited*

STEPHEN ALLEN

## I. INTRODUCTION

TRADITIONAL FISHING RIGHTS have long been recognised in customary international law, but the advent of the Law of the Sea Convention (LOSC) seemed to cast doubt on their continuing importance at a general level.[1] Nevertheless, a number of recent arbitral decisions – including *Chagos Award* and *South China Sea Award* – appear to have created the conditions which foster the juridical connections between traditional (or artisanal) fishing rights and the Convention.[2] This chapter explores the evolving jurisprudence concerning these non-exclusive fishing rights. In particular, it scrutinises their origins in the doctrine of vested rights before examining the consequences on the plane of international law. It goes on to assess the manner in which the LOSC regulates artisanal fishing rights and the limits of its framework as far as the protection of these communal entitlements are concerned. It concludes by considering the role that other bodies of law may perform in safeguarding marine resource entitlements for the benefit of artisanal fishing communities and coastal-based Indigenous peoples alike.

Artisanal fishing communities are, typically, distinguishable from Indigenous peoples, but they can, and do, overlap in concrete settings.[3] Moreover, artisanal

[1] United Nations Convention on the Law of the Sea (adopted 10 December 1982, entered into force 16 November 1994) 1833 UNTS 396. The LOSC does provide for the continuity of traditional fishing rights in the waters of archipelagic states: see arts 47 and 51.

[2] *Chagos Marine Protected Area Award (Mauritius/UK)*, Annex VII LOSC Tribunal, PCA (18 March 2015); and *South China Sea (Merits) Award (Philippines/People's Republic of China)*, Annex VII LOSC Tribunal, PCA (12 July 2016).

[3] eg, the Chagos Islanders qualify as both an Indigenous people and a community of artisanal fishers. See the Divisional Court's judgment in *R (Bancoult No 3) v Secretary of State for Foreign and Commonwealth Affairs* [2013] EWHC 1502 (Admin); Stephen Allen, *The Chagos Islanders and International Law* (Hart Publishing, 2014); and Amy Schwebel, 'International Law and Indigenous

fishing communities and Indigenous peoples often experience similar problems, including in relation to the issues of how sub-state groups can secure recognition of their traditional rights in marine settings, and how such entitlements can be maintained, given the strong tendency of state legal systems to restrict the extent to which historical harvesting methods can be altered and/or changes in the nature and scale of harvesting activities (ie, commercialisation) can be made without losing their 'traditional' character. As a number of contributions to this volume show, these matters generate fundamental questions about how the international legal system (and national legal systems) recognise and accommodate ancient, distinct normative orders. Against this background, there is scope for both sets of rights-holders to make a common cause as sub-state groups in key respects. Nevertheless, some scholars have drawn a conceptual divide between artisanal fishing rights and Indigenous marine resource rights by pointing out that although artisanal rights can be pressed into action at the inter-state level, indigenous entitlements are exercisable against their 'own' state.[4] Such a binary divide is clearly questionable in principle because categorising Indigenous claim-rights as, essentially, domestic in application has the effect of reinforcing the statist character of the international legal order.

To be sure, Indigenous peoples may be more focused on the job of ensuring that those states which have enveloped them give effect to their marine rights than on advancing claims against neighbouring states. Even so, in certain situations, Indigenous peoples are capable of asserting such entitlements against *another* coastal state as well. Of course, a state may take up the claim of one or more of its nationals at the inter-state level via the mechanism of diplomatic protection.[5] However, this approach has been initiated only rarely in connection with the protection of the rights of Indigenous peoples in marine areas.[6] Further, this chapter considers whether the exercise of diplomatic protection – which gives rise to state rights in keeping with the 'Mavrommatis fiction'[7] – is necessarily the best way forward in such situations, given that it raises wider questions about the normative character of the rights of Indigenous peoples (and those belonging to other sub-state societal groups) within the international legal order.

Peoples' Rights: What Next for the Chagossians' in Stephen Allen and Chris Monaghan (eds), *Fifty Years of the British Indian Ocean Territory: Legal Perspectives* (Springer, 2018).

[4] See, eg, Polite Dyspriani, *Traditional Fishing Rights: Analysis of State Practice* (UN, 2011); and Endalew Enyew, 'The South China Sea Award and the Treatment of Traditional Fishing Rights within the Territorial Sea', 10 August 2016, http://site.uit.no/jclos.

[5] See section III.C below.

[6] This was demonstrated, in the Indigenous context, by the conclusion of the 1984 Torres Strait Treaty between Australia and Papua New Guinea. See SB Kaye, 'Jurisdictional Patchwork: Law of the Sea and Native Title Issues in the Torres Strait' (2001) 2 *Melbourne Journal of International Law* 381. See also the *Behring Sea Arbitration Award* (Great Britain/USA) 15 August 1893, 179 CTS No 8, 97,103 [8].

[7] See section III.C below.

## II. THE CHARACTER OF TRADITIONAL/ARTISANAL FISHING RIGHTS

Traditional fishing rights have been acknowledged to exist in situations where states have been engaged in processes of maritime delimitation. In such cases, the exercise of non-exclusive fishing rights which have long persisted in a given maritime area have been interpreted as a legitimate – but exceptional – factor in determining the position of maritime boundaries.[8] Such rights may also be recognised when an area that was formerly part of the High Seas has been enclosed as a result of the introduction of new maritime zones by a coastal state.[9] Nevertheless, there has been a marked shift in the perceived character of these traditional fishing entitlements in recent years. Specifically, during the last two decades, greater importance seems to have been attached to the type of the fishing being undertaken for the purpose of qualifying as 'traditional fishing' rather than simply determining the duration of the fishing activity in question. Advocates of Indigenous rights are familiar with debates about what is meant by the adjective 'traditional'. Does it connote a practice that has survived across the generations, perhaps since time immemorial (ie, is it a temporal signifier)? Does it require participants to use historical methods when carrying out a given activity? Or does the practice amount to a culturally symbolic performance which is intimately bound up with communal identity and livelihood rather than one which is undertaken principally for commercial purposes?

In the 1974 *Fisheries Jurisdiction Cases*, the International Court of Justice (ICJ) decided that Iceland's newly extended Exclusive Fishing Zone had to accommodate the traditional fishing rights of the UK and the Federal Republic of Germany on the grounds that their non-exclusive fishing rights in the maritime area in issue had been established for a long period of time.[10] Nonetheless, it was clear that the fishing activities in question were being conducted on an industrial scale. The nature of the fishing practices involved was not a material factor as far at the ICJ was concerned. It was satisfied that the withdrawal of such entitlements would have a substantial and detrimental impact on the livelihoods

[8] An ICJ Chamber observed that traditional fishing activities could only amount to a relevant circumstance for the purpose of maritime delimitation if the standard methodology would produce a 'radically inequitable' result, ie, one that is 'likely to entail catastrophic repercussions for the livelihood and economic well-being of the population of the countries concerned': *Delimitation of the Maritime Boundary in the Gulf of Maine Area (Canada/USA)* (1984) ICJ Reps 329 [237]. See also the *Jan Mayen Case (Denmark/Norway)* (1993) ICJ Reps 38. The exceptional nature of moving a boundary on the basis of traditional fishing activities was reiterated in the *Delimitation of Maritime Boundary Award (Barbados/Trinidad and Tobago)*, Annex VII LOSC Tribunal, PCA (11 April 2006) [266]–[269].

[9] The *Fisheries Jurisdiction Cases (UK/Iceland) and (Federal Republic of Germany/Iceland)* (1974) ICJ Reps 3 and 175. More recently, this issue has become significant in situations where a coastal state declares new maritime zones pursuant to the LOSC's introduction. See W Michael Reisman and Mahnoush Arsanjani, 'Some Reflections on the Effect of Artisanal Fishing on Maritime Boundary Delimitation' in M Ndiaye and R Wolfrum (eds), *Law of the Sea, Environmental Law and Settlement of Disputes* (Brill 2007) 629–65.

[10] *Fisheries Jurisdiction Cases* (n 9) [61].

of those fishers who depended on continued access to these fishing grounds. It is highly improbable that the British and German fishers had been fishing in the waters claimed by Iceland since time immemorial, given the distance involved. Consequently, in the *Fisheries Jurisdiction Cases*, the notion of traditional fishing rights was understood in a purely temporal sense and even then only by recourse to a relatively short timeframe and not by reference to the type of fishing methods which were being observed.

In sharp contrast, artisanal fishing practices invariably involve fishing on a small commercial scale using rudimentary methods that have been followed in a given maritime area often since time immemorial. In many ways, the *Eritrea/Yemen Awards* constituted a pivotal moment for the jurisprudence of artisanal fishing rights.[11] The Eritrea/Yemen Tribunal was significantly influenced by the United Nations (UN) Food and Agriculture Organisation's 1995 Fisheries Infrastructure Development Project Report, which stressed the importance of a number of key requirements for inter-generational fishing activities to qualify as 'artisanal fishing'.[12] Further, the Tribunal was anxious to distinguish this type of fishing from industrial fishing. It noted that:

> 'Artisanal fishing' is used in contrast to 'industrial fishing'. It does not exclude improvements in powering the small boats, in the techniques of navigation, communication or in the techniques of fishing; but the traditional regime of fishing does not extend to large-scale commercial or industrial fishing nor to fishing by nationals of third States in the Red Sea, whether small-scale or industrial.[13]

The character and scope of artisanal fishing rights were closely scrutinised in the *Barbados/Trinidad and Tobago Arbitration Case* and the analysis undertaken in the parties' pleadings has contributed to our understanding of the concept of artisanal fishing rights in key respects.[14] At a definitional level, Barbados observed in the pleadings that 'traditional artisanal fishing may be broadly conceived as akin to an irrevocable licence available to certain members of a functional, intergenerational group, defined cumulatively in terms of nationality, occupation, and prior exploitation of the resources of a specific maritime region'.[15] This led Barbados to conclude that: 'In the lexicon of international law … artisanal fishing denotes traditional fishing.'[16]

[11] *First Award in the Eritrea/Yemen Case (Territorial Sovereignty)*, PCA, 9 October 1998; and its *Second Award (Maritime Delimitation)*, PCA, 17 December 1999.

[12] UN FAO's Fisheries Infrastructure Development Project Report on Fishing in Eritrean Waters (1995), cited in the *Second Eritrea/Yemen Award* (n 11) [105].

[13] ibid [106].

[14] *Barbados/Trinidad and Tobago Award* (n 8). The Tribunal did not engage fully with the substantive arguments advanced by the parties on this issue due to its finding that the factual basis underpinning Barbados' claim had not been established.

[15] Barbados' Reply (n 8) [409].

[16] ibid.

In its 2016 *South China Sea Award*, the Tribunal endorsed the artisanal/industrial fishing distinction adopted by the *Eritrea/Yemen Awards*,[17] but it went further by observing that:

> Artisanal fishing has been a matter of concern in a variety of international fora without any common definition having been adopted ... Despite this attention, the essential defining element of artisanal fishing remains, as the tribunal in *Eritrea v Yemen* noted, relative. The specific practice of artisanal fishing will vary from region to region, in keeping with local customs. Its distinguishing characteristic will always be that, in contrast with industrial fishing, artisanal fishing will be simple and carried out on a small scale, using fishing methods that largely approximate those that have historically been used in the region.[18]

The increasing attention paid by arbitral tribunals to the fishing methods used in situations where traditional fishing claims are asserted has had a discernible impact on both the nature and scope of this kind of non-exclusive activity. Consequently, it seems reasonable to conclude that, for the most part, traditional fishing rights are largely equated with artisanal fishing rights nowadays.

## III. THE DOCTRINE OF VESTED (OR ACQUIRED) RIGHTS

### A. The General Concept and Scope of Vested Rights

The doctrine of vested, or acquired, rights originated as a response to situations of state succession and has achieved the status of a general principle of law.[19] The principle holds that private rights acquired in, or recognised by, one legal system survive the changes that come about with a transfer of sovereignty by ensuring that they retain their legal validity in the succeeding legal system. More recently, the doctrine has also been considered to be relevant in situations where maritime areas, such as the High Seas, are enclosed pursuant to claims made by coastal states.[20] In particular, the doctrine of vested rights seems to have gained resonance for the purpose of establishing traditional fishing rights in relation to processes initiated to establish maritime boundaries and the declaration of maritime zones. For instance, the South China Sea Tribunal was

[17] *South China Sea Award* (n 2) [795]–[796].

[18] ibid [797].

[19] See Reisman and Arsanjani (n 9) 658–59.

[20] The doctrine of vested rights has also been used to account for the recognition of certain rights belonging to Indigenous peoples, at least within common law jurisdictions. See PG McHugh, *Aboriginal Title: The Modern Jurisprudence of Tribal Land Rights* (Oxford University Press, 2011). But, as discussed below, such grand-parented rights are vulnerable to the sovereign authority of the successor state in the absence of constitutional protection.

keen to embrace the vested rights argument advanced by the Philippines. Specifically, it understood that:

> The legal basis for protecting artisanal fishing stems from the notion of vested rights and the understanding that, having pursued a livelihood through artisanal fishing over an extended period, generations of fishermen have acquired a right, akin to property, in the ability to continue to fish in the manner of their forebears. Thus, traditional fishing rights extend to artisanal fishing that is carried out largely in keeping with the longstanding practice of the community, in other words to 'those entitlements that all fishermen have exercised continuously through the ages' … *Importantly, artisanal fishing rights attach to the individuals and communities that have traditionally fished in an area. These are not the historic rights of States, as in the case of historic titles, but private rights, as was recognised in* Eritrea v Yemen. (Emphasis added)[21]

In support of its analysis, the Tribunal relied on treatment of the Permanent Court of International Justice (PCIJ) of this doctrine in the *Certain German Interests in Polish Upper Silesia* case.[22] Specifically, in its judgment, the Court noted that:

> Private rights acquired under the existing law do not cease on a change of sovereignty … [E]ven those who contest the existence in international law of a general principle of State succession do not go as far as to maintain that private rights including those acquired from the State as the owner of the property are invalid against a successor in sovereignty.[23]

This authority has been marshalled in support of the stability and continuity of legal orders by many eminent international lawyers.[24] However, there are certain difficulties with harnessing the idea of vested rights, as it was elaborated in the *German Interests* case, for the purpose of sustaining artisanal fishing claims. In that case, the Court was confronted with a state of affairs where Poland – the successor state – was seeking to invalidate contracts entered into by representatives of the German state and individual German settlers, who had subsequently become Polish citizens. Accordingly, in the *German Interests* case, two comparable municipal legal systems were involved, the argument in favour of continuity was seen as overwhelming, and the means of giving effect to such rights was relatively straightforward.

In any event, the doctrine's contours have remained contested at a general level.[25] It has been claimed that the principle mandates that the transfer of

[21] *South China Sea Award* (n 2) [798].

[22] *Certain German Interests in Polish Upper Silesia*, Merits, Judgment of 25 May 1926, PCIJ Series A, No 7, 4, 42, cited in ibid [808].

[23] *German Interests Case* (n 22) 36.

[24] See Hersch Lauterpacht, *Private Law Sources and Analogies in International Law* (Longman, 1927); and DP O'Connell, *State Succession in Municipal Law and International Law*, vol 1 (Cambridge University Press, 1967); and Reisman and Arsanjani (n 9) 658–59.

[25] Lauterpacht acknowledged that the principle was problematic in certain respects and was ripe for codification. See Eli Lauterpacht (ed), *Hersch Lauterpacht: International Law: Collected Papers*,

sovereignty has no bearing on pre-existing private rights, which must be fully respected by a new sovereign's legal system; however, even the doctrine's leading proponents have adopted a more qualified approach. For example, O'Connell admitted that it amounts to 'no more than a principle that a change in sovereignty should not touch the interests of individuals more than is necessary' and that international minimum standards would need to be observed in the event of the alteration or termination of vested rights in any given case.[26] Accordingly, while a new sovereign may be capable of introducing new laws which may affect, or abrogate, pre-existing entitlements belonging to foreign nationals, such a course of action would not be tenable if it compromised the applicable human rights law.[27]

### B. Vested Rights and the 'Mavrommatis Fiction'

Another case concerning vested rights, which is especially significant for the present purposes, is the *Mavrommatis Palestine Concessions Case*.[28] Mavrommatis, a Greek national, was granted certain concessions relating to Palestine by the Ottoman Empire. However, after the First World War, Britain (the mandatory authority) granted overlapping concessions to someone else. Mavrommatis complained that Britain had expropriated his property and, ultimately, Greece initiated proceedings against Britain. At one level, the case involved an unremarkable exercise of diplomatic protection, a mechanism which allows a state to take up the case of one of its nationals where the individual concerned has been injured by the internationally wrongful conduct of another state. Nevertheless, at the jurisdiction stage, the PCIJ famously observed that through the exercise of diplomatic protection, 'a State is in reality asserting its own rights – its right to ensure, in the person of its subjects, respect for the rules of international law'.[29] Therefore, according to the Court, by taking up the claim of one of its nationals at the inter-state level, a state

vol 1 (Cambridge University Press, 1970) 479–80. The ILC considered certain aspects of the doctrine to be 'extremely controversial'; Second Report of the Special Rapporteur on State Succession, *ILC Yearbook* (1969) vol 2, 228–29.

[26] See O'Connell (n 24) 266; and RY Jennings and A Watts (eds), *Oppenheim's International Law*, vol 1, 9th edn (Longman, 1992) 216. Others have pointed out that a succeeding state possesses the same freedom to change the law as its predecessor once exercised: see James Crawford, *Brownlie's Principles of Public International Law*, 8th edn (Oxford University Press, 2012) 429.

[27] MN Shaw, *International Law*, 8th edn (Cambridge University Press, 2017) 758. See, eg, *Mabo v Queensland [No 1]* (1988) 166 CLR 186.

[28] See Michael Waibel, 'Mavrommatis Palestine Concessions Case (Greece v Great Britain) (1924–1927)' in Eirik Bjorge and Cameron Miles (eds), *Landmark Cases in Public International Law* (Hart Publishing, 2017) 33–59.

[29] *Mavrommatis Palestine Concession Case* (1924) PCIJ Rep Series A No 2 (Jurisdiction), 12. This position was echoed by the ICJ in the *Nottebohm Case (Liechtenstein/Guatemala)* (1955) ICJ Reps 4, 24.

is – *in effect* – transforming that individual's private rights into state rights. This interpretation has become known as the Mavrommatis fiction. The ICJ has subsequently observed that this entitlement is not counter-balanced by the existence of a concomitant international legal obligation; instead, the state in question is the sole judge of whether to grant diplomatic protection and an affected national has no recourse as a matter of international law if that state chooses not to act.[30]

The Mavrommatis fiction has attracted serious criticism over the years, but it has been defended on the ground that it provides individuals with a vital remedial device through which their rights can be vindicated on the international plane.[31] But Pellet points out that the approach articulated in the *Mavrommatis* case fails to accord with reality, not least the fact that the trigger for the exercise of diplomatic protection is the violation of a given individual's private rights.[32] He attributes the fiction to an ideological commitment to the current structure of the international legal order. In particular, by maintaining that diplomatic protection involves the exercise of state right, individuals (and, by implication, sub-state groups) are denied international legal personality by a system that evolved to regulate – exclusively – relations between states.[33] Consequently, Pellet argues that the existing approach should be abandoned in favour of one which recognises that the rights involved belong to the individuals concerned and that the state is acting in a purely representative capacity when it invokes the mechanism of diplomatic protection.[34] But, as things stand, although certain remedial advantages arise from the continued observance of the Mavrommatis fiction, the implications cannot be ignored for individuals. This fiction has special resonance in relation to the protection of traditional fishing rights, given their grounding in the doctrine of vested rights. Clearly, the current approach leaves any rights that non-state actors may have at the international level vulnerable to state discretion and, for obvious reasons, this is hardly a satisfactory position for marginalised minorities and Indigenous peoples to be in. In contrast, the approach championed by Pellet not only has the advantage of according with reality, but would also have the effect of strengthening the international legal personality of the individuals and societal groups involved.

[30] See the *Barcelona Traction Case (Belgium/Spain)* (1970) ICJ Reps 3, 44; and the ILC's 'Draft Articles on Diplomatic Protection with Commentaries' (UN, 2006) 28.

[31] See the ILC's Commentary in art 1 of the 'Draft Articles' (n 30) 27. There has been increasing support for the 'two rights' thesis, with international courts now being more sympathetic to the idea that, in cases of diplomatic protection, the state is invoking its own right *and* those of the affected individuals. See Waibel (n 28) 54. However, the ILC's Draft art 1 does not explicitly endorse such an approach, preferring instead to follow an open-ended approach: see Commentary 27[5].

[32] A Pellet, 'The Second Death of Euripide Mavrommatis? Notes on the ILC's Draft Articles on Diplomatic Protection' (2008) 7 *Law and Practice of International Courts and Tribunals* 33, 37.

[33] ibid 37–38.

[34] ibid 51–52.

## C. Vested Rights and Traditional/Artisanal Fishing

The question for present purposes is whether and how ideas of vested rights developed in the context of state succession are applicable to the case where a given maritime area, which previously formed part of the High Seas, becomes subject to the sovereignty, or jurisdiction, of a given coastal state. In such circumstances, it is clear that the doctrine's general interpretation is open to question on the basis that the relationship between the two legal systems involved – international law and the domestic legal system of the coastal state in issue – are not, prima facie, comparable for the purpose of the operation of the vested rights doctrine. Gerald Fitzmaurice addressed the manner in which the doctrine of vested rights operates in relation to traditional fishing rights as state entitlements by way of his analysis of the *Anglo-Norwegian Fisheries Case*.[35] His insight on this point is worth quoting at length:

> Thus if the fishing vessels of a given country have been accustomed from time immemorial, or over a long period, to fish in a certain area, on the basis of the area being high seas and common to all, it may be said that *their country has through them* (and although they are private vessels having no specific authority) *acquired a vested interest* that the fisheries of that area should remain available to its fishing vessels (of course on a non-exclusive basis) – so that if another country asserts a claim to that area as territorial waters, which is found to be valid or comes to be recognized, this can only be *subject to the acquired rights of fishery in question*, which must continue to be respected. (Emphasis added)[36]

A number of points are worth noting at this stage. First, it is clear that, in this passage, Fitzmaurice is concerned with the acquisition of non-exclusive rights – which he asserts belong to states – rather than exclusive historic rights.[37] Second, in discussing the significance of the notion of vested rights pursuant to traditional fishing claims in situations where a coastal state asserts that a given maritime area forms part of its territorial waters, Fitzmaurice argues that such traditional rights are binding on a coastal state because they constitute the stronger rights in question (as they are pre-existing entitlements).[38]

Third, from Fitzmaurice's careful formulation, it appears he is saying that *before* a coastal state makes a new claim that a certain marine area comes within its territorial waters, another state which subsequently asserts non-exclusive fishing rights in those waters (which were previously part of the High Seas)

[35] *Anglo-Norwegian Fisheries Case (UK/Norway)* (1951) ICJ Reps 116.

[36] G Fitzmaurice, 'The Law and Procedure of the International Court of Justice, 1951–1954. General Principles and Sources of Law' (1953) 30 *British Year Book of International Law* 1, 51.

[37] ibid 47–50. See also Zhou Keyuan, 'Historic Rights in International Law and in China's Practice' (2001) 32 *Ocean Development & International Law* 149.

[38] Fitzmaurice (n 36) 51.

has no rights until those waters are claimed and enclosed. It may be supposed that, until that moment, the other state possesses nothing more than the freedoms it enjoys in common with other states. Such an initial impression might be supported by the view that no individual, or state, can have enforceable property or private rights in the High Seas, as it constitutes *res communis*. This view might also make sense when this matter is considered by reference to the way in which the doctrine of acquired rights works in general as it facilitates the continuity of rights conferred, or recognised, by one legal system when it has been superseded by another legal system. The difficulty with the general account, when applied in the context of traditional fishing rights, is that it purports to turn a freedom into a right which is then opposable against all other states. Fitzmaurice does not seem to appreciate the full implications of his analysis in this respect. Instead, he notes that:

> In the case of the sea, which is *res communis*, international law confers a positive right on all to exploit its resources – and anyone who does so is exercising a substantive right, and not merely availing himself of a faculty to do something which international law does not prohibit.[39]

He goes on:

> [A]nd if this right is actually exercised for sufficiently long in a particular area, this may lead to the formation of a vested interest, conferring special rights in relation to that area as such, i.e. to continue the exploitation there, even though the area passes under the jurisdiction of a coastal State.[40]

This observation prompts reflection on the relationship between the private rights in question and the claimant state. In this context, as will be discussed in the next section, it is worth noting that, for instance, in the *Eritrea/Yemen Case*, the private rights in question were not comprehensible by reference to the national laws of Eritrea or Yemen, respectively. Indeed, the non-exclusive entitlements exercisable by the fisher-folk in issue had emerged long before the states parties to the dispute came into existence, so they were not underpinned by modern conceptions of state sovereignty or indeed the idea that the High Seas constitute *res communis*.

In the circumstances, as Fitzmaurice's reasoning shows, international law – as a distinct normative regime – cannot account for the creation of traditional fishing rights or at least not on its own. Instead, it must rely on another normative system (eg, a municipal legal order or, as discussed below, a hybrid normative order) by which the prior legal validity of private rights can be established pursuant to the operation of the doctrine of vested rights.

[39] ibid 52.
[40] ibid.

## IV. THE HYBRID NATURE OF ARTISANAL FISHING RIGHTS

In its *First Award*, the Eritrea/Yemen Tribunal declared that its finding that Yemen possessed sovereignty over certain islands in the Red Sea did not prevent the ancient traditional fishing regime, which entitled artisanal fishers from both Eritrea and Yemen to access and harvest resources in this marine area, from continuing.[41] In its *Second Award*, the Tribunal sought to elaborate on the content and ambit of this regime which, it resolved, would straddle any maritime boundaries delimited.[42] It justified this regime by recourse to wider Islamic concepts which had, in its view, acquired the status of a regional tradition.[43] Further, it fully acknowledged the intermediate character of the artisanal fishing rights in issue and although it ruled that these *private* inter-generational rights could be asserted at the inter-state level, it understood that their normative origins were not to be found in the municipal legal orders of the states involved, nor were they derived from international law. In the circumstances, it based its *Second Award* on the recognition of the existence of a hybrid normative order – a *lex pescatoria* – that was sustained by regional traditional practices which had been followed on either side of the Red Sea since time immemorial.[44] This approach chimes with contemporary thinking that champions the existence of a plurality of normative orders, but it fits rather uncomfortably with the LOSC's avowed statist character.

In his analysis of the *Second Award*, Antunes applauds the way in which the Tribunal managed to superimpose a traditional fishing regime onto the state-centric processes established to determine the allocation of territorial sovereignty and to delimit the maritime boundaries between the parties.[45] In so doing, he commends the Tribunal for looking beyond Western constructions of sovereignty in an effort to find a juridical solution that would give effect to historical artisanal fishing practices. But despite the Tribunal's apparent willingness to move beyond the structural confines of the international legal order and those of the national legal systems involved, Antunes is rightly troubled by the unintended consequences of this otherwise welcome shift. First, he is concerned by the Tribunal's preparedness to ground its findings in the Islamic tradition on the basis that such an approach is, inevitably, geographically and culturally limiting – how could a pluralistic approach to artisanal rights be justified outside of the Islamic world? Second, he worries about the

[41] *Eritrea/Yemen Case*, *First Award* (n 11) [526].
[42] *Eritrea/Yemen Case*, *Second Award* (n 11) [94].
[43] ibid [94]–[95].
[44] Antunes applied the term 'lex pescatoria' in this context. See NSM Antunes, 'The 1999 Eritrea/Yemen Maritime Delimitation Award and the Development of International Law' (2001) 50 *International & Comparative Law Quarterly* 299, 306.
[45] ibid.

Tribunal's ruling that the traditional fishing regime established in the Red Sea qualifies as an international servitude,[46] which, logically, imposes an obligation on the burdened state in respect of the maritime area concerned – like some kind of internationally recognised prescriptive easement or usufruct entitlement.[47] As he points out that the central difficultly with this conception of artisanal fishing rights is that it endeavours to convert the *private* entitlements in question directly into state rights and, in so doing, fails to appreciate the full implications of the fact that artisanal fishers are non-state actors.[48]

It is worth noting that the Eritrea/Yemen Tribunal was not constituted under the terms of Annex VII of the LOSC as Eritrea was not a party to the Convention at the material time. Consequently, the Tribunal was not bound to observe its applicable law provision.[49] Instead, the 1996 Arbitration Agreement empowered it to take the LOSC into account along with any other pertinent factors.[50] As a result, it could afford to take a more expansive view of traditional fishing rights for the purpose of rendering its awards. Indeed, in its Second Award, it was prepared to adopt a reflective approach to the question of the rights of non-state actors in the international legal order when it observed that:

> As the Tribunal has indicated in its Award on Sovereignty, the traditional fishing regime [in the Red Sea] is one of free access and enjoyment for the fishermen of both Eritrea and Yemen. It is to be preserved for their benefit. This does not mean, however, that Eritrea may not act on behalf of its nationals, whether through diplomatic contacts with Yemen or through submissions to this Tribunal. There is no reason to import into the Red Sea the *western legal fiction – which is in any event losing its importance – whereby all legal rights, even those in reality held by individuals, were deemed to be those of the State. The legal fiction served the purpose of allowing diplomatic representation (where the representing State so chose) in a world in which individuals had no opportunities to advance their own rights*. It was never meant to be the case however that, were the right to be held by an individual, neither the individual nor his State should have access to international redress. (Emphasis added)[51]

This paragraph acknowledges that states are not the only holders of rights as a matter of international law, as individuals may possess such entitlements too. However, this recognition is accompanied by the observation that Eritrea possesses broad rights to represent its nationals – via the mechanism of diplomatic protection – regarding the assertion and protection of artisanal fishing

[46] *Eritrea/Yemen Case, First Award* (n 11) [126].

[47] See the *Abyei Arbitration Award (Sudan/Sudan People's Liberation Movement)*, Arbitration Award, 22 July 2009 [754].

[48] Antunes (n 44) 310. In this respect, the Tribunal's conception of traditional fishing rights appears to be consistent with the one advanced by Fitzmaurice, as discussed in the previous section.

[49] Article 293(1) LOSC provides that: 'A court or tribunal having jurisdiction under this section shall apply this Convention and other rules of international law not incompatible with this Convention.'

[50] Article 2(3) of the 1996 Agreement, annexed to the First Award (n 11).

[51] *Eritrea/Yemen Case, Second Award* (n 11) [101].

rights in the Red Sea. However, the Award does not address the way in which such entitlements could be asserted by the Eritrean fisher-folk themselves in the event of dispute, other than through the Eritrean state. In short, at a remedial level, the practical significance of the observation that individuals (or sub-state groups) have certain rights is extremely limited.[52] Accordingly, while the Tribunal showed its awareness of the hybrid character of artisanal fishing rights, the Awards could be seen as a missed opportunity to significantly advance the concept of artisanal fishing rights as collective rights belonging to non-state groups.

## V. ARTISANAL FISHING RIGHTS IN THE TERRITORIAL SEA

Traditional fishing rights have long been acknowledged in relation to a coastal state's internal and territorial waters. And, as the *Anglo-Norwegian Fisheries Case* showed, in appropriate cases, they may constitute a legitimate factor for the purpose of establishing the parameters of these maritime areas pursuant to the practice of drawing of straight baselines.[53] In that case, while the traditional fishing activities in issue were being undertaken by Norway's coastal-based inhabitants rather than by the claimant state's fisher-folk, the ICJ was prepared to take into consideration 'the vital [economic] needs of the population' which had been established by 'very ancient and peaceful usage',[54] especially as the inhabitant of 'this barren region … derive[d] their livelihood essentially from fishing' in this context.[55]

As far as the maritime zone of the territorial sea is concerned, Article 2(3) of the LOSC provides that a coastal state's 'sovereignty … is exercised subject to the Convention and to other rules of international law'. While it appeared that a coastal state's territorial waters amounted to a straightforward seaward extension of its sovereign authority – save for the exception of the right of innocent passage – the *renvoi* in the text of this provision evidently created the scope for a coastal state's sovereignty to be perforated by a wide range of international legal rules both inside and outside the Convention. The validity of such a holistic interpretation did not fall to be determined by courts and tribunals in the years immediately following the LOSC's entry into force. However, more recently, the meaning of Article 2(3) has been revisited in the *Chagos Marine Protection Area Award* and *South China Sea Award*. These cases will now be considered in turn.

[52] However, the limits of the Tribunal's approach in this regard may be explicable by reference to the Mavrommatis fiction; see section III.C above.

[53] See *Anglo-Norwegian Fisheries Case* (n 35).

[54] ibid 133 and 142.

[55] ibid 128.

## A. The *Chagos Marine Protection Area Award*

The Chagos Islands were detached from the British colony of Mauritius in November 1965 to form the British Indian Ocean Territory (BIOT), a step that was intimately connected with the achievement of Mauritian independence. Mauritius' consent to the act of excision was negotiated during the Constitutional Conference on Mauritius, which was held at Lancaster House in September 1965. During this Conference, a series of commitments – the 'Lancaster House Undertakings' – were hammered out by the UK government and certain high-level Mauritian delegates.[56] They formed the basis on which the Chagos Archipelago was detached from the Mauritian colonial unit and included an undertaking to respect Mauritian fishing rights in the Archipelago's waters. In the *Chagos Award*, the Tribunal understood that determining the nature and effect of the 1965 Undertakings was pivotal to the task of settling the dispute.[57] The Tribunal decided that the Undertakings implicated Article 2(3) of the LOSC, but it did not find that they had *direct* application in relation to the BIOT's Territorial Sea.[58] To this end, it examined the drafting history of the corresponding provision in the 1958 Geneva Convention on Territorial Sea and the Contiguous Zone,[59] which, in the Tribunal's view, led to the conclusion that a coastal state's sovereignty could only be constrained by *general* norms of international law in this maritime zone.[60] Accordingly, the Tribunal decided that, as the Undertakings did not form part of the general corpus of international law, they could not generate an obligation on the UK which could be read into Article 2(3).[61] Nevertheless, the Tribunal acknowledged that general international law requires that states act in good faith in their international relations and, as a result, it held that the UK was bound to honour the Undertakings in its dealings with Mauritius in the context of the BIOT's Territorial Sea.[62]

In their Dissenting and Concurring Opinion, Judges Kateka and Wolfrum reached the opposite conclusion on the issue of whether the 1965 Undertakings engaged Article 2(3) directly.[63] They harnessed the International Law Commission (ILC)'s Draft Articles concerning the Law of the Sea (and its 1956 Commentaries) in support of a more extensive reading of those international legal norms which could be read into what became Article 1(2) of the 1958 Convention and, in turn, Article 2(3) of the 1982 Convention. Specifically, the

[56] *Chagos Award* (n 2) [77]; and Allen (n 3).

[57] *Chagos Award* (n 2) [417], [534], [535] and [536].

[58] ibid [514].

[59] Article 1(2) of the 1958 Convention, which found its origins in the ILC's Draft Articles. See ILC's Draft Articles on the Law of the Sea and Commentaries, Eight Session (1956) UN Doc A/3159 265.

[60] *Chagos Award* (n 2) [515]–[517].

[61] ibid [517].

[62] ibid [517] and [520].

[63] Dissenting and Concurring Opinion appended to the *Chagos Award* (n 2) [94].

minority noted that the ILC anticipated that any such rights and obligations could arise 'by reason of some special relationship, geographical or other, between two States, rights in the territorial sea of one of them are granted to the other in excess of the rights recognised in the present draft'.[64] Consequently, the minority concluded that the reference to 'other rules of international law' in Article 2(3) encompassed international legal obligations that could be created by means of bilateral, or unilateral, commitments; as a result, they were of the view that the Undertakings must 'be read directly into Article 2(3) of the Convention'.[65] In sum, both the approach adopted in the *Chagos Award* and the minority's view allow for the possibility that, in principle, a traditional fishing regime could exist within the Territorial Sea.

As noted above, in the *Chagos Award*, both the majority and the minority took the view that Mauritius' fishing rights in the BIOT's Territorial Sea were recognised in the 1965 Undertakings, which created international legal obligations for the UK.[66] As a consequence, the Tribunal ruled that there was no need to examine whether a traditional fishing regime existed in this maritime zone via the traditional activities of Mauritian (ie, Chagossian) fishers in these territorial waters.[67] In its pleadings, Mauritius went to great lengths to show the degree to which the UK government, and its colonial administrations in Mauritius and the Seychelles, acknowledged that the artisanal fishing activities which were carried out in the BIOT's Territorial Sea would continue to be respected after the Chagos Islands were detached from the Mauritian colonial unit.[68] However, in this respect, Mauritius failed to highlight the extent to which the traditional fishing undertaken in this maritime zone was largely conducted by the Chagos Islanders themselves rather than by fishers from the island of Mauritius, which was located over 1,000 miles away from the Archipelago.[69] Thus, while the fishing rights expressed in the 1965 Undertakings were negotiated by Mauritian ministers, they were largely informed by the exercise of traditional fishing activities undertaken in and around the Archipelago by the Chagossians themselves.[70] In any event, as the Chagos Archipelago formed part of the Mauritian colonial unit before it was excised to create the BIOT, even if non-exclusive fishing rights had not been protected via the Lancaster House Undertakings, the Mauritian state could have used the mechanism of diplomatic protection in

[64] ILC's 1956 Report, 265 [5]; ibid [93–94].

[65] Dissenting and Concurring Opinion (n 63).

[66] Mauritius claimed that traditional fishing rights *and* the Lancaster House Undertaking regarding Mauritius' fishing rights were both compatible with the LOSC. Mauritius' Memorial (n 2) 125–33.

[67] *Chagos Award* (n 2) [456].

[68] See Mauritius' Memorial (n 2) 125–29 and Reply, 56–58 and 170–73.

[69] See Allen (n 3).

[70] See the Divisional Court's judgment in *Bancoult (No 3)* (n 3); Dunne's witness statement, Mauritius' Reply, Annex 172; and R Dunne, N Polunin and P Sand, 'The Creation of the Chagos Marine Protected Area: A Fisheries Perspective' (2014) 29 *Advances in Marine Biology* 79.

order to protect the traditional fishing activities of the Chagos Islanders on the basis that they were Mauritian nationals. Consequently, by only addressing the non-exclusive fishing rights enumerated in the Lancaster House Undertakings in its Award, the Tribunal overlooked the customary international law relating to artisanal fishing rights and its significance for non-state actors.[71]

## B. The *South China Sea Arbitration Award*

The South China Sea dispute arose from the claim by the People's Republic of China to exercise sovereignty over much of the South China Sea as a result of its possession of exclusive historic rights in this area. The South China Sea Tribunal decided that China's exclusive historic rights argument could not satisfy the requirements for a valid historic title claim relating to the South China Sea under the terms of the Convention.[72] The Tribunal turned to consider whether the PRC and/or the Philippines could have acquired non-exclusive artisanal fishing rights in the waters surrounding Scarborough Shoal. Scarborough Shoal was a maritime feature over which both the Philippines and the PRC claimed sovereignty.[73] The South China Sea Tribunal indicated that the existence of traditional fishing rights in the Territorial Sea is particularly important for artisanal fishers because 'the vast majority of traditional fishing takes place in close proximity to the coast'.[74]

The Philippines claimed, inter alia, that China had prevented Filipino fishers from exercising their artisanal fishing rights in the Territorial Sea surrounding Scarborough Shoal in violation of the LOSC's provisions.[75] The Tribunal chose to apply the interpretation favoured in the *Chagos Award*, ie that, in principle, a coastal state's rights in the Territorial Sea are subject to the general rules of international law, in accordance with the terms of Article 2(3). To this end, it held that the vested rights of the artisanal fishers from both the Philippines and China could generate traditional entitlements in the Territorial Sea surrounding

[71] It could be argued that, in accordance with the 'Mavrommatis fiction', the exercise of diplomatic protection has the effect of transforming private rights into state rights unless a more enlightened view of the normative basis for the operation of diplomatic protection is adopted. See section III.C above.

[72] *South China Sea Award* (n 2) [228]–[229]. See Zhiguo Gao and Bing Bing Jia, 'The Nine-Dash Line in the South China Sea: History, Status and Implications' (2013) 107 *American Journal of International Law* 98; and Stephan Talmon, 'The South China Sea Arbitration: Is There a Case to Answer?' in Stephan Talmon and Bing Bing Jia (eds), *The South China Sea Arbitration: A Chinese Perspective* (Hart Publishing, 2014) 48–54.

[73] *South China Sea Award* (n 2) [761].

[74] ibid [804].

[75] The Tribunal classified this maritime feature as a rock for the purpose of determining a coastal state's entitlements under the LOSC. Consequently, Scarborough Shoal was only deemed to have a Territorial Sea.

Scarborough Shoal as a matter of customary international law.[76] Specifically, the Tribunal said:

> Traditional fishing rights constitute a vested right, and the Tribunal considers the rules of international law on the treatment of the vested rights of foreign nationals to fall squarely within the 'other rules of international law' applicable in the territorial sea [pursuant to Article 2(3)].[77]

The Tribunal's full endorsement of artisanal fishing rights as vested rights, its readiness to view them as compatible with the Convention's provisions concerning the Territorial Sea, and its concrete findings concerning the rights of Filipino and Chinese fisher-folk in this maritime zone constitute an important moment in the Convention's interpretative development and, specifically, the *renvoi* contained in Article 2(3).

## VI. ARTISANAL FISHING RIGHTS IN THE EXCLUSIVE ECONOMIC ZONE

In its *Second Award*, the Eritrea/Yemen Tribunal decided that the traditional fishing regime in the Red Sea was, in principle, applicable throughout the parties' respective maritime zones.[78] However, such a finding conflicts with the Convention's provisions, which provide that coastal states possess exclusive sovereign rights over living resources (including fisheries) in the Exclusive Economic Zone (EEZ).[79] It has been suggested that the wider significance of this Tribunal's observation regarding the geographical ambit of the fishing regime existing in the Red Sea may be over-stated. In particular, in its *Merits Award*, the South China Sea Tribunal pointed out that the Eritrea/Yemen Tribunal was not constituted under the terms of Annex VII of the LOSC and so it was not bound to observe the Convention's applicable law provision.[80] This led the South China Sea Tribunal to observe that the Eritrea/Yemen Tribunal 'was thus empowered to – and in [its] view did – go beyond the law on traditional fishing as it would exist under the Convention'.[81] But can the Eritrea/Yemen Tribunal's position on this issue be attributed to the breadth of the applicable law or to its reading of the normative reach of artisanal fishing rights? This question can only be answered by assessing the way in which the relationship between artisanal fishing rights and the Convention's provisions on the EEZ have been interpreted in the subsequent case law.

In the *Barbados/Trinidad and Tobago Arbitration* case, Barbados claimed that although Part V of the LOSC regulates the operation of EEZs, it does not

[76] *South China Sea Award* (n 2) [805]–[808]. This meant that such rights would be capable of binding the coastal state in issue, regardless of whether, ultimately, that was the Philippines or China.

[77] ibid [808].

[78] *Eritrea/Yemen Case, Second Award* (n 11) [109].

[79] See art 56 LOSC.

[80] *South China Sea Award* (n 2) [259].

[81] ibid; and see the text accompanying nn 49 and 50 above.

seek to abolish pre-existing artisanal fishing rights.[82] Specifically, Barbados argued that the Convention could not have extinguished such rights because none of its provisions abrogate them expressly. In support of this contention, Barbados alluded to the observation, made by an ICJ Chamber in its *ELSI* decision, that as a matter of interpretation, an intention to extinguish existing rights cannot be inferred from a treaty provision.[83] However, it should be recalled that Barbados was seeking to use artisanal fishing rights, which it claimed had been acquired by its nationals, to justify the redrawing of the maritime boundary between the parties in its favour (ie, in support of a claim for *exclusive* rights). In response, Trinidad and Tobago argued that such a claim was not made out on the facts and the only way to give effect to *non-exclusive* artisanal fishing rights was via an access regime.[84] To this end, it argued that Article 62(3) of the LOSC provides that, in giving access to other states for the purpose of harvesting living resources in its EEZ, a coastal state should take into account 'the need to minimize economic dislocation in states whose nationals have habitually fished in the zone'.[85] Barbados replied that, Article 62(3) sets out a number of factors a coastal state should take into account when exercising its discretion to allocate any surpluses that may exist and the requirement to have 'due regard' to a wide range of considerations provides a means of structuring a coastal state's discretion to allocate surpluses rather than providing a way of grounding an obligation to give effect to pre-existing artisanal fishing rights which must now be exercised within a newly formed EEZ.[86]

Barbados' reading of this provision is undoubtedly correct. Article 62(3) does not endeavour to protect artisanal fishing rights as Part V of the LOSC is silent on the question of the ongoing validity of traditional fishing rights in this maritime zone. Barbados was anxious to point out that Part IV of the LOSC expressly protects traditional fishing rights in the waters of archipelagic states.[87] Therefore, it argued that the Convention's drafters must have intended artisanal fishing rights to persist in other LOSC zones too.[88] However, this strategy is potentially double-sided as it could also be contended that the Convention's silence as to the continuity of artisanal fishing rights in the EEZ in contrast to its effort to regulate this type of fishing archipelagic waters might suggest that the drafters did not intend such entitlements to survive the creation of EEZs.

In its *Chagos Award*, the Annex VII Tribunal decided that it only had jurisdiction to adjudicate Mauritius' fishing rights in relation to the BIOT/Chagos

[82] Barbados' Memorial (n 8) [131].

[83] *ELSI Case (US/Italy)* (1989) ICJ Reps 15 [50]; and Barbados' Memorial (n 8)[132].

[84] The Tribunal did not have jurisdiction to adjudicate the issue of an access regime, but it did record the undertakings made by Trinidad and Tobago in this regard: *Barbados/Trinidad and Tobago Award* (n 8) [286]–[293].

[85] Trinidad and Tobago's Counter-Memorial, ibid [213].

[86] Barbados Reply, ibid [398]–[404].

[87] See arts 47 and 51 LOSC.

[88] Barbados Reply (n 8) [403].

Archipelago's Territorial Sea.[89] It took this stance because, in its view, Article 297(3)(a) provides that a coastal state is not obligated to submit to section 2 procedures, under Part XV, in cases where a dispute relates to the exercise of its sovereign rights in respect of those living resources found in its EEZ.[90] This did not prevent the Tribunal from finding a way forward as far as Mauritius' rights in the BIOT's EEZ were concerned. It held that the rights and obligations of a coastal state in the EEZ are expressly qualified by the requirement to 'have due regard to the rights and duties of other States' and, as a result, this duty had the effect of engaging the Lancaster House Undertakings on the facts.[91] Nonetheless, the Tribunal was reluctant to establish a universal standard of conduct for coastal states in this context, but it indicated that what would qualify as a duty to have due regard would depend on the circumstances. But it expressed the view that 'in the majority of cases [the obligation] will necessarily involve at least some consultation with the rights-holding State'.[92] It is possible to argue that the Tribunal's approach on this issue may have created a degree of symmetry, as far as traditional fishing rights are concerned, between the Territorial Sea and the EEZ.[93] However, as things stand, any protection afforded to such rights relating to the EEZ would inevitably be contingent in nature.

The issue of whether artisanal fishing rights could survive the introduction of an EEZ pursuant to the application of the LOSC was directly confronted in the *South China Sea Award*, where the Tribunal revisited the importance of the way in which Part V's provisions were drafted when compared with the way in which traditional fishing rights were protected in relation to archipelagic waters in Part IV. Specifically, it addressed the importance of Article 62(3) in this regard, observing that 'the inclusion of this provision – which would be entirely unnecessary if traditional fishing rights were preserved in the exclusive economic zone – confirms that the drafters of the Convention did not intend to preserved such rights'.[94] The Tribunal's approach strengthens the conclusion that the LOSC has the effect of extinguishing artisanal fishing rights in the EEZ. It acknowledged that it was open to neighbouring states to negotiate fishing rights regimes on a bilateral basis, or coastal states could choose to protect such entitlements unilaterally.[95] Accordingly, the implication is obvious – artisanal fishing rights are not safeguarded by the LOSC alone, or in combination with

[89] *Chagos Award* (n 2) [455].

[90] Stephen Allen 'Article 297 of the United Nations Convention on the Law of the Sea and the Scope of Mandatory Jurisdiction' (2017) 48 *Ocean Development and International Law* 313.

[91] *Chagos Award* (n 2) [519]. Article 56(2) provides: 'In exercising its rights and performing its duties under this Convention in the [EEZ], the coastal State shall have due regard to the rights and duties of other States and shall act in a manner compatible with the provisions of this Convention.'

[92] ibid.

[93] See N Bankes and E Enyew, 'Interaction between the Law of the Sea and the Rights of Indigenous Peoples' forthcoming (on file with the author).

[94] *South China Sea Award* (n 2) [804(b)].

[95] ibid. Such negotiations would be required in situations where 'due regard' obligations are engaged.

the vested rights doctrine. A least in relation to the EEZ additional protection is required.

Together, the *Chagos* and the *South China Sea Awards* represent a decisive moment in the Convention's development as far as the recognition of artisanal fishing rights in the Territorial Sea and EEZ are concerned. In respect of the BIOT's Territorial Sea, the Chagos Tribunal was not prepared to read the Lancaster House Undertakings directly into Article 2(3) because, in its view, they did not constitute general norms of international law. Nonetheless, it harnessed the obligation to act in good faith as an interpretative device by which the Undertakings could be given indirect effect. There was no need for the South China Sea Tribunal to disturb this finding, given its ruling that the established artisanal fishing rights in Scarborough Shoal's Territorial Sea were general international norms. However, it is apparent from both Awards that bilateral arrangements are significant with regard to the ongoing validity of artisanal fishing rights in the EEZ. In particular, the Chagos Tribunal relied on the 1965 Undertakings in support of the existence of 'due regard' obligations, while the absence of any comparable inter-state arrangements negotiated between the parties in the *South China Sea* case led that Tribunal to conclude that, in principle, pre-existing artisanal fishing entitlements could not survive in this maritime zone without the coastal state's consent. Accordingly, when taken together, these two Awards complement one another and contribute to our understanding of artisanal fishing rights in the Territorial Sea and the EEZ.

## VII. THE LOSC AND THE LIMITS OF SUBJECT-MATTER JURISDICTION

Another difficulty that may arise, particularly in the context of proceedings initiated under Part XV of LOSC, is subject-matter jurisdiction pursuant to the application of Article 293.[96] Article 293 enables a court or tribunal, constituted under Article 287, to interpret and apply the Convention and any other sources not incompatible with it in accordance with the jurisdictional clause set out in Article 288.[97] There has been some debate about the inter-relationship between the notion of applicable law and the matter of a court or tribunal's jurisdiction pursuant to the operation of Part XV. In this respect, it is worth noting the Annex VII Tribunal's observation in the *Guyana/Suriname Award* that Article 293 gives a court or tribunal the competence to apply not only the Convention but also the relevant norms of customary international law.[98]

[96] See n 49.

[97] Article 288(1) LOSC holds that: 'A court or tribunal … shall have jurisdiction over any dispute concerning the interpretation or application of this Convention which is submitted to it in accordance with this Part.'

[98] Delimitation of the Maritime Boundary between Guyana and Suriname Award, 17 September 2007, 30 RIAA 1 [404]–[406]. The Tribunal thought that its position was consistent with the

In a recent article, Parlett assessed whether Article 293 has the capacity to expand the scope of compulsory jurisdiction pursuant to Part XV.[99] While she acknowledged the extensive interpretations favoured in the previously mentioned cases, she drew attention to the guarded approaches followed by Annex VII Tribunals in more recent decisions, including the *Arctic Sunrise Award*,[100] and the *South China Sea Award*.[101] In the former Award, the Tribunal cautioned that Article 293 was designed to enable a Part XV court or tribunal to give full effect to the Convention's provisions rather than as a means of expanding its jurisdiction. Accordingly, in its view, Article 293 facilitates the proper exercise of the jurisdiction conferred by Article 288.[102] In particular, the Tribunal observed that this provision does not permit external sources, especially treaties, to be read into the Convention's provisions and directly applied, unless they have been specifically incorporated by reference.[103] In this context, it noted that:

> The Tribunal considers that, if necessary, it may have regard to general international law in relation to human rights in order to determine whether law enforcement action such as the boarding, seizure, and detention of the Arctic Sunrise and the arrest and detention of those on board was reasonable and proportionate. This would be to interpret the relevant Convention provisions by reference to relevant context. This is not, however, the same as, nor does it require, a determination of whether there has been a breach of Articles 9 and 12(2) of the ICCPR as such. *That treaty has its own enforcement regime and it is not for this Tribunal to act as a substitute for that regime*. (Emphasis added)[104]

But, as far as customary international law was concerned, the Tribunal added:

> In determining the claims by the Netherlands in relation to the interpretation and application of the Convention, the Tribunal may, therefore, pursuant to Article 293, have regard to the extent necessary to rules of customary international law, including international human rights standards, not incompatible with the Convention, in order to assist in the interpretation and application of the Convention's provisions.[105]

approach adopted in *M/V Saiga No 2 (Saint Vincent and Grenadines/Guinea)* (1999), where the International Tribunal for the Law of the Sea (ITLOS) had recourse to art 293 for the purpose of applying the canon of international law concerning the use of force, notwithstanding the absence of any express reference to this body of law within the Convention itself. See ITLOS Reports 1999 7 [155], [159] and [183(9)]. Subsequently, in the *Chagos Marine Protected Area* (MPA) proceedings, Mauritius advanced a broad compatibility argument by reference to art 293. See Mauritius' Memorial (n 2) [6.4].

[99] Kate Parlett, 'Beyond the Four Corners of the Convention: Expanding the Scope of Jurisdiction of Law of the Sea Tribunals' (2017) 48 *Ocean Development and International Law* 284.

[100] *Arctic Sunrise Arbitration Award (Netherlands/Russia)*, Annex VII LOS Tribunal, Permanent Court of Arbitration (14 August 2015).

[101] In the *Chagos Award* (n 2), the Tribunal did not think it necessary to rule on the relevance of art 293 for its purposes.

[102] *Arctic Sunrise Award* (n 100) [188].

[103] ibid [192].

[104] ibid [197].

[105] ibid [198].

The problem with trying to use Article 293 in order to activate those artisanal fishing rights recognisable by customary international law within a coastal state's EEZ is that such an approach would directly contradict the scope of the sovereign rights belonging to that state, as set out in Article 56, and the limits upon compulsory jurisdiction, as enumerated in Article 297. On this point, the South China Sea Tribunal confirmed that customary norms will only be deemed to be compatible with the Convention where they do not conflict with its provisions.[106] Accordingly, as far as the operation of Part XV of the LOSC is concerned, artisanal fishing rights do not survive in the EEZ in the absence of bilateral arrangements (which may be driven by 'due regard' obligations) without the consent of the coastal state.

## VIII. ARTISANAL FISHING COMMUNITIES AND HUMAN RIGHTS TREATIES

As discussed above, it is open to a state to take up the claim of one or more of its nationals, via the exercise of *its right* of diplomatic protection, in keeping with the Mavrommatis fiction.[107] Thus, in the present context, a claimant state seeks to harness the LOSC's dispute settlement provisions in order to protect its artisanal fisher-folk where they possess private rights to access and harvesting resources in the defendant (coastal) state's territorial waters. However, it cannot invoke the provisions of applicable human rights treaties directly through this process for jurisdictional reasons. Against this background, it is worth considering other ways in which artisanal fishing communities may be able to trigger the adjudication of their entitlements to access and harvest resources in a disputed maritime area. To this end, it is clear that they are capable of harnessing human rights treaties directly for this purpose. For instance, in the *Barbados v Trinidad and Tobago* case, Barbados argued that artisanal fishing rights belong not only to states but also vest in individuals and communities too.[108] Specifically, it relied on certain multilateral human rights treaties – including the International Covenant on Civil and Political Rights (ICCPR),[109] the European Convention on Human Rights (ECHR)[110] and the American Convention on

[106] *South China Sea Award* (n 2) [238]. Thus, the Tribunal decided that the claim that China possesses exclusive historic rights to living and non-living resources in the EEZ was incompatible with the Convention as it had superseded any prior maritime regime that may have existed in the region (at [239]).

[107] See section III.C above.

[108] Barbados' Memorial (n 8) [126]; the *Eritrea/Yemen Case, Second Award* (n 11); and the *South China Sea Award* (n 2) [798].

[109] International Covenant on Civil and Political Rights, concluded on 16 December 1966, entered into force 23 March 1976, 999 UNTS 171.

[110] European Convention for the Protection of Human Rights and Fundamental Freedoms, concluded on 4 November 1950, entered into force 3 September 1953, 213 UNTS 2.

Human Rights[111] – in support of its contention that fishing rights constitute actionable individual and/or communal property rights.[112] It is clear that Indigenous peoples and national minorities can rely on the ICCPR's provisions and the Human Rights Commission's (HRC) concomitant jurisprudence, as well as the terms of the International Convention on the Elimination of All Forms of Racial Discrimination (ICERD) and the jurisprudence of the Committee on the Elimination of Racial Discrimination (CERD) in this regard.[113] Consequently, it would appear that a compelling way forward would be for artisanal fishing communities to invoke applicable human rights treaties *directly against the coastal state involved* because it exercises jurisdiction in the area in question – not only within its Territorial Sea but within its EEZ as well – rather than relying on their own state to take up their claim via the LOSC's dispute resolution mechanisms.[114] Such an approach is reminiscent of the way in which minorities and Indigenous peoples have utilised the quasi-judicial functions of the HRC and the CERD in a number of pivotal cases, a strategy which has led to the development significant bodies of law as far as their rights, and the corresponding obligations of their states, are concerned.[115] However, it is important to appreciate that the crucial difference here is that the tactic being mooted would necessitate the assertion of such rights against another coastal state rather than against the individual or community's state of nationality.

## IX. CONCLUSION

This chapter has explored the juridical foundations of artisanal fishing rights and the manner in which these customary entitlements are grounded in the doctrine of vested rights – a characteristic which they share with the rights of

[111] American Convention on Human Rights, concluded on 22 November 1969, entered into force 18 July 1978, 1144 UNTS 143.

[112] Barbados sought to rely on the property rights protections contained in international and regional human rights treaties, including art 17 ICCPR; art 21 of the American Convention on Human Rights; and art 1 of Protocol 1 to the ECHR. It also referred to *Baner v Sweden* (1989) App No. 11763/85, where the European Commission on Human Rights held that fishing rights qualify as property rights. Barbados' Memorial (n 8).

[113] International Convention on the Elimination of All Forms of Racial Discrimination, concluded on 21 December 1965, entered into force 4 January 1969, 660 UNTS 195. See, eg, Ben Saul, *Indigenous Peoples and Human Rights* (Hart Publishing, 2016); and Patrick Thornberry, *Oxford Commentary on the International Convention on the Elimination of Racial Discrimination* (Oxford University Press, 2017).

[114] Article 2(1) ICCPR provides that: 'Each State Party to the present Covenant undertakes to respect and to ensure to all individuals within its territory and subject to its jurisdiction the rights recognized in the present Covenant.' See the HRC's General Comment No 31 'The Nature of the General Legal Obligation Imposed on States Parties to the Covenant' (29 March 2004). Article 1 ECHR provides that: 'The High Contracting Parties shall secure to everyone within their jurisdiction the rights and freedoms defined in Section I of this Convention.' The ICERD does not contain a jurisdictional clause.

[115] See Enyew (ch 2 in this volume).

Indigenous peoples, at least within common law settings. In addition, it has analysed the way in which the hybrid nature of artisanal fishing rights has made their recognition problematic, especially within the context of the LOSC's provisions, but also as a consequence of international law's continuing adherence to the 'Mavrommatis fiction' in relation to the exercise of diplomatic protection. It has examined a number of arbitral decisions, delivered over the last two decades, which have upheld the continuity of artisanal fishing rights in specific settings. These decisions have shown that such entitlements have been deemed to be compatible with the LOSC's provisions (especially those governing a coastal state's territorial waters), but artisanal rights in the EEZ have been largely compromised by the Convention's provisions concerning this maritime zone. Notwithstanding the LOSC's somewhat uneven framework as far as these non-exclusive rights are concerned, artisanal fishing communities do possess other means of asserting their rights across a range of maritime zones because artisanal fishing entitlements are not essentially rights that belong to states. In this respect, applicable international and regional human rights treaties – and their supervisory and/or enforcement mechanisms – have an important role to play in the protection of such communal rights. Moreover, it is important to acknowledge that such rights may not be actionable only against an artisanal fishing community's own state, as long as it can be shown the defendant state exercises jurisdiction over the marine area in question. The categories of artisanal fishing communities and Indigenous peoples are not mutually exclusive, and it is clear that gains made in the context of artisanal fishing rights will, in principle, be applicable to the growing jurisprudence concerning the marine resources of Indigenous peoples. Further research needs to be undertaken regarding the ways in which Indigenous peoples can make the most of these developments and, in turn, contribute to them.

# Part III

# Indigenous Rights in Marine Areas in Different Jurisdictions

# 5

# *The Evolving Governance of Aboriginal Peoples and Torres Strait Islanders in Marine Areas in Australia*

LEE GODDEN

## I. INTRODUCTION

GROWING ACKNOWLEDGEMENT OF the connection to country of Saltwater peoples that is captured in songlines has transformed the legal understanding of how Aboriginal peoples and Torres Strait Islanders across northern Australia relate to marine areas.[1] Traditional knowledge, made explicit in songs, tells a story of a cultural geography of marine places, a knowledge largely supressed since colonisation.[2] The revelation of that geography has been the catalyst for enhancing indigenous participation in marine governance. Even so, the inter-relationships of Aboriginal peoples and Torres Strait Islanders in 'sea country' (marine areas) across Australia are still shaped by complex legal and normative patterns that filter how that participation occurs. The patterns reflect a matrix of formal legal rights derived from native title law and statutory land and resource rights, as well as governance models arising from Indigenous partnerships in marine areas for environmental conservation purposes. These patterns can be overlain by more informal models of consultation and representation with Aboriginal peoples and Torres Strait Islanders.

In examining the evolution of Indigenous peoples' governance of marine areas in Australia, this chapter first outlines the legal system that has mediated the inclusion or exclusion of Indigenous peoples. Second, given the sheer size of the continent, the chapter provides a selective overview of the rights of Aboriginal peoples and Torres Strait Islanders to access marine areas and

[1] See Margaret Somerville and Tony Perkins, *Singing the Coast* (Aboriginal Studies Press, 2010).

[2] Nonie Sharp, 'Saltways' in *Saltwater People: The Waves of Memory* (University of Toronto Press, 2002) 140.

to gather and manage resources along its coastlines and surrounding seas. It discusses the 2013 Torres Strait Islander Sea Claim, where the Australian High Court recognised a right for Indigenous peoples to take marine resources for commercial purposes. In the same year, the High Court considered the interaction of customary rights and endangered species legislation in respect of marine areas. Despite growing formal legal recognition, Indigenous peoples' rights in marine areas remain largely confined to a customary, subsistence basis. The analysis concludes with an evaluation of the prospects for ensuring more equitable participation by Indigenous peoples in marine governance in Australia by re-shaping contested ideas of indigenous sovereignty.

## II. ABORIGINAL PEOPLES AND TORRES STRAIT ISLANDERS

When exploring the involvement of Aboriginal peoples and Torres Strait Islanders in marine governance, the diversity and uniqueness of communities must be understood. While the generic terms 'Indigenous peoples', 'Aboriginal peoples' and 'Torres Strait Islanders' are used, most communities identify more closely with local places or 'country'. Aboriginal peoples of the mainland have distinct characteristics from the Melanesian traditional owners of the islands and seas of the Torres Strait.[3]

Ties to local places, both terrestrial and marine, for all communities are expressed and differentiated for each group through cultural designations based on language, connection to land, waters, and group membership.[4] Integral to such designation is cultural knowledge (traditional ecological knowledge), which is inherent to the law and custom of Aboriginal peoples and Torres Strait Islander communities. 'Cultural knowledge' signifies a connection where 'places are discursively acknowledged as being essentially and primarily particular things in place, things that are resonances and signs of the ancestral past'.[5] European legal systems, by contrast, bifurcate place relationship through diverse forms of separate regulation. Relevant to indigenous marine resources, the Australian legal system separates cultural heritage law from native title, land title regulation from marine governance, and issues of control over access to biological and genetic resources from their actual use in marine areas.[6]

[3] References to Aboriginal peoples indicate traditional owners or First Nations where relevant to the context.

[4] For language groups, see Australian Institute of Aboriginal and Torres Strait Islander Studies, 'AIATSIS Map of Indigenous Australia', https://aiatsis.gov.au/explore/articles/aiatsis-map-indigenous-australia.

[5] Marcia Langton, 'The Estate as Duration: "Being in Place" and Aboriginal Property Relations in Areas of Cape York Peninsula in North Australia' in Lee Godden and Maureen Tehan (eds), *Comparative Perspectives on Communal Lands and Individual Ownership: Sustainable Futures* (Routledge, 2010) 87.

[6] Genetic resources are included within the Convention on Biological Diversity (adopted 22 May 1992, entered into force 29 June 1993) 1760 UNTS 79.

By contrast, intangible Indigenous cultural heritage encompasses performative expressions of the knowledge of places (and seascapes) – in dance, art, stories and ceremonies. Much of the knowledge is not openly shared, but is transmitted through genealogically and spatially referenced practices. These complex inter-relationships of Aboriginal peoples and Islander groups to sea country have been given specific legal crystallisation in the land rights and sea claim processes.

The recognition of Indigenous law and custom had significant ramifications for marine governance in Australia.[7] Since 1992, comprehensive native title legislation has been enacted, along with significant case law around native title sea claims and partnerships built around Indigenous marine governance.[8] Yet, the law has continued to disappoint the expectations of many Indigenous peoples for a more comprehensive role in marine governance, particularly in southern Australia. There are major gaps in terms of how laws support Indigenous peoples to protect local places and heritage sites, and to sustain social and economic relationships. Further, the capacity of Aboriginal peoples to harvest marine resources has been strongly contested through the criminal law. These constraints mirror the unevenness in the legal and constitutional systems in according recognition to Indigenous peoples as a polity within Australia.[9]

## A. Deep Colonisation

Many parts of coastal and marine Australia are characterised by a history of 'deep colonisation'[10] and frontier violence, particularly along the southeastern coastal margin. Frontier conflicts, disease and forced movements of Aboriginal peoples into reservations greatly decreased access to marine areas and resources. A small minority of reservations were located in coastal areas[11] – well away from the expanding European settlements, which were focused on coastal port cities. Even in remote areas, Aboriginal peoples had to compete with an exploitative whaling and sealing industry that was a substantial component of early colonial economies along the southern coasts.

[7] See Gary Meyers et al, *A Sea Change in Land Rights Law: The Extension of Native Title to Australia's Offshore Areas* (Australian Institute of Aboriginal and Torres Strait Islander Studies, 1996).

[8] Lauren Butterly and Erica Techera, 'Critical Linkages: Trans-jurisdictional Approaches to Advancing Indigenous Marine Governance' in Cameron Holley, Rosemary Rayfuse and Janice Gray (eds), *Trans-jurisdictional Water Law and Governance* (Routledge, 2016).

[9] Dylan Lino, 'Thinking outside the Constitution on Indigenous Constitutional Recognition: Entrenching the Racial Discrimination Act' (2017) 91(5) *Australian Law Journal* 381.

[10] See Marcia Langton, 'Self-determination: Overhauling the Administrative Practices of Colonisation' in Peter Jull et al (eds), *Surviving Columbus: Indigenous Peoples, Political Reform and Environmental Management in North Australia* (North Australia Research Unit, Australian National University, 1994).

[11] See now, eg, the Lake Tyers Aboriginal Trust under the Aboriginal Lands Act 1970 (Vic).

The political and economic subjugation of Aboriginal peoples continued over the twentieth century with highly repressive and paternalistic legislative measures,[12] with Aboriginal peoples often being heavily supervised in every aspect of their life. In northern Australia, the impacts of European colonisation were experienced later, as typically first land contact was in the early twentieth century. Yet along northern coastlines, fishing and pearling were well established by the late nineteenth century.[13] The Torres Strait Islands in a remote northern location experienced European settlement more sporadically.[14] The Islanders were not physically dispossessed from land and seas as occurred over much of mainland Australia.[15]

However, in the late twentieth century, the conservative Bjelke-Petersen Queensland government enacted discriminatory legislation in respect of these islands, which precipitated *Mabo v Queensland (No 1)*.[16] The Coastal Islands Declaratory Act was designed to allow the state to acquire Indigenous land in the Torres Strait Islands. With respect to that legislation, the High Court found that it was discriminatory in its treatment of Torres Strait Islanders' interests. A subsequent native title action resulted in *Mabo v Queensland (No 2)*.[17] In this seminal case, the Australian High Court 'recognised' the prior occupation of the Australian continent by Aboriginal peoples and Torres Strait Islanders 200 years after the British assertion of sovereignty and colonisation.[18]

### B. Legal Recognition in the Australian Legal System

Australia remains anomalous in not affording robust legal and constitutional protections to its Indigenous peoples. Despite First Nations' long agitation for a comprehensive, national settlement to the historic injustice of colonisation, Australia remains without a national treaty process.[19] Comparable jurisdictions

[12] Lauren Butterly, 'Before the High Court: Clear Choices in Murky Waters: Leo Akiba on Behalf of the Torres Strait Regional Seas Claim Group v Commonwealth of Australia' (2013) 35 *Sydney Law Review* 237, 237.

[13] See generally Yawuru, 'Lustre and Pearling Exhibition', 2018, www.yawuru.com/lustre-pearling-australia.

[14] *Queensland v Mabo: Determination of Facts* (Moynihan J, Supreme Court of Queensland, 16 November 1990).

[15] Lauren Butterly, 'Changing Tack: *Akiba* and the Way Forward for Indigenous Governance of Sea Country' (2013) 17 *Australian Indigenous Law Review* 2.

[16] *Mabo v Queensland (No 1)* (1988) 166 CLR 186 (*Mabo (No 1)*).

[17] *Mabo v Queensland (No 2)* (1992) 175 CLR 1 (*Mabo (No 2)*).

[18] Terra Nullius was invoked by colonial courts in respect of the Australian mainland; see *Milirripum v Nabalco* (1971) 17 FLR 141. While some scholars used the term 'mare nullius' to refer to offshore areas following *Mabo (No 2)*, strictly, the legal status of indigenous rights in the offshore was not authoritatively decided until *Commonwealth of Australia v Yarmirr* (2001) 208 CLR 1.

[19] There are various 'theories' as to why no historic treaties were concluded with Australia's Aboriginal peoples (see, eg, Lisa Ford, 'Locating Indigenous Self-Determination in the Margins of Settler Sovereignty: An Introduction' in Lisa Ford and Tim Rowse (eds), *Between Indigenous and Settler Governance* (Routledge, 2013). Australia as a 'settled' state is discussed in Australian Law

such as New Zealand, Canada and the US have well-entrenched constitutional protections or foundational treaty systems between the state and Indigenous peoples. In the US, the Marshall doctrine established American native peoples as 'domestic dependent nations'.[20] Unlike Canada, Australia does not have a regional agreements model or a system of compensation and transitional justice that distinguishes the Treaty of Waitangi process in New Zealand. Australia does have a consent determination and agreement-making model embedded into the Native Title Act 1993 in respect of claims extending to offshore.

While 'customary' law systems operating independently or semi-autonomously from the nation-state are apparent in postcolonial countries across the world, the degree of legal pluralism varies significantly. Australian jurisprudence has stepped around the thorny issues of Indigenous peoples' sovereignty and a plural legal system by deploying concepts of doctrinal recognition. This doctrinal model effectively excises from scrutiny the prior question of the assertion of British sovereignty.[21] Instead, the jurisprudence promotes 'economic and cultural' co-existence, especially in native title law. Indeed, the Federal Court determined the relationships of the Torres Strait Islanders to the seas to be one of 'utility and practicality'.[22] In the offshore, the co-existence model translates to non-exclusive rights for Indigenous peoples, unless aligned to fee simple rights pertaining to land tenure.[23]

In place of treaty systems, agreement making in Australian jurisdictions can cover both land and marine territories.[24] Agreements are a relatively flexible tool for Indigenous marine governance, but are constrained by the inherent requirement for consensus among the parties. Agreement making also is frequently characterised by power imbalances and resource inequalities between indigenous and non-indigenous parties.[25] This situation renders Indigenous marine governance vulnerable to changing policy directions and the vagaries of government funding.[26] Indigenous peoples within Australia remain subject to a postcolonial

Reform Commission, *Connection to Country: Review of the Native Title Act 1993 (Cth)* (ALRC Report 2015) ch 2.

[20] After two centuries, the State of Victoria has entered a treaty process with traditional owners in Victoria.

[21] The 'act of state' doctrine propounded by Justice Brennan draws a distinction between the acts of executive government in asserting sovereignty and the jurisdiction of the courts to examine its proprietary consequences in *Mabo (No 2)* (n 17) 31 (Brennan J); see also Peter Fitzpatrick '"No Higher Duty": *Mabo* and the Failure of Legal Foundation' (2002) 13 *Law and Critique* 233.

[22] *Akiba v Queensland (No 3)* (2010) 204 FCR 1, 20 [6].

[23] See *Gumana v Northern Territory* (2005) 141 FCR 457; *Gumana v Northern Territory (No 2)* [2005] FCA 1425.

[24] Lee Godden and Maureen Tehan, 'Legal Forms and Their Implications for Long-Term Relationships and Economic, Cultural and Social Empowerment: Structuring Agreements in Australia' in Marcia Langton and Judy Longbottom (eds), *Community Futures, Legal Architecture: Foundations for Indigenous Peoples in the Global Mining Boom* (Routledge, 2012).

[25] ibid 121.

[26] Butterly (n 15).

economic and legal regime that very reluctantly concedes marine space and resources to Aboriginal peoples and Torres Strait Islanders.

## C. The Constitutional Position

While other settler nations have accorded legally entrenched rights to Indigenous peoples, Australia has no constitutional protections for its First Nations. Aboriginal peoples and Torres Strait Islanders did not achieve Australian citizenship status until 1967.[27] Since then, attempts to recognise Australia's Indigenous peoples in the national constitution have failed.[28] Castan contends that:

> [T]he formation of the constitutional system, and the Australian Constitution itself speaks as much to what the distinctive new nation of Australia was to be, and what it remains; a land acquired by the British as terra nullius now with an Anglo-Australian legal system deeply vested in the denial of Indigenous rights and sovereignty.[29]

The federation of British colonies to form Australia occurred in 1901 with limited reference to Indigenous peoples. Section 51(xxvi) of the Constitution provided the Commonwealth with power to make 'special laws' for the Aboriginal race.[30] Subsequently, there has been contestation as to whether those laws are to be, 'beneficial or detrimental, wholly or partially'.[31] As Kirby J noted: 'History, and not only ancient history, teaches that there are many dangers in enacting special laws that target people of a particular race and disadvantage their rights to liberty, property and other entitlements by reference to that criterion.'[32] By contrast, in New Zealand and Canada, the courts acknowledge that the Crown owes fiduciary obligations to Indigenous peoples with respect to dealings with their land and waters.[33] Australian courts have generally declined to find such a relationship.[34]

Recent efforts to acknowledge Indigenous peoples within the Constitution crystallised in the Aboriginal and Torres Strait Islander Peoples Recognition Bill 2013 (Cth). Despite extensive consultation, the process for constitutional amendment foundered.[35] In turn, Indigenous peoples unsuccessfully sought an

[27] See John Chesterman and Brian Galligan, *Citizens without Rights: Aborigines and Australian Citizenship* (Cambridge University Press, 1997) 71.
[28] Melissa Castan, 'Competing Frameworks for Indigenous Recognition: International, Australian and Victorian Approaches', PhD thesis, Monash University, 2017, 1.
[29] ibid 2.
[30] ibid 69.
[31] ibid 72.
[32] *Wurridjal v Commonwealth* (2009) 237 CLR 309, 393.
[33] Kirsty Gover, 'The Honour of the Crowns: State–Indigenous Fiduciary Relationships and Australian Exceptionalism' (2016) 38 *Sydney Law Review* 339, 368.
[34] ibid; and see Bankes (ch 6 in this volume) and Erueti (ch 10 in this volume).
[35] See Melissa Castan, 'Closing the Gap on the Constitutional Referendum' (2013) 8 *Indigenous Law Bulletin* 13.

advisory 'Voice' in Federal Parliament – an approach reflecting the Australian preference for consultative models rather than rights-based models. Nonetheless, the later Uluru Statement by First Nations embeds Indigenous sovereignty in an authority sourced in the 'ancestral tie' of First Nations to the land and waters that 'co-exists with the sovereignty of the Crown'.[36] Such an approach, if accepted by the Australian nation-state, has clear ramifications for Indigenous peoples' sovereignty and governance in marine areas.

### D. Influence of International Law

The growing involvement of Aboriginal peoples and Torres Strait Islanders in marine governance parallels trends across the globe[37] and reflects the expansion of human rights norms. Yet Indigenous peoples' rights in international law remain contested.[38] Nationally, these supra-national legal orders compound already complex relationships within former colonial states.[39] Although Indigenous academic Irene Watson welcomes the moves to decentre, she identifies 'the usual analytical tendency to privilege the dominant structure and concepts of Western law'.[40]

Modern agreement making arises from the legacy of the colonial era, but it has been progressively adapted due to the re-assessment of the relationship between First Nations' peoples and governments. This revision has been fostered by Indigenous peoples' rights in international law.[41] Formal agreement making has been matched by a rapid expansion in normative principles whereby corporate actors must demonstrate their legitimacy in dealing with Indigenous peoples, typically termed as gaining a 'social licence' to operate in environmental and resource fields.[42]

[36] Referendum Council, 'Final Report Uluru Statement from the Heart', June 2017, https://www.referendumcouncil.org.au/sites/default/files/2017-5/Uluru_Statement_From_The_Heart_0.PDF.

[37] Graeme Kelleher, Chris Bleakley and Sue Wells, *A Global Representative System of Marine Protected Areas* (Great Barrier Reef Marine Park Authority, World Bank and World Conservation Union, 1995).

[38] Benedict Kingsbury, 'Reconciling Five Competing Conceptual Structures of Indigenous Peoples' Claims in International and Comparative Law' (2001) 34 *New York University Journal of International Law and Politics* 189.

[39] Karen Engle, *The Elusive Promise of Indigenous Development: Rights, Culture, Strategy* (Duke University Press, 2010) 18.

[40] Irene Watson, *Aboriginal Peoples, Colonialism and International Law: Raw Law* (Routledge, 2014) 6.

[41] Endalew Lijalem Enyew, 'Application of the Right to Permanent Sovereignty over Natural Resources for Indigenous Peoples: Assessment of Current Legal Developments' (2017) 8 *Arctic Review on Law and Politics* 222; and ch 2 of this volume.

[42] 'Social licence' refers to the need for corporate entities that extract resources or damage environments to gain legitimacy with surrounding communities by acting in a socially responsible manner. See The Hon Justice Brian Preston, 'The Adequacy of the Law in Satisfying Society's Expectations for Major Projects' (2015) 32 *Environmental and Planning Law Journal* 182, 183–84.

### *i. International Environmental Law*

Historically approaches to marine conservation have reflected a Eurocentric relationship with marine areas – not unsurprisingly, given Western conceptions of oceans as 'the commons'.[43] Marine 'commons', like Indigenous peoples' lands, were regarded by colonial nations as open to appropriation.[44] In a postcolonial world, international law has now proved to be a foundation for environmental and cultural heritage protection within Australia,[45] while not displacing the underlying colonial appropriation of land and surrounding seas. The Australian government, without a direct legislative power for environmental matters, has relied on the 'indirect' legislative powers (principally the external affairs power) to give effect to international obligations within the nation.

International environmental treaties thus play an important translational role in Australian laws, especially the World Heritage Convention. Significantly, the Convention acknowledges Indigenous peoples as partners in the conservation of World Heritage properties.[46] World Heritage management principles[47] include special provision for 'indigenous heritage values'.[48] World Heritage sites recognise the cultural heritage significance of both the Great Barrier Reef and Ningaloo Reef. The Ramsar Convention[49] acknowledges Indigenous peoples' interest in wetland management.[50] Guidelines support the strengthening of Indigenous peoples' participation in managing wetlands, many of which are located in coastal environments.[51]

The 1992 Convention on Biological Diversity (CBD) commits the contracting parties to 'respect, preserve and maintain' Indigenous Peoples' 'knowledge, innovation and practices … relevant for the conservation and sustainable use of biological diversity'.[52] The obligations are 'soft law'. Australia, an early

[43] See, eg, Madeleine Heyward, 'Common Ownership and Colonial Mentality: The Conceptual Barriers to Effective Management of Sea Country' (2008) 2 *Ngiya: Talk the Law* 34; Enyew (n 41).

[44] Erica Techera, 'Legal Pluralism, Indigenous People and Small Island Developing States: Achieving Good Environmental Governance in the South Pacific' (2010) 42 *Journal of Legal Pluralism* 61.

[45] Lee Godden and Jacqueline Peel, *Environmental Law: Scientific, Policy and Regulatory Dimensions* (Oxford University Press, 2018) ch 3.

[46] UNESCO World Heritage Committee, 'Decisions Adopted by the World Heritage Committee at its 39th Session' (8 July 2015) WHC-15/39.COM/19, 243.

[47] Environment Protection and Biodiversity Conservation Act 1999 (Cth), s 137.

[48] ibid s 324Y.

[49] ibid s 138.

[50] Meeting of the Conference of the Contracting Parties, 'Recommendation 6.3 at the Proceedings of the 6th Meeting', 19–27 March 1996, www.ramsar.org/sites/default/files/documents/library/key_rec_6.03_e.pdf.

[51] 'Guidelines for Establishing and Strengthening Local Communities' and Indigenous People's Participation in the Management of Wetlands' (adopted as an annex to Resolution VII.8, adopted by the 7th Meeting of the Conference of the Contracting Parties to the Convention on Wetlands, 10–18 May 1999), www.ramsar.org/sites/default/files/documents/pdf/participation-guidelines.pdf.

[52] Convention on Biological Diversity (n 6) art 8(j).

signatory to the Convention, has adopted many principles in the Environment Protection and Biodiversity Conservation Act 1999 (hereinafter 'EPBC Act').[53] The Act also incorporates other international environmental agreements to develop an extensive cetacean and fisheries management regime in coastal waters. Australian states and territories have fisheries and coastal management legislation, although effective implementation is often lacking.

The Akwe: Kon guidelines, promulgated under the CBD, guide impact assessment, where projects affect Indigenous lands, waters and sacred sites. Australia incorporated the guidelines into the EPBC Act, although it is not specific to marine areas.[54] Further, when deciding whether to approve projects, the relevant minister must consider international treaties and principles, many of which have relevance to Aboriginal and Torres Strait Islander values. The EPBC Act expressly acknowledges the role of Aboriginal peoples and Torres Strait Islanders in environmental protection, although the legislation is selective in its practical implementation.[55] The Act explicitly recognises 'a partnership approach to environmental protection and biodiversity conservation'.[56] Indigenous marine protected areas rely on the underpinning EPBC Act.[57]

Some environmental statutes include Indigenous consultation bodies,[58] but few consultative mechanisms are expressly dedicated to marine areas. However, consultative mechanisms form an important conduit for international principles into the national space. Australia was involved in the establishment of the World Indigenous Network of Land and Sea Managers at the UN Conference on Sustainable Development (Rio+20).

### *ii. Law of the Sea*

The Law of the Sea Convention interacts with the national and international environmental frameworks and provides an overarching, but impinging framework in respect of Indigenous governance in marine areas. Australia has a large Exclusive Economic Zone (EEZ) due to its extensive coastline. The inner coastal waters are subject to a complex regime of federal 'cooperative management' under the 'Offshore Constitutional Settlement'.[59] State and Northern Territory governments have the primary responsibility for governing marine environments (and coastal sea beds) up to three nautical miles from the territorial sea baseline.

[53] EPBC Act, ss 3 and 3A.

[54] Chris McGrath, *Does Environmental Law Work?: How to Evaluate the Effectiveness of an Environmental Legal System* (Lambert Academic Publishing, 2010).

[55] EPBC Act, s 3(1)(f) and (g).

[56] ibid s 3(2)(g)(iii).

[57] See below.

[58] See Indigenous Advisory Committee; EPBC Act, s 505B(1).

[59] Coastal Waters Act (State Powers) Act 1980 (Cth); Attorney-General Australia, 'Offshore Constitutional Settlement', https://www.ag.gov.au/Internationalrelations/InternationalLaw/Pages/TheOffshoreConstitutionalSettlement.aspx.

The Commonwealth Government's responsibility extends from the State or Territory limit to the limit of the Australian EEZ (ie, 200 nautical miles). The Great Barrier Reef Marine Park in northern Queensland is an exception due to its World Heritage status. The EPBC Act requires such reserves to be managed in accordance with the Australian International Union for the Conservation of Nature (IUCN) Reserve Management Principles. Other initiatives in transjurisdictional marine management, such as land-based marine pollution controls, do not comprise comprehensive frameworks.[60]

Within this elaborate governance regime, Aboriginal peoples have often been marginalised. Consultation with them can be tokenistic, although notable exceptions are the interactions between governments and Indigenous organisations such as NAILSMA.[61] While not totally displacing the view of the natural world as 'physical rather than metaphysical spaces',[62] there have been clear moves to adopt Indigenous values in environmental legislation. Nevertheless, growing acceptance of knowledge pluralism has not been matched by enhanced legal pluralism.

### E. Human Rights Norms

Legal pluralism comprehends the interplay of formal and informal rules in mediating the legal, political and cultural relations between the state and 'polities' within the nation.[63] Human rights principles and non-binding norms have contributed strongly to the evolution of Indigenous participation in marine governance as a narrow form of pluralism.[64] Despite some scepticism remaining – at the moment there is optimism that Indigenous peoples' rights in marine areas are at a point when 'the concept and practice of human rights have the potential to become more capacious embracing norms of equality and self-determination'.[65] Within Australia, human rights principles based on equality and non-discriminatory treatment have enabled legislative change for greater recognition for Indigenous peoples' rights.[66] Australia became a party to a range of international human rights instruments with many

[60] Holley, Rayfuse and Gray (n 8) 7.

[61] North Australian Indigenous Land and Sea Management Alliance, https://www.nailsma.org.au.

[62] Ambelin Kwaymullina and Blaze Kwaymullina, 'Learning to Read the Signs: Law in an Indigenous Reality' (2010) 34 *Journal of Australian Studies* 195, 201.

[63] Shane Chalmers, 'Law's Pluralism: Getting to the Heart of the Rule of Law' *Law, Culture and the Humanities* (16 May 2017), https://doi.org/10.1177/1743872117707276.

[64] Butterly and Techera (n 8) 79–99.

[65] Kristen Carpenter and Angela Riley, 'Indigenous Peoples and the Jurisgenerative Moment in Human Rights' (2014) 102(1) *California Law Review* 173.

[66] Russell Barsh, 'Indigenous Peoples in the 1990s: From Object to Subject of International Law?' (1994) 7 *Harvard Human Rights Journal* 33.

provisions incorporated into domestic laws, such as the Racial Discrimination Act 1975 (Cth).

### *i. The International Covenant on Civil and Political Rights*

Foremost in influence was the International Covenant on Civil and Political Rights (ICCPR),[67] which addresses self-determination and minority cultural rights,[68] although its domestic implementation is not without limitations.[69] Self-determination has continued to be advocated by Indigenous peoples in Australia, although it is often associated with a moderate position on Indigenous sovereignty. To the extent that self-determination necessitates the establishment and maintenance of institutional frameworks that include Aboriginal and Torres Strait Islander peoples in the decisions, processes, law making and administration that impact upon their lives,[70] it has clear import for indigenous marine governance. Australia is not a party to the Indigenous and Tribal Peoples Convention 1989 (No 169), but its influence is felt beyond the ratifying states.[71] The Inter-American jurisprudence articulates procedural measures and standards, directed to Indigenous participation, consultation or consent, that operate as protective devices for Indigenous communities in relation to territories, property and resources.[72] These principles are persuasive in Australia.

### *ii. The Duty to Consult and FPIC*

In Australia, free, prior and informed consent (FPIC) and any 'duty to consult' have an ambivalent status. Although it has no unequivocal legislative basis, FPIC has become a default standard in many agreement-making contexts. The Native Title Act 1993 sets out good faith procedures for negotiation of agreements which apply to the offshore, and limited protections are offered by the future acts regime under the Native Title Act, although Indigenous groups have no power of veto over projects.

[67] International Covenant on Civil and Political Rights, opened for signature 16 December 1966, 999 UNTS 171 (entered into force 23 March 1976).

[68] See also International Covenant on Economic, Social and Cultural Rights (adopted 19 December 1966, entered into force 3 January 1976) 999 UNTS 3, art 1.

[69] See, eg, obstacles to group complaints; see Melissa Castan 'DRIP Feed: The Slow Reconstruction of self-Determination for Indigenous Peoples' in Sarah Joseph and Adam McBeth (eds), *Research Handbook on International Human Rights Law* (Edward Elgar, 2010) 499.

[70] ibid 501.

[71] Alexandra Xanthaki, 'Indigenous Rights in International Law over the Last Ten Years and Future Developments' (2009) 10 *Melbourne Journal of International Law* 27, 32.

[72] See Mauro Barelli, 'Free, Prior and Informed Consent in the Aftermath of the UN Declaration on the Rights of Indigenous Peoples: Developments and Challenges Ahead' (2012) 16 *International Journal of Human Rights* 1, 1.

In 2007, the United Nations Declaration on the Rights of Indigenous Peoples (UNDRIP) gave expression to 'third-generation' rights built around culture and communal identity.[73] The Declaration relates to 'lands, territories, waters and coastal seas and other resources' and customary practices.[74] As a Declaration, the binding effect on nations is debated.[75] Australia has been equivocal. In 2007, the 'federal government still felt incapable of recognising Indigenous Australians … by voting against the UN Declaration on the Rights of Indigenous Peoples',[76] but later issued a Statement of Support.[77] Such equivocation relates to the strong language of self-determination and sovereignty over traditional territories, natural resources and coastal seas in the Declaration. As a settler nation, Australia largely maintains a position of unilateral sovereignty, which is difficult to reconcile with these articles.

The UNDRIP does not specifically address marine areas and resources,[78] but an expansive interpretation would clearly cover marine governance.[79] Domestically, self-determination is linked to sustainable development and Indigenous peoples' rights.[80] The UNDRIP is a 'very clear exercise in translating the right to self-determination from international law into the domestic context'.[81] Consequently, self-determination encompasses measures to protect the environment for future generations and culturally appropriate economic development.[82] Indigenous advocacy also seeks to secure subsistence for communities and engagement in traditional activities in marine areas.[83]

Articles that require Indigenous peoples' participation in decisions 'affect[ing] their rights' apply, for example, to offshore native title rights. Similarly, the rights to 'maintain and strengthen' spiritual relationships with 'traditionally owned … lands, territories, waters and coastal seas and other resources'[84] have clear application to marine governance, given the rights to determine and develop strategies for the development or use of these lands, territories and resources.[85] While these principles are advocated by the First Nations in Australia, their formal incorporation in national legislation has not been significant.

[73] United Nations Declaration on the Rights of Indigenous Peoples (adopted 13 September 2007 UNGA Res 61/295 (hereinafter 'UNDRIP').

[74] See below re commercial native title in the offshore.

[75] Megan Davis, 'To Bind or Not to Bind: The United Nations Declaration on the Rights of Indigenous Peoples Five Years on' (2012) 19 *Australian International Law Journal* 3, 17.

[76] Castan (n 28) 13.

[77] Jenny Macklin, 'Statement on the United Nations Declaration of Indigenous Peoples', 3 April 2009, www.un.org/esa/socdev/unpfii/documents/Australia_official_statement_endorsement_UNDRIP.pdf.

[78] See Enyew (n 41); and ch 2 of this volume.

[79] Butterly (n 15) 5–6.

[80] See, eg, UNDRIP, arts 20, 23 and 32.

[81] Megan Davis, 'Indigenous struggles in standard-setting: The United Nations Declaration on the Rights of Indigenous Peoples' (2008) 9 *Melbourne Journal of International Law* 439, 461.

[82] UNDRIP, preamble.

[83] ibid art 20.

[84] ibid art 25.

[85] ibid arts 26 and 32; see also art 29(1).

## III. INDIGENOUS RIGHTS AND NATIVE TITLE

Indigenous peoples across the globe have sought legal rights to their ancestral lands, waters and marine spaces. The responses take different legal forms, but developed from a shared jurisprudential basis.[86] In British Commonwealth countries, customary rights to traditional territories and resources derive from their laws, but are recognised at common law in tightly defined circumstances.[87] Aboriginal leader Noel Pearson commented:

> [N]ative title is not a common law title but is instead a title recognised by the common law. What they failed to tell us … is that neither is native title an Aboriginal law title. Because patently Aboriginal law will recognise title where the common law will not. Native title is therefore the space between the two systems, where there is recognition.[88]

In the unfolding iteration between the two systems, critical research into Indigenous marine governance provides a window into the relationships between marine areas, land, culture and economies previously ignored in legal analyses. *Mabo (No 2)* precipitated interest in Indigenous marine governance that had subsisted for tens of thousands of years.[89] The initial claim in *Mabo*, although ultimately limited to land areas, was made over Mer, a tiny island in the Torres Strait. Fishing, collecting marine resources and trading them, as much as gardening and cultivating crops on land were all part of the customary practices of its peoples. The legal team did not pursue a sea claim,[90] despite the Islanders' practices transcending land and water boundaries.[91] A sea claim in the Torres Strait was to re-appear 20 years later.

### A. The Elements of Native Title

Following a tortuous negotiation, the Native Title Act 1993 (Cth) became the central mechanism for determining Aboriginal and Torres Strait Islander peoples' rights and interests in marine areas. To date, there is an uneven

[86] Noel Pearson, 'The Concept of Native Title at Common Law', *Australian Humanities Review*, 1997, http://australianhumanitiesreview.org/1997/03/01/the-concept-of-native-title-at-common-law.

[87] The scholarship is extensive: see, eg, Robert Miller et al, *Discovering Indigenous Lands* (Oxford University Press, 2010); Paul McHugh, *Aboriginal Title: The Modern Jurisprudence of Tribal Land Rights* (Oxford University Press, 2011).

[88] See Noel Pearson, 'The Concept of Native Title at Common Law' in Galarrwuy Yunupingu (ed), *Our Land is Our Life: Land Rights: Past, Present and Future* (University of Queensland Press, 1997) 150. See also Ulla Secher, *Aboriginal Customary Law: A Source of Common Law Title to Land* (Hart Publishing, 2014) 307.

[89] See above n 17. The High Court decision overturned the finding that Australia was *terra nullius*, although not the point that Australia was a settled colony.

[90] Bryan Keon Cohen, 'The Mabo Litigation: A Personal and Procedural Account' (2000) 24(3) *Melbourne University Law Review* 893.

[91] Sharp (n 2) 140.

geographical distribution to offshore native title determinations, with growing numbers of native title sea claims in southern Australia. Despite the nomenclature, the courts have held that native title is a 'bundle of rights'. The Act is the 'starting point' for interpreting native title.[92] Section 223(1) provides that 'native title' means rights in relation to land or waters, where:

(a) the rights and interests are possessed under the traditional laws acknowledged, and the traditional customs observed, by the Aboriginal peoples or Torres Strait Islanders; and
(b) the Aboriginal peoples or Torres Strait Islanders, by those laws and customs, have a connection with the land or waters; and
(c) the rights and interests are recognised by the common law of Australia.

Section 223(2) provides a non-exhaustive listing of native title rights and interests.[93] The interpretation of these two sections has proved critical in terms of the availability of Indigenous rights of a commercial nature in marine areas.[94] Whether native title includes rights to trade and to take resources such as fish for commercial purposes raises pivotal questions about the scope of Indigenous marine governance.

Native title refers to the legal character of the rights and interests,[95] but the specific content of native title for any claimant group depends on 'the factual matrix' of evidence of the law acknowledged and custom practiced since prior to the assertion of British sovereignty. The factual matrix is determined through litigation in the Federal Court or can be a consent determination based on agreement between the claimants, governments and third parties.[96]

Moreover, only rights are recognised in a native title determination – not the complex of law, custom and society.[97] This elaborates Pearson's point that native title does not comprehend an expansive legal plurality, but is a narrow point of system intersection where the parameters of the interaction are set by the dominant legal system. Moreover, disentangling native title rights from the culture and society requires a complex fracturing of the traditional laws and customs.[98] By implication, native title does not extend to rights to protect cultural knowledge,[99] although it can comprise rights of access to marine sacred

[92] *Western Australia v Ward* (2002) 213 CLR 1 [228] (Gleeson CJ, Gaudron, Gummow and Hayne JJ).

[93] Section 223(2) of the Native Title Act 1993 (Cth) states: 'Without limiting subsection (1), rights and interests in that subsection includes hunting, gathering, or fishing, rights and interests.'

[94] See below re commercial native title.

[95] *Western Australia v Brown* (2014) 306 ALR 168 [34]; *Akiba v Commonwealth* (2013) 250 CLR 209 [61] (Hayne, Kiefel and Bell JJ), citing *Western Australia v Ward* (n 92) [468].

[96] Section 225 of the Native Title Act 1993 (Cth) defines a 'determination of native title'. It requires the listing of the native title rights in the determination area and their relationship to other rights and interests.

[97] Australian Law Reform Commission, *Defining Native Title, Connection to Country: Review of the Native Title Act 1993 (Cth)* (ALRC Report, 2015) ch 4.

[98] ibid.

[99] *Western Australia v Ward* (n 92) [468].

sites and to conduct ceremonies on sea country. Further, the proof of native title requires elaborate anthropological and historical investigation in order to meet the stringent evidential threshold set in *Yorta Yorta v Victoria*.[100] In sum, these constraints significantly limit the relationships with sea country that can be realised through the native title process.

Yet, conversely, evolution in the judicial conception of native title occurred, in part, due to the offshore claims. In *Mabo (No 2)*, Justice Brennan described native title as 'burdening or qualifying' the radical title of the Crown, ie, the sovereign title to territory the British government asserted at colonisation.[101] Radical title was a form of constitutional power to deal with territory, which did not automatically extinguish prior interests, although subsequent Crown grants could do so.[102] This model of co-existence was further articulated in the *Wik* decision,[103] but later High Court cases curtailed the scope of native title rights and interests. Simultaneously, these decisions expanded the circumstances where rights and interests were extinguished or infringed.[104]

### B. Native Title in the Offshore

In *Commonwealth v Yarmirr*, the High Court developed native title jurisprudence in respect of marine areas.[105] The applicant, Mary Yarmirr, represented a claimant group whose traditional sea country extended around Croker Island in the Northern Territory. The claimant group held land tenure under the Aboriginal Land Rights (Northern Territory) Act 1976 (Cth)[106] and sought recognition of comparable rights in the offshore. The courts at all levels confirmed that native title could be recognised in the offshore, but only as non-exclusive rights and interests, ie, native title did not confer 'possession, occupation use and enjoyment' of the sea or seabed to the exclusion of all others.[107] As a finding on the evidence, the first instance decision set out rights of access to sea country for cultural and spiritual purposes, and to fish and hunt on a personal, domestic or subsistence basis.

On appeal, the High Court further transfigured the legal construction of co-existence.[108] Native title became the rights and interests that 'survived annexation' by the Crown.[109] Uncertainty over whether sovereign 'territorial'

[100] *Yorta Yorta v Victoria* (2002) 214 CLR 422.
[101] See *Mabo v Queensland (No 2)* (n 17) [51] (Brennan J).
[102] ibid.
[103] Lee Godden, 'Wik: Legal Memory and History' (1997) 6 *Griffith Law Review* 122, 123.
[104] Maureen Tehan, 'A Hope Disillusioned, an Opportunity Lost? Reflections on Common Law Native Title and Ten Years of the Native Title Act' (2003) 27 *Melbourne University Law Review* 523.
[105] *Commonwealth of Australia v Yarmirr* (n 18).
[106] Note that the land rights legislation confers a fee simple equivalent title.
[107] *Yarmirr and Others v Northern Territory* (1998) 82 FCR 533 (Olney J).
[108] See generally above n 88.
[109] *Commonwealth v Yarmirr* (n 105) [47].

title extended beyond the low-water mark was pivotal to the change. Thus, the test of native title rights came to rest on 'inconsistency'. In relation to Australia's territorial seas, the High Court noted:

> [T]here was no necessary inconsistency between the rights and interests asserted by Imperial authorities and the continued recognition of native title rights and interests. The qualification is required because the rights and interests asserted at sovereignty carried with them the recognition of public rights of navigation and fishing and, perhaps, the concession of an international right of innocent passage. Those rights were necessarily inconsistent with the continued existence of any right under Aboriginal law or custom to preclude the exercise of those rights … however, there was no necessary inconsistency and there is no need to resort to notions of radical title to explain why that is so.[110]

Justice McHugh in dissent held that there could be no recognition of offshore native title.[111] The interaction between public rights of fishing and navigation and native title was resolved by a finding of fundamental inconsistency between exclusive possession native title and fishing and navigation.[112]

Eurocentric law could not easily make the translation between land and sea, precipitating a further weakening of native title. The courts reinforced the dominance of national sovereignty in the offshore (with an eye to the Law of the Sea Convention) by conceding rights over sea country to Indigenous communities that were limited to cultural and subsistence bases. Such findings obscured the long history of marine governance and seafaring practised for millennia by the Aboriginal peoples of Croker Island.

Setting its face against such histories, the path set in *Yarmirr* was followed in later cases.[113] Together with the need for claim groups to bring evidence of a continuing pre-sovereign normative system, it locked native title into a model of 'traditional' usufructuary rights. In the marine context, however, the nature of native title was to come before the High Court again in the Torres Strait Sea Claim in 2013.

### *i. Blue Mud Bay and Controlling Access*

In the intervening period, the Blue Mud Bay case was decided – in respect of the Aboriginal Land Rights Act (Northern Territory) 1976 (Cth) rather than native title.[114] Here, the High Court found that the freehold title held by an Aboriginal Land Trust for the Yolgnu people included the right to make decisions about

[110] ibid [61] (Gleeson CJ, Gaudron, Gummow and Hayne JJ).

[111] ibid [179].

[112] Lisa Strelein, *Compromised Jurisprudence: Native Title Cases since Mabo*, 2nd edn (Aboriginal Studies Press, 2009) 52.

[113] ibid 55.

[114] *Northern Territory of Australia v Arnhem Land Aboriginal Land Trust* (2018) 236 CLR 24 (Blue Mud Bay).

who entered the associated tidal waters, irrespective of the operation of the Northern Territory Fisheries Act 1988 (NT).[115] The High Court determined that extensive statutory regulation of fishing had removed any public right to fish in these tidal waters.

The Northern Territory allows traditional owners to apply for 'sea closures' whereby a group can apply to prevent outsiders from entering and fishing in seas within two kilometres of their land without permission.[116] The capacity for Aboriginal peoples along the northern coast to control access to coastal waters has significant economic and political implications for commercial fisheries and recreational fishing.[117] The platform was set for other sea claims.

## IV. COMMERCIAL NATIVE TITLE RIGHTS AND INTERESTS IN MARINE RESOURCES

Stories from traditional owners, together with anthropological and historical evidence, reveals that Aboriginal and Torres Strait Islanders have long been engaged in trading marine resources.[118] The Torres Strait Sea Claim raised the critical issue of whether native title rights to commercial fishing had been extinguished, and the effect of the regulation of marine resources. The Queensland and Commonwealth governments argued that commercial native title fishing rights should not be recognised due to inconsistency[119] or were extinguished by comprehensive legislation.[120]

The Torres Strait Sea Claim initiated a long trajectory of litigation, with the evidential findings by the trial judge in *Akiba v Queensland (No 2)* raising debate.[121] The relevant native title claimed was 'to take for any purpose resources in the native title areas' based on a 'long and well chronicled history' that 'marine products were historically, and are today, taken for the purpose of exchange and sale'.[122] The judge commented that 'the evidence establishes beyond question that the Islanders sold marine resources for money ... The Islanders were, and are, trading fish'.[123] Justice Finn determined that the Sea Claim Group enjoyed non-exclusive rights to access, remain in and use their maritime territories, and to access resources and take resources for any purpose

[115] The significance of this finding becomes more apparent given the extreme tidal range along this coastline.

[116] There are two sea closure areas in the Northern Territory, but groups have difficulty in enforcing them.

[117] *Akiba v Queensland (No 2)* (2010) 204 FCR 1 [847].

[118] See Butterly (n 12) 240–41.

[119] ibid.

[120] Butterly (n 15).

[121] Above (n 117) [932].

[122] Butterly (n 12) 243.

[123] *Akiba v Queensland (No 2)* (n 117) [528].

(ie, including commercial uses).[124] This finding stood against *Yarmirr*, where the High Court found a non-exclusive right to take resources,[125] excluding sea-bed mineral and petroleum resources. An interplay between 'inconsistency and extinguishment' re-appeared in the subsequent litigation.

In *Akiba (No 3)*,[126] the High Court majority, while determining issues of extinguishment and regulation, also openly engaged on the 'purposes' of native title rights, reinvigorating a broader, relationship-focused concept of native title.[127] French CJ and Crennan J held that:

> A broadly defined native title right such as the right 'to take for any purpose resources in the native title areas' may be exercised for commercial or non-commercial purposes. The purposes may be well defined or diffuse … But none of those propositions requires a sectioning of the native title right into lesser rights or 'incidents' … A native title right or interest defines a relationship between the native title holders and the land or waters to which the right or interest relates.[128]

The native title right subsequently determined was 'the right to access resources and take for any purpose'.[129] This decision precipitated several 'test' claims around rights to take resources for 'any purpose'. Again, the Torres Strait decision provided a legal model that was translated to other areas of Australia. In December 2017, for example, a native title determination in northern New South Wales recognised commercial native title rights to resources. The consent determination for the Gumbaynggirr people, resolved after 19 years, recognised native title rights over 130 hectares of land and sea.[130] Such legal developments will give impetus for the resolution of other native title sea claims in southern Australia.[131]

### A. Section 211 of the Native Title Act: Protecting Customary Rights and Interests

The substantive provisions for establishing offshore native title should be read alongside section 211 of the Native Title Act. This section operates so that certain 'customary' activities by native title holders or claimants that otherwise are contrary to national, state or territory laws are not prohibited or restricted.

[124] ibid (xiii) (xv), [13].

[125] *Commonwealth of Australia v Yarmirr* (n 18) (iii).

[126] See *Akiba v Queensland (No 3)* (n 22).

[127] See Paul Finn, '*Mabo* into the Future: Native Title Jurisprudence' (2012) 8 *Indigenous Law Bulletin* 5, 8.

[128] *Akiba v Commonwealth* (n 95) [21].

[129] ibid.

[130] Gumbaynggirr People Native Title Determination (15 August 2014, NCD2014/001), www.nntt.gov.au/searchRegApps/NativeTitleClaims/Pages/Determination_details.aspx?NNTT_Fileno=NCD2014/001.

[131] The National Native Title Tribunal has maps detailing native title sea claims; see www.nntt.gov.au/Maps/SA_NTDA_Schedule.pdf.

Prominent among such laws are statutory regimes that regulate fisheries and marine resources such as abalone,[132] as well as environmental protections for endangered species. In *Western Australia v Commonwealth*, the High Court held that such laws are suspended to allow the enjoyment of the native title rights and interests.[133]

Three elements must be satisfied for the 'shield' to become operative. First is the exercise or enjoyment of rights and interests such as traditional fishing or gathering of resources such as shellfish. Second, the respective activities are prohibited for everyone unless authorised by 'a licence, permit or other instrument' and, third, the activity is for satisfying 'personal, domestic or non-commercial needs'. Meeting the third element has been a source of conflict between Aboriginal peoples and regulatory authorities. The regulators have also prosecuted Aboriginal peoples for 'taking' marine resources without requisite permits.[134]

Overarching legal issues around section 211 relate to whether environmental conservation legislation merely regulates or extinguishes native title rights. Generally, regulation does not extinguish native title, but may have effects such as suspension of rights and interests. Section 211 as a defence to prosecutions for taking marine resources has come before the High Court in *Yanner v Eaton*[135] (northern Queensland Gulf Country) and *Karpany v Dietman*[136] (southern Australian 'Bight'). In *Yanner v Eaton*, the appellant, Marandoo Yanner, a local Aboriginal leader, was charged with the taking of juvenile saltwater crocodiles (an endangered species) without a permit as required by section 54(1)(a) of the Fauna Act 1974 (Qld). The appellant argued successfully before the magistrate that section 211 applied. This finding, which was overturned on appeal, was ultimately upheld by the High Court. Central to the reasoning was that the Native Title Act was federal legislation:

> Accordingly, by operation of s 211(2) of the Native Title Act and s 109 of the Constitution, the Fauna Act did not prohibit or restrict the appellant, as a native title holder, from hunting or fishing for the crocodiles he took for the purpose of satisfying personal, domestic or non-commercial communal needs.[137]

This priority accorded to the exercise of native title rights within the Australian federal structure stands in contrast to jurisdictions where endangered species legislation has taken priority over traditional rights.

[132] Aboriginal peoples in southern Australia have long harvested marine resources including abalone. See Beryl Cruse, Liddy Stewart and Sue Norman, *Mutton Fish: The Surviving Culture of Aboriginal People and Abalone on the South Coast of NSW* (Aboriginal Studies Press, 2005).

[133] *Western Australia v Commonwealth* (1995) 183 CLR 373, 474.

[134] See, eg, *Lewis (Department of Primary Industries-Fisheries) v Wanganeen and Harradine* [2005] SASC 36; *Police v Graeme William Sydney Talbot* [2013] NTMC 033 (17 December 2013).

[135] *Yanner v Eaton* (1999) 201 CLR 351.

[136] *Karpany v Dietman* (2013) 88 ALJR 90.

[137] *Yanner v Eaton* (n 135) [40] (Gleeson CJ, Gaudron, Kirby and Hayne JJ).

*Yanner v Eaton* is also cited extensively on the adaptation and evolution of the traditional practices that ground native title rights and interests.[138] When hunting the juvenile crocodile, Yanner used 'modern' weapons (ie, a shotgun) to kill the saltwater crocodile and what is colloquially known as a 'tinnie' – a small metal boat rather than a dugout traditional canoe. The issue turned upon whether such practices could still be regarded as traditional and therefore fall within the definition of native title.[139] *Karpany v Dietman* concerned a prosecution of Karpany (father and son) members of the Narrunga people for taking undersized abalone contrary to the Fisheries Management Act 2007 (SA).[140] The Karpanys argued that as native title holders, section 211 exempted them from size restrictions on abalone. It was accepted that the appellants had acted in accordance with the traditional laws and customs of the Narrunga People and that the abalone was for 'bona fide non-commercial, or communal need'.[141] The High Court found that the native title rights were not impacted by the restrictions in the fisheries legislation. This decision clarified situations where Aboriginal peoples were often prosecuted for the exercise of traditional rights to take marine resources. Yet in many coastal regions, it has not dispelled persistent attitudes that Aboriginal peoples are acting either illegally or are in competition with more 'legitimate' stakeholders in the marine space. Long-term change in normative values requires not only legal rules to be enforced, but also negotiation and trust to be built between parties in marine governance. Agreement making plays a pivotal role in that regard.

## V. AGREEMENT MAKING

Agreement making is a widespread model of 'engagement, recognition and co-existence' with Indigenous peoples in Australia.[142] These models occur within designated statutory frameworks and as informal arrangements. Such approaches may be more significant in terms of relationship-building and addressing power imbalances than in giving strict effect to legal frameworks. In particular, such measures may allow third parties and agencies to deal with First Nations as 'polities' in a manner rarely openly acknowledged within the formal, constituted nation-state.

[138] See, eg, *Members of the Yorta Yorta Aboriginal Community v Victoria* (2002) 214 CLR 422 [187] (Gleeson CJ, Gummow and Hayne JJ).

[139] *Yanner v Eaton* (n 135) [132].

[140] Fisheries Management Act 2007 (SA), s 72(2)(c). Several state environmental regulatory agencies were joined to the action. Abalone is a valuable export commodity and customary food species.

[141] *Karpany v Dietman* (n 136), [46].

[142] Maureen Tehan, 'Negotiating Co-existence' in Marcia Langton et al (eds), *Honour among Nations? Treaties and Agreements within Indigenous People* (Melbourne University Press, 2004) 174; Marcia Langton et al (eds), *Settling with Indigenous People: Modern Treaty and Agreement-Making* (Federation Press, 2006).

Native title laws blend prescriptive substantive provisions with negotiation and consent regimes. Other statutory regimes allow more open-textured agreements. The Traditional Owner Settlement Act 2010 (Vic) addresses concerns that rendered successful native title claims difficult in areas of extensive colonisation and the dispossession of Aboriginal peoples. The Act provides for recognition of traditional owner rights in land and waters by means of a recognition and settlement agreement negotiated with the government. A traditional owner group may enter a 'natural resource agreement' as part of a 'recognition and settlement agreement'.[143] Several settlements over Crown lands in coastal Victoria have co-management agreements whereby traditional owners have rights to harvest subsistence-level marine resources.

Beyond native title and statutory settlements, access to coastal resources and Indigenous participation in marine governance derives from a multi-layered mix of legal rights (proprietary and non-proprietary) strategic planning frameworks, representative committees and institutional management responsibilities. Agreement making and partnerships with Indigenous peoples characterise much offshore environmental management in Australia. Initially, co-management was focused on wilderness protection, but this was progressively displaced by more culturally inclusive models.[144]

## VI. ENVIRONMENTAL CO-MANAGEMENT OF MARINE AREAS

Even so, there is long-standing critique of the 'protected areas' approach in marine areas.[145] Instituting protected areas quarantined from human inhabitants or use,[146] such as 'no-take' zones, may occlude the complex inter-relationships between indigenous people and marine areas. Under traditional laws, many Indigenous communities create spaces and sites from which their members are excluded to manage 'special places'. This occurred within the horizon of socially sensitive forms of Indigenous marine governance. By contrast, marine protected areas based in Western conservation philosophies can be implemented with little or no Indigenous community consultation or involvement in management.[147] However, in the face of environmental and biodiversity decline, there have been strong calls from Indigenous communities for greater involvement in managing marine areas.[148]

[143] Traditional Owner Settlement Act 2010 (Vic), ss 8, 80.

[144] Lee Godden and Stuart Cowell, 'Conservation Planning and Indigenous Governance in Australia's Indigenous Protected Areas' (2016) 24 *Restoration Ecology* 692.

[145] Donald Rothwell and David Vanderzwaag (eds), *Towards Principled Oceans Governance: Australian and Canadian Approaches and Challenges* (Routledge, 2006).

[146] Alex Caveen et al, *The Controversy over Marine Protected Areas: Science Meets Policy* (Springer, 2014).

[147] Dermot Smyth, 'Just Add Water? Taking Indigenous Protected Areas into Sea Country' in Dermot Smyth and Graeme Ward (eds), *Protecting Country: Indigenous Governance and Management of Protected Areas* (Australian Institute of Aboriginal and Torres Strait Islander Studies, 2008).

[148] See Heyward (n 43).

More culturally appropriate forms of co-management have evolved as Aboriginal and Torres Strait Islander peoples have asserted native title and their rights to be involved in marine governance.[149] In Australia, co-management has shifted slowly from a 'parks perspective' to placing decision making more firmly in the hands of Aboriginal peoples and Torres Strait Islanders.[150] A formative, early analysis of the inadequacies of conventional environmental management regimes for marine areas was initiated by Aboriginal Land Councils in northern and western Australia.[151] Momentum built over the following decades for more engaged and respectful models for Indigenous communities' participation in marine governance in northern Australia. Ultimately that concern saw expression in tangible management regimes, for example, as Sea Country Indigenous Protected Areas. In southern Australia, individual settlements and native title agreements are building a mosaic of Indigenous participation in marine governance in coastal regions.

### A. Indigenous Marine Protected Areas

In 1994, the IUCN defined protected areas as an 'area of land and/or sea especially dedicated to the protection and maintenance of biological diversity and associated cultural resources, and managed through legal or other effective means'.[152] In 2010, Nursey-Bray asserted that, in Australia, the primary function of a marine protected area (MPA) is for biodiversity conservation.[153] There was consternation that 'Indigenous peoples that live along or within MPAs in Australia still harvest various fish species, including in some instances those that are endangered or threatened like turtle or dugong'.[154] Such a view of Aboriginal people as impacting biodiversity downplays initiatives such as Indigenous coastal ranger projects and increasing cooperation between environmental organisations and Aboriginal peoples in managing marine areas.

Negotiations around the function of marine protected areas centre on decision-making powers and the extent to which traditional knowledge features in those decisions. For non-Indigenous stakeholders and managers, an MPA prioritises environmental sustainability in a marine commons, which, while managed according to a set of norms and rules, is defined by the public interest.[155]

[149] Hanna Jaireth and Dermot Smyth (eds), *Innovative Governance: Indigenous Peoples, Local Communities, and Protected Areas* (Ane Books, 2003).

[150] Godden and Cowell (n 144).

[151] Peter Jull et al (eds), *Surviving Columbus: Indigenous Peoples, Political Reform and Environmental Management in North Australia* (Australian National University, 1994). Such research also set the groundwork for a number of later sea claims.

[152] Smyth (n 147).

[153] Melissa Nursey-Bray, 'Social Contexts and Customary Fisheries: Marine Protected Areas and Indigenous Use, Australia' (2011) 47 *Journal of Environmental Management* 671.

[154] ibid 672.

[155] ibid 677.

Traditional owners relate to marine areas as a suite of connected but distinct sea estates or country, with duties and obligations arising from relationships embedded in those marine places.[156] Indigenous Protected Marine Areas seek to coalesce the differing perspectives.

### B. Marine Governance: IPA Case Study

The Indigenous Protected Areas (IPA) Program comprises areas of Indigenous controlled land or sea where traditional owners have entered into an agreement with the Australian government to promote biodiversity and cultural resource conservation. Although an IPA may exist over land or sea, declarations in the first decade focused on land.[157] The establishment of marine IPAs was regarded as problematic due to the lack of an Indigenous 'tenure' and exclusive authority in the sea. Native title rights and interests are not regarded as 'tenure'. The non-exclusive nature of native title rights and interests in the offshore gave rise to a perception that this denoted a lack of authority, a view that has had long-term repercussions for the ability of Aboriginal peoples and Torres Strait Islanders to control and manage sea country.

In 2008, Smyth identified that: 'The capacity to include marine areas within a declared IPA is a significant issue for Indigenous groups whose traditional country includes coastal, island and marine environments all around Australia.'[158] Following a 2006 review, this constraint was overcome at a practical level by adopting a sea country management framework rather than a 'legal rights basis'. Subsequently, a wide range of marine IPAs or joint land and sea IPAs have been declared. IPAs do not necessarily have a formal legal foundation. The areas come into existence when Indigenous communities declare or dedicate their land or sea for a conservation purpose that reflects cultural obligations to care for country.[159]

Governments then 'recognised' (but not in a legal pluralist sense) the IPAs as a part of the National Reserve System. This can be accorded formal legal status or, as occurs with marine areas, can be achieved by 'other effective means'.[160] Alignment of sea country IPAs to cultural obligations and managerial functions provides less certainty than 'tenure' models. Even so, given the non-exclusive character of offshore native title, this model, which allows Indigenous groups to negotiate beyond strict legal rights, represents a positive engagement.[161]

[156] ibid.
[157] Smyth (n 147) 97.
[158] ibid 99.
[159] Bruce Rose, 'Indigenous Protected Areas – Innovation beyond the Boundaries', http://aciucn.org.au/wp-content/uploads/2015/09/08_Rose.pdf.
[160] ibid.
[161] Butterly (n 15) 2, 3.

Indigenous communities engaged in marine IPAs can secure funding, especially from the 'Working on Country' Indigenous rangers programme. Increasingly, Indigenous groups are seeking to diversify funding sources to support their marine governance by working in partnerships with state and local governments, non-government organisations, and philanthropic and research organisations.

Despite such agreement-based models being instituted, there remain difficulties for Indigenous communities in negotiating robust participation in marine governance in protected areas. A 2016 review acknowledged the importance of Indigenous management in marine reserves and the opportunities offered for culturally appropriate economic development.[162] Ironically, Australia's marine reserves were extended and then reduced by the subsequent federal government thereby impacting Indigenous governance, which is dependent in many ways upon the vagaries of the political system and resource availability.

## VII. FUTURE PROSPECTS

Many governance frameworks now exist for marine areas in Australia. Yet, there are few models that clearly and directly prioritise the legal and customary relationships that Aboriginal peoples and Torres Strait Islanders have with marine places. As Lauren Butterly argues:

> A different paradigm is needed to consider Indigenous governance of sea country. We need to 'change tack' and promote a discussion that straddles Indigenous rights (including native title) and governance and environmental law and governance. In this space, native title rights are complementary but are not the focus. Rather, they are one of a number of blocks to build upon.[163]

This convergence of formal rights with transformative environmental agendas reinforces the fact that Indigenous participation in marine governance in Australia is shaped by a complex matrix of native title rights to sea country and marine places, environmental legislation and policy, human rights and procedural norms. These complexes have evolved in the absence of substantive constitutional rights and protections for Australia's Indigenous peoples, let alone a formal concession to indigenous sovereignty – or at least as that term is conventionally understood.[164] Moves to acknowledge Indigenous sovereignty

[162] Colin Buxton and Peter Cochrane, 'The Story behind Australia's Marine Reserves, and How We Should Change Them' (*The Conversation*, 3 October 2016), https://theconversation.com/the-story-behind-australias-marine-reserves-and-how-we-should-change-them-65220.

[163] Butterly (n 15) 2.

[164] Webber argues that there are five different ways to conceive sovereignty and suggests a relational model might be most productive; see Jeremy Webber, 'We are Still in the Age of Encounter: Section 35 and a Canada beyond Sovereignty' in Patrick Macklem and Douglas Sanderson (eds), *From Recognition to Reconciliation: Essays on the Constitutional Entrenchment of Aboriginal and Treaty Rights* (University of Toronto Press, 2016) 77–79 and 84.

in marine places are unlikely to gain mainstream political acceptance and the prevailing model of co-existence is likely to continue. The co-existence model privileges settler law. Aboriginal peoples and Torres Strait Islander law is counterpoised to the dominant legal system;[165] it is cast as traditional and/or 'normative'. In marine areas, this designation of customary law as a normative framework has the consequence that the rights and interests that inhere in that system must give way to government and third-party interests. Even if this minimal position on Indigenous rights to manage marine resources is accepted as the prevailing constitutional model, it can be strengthened to more fully acknowledge Indigenous marine governance by providing a statutory basis for the many programmes that currently rest on insecure policy and discretionary funding regimes.

Indigenous MPAs are an important 'first step' in moving towards more equal partnerships in marine governance, although they are still representative of the model of economic and cultural co-existence that characterises Australia's response to Indigenous self-determination and cultural rights.[166] Similarly, the convergence of legal recognition models, such as native title with environmental and economic measures, largely relies for its implementation on policy guidelines and practices such as 'Healthy Country' protocols rather than robust affirmation of Indigenous participation in the Australian polity.

The laws pertinent to Indigenous marine governance have been extended by landmark High Court decisions on commercial offshore native title rights and the reinforcement of the protections offered by section 211 of the Native Title Act. These cases provide a platform for further sea claims to be determined that can continue to build positive forms of collaborative governance in marine areas that begin to approach forms of pluralism and 'shared sovereignty'. Such models of incipient shared sovereignty can be found in the Haida Gwaii Reconciliation Act of 2010 (BC Canada), which Webber argues is an incremental step in the reconciliation of the Haida and Crown title and a framework 'to guide joint decision-making regarding land and natural resource management on Haida Gwaii'.[167] In New Zealand, the articulation between resource management, legal pluralism and shared sovereignty is expressed most directly in the river co-management institutions that derive from settlements under the Treaty of Waitangi process.[168] Australia has developed expansive shared governance and

[165] See above n 100. In this decision, the High Court reinforced the dominance of common 'law' by its construction of Aboriginal law as 'normative'; for discussion, see Strelein (n 112) 76–80.

[166] For an early discussion, see Lisa Strelein, 'Symbolism and Function: From Native Title to Aboriginal and Torres Strait Islander Self-Government' in Marcia Langton et al (ed), *Honour among Nations: Treaties and Agreements with Indigenous People* (Melbourne University Press, 2004) 189.

[167] See the discussion in Webber (n 164) 84–85.

[168] See Co-Management Agreement for Waikato River Related Lands, Waikato Raupatu River Trust and Waikato Regional Council (2012) (NZ); and for discussion, see, eg, Samuel Wevers, 'Recognising Rangatiranga through Co-management: The Waikato River Settlement' (2013) *New Zealand Law Review* 689; and Te Awa Tupua (Whanganui River Claims Settlement) Act (2017) (NZ).

co-management models under the Noongar settlement in Western Australia,[169] and the State of Victoria is in treaty negotiations with Aboriginal people, a significant component of which will be negotiations over management of country.

In tandem, in Australia the expansion of private sector agreements and local partnerships also represents a foundation for cooperative marine governance solutions to extend the basis on which formal legal rights to sea country are realised. If we conceive legal pluralism more flexibly as not constrained to constitutional and sovereign modes, it has the potential to give recognition to the multiple, often uncoordinated, co-existing, overlapping systems of law, normative regimes and 'practices' that meet in marine places. Where Indigenous and non-Indigenous laws meet in marine places, it remains a contested and artificial recognition space for Indigenous peoples. Nonetheless, this space also creates opportunities for Indigenous communities within Australian society to select, opportunistically, pathways among legal and policy models that range from litigation, native title and environmental partnerships, and cultural heritage, to financial leverage and business models in order to advance their objectives in marine governance. Transnational principles derived from the UNDRIP and human rights regimes are enlivened in such plural marine spaces, strengthening the resilience of 'customary' law and 'harmonising' relations between state and non-state systems. The renewed attention to Indigenous rights in marine areas, including moves to strengthen commercial native title, adds a new dimension to this effort. The practicalities of distributing power between Aboriginal peoples and Torres Strait Islanders, and the constituent institutions of the Australian nation (and the overarching international legal regimes of trade, navigation and resource exploitation) in managing marine areas, while difficult, are being addressed. The challenge for evolving marine governance models will be to more fully realise the 'waves of memory' and cultural obligation that underpin Indigenous participation in sea country governance.

[169] See, eg, Ballardong People Indigenous Land Use Agreement.

# 6

# *Modern Land Claims Agreements in Canada and Indigenous Rights with Respect to Marine Areas and Resources*

NIGEL BANKES

## I. INTRODUCTION

THIS CHAPTER EXAMINES the way in which modern land claims agreements between the Government of Canada and Indigenous nations and communities have addressed Indigenous rights with respect to marine areas and resources. It begins with some historical background describing the Crown's treaty-making practices with Indigenous nations and communities, and then provides a short summary of the case law with respect to Indigenous rights to marine areas, drawing upon treaty rights, Aboriginal rights and Aboriginal title. It then turns to examine the modern generation of land claims agreements, focusing on one agreement in particular, the Nunavut Agreement,[1] but also referencing the Labrador Inuit Agreement[2] and the Inuvialuit Agreement.[3]

The chapter demonstrates that the case law with respect to Aboriginal title in the offshore in Canada remains undeveloped. The case law on treaty-based fishing rights now offers considerable guidance, but the case law with respect to an Aboriginal right to fish is also still under development, especially with respect to

[1] Agreement between the Inuit of the Nunavut Settlement Area and Her Majesty the Queen in Right of Canada, 23 May 1993 (NA). The text of this agreement and all other land claim agreements are available on line through this portal https://www.aadnc-aandc.gc.ca/eng/1100100030583/1100100030584.

[2] Land Claims Agreement between the Inuit of Labrador and Her Majesty the Queen in Right of Newfoundland and Labrador and Her Majesty the Queen in Right of Canada, 22 January 2005 (LIA).

[3] The Western Arctic Claim, the Inuvialuit Final Agreement, 5 June 1984 (IFA). For a map of modern land claims agreement settlement areas, see https://www.aadnc-aandc.gc.ca/DAM/DAM-INTER-HQ-AI/STAGING/texte-text/mprm_pdf_modrn-treaty_1383144351646_eng.pdf.

commercial activities. The chapter shows that modern land claims agreements between Canada and coastal Indigenous peoples often contain large marine areas within the settlement boundaries. This allows the co-management bodies established by these agreements to exercise considerable authority in these marine areas. At the same time, these agreements generally do not recognise Aboriginal title in marine areas.

## II. THE HISTORICAL BACKGROUND

The Imperial Crown acquired sovereignty over the territory now known as Canada over a period of centuries through occupation and settlement and in some cases by succession to the claims of the French Crown. The Imperial Crown established a number of separate colonies within British North America: four of those colonies (Canada (as the union of Upper and Lower Canada or Ontario and Quebec), Nova Scotia and New Brunswick) formed the confederation of Canada in 1867.[4] Other colonies subsequently joined that confederation (British Columbia in 1871, Prince Edward Island in 1873 and Newfoundland and Labrador in 1949) and in 1870 the Imperial Crown also transferred to Canada the vast area known as Rupert's Land and the Northwest Territory, followed by the Arctic Islands in 1880 and 1897. The prairie provinces of Manitoba, Saskatchewan and Alberta were created out of these territories between 1870 and 1930. This left the two northern territories of Yukon and the Northwest Territories until the Northwest Territories was divided to create a third territory, the Inuit territory of Nunavut, in 1999.

The general policy of the Crown was to negotiate treaties with the Indigenous peoples of British North America, but the character of these treaties changed over time. The first such treaties were negotiated between 1722 and 1786 with the Mi'kmaq and Wuastukwiuk nations of the east coast. These treaties are generally referred to as 'peace and friendship treaties'.[5] Further treaties were negotiated as settlement moved west, first in Ontario and later with the so-called numbered treaties on the prairies.[6] Unlike the earlier peace and friendship treaties, all of these treaties involved cessions of land from First Nations to the Crown. But there were also significant gaps in the treaty-making process by the time that process came to an end in the 1920s. Thus, with some limited exceptions, there were no treaties in British Columbia, in the eastern Arctic, on the Labrador coast or in much of Quebec.

[4] Constitution Act, 1867.

[5] William Wicken, 'The Mi'kmaq and Wuastukwiuk Treaties' (1994) 44 *University of New Brunswick Law Journal* 241. See also the discussion in Hamilton (ch 1 in this volume).

[6] For a general review of treaty making, see DN Sprague, 'Canada's Treaties with Aboriginal Peoples' (1996) 23 *Manitoba Law Journal* 341. Treaty texts are available at: https://www.aadnc-aandc.gc.ca/eng/1100100030583/1100100030584.

None of these historic treaties had much to say about Indigenous use of marine space, although they did generally provide for the continuation of fishing activities, directly or indirectly,[7] in both freshwater rivers and lakes and marine areas. For example, a treaty of peace and friendship of 1752 with the Mi'kmaq provided that the Mi'kmaq should continue to have 'free liberty of hunting and Fishing as usual',[8] the numbered treaties of the prairies generally provided that the signatory nations could continue to engage in fishing activities throughout the lands surrendered, subject to regulation,[9] and the so-called Douglas treaties negotiated with some First Nations on Vancouver Island assured the signatories of their ability to 'carry on their fisheries as formerly'.[10]

Following the last 'historic' treaties of the 1920s, there followed a period during which the status of Indigenous title claims remained uncertain and contested. Treaty making began again in the mid-1970s under the rubric of modern land claims agreements, partly in response to the Supreme Court of Canada's 1973 decision in the Nisga'a case (*Calder v British Columbia*)[11] which confirmed the existence of Aboriginal title in Canadian law, and partly to provide greater legal certainty for resource development. Geographically, these negotiations focused on those areas where treaties had not been negotiated (or if negotiated not implemented)[12] with an initial focus on northern Quebec and the two (subsequently three) northern territories. Other land claims agreements cover areas of British Columbia and Labrador. Many of these agreements have been negotiated with coastal peoples and this chapter examines how these agreements have recognised (or not) Indigenous rights in relation to marine space. But first, the chapter analyses the case law with respect to treaty rights, Aboriginal rights and Aboriginal title as each pertain to the Indigenous use of marine space.

## III. THE CASE LAW ON TREATY RIGHTS, ABORIGINAL RIGHTS AND ABORIGINAL TITLE AS APPLIED TO MARINE SPACE

Over the years, and in many cases in parallel to the treaty negotiations outlined above, there has been extensive litigation with respect to Indigenous rights to the use of marine resources. This litigation has been based on treaty rights, Aboriginal rights and, to a lesser extent, Aboriginal title. Since all negotiations

[7] For an example of indirect or implied continuation of fishing rights, see *R v Marshall* [1999] 3 SCR 456, which is discussed further below.

[8] *Simon v R* [1985] 2 SCR 387 (SCC).

[9] See, eg, the texts of all the numbered treaties except Treaty 7; see the weblink in n 6.

[10] See, eg, *Saanichton Marina Ltd v Claxton* [1989] 5 WWR 82 (BC CA); *R v Ellsworth* 1992 CanLII 1034 (BC SC).

[11] *Calder v British Columbia* [1973] SCR 313 (SCC).

[12] eg, the Canadian government agreed to negotiate treaties with First Nations in Yukon and the Northwest Territories notwithstanding the fact that Treaties 8 and 11 covered significant parts of these territories.

occur 'in the shadow of the law', it is useful to identify the key principles arising out of the leading cases under each of these three headings.

### A. Treaty Rights

The leading decision on treaty rights in the context of marine resources is the Supreme Court of Canada's majority decision in *R v Marshall*.[13] *Marshall* involved the interpretation of a 1760 treaty of peace and friendship between the Mi'kmaq and the representative of the Crown. The text of the treaty was hardly promising insofar as the most textually relevant clause simply committed the Mi'kmaq to trade through facilities ('truck houses') established by the Crown. Nevertheless, viewing the treaty in its historical context along with other contemporaneous treaties, the majority of the Court found that it was implicit in this undertaking that the Crown would assure the Mi'kmaq of continued access to the resources of the country so as to make trade possible. However, the right to fish that this implied was not unlimited. Drawing again on the context of the treaty discussions, the majority of the Court concluded that the treaty right was 'a right to trade for necessaries' or for a 'moderate livelihood' and not 'a right to trade generally for economic gain'.[14] As a constitutionally protected right, a treaty right to fish is entitled to priority over the harvesting rights of non-Indigenous communities.[15] *Marshall* involved the harvesting of eels, but the logic of the decision extends to more economically valued resources such as lobster. Other cases involving different treaties have interpreted a treaty right 'to carry on our fisheries as formerly' as entitling the signatory community to enjoin activities (the construction of a marina) that might prejudice essential habitat of marine resources.[16]

As a constitutionally protected right, a treaty right, in common with an Aboriginal right or title, can only be infringed if the government can show that the infringement can be justified.[17] In order to meet that burden, the government will first need to demonstrate that the infringing regulatory scheme taken as a whole (or another more specific infringement) had a legitimate objective (for example, a rule for the conservation and management of a resource).[18]

Second, the government will need to demonstrate that the infringement is consistent with its fiduciary obligations owed to that community.[19] In *Sparrow*,

[13] *Marshall* (n 7).

[14] ibid [58].

[15] Constitution Act, 1982, s 35. Section 35 provides that: 'The existing aboriginal and treaty rights of the aboriginal peoples of Canada are hereby recognized and affirmed.' On the priority issue see the discussion of *R v Sparrow* [1990] 1 SCR 1075 below.

[16] *Saanichton Marina* (n 10).

[17] *R v Sparrow* [1990] 1 SCR 1075 (SCC); *R v Gladstone* [1996] 2 SCR 723 (SCC).

[18] *Sparrow* (n 17) 1113. For a much longer list of legitimate objectives in the context of an Aboriginal rights fisheries case, see *Ahousaht Indian Band v Canada (Attorney-General)* [2018] BCSC 633 [769].

[19] *Sparrow* (n 17) 1114.

the first fisheries case to come before the Court following the constitutional entrenchment of Aboriginal rights, the Court interpreted the Crown's fiduciary obligation not in terms of an undivided duty of loyalty, but in terms of a priority of allocation.[20] That priority favoured an allocation for resource conservation, followed by the Indigenous food fishery, followed by commercial and sports fishing.[21] The necessary consequence of such an allocation is that non-Indigenous fishers may be completely excluded from access to the resource, depending upon its conservation status.[22] However, the Court has modified the scope of the priority in the case of a commercial fishery on the grounds that the exercise of such a right has no internal limit.[23] The implications of this modified form of priority are still being worked out by the courts.[24]

Third, the Court has referred to other considerations that will be relevant to justifying an infringement including as little infringement as possible given the objective, the availability of compensation and procedural requirements such as consultation.[25]

### B. An Aboriginal Right to Fish

The modern case law on an Aboriginal right to fish focuses on the constitutional protection extended to Aboriginal rights, including fishing rights, in 1982.[26] Thus, beginning with a trilogy of cases in 1996 (*R v Van der Peet*,[27] *R v NTC Smokehouse*[28] and *R v Gladstone*)[29] and continuing through to *Lax Kw'alaams* in 2011,[30] the Supreme Court of Canada has articulated a set of tests to govern when an Indigenous practice, custom or tradition qualifies for constitutional protection. The Court has paid particular attention to the question of whether or not a right to harvest based upon a traditional practice is a right that is confined to harvesting for food (and cultural or ceremonial purposes) or whether it extends to harvesting for trading purposes, and, if so, what might be the limits of any such commercial harvesting. These efforts by the Court to

[20] ibid 1115–18.

[21] ibid 1116.

[22] ibid; *Gladstone* (n 17) [38].

[23] *Gladstone* (n 17) [62]–[64]. See also *Haida Nation v British Columbia (Minister of Forests)* [2004] 3 SCR 511 [18].

[24] *Ahousaht* (n 18) [811]–[837], emphasising the complexity of giving effect to the principle of priority but also ruling (at [918], [925] and [1251]) that a recreational fishery was not entitled to priority over an Aboriginal right to fish even if described as a commercial right; see also [1477] re halibut, [1596], [1598] and [1560] re crab and [1702] [1709] re prawn.

[25] *Sparrow* (n 17).

[26] Constitution Act, 1982, s 35. Prior to 1982, most Indigenous fishing rights were vulnerable to regulation and abrogation by federal legislation: *R v Derriksan* 1976 CanLII 1270 (SCC).

[27] *R v Van der Peet* [1996] 2 SCR 507 (SCC).

[28] *R v NTC Smokehouse* [1996] 2 SCR 672 (SCC).

[29] *Gladstone* (n 17).

[30] *Lax Kw'alaams Indian Band v Canada (Attorney-General)* [2011] 3 SCR 535.

categorise Indigenous practices as entitled (or not) to constitutional protection have been much criticised, but that has not swayed the Court from this endeavour.[31] In general, the courts have emphasised that the right does not include a right to manage the fishery.[32] Thus, the federal government retains overall responsibility for the management of the fishery, taking into account Indigenous and non-Indigenous interests and subject to an ongoing duty to consult with respect to those decisions and plans.[33]

In its most recent decision in *Lax Kw'alaams*, the Supreme Court articulated a four-step process that a trial judge must follow in adjudicating rights-based fishing claims.[34] First, the court must characterise the precise claim of the Indigenous community based on the pleadings. That characterisation might be refined in the course of the trial in light of the evidence. Second, based on the evidence adduced, the court must determine whether the Indigenous community has proved: '(a) the existence of the pre-contact practice, tradition or custom advanced in the pleadings as supporting the claimed right; and (b) *that this practice was integral to the distinctive pre-contact Aboriginal society*' (emphasis added).[35] Third, the Court must determine 'whether the claimed modern right has a reasonable degree of continuity with the "integral" pre-contact practice'.[36]

Taken together, these first three tests seem to require a community to prove its case on a species-specific basis. For example, in *Lax Kw'alaams*, the community argued that it had the right to the commercial harvesting and sale of all species of fish. The trial judge rejected this claim and the Supreme Court of Canada upheld this conclusion. The trial judge concluded that while the Coastal Tsimshian had established that they harvested a range of fish for sustenance purposes,[37] they had not been able to establish, save with respect to one particular species (eulachan), that trade in the species harvested was 'a central and significant part of the society's distinctive culture'.[38] While harvesting rights should not be frozen in time (and thus the community should be able to adopt new methods of harvesting and preserving the products), this approach is subject to both qualitative and quantitative limits. Accordingly, any effort to extend a culturally significant trade in a single species could not be extended to a modern right to harvest all species for commercial purposes, since this would be 'qualitatively different from the pre-contact activity.'[39]

[31] For criticisms, see, eg, R Mainville, *An Overview of Aboriginal and Treaty Rights and Compensation for Their Breach* (Purich Publishing, 2001) 28–31; and L Rotman, 'Creating a Still-Life out of Dynamic Object: Rights Reductionism at the Supreme Court of Canada' (1997) 36 *Alberta Law Review* 1.

[32] *Sparrow* (n 17) 1119; *Gladstone* (n 17) [65]; and *Ahousaht* (n 18) [985]–[992] and [1221].

[33] *Ahousaht* (n 18) [985]–[992], [1221] and [1253].

[34] *Lax Kw'alaams* (n 30) [46].

[35] ibid.

[36] ibid.

[37] ibid [52].

[38] ibid [28] and quoting *Van der Peet* (n 27) [53].

[39] *Lax Kw'alaams* (n 30) [56].

The fourth step is only engaged if the court concludes that the proven Aboriginal right includes a right 'to trade *commercially*'.[40] In such a case, the court must have regard to the interests of non-Indigenous Canadians and this consideration should somehow relate back to the 'delineation of the right'.[41] The precise implications of this fourth step are far from clear and have caused significant challenges for lower courts attempting to follow this direction.

These challenges have been exemplified in a case brought by the Ahousaht First Nation and related communities on the west coast of Vancouver Island.[42] In *Ahousaht*, the plaintiff First Nations sought a declaration of fishing rights in their traditional territory as well as a declaration to the effect that Canada's fisheries regime represented an unjustifiable infringement of those rights. The original trial judge elected to split the trial into two stages. In the first stage, Justice Garson issued a declaration that the First Nations had a right to fish any species of fish within their fishing territories and to sell their catch.[43] The fishing territories were held to extend nine miles from the coast as measured from lines drawn from headland to headland.[44] Justice Garson also declared that the federal fisheries regime constituted a prima facie infringement of that commercial right. However, she refrained from ruling as to whether Canada could justify that infringement. She considered that Canada was not in a position to make its case with respect to justification absent a declared right. In the end, she directed the parties to consult and negotiate, with leave to apply for a determination as to justification should they be unable to reach agreement.

Negotiations failed and the First Nations brought the matter back before the court (but a different judge). In the meantime, the Supreme Court of Canada had rendered its judgment in *Lax Kw'alaams*.[45] The principal

[40] ibid (the emphasis is Justice Binnie's).

[41] ibid [46] The reference to the interests of other Canadians and broader social and economic agendas comes from Chief Justice Lamer's decision in *Gladstone* (n 17) [75]. In quoting that text here, Justice Binnie acknowledges that Chief Justice Lamer refers to these broader interests in the context of justifiable infringement. It is not clear what such external interests have to do with the characterisation of the Indigenous right.

[42] *Ahousaht Indian Band v Canada (Attorney-General)* 2009 BCSC 1494; and *Ahousaht* (n 18).

[43] ibid.

[44] ibid [414]. Justice Garson concluded that the evidence did not support the plaintiffs' claim that their rights extended out 100 nautical miles. Justice Garson did not specify whether the nine-mile fishing territory was measured in statute miles or nautical miles. That led to some confusion between the parties, but in phase 2 of the trial (2018 BCSC 633), Justice Humphries concluded that the fishing territory should be measured in nautical miles. That was the way in which the parties had originally interpreted Justice Garson's judgment (at [467]) and it was the customary way (at [468]) of stating measurements at sea.

[45] In fact, the matter was even more complicated. Canada had appealed the trial judgment. By majority, the Court of Appeal affirmed 2011 BCCA 237 (although concluding that the commercial fishing right did not extend to geoduck clams). The SCC denied leave to appeal (2011 SCAA 353), but instead sent the matter back to the Court of Appeal to have that court reconsider its decisions in light of *Lax K'alaams*. The Court did so, but declined to vary its decision (2013 BCCA 300). A further application for leave was denied (2011 SCAA 35).

challenge for the new trial judge was to assess the extent to which the justifiable infringement analysis might affect the contours of the declared right, ie, the fourth step in the analysis demanded by *Lax Kw'alaams*. Naturally, the parties had competing views on this question. The First Nations argued strenuously that the declaration as to the commercial right to fish was final. Canada and intervenors representing commercial fishery interests argued that this would be inconsistent with *Lax Kw'alaams*. In the end, Justice Humphries felt bound by the existing declaration. In a detailed analysis of the different fisheries (salmon, groundfish – including halibut and sablefish – crab and prawn), she found that Canada had been unable to justify certain elements of its policies, but had adequately justified others (especially with respect to species for which there was little evidence of historic and cultural connection to the fishery – eg, crab, prawn and sablefish). In determining the appropriate relief to be granted for those cases for which the infringements could not be justified, Justice Humphrey declined simply to exempt the First Nations from the federal regulations. She also declined to remain seised of the case, remarking, as she had done many times in her lengthy judgment, that it would exceed the judicial role to prescribe the terms of a fishery or to make any particular allocation.[46] In effect, therefore, the ultimate order will require the federal government to develop new regulations and policy that brings them into compliance. While the parties no doubt have much more guidance than before as to the protections and priority to be afforded to Indigenous commercial fisheries, the pattern of litigation here also confirms the importance (if not ultimately the necessity) of negotiated solutions.

### C. Aboriginal Title to Marine Spaces

It is possible to deal with the Canadian case law on claims to indigenous title to marine spaces briefly, if only because the courts have yet to provide any definitive rulings,[47] notwithstanding that the issue has been raised in at least three cases: *Ahousaht*,[48] *Lax Kw'alaams*[49] and *Haida Nation v British Columbia*.[50]

*Ahousaht* was the first of these cases to come to trial. In addition to the commercial fishing right discussed above, the plaintiff First Nations claimed

[46] See, eg, *Ahoushat* (n 18) [668], [758], [867], [981] and [984].

[47] The leading decision on Aboriginal title with respect to land territory is *Tsilhqot'in Nation v British Columbia*, [2014] 2 SCR 257; 2014 SCC 44. For two surveys of Indigenous title law in the context of marine spaces in Canada, see CR Brown and JI Reynolds, 'Aboriginal Title to Sea Spaces: A Comparative Study' (2004) 37 *University of British Columbia Law Review* 449; and Paula Quig, 'Testing the Waters: Aboriginal Title Claims to Water Spaces and Submerged Land: An Overview' (2004) 45 *Les Cahiers de Droit* 659.

[48] *Ahoushat* (n 42); *Ahousaht* (n 18).

[49] *Lax Kw'alaams* (n 30).

[50] *Haida Nation v British Columbia* 2018 BCSC 277.

title to the adjacent marine territory out to 100 nautical miles.[51] However, the only economic element of that title that was pleaded was the right to the fishery.[52] Since Justice Garson had concluded that the plaintiffs had established a commercial fishing right, she further concluded that it was not necessary to decide the title claim: 'Even assuming that a claim to submerged lands is legally tenable, of which I have some doubt.'[53]

In the second case, *Lax Kw'alaams*, the plaintiff community also claimed title to various lands as well as 'off-shore and in-shore water bodies',[54] in addition to the right to harvest all species of fish and trade on a commercial basis as referenced above. However, shortly before the matter was to go to trial, the province brought a successful application to sever the title claim so as to have the parties proceed to trial only with respect to the Aboriginal rights claim.[55]

The final case in the group is the claim brought by the Haida Nation for a declaration that the Nation has Aboriginal title and rights to Haida Gwaaii, including 'the land, inland waters, seabed, archipelagic waters, airspace and everything contained thereon and therein'. The case has yet to go to trial. The claim was particularised in a recent case management decision as follows:

> [T]he plaintiffs seek a declaration of Aboriginal title to the terrestrial portions of Haida Gwaii including its inland waters, to the waters and submerged lands within the surrounding territorial sea (12 nautical miles from the coastal baseline) and to all living creatures such as fish and birds during times when they are present in the claim area …
>
> The plaintiffs also seek a declaration of aboriginal rights within the claim area which is from the top of Haida Gwaii to the US border in the north, to the limits

[51] *Ahousaht* (n 42) [491].

[52] ibid. More specifically (at [494]), the claim was: 'That each of the Nuu-chah-nulth Bands or, in the alternative, each of the Nuu-chah-nulth Nations, hold aboriginal title to the Fishing Territories, or portions thereof, and the right or rights, as a component of that aboriginal title, to harvest for any purpose, including any or all of those purposes referred to in paragraph (a) and sell all species of Fisheries Resources or, in the alternative, one or more of those species of Fisheries Resources, harvested from territories to which they have aboriginal title.'

[53] ibid [502].

[54] *Lax Kw'alaams Indian Band v Canada (Attorney-General)* 2008 BCSC 447 [93].

[55] *Lax Kw'alaams Indian Band v Attorney-General of Canada* 2006 BCSC 1463. The title claim has yet to be adjudicated. In support of its application to sever, the province offered a list of issues that would not need to be considered as part of an Aboriginal rights claim that would be relevant to a title claim (at [11]): '(a) whether a right to a commercial fishery is or was an ancillary right to aboriginal title to lands or lands covered by waters; (b) whether there can be a right to an exclusive fishery that displaces the public right to a fishery in lands covered by tidal waters; (c) whether aboriginal title can exist in the seabed specifically or in lands covered by water generally; (d) whether aboriginal title in lands covered by water would carry with it any rights in the nature of title or ownership to the waters themselves; (e) whether exclusive occupation of lands covered by waters could co-exist with an unfettered right of navigation, whether from time immemorial or more recently; (f) whether aboriginal title to lands covered by waters and to the waters themselves can give a possessory right in the fish resources in, on or passing by or over the lands covered by waters and the waters; (g) whether such a possessory right in fish resources, if so determined, would be different for migratory and non-migratory fish resources; and (h) what is the constitutional status of lands covered by water, the waters and the fish resources, should all or some be subject to aboriginal title'.

> of Canada's [EEZ] to the west, to the mid-point of Hecate Strait to the east and to the mid-point between the south end of Haida Gwaii and the northern tip of Vancouver Island.[56]

In sum, Canadian courts have yet to grapple in any serious way with the idea of extending the doctrine of Indigenous title to marine areas. As a result, we cannot be sure how Canadian courts will respond to the common objections identified to the recognition of an Indigenous title identified in other jurisdictions and in the literature, including objections based on common law and international freedoms relating to fisheries and navigation.[57]

## IV. MODERN LAND CLAIMS AGREEMENTS

This section of the chapter examines the way in which modern land claims agreements deal with Indigenous rights in marine areas. While there are at least eight such agreements with marine components, this chapter principally draws examples from the Nunavut Agreement,[58] but also references the Labrador Agreement[59] and the Inuvialuit Final Agreement.[60] This section examines how the agreements address some key questions, specifically: (1) the connection of the Indigenous signatories to marine space; (2) the categorisation of marine space; (3) governance rights (both law making and co-management) in relation to marine space; (4) harvesting rights with respect to marine species; (5) other rights in marine areas; (6) recognition of title in marine areas; and (7) treatment of international freedoms.

### A. Recognition of Connection to Marine Space

The Inuit signatories to the Nunavut Agreement are fundamentally a marine people.[61] All but one of the Inuit communities in Nunavut has a coastal

[56] *Haida Nation* (n 50). The decision further informs (at [7]) that "Canada denies the plaintiffs' claim of Aboriginal title to submerged lands excepting, perhaps, some inter-tidal lands and submerged lands in the mouths of some rivers', and Justice Mayer (at [27] and [29]) noted that both Canada and British Columbia characterised the claim to title over submerged lands as 'novel'.

[57] Both Quig (n 47) and Brown and Reynolds (n 47) discuss the main objections; for further discussion, see the Introduction to this volume and Godden (ch 5 in this volume) on Australia.

[58] NA (n 1).

[59] LIA (n 2).

[60] IFA (n 3). In addition to these three agreements, see also the Eeyou Marine Region Claims Agreement, the Nunavik Inuit Land Claims Agreement and four agreements in British Columbia with marine elements: the Nisga'a Final Agreement, the Tsawwassen First Nation Final Agreement, the Maa-nulth First Nations Final Agreement and the Tla'amin Final Agreement (see n 1 for the weblink for these agreements).

[61] See generally MMR Freeman (ed), *Inuit Land Use and Occupancy Project*, 3 vols (Ottawa, Supply and Services Canada, 1976); more recently, see Inuit Circumpolar Council – Canada, *The Sea Ice is Our Highway*, March 2008, https://www.inuitcircumpolar.com/project/the-sea-ice-is-

location. A report prepared for the Nunavut Marine Council observes that the Inuit of Nunavut consider themselves to be 'an integral part of the ecosystems in which they live and carry out their traditional activities. The land, sea and ice of Nunavut form one continuous area of activity in which Nunavummiut enjoy – and will continue to seek – cultural, social and economic fulfillment'.[62] At least some of these ideas are carried through into the Nunavut Agreement. For example, the Preamble recites that the Inuit of Nunavut assert an Aboriginal title to the Nunavut Settlement Area (NSA) 'based on their traditional and current use and occupation of the *lands, waters and land-fast ice therein in accordance with their own customs and usages*' (emphasis added).[63] The Preamble further acknowledges that the Agreement was designed 'to provide for certainty and clarity of rights to ownership and use of lands and resources, and of rights for Inuit to participate in decision-making concerning the use, management and conservation of land, water and resources, *including the offshore*' (emphasis added). Beyond this, Article 15 (Marine Areas) recognises the fundamental connection between land and marine territory in a statement of principles:

> (a) Inuit are traditional and current users of certain marine areas, especially the land-fast ice zones;
> (b) the legal rights of Inuit in marine areas … are based on traditional and current use;
> (c) Canada's sovereignty over the waters of the Arctic archipelago is supported by Inuit use and occupancy;
> (d) Inuit harvest wildlife that might migrate beyond the marine areas;
> (e) an Inuit economy based in part on marine resources is both viable and desirable;
> (f) there is a need to develop and co-ordinate policies regarding the marine areas; and
> (g) there is a need for Inuit involvement in aspects of Arctic marine management, including research.

## B. The Categorisation of Marine Space

All land claims agreements inevitably describe the geographical reach or ambit of the agreement. To the extent that marine areas are included within their reach, these descriptions recognise an Indigenous interest in marine

our-highway-an-inuit-perspective-on-transportation-in-the-arctic. See in particular at 2: 'The Inuit concept of land … When defining our "land", Inuit do not distinguish between the ground upon which our communities are built and the sea ice upon which we travel, hunt, and build igloos as temporary camps. Land is anywhere our feet, dog teams, or snowmobiles can take us.'

[62] Nunavut Marine Council, Business Case, February 2012, at 2, www.nunavutmarinecouncil.com/admin_dms/db.php?command=download&fileid=38.

[63] FA (n 1) Preamble; and see also LIA (n 2) Preamble. Land-fast ice refers to ice that is literally connected or fastened to the shore. It may extend many miles from land.

territory, although not the scope of that interest. For example, the Inuvialuit Final Agreement applies to the Inuvialuit Settlement Region (ISR), which refers to portions of Yukon, the Northwest Territories and a massive adjacent offshore area that embraces the entirety of Canada's share of the Beaufort Sea.[64] Therefore, this includes not just the territorial sea but also Canada's Exclusive Economic Zone (EEZ). Similarly, the NSA under the Nunavut Agreement embraces, inter alia, all the marine areas within the central and eastern part of Canada's Arctic Archipelago as well as the territorial sea along the east coast of the Ellesmere, Devon, Bylot and Baffin Islands.

Many of the lines of recognition drawn in these agreements are straight lines referencing lines of latitude and longitude and official government maps, charts and baselines. But in at least one case, the resulting line draws heavily on Indigenous knowledge and experience. This is the Outer Land Fast Ice Zone (OLFIZ) on the east coast of Baffin Island under the terms of the Nunavut Agreement. As definitively shown in Inuit land use and occupancy studies, Inuit use sea ice for travel and as an important platform for their harvesting and related cultural activities.[65] The interface between land-fast ice and open water is especially biologically productive and a focus for harvesting activities.[66]

Given the importance of this zone, the Nunavut Inuit successfully negotiated for the recognition of the OLFIZ and a special regime for that zone.[67] The zone is defined as commencing at the *outer* limit of the territorial sea boundary off the east coasts of the Bylot and Baffin Islands and extending seawards to the maximum limit of land fast ice as documented between 1963 and 1989.[68] Thus, the OLFIZ overlaps with Canada's EEZ. The OLFIZ is not part of the NSA, but it is an area within which the Nunavut Agreement recognises that Inuit have additional rights.[69]

[64] IFA (n 3) s 2 definitions and Annex A and A-1. Annex A is a map depicting the ISR. In the west, the region is delineated by an extension of the 141st meridian of latitude as far north as 80 degrees north. Canada and the US disagree as to the maritime delimitation in the Beaufort Sea. While Canada's claim is based on an extension of the 141st meridian, the US favours an equidistance line which at least initially would push the boundary further east. The Inuvialuit and the Inupiat of Alaska have cooperative arrangements between them with respect to the management and harvesting of wildlife resources, including marine resources such as polar bears and beluga whales: Inuvialuit Inupiat Beaufort Sea Beluga Whale Agreement, http://fishfp.sasktelwebhosting.com/publications/Inuvialuit_Inupiat%20Beluga%20agreement.pdf; and Inuvialuit Inupiat Polar Bear Management Agreement in the Southern Beaufort Sea, 2000, http://pbsg.npolar.no/en/agreements/USA-Canada.html.

[65] See Freeman (ed) n 61; and Inuit Circumpolar Council – Canada (n 61). There is a map of the OLFIZ in sched 16.1 to the NA (n 1).

[66] I Stirling, 'The Importance of Polynyas, Ice Edges and Leads to Marine Mammals and Birds' (1997) 10 *Journal of Marine Systems* 9.

[67] NA (n 1) art 16.

[68] ibid s 1.1.1 (definitions) and art 16. The area of the OFLIZ is depicted on a map deposited with the agreement and shown at small scale in sched 16.1.

[69] NA (n 1) art 16; and see the discussion below of Inuit harvesting rights in marine areas beyond the NSA.

Since the OLFIZ is not part of the NSA, its recognition also demonstrates that these agreements contain multiple categories of marine space. These different categories have a material impact on the forms and level of entitlement of beneficiaries. The Federal Court of Appeal acknowledged this in *Nunavut Tunngavik Inc v Canada (Minister of Fisheries and Oceans)*[70] (discussed in more detail below) when it stated that: 'Under the Agreement, the level of constraints imposed upon the Minister varies with the area where the ministerial decision is to take effect.'[71]

### C. Governance Rights in Marine Areas

This section examines the extent to which these Agreements recognise Indigenous governance rights in marine areas. By governance rights I mean law-making and decision-making authority with respect to marine areas. None of the agreements affords Indigenous communities exclusive governance rights with respect to marine resources, but there is some limited recognition of law-making and decision-making authority, whether through Indigenous institutions or through the institutions of public government as in Nunavut. There is a much broader recognition of the role of Indigenous communities in co-management institutions.

#### *i. Law-Making Authority*

The Nunavut Agreement did not expressly deal with the law-making authority of Inuit Indigenous institutions, although it does confirm an important role for community Hunters and Trappers Organizations (HTOs) to apply community-based norms.[72] HTOs have the responsibility for the regulation of harvesting and allocation of quotas at the community level.

A principal reason for the silence of the Agreement itself on the law-making authority of Indigenous institutions was the political commitment embodied in the Agreement to create the new territory of Nunavut with a large majority Inuit population within that territory.[73] As a territory, the Government of Nunavut has significant law-making powers, including the power to make laws with respect to property and civil rights and wildlife.[74] While a territory (much as with a province) cannot make laws for areas outside the territory, the territory

[70] *Nunavut Tunngavik Inc v Canada (Minister of Fisheries and Oceans)* [1998] 4 FC 405 (FCA).
[71] ibid [17].
[72] NA (n 1) art 5, pt 7.
[73] NA (n 1) art 4. Nunavut was established as a separate territory in 1999 in fulfilment of this political commitment.
[74] The law-making powers of Nunavut's legislature are laid out in the Nunavut Act, SC 1993, c 28 s 23.

of Nunavut is defined in extraordinarily broad terms to include all that 'part of Canada' north of 60 degrees that is not included within any other provincial or territorial jurisdiction.[75] Since the Oceans Act[76] defines both Canada's internal waters and its territorial sea as being part of Canada, it must follow that all of these marine areas are within Nunavut. However, this does not confer as much authority as one might anticipate for several reasons. First, the federal government has exclusive law-making authority in relation to a number of heads of power concerning marine areas including fishing and navigation and shipping.[77] Second, to this point, the federal government has retained administration and control over publicly owned land and resources within Nunavut, whether onshore or within the marine part of the territory,[78] and, finally, federal laws override inconsistent territorial laws.[79]

The Labrador Agreement expressly addresses the law-making authority of the Government of Nunatsiavut.[80] While some of its law-making powers are not subject to strict territorial limitation (eg, the provision of social and other services to Inuit residents anywhere within Newfoundland and Labrador),[81] most of its law-making powers are geographically narrowly circumscribed and typically apply only to 'Labrador Inuit Lands and the Inuit Communities'.[82] Thus, the Government of Nunatsiavut does not have broad law-making powers with respect to the Settlement Area generally. That said, and as noted further below, Labrador Inuit Lands do extend in some cases to 'water lots' (lands covered by tidal waters) and thus in these limited cases, the law-making powers of the Government of Nunatsiavut would extend to these areas. Relevant powers might include powers in relation to environmental protection and land use.

To the extent that other orders of government may exercise concurrent law-making powers with respect to the same matters, the Labrador Agreement establishes a series of paramountcy rules. For laws in relation to the administration and control of Labrador Inuit Lands (including the water lots) and access to or use of those lands, the Inuit law will prevail over an inconsistent federal or provincial law to the extent of the conflict.[83] However, in the case

[75] Nunavut Act, s 3. By contrast, the territory of most provinces ends at the low-water mark. There are exceptions to this proposition based on the constitutional instruments creating the individual provinces. For example, the province of British Columbia includes the waters between the mainland and Vancouver Island: *Reference Re Georgia Strait* [1984] 1 SCR 388.

[76] Oceans Act, SC 1996, c 31, s 6 (internal waters), s 7 (territorial sea).

[77] Constitution Act, 1867, s 91.

[78] However, the federal government has transferred administration and control of land and resources to each of Yukon and Northwest Territories.

[79] See the opening words of s 23(1) of the Nunavut Act: 'Subject to any other Act of Parliament …'

[80] LIA (n 2) ch 17, Labrador Inuit Self-Government.

[81] ibid s 17.6.1.

[82] ibid ss 17.8.1, 17.9.1 and 17.11.1 (dealing with laws in relation to environmental protection).

[83] Part 8 of ch 4 of the LFA list some 10 heads of power directly related to the use of Labrador Inuit Lands that benefit from this paramountcy provision.

of more general law-making authority, such as the right to make laws for the protection of the environment, the relevant federal or provincial law will prevail to the extent of the conflict with Inuit law.[84]

In sum, both the Nunavut and Labrador Agreements offer only limited recognition of an Indigenous law-making capacity with respect to marine areas.

### *ii. Co-management Approaches*

The Nunavut Agreement emphasises a co-management approach with respect to both terrestrial and marine areas.[85] It creates a number of different co-management bodies, including a planning authority and an environmental assessment regime, but for the purposes of this volume, the most important co-management institution is the Nunavut Wildlife Management Board (NWMB).

The approach of the Nunavut Agreement to co-management in marine areas has three main elements. First, Article 15 (Marine Areas) expressly provides that certain articles of the Agreement shall apply to marine areas of the NSA.[86] Second, the Agreement provides that Inuit have additional management and harvesting rights in marine areas beyond the NSA. Third, the Agreement provides for the creation of the Nunavut Marine Planning Council (NMC). The following sub-sections sections will deal with each of these elements in turn.

#### a. Application of Articles of the Agreement to Marine Areas

Article 15 of the Agreement expressly provides that certain articles shall apply to the large marine areas of the NSA. These articles include the articles pertaining to wildlife (Article 5), wildlife compensation (Article 6), land use planning (Article 11), environmental impact assessment (Article 12), certain employment and economic matters (Articles 23–25), and archaeological and ethnographic matters (Articles 33 and 34).

The significance of this can perhaps best be illustrated by considering Article 5, which deals with wildlife. Article 5 addresses both Inuit rights in relation to wildlife and the co-management responsibilities of the NWMB with respect to wildlife. Of the nine members of the NWMB, four are appointed by different Inuit organisations, three are appointed by the federal government, one is appointed by the territorial government and a further member is appointed by the federal government from nominations

[84] LIA (n 2) s 17.11.3.

[85] See generally Nigel Bankes, 'Implementing the Fisheries Provisions of the Nunavut Claim: Re-capturing the Resource?' (2003) 12 *Journal of Environmental Law and Policy* 141; Stephanie Boudreau and Lucia Fanning, 'Nunavut Fisheries Co-management and the Role of the Nunavut Land Claims Agreement in Fisheries Management and Decision-Making' (2016) 30 *Ocean Yearbook* 207.

[86] NA (n 1) s 15.2.2.

provided by the NWMB.[87] 'Wildlife' is defined broadly to mean 'all terrestrial, aquatic, avian and amphibian flora and fauna *ferae naturae*, and all parts and products thereof'.[88] Article 5.2.33 recognises that the NWMB is the 'main instrument of wildlife management' in the NSA and 'the main regulator of access to wildlife'. Its functions include establishing needs levels and total allowable harvests (TAHs), where necessary, for conservation reasons. The NWMB has established TAHs for a number of marine species including narwhal, bowhead whale, walrus, polar bear and some distinct populations of Arctic char. The Board is also involved in approving management plans for a number of marine species including turbot, shrimp and Arctic char.[89] It also has the authority to approve the designation of rare, threatened and endangered species.[90] However, the government 'bears the ultimately responsibility for wildlife management' and accordingly the decisions of the NWMB may be disallowed by the relevant federal or territorial minister (subject to the duty to provide reasons).[91]

### b. Inuit Management and Harvesting Rights in Marine Areas beyond the NSA

Article 15 of the Nunavut Agreement recognises that Inuit have additional (albeit attenuated) management and harvesting rights in marine areas beyond the NSA. These areas include waters north of 61 degrees subject to Canada's EEZ jurisdiction as well as waters within James Bay, Hudson Bay and Hudson Strait.[92] In these waters, the Agreement commits Canada to seek the advice of the NWMB with respect to any management decisions concerning these waters that might 'affect the substance and value of Inuit harvesting rights and opportunities' within the NSA.[93] Canada also committed to give 'special consideration' to 'the principles of adjacency and economic dependence of communities in the NSA on marine resources' when allocating fishing licences within these waters. The principles were to be applied in such a way as to 'promote a fair distribution of licences between the residents of the NSA and the other residents of Canada and in a manner consistent with Canada's interjurisdictional obligations'.[94] Both the advisory function and the application of the principles of adjacency and economic dependence have been subject to litigation.

*Nunavut Tunngavik Inc v Canada (Minister of Fisheries and Oceans)*[95] dealt with the Minister's decision to issue licences for turbot in Canada's EEZ off the

[87] ibid s 5.2.1.
[88] ibid s 1.1.1.
[89] See Boudreau and Fanning (n 85).
[90] NA (n 1) s 5.2.34(f).
[91] ibid s 5.3.11 and s 5.3.18.
[92] These waters are referred to in the Agreement as Zones I and II, both of which are defined terms.
[93] NA (n 1) s 15.3.4.
[94] ibid s 15.3.7.
[95] *Nunavut Tunngavik Inc* (n 70).

coast of Baffin Island under the terms of the federal Fisheries Act.[96] Nunavut Tunngavik Inc (NTI) sought judicial review of the Minister's decision. While the Minister argued that the Fisheries Act conferred upon him close to an unlimited discretion in granting licences,[97] the Federal Court of Appeal concluded that the Nunavut Agreement and its implementing legislation:

> [I]mposes upon the Minister *both procedural and substantive requirements* which affect the manner in which the decision-making process, including the ministerial discretion to fix fishing quotas, is to be exercised. In our view, the Minister's discretion in section 7 of the *Fisheries Act* is no longer absolute when the exercise of that discretion affects the wildlife and the marine areas of the NSA and the wildlife management in Zones I and II. (Emphasis added)[98]

This is a significant statement as to how the terms of a land claims agreement might modify and limit the executive authority of the Crown.

The Minister's principal procedural obligation was to seek the advice of the NWMB and to consider that advice,[99] but he was not obliged to follow that advice or (subject to the further discussion below) to provide reasons should he fail to do so.[100]

The substantive issue that arose was the Minister's duty to give special consideration to the principles of adjacency and economic dependence. NTI argued that these principles should have resulted in the Minister according significant priority to Nunavut interests over the interests of southern-based fishers. The Court largely rejected those submissions as well as analogies between the position under the Agreement and the priority accorded to an Aboriginal food and ceremonial fishery based on the constitutional protection of Aboriginal rights.[101] The Court reasoned that this case concerned a commercial fishery and not a food fishery, and that in any event, Inuit rights were established by the terms of the Agreement and not on the basis of Aboriginal rights.[102] The language of the Agreement made it clear that the parties had chosen to reflect (at least in these areas beyond the NSA) 'a principle of equity, not one of priority'. Had the parties meant to adopt the principle of priority, the provision would have been quite different:

> First, the provision would have spoken in terms of priority of access. Second, it would have clearly given such priority to the communities of the NSA and would not have extended it, as it does, to all those who are within a reasonable geographic distance of the zone in question. Third, it would not have adopted a principle of fair distribution of licences between the residents of the NSA and the other

[96] RSC 1985, c F-14. For further discussion of the case and of the status of the principles of adjacency and economic dependence in Canadian law and policy, see Bankes (n 85) 191–200.

[97] *Nunavut Tunngavik Inc* (n 70) [13].

[98] ibid [16].

[99] ibid [35].

[100] ibid [35] and [36].

[101] See discussion of priority in section III.A above.

[102] *Nunavut Tunngavik Inc* (n 70) [48].

> residents of Canada. Finally, as previously mentioned, it would not have subjected the fair distribution principle to an obligation to respect Canada's interjurisdictional obligations.[103]

Nevertheless, the Court still found that the Minister was in breach of his more limited obligation to afford special consideration to the principles of adjacency and economic dependence. The Court reached this conclusion principally on the basis of the actual result of the Minister's licensing decisions, which accorded other fishers an *enhanced* percentage of the total allowable catch, while that of Nunavut Inuit interests actually declined. Absent some reasoned explanation as to how the Minister had been able to reach this conclusion, the Court preferred to draw the 'reasonable inference that the Minister either did not give special consideration to the adjacency and economic dependence principles as required by the Agreement or misconstrued these principles when allocating commercial fishing licences to areas outside the NSA'.[104]

In evaluating this decision, it is important to keep in mind that it deals with marine areas beyond the NSA, ie, beyond Canada's 12 nautical mile Territorial Sea. Within the NSA, there can be no doubt that the NWMB plays the dominant role (subject to ministerial disallowance). The decision therefore illustrates how the Inuit role in management covers a spectrum depending upon the classification of the marine area. Nevertheless, even in the EEZ, the decision recognises that the terms of the Agreement constrain the Minister's discretion and that the Minister must have regard to the principles of adjacency and economic dependence, even though such principles do not afford a hard priority to Nunavut fishing interests.

### c. Nunavut Marine Council

Article 15 of the NA contemplates that the four main co-management organisations of the Agreement might individually, or collectively as the Nunavut Marine Council, 'advise and make recommendations' to government agencies 'regarding marine areas'.[105] For many years, the NMC was nothing more than a possibility, but in 2010, these four organisations agreed to formalise the establishment of the NMC. They were motivated to do so by the rate of change affecting Arctic marine areas, including such things as: depletion of Arctic multi-year sea ice; increased shipping in Arctic waters for destination traffic, resource development, tourism and other commercial navigation; oil and gas exploration in Arctic waters offshore of Greenland and in the Beaufort Sea, and proposed seismic testing in Lancaster Sound; increased fisheries activities; mapping of the sub-sea continental margins to support extended shelf claims

[103] ibid [51].
[104] ibid [64].
[105] NA (n 1) s 15.4.1.

under the Law of the Sea Convention; and military and other security activities to support and enforce Canadian sovereignty.[106] The NMC has adopted a number of principles derived from the Agreement as well as the principles of Inuit Qaujimajatuqangit (traditional Inuit values, knowledge, behaviour, perceptions and expectations).[107] The four co-management authorities saw the NMC as a potential vehicle to offer a more 'strategic and holistic approach' to Arctic marine issues going beyond the sectoral interests of the particular co-management authorities. The NMC's website suggests that it has engaged in a relatively small number of issues, perhaps the most significant being proposals for seismic testing in Lancaster Sound.[108]

### D. Indigenous Harvesting Rights in Marine Areas

The Agreement defines Inuit harvesting rights in relation to wildlife as the right of an Inuk to harvest any stock or population of wildlife within the NSA 'up to the full level of his or her economic, social, and cultural needs'.[109] This right is qualified where a species, for conservation needs, is subject to a TAH by the NWMB, but in such a case, Inuit are entitled to a priority allocation of that TAH up to 'the basic needs level' (BNL).[110] The BNL is based on actual harvest levels by Inuit, understanding that it may be adjusted by the NWMB to acknowledge increased consumption by Inuit. Crucially, the Agreement acknowledges that the BNL may encompass the entire TAH for a stock or population.[111] In sum, within the NSA, Inuit enjoy extensive harvesting rights in relation to marine species with the benefit of a strong priority entitlement, which in some cases will afford Inuit exclusive harvesting rights with respect to a particular species.[112]

### E. Other Rights in Marine Areas

The discovery of the wrecks of *HMS Erebus* and *HMS Terror* offers an unusual application of the NA in marine areas. These two vessels, engaged as part of

[106] Nunavut Marine Council, Business Case (n 62) 6–7.

[107] ibid 19. These include principles dealing with stewardship and respect as well as flexibility and creativity.

[108] Although even here, the principal burden for opposing this activity seems to have been assumed at a local level by the Hamlet of Clyde River: see *Clyde River (Hamlet) v Petroleum Geo-Services Inc* 2017 SCC 40.

[109] NA (n 1) s 5.6.1.

[110] NFA, s 5.6.20.

[111] NA, ss 5.6.20 and 5.6.29.

[112] Other rules may reinforce this priority. For example, s 4(2) of the Marine Mammal Regulations, SOR 93/56 effectively provides that no person other than an Inuk shall take narwhal.

Sir John Franklin's ill-fated expedition which set sail in 1845 in search of a Northwest Passage between Europe and Asia, were lost when they became trapped and destroyed by pack ice. While their precise location remained a mystery until 2014, the two vessels had already been designated a National Historic Site (NHS) by Canada in 1992.[113] Inuit traditional knowledge provided key information that narrowed down the search area.

The NHS designation and the discovery of the wrecks directly engages several articles of the NA, including Article 9 dealing with 'conservation areas' and Article 33 dealing with archaeology.[114] Both articles are listed in section 15.2.2 of the NA as being applicable to marine areas. 'Conservation area' is defined broadly in the NA to include NHSs, National Historic Parks and Historic Places, and other areas 'when established under legislation' as an area 'of particular significance for ecological, cultural, archaeological, research and similar reasons'. The designation as an NHS therefore triggered an obligation on the part of the Government of Canada to negotiate an Inuit Impact and Benefit Agreement (IIBA) with respect to the site.

Article 33 provides that any archaeological specimens found within the NSA shall be jointly owned by government and the Inuit Heritage Trust (IHT), subject to the proviso that this not apply to 'the private property of any person'.[115] It seems fairly clear that the two wrecks fall within the definition of archaeological specimen as that term is defined in the Agreement.[116] However, under both international law and Canadian domestic law, ownership of a vessel does not change as a result of its being wrecked. The British and Canadian governments recognised this in a Memorandum of Understanding (MoU) agreed to in 1997 following Canada's initial NHS designation.[117] Under the MoU, Britain recognised Canada's 'custody and control of the wrecks', but also contemplated that, subject to some exceptions and once the wrecks had been positively located and identified, Britain would 'assign to Canada ownership of everything recovered from the wreck and its contents'.

Canada has acknowledged its obligations to Inuit under both Articles 9 and 33 of the NA. For example, in the Regulatory Impact Assessment Statement (RIAS) supporting the Order protecting *HMS Erebus*, the government indicated it would 'engage with designated Inuit organizations (Kitikmeot Inuit

[113] See Directory of Heritage Designations, https://www.pc.gc.ca/apps/dfhd/page_nhs_eng.aspx?id=334.

[114] In addition, activities at the site have also been subject to review under art 11 (the land use planning provisions of the claim) and under art 12, which establishes the Nunavut Impact Review Board (NIRB).

[115] NA (n 1) s 33.7.1.

[116] ibid s 33.1.1.

[117] Memorandum of Understanding between the Governments of Great Britain and Canada Pertaining to the Shipwrecks *HMS Erebus and HMS Terror*, 5 and 8 August 1997, www.ric.edu/faculty/rpotter/mou.pdf.

Association, Nunavut Tunngavik Inc, Kivalliq Inuit Association and Qikiqtani Inuit Association), as required, on this measure as well as the negotiation of an IIBA'.[118] The RIAS for the subsequent Order protecting *HMS Terror* further elaborated on the ongoing steps to negotiate an IIBA.[119] These steps included the creation of the Franklin Interim Advisory Committee, which amongst other things supported the creation of an Inuit Guardians Program to help protect the wrecks. Negotiations for an IIBA are ongoing, but it is contemplated that the agreement might include improvements to the Nattik Centre in Gjoa Haven (the closest Inuit community) to make it suitable to receive original artefacts (temperature controlled facilities etc).[120] In the most recent development, Canada and the UK signed an additional agreement on 26 April 2018 indicating that Britain would be entitled to keep the 65 items already discovered, but would transfer to Canada title to the vessels and all artefacts subsequently recovered from the site.[121] Canada in turn has acknowledged that all of these artefacts will be jointly owned by Canada and the IHT.[122]

This example illustrates that the co-management approach of the NA extends to the marine area of the NSA across a range of subject matters conferring political leverage and economic benefits perhaps unanticipated at the time that the NA was negotiated. As such, it emphasises the importance of residual provisions like Article 15, Article 33 and Article 9, which recognise (in turn) the applicability of substantive provisions of the agreement in marine areas, the co-ownership of archaeological specimens, and the duty to negotiate an IIBA with respect to a conservation area whenever the creation of such an area may create a detrimental impact for Inuit or could reasonably confer a benefit.

## F. Recognition of Title in Marine Areas

Canada has been reluctant to recognise Indigenous title in marine areas as part of land claims agreements. Section 19.2.6 of the NA, for example, bluntly provides that 'Inuit Owned Lands shall not include … marine areas'.[123] Other

[118] Available at: www.gazette.gc.ca/rp-pr/p2/2015/2015-04-22/html/sor-dors88-eng.html. It is worth mentioning that Nunavut Tunngavik Inc (NTI), the Inuit representative organisation under the NA, considered that it was entitled to be involved directly in the negotiations with the UK.

[119] Available at: www.gazette.gc.ca/rp-pr/p2/2017/2017-12-27/html/sor-dors273-eng.html.

[120] For an update, see Jane George, 'Inuit, Parks Canada Close to Deal on Franklin Wrecks National Historic Site' *Nunatsiaq News* (18 October 2018), https://www.arctictoday.com/inuit-parks-canada-close-deal-franklin-wrecks-national-historic-site.

[121] Deed of Gift, 26 April 2018 between the Secretary of States for Defence of the United Kingdom of Great Britain and Northern Ireland and the Parks Canada Agency (on file with the author).

[122] 'Britain Officially Gifts Two Long-Lost Ships from Franklin Expedition to Canada, Inuit' *Globe and Mail* (25 April 2018), https://www.theglobeandmail.com/canada/article-britain-officially-gifts-two-long-lost-ships-from-franklin-expedition.

[123] See also NA (n 1) s 15.2.3: 'There shall be no Inuit Owned Land in marine areas.'

agreements are not quite so definitive. For example, the Labrador Agreement contemplates that Inuit title extends to certain water lots defined in the Agreement, generally adjacent to communities and other Labrador Inuit lands.[124] The Nunatsiavut government may make laws in relation to such lands, dealing with, inter alia, access to or use of those lands,[125] and in the event of any conflict between an Inuit law and a federal or provincial law, the Inuit law shall prevail to the extent of the inconsistency.[126]

## G. Treatment of International Freedoms

As noted in the Introduction to this volume and in several of the individual chapters, states (and domestic courts) have in some cases relied upon obligations arising under the international law of the sea as a reason for not recognising Indigenous rights and title in marine areas.[127] It is therefore useful to examine how, if at all, these issues are dealt with in Canada's land claim agreements. Perhaps of most interest is Article 16 of the NA dealing with the OLFIZ. As noted above, this area lies within Canada's EEZ. Various provisions of the NA apply to the OLFIZ subject to the caveat that they do so 'in a manner consistent with Canada's sovereignty, sovereign rights and jurisdiction, *and with Canada's international obligations*' (emphasis added).[128] Within the OLFIZ, Canada undertakes to manage fisheries 'so as not to deplete the marine mammal population'.[129]

However, these agreements also recognise the potential that exists for the federal government to prejudicially affect (or benefit) Indigenous communities in conducting treaty negotiations with other states. Thus, Article 5 of the NA (concerning wildlife) contemplates that Canada shall include Inuit representation 'in discussions leading to the formulation of government positions in relation to an international agreement relating to Inuit wildlife harvesting rights'[130] in the NSA and that in negotiating domestic inter-jurisdictional agreements, the NWMB should be involved commensurate with its status and responsibilities for the management of wildlife in the NSA.[131] Section 15.3.5

[124] LIA (n 2) s 4.4.3.

[125] ibid s 4.8.1.

[126] ibid s 4.8.2.

[127] See Godden (ch 5 in this volume); see also the reviews in Quig (n 47) and Brown and Reynolds (n 47).

[128] NA (n 1) s 16.1.1. See also s 15.5.1, which provides that: 'This Article shall be interpreted in a manner consistent with Canada's sovereignty, sovereign rights and jurisdiction and with Canada's international obligations.' There is a similar provision in LIA (n 2) s. 6.2.1(a).

[129] NA (n 1) s 16.1.3.

[130] ibid s 5.9.2.

[131] ibid s 5.9.5.

extends these requirements to any international or domestic inter-jurisdictional agreement relating to wildlife management *in marine areas beyond the NSA*.

## V. CONCLUSIONS

Indigenous peoples in Canada have been able to assert rights to marine resources based on Aboriginal rights, treaty rights and through modern land claims agreements. Up to this point in time, no Indigenous community has successfully litigated an Indigenous or Aboriginal title to marine areas. Modern land claims agreements may recognise an Indigenous title to small water lots, but not to larger areas of traditional territory. Indigenous communities have been more successful in re-asserting traditional fishing rights both through litigation and through negotiated land claims agreements. Rights secured in this way are entitled to priority and, in some cases, that priority amounts to the exclusive use of a particular resource. The nature of the priority is more clearly defined in land claims agreements than it is through litigation. Land claims agreements have also facilitated Indigenous engagement in resource management and governance, although typically through co-management arrangements rather than through the direct application of Indigenous laws. These co-management arrangements cover a range of different subject matters and extend over large marine areas, in some cases extending beyond Canada's Territorial Sea.

# 7

# *Indigenous Fishing Rights in Colombia*

# A Case of Dispossession and Invisibility

ISABELA FIGUEROA

## I. INTRODUCTION

In Colombia, the rights of Indigenous peoples were first recognised in the 1991 Constitution. Since then, the Colombian Constitutional Court has gradually incorporated the jurisprudence of the Inter-American Court on Human Rights (ICtHR) in its decisions relating to the rights of these peoples. However, this process has not included the rights of Indigenous peoples living in coastal areas whose traditional ways of life include small-scale fishing. While the Court itself has stated that small-scale fishing is one of the most marginalised economic activities in the country, judicial inertia in protecting Indigenous fishing communities has left them vulnerable to outside forces. Climate change, loss of biodiversity, invasion of alien species, and the destruction of coastal and marine habitat by human activity have created catastrophic problems for coastal regions throughout Latin America and the Caribbean. The crisis in Colombia is deepened by drug trafficking and a weak state fishery administration. Furthermore, thousands of Colombians displaced by the civil war have turned to small-scale fishing for survival. All these factors have converged to create social and territorial conflicts for Indigenous peoples, which the Colombian state has yet to address.

In this chapter, I will present some of the conflicts faced by traditional fishing communities in the coastal areas of Colombia: the Afro-Colombian traditional communities; the Wayúu people of La Guajira; and the Raizal population of the Archipelago of San Andrés, Providencia and Santa Catalina. I will also discuss the case of the Taganguero fishing community, whose ancestral land now falls within the Tayrona National Natural Park, an area of 15,000 ha of land and 4,500 ha of the Caribbean Sea.

## II. MULTI-CULTURALISM AND THE 1991 CONSTITUTION

During the 1980s, Colombians witnessed with horror the rapid expansion of the drug trade and its devastating consequences for the country: the killing of hundreds of political observers and leaders, the random violence of the war between the cartels, and the proliferation of paramilitary organisations. By the end of the decade, more than 120 judges had been murdered, and organised violent groups had exterminated hundreds of left-wing leaders, especially members of the Unión Patriótica, a political party founded by left-wing activists in 1985. As a result, the emerging power of the Revolutionary Armed Forces of Colombia (FARC), the National Liberation Army (ELN), the Popular Liberation Army (EPL) and the 19th of April Movement (M19) grew stronger.[1]

At the same time, Colombia was being governed by a corrupt and exclusive system resulting from the 1958 National Front. The state seemed to be over-centralised and there was a consensus among the population on the need to grant more decision-making powers to local authorities. The government's efforts to end the country's violence and political crisis were failing, and civil society pushed for comprehensive, radical institutional change to enable a peace process to begin. This sentiment was channelled by a student protest in Bogotá, which organised an additional element to the official electoral ballot of 1990, through which more than two million people voted extra-officially to establish a Constituent Assembly.[2] Two months later, President Virgilio Barco submitted to popular opinion by forming a Constituent Assembly, which yielded positive results.[3]

The Constituent Assembly was convened in August 1990 by presidential decree. Despite the formality of the national electoral system, the vulnerability of the political affiliation process on Indigenous reserves and the low number of identification cards issued to them, the Indigenous movement managed to present five candidates for the election of 100 Assembly members, and two of their candidates were elected to the Constituent Assembly. Embracing some of the Indigenous movement's proposals, the Assembly finally amended the Constitution to include Indigenous *peoples* as legal subjects (although it also defined them as 'ethnic groups') and to protect Indigenous peoples' rights to their language, their 'cultural heritage', bilingual education and political

[1] Julieta Lemaitre Ripolli, *El derecho como conjuro* (Siglo del Hombre Editores, 2009).
[2] ibid 110.
[3] ibid 114.

participation in the Congress. It also recognised their inalienable right to their territories, established Indigenous Territorial Entities, and affirmed Indigenous peoples' right to self-government and traditional forms of carrying out justice under their own regulations.[4]

Including the *peoples* as such, as political actors, involved the recognition of a certain degree of autonomy. However, even though Colombia was about to ratify Convention No 169[5] of the International Labour Organization (ILO), the constitutional text did not cover the state's duty of consultation with Indigenous peoples. Since then, the Colombian Constitutional Court has developed significant legal precedents on Indigenous rights. Between 1993 and 2006, 'the constitutional court found approximately 18 times in favour of Indigenous peoples in cases where their land rights were being violated by intrusive initiatives or large infrastructure projects'.[6] The Constitutional Court's rulings have been based on the theory of the block of constitutionality,[7] enforcing some international treaties domestically. However, this has not prevented several attempts from national governments to undermine the mechanism of consultation in different ways. Currently, there is a proposal for legislation[8] under congressional revision that would establish a mechanism for consultation that is not in accordance with international standards.

There are two major laws that protect Indigenous and Afro-Colombian peoples' rights: Law 21 (1991), which enforces ILO C169 in Colombia, and Law 70, which specifically regulates the 'tribal' rights of Afro-Colombian communities descended from African slaves who still maintain their traditional political and cultural values.

Colombia has also ratified the International Covenant on Civil and Political Rights (ICCPR)[9] and the International Covenant on Economic, Social and Cultural Rights (ICECSR),[10] and has welcomed both the United Nations

[4] Libardo José Ariza, *Derecho, saber e identidad indígena* (Siglo del Hombre Editores, 2009).

[5] Convention (No 169) Concerning Indigenous and Tribal Peoples in Independent Countries (1989) 72 ILO Official Bull 59.

[6] UNGA, 'Report of the Special Rapporteur on the Situation of Human Rights and Fundamental Freedoms of Indigenous People, Mr. James Anaya. Addendum. The Situation of Indigenous Peoples in Colombia: Follow-up to the Recommendations Made by the Previous Special Rapporteur', UN HRC 15th Session UN Doc A/HRC/15/37/Add.3 (2010) [41].

[7] Article 93 of the Colombian Constitution establishes that: 'International treaties and agreements ratified by the Congress that recognise human rights and that prohibit their limitation in states of emergency have priority domestically' (author's translation). According to this and to the Constitutional Court jurisprudence, the 'Constitutional Block' is a set of norms that have been integrated into the Constitution by the mandate of the Constitution itself.

[8] Congress of the Republic of Colombia, Proyecto de Ley, 'Por el cual regula el derecho fundamental a la Consulta Previa y se dictan otras disposiciones' (2018).

[9] International Covenant on Civil and Political Rights, UNGA Res 2200A (XXI) (16 December 1966).

[10] International Covenant on Economic, Social and Cultural Rights, UNGA Res 2200A (XXI) (16 December 1966).

and the Organization of American states Declarations on the Rights of Indigenous Peoples.[11] Despite these developments in international law and the efforts of the Constitutional Court, the tension between Indigenous peoples and the Colombian government over issues relating to property and natural resources has not decreased since the 1991 Constitution. Due to a lack of political will, inconsistent legislation and the absence of a specific law on consultation, Colombia has yet to fully meet its obligations regarding Indigenous peoples' rights. In 2010, the United Nations (UN) Special Rapporteur for Indigenous Issues pointed out:

> [T]he need to bring Colombia's public policy relating to economic development of the country (particularly in regard to natural resource extraction and agro-industry and tourism infrastructure 'megaprojects') in line with Indigenous peoples' rights to land and natural resources, in accordance with the provisions of ILO Convention No. 169 and the United Nations Declaration on the Rights of Indigenous Peoples.[12]

In 2017, the Colombian government signed a peace agreement with the FARC guerrillas, formally ending a 50-year-long civil war. The agreement foresees the implementation of different programmes to secure the protection of the environment and civil participation in the decision-making process. It also includes a special chapter on the rights of the 'ethnic groups' such as Afro-Colombian and Indigenous peoples, in which both the Colombian government and the guerrillas recognise these peoples' rights to collective ownership of land, self-government and consultation.

As a state party to both the ICCPR and the ICESCR, Colombia has a responsibility to comply with the guidelines of the two supervisory bodies for these covenants with respect to the protection of the cultures of minority groups, including the different ways in which such groups use their territories and carry out their hunting and fishing practices.[13]

## III. FISHING LAW AND SOCIAL CONFLICT

In Latin America and the Caribbean, 12 countries face especially severe fishing problems, including: fishery resource depletion; an increase in fishing activities; poor scientific knowledge of the fisheries and their associated ecosystems in particular; limited financial support for fishing institutions; weak government structures; and over-fishing stimulated by inappropriate subsidies and incentives,

[11] American Declaration on the Rights of Indigenous Peoples, OASAG Res 2888 (XLVI-0/16) (15 June 2016).

[12] UNGA (n 6).

[13] See in particular UNHRC 'Comment No. 23: The Rights of Minorities (Art. 27)', UN HRC 50 Session UN Doc CCPR/C/21/Rev.1/Add.5 [7].

as well as by desperately poor living conditions in coastal communities.[14] Fishing activities suffer further from such diverse impacts as climate change, loss of biodiversity, invasion of alien species, and human destruction of coastal and marine habitats. These difficulties in resource management are common in countries around the world, but they are exacerbated in Colombia, where civil war has displaced thousands of people, many of whom have turned to fishing for their survival. Drug trafficking and an extremely weak state fishery administration are also exacerbating factors.[15]

National laws in Colombia for small-scale fishing are highly inconsistent. For decades, as many as five state institutions have been charged with governing small-scale fishing in Colombia.[16] Currently there are six ministries involved in governing small-scale fishing, the most important of these being the Rural Development and Agriculture Ministry. The poor coordination among various offices prevents proper governance and makes it difficult for local actors to understand fishery policies.

The Colombian Constitution establishes that renewable and non-renewable natural resources belong to the state,[17] and that the state is responsible for their conservation and sustainable use. The Colombian state also has dominion over the hydrobiological resources of its territorial sea, of its Exclusive Economic Zones and of the continental shelf. Fishing activities such as research, harvesting, cultivation, processing and commercialisation are declared to be a matter of public utility and social interest, and are also administered by the state.[18] The Colombian Constitutional Court has ruled that fishing resources are analogous to *res nullius* – common goods that are not subject to property law – and that it is a duty of the state to watch over their administration and create rules and conditions for access to those resources.[19] Furthermore, the state has the duty to protect food production, giving priority to agricultural policies, which includes fishing.[20]

In Colombia, the law differentiates continental from coastal fishing. Continental fishing is performed in rivers or lakes; coastal fishing in the ocean.[21] Coastal marine fishing is classified in one of the following ways: subsistence, research, sport or commercial. Subsistence fishing, allowed on all Colombian territory, refers to harvesting fish for the fisher and families, but not for profit.[22]

[14] Lina M Saavedra-Díaz, Andrew A Rosenberg and Berta Martín-López, 'Social Perceptions of Colombian Small-Scale Marine Fisheries Conflicts: Insights for Management' (2015) 56 *Marine Policy* 61.

[15] ibid.

[16] ibid 64.

[17] Colombian Constitution (1991) art 332.

[18] Colombia, Ley 13 (1990) arts 2 and 3.

[19] Constitutional Court (Colombia), *Acción de tutela interpuesta por Jónatan Pachechpo Yanez contra el Ministerio de Ambiente y Desarrollo Sostenible, la Unidad Administrativa del Sistema de Parques Nacionales Naturales y otros* [2015] T-606.

[20] Colombian Constitution (1991) art 65.

[21] Colombia, Ley 13 (1990) art 8.

[22] ibid art 47.

Commercial fishing is defined by the sale of the catch with the goal of reaching internal and external markets, and small-scale artisanal fishing entitlements are established by different national decrees and regulations. The sport fishery is not economically significant in Colombia, and most of the research fishing is performed by or in collaboration with the state.[23]

Inland fishing – which is performed in rivers, lakes and bodies of waters other than the ocean – is classified as either industrial or artisanal (small-scale).[24] Artisanal fishing is practised by coastal communities using wood or fibreglass boats, oars and sails. The main products include shallow-water shrimp, tuna, sea bass, sawfish, *picuda*, shark, black shells, clams, lobster and snails.[25] Fisherman work through the whole day and their vessels carry up to three sailors who fish within five nautical miles of the coast. The fishing gear employed is the trammel net and gill net, and the throw net for shrimp and white fish. Fishermen also use hand lines and hand nets to catch white fish, and traps and pots to catch lobster, snails, and other kinds of fish and crustaceans.[26]

Traditional communities cannot impose restrictions or limitations on any coastal fishing area other than those which are imposed by national law. A consequence of this is that novice fishermen, especially those displaced by war, have open access to any fishing area and, with no previous experience in fishing, they tend to use destructive equipment and methods. This leads to social conflicts and disputes.[27] From the government's perspective, the ocean is an economic, biological and geopolitical resource. Fishing regulations do not incorporate Indigenous, Afro-Colombian or any other traditional communities' integrated points of view. Consequently, Indigenous ancestral technologies and practices for fishing and trade are not protected by Colombian law.

Saavedra-Días and Jentoff note that fishermen on both the Pacific and Caribbean coasts of Colombia describe themselves as being victims of corruption by politicians and local administrators. Furthermore, and in addition to all the problems related to violence from the war and drug trafficking, 'illegal groups own and use fishing equipment for the drug trade, thus tarnishing the image of small-scale fishers and affecting family and communal values'.[28] War-related attacks on national pipelines have also affected rivers, mangroves and estuarine zones where traditional fishing takes place, especially affecting the women who collect *piangua* in mangrove roots.[29]

[23] UNFAO, 'República de Colombia. Datos económicos generales', 2003, www.fao.org/fi/oldsite/FCP/es/col/profile.htm.

[24] Colombia, Ley 13 (1990) art 8.

[25] UNFAO (n 23).

[26] ibid.

[27] Lina M Saavedra-Díaz, Andrew A Rosenberg and Berta Martín-López, 'Social Perceptions of Colombian Small-Scale Marine Fisheries Conflicts: Insights for Management' (2015) 56 *Marine Policy* 63.

[28] Lina María Saavedra-Díaz and Svein Jentoft, 'Guidelines in Reclaiming Human Rights for Small-Scale Fishing People in Colombia' in Svein Jentoft et al (eds) *The Small-Scale Fisheries Guidelines. Global Implementation* (Springer, 2011) 580.

[29] ibid.

## IV. INDIGENOUS COMMUNITIES WHO HARVEST MARINE RESOURCES IN COLOMBIA

Colombia has a total coastline of 3,240 km distributed between the Pacific Ocean and the Caribbean Sea.[30] Fishing in Colombia involves fish products in both coastal zones and in innumerous pluvial and lacustrine bays. The University of Magdalena inventoried the artisanal fishing entities in the country and, setting aside the Archipelago of San Andrés, Providencia and Santa Catalina, and the Ciénaga Grande of Santa Marta, registered some 21,885 such entities, 17 per cent of them located in the Caribbean Sea and 15 per cent in the Pacific Ocean.[31] Other entities engage in inland fishing. Artisanal fishing may not be significant in terms of gross domestics product (GDP), but it is an important activity for around 10,000 families, providing them with an important source of protein and ensuring their rights to food and food sovereignty.

In 1992, in a constitutional injunction decision related to fishing rights, the Constitutional Court reasoned that although artisanal fishing sustains national fish consumption, it is one of the most marginalised activities in the country's economy. Artisanal fishers make less than the minimum wage and live on the margins of the nation's economic and cultural life.[32] According to the Court:

> Small-scale fishing is practiced by different ethnic and cultural groups on the shores of both oceans, on the river banks and margins of swamps and estuaries. Artisanal fishermen throughout the country are affected by common problems that make them have a low quality of life. Industrial water pollution, riverside landowners blocking free passage to riverbanks or beaches, the drying of swamps for farming or agriculture, the uncontrolled intensive fishing by national and foreign vessels, and the use of intermediaries are some of the problems that make Colombian fishermen one of the poorest human groups, with little means to generate income.[33]

The Court's reasoning describes a reality apparent to all in the fishing areas of Colombia's coastal areas. However, there is no scientific or governmnental data documenting the social and economic situation of artisanal fisherman. Montalvo and Silva note that less than five per cent of more than 2,000 research projects on this subject in Colombia consider marine areas from a social perspective. A total of 95 per cent of these academic papers have a commercial or biological point of view.[34] The dynamics of local human communities are rendered invisible,[35] especially the dynamics of Indigenous communities. There is no ethnographic study that provides accurate information on the Indigenous populations and

[30] UNFAO, 'Fishery Country Profile' (2003) FID/CP/Col Rev 6, www.fao.org/fi/oldsite/FCP/es/col/profile.htm.

[31] ibid.

[32] Constitutional Court (Colombia), *Tutela. Lucio Quintero Rincón, José Torregosa Mercado* [1992] T-605.

[33] ibid (author's translation).

[34] Alfonso Julian Montalvo and Fabio Silva, 'El mar ¿territorio de quién? Algunos elementos para una propuesta de una antropología del litoral' (2009) 68 *Universitas humanística* 248.

[35] ibid 250.

traditional communities who include parts of the coast in their territoriality, or on the way in which national policies affect the rights of those populations.

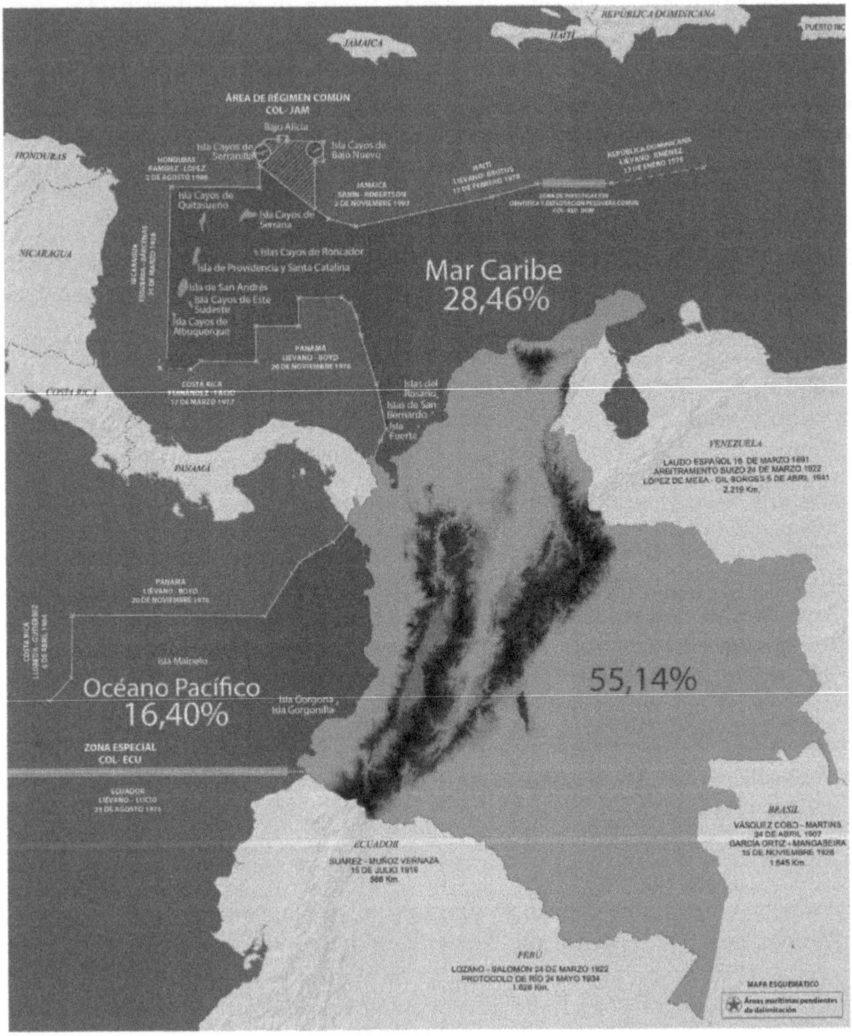


**Figure 7.1** Map of Colombia

*Source*: Colombian Ocean Commission, www.cco.gov.co/cco/publicaciones/83-publicaciones/262-mapa-esquematico-de-colombia.html.

## A. Indigenous Populations in Coastal Areas: Resisting as a Profession

In a document that provides an overview of the violence in Indigenous populations, the UN identified various Indigenous communities on the coast and on riverbanks in which fishing is an important element of their diet and culture. Among them are the Awá Kaiker people (Nariño, Pacific region); the Tule/Cuna people (Urabá from Antioquia and Chocó, Pacific region); the Embera Chamí people (Risaralda, Pacific region); the Emebrá Dobidá people (Chocó, Pacific region); the Zenú people (Córdoba, Pacific region); the Emberá Katio people (Antioquia, Córdoba and Chocó, Pacific region); the Wounnan people (Chocó, Pacífic region); the Kogui people (Magdalena, Caribbean); the Arhuaco people (Magdalena, Pacific region); and the Wayúu people (Guajira, Caribbean).[36] The Taganqueros (Magdalena, Caribbean) are not recognised as an Indigenous people either by this UN document or by the Colombian government. However, they are fighting to be considered Indigenous and to receive specific protection for their fishing rights, as I will discuss later on in this chapter.

The next section discusses some of the fishing conflicts faced by traditional communities and the few court decisions dealing, in limited ways, with their fishing rights.

## B. The Wayúu People from La Guajira and Indigenous Rights over the Coastal Areas

The Wayúu people inhabit the Guajira Peninsula in northern Colombia and northwestern Venezuela. Their traditional territory covers around 1,080,336 ha of land, located in the reserve of Alta and Media Guajira, containing the largest Indigenous population in Colombia. Their maritime territory is not recognised by national law and there is no accurate data describing their relationship with the Caribbean. They also inhabit the desert, where their territoriality is established around a water source or another resource such as a swamp, a salt mine, or a plaster or talc deposit.[37] Artisanal fishing and the grazing of goats are the main components of the Wayúu economy.

In addition to displacement caused by agricultural colonisation, this population has recently faced the terrible impact on their territory of El Cerrejón, Latin America's largest open-pit coal mine, covering 69,000 ha (170,502 acres). Some communities directly affected refused to leave their lands, and now their members are suffering from skin rashes, deafness, nutritional deficiencies, and restrictions on their rights to come and go as they wish. The Wayúu houses at that location are made with the mine's residues, since the materials they traditionally used to build their houses fall partially on land closed by the mine. In addition, the building and operation of the El Cerrejón mine caused the Ranchería River (the largest river in that area) to change its course, thereby

[36] UNHCR, 'Comunidades indígenas', 2011, www.acnur.org/t3/fileadmin/Documentos/Pueblos_indigenas/2011/Comunidades_indigenas_en_Colombia_-_ACNUR_2011.pdf?view=1.ONU.

[37] Ministry of Government (Colombia), 'Pueblos Wayúu', https://www.mininterior.gov.co/sites/default/files/upload/SIIC/PueblosIndigenas/pueblo_way_u.pdf.

worsening the drought on their land and resulting in the severe malnutrition of their people. Consequently, there exists an epidemic of high child mortality. In 2015, the Inter-American Commission on Human Rights (IACHR) recommended that Colombia provide accessible and better-quality health services for the Wayúu community's children and youth, as well as immediate access to safe drinking water and nutritional food for children.[38] In 2017, the IACHR extended the scope of these precautionary measures to pregnant and lactating women.[39] So far, however, the Colombian government has not been able to reduce the epidemic levels of child mortality.

For the Wayúu people, the sea is closely linked to their spirituality. They have diverse ways of navigation and fishing, ancestral knowledge of daytime and night-time fishing, and worldviews that represent a complex idea of territoriality, all of which are completely ignored by the state. In interviews with University of Magdalena anthropologists, members of the Wayúu have stated that while national law prevents them from fishing offshore, it allows the operation of large fishing vessels which damage their entire territory and put their lives at risk.[40]

The state's inaction regarding environmental damage on Indigenous inland territories has been assessed by the Colombian Constitutional Court in a deforestation injunction case in the Emberá-Catío lands on the border of the Caredajó River (Pacific region). The Court stated that due to the inter-dependence between the human population and the river's ecosystem, the state's inaction could amount to ethnocide, and it demanded that the private company 'restore the natural resources affected by the illegal forest utilization'.[41] The Court's reasoning was as follows:

> The close relationship between balanced ecosystem and the survival of Indigenous communities that inhabit the tropical rainforests transforms the environmental damage produced by deforestation, sedimentation and pollution of the rivers … into a potential danger to the life and cultural, social and economic integrity of minority groups that require a special protection from the state due to their ethnic and cultural diversity … The state's inaction after severe environmental damage caused to an ethnic group may passively contribute, due to the ecosystem's biological interdependence, to the commission of an *ethnocide*, which is the forced disappearance of an ethnicity … due to the destruction of their living conditions and system of beliefs. (Emphasis in original)[42]

[38] *Niñas, niños y adolescentes de las comunidades de Uribía, Manaure, Riohacha y Maicao del pueblo Wayúu, asentados en el departamento de la Guajira, respecto de Colombia* (2015) IACHR CM 51-15.

[39] *Ampliación de beneficiarios a favor de las mujeres gestantes y lactantes de la Comunidad Indígena Wayúu en los municipios de Manaure, Riohacha y Uribía respecto de Colombia* (2017) IACHR CM 51-15.

[40] Montalvo and Silva (n 34).

[41] Constitutional Court (Colombia), *Comunidad indígena/derechos fundamentales/derecho a la vida/derecho a la subsistencia* [1993] T-380.

[42] ibid (translated by the author).

In a separate case in which landowners sought to block access to the sea of traditional fishermen on the Caribbean coast of Magdalena, the Court considered that the chronic neglect and poverty of the country's artisanal fishermen is an obstacle to a proper and timely defence of their rights.[43] Ruling in favour of their right to access the sea, the Court added that when two visions of progress are competing (hotel owners versus traditional fishermen, for example), the conflict of interests should be resolved in accordance with the principles of pluralist democracy and the participation of all parties in the overall prosperity of the country.[44]

Although there exists solid jurisprudence for the defence of Indigenous peoples' rights to land – including access to the ocean and sea – the Constitutional Court has yet to decide a single case regarding the territorial rights of Indigenous populations over a coastal area. To the best of my knowledge, this is because no case of this kind has yet been brought on behalf of coastal peoples. As a result, decisions protecting the rights of coastal traditional fishers have been based on the narrow right to exercise a profession rather than the territorial rights upon which their cultures and livelihoods depend.

### C. Afro-Colombian Traditional Communities

At the end of the sixteenth century, a significant number of Africans were brought as slaves to the Pacific coast of what is today Colombia, especially to work in the gold mines of Chocó. Descendants of these slaves currently maintain distinct socio-cultural, economic and tribal policies in their communities, and many of them maintain their traditional fishing practices.[45] In 1996, while examining the rights of communities affected by several oil spills on the Pacific coast, the Constitutional Court acknowledged the enormous impact of these spills on fishers' right to work, especially when fishing is part of an ethnicity's cultural practices.[46] However, the Court did not further examine the community's use rights over the coastal zone or the territorial aspects of that relationship.

### D. The Raizal Population of the Archipelago of San Andrés, Providencia and Santa Catalina

In the Caribbean Sea, 770 km (478 miles) from Cartagena, Colombia, and 180 km (111 miles) from the Nicaraguan coast, there live approximately 30,000

[43] *Tutela* (n 32).
[44] ibid.
[45] Ministry of Environment (Colombia), 'Documento base para la elaboración de la "Política Nacional de Ordenamiento Integrado de las Zonas Costeras Colombianas"' (1997) 6–49.
[46] Constitutional Court (Colombia), *Pescadores de Salahonda* [1996] T-574.

Raizal people inhabiting the 46 sq km (17.76 sq miles) of mainland in the Archipelago of San Andrés, Providencia and Santa Catalina. Although it is the smallest political territorial division in Colombia, it includes 250,000 sq km (96,525 sq miles) of the Caribbean Sea. The Raizal people are descendants of African slaves brought to the islands by the British. They are a population characterised by the interweaving of Anglo-African-Antillean identities who continue to maintain their own traditions and language (Creole), distinguishing them from the rest of the Colombian population. The term 'Raizal' allows the state and Colombian society to set the San Andrés African descendants apart from the rest of the Afro-Colombian population of the Pacific region.[47] While the African descendants of Colombia's Pacific coast built a social resistance movement forcing the state to recognise their lands and other collective rights, the San Andrés Raizal people have no recognition for their collective rights, and they must contend with a growing tourism industry that employs them as cheap labour in San Andrés and, to a lesser extent, in Providencia.[48]

The Raizal were originally brought to the islands as slaves to work on cotton plantations, and when this activity was no longer profitable for the landlords, they were left on their own. The Raizal survived through a subsistence economy based primarily on fishing and gathering shellfish, the products of which they sold to restaurants in local resorts. Importantly, traditional communal fishing practices helped them survive. According to Londoño and Gonzales:

> Men spent much of the day, almost sixteen hours, at sea, collecting lobsters or harpooning different species to meet family needs. In fact, some reports point out that in order to keep lobster and fish populations stable, social convention amongst Raizals banned the use of oxygen tanks or large nets. Fishing is limited by the immersion capacity of the fishermen. A recurring expression when the Raizals are questioned about their fishing systems is that 'you get what you can get'. That is, the longer the fisherman can be submerged, the more resources he can get. Amongst fishermen, breaking this rule brings dishonor, while those who are able to spend more than five minutes underwater are distinguished as heroes.[49]

The archipelago was successively colonised by the Netherlands, France, Spain and England. It maintained a certain autonomy until 1822, when it was finally annexed to Colombia by means of treaties between the local authorities of the archipelago and Colombian patriots. In 1912, Colombia introduced a colonisation policy with an administrative scheme for the archipelago.[50] In 1959, the archipelago was turned into a free port,[51] which brought a significant influx of

[47] Wilhelm Londoño and Pablo Alonso Gonzales, 'From Plantation to Proletariat: Raizales in San Andrés, Providencia and Santa Catalina' (2017) 59 *Race and Class* 84.

[48] ibid 87.

[49] ibid 87–88.

[50] Colombia, Ley 52 (1912).

[51] Colombia, Ley 127 (1959).

migrants from the continent, causing the current over-population and a deterioration in the quality of life of its inhabitants.

In 1999, the Colombian Constitutional Court decided that the conclusion of a maritime boundary delimitation treaty between Colombia and Honduras did not create any duty for the state to consult with this population, even though the treaty affected the fundamental rights of the San Andrés Raizal.[52] Due to the neglect of the islanders' claims by successive national governments, a group of Raizal declared their self-determination in 2002,[53] but this had a more political than a legal effect.

In 2012, the International Court of Justice (ICJ) settled a border dispute between Nicaragua and Colombia regarding the archipelago's maritime area. The Court's judgment affected the rights of the Raizal fishermen by reducing their maritime territory. The largest part of the Raizal fishing area is beyond the coral reef surrounding the islands, which were recognised as being part of Nicaragua.[54] In 2014, the Colombia Workers' Union (CGT – its acronym coming from its Spanish name) expressed its concern regarding the Raizal's rights under ILO 169. The CGT pointed out that during the international judicial process, the Colombian state never bothered to consult with the Raizal. To date, there has yet to be any type of proper consultation with the Raizal as required by ILO 169, and the current situation of the fishers of San Andrés, Providencia and Santa Catalina has never been more daunting, primarily due to intensive tourism and loss of territory.

## V. INDIGENOUS HARVESTING RIGHTS IN MARINE PROTECTED AREAS

National Nature Parks are defined by the national government through presidential decrees.[55] The allocation of uncultivated lands, land sales, hunting, fishing and any industrial, livestock or agricultural activity are all forbidden within National Nature Parks.[56] One exception to these prohibitions is subsistence fishing,[57] so long as the national zoning authority is respected – zoning that so far has not taken Indigenous traditional practices into consideration. The relevant decree also restricts subsistence fishing along beaches identified as National Nature Parks, public beaches or reproductive areas for wildlife species.[58]

[52] Constitutional Court (Colombia), *Tratado de Delimitación Fronteriza y Tratado de Modificación de Fronteras* [1999] C-1022.

[53] San Andrés (Colombia), *Declaración de Autodeterminación*, 2002, www.urosario.edu.co/jurisprudencia/catedra-viva-intercultural/Documentos/DeclaracionAutodeterminacionRaizal.pdf.

[54] Londoño and Gonzales (n 47) 90, 91.

[55] Colombia, Ley 2 (1959) art 13.

[56] Constitution of Colombia (1991) art 63; Colombia, Ley 2 (1959) art 13.

[57] Colombia, Decreto 622 (1977) art 30.

[58] Colombia, Decreto Ley 2811 (1974) art 278.

The Aquaculture and Fishing National Authority (AUNAP – its acronym coming from its Spanish name) is the government body that implements fishing and aquaculture policy, grants authorisations for fishing activities, and establishes control mechanisms and compliance with regulations. On the other hand, the National Nature Parks of Colombia (PNNC – its acronym coming from its Spanish name) is the entity in charge of the administration and management of the Natural National Parks System and coordination of the National Protected Areas System.[59] The activities allowed in national parks are regulated jointly by the AUNAP and the PNNC, but as these entities employ two very different management systems, confusing and inefficient administration of the parks make it almost impossible to determine which activities are forbidden and why.

I have noted above that the Colombian Constitution recognises and protects the nation's ethnic and cultural diversity.[60] Likewise, national legislation and Constitutional Court jurisprudence repeatedly acknowledge that cultural diversity includes worldviews that fall outside the predominant political and juridical customs.[61] Even before the 1991 Constitution, Decree 622 (1977), which is still relevant to the Parks Law of 1974, had already recognised that it is not inconsistent to have a national park and an Indigenous reserve in the same area. In these cases, the national authorities are responsible for establishing governance that benefits the Indigenous population by respecting their communities' permanence and their right to utilize the area's renewable natural resources.[62] This is the case in Tayrona Park, for instance, but not in oceanic part of the Park, where, as I have noted previously, Indigenous territorial rights are not recognised.

According to the law that regulates the National Development Plan, all national development plans should be made in collaboration with the Indigenous and Afro-Colombian territorial entities.[63] Many different development plans recognise this normative requirement.[64] It is therefore clear that the delimitation of coastal areas and national park preservation policies should take Indigenous traditional norms into account. However, this is still far from the case in Colombia.

[59] Colombia, Decreto 3572 (2011).

[60] Constitution of Colombia (1991) art 8.

[61] Constitutional Court (Colombia), *Acción de tutela ejercida por Oscar Carupia Domicó y otros, a nombre de los resguardos Chidima-Tolo y Pescadito pertenecientes a la etnia Embera-Katío contra los Ministerios de Transporte, Ambiente, Vivienda y Desarrollo Territorial, Interior y de Justicia, de Minas y Energía, de Agricultura, de Defensa, el Consejo Asesor de Regalías adscrito al Departamento Nacional de Planeación, las alcaldías de Unguía y Acandí, la Corporación Autónoma Regional del Chocó (Codechocó), el Ejército Nacional, la Brigada XVII y la Agencia Logística de las Fuerzas Militares* [2011] T-129.

[62] Colombia, Decreto 622 (1977) art 7.

[63] Colombia, Ley 152 (1994).

[64] The Municipality of Orucue's Development Plan in the department of Cesanare is an example of this collaboration.

### A. The Case of the Magdalena Taganguero

The Taganga fishing community is located north of the city of Santa Marta in the department of Magdalena. Its citizens are called Tagangueros, which is significant in terms of cultural identity but devoid of any legal significance. Members of the Taganga (*taguangua* means 'land and sea' in their native language) community are descendants of ancient Caribbean peoples, and currently on the front lines of the movement to assert Indigenous identity and obtain constitutional protection. The Colombian state opposes this since it would require them to recognise the large area of land area that was reserved for the Taganga people during the era of the Spanish Empire. The Tagangueros' ancestral land now falls within the Tayrona National Natural Park, with a total area of 15,000 ha of land and 4,500 ha of sea. When it was created in 1964, the park was also inhabited by other Indigenous and peasant communities. Strict park regulations forbidding fishing have now displaced the traditional fishers from the area.

The fishers, including Indigenous peoples and Tagangueros, demand from the national government decent living conditions, recognition of their cultural knowledge and decriminalisation of their activities.[65] The main problem for the community involves the concept of territoriality, in which, according to the Taganguero Cantillo:

> [F]or many centuries, social relationships have been built upon a territorial identity that we need to keep in order to continue with the fishing activities considered ancestral to us. What the *taganguero* fishermen are demanding is that before making any decisions on the territory that we have always controlled, we should be consulted, because we have been in these areas since long before the arrival of the settlers or the creation of Tayrona Park.[66]

The Tagangueros consider that all the beaches in Tayrona Park are part of their territory. However, the Colombian Constitutional Court has a different view.[67] In a case in which the environmental authority had confiscated the fishing gear of Taganguero fishers, the Court focused on the state's responsibility for not implementing compensatory measures to mitigate damage caused by a fishing ban rather than whether the ban was lawful.

The Court noted that in 2004, almost all the maritime area of Tayrona Park had been categorised as a natural recovery area, thereby preventing fishing activities. According to the Court, the ban on artisanal fishing in the Park was not an arbitrary measure, but a measure to protect the reproduction of marine species.

[65] Ayrton David Cantillo Matos, 'Bogando en un mar de incertidumbre' [2017] *Oraloteca* 8.

[66] ibid 37 (author's translation).

[67] Constitutional Court (Colombia), *Acción de tutela interpuesta por Jónatan Pachechpo Yanez contra el Ministerio de Ambiente y Desarrollo Sostenible, la Unidad Administrativa del Sistema de Parques Nacionales Naturales y otros* [2015] T-606.

The ban serves to protect the ecosystem's environmental services and contributes to the guarantee of the right of all Colombians to food.

Ironically, the Court also concluded that the loss of marine species was not caused by artisanal fishing, but by much more damaging activities such as coal extraction and transport, illegal construction and the extension of port facilities. In the end, the Court did not take any measure to reconcile traditional fishing activities with Park preservation. In its verdict, the Court merely asked the state authorities to establish compensatory measures for the fishers prevented from engaging in fishing by the creation of the National Park. According to the Court, the damages suffered by the fishers could be overcome through relocation and fishing training programmes led by governmental authorities.

The Constitutional Court's significant jurisprudence regarding Indigenous territorial rights contrasts sharply with its naïve reasoning in this case. The Court also ordered the creation of a roundtable to negotiate compensation for the Tayrona National Nature Park artisanal fishermen. The roundtable should include the Ministry of Environment and Land Development, the Special Administrative Unit of the Colombia's Natural National Parks System, the Colombian Rural Development Institute, the Regional Autonomous Corporation of Magdalena, the National Learning Service, Magdalena's Ombudsman, the Attorney's General Office, the Magdalena government and the different artisanal fishing associations of the Tayrona National Nature Park. In short, the Court ordered various national actors with diverse and competing interests to negotiate with an historically ignored and marginalised community, demonstrating its ignorance of the lives and challenges of the traditional fishermen. By July 2018, no substantial agreement had been reached.[68]

The ICtHR understood in the *Sawhoyamaxa* case that the loss of material possessions or the prohibition of access to traditional territory should not be obstacles to the survival of Indigenous traditional rights.[69] It is odd that in this case the Constitutional Court, which has historically decided cases of Indigenous rights conflicts in accordance with the ICtHR's jurisprudence, failed to analyse the case in terms of the collective rights of the Indigenous populations, but focused instead on the right to work and to perform a job.

In closing, the Court established a 60-day deadline for the PNNC to design a compensation plan that guarantees the fulfilment of the fundamental rights to work, food sovereignty and essential conditions to life to the artisanal fishermen affected by the Park. It also determined that it is the responsibility of the Magdalena government to provide nutritional and economic support to the people who traditionally practised fishing. According to the Santa Marta Ecotourism Fishing Association, the Magdalena government has provided

[68] 'Pescadores reclaman auxilios económicos a la Gobernación' *Hoy Diario del Magdalena* (Santa Marta, 15 July 2018), www.hoydiariodelmagdalena.com.co/new/archivos/64980.

[69] *Case of the Sawhoyamaxa Indigenous Community v Paraguay* (2006) IACtHR C 146 [132].

compensation to just 33 fishermen, while it is estimated that 400 fishermen have been affected by the Park and lack the necessary resources to fulfil their essential right to decent living conditions, including the right to perform a job.[70]

## VI. CONCLUSIONS

Respect for Indigenous rights requires that traditional knowledge be made visible and incorporated into national policies governing the physical and ontological space that we non-Indigenous people call 'nature'. It is essential to the survival of cultural diversity – and thus the survival of all Colombians – to articulate and respect the knowledge of ethnic groups whose territories overlap areas declared as protected or which form part of the system of natural parks. Colombian legislation and jurisprudence provide the tools to do this, but there has not been sufficient will on the part of the government to establish mechanisms of co-management, not only in the protected areas, but also in all the coastal areas where traditional collective rights apply.

All of this indicates an urgent need for a reconceptualisation of artisanal and subsistence fishing to include the cosmology of the traditional fishing communities. Commercial fishing in many cases is also subsistence fishing. For example, small-scale trading is part of a traditional community's culture, a vital part of its peoples' identity and sense of dignity.

It is critical for traditional people who live from fishing that the national government and courts recognise that ancestral territory consists of parts of the ocean, and that traditional peoples have governance rights over that territory. In the cases of the Tagangueros and the Raizal, the Colombian state still has a long way to go to correct its injustices, starting with its recognition of them as peoples with collective rights, including self-determination.

[70] 'Pescadores reclaman auxilios económicos a la Gobernación' (n 68).

# 8

# *Marine Protected Areas and Indigenous Peoples' Rights*

## A Case Study of the National Park of the Coral Sea in New Caledonia

DOROTHÉE CAMBOU, JÉRÉMIE GILBERT AND MARLÈNE DÉGREMONT

### I. INTRODUCTION

IN APRIL 2014, the Government of New Caledonia established the Natural Park of the Coral Sea. Covering a vast 1.3 million sq km area of the South Pacific, the park was established to protect the world's second-largest coral reef and its attendant lagoon.[1] The park is considered the fourth-largest marine protected area (MPA) in the world and falls within the International Union for Conservation of Nature (IUCN) category VI.[2] Geographically, the park covers all of New Caledonia's Exclusive Economic Zone (EEZ) as well as the islands located in this area and their territorial waters.[3] As such, the creation of the park significantly increased France's contributions to the protection targets set by the United Nations (UN) for 2020. It also constitutes France's first contribution to the Pacific Oceanscape, a collaboration by 16 Pacific Island states and six territories dedicated to sustainably manage nearly 40 million sq km of ocean. In effect, this area of the Coral Sea is a nursery for an exceptional level of biodiversity, including 25 kinds of marine mammals, 48 species of shark, 19 species of nesting birds and five different marine turtles. It also spawns vast

[1] République Française, Arrêté créant le Parc Naturel de la Mer de Corail, N2014-1063GNC, 23 April 2014 (hereinafter 'decree of adoption').

[2] The International Union for Conservation of Nature is an international organisation working in the field of nature conservation and sustainable use of natural resources.

[3] However, the park excludes territorial waters between the shoreline and 12 nautical miles.

numbers of pelagic fish, 3,000 tons of which make it into the Pacific every year – an important food source for millions of people and a source of employment for thousands of people living in the region.[4] While the extent of non-biological resources in the park is not known, it has also been argued that given the region's geological context, New Caledonia's vast EEZ presents some potential for oil and mineral resources, including phosphates, polymetallic nodule and ferromanganese crust, that are essential for modern technology.[5]

However, the establishment of the park also raises important issues. From an ecological perspective, it is questionable whether the park can meet expectations, especially as it constitutes a managed marine area that still awaits the formal definition of its protection levels and the establishment of the zones to be included in an MPA network.[6] In this regard, researchers have cast general doubts as to whether so-called large-scale MPA are anything more than 'paper parks', which exist only in legislation, but not in practice.[7] Others also 'assert that large scale MPAs are ineffective in protecting the ocean because the capabilities of most management and enforcement agencies are insufficient'.[8] Finally, from a socio-economic perspective, existing concerns include the fact that large-scale MPAs 'do not address wider links to key social issues, including negative impacts on local communities, Indigenous peoples' rights, benefit-cost sharing, poverty, gender equity, food security and livelihoods'.[9] In the New Caledonian context, where huge inequities exist between the three provinces of the territory and the question of the decolonisation process is still an open-ended process, historical, political, legal and socio-economic issues loom large in the midst of the current establishment of the natural park.

The purpose of this chapter is to discuss more specifically the significance of the creation of the Natural Park of the Coral Sea for the protection of Indigenous peoples' rights.[10] The Kanak people (the Indigenous people of New Caledonia) have developed over the centuries a livelihood system that is closely inter-connected with the maritime ecosystem. Historically and to a great extent

[4] Government of New Caledonia, 'Management Plan 2017–2021' (2017), https://mer-de-corail.gouv.nc/sites/default/files/atoms/files/management_plan_21th_december.pdf.

[5] ibid 30, 93.

[6] It may be better to consider the park as a large marine managed area rather than a protected area.

[7] Pierre Leenhardt et al, 'The Rise of Large-Scale Marine Protected Areas: Conservation or Geopolitics?' (2013) 85 *Ocean & Coastal Management* 112, 2; EM de Santo, PJS Jones and AMM Miller, 'Fortress Conservation at Sea: A Commentary on the Chagos Marine Protected Area' (2011) 35 *Marine Policy* 258.

[8] Nicholas K Dulvy, 'Super-Sized MPAs and the Marginalization of Species Conservation' (2013) 23 *Aquatic Conservation: Marine and Freshwater Ecosystems* 357; Rebecca L Singleton and Callum M Roberts, 'The Contribution of Very Large Marine Protected Areas to Marine Conservation: Giant Leaps or Smoke and Mirrors?' (2014) 87 *Marine Pollution Bulletin* 7.

[9] Nai'a Lewis et al, *Large-Scale Marine Protected Areas Guidelines for Design and Management* (Teresa Catle et al, IUCN, 2017) vii, http://bigoceanmanagers.org/best-practice-guidelines.

[10] More generally on the implications of MPA for the rights of Indigenous peoples, see Farran (ch 14 in this volume).

currently, the Kanak people have relied on fishing, gathering and agriculture. In effect, Kanak communities identify as either 'land' or 'sea' clans. For some clans, the sea is an important part of their identity.[11] In this regard, sea access is important to the Kanak people for subsistence fishing and shellfish harvesting and for customary ceremonies. Thus, although many Kanak today seek opportunities in the more urban market economy, the marine environment still represents a significant aspect of their livelihood. However, the Kanak's access to and use of their marine resources is not always sufficiently or adequately respected. According to the UN Special Rapporteur on the Rights of Indigenous Peoples, several Kanak sources complain that their access to fishing areas in some places is blocked by owners of private property adjacent to coastal areas.[12] In addition, there are also concerns about the environmental impacts of mining operations on the environment and important frustration have been expressed by Kanak sources 'over the absence of economic benefits to their people from the enormous nickel wealth being generated in the country'.[13] More generally:

> [I]t is evident that the Kanak people face ongoing challenges to maintain and develop on their own terms the multiple aspects of their cultural identity, to fully participate in political processes and government, to improve the economic and social conditions of daily life, and to be free from discrimination.[14]

While these issues are at the heart of the decolonisation process, they are also more singularly connected with the establishment of the park. The creation of the park and its asserted goals to protect and develop sustainably the resources located in the area will affect the livelihoods of the Kanak people and other Indigenous communities living in the vicinity of the park. This impact can either be positive or negative. On the one hand, researchers claim that the creation of MPAs has the potential to catalyse 'indigenous claims to preserve their traditional and future rights forcing States to make sovereignty compromises on traditional rights'.[15] On the other hand, an MPA can also undermine Indigenous rights, while depriving community users of their resources, undermining their access to areas that have been historically important to them or excluding them from the decision-making process concerning the conservation and development of resources.[16]

Against this background, this chapter offers some reflections on the challenges that the governance and management of the Natural Park of the Coral

[11] Report of the Special Rapporteur on the Rights of Indigenous Peoples, James Anaya, 'The Situation of Kanak People in New Caledonia, France' (2011) UN Doc A/HRC/18/35/Add 6, 10.

[12] ibid.

[13] ibid 12.

[14] ibid.

[15] Leenhardt et al (n 7) 1.

[16] Nathan James Bennett, Hugh Govan and Terre Satterfield, 'Ocean Grabbing' (2015) 57 *Marine Policy* 61; Natalie C Ban and Alejandro Frid, 'Indigenous Peoples' Rights and Marine Protected Areas' (2018) 87 *Marine Policy* 180.

Sea raise, more particularly in relation to the customary rights of Indigenous peoples. While New Caledonia currently follows a process within the UN decolonisation regime as described in the next section, the Kanak people benefit from a distinct regime of rights pursuant to their identity as an Indigenous people. Accordingly, this context leads to the question of how the management of the park can meet such challenges to ensure the rights of the Kanak as an Indigenous people. In order to answer this question, the analysis is divided into four main sections. Section II provides a general background describing the legal status of the Kanak people under domestic law and their rights to marine resources. Section III outlines the establishment of the Natural Park of the Coral Sea. Section IV examines the recognition of the Kanak dimension within the governance of the park and section V explores the relevance of the application of Indigenous peoples' rights in New Caledonia. Finally, section VI examines how the establishment of the park strengthens sovereignty issues over the Coral Sea. Ultimately, a brief conclusion is provided, which underscores the relevance of the application of the rights of Indigenous peoples in the management of the park to adequately secure its Indigenous dimensions and ensure its compliance with human rights law.

## II. THE KANAK PEOPLE IN NEW CALEDONIA: A SHORT BACKGROUND

The Kanak people make up approximately 45 per cent of New Caledonia's population of 275,000. New Caledonia is a sui generis collective territory of France located in the southwest Pacific Ocean to which France has gradually transferred certain powers. In 1986, the UN Committee on Decolonisation re-inscribed New Caledonia on the list of Non-Self-Governing Territories and since then, it has constantly monitored the implementation of the right to self-determination of the Kanak people.[17] With the Matignon Accords of 1988,[18] the preparatory stages for the referendum of self-determination were organised. Subsequently, the Nouméa Accord was signed on 5 May 1998 and scheduled the possible transfer of sovereignty for 2018.[19] As a consequence, a referendum was organised in order to decide whether New Caledonia should gain full sovereignty and become independent. On 4 November 2018, the Territory's population voted narrowly against independence (56.4 per cent to 43.6 per cent). However, a second referendum could be held in 2020.

[17] See especially the work of the Special Committee on the Situation with Regard to the Implementation of the Declaration on the Granting of Independence to Colonial Countries and Peoples (26 March 2003) A/AC.109/2003/7.

[18] Accords de Matignon-Oudinot du 26 juin 1988, www.mncparis.fr/uploads/accords-de-matignon_1.pdf.

[19] Accord de Nouméa, 5 May 1998, JORF, Lois et Décrets, 130ème année, no 121, 27 mai 1998, 8039–44.

The Matignon and Nouméa Accords of 1988 and 1998 were adopted after a long-term conflict between the French government and the Kanak pro-independence movement. Together, the agreements aimed to incrementally transfer competences to the local government leading to eventual independence. Therefore, the Accords constitute a defining moment. They laid the foundation for a new legal relationship between the French government and the Kanak people based on the notion of 'shared sovereignty'. They include the transfer of governmental functions from metropolitan institutions, except for certain reserved powers, including the administration of justice, the maintenance of public order, security and defence, nationality, currency and budgeting, and international relations.

More specifically regarding land and natural resources, the Nouméa Accord recognises some of the harms done by colonisation and tries to address the lack of respect for, and recognition of, the Kanak identity. The preamble states:

> Large-scale land colonisation caused considerable population movements, in which Kanak clans saw their subsistence resources depleted and their places of memory lost. This process of dispossession engendered a loss of identity markers.[20]

On this basis, the accords established an agenda to redress some of the loss of land and natural resources suffered by the Kanaks. One important aspect concerns the relationship between customary rights and the formal legal system. In the past, customary rights were ignored and trumped by formal rights; the accords try to change this dynamic by providing more space for customary rights and customary institutions.[21] With the adoption of the Matignon Accords, eight customary areas were established which comprise the 4,000–5,000 family-based clans of the territory. Each customary area is represented by a customary council and is competent for issues concerning private matters, customary areas and questions relating to Kanak language and cultures.[22] In this regard, Kanaks may have recourse to customary authorities regarding civil matters such as marriage, adoption, inheritance and certain land issues.[23] In addition, the Nouméa Accord provided for a survey and the registration of all lands in New Caledonia that would be classified as either customary land or land held under ordinary civil law.[24] While there is an important focus on customary land rights, customary rights to the sea and marine resources have not received as much attention. One of the reasons for this has to do with the classification of marine resources as part of the overall public domain. This leaves little room for management methods and practices inspired by local norms. However, it is also due to the

[20] ibid Préambule (authors' translation).

[21] See Oona Le Meur, 'Customary Law and Custom in New Caledonia: Legal Pluralism, Citizenship and the External/Internal Sovereignty Issue' (2015) 2 *SOAS Law Journal* 230.

[22] Accords de Matignon-Oudinot (n 18).

[23] See Régis Lafargue, *Le droit coutumier en Nouvelle Calédonie* (Maison de la Nouvelle-Calédonie, 2012).

[24] This is being carried out by the Rural Development and Land Management Board (ADRAF).

lack of recognition and understanding of the profound connections that exist between land and marine resources in the Kanaks' traditions and customs.[25] This has led to a general lack of recognition of customary rights over marine resources, or at least less recognition than that accorded to customary rights to land.[26]

The Nouméa Accord is operationalised by an organic law (fundamental law) adopted in 1999, which provides more specific guidance regarding the management of marine resources.[27] The law notably organises the decentralisation of powers between different institutions, including the government of New Caledonia and three provinces (South, Loyalty Islands and North).

The Government of New Caledonia has the right to legislate in matters of the public domain, while the provinces have the power to regulate the exercise of the rights of management and conservation of natural resources. As a general principle, the public domain is governed by the principle of equality of users. Hence, maritime and coastal areas are often under the public domain of France, despite traditional Kanak resource use and ancestral cultural connections in these areas.[28] Regarding exploration rights, exploitation and the management and conservation of natural resources, the Government of New Caledonia has rights over the EEZ, whereas the provinces regulate and exercise the rights to explore, exploit, manage and conserve the biological and non-living natural resources of inland waters, including those of bays and lagoons, their soil and subsoil, and ground, subsoil and adjacent waters of the Territorial Sea.[29] There is some space for the eventual recognition of customary rights, as the provinces, after consultation with the customary council concerned, can make the special arrangements necessary to take customary practices into account. Several MPAs have been implemented to formalise customary rules over a sacred place or customary reserves.[30]

[25] See Isabelle Leblic, *Vivre de la mer, vivre avec la terre … en pays kanak. Savoirs et techniques des pêcheurs kanak du sud de la Nouvelle-Calédonie* (Société des Océanistes, 2008).

[26] Pierre-Yves Le Meur et al, *Les enjeux de la gouvernance locale des ressources marines en Nouvelle-Calédonie: contribution à la réflexion sur le 'foncier maritime' à partir de deux études de cas* (Bruylant, 2012) 235.

[27] Loi organique n° 99-209 du 19 mars 1999.

[28] See Article 3 of la Loi du Pays of 11 January 2002 on the public maritime domain of New Caledonia and the provinces, which states that 'pedestrian access to shores and beaches is free unless justified by reasons of security, defence protection of the environment or respecting customary uses of enjoyment require special provisions. Free and free use by the public is the fundamental destination of shorelines and beaches as well as their allocation to fishing and marine farming activities' (translation by the authors). However, in some cases, the public domain status has been suspended on the request of the customary authorities.

[29] Loi organique (n 27) arts 45–46.

[30] See Marlène Dégremont, 'Services écosystémiques et Enjeux de Gouvernance à Hienghène' (2015) Final Report, Best Corail Programme; Samuel Cornier and Isabelle Leblic, 'Kanak Coastal Communities and Fisheries Meeting New Governance Challenges and Marine Issues in New Caledonia' in Elodie Fache and Simonne Pauwels (eds), *Fisheries in the Pacific: The Challenges of Governance and Sustainability* (Pacific-credo Publications, 2018) 119.

The three provinces are also responsible for their own environmental laws and policies. This results in differentiated environmental policies between the provinces, as evidenced by the adoption of an Environmental Code by the North Province in 2008 and the South Province in 2009. Significantly, the environmental code of the North Province specifically mentions the relationship between marine resources and the Kanaks. It states:

> The spaces, resources and natural environments, sites and landscapes, animal and plant species, indigenous, diversity and the biological balances in which they participate are part of the common heritage. Kanak identity, in particular, is based on a specific link to land and sea.[31]

This represents one of the most direct legal recognitions of the Kanaks' connections to marine resources. However, as noted by David, this has not led to any meaningful integration of specific rights or customary practices regarding resources for the Kanaks.[32] The only potential connection relates to the requirement to conduct a cultural survey, including Kanak oral heritage, when undertaking development of customary territories.[33] In 2016, the Loyalty Islands Province adopted its Environmental Code following a three-year participatory process that included consulting with the customary authorities as well as the local population. However, the focus of that Code is mainly on the relationship between protected natural areas and customary areas with little indications of the potential role and place of the Kanaks' customary marine resources and cultural connection to the sea.[34]

One of the complexities of the overall legal framework governing marine resources lies in the extreme diversity of situations between the different provinces and islands, with areas of high density, areas impacted by mining exploitation and areas inhabited mainly by Kanak populations. This extreme diversity results in the overlapping of several customary institutions since all of these institutions oversee the use of marine resources. This overlap and the multiplying number of institutions and norms has led to a confused overall framework governing marine resources, usually with a lack of proper understanding and integration of customary practices. Overall, what becomes evident is that the different levels of regulation of marine resources form complex layers of norms (public domain, protected areas, environmental, fishing, extraction)

[31] Authors' translation: Code de l'environnement de la province Nord (JONC 29 décembre 2008) art 110-2: 'Les espaces, ressources et milieux naturels, les sites et paysages, les espèces animales et végétales, autochtones, la diversité et les équilibres biologiques auxquels ils participent font partie du patrimoine commun. L'identité Kanak, en particulier, est fondée sur un lien spécifique à la terre et à la mer.'

[32] Victor David, 'La lente consécration de la nature, sujet de droit' (2012) 37 *Revue juridique de l'environnement* 469.

[33] See arts 220–23 of the Environmental Code.

[34] For analysis, see Victor David, 'Le Métissage de la Norme par la Co-construction du Droit : L'exemple du Code de L'environnement de la Province des Iles Loyauté' (2017) 30 *Revue Juridique Politique, Économique de Nouvelle-Calédonie* 102.

and institutions (government, provinces, customary authorities), which usually ignore the more traditional and customary marine uses and traditions.[35] Indeed, the UN Committee on the Elimination of Racial Discrimination (CERD) has observed that the government needs to address the lack of clarity on fishing rights and access to marine resources.[36]

With this as background, we are now in a position to examine the establishment of the Natural Park of the Coral Sea.

## III. THE ESTABLISHMENT OF THE NATURAL PARK OF THE CORAL SEA

The 'Parc Naturel de la Mer de Corail' was designated an MPA in 2014. At the time, the park was the largest protected area anywhere in the world,[37] making an important contribution to meeting France's conservation objectives under the Aichi Targets.[38] The park's establishment was facilitated by the far from restrictive status of a marine natural park, which allows the delegation of competence for the administration of the park and the adoption of rules restricting the use of the marine environment to the New Caledonian government.[39] This marked the culmination of a process, which started in 2012, supported by the French MPA Agency and the Pew Charitable Trust. The stated objectives of the park are to protect the marine environment, to maintain ecosystem services benefiting human kind and to contribute to the sustainable development of marine activities within the park's perimeters.[40] Three principal underlying purposes justify the creation of the park: to place the human factor at the heart of the park's priorities, to make New Caledonia a driver of regional dynamics for sustainable development and to create the conditions for sustainable development.[41] From the outset, it was established that these objectives would be further specified by the representatives of the

[35] On the lack of integration of the Kanaks norms on marine resources by the formal legal system, see Marie-Hélène Teulières-Preston, 'Le droit maritime kanak et ses transformations Ethnologie, linguistique, archéologie, histoire de la Nouvelle Calédonie' in Alban Bensa and Isabelle Leblic (eds), *En Pays Kanak: Ethnologie, linguistique, archéologie, histoire de la Nouvelle Calédonie* (Maison des sciences de l'homme, 2000).

[36] Committee on the Elimination of Racial Discrimination: concluding observations on the combined twentieth and twenty-first periodic reports of France (June 2015) UN Doc CERD/C/FRA/CO/20-21 [13].

[37] Since 2014, three larger-scale MPAs have been adopted, namely Marae Moana in the Cook Islands, Ross Sea in Antarctica and Papahānaumokuākea Marine National Monument in Hawaii.

[38] The park's creation increases significantly the surface of the French MPAs – 16 per cent of waters under French jurisdiction are now under MPA status, as opposed to four per cent before.

[39] OECD, *OECD Environmental Performance Reviews: France 2016* (OECD Publishing, 2016) 233.

[40] Decree of adoption (n 1).

[41] Government of New Caledonia, 'Le Parc Naturel de La Mer de Corail' (2014), 64, https://mer-de-corail.gouv.nc/sites/default/files/atoms/files/livret_le_parc_naturel_de_la_mer_de_corail_.pdf.

management committee appointed in 2015 to supervise the implementation of the park for the next five years.[42] It was also decided that the committee would have three years to build a management plan for the new park that would divide it into different zones based on the kinds of activities and levels of protection that are allowed in each zone.

In 2017, the management committee, co-presided over by the High Commissioner of the Republic (representing the French government) and the President of New Caledonia and including Kanak presidents from the different customary clans as well as researchers and members of the civil society, adopted the first strategic plan.[43] Among the 15 listed objectives, the plan mentions the need to protect the ecosystem, including both its natural and cultural heritage.[44] In accordance with its ecological objectives for conservation, the plan also notes the need to recognise sustainable and responsible use of the marine area.[45] This is implemented by objectives that guarantee responsible tourism and sustainable fisheries, and diminish the negative impact of maritime transport. Another objective is to prepare for future uses of the marine area, including the secondary goal of gaining a better understanding of the issues and risks associated with deep resource exploration before considering new prospecting or geological exploration in the area.[46] In order to ensure good governance of the area, the management plan indicates that the effectiveness of the park should be maintained and that the population should be able to participate in its management, notably via their inclusion in the monitoring mechanisms of the park.[47] Ultimately, the plan also indicates the objective of improving knowledge to guarantee the proper management of the park. It is indeed admitted that there is a lack of data in many fields, as well as insufficient financial resources, limitations that need to be addressed in order to meet the stated objectives.[48]

The park was established through a concerted process based on a strategic analysis and a multi-institutional committee, but its creation was also criticised. First, unlike the situation required by law in France (under the Environment Charter), in New Caledonia there was no legal requirement for a public inquiry and the proposal did not fall under the separate Environmental Codes of the three provinces of New Caledonia.[49] Control thus lay solely with the central New Caledonian government and it has been suggested that 'the project rapidly faced opposition from local actors and environmental organisations, calling into question the concerted approach on which the management process of the

[42] Decree of adoption (n 1).
[43] The park's management plan was approved by all committee members save one.
[44] Government of New Caledonia (n 4) 12.
[45] ibid.
[46] ibid 56.
[47] ibid 58.
[48] ibid 59.
[49] Cornier and Leblic (n 30) 155.

future Coral Sea Natural Park was supposed to be based'.[50] It would also appear that the decree establishing the park was not discussed with the Environment Consultative Committee, thereby denying local representatives the chance to raise concerns or express opposition.[51] Finally, the fact that no adequate public inquiry was initiated also raised suspicions about hidden economic stakes within the project, more particularly concerning the fact that deep-sea mining would be permitted.[52] Given New Caledonia's mining history, the identification of the Pacific region as geologically rich, and the collaboration between scientific research institutes and the New Caledonian Geological Service, the grounds for such suspicions are by no means unreasonable.

Local organisations and inhabitants were not the only ones to oppose the creation of the park or to criticise its establishment. The Vanuatu government also raised strong concerns about 'the unilateral decision' by the New Caledonia government to establish a natural park that includes the Matthew and Hunter Islands, south of Tafea Province, the sovereignty of which is still being disputed.[53] Whether the declaration of an MPA will cause this long-running sovereignty dispute to go to an international arbitration tribunal, as happened in the Chagos Archipelago/British Indian Ocean Territory MPA case,[54] remains to be seen.

Finally, it is also noteworthy that even three years after its creation, criticisms of the park have not disappeared. In particular, there is concern that the existing management plan stipulates general objectives that are devoid of strict regulation and therefore fails to specify how to effectively manage and protect the marine environment of the park in practice.[55] There is also the question of whether New Caledonia has the resources to police an MPA of this size in practice. The task is massive, not only due to the surface area of the park, but also to the sheer size and diversity of resources in the area, its economic importance and the diverse political interests and jurisdictional complexities marked more specifically by the different legal frameworks governing the territory and its customary areas.

Thus, a number of question marks hang over the park, and it is clear that much remains to be done to operationalise it in practice. Besides, there is still the possibility of a new national referendum on independence in 2020,

[50] ibid 154.

[51] ibid.

[52] ibid.

[53] Jonas Cullwick, 'Vanuatu Objects to Marine Natural Park Established by New Caledonia' *Vanuatu Daily Post* (4 May 2014).

[54] *Chagos Marine Protected Area Arbitration (Mauritius v United Kingdom) Final Award*, ICGJ 486 (PCA 2015).

[55] Interview with Christophe Chevillon, 'La Consultation Publique sur le Plan de Gestion du Parc Naturel de la Mer de Corail Fait Polémique – Nouvelle Calédonie la 1ère' (2017), https://la1ere.francetvinfo.fr/nouvellecaledonie/consultation-publique-plan-gestion-du-parc-naturel-mer-corail-fait-polemique-443759.html.

which may lead to questions as to the future governance and policy regarding the country's marine resources and EEZ should independence from France be the eventual outcome. The referendum outcome notwithstanding, given the range of users and interest groups competing with each other, the need for equity and fairness in facilitating use and access to the marine park calls for the specific recognition of the Kanak communities' interests.

## IV. MANAGEMENT OF THE NATURAL PARK OF THE CORAL SEA AND THE CUSTOMARY RIGHTS OF THE KANAK

Although the establishment of the Natural Park of the Coral Sea is largely intertwined with French national ambitions to improve the sustainable development of the Coral Sea, the importance of Kanak culture and their customary rights and interests at the local level are also recognised to some extent in the management plan of the park. First, the 2017–21 management plan highlights the importance of the Kanak culture by granting each Kanak representative from the eight customary areas of New Caledonia a seat on the management committee of the park. The Kanak customary representatives therefore constitute one of the four equally balanced pillars of the management committee which is also comprised by the groups representing the governmental institutions, socio-professional and civil society members. In addition, the plan notes that the park's management must be in compliance with the principle of good governance, which not only implies that decisions must be efficient, but also that they must 'satisfy criteria like participation, transparency, responsibility and even respect for practices and customs'.[56] In this regard, the management plan recognises the importance of customary law. This aspect is buttressed in other parts of the plan. For instance, the management plan recognises that the park 'must also tailor its management to provincial regulations and customary rules',[57] thereby acknowledging once again the significance of Kanak customary legal systems. Furthermore, one of the objectives of the park is to include customary representatives in the decision-making process and to take local knowledge and expertise about species and the marine area into account in order to operationalise coherent management of the park.[58] The importance of the ocean as an element of the Kanak culture is also recognised.[59] It is more specifically acknowledged that 'in Kanak culture, the sea is represented and appropriated in the same way as other natural systems (mountains, forests, rivers etc.)', which confirms the specific importance of the park for the Kanak people.[60]

[56] Government of New Caledonia (n 4) 56.
[57] ibid 60.
[58] ibid 108.
[59] ibid 32.
[60] ibid.

Existing research also supports the existence of a Kanak relationship with the marine area and resources located in the park.[61] Terrestrial elements include rocks, capes and caves that are named by the inhabitants and are therefore socially marked. As for marine areas and places, inhabitants have also named coral heads, reefs and islets with toponyms, which indicates a specific relationship with Kanak clans or tribes. Furthermore, certain marine areas, including sacred sites, specific fishing areas and marine cemeteries, are significant in the culture and economy of Kanak communities. There is, for instance, a 'traditional link between the islands and Entrecasteaux reefs and the Kanak population of Bélep'.[62] In addition, 'the people of the Pacific were present for an extended period in the past on Walpole'.[63] In fact, 'in spite of difficulties in precisely defining the maritime property and its limits, it is now recognised that some reefs and remote islands of the Coral Sea Natural Park have been used by the local Melanesian communities'.[64] Considered to be an integral part of the customary territorial organisation, the ocean therefore plays an important role in the social and political organisation of Kanak societies.

From a cultural perspective, the strong connection of the Kanak to the sea also relies on mythic and genealogic narratives passed down from generation to generation.[65] In this context, local knowledge related to coastal areas regarding fishing practices and customary rules is quite dense. The complex organisation of marine uses and activities follows a territorial organisation based on a continuum between land and sea. The customary exchanges of products from land and sea illustrate the inter-dependence between these two elements. For example, in Hienghène, a village on the north-east coast of the main island of New Caledonia, the 'clans of the sea' provide fish to the clans of the mountains, while the latter offer them yams and other tubers during customary exchanges. According to Kanak views, land and sea are also crossed by invisible pathways, which unite Kanak social groups. From a geographical perspective, the customary paths used by ancestors, navigators and symbolically followed by the ancestors' souls extend from the mountain ridge to the open ocean and connect islands in the wider Pacific area. Similar names, myths and languages connected with the sea and its environment are found in different parts of New Caledonia as well as in Vanuatu, Tonga, Wallis and Futuna, especially around reef barriers, channels and islets, where people have met and exchanged goods for centuries. In Ouvea, several toponyms refer to Uvea, one of the three realms of Wallis

[61] Marlène Dégremont, 'Étude de la dimension culturelle du Parc naturel de la mer de Corail' (2016) Institut de Recherche pour le Développement – Conservation International – Direction de l'Agriculture, de la Forêt et de l'Environnement. This anthropological research was conducted at the request of the management committee, in close collaboration with the customary authorities of New Caledonia.

[62] Government of New Caledonia (n 4) 32.

[63] ibid.

[64] ibid.

[65] These paragraphs draw on the analysis of Dégremont (n 61).

and Futuna. In Belep, according to one tribal chief, the name *Pooc* refers to a place located between two reefs, where boats usually cross and is also associated with an ancestor's name coming from Samoa. Through the narrative and social representations of the ocean, the coastal and pelagic areas carry strong cultural values, as they connect different groups of people and symbolise the meeting place between the human and invisible worlds. In this regard, the conservation of the sea is an important issue for local people. According to inhabitants along the north-east coast of New Caledonia, the ocean must be preserved since it hosts the ancestors' souls and has always been part of Kanak everyday life, as well as of all peoples in Oceania.

Yet, despite the existence of this natural and cultural heritage, many issues still need to be addressed to consolidate the customary relations of the Kanak people with the park. First, there is a knowledge gap concerning the natural and cultural heritage of the Kanak in relation to the park that still must be resolved. While existing research supports the existence of Kanak's cultural ties with the park, more research is needed to understand the extent of their heritage in this context. Second, the involvement of the Kanak with the management of the park will need to be strengthened in accordance with their customs. However, it is unclear whether the existing decision-making process is adequate. While the management structure supports a co-management model of governance with the inclusion of different stakeholders and a decision-making process based on consensus, this structure is rooted in a top-down managerial approach with a decision-making process that is also centralised in Nouméa. Ultimately, this may run the risk of undermining and complicating the participation of customary representatives scattered throughout the main island and the Loyalty Islands.

Finally, in spite of the strategic plan's references to the Kanak people's culture, territory and knowledge, most regulations concerning the management of the park are still in the making, and it remains unclear how those regulations will uphold Kanak interests and customary rights. For example, the goal is to establish strict reserves or nature reserves to protect the whole park's ecosystems,[66] yet the levels of protection of the different zones and how they will be used still need to be defined.[67] Since the park is a multiple-use MPA, certain areas may be open to economic activities while others may be considered no-take zones. In this regard, the new management framework and regulations have the potential to restrict local access to certain areas and to affect the use of resources, especially if exploration and exploitative activities on the seabed are allowed. However, no concrete zoning plan and regulation, or even guidelines, concerning the rights of Kanak communities have yet been defined. Nor has anything been specified about the way in which traditional Kanak knowledge will be included to support

[66] Decree of adoption (n 1) art 2.

[67] Except for the natural reserve that includes the Entrecasteaux reefs, which was classified as a World Heritage Site in 2008.

the implementation and monitoring mechanisms of the park. This regulatory gap is a significant issue that needs to be addressed in compliance with the customary interests and rights of the Kanak people. From this perspective, the international legal framework on the rights of Indigenous peoples constitutes a relevant tool for upholding these rights in the Coral Sea Park.

## V. THE RIGHTS OF INDIGENOUS PEOPLES AND THEIR APPLICATION IN THE CORAL SEA PARK

Kanak livelihoods are closely intertwined with land and sea. Yet, their customary relations to the sea, especially areas beyond territorial waters, are still inadequately recognised.[68] From a legal perspective, there are two main reasons that explain this situation. First, France's position on the recognition of minority and Indigenous rights is fairly weak. The lack of integration of Indigenous peoples' rights by the French authorities is not specific to New Caledonia, but is part of a larger rejection of any type of minority or specific groups' rights under the French legal system. This rejection extends to rights over natural resources.[69] At the international level, France is one of the few countries that have made a reservation to Article 27 of the ICCPR on the right of minorities to their own culture.[70] In addition, although the government supported the adoption of the United Nations Declaration on the Rights of Indigenous Peoples (UNDRIP) in 2007, it has yet to ratify ILO Convention 169 concerning Indigenous and Tribal Peoples in Independent Countries.[71] Second, under French law, the maritime and coastal areas are considered to be the public domain and the principle of state sovereignty does not provide space for recognition of the customary rights of Indigenous communities.[72] Historically, the position of France is the result of a strong republican legal tradition that puts great emphasis on the principle of equality before the law and the indivisibility of the French people, but also allows little room to recognise and accommodate the collective rights of minorities and Indigenous peoples.

This position has not gone without criticism. Several international human rights bodies have raised concerns about the lack of recognition of the rights of indigenous peoples in French overseas territories, including New Caledonia.

[68] Anaya (n 11) paras 32–34.

[69] See Jérémie Gilbert and David Keane, 'Equality versus fraternity? Rethinking France and its Minorities' (2016) 14 *International Journal of Constitutional Law* 883.

[70] When endorsing the ICCPR in 1980, France made the following reservation: 'In the light of article 2 of the Constitution of the French Republic, the French Government declares that article 27 is not applicable so far as the Republic is concerned': 999 UNTS 171, Declarations and Reservations, Chapter IV, 6, https://treaties.un.org/doc/Publication/MTDSG/Volume%20I/Chapter%20IV/IV-4.en.pdf.

[71] International Labour Organization, Indigenous and Tribal Peoples Convention, 1989 (No 169).

[72] Committee on the Rights of the Child, 'Concluding Observations of the Committee on the Rights of the Child: France' (2009) UN Doc CRC/C/FRA/CO/4 [101].

In 2015, the CERD expressed, for instance, its concern at 'the failure (of France) to fully recognize the existence of indigenous peoples in the overseas territorial collectivities' and 'fears that this may prevent the State party from adopting the most appropriate, targeted measures to respond to the specific needs and concerns of indigenous peoples'.[73] In relation to New Caledonia, the CERD also expressed its ongoing concerns regarding the situation of the Kanak people, noting that 'the land issues of concern to the Kanaks have not been entirely settled', 'the Kanaks are underrepresented in public administration', 'disparities in terms of enjoyment of economic, social and cultural rights persist' and, more importantly for the purposes of this study, 'access to fishing grounds and to the sea is impeded'.[74] With respect to the last issue, the CERD also recommended that France 'find definitive solutions for the remaining land issues in New Caledonia, including the issue of how to guarantee access to fishing grounds and to the sea'.[75] In addition to this criticism, the Special Rapporteur on the Rights of Indigenous Peoples also noted in a 2011 report on the situation of the Kanak people and their access to the sea 'a potential incompatibility between the State [of France] legal system, under which maritime and coastal areas are public domain, and traditional Kanak resource and land use in these areas'.[76] Together, these observations clearly underline the shortcoming of the French system in accommodating the rights of the Kanak people, particularly their rights to marine resources.

Although none of the human rights bodies provided clear specification about what type of solution could help to resolve the land issue and guarantee access to the sea, the corpus of human rights law and environmental law recognise that the rights of Indigenous peoples extend to protected areas.[77] Furthermore, while the recognition of Indigenous rights in relation to water and marine areas is more limited in comparison to rights attaching to land, it is also acknowledged that the rights of Indigenous peoples to their traditional territories and resources encompass rights over their waters and coastal seas.[78] This has been recognised by international instruments focusing on the rights of Indigenous peoples, such as ILO Convention 169 or the UNDRIP,[79]

[73] CERD, 'Concluding Observations on the Combined Twentieth and Twenty-First Periodic Reports of France' (2015) UN Doc CERD/C/FRA/CO/20-21 [11].

[74] ibid [12].

[75] ibid.

[76] Anaya (n 11) [33].

[77] For instance, the 'IUCN has recognized the importance of human rights instruments and processes in a number of resolutions and other policy initiatives, particularly in relation to indigenous peoples. Without binding legal effect for IUCN members, this provides however, a body of policy particularly relevant for the CBD discussions, the reform of protected area policies and the wider conservation community'. Peter Bille Larsen, *Reconciling Indigenous Peoples and Protected Areas: Rights, Governance and Equitable Cost and Benefit Sharing* (IUCN, 2006) 19.

[78] See Enyew (ch 2 in this volume).

[79] See in particular ILO Convention 169, art 23; and United Nations Declaration on the Rights of Indigenous Peoples, Resolution 61/295, 2007, arts 25 and 32.

as well as human rights jurisprudence.[80] The application and importance of active, ecologically sustainable participation of local, traditional and Indigenous peoples has also been recognised within the context of marine protected areas by several international instruments.[81] Despite the park's location in the EEZ at some distance from the coastlines, there can be no doubt that the existence of a relationship between the Kanak people and areas within the park justifies the application of the rights of Indigenous peoples to the management of the park.

In this context, it is important to highlight the significance of the rights of Indigenous peoples to participate in the development of subsoil resources. While the rights of Indigenous peoples include the right to own, control and use their traditional lands and resources,[82] international law also recognises their right to participate in the development of resources, including subsoil mineral and oil and gas deposits. This right directly stems from Article 15 of ILO Convention 169 and Article 32 of the UNDRIP, which specifically reference the duty of the state to consult in good faith with the Indigenous peoples concerned prior to the approval of any project affecting their lands or territories and other resources, particularly in connection with the development, utilisation or exploitation of mineral, water or other resources.[83] Although Article 32 does not single out marine areas, the fact that it recognises that subsoil activities have the potential to significantly impact Indigenous peoples' lands, territories and natural resources gives rise, reciprocally, to the duty of the state to consult with Indigenous communities in the development of activities affecting them at sea. Considering the potential for deep-sea oil and mining resources exploitation, which could also affect the integrity of nature and ecosystem services in the Coral Sea, the need to secure and enforce the rights of Kanak communities in the management and potential development of resources located in the park should therefore be seriously taken into account.

Importantly, when viewed through the lens of human rights law, the rights of the Kanak people are also not limited to mere consultation in the development of resources affecting their traditional lands and resources. The right to free, prior and informed consent (FPIC), as outlined in Articles 18 and 32 of the UNDRIP and in various other international instruments and jurisprudence, requires the state to obtain Indigenous peoples' informed consent prior to approving any project affecting their traditional lands and territories. This would include projects in the park which are likely to affect the rights of the

[80] See, for instance, HRC, *Apirana Mahuika et al v New Zealand*, Communication No 547/1993 (2000) UN Doc CCPR/C/70/D/547/1993.

[81] See, for instance, OSPAR Recommendation 2003/3 on a Network of Marine Protected Areas, s 3. See also Annex I.B. Caribbean Protocol, arts 4 (2) and 14; and Protocol Concerning Protected Areas of Wild Fauna and Flora in the Eastern African Region. For an analysis of these instruments, see Alexander Gillespie, *Conservation, Biodiversity and International Law* (Edward Elgar, 2013) 171–73.

[82] See, for instance, UNDRIP, article 26; ILO Convention 169, art 14.

[83] UNDRIP, art 32.

Kanak.[84] Furthermore, even if consent is not strictly required, it is established that in all instances of proposed projects that might affect Indigenous peoples, consultations with them should take place and consent should at least be sought,[85] and an emerging international human rights jurisprudence recognises that where large-scale projects significantly affect the livelihoods of Indigenous communities, consent must not only be sought but is also required.[86] Thus, the application of the duty to consult with Indigenous peoples based on the principle of FPIC will vary in accordance with the significance of the relevant project.[87]

Finally, another important element of the international legal framework that could be significant in New Caledonia relates to the principle of benefit-sharing, an element currently missing in the management of the park. The principle of fair and equitable benefit-sharing has primarily emerged within the sphere of international environmental law and more specifically within the field of biodiversity law.[88] The increased connection between the use of biological resources and benefit-sharing has also paved the way for the emergence of a human rights-based approach to benefit-sharing.[89] The recognition of a right to benefit-sharing over marine resources, including deep seabed minerals, for Indigenous peoples could have significant impact on the future management of the park in New Caledonia. So far, there has yet to be any engagement on the issue of future benefit-sharing in the management plans, and this is in spite of the general frustration raised by a number of Kanak chiefs and representatives 'over the absence of economic benefits to their people from the enormous nickel wealth being generated in the country'.[90] From this perspective, a better integration of international legal standards on Indigenous peoples' rights therefore appears to be relevant. These standards could also more specifically support the integration of future plans for benefit-sharing agreements in the park in order to ensure that Indigenous communities directly benefit from the development of all types of exploitation, whether from mineral development, fishing or tourism.

[84] See ibid art 19; ILO Convention 169, art 6(2).

[85] Report of the Special Rapporteur on the Rights of Indigenous Peoples, James Anaya, 'Extractive Industries and Indigenous Peoples', UN Doc A/HRC/24/41 9.

[86] Inter-American Court of Human Rights, *Saramaka People v Suriname*, judgment of 28 November 2007 [129]–[137]; HRC, Communication No 1457/2006, *Poma v Peru*, 27 March 2009 [7.5], [7.7].

[87] James Anaya, 'Indigenous Peoples' Participatory Rights in Relation to Decisions about Natural Resource Extraction: The More Fundamental Issue of What Rights Indigenous Peoples Have in Lands and Resources' (2005) 22 *Arizona Journal of International and Comparative Law* 16.

[88] The Convention on Biological Diversity requires states parties to ensure 'the equitable sharing of the benefits' that arise as a result of the utilisation of indigenous and local communities' traditional knowledge (art 8(j)): Convention on Biological Diversity (adopted 5 June 1992, entered into force 29 December 1993) 1760 UNTS 69. See also the Nagoya Protocol on Access to Genetic Resources and the Fair and Equitable Sharing of Benefits Arising from Their Utilization (29 October 2010) UNEP/CBD/COP/DEC/X/1.

[89] See Jérémie Gilbert, *Natural Resources and Human Rights: An Appraisal* (Oxford University Press, 2018).

[90] Anaya (n 11) [38].

## VI. PERSPECTIVES ON SOVEREIGNTY

While the strong cultural ties between the Kanak people and the park are recognised, and legitimately give rise to the recognition of their participatory rights in the management of the park, a more controversial question concerns the recognition of the rights of other indigenous communities, more particularly those of the Vanuatu people. As mentioned above, sovereignty over the Matthew and Hunter Islands, both of which are located within the park, is currently contested.[91] Both Vanuatu and France lay claim to the remote volcanic islands, which lie to Vanuatu's south and to the east of the French territory of New Caledonia.[92] Although the islets themselves would not seem to represent much in the form of resources, rights to the waters around them could offer significant potential wealth in marine resources, including fishing spots, rare earth minerals and oil deposits. As a result, there are important economic factors at stake in the affirmation of traditional and customary ties with the two small islands.

The inclusion of the two islands within the Coral Sea Park led to its rejection by the Government of Vanuatu. According to Edward Natapei, Vanuatu's former Prime Minister, the creation of the park 'does not promote respect for Vanuatu's national sovereignty and its traditional heritage and cultural rights, which is deeply revered by the Indigenous people of Vanuatu and the Kanak people of New Caledonia'. The Matthew and Hunter Islands are indeed places that have been used since ancient times by the inhabitants of Anatom, the southern island of the archipelago, and bear the Ni-Vanuatu names of Leka and Unmaenupne.[93] In Ni-Vanuatu tradition, Matthew Island is also called the House of the Gods, the place where the spirits of the dead go to rest, and oral customs speak of the Ni-Vanuatu travelling regularly from the islands of the Vanuatu archipelago to the Hunter and Matthew Islands.

In 2009, Victor Tutugoro, a representative of the Kanak people and the Socialist National Liberation Front, secured the agreement of the New Caledonian Senate to recognise Vanuatu's sovereignty over the island while adopting the Kéamu Declaration.[94] In the Kéamu Declaration, it was also agreed together with the Melanesian Spearhead Group, a Melanesian organisation composed

[91] The islands were successively in the possession of France (1929) and Britain (1965). Given that the Matthew and Hunter Islands lie in the New Hebrides island arc, the British government requested that the islands be attached to the New Hebrides, but France contested this and claimed sovereignty over them in 1975. To assert its sovereignty, France set up infrastructure on the islands. Soon after attaining independence, Vanuatu claimed the islands as a part of Vanuatu territory on both geological and historical grounds. See also Denise Fisher, *France in the South Pacific: Power and Politics* (ANU E Press 2013) 145.

[92] France applied for an extended continental shelf in the area. Vanuatu's Prime Minister objected to this submission before the UN, but France keeps undertaking activities (mostly scientific) on and around the islands to maintain its sovereignty; Fisher (n 91).

[93] Gilbert David, 'Le Vanuatu côté océan : La révolution bleue et les premières années de l'indépendance' (2011) 133 *Le Journal de la Société des Océanistes* 353.

[94] Fisher (n 91) 146.

of Fiji, Papua New Guinea, the Solomon Islands and New Caledonia, that the islands must be 'given back' to Vanuatu, a position evidently rejected by the French government of New Caledonia.[95] This declaration, which highlighted the strengthening of a customary alliance between the traditional representatives of the Malvatumauri of Vanuatu and the New Caledonia's Customary Senate, was based on the fact that more traditional and cultural ties exist between the Vanuatu people and the islands than the Kanak Vanuatu people. As such, the customary authorities of New Caledonia contest France's sovereignty rights over these two islands, while instead highlighting the importance of customary rights in the area.

The historical ties of the Vanuatu people with the islands raises the question of the need to accommodate their rights and interests in the park. This question is particularly timely considering the recent China Sea Award that recognises the traditional foreign fishing rights of artisanal fishermen within territorial seas.[96] However, the reasoning in the Award may not affect the recognition of Vanuatu's customary rights in the Coral Sea since the Award applies to traditional fishing rights in the territorial sea, as opposed to the EEZ.[97] New Caledonia's exclusive rights necessary for the exploration and exploitation of resources as well as other activities for the economic exploitation and exploration of the zone should therefore remain unburdened by these historic rights. As a result, without any legal recognition, the Matthew and Hunter area remains a 'grey zone' where conflicts of governance still exist.[98] To resolve this issue, some members of the management committee of the park advocate the establishment of a 'peace Park' to support a co-management area.[99] While it is still uncertain whether such a proposal will be accepted, it could constitute an effective way to resolve the sovereignty issue, while guaranteeing the cultural, ecological and economic interests of the different parties involved. This proposal is also in compliance with the rights of Indigenous peoples to maintain and strengthen their distinctive spiritual relationship with the coastal sea and their right to participate in the development of resources located within their traditional territories.[100] Behind sovereignty issues, the rights of indigenous peoples therefore appear once again to be a necessary factor to take into account, formalising the effective management of the Coral Sea Park.

[95] Paul Giacobbi, Didier Quentin and commission des affaires étrangères, *Rapport d'information sur la diplomatie et la défense des frontières maritimes de la France : Nos frontières maritimes : pour un projet politique à la hauteur des enjeux* (Assemblée nationale, 2016) 117.

[96] *South China Sea Arbitration (Philippines v China) Award* PCA Case No 2013-19, ICGJ 495 (PCA 2016). See also Allen (ch 4 in this volume).

[97] *South China Sea Arbitration (Philippines v China) Award* (n 96)[407].

[98] See in particular the 2004 and 2013 incidents concerning the seizure by the French Navy of Chinese fishing boats in the Matthew and Hunter area.

[99] Information based on the analysis of Marlène Dégremont established during the internal meetings of the management committee of the Natural Park of the Coral Sea.

[100] See in particular UNDRIP, arts 25 and 32.

## VII. CONCLUSION

In 2014, New Caledonia strengthened protections of the Coral Sea with the establishment of a multiple-use MPA covering New Caledonia's entire EEZ. The creation of this park represents a unique opportunity to protect the exceptional biodiversity of New Caledonia's maritime space, while also allowing for sustainable and responsible economic development. This chapter has examined whether the creation of the park has allowed for the recognition and protection of the customary rights of the Kanak people. As the Indigenous people of New Caledonia, the Kanak people have historical and cultural ties to the marine environment. Yet, the protection of Kanak interests and rights in the management of the park needs to be reinforced. It is first suggested that more research is needed in order to understand the nature and extent of Kanak's relationship with the park. As stated in the management plan, 'knowledge of this heritage is a first step towards recognising the important place the marine environment occupies in the organisation of Kanak society'.[101] Second, there is still an important regulatory gap that needs to be filled. As indicated in this analysis, despite the recognition of Kanak customary ties with the park, no clear regulations have yet been adopted for the protection of Kanak interests and rights in the management of the park. The recognition and protection of the customary rights of the Kanak people must be consolidated in the regulatory framework of the park.

This analysis has also argued that the application of the rights of indigenous peoples constitutes a relevant and important tool for securing the rights of the Kanak people in the management of the park. Although New Caledonia is advancing in a process that falls within the UN decolonisation regime, the Kanak people also benefit from the specific protections of the rights of Indigenous peoples as recognised under the UNDRIP[102] and various other instruments. The relevance of this corpus of law continues to grow at the international level and constitutes an important element to guide the future management of the park on several issues. This concerns more specifically the protections of the rights of the Kanak people to the marine environment in the park and their right to participate in the management of its resources, including the potential exploration and exploitation of mineral resources. Besides, the application of the rights of Indigenous peoples also appears relevant for protecting the interests and rights of other Indigenous communities, such as the Vanuatu people. By contrast, looking at management issues through the lens of sovereignty could exacerbate tensions and undermine local interests.

Irrespective of the results of the referendum on independence and sovereignty issues, the creation of the park provides important momentum in

[101] Government of New Caledonia (n 4) 50.
[102] Anaya (n 11) [14]–[15].

pushing the government, either in Nouméa or Paris, to enforce and respect the international legal framework protecting Indigenous peoples' rights over their natural resources. Although the management of the park is extremely complex due to a multi-layered mosaic of different levels of governance and the interweaving of various interests, the application of the rights of Indigenous peoples could make a significant contribution to ensuring that customary relations and rights are adequately recognised and protected in the management of the Natural Park of the Coral Seal. By linking the management of the park with the rights of Indigenous peoples, there is indeed a chance to achieve the protection of the natural and cultural heritage of the park, while affirming the history and identity of the park in its human and Indigenous dimensions. Implementing the rights of Indigenous peoples to manage the Natural Park of the Coral Sea would thus help to fulfil its objectives and also more generally ensure protection of the human rights of the Kanak people in New Caledonia.

# 9

# *Legal Protection of Coastal Sámi Culture and Livelihood in Norway*

ØYVIND RAVNA AND LINE KALAK

## I. INTRODUCTION

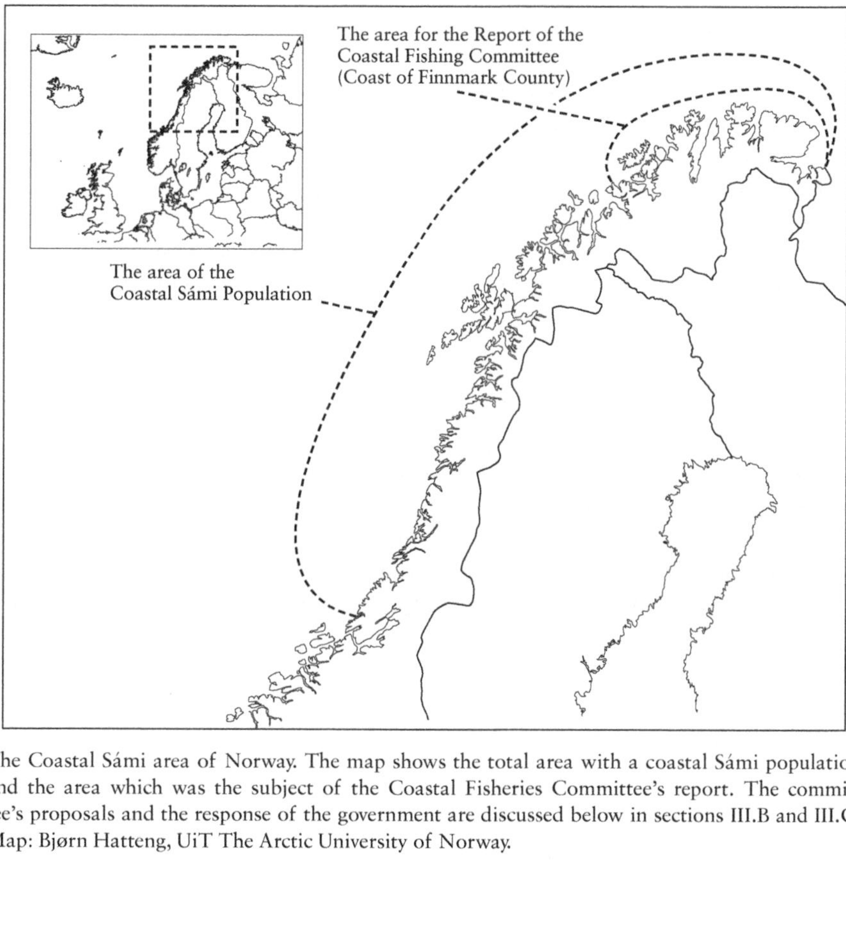


The Coastal Sámi area of Norway. The map shows the total area with a coastal Sámi population and the area which was the subject of the Coastal Fisheries Committee's report. The committee's proposals and the response of the government are discussed below in sections III.B and III.C. Map: Bjørn Hatteng, UiT The Arctic University of Norway.

## A. The Topic

The Sámi people constitute an Indigenous minority with their homelands in northern Scandinavia, including Finnish Lapland and the Kola Peninsula in the Russian Federation. They are mostly known as reindeer herders, who follow their herds over the cold, Nordic tundra. Nevertheless, the Sámi are also a coastal culture with salt-water fishing as an important part of their livelihood and subsistence. Sámi coastal fishing takes place in the fjords, along the coastline and on the coastal banks, as opposed to bank and ocean fishing, where the pelagic fishing fleet have the gear and supplies to stay out in the open ocean for long periods.

This chapter deals with the legal aspects of the coastal Sámi culture and livelihood, in other words Sámi rights in the fishery and for other marine resources. The coastal Sámi culture in Norway survives primarily along the coastline from Helgeland to the border of Russia (see map on page 213). Living together with the expanding Norwegian coastal communities, the coastal Sámi have long been subject to an assimilation policy that has meant that many of them have lost their language and particular cultural characteristics. The assimilation policy has also meant that their rights to natural resources are poorly safeguarded and consequently marginalised.

It is natural to address the issue of Sámi rights to coastal resources in Norway since Norway has the largest contingent of Sámi people, it is the only country with a living Sámi coastal culture, and it is the only country with a Sámi population that has ratified International Labour Organization (ILO) Convention 169.[1]

Norway is a constitutional monarchy with the King, in practice the government, as executive authority. It is also a unitary state. The Norwegian Parliament, the Storting, is the only legislative power.[2] However, Norway has established a Sámi Parliament. Its responsibilities include 'any matter that in the view of the [Sámi] parliament particularly affects the Sámi people'.[3]

Norway is considered a civil law country, but the case law of the Supreme Court is also of great importance. The Norwegian judicial system is therefore something between a civilian law system and the common law system. This chapter draws on the current, national legal protection of the Indigenous Sámi cultures, as well as international commitments endorsed by Norway. It then considers whether the Norwegian state complies with its commitment to protect the coastal Sámi culture in a legally acceptable way.

[1] ILO Convention No 169, Convention Concerning Indigenous and Tribal Peoples in Independent Countries, adopted 27 June 1989, entered into force 5 September 1991.

[2] Norwegian Constitution 1814, s 49.

[3] Lov 12 juni 1987 nr 56 om Sametinget og andre samiske rettsforhold (sameloven) (Sámi Act of 1987 No 56 Concerning the Sámi Parliament and Other Sámi Legal Matters (hereinafter the Sámi Act)) s 2-1. An English translation of the Act is available at: https://www.regjeringen.no/en/dokumenter/the-Sámi-act-/id449701.

Due to the long co-existence between Norwegians and Sámi along the coast of northern Norway, it is difficult to make distinct ethnic divisions between Sámi and non-Sámi fishermen. Furthermore, any effort to do so would create conflict. The Parliamentary Standing Committee of Justice emphasised in 2005 that any rights, and any corresponding obligations for the authorities, must be linked to geographically defined communities and not to persons or groups on an ethnic basis.[4] This has been the starting point for subsequent investigations and legislative proposals,[5] and is consequently also the starting point for this chapter.

## B. Background

The ocean trawler fleet (also known as the pelagic fishing fleet) began to make significant catches of coastal fishery stocks as early as the beginning of the 1900s, leading to disputes with coastal fishing communities. These disputes continued during the post-war years. By the last decades of the twentieth century, the Sámi Rights Committee, which was established in 1980, was mandated to investigate the conflicts as well as the protection of coastal fishing rights of the Sámi as part of the umbrella topic of 'the natural basis for Sámi culture'.[6]

The introduction of a new fishing regulation in 1990 caused the coastal Sámi to lose many of their rights established during more than 1,000 years of fishing. The new regulation was introduced in response to over-exploitation and created individual transferrable vessel quotas, but only a few fishermen in the Sámi areas obtained a quota.[7] With the transferrable vessel quota, the resources are in fact privatised.[8] This contributed to a perception of unfair distribution of access to the resource among the coastal people, making it more important for a Sámi Rights Committee investigation.

[4] Innst O nr 80 (2004–2005) *Innstilling fra justiskomiteen om lov om rettsforhold og forvaltning av grunn og naturressurser i Finnmark fylke (finnmarksloven)* (Bill from the Standing Parliamentary Committee of Justice Relating to Legal Relations and Management of Land and Natural Resources in the County of Finnmark), 30.

[5] NOU (Norwegian Public Report) 2008: 5 *Retten til fiske i havet utenfor Finnmark* (*The Right to Fish in the Sea off Finnmark*) 19 (the translation of quotations here and below is that of the authors).

[6] NOU 1997: 4 *Naturgrunnlaget for Samisk kultur* (*The Natural Basis for Sámi Culture*) s 5(6). The Sámi Rights Committee was established by the government in 1980 with a four-point mandate; see NOU 1984: 18 Om samenes rettsstilling (The Sámi Legal Position). The first two points were to examine: (1) 'the question about the Sámi people's legal position in relation to land and water'; and (2) to evaluate and suggest 'how to secure the Sámi population opportunities to utilize natural resources in their areas of habitation, while also recognizing the non-Sámi population's interests'.

[7] NOU 2008: 5 (n 5) 45, with further references to the report *Sametingets melding om fiske som næring og kultur i kyst- og fjordområdene* (*The Sámi Parliament's Report on Fishing as Livelihood and Culture in Coastal and Fjord Areas*) (2004). The expanding seal population in the 1980s was a significant cause of the low catch in many fjords and dramatically affected the coastal Sámi fishery.

[8] Susann Funderud Skogvang, 'Local Community Rights to Fish: A Sami Perspective' in Christina Allard and Susann Funderud Skogvang (eds), *Indigenous Rights in Scandinavia* (Juris Diversitas, 2015) 131.

In 1997, the Sámi Rights Committee proposed that the most appropriate way to facilitate Sámi coastal fishing in Finnmark was to provide administrative priorities including free fishing for vessels less than 10 metres in length (which would largely cover the coastal Sámi fishermen).[9] The Committee also proposed greater local participation in the management of the fisheries. These proposals contained in the original bill that later became the Finnmark Act of the Bondevik government of 2003 were rejected.[10] They thus became the subject of subsequent negotiations.

## II. PROTECTION OF SÁMI RIGHTS TO LAND AND WATERS IN NORWAY

### A. The Legal Bases for Protection of Sámi Culture in Norway

As an ethnic minority and an Indigenous people, the Sámi enjoy legal protection for their culture and way of life in both national and international law. The discourse on coastal Sámi rights and livelihood following the Coastal Fishery Committee's report in 2008 might lead to the conclusion that Norway is less willing to protect the coastal elements of Sámi culture than other parts of that culture, particularly the Sámi reindeer husbandry. Before examining the legal situation of the coastal Sámi further, it is beneficial to briefly consider the legal basis for protection of Sámi substantive culture and way of life in Norway more generally.

The legal bases for protection of Sámi culture stands on several foundations. First, there is the constitutional protection of Sámi Culture through Article 108 of the Constitution:

> It is the responsibility of the authorities of the State to create conditions enabling the Sámi people to preserve and develop its language, culture and way of life.

This protection is filled out by other pieces of national legislation, including the Sámi Act of 1987 (which established the Sámi Parliament in 1989 and states that the Sámi language is formally equal to Norwegian),[11] the Reindeer Husbandry Act[12] and the Finnmark Act.[13]

[9] NOU 2008: 5 (n 5) 40 and see also Innst O nr 80 (n 4) 30.

[10] Ot prp nr 53 (2002–2003) *Om lov om rettsforhold og forvaltning av grunn og naturressurser i Finnmark fylke* (Government Bill for the Finnmark Act) (*Relating to Legal Relations and Management of Land and Natural Resources in the County of Finnmark*).

[11] Sámi Act (n 3).

[12] Lov 15 juni 2007 nr 40 om reindrift (reindriftsloven) (Act of 15 June 2007 No 40 on Reindeer Husbandry (hereinafter the Reindeer Husbandry Act)) s 4, where it is stated that Sámi reindeer husbandry is based on immemorial usage.

[13] Lov 17 juni 2005 nr 85 om rettsforhold og forvaltning av grunn og naturressurser i Finnmark fylke (Finnmarksloven) (Act of 17 June 2005 No 85 Relating to Legal Relations and Management of Land and Natural Resources in the County of Finnmark (hereinafter the Finnmark Act)). An English translation of the Act of the Act is available at: http://www.ub.uio.no/ujur/ulovdata/lov-20050617-085-eng.pdf.

In addition, the legal protection of Sámi culture and way of life is clarified through case law. Furthermore, Sámi culture enjoys legal protection under the international human rights obligations that commit Norway, including the International Covenant on Civil and Political Rights (ICCPR),[14] ILO Convention 169[15] and the United Nations (UN) Declaration on the Rights of Indigenous Peoples.[16] The increased significance of international law affords Sámi customary law a foundation to protect the Sámi culture and way of life.

### B. National Legislation and Case Law

Among national law, the Finnmark Act of 2005 is of general interest. The Act is a land code for governing land in Finnmark and at the same time establishes a genuine process for identifying and recognising Sámi rights to land and on-shore land resources. The purpose of the Act, according to section 1, is to facilitate the management of land and natural resources in the county of Finnmark in a balanced and ecologically sustainable manner for the benefit of the residents of the county and particularly as a basis for Sámi culture, reindeer husbandry, the use of non-cultivated areas, commercial activity and social life. Section 3 states that the Act shall apply within the framework of ILO Convention 169.

The first paragraph of section 5 acknowledges that through prolonged use of land and water areas, the Sámi have collectively and individually acquired rights to land in Finnmark. This is an important principle and constitutes political recognition that such rights exist.[17] The majority of the Standing Committee of Justice also recognised that the identification of existing land rights must be included as a key element in the Finnmark Act and therefore proposed to establish 'a surveying commission and a judging tribunal to identify existing rights to land and water in Finnmark'.[18] This is reflected in Chapter 5 of the Act.

The question of the coastal Sámi rights to fishing was raised during the consultations on the Act, but there was a consensus to defer this subject to an independent investigation by an expert committee.[19] We will revert to that investigation, performed by the Coastal Fishing Committee, below. For the present, we mention that section 29 of the Finnmark Act was amended in

[14] International Covenant on Civil and Political Rights, by General Assembly Resolution 2200A (XXI) of 16 December 1966, entry into force 23 March 1976.

[15] ILO Convention No 169 (n 1).

[16] United Nations Declaration on the Rights of Indigenous Peoples, adopted by the General Assembly 13 September 2007 (UNDRIP).

[17] Innst O nr 80 (n 4) 15, 37.

[18] Innst O nr 80 (n 4) 17.

[19] ibid 30–31. See more about this in section III.A below.

2012 to allow claims to rights to fishing grounds to be heard by the Finnmark Commission.[20]

The Finnmark Act has been held up as an example of good practice and a response to Norway's ratification of ILO Convention 169. The former UN Special Rapporteur on the Rights of Indigenous Peoples, emphasising the Norwegian adoption of the Finnmark Act in 2005 as a kind of best practice, stated that the Act 'offers important protections for the advancement of Sámi rights to self-determination and control over natural resources at the local level, setting an important example for the other Nordic countries'.[21]

Today, 13 years after its adoption, it can be said that the Finnmark Act has not delivered what many Sámi expected. The mapping of rights to land and waters has, after 10 years of investigation, not led to the recognition of any Sámi collectively owned land areas, and the new landowner, the Finnmark Estate (FeFo), largely governs the land in the same way as the previous State Forest Company did. Recently, the Supreme Court of Norway, in the *Nesseby* case, has ruled that the residents of a Sámi settlement do not have the right to manage their own outlying field resources. In the 2016 country report for the Sápmi Region, the current UN Special Rapporteur of the Human Rights of Indigenous Peoples was critical of the process of identifying and recognising Indigenous peoples' land and resource rights in Finnmark.[22]

Case law establishes an independent legal basis for Sámi land rights. In the preparatory work of the Finnmark Act, the majority of the Standing Committee of Justice emphasised the importance of case law on historical use or immemorial usage, stating that:

> Assessment of evidence in the recent case law has been satisfactory. Modern Norwegian case law, particularly the Selbu and Svartskog cases, have given instruction on how traditional Sámi use shall be considered as a basis for acquisition. These will be important sources of law for the Commission and Court.[23]

In these cases, the Supreme Court considered rules on immemorial usage in light of Sámi traditional uses of the landscape, including reindeer husbandry and

[20] Prop 70 L (2011–2012) Endringar i deltakerloven, havressurslova og finnmarksloven (kystfiskeutvalet) (Changes in the Participation Act, the Marine Resources Act and the Finnmark Act (Coastal Fishing Committee)), (a parliamentary bill) 115, 125. Skogvang (n 8) 128.

[21] Human Rights Council, 'The Situation of the Sámi People in the Sápmi Region of Norway, Sweden and Finland' (2011) [44], http://unsr.jamesanaya.org/docs/countries/2011-report-sapmi-a-hrc-18-35-add2_en.pdf. The UN Special Rapporteur (at [14]–[20]) highlighted Norway's compliance with its obligations to protect Sámi culture and way of life arising from constitutional and international law, also noting that Norway was the first country to ratify ILO Convention 169.

[22] Human Rights Council, 'Report of the Special Rapporteur on the Rights of Indigenous Peoples on the Human Rights Situation of the Sami People in the Sápmi Region of Norway, Sweden and Finland' (2016), https://documents-dds-ny.un.org/doc/UNDOC/GEN/G16/175/50/PDF/G1617550.pdf?OpenElement.

[23] Innst O nr 80 (n 4) 36. The *Selbu* and *Svartskog* cases are published in Norsk Retstidende (NRt) 2001,759 and Rt 2001, 1229, respectively. NRt is a Norwegian court record, publishing Supreme Court judgments.

harvesting of outfields. The most important norms of these cases are that the court emphasised the significance of Sámi cultural features and particular ways of using the land when applying the rules of immemorial usage.[24]

## C. International Human Rights Commitments

Enyew's chapter in this volume canvasses the main international instruments with relevance for the rights Indigenous peoples including the ICCPR and ILO Convention 169. The ICCPR came into effect as Norwegian law in 1999 with the adoption of the Human Rights Act. This Act incorporated the ICCPR with precedence. However, up to this point, it seems that the domestic recognition of these instruments has had a broader impact politically than judicially.

As Enyew shows, the decisions of the Human Rights Committee on Article 27 along with General Comment No 23 make it clear that states must take positive measures in support of minority language and culture, including the material basis of the minority culture.[25] In relation to the Sámi, this means that Sámi use of lands and access to pastures, waters and other natural resources that can be considered as cultural expressions or constitute a material basis for Sámi culture and can enjoy legal protection. Although Article 27 does not compel the recognition of property rights over land and resources, the Human Rights Committee interprets it 'as obliging states to recognize and respect the sense of identity that Indigenous peoples feel in connection with their traditional lands'.[26] The Norwegian government recognises all of this, endorsing a statement of the Ministry of Labour and Social Inclusion to the effect that Article 27 'includes the substantive bases for the Sámi total cultural practices, also referred to as a natural basis for Sámi culture'.[27]

Case law from the Human Rights Committee also confirms that modern ways of exercising traditional culture-related industries, such as fishing with modern gear, are protected under Article 27 of the ICCPR.[28] As noted by Carsten Smith, the former Chief Justice of the Norwegian Supreme Court and head of

[24] In addition, the case law places greater emphasis on oral sources in cases where the Sámi people are parties, since the Sámi culture is based upon traditions passed down orally through generations; see (NRt) 2001, 769, 792–93.

[25] *Ivan Kitok v Sweden*, Comm No 197/1985, views adopted 27 July 1988; *The Lubicon Lake Band v Canada*, Comm No 167/1984, views adopted 26 March 1990; *Ilmari Länsman et al v Finland*, Comm No 511/1992, views adopted 26 October 1994; and *Jouni E. Länsman et al v Finland*, Comm No 671/1995, views adopted 30 October 1996; Report of the Human Rights Committee, vol 1, General Assembly Official Records, 49th Session, Supplement No 40 (A/49/40). General Comment No. 23, adopted on 50th Session, 8 April 1994 [6.2].

[26] Ghislain Otis and Aurélie Laurent, 'Indigenous Land Claims in Europe: The European Court of Human Rights and the Decolonization of Property' (2013) 4 *Arctic Review on Law and Politics* 156, 164.

[27] St meld nr 28 (2007–2008) *Samepolitikken* (White Paper on the Governmental Sámi Policy, a Recommendation from the Ministry of Labor and Social Inclusion) 33.

[28] *Apirana Mahuika et al v New Zealand*, Comm No 547/1993, views adopted 27 October 2000.

the Coastal Fishing Committee, in his ironic reply to the Attorney-General's submission to the report (NOU 2008: 5) of the Coastal Fishing Committee,[29] it cannot be required that the coastal Sámi shall continue to use oars and sails to enjoy legal protection for their coastal fishing.

ILO Convention 169 is of particular importance in Norway.[30] Notable here are the rights of Indigenous peoples to be consulted in Article 6, the right to decide their own priorities and to participate in Article 7, and the protection of Indigenous customs and customary law in Article 8. However, Article 14 is most significant with respect to Indigenous traditional lands.[31] Article 14(1) reads as follows:

> The rights of ownership and possession of the peoples concerned over the lands which they traditionally occupy shall be recognised. In addition, measures shall be taken in appropriate cases to safeguard the right of the peoples concerned to use lands not exclusively occupied by them, but to which they have traditionally had access for their subsistence and traditional activities. Particular attention shall be paid to the situation of nomadic peoples and shifting cultivators in this respect.

Despite its unambiguous wording, there has been some discussion as to whether Article 14 requires states to recognise ownership rights of Indigenous peoples to traditional lands.[32] Among scholars, the better view is that the language is clear and that Indigenous communities have rights to collectively own and use their traditional lands.[33]

Although Article 15 has not received the same attention as Article 14, it is no less important for safeguarding natural resources, particularly when planning and establishing extractive industries within Indigenous traditional lands. Article 15(1) states that the rights of Indigenous peoples to the natural resources pertaining to their lands shall be specially safeguarded and that these rights include the right to participate in the use, management and conservation of these resources.[34]

Article 15(2) highlights the duty of the government to consult Indigenous peoples when planning extraction of mineral or sub-surface resources or 'rights

[29] Carsten Smith, 'Retten til fiske i havet utenfor Finnmark' (2010) 1 *Arctic Review on Law and Politics* 4, 22.

[30] ILO Convention 169 (n 1).

[31] NOU 1993: 34 *Rett og forvaltning av land og vann i Finnmark* (*Rights and Management of Land and Water in Finnmark*), 70.

[32] Geir Ulfstein, 'Indigenous Peoples Right to Land' (2004) *Max Planck Yearbook of United Nations Law* 8, 21–23. See also NOU 1993: 34, 70–72; and NOU 1997: 5 *Urfolks landrettigheter etter folkerett og utenlands rett* (*Land Rights of Indigenous Peoples by International Law and Foreign National Law*), 33–37.

[33] James Anaya, *Indigenous Peoples in International Law*, 2nd edn (Oxford University Press, 2004) 143; Mathias Åhren, *Indigenous Peoples' Status in the International Legal System* (Oxford University Press, 2015) 174.

[34] And it is worth emphasising that art 13(2) of the Convention provides that the term 'lands', as used in arts 15 and 16, includes 'territories', which refers in turn to the total environment that the people occupy or use. For further discussion, see Enyew (ch 2 in this volume).

to other resources pertaining to lands' over which the state retains ownership. Both for mineral and renewable recourses, this is the case in Norway.[35] In addition, it ensures a benefit-sharing commitment, stating that Indigenous peoples 'shall wherever possible participate in the benefits of such activities'. This extends beyond the obligation to compensate economically for damage to the lands, which is ensured in the following sentence, stating that Indigenous peoples 'shall receive fair compensation for any damages which they may sustain as a result of such activities'.[36]

Although the UN Declaration on the Rights of Indigenous Peoples of 2007 is not a binding treaty,[37] it is an important instrument in protecting Indigenous peoples' rights to land and waters principally, as many of its provisions can be regarded as international customary law. This was emphasised by the Norwegian Supreme Court in the *Nesseby* case, where the Court observed that the declaration 'reflects international law principles in the area [of Indigenous Peoples' law] and has received support from many states'.[38]

For Norway, the endorsement carries particular obligations since Norway had worked actively in order to get the declaration adopted by the UN.[39] The Stoltenberg government pointed out that the Declaration, although not legally binding, will 'put important guidelines in further work to determine the rights of indigenous peoples'.[40] Enyew's chapter in this volume contains a detailed exposition of provisions of the Declaration that are particularly relevant to the use of marine resources by Indigenous communities.

## D. Sámi Customary law

Sámi law, or more precisely Sámi customary law, also provides a basis for Sámi land rights and a legal source to protect traditional Sámi livelihood. That said, there are few examples in the Supreme Court of Norway where the Court has applied Sámi customs where they conflict with Norwegian statutory law. However, in the *Selbu* and the *Svartskog* cases, the Supreme Court emphasised Sámi customs and traditional use of land.[41] Both Article 8 of

[35] See lov 19 June 2009 nr 101 om erverv og utvinning av mineralressurser (mineralloven) (the Mineral Act) s 7; lov 6 June 1975 nr 6 om utnytting av rettar og lunnende m.m. i statsallmenningane (fjellova) (the Mountain Act) s 1; Finnmark Act, s 6.

[36] When it comes to compensation for damages, loss and inconvenience as a result of state intervention, the Sámi like others are covered by s 105 of the Constitution, the Expropriation Act (23 October 1959 no 3) and Article 1 of Protocol 1 of the European Convention on Human Rights to receive full compensation for infringement. This is not discussed further here. The text of the Protocol is available at: https://www.echr.coe.int/Pages/home.aspx?p=basictexts&c.

[37] UNDRIP (n 16).

[38] HR-2018-456-P *Nesseby* (*Nesseby bygdelag v The Finnmark Estate*) [97].

[39] St meld nr 28 (n 27) 35.

[40] ibid 34.

[41] *Selbu* and *Svartskog* (n 23).

ILO Convention 169[42] and Article 40 of the United Nations Declaration on the Rights of Indigenous Peoples (UNDRIP)[43] oblige states to apply Indigenous customs and customary law as sources of law entitled to due consideration. Some Norwegian laws such as the Reindeer Husbandry Act do afford some role for Sámi customs and law.[44] Nevertheless, it seems important to map customary law and to give it greater standing and respect within the dominant legal system.[45]

## III. RIGHTS TO MARINE RESOURCES

### A. The Historical Background

Marine resources in the coastal waters, particularly codfish, herring and saithe, have historically been of great importance for the Sámi. The oldest historical record of Sámi coastal fishing is chieftain Ottar's narrative to King Alfred of England from the end of the ninth century. Ottar recounted a journey along the coast of Finnmark up to the White Sea (currently part of Russia) during which he saw only Finns engaged in fishing, hunting and trapping.[46] 'Finn' is an older denomination of Sámi (and the source of the name for Finnmark County). Until the thirteenth century, the coastal Sámi were left alone to utilise the marine resources of the northern coastal waters. Later, the appearance of the European stock fish market caused Norse settlers and seasonal fishermen to move northwards.

Sámi fishing activities involved both local home fishing and seasonal fisheries such as cod fishing in the Lofoten archipelago. Hans Paus, a well-known historian and chief justice of Finnmark, wrote in 1769 that the Sámi were not only the equal of the Norwegians on the sea, but were often far better, especially when it came to navigation in Arctic waters.[47]

The fishing gear utilised by the coastal fleet is small-scale and not capable of over-fishing the stocks. This is still the case today. By contrast, the well-capitalised pelagic fishing fleet was able to take significant catches as early as the 1900s. As mentioned above, this caused disputes and, over time, over-exploitation. During the 1980s, the resource situation became so critical that in 1990, the

[42] ILO Convention 169 (n 1).

[43] UNDRIP (n 16).

[44] Reindeer Husbandry Act (n 12) ss 1, 27–31.

[45] For additional references, see Øyvind Ravna, 'Sámi Legal Culture – and its Place in Norwegian Law' in Jørn Øyrehagen Sunde and Knut Einar Skodvin (eds) *Rendevous of European Legal Cultures* (Fagbokforlaget, 2010) 149–65; and Susann Skogvang, *Samerett*, 3rd edn (Universitetsforlaget, 2017) 63, 92.

[46] Håvard Dahl Bratrein in *Store norske leksikon*; see https://nbl.snl.no/Ottar.

[47] Hans Paus, *Indberetning av 1769 om Finmarkens økonomiske tilstand med forslag om dens forbedringer* (Vadsø, 1908) 6.

Ministry of Fisheries introduced a temporary regulation of the important cod-fisheries north of the 62nd parallel north, which to a large extent includes the coastal Sámi area. To qualify for access under the new regulation, vessels had to meet certain activity levels in previous years.[48] Because of the critical resource situation during those years, most of the Sámi small-scale actors did not fulfil the terms. This regulation was meant to be a temporary emergency measure, but became permanent. The introduction of the vessel quota became a fact and it put most of the Sámi vessel fleet out of business. The regulation of 1990 brought about a paradigm shift within the fisheries, as the open fisheries became closed; some actors obtained a privatised right through the vessel quota, at the expense of the loss of access by many others. The coastal Sámi lost a significant proportion of their rights, established over the centuries, because of low 'historical catch' in these previous years.[49]

As recounted above, Sámi rights to coastal fishing were considered by the Sámi Rights Committee. While the Committee's proposals to protect the Sámi coastal fishing in Finnmark were not included in the bill that became the Finnmark Act of 2003, the question of fishing rights became a subject of consultations between the Parliamentary Standing Committee of Justice, the Sámi Parliament and the Finnmark County Council before the Finnmark Act was adopted in 2005. In the preparatory work, the majority of the Standing Committee acknowledged that the Sámi Rights Committee's proposals had not been implemented. It went on to state that:

> It cannot be ruled out that there are guidelines both in International and Norwegian law for paying particular attention to fishing in coastal Sámi areas in establishing and practicing fisheries management. However, in relation to the current situation, it has not been specifically investigated how these considerations can be safeguarded most efficiently and appropriately in the ongoing fisheries management.[50]

Based on these acknowledgements, the majority of the Parliamentary Standing Committee of Justice suggested that:

> The Parliament calls on the Government, as soon as possible, to investigate the Sámi and others' right to fishing in the sea, including a minimum quota for boats less than ten meters, and promote a subsequent case for this to the Parliament.[51]

With the guarantee that such an independent investigation would be undertaken in the aftermath of the adoption of the Finnmark Act, the parties agreed to remove this issue from the Finnmark Act negotiations.[52]

[48] Susann Funderud Skogvang, 'Innføringen av fartøykvoter for torsk i kystfiskeflåten i 1990' (2010) 5 *Natur, rett, historie* 211, 217.

[49] NOU 1997:4, 308; and Øyvind Ravna, 'The Fulfilment of Norway's International Legal Obligations to the Sámi – Assessed by the Protection of Rights to Lands, Waters and Natural Resources' (2014) 21 *International Journal on Minority and Group Rights* 297, 313.

[50] Innst O nr 80 (n 4) 30.

[51] ibid 30–31.

[52] ibid. On the consultation, see ibid 15.

### B. The Effort to Establish a Sámi Fishing Act

Based on the proposal by the Standing Committee of Justice and consultations with the Sámi Parliament, the Norwegian government appointed the Coastal Fishing Committee (CFC) in 2006 with a mandate to investigate the rights of the coastal Sámi and others to fish in the sea off the coast of Finnmark.[53]

The Committee submitted its unanimous report in February 2008, in which it concluded that the peoples living around the fjords and along the coast of Finnmark have legal rights to fish in the coastal seawaters outside Finnmark.[54] The report contributed significantly to the ongoing debate about the Sámi and other locals' rights to fish in coastal seawaters of Finnmark. For the Committee, these rights were based on historical use and obligations under international law to protect the exercise of culture of Indigenous peoples and minorities as codified in the Article 27 of the ICCPR.[55] These rights apply regardless of governmental fisheries regulations.

To support its conclusions, the Committee presented research by Kirsti Strøm Bull that documented that coastal fishing has long been considered an exclusive right of the local population. According to Bull:

> The use that the Sámi people from olden times exercised in the fjords was by the beginning of 1800s of such a nature that it constituted grounds for established rights. Thus, there is no reason to estimate their use differently from the use that reindeer herders and others exercised on the mainland.[56]

In addition, Bull argued that: 'In accordance with the opinion that there may be local rights to fish in sea waters, this use has been of such a nature that people in the fjords had acquired a right to this fishery.'[57]

The CFC proposed that specific rights of fishing, which it named 'fjord rights', should be implemented in a Finnmark fishing act. It recommended the inclusion of a right to fish for personal consumption, a right to take up fishing as a livelihood and a right for professional fishermen to catch in order to provide the financial basis for a household, either as the fisher's main subsistence or together with another livelihood.[58] The proposed fjord right (comparable to rights in, eg, Canada)[59] was drafted as a right relative to *a geographically defined area*. Such a right would mean that persons living around a fjord have the right to fish in that particular fjord, irrespective of their ethnicity.[60]

[53] NOU 2008: 5 (n 5) 13.
[54] ibid 5, 13, 14.
[55] ibid 5, 250.
[56] ibid 156.
[57] ibid.
[58] ibid 5, 14.
[59] Douglas Harris and Peter Millerd, 'Food Fish, Commercial Fish …: Characterizing Aboriginal and Treaty Rights to Canadian Fisheries' (2010) 1 *Arctic Review on Law and Politics* 82.
[60] NOU 2008: 5 (n 5) 14.

In relation to the necessary governmental regulations or restrictions on fishery resources, the CFC also recommended that the coastal population's right to fish to a sufficient degree should be completed by quotas. In determining such quotas, the substantive basis for the coastal Sámi culture and other coastal cultures in Finnmark would be secured by statutory rules. The CFC's report also included a proposal to establish a regional governing body, the Finnmark Fisheries Management, to determine the framework of the fjord right in each fjord according to specific terms, including the resource base.[61] According to the draft, the governing body might, after a further assessment, let 'outsiders' catch fish in the particular fjord. Outside the fjords, the CFC concluded that the Finnmark fishermen had not enjoyed any customary special position and should not do so in the future.

## C. The Response of the Norwegian Government

The draft of the CFC received a diverse range of feedback and was regarded as controversial. Sámi and local fishermen's organisations in Finnmark largely approved the draft. However, ocean trawlers and the central fishermen's association considered that the draft challenged their access to marine resources allocated to them under the government-approved quota system. The government apparatus, including the Ministry of Fishery and Coastal Affairs, supported the ocean trawlers, relying on the doctrine that 'the wild living marine resources belongs to the community of the country as a whole'.[62]

By the autumn of 2009, the then Minister of Fishery and Coastal Affairs, Helga Pedersen, despite her initial support, now opposed the draft. In an interview with a local Sámi newspaper, she stated that:

> It is time to take the Sámi policy out of the lawyers' claws, so that the discussion to a larger extent will be on concrete and practical solutions that benefit the fishermen in the Finnmark fjords, instead of discussing paragraphs and commitments.[63]

Such a statement from a cabinet minister suggesting that politicians stood free to design both Sámi policy and fishery policy without looking much to international law and historical customary rights was a warning of what was to come.

One of the strongest opponents of the CFC's recommendation, and a spokesperson for the government, was the Attorney-General, who, several months after the deadline for submissions closed, filed a negative submission that

[61] ibid 5, 15.

[62] Marine Resources Act 2008 (Lov 6 Juni 2008 nr 6 om forvaltning av viltlevande marine ressursar (Law of 6 June 2008 No 6 on the Management of Wild Living Marine Resources)) s 2.

[63] *Ságat*, 7 October 2009, 3.

ended any chance of the draft becoming a law bill.[64] In doing so, the Attorney-General questioned whether Article 27 of the ICCPR protected fishing with modern gear.

## D. Norway Fails to Recognise Sámi Rights to Fish in the Sea off Finnmark

Despite the position of the local communities of the Finnmark coastline and local fishermen's associations, the government rejected the CFC's draft. In doing so, it was not deterred by the recommendations of the then UN Special Rapporteur on the Rights of Indigenous Peoples, James Anaya, who had recommended in his 2011 report that Norway consider the findings of the CFC and take effective measures to secure fishing rights for the coastal Sámi.[65]

In the final consultations in 2011, the Sámi Parliament accepted an agreement in which their historical rights were set aside in return for an annual quota of 3,000 tonnes of cod.[66] However, the agreement did not allay the sense of injustice among the coastal population arising from the fishery regulations of the 1990s, and the Sámi Parliament did not consider the consultation to be a final resolution of the issues raised by the CFC.[67] The 'cod agreement', from the view of the Sámi Parliament, was instead an interim action to help alleviate the critical situation coastal Sámi communities faced at the time rather than correcting the injustice of 1990s fisheries policy.

Finally, in March 2012, the Ministry of Fisheries and Coastal Affairs submitted the bill on the coastal fishing issues as the government's response to the CFC's draft and as the final legal outcome of the long-lasting political and legal debate introduced in the mandate of the Sámi Rights Committee back in the 1980s. In submitting the bill, the Ministry made it clear that it had its own interpretation of international law and historical usage, and that it did not share the CFC's opinion. Instead, it emphasised that the new regulations were consistent with Norway's international legal obligations to the Sámi.[68]

[64] Regjeringsadvokaten, submission 2009. NOU 2008: 5 Retten til fiske i havet utenfor Finnmark – Høyring (The Right to Fish in the Sea outside Finnmark: Hearing), available at: https://www.regjeringen.no/globalassets/upload/fkd/vedlegg/hoeringer/2008/horing---retten-til-fiske-i-havet-utenfor-finmark/regjeringsadvokatene.pdf.

[65] James Anaya, 'The Situation of the Sámi People in the Sápmi Region of Norway, Sweden and Finland', 6 June 2011, http://unsr.jamesanaya.org/docs/countries/2011-report-sapmi-a-hrc-18-35-add2_en.pdf, [80].

[66] Utkast til protokoll fra konsultasjoner om oppfølging av Kystfiskeutvalget mellom Sametinget og Fiskeri- og kystdepartementet (Draft Minutes of Consultations on the Following-up of the Coastal Fishing Committee between the Sámi Parliament and the Ministry of Fisheries and Coastal Affairs), 9 May 2011.

[67] ibid.

[68] Prop 70 L (n 20) 7.

## E. Current Legislation on the Rights to Fish in the Sea off Finnmark

Although the Norwegian government rejected the CFC's draft Finnmark Fishing Act, and consequently failed to recognise the historical rights of the coastal Sámi, it did propose amendments to the Marine Resources Act and the Fisheries Participation Act.[69] These amendments intend to secure Sámi rights to marine resources.[70] The Norwegian Parliament approved the bill in the autumn of 2012.[71]

In the preparatory works, the Ministry declared in accordance with the CFC that the concept of culture in Article 27 of the ICCPR covers Sámi coastal fishing rights. At the same time, it emphasised that such fishing must be a continuation of traditional fishing, particularly Sámi home-based coastal and fjord fishing, using small vessels and passive gear. However, it did acknowledge that the use of modern technology and gear does not take the activity outside the protection offered by Article 27.[72]

Yet, the consensus ends there. Unlike the CFC, the Ministry considers the coastal fishery to be an issue of regional policy rather than an international legal obligation imposed on Norway. It concluded that the CFC's proposal went beyond the scope of international law[73] and it did not agree with the CFC's opinion that there exist particular Sámi rights for fishing along the coastline of Finnmark:

> There is no legal basis for saying for the fishermen of the fjords in Finnmark, that there is a rule of law on historical bases of a general character, which gives them a protected right to fish in the fjords of Finnmark.[74]

Instead, the Ministry argued that the fish resources, as living resources, belong to the community as a whole and that the current regulation is consistent with both historical rights and international legal obligations owed to the Sámi.

Nevertheless, the Ministry did propose new provisions to safeguard the rights of the Sámi coastal population to fish resources. These provisions are now a part of the Norwegian fishery legislation as amended in the Fisheries Participation Act and the Marine Resources Act.[75] The Participation Act includes

[69] Act 26 March 1999 No 15 on the Right to Take Part in Fishing and Hunting (the Participation Act).

[70] Prop 70 L (n 20) 7.

[71] Lov 21 September 2012 nr 66 om endringar i deltakerloven, havressurslova og finnmarksloven (Amendment 21 September 2012 No 66 of Fisheries Participation Act, Marine Resources Act and Finnmark Act).

[72] Prop 70 L (n 20) 88.

[73] ibid 89.

[74] ibid 99.

[75] Lov 26 mars 1999 nr 15 om retten til å delta i fiske og fangst (deltakerloven) (Act 26 March 1999 no 15 Relating to the Right to Participate in Fishing and Catching); and lov 6 juni 2008 nr 37 om forvaltning av viltlevande marine ressursar (havressurslova) (Act 6 June 2008 no 37 Relating to the Management of Wild Living Marine Resources (Marine Resources Act)), respectively.

new provisions intended to raise awareness of the international legal obligations owed to the Sámi. The new section 1(a) declares that 'the act shall be interpreted in accordance with international law of Indigenous peoples and minorities'. It is not clear whether this provision serves to incorporate ILO Convention 169 into Norwegian fisheries law, but there might be reasons to interpret it this way. However, the provision does not entail any changes to the Act beyond referring to existing international legal obligations.[76]

The amendment to the Fisheries Participation Act also includes a right to fish for persons living in Finnmark, North Troms and other areas with coastal Sámi settlements with a registered vessel less than 11 metres in length. The old idea of free fishing for boats of 10 metres in length or less, as proposed by the Sámi Rights Committee in 1997, has thus largely been met. The amendment, section 21(4), provides that:

> Notwithstanding provisions made pursuant to the first paragraph, persons living in Finnmark, the municipalities of Kåfjord, Skjervøy, Nordreisa, Kvænangen, Karlsøy, Lyngen and Storfjord and those areas with sea-Sámi features in the rest of Troms and Nordland as determined by the King, shall be entitled to fish cod, haddock and saithe with conventional tools. The right after the first sentence applies only those who are listed in the fisherman census.

In order for the protection of this vessel group to be effective, access to resources must be safeguarded as well. In addition to a quota or free fishing, access to the resource requires protection against competition on the same fish stock from larger vessel groups with more effective fishing capacity. A new paragraph 6 added to section 11 of the Marine Resources Act addresses this issue. It reads as follows:

> In the area covered by the Participation Act section 21, third paragraph, the allocation of quotas of wild marine resources and by other forms of regulation of these resources, will place considerable emphasis on Sámi use and what this use means for the Sámi local communities.

The provision expresses the state's intention to safeguard the Sámi fishery and gives interpretative guidance for the balance of the statutory provisions and any subsequent regulations. The preparatory works confirm that this is the intention of the Ministry. At the same time, the preparatory works suggest that the provision is not meant to place any specific guidelines on fishery policy making or prescribe the weight to be accorded to the needs of Sámi culture and communities.[77]

Section 7(2)(g) also acknowledges the state's responsibility for the Sámi communities, stating that: 'In managing wild living marine resources … it shall be emphasised that … the management measure is ensuring the material basis

[76] Prop 70 L (n 20) 122.
[77] ibid 124.

for Sámi culture.' This provision adds an additional dimension to the management of the fishery by emphasising Sámi use of these resources and supports the argument that Sámi coastal communities should be prioritised in the allocation of quotas. The provisions will support the allocation of additional quotas to vessels participating in the open group.[78] According to the Ministry, this provision, in combination with other regulations, intends to contribute to ensuring that future Norwegian fisheries law will be consistent with Norway's obligations under international law.

Safeguarding the rights of the small vessel group against financially strong competitors who fish the same resources may also requires other measures. For example, competition could be prevented by forbidding the ocean fleet from fishing in the fiords and by giving the small-scale fleet sufficient participation in the decision-making processes affecting their fishery. The expanding salmon farming industry is also seen as a competing activity for the space within the fiords, or even a threat to the fiord fisheries.[79] It may be necessary to curb such activities within the fiords to protect the small-scale fisheries.

### F. The Fjord Fishing Board

A new section 8(b) in the Marine Resource Act provides for the establishment of the Fjord Fishing Board (Fjordfiskenemda) for Finnmark, Troms and Nordland.[80] The purpose of the board is to enhance Sámi participation in the decision-making processes affecting the fishery in a manner consistent with Norway's international law commitments.[81] The board is composed of representatives from the Sámi Parliament and the three northernmost county municipalities. However, the board's recommendations are advisory in nature and are not binding for any final decisions and regulations. The board is modelled on the scheme chosen for the board of the Finnmark Estate and the proposal of the CFC.[82]

### G. Developments since the Adoption of the 2012 Amendments

The government's conclusion that the amendments reviewed above end the work to recognise Sámi rights undertaken over almost 40 years has not been accepted by all. While the Sámi Parliament undeniably approved the increased quota and

[78] ibid.

[79] The Sámi Parliament refers to the salmon farming industry as a threat to Sámi societies, both because of its pollution and the conflict of interests the industry represents when it comes to use of spaces. Sametinget, *Næringsutvikling i sjøsamiske samfunn*, 7 December 2017, https://www.sametinget.no/content/download/2267/34194, 3.

[80] Prop 70 L (n 20) 122.

[81] ibid 115.

[82] ibid 115; *cf* Finnmark Act, s 6.

other legislative amendments in 2012, it did not (as already noted) consider that this was the end of the matter and of the CFC's recommendations. Instead, it stated that the measures were only a 'first important step into a full safeguarding and recognition of the Sámi and other local people's right to the marine resources'.[83] It also declared that it did not support the Ministry's legal basis for these measures and that a continued process had to result in solutions consistent with international law. In particular: 'Sámi participation in the governmental management of fishery-resources and the Sámi Parliament's claim that the Sámi rights, based on immemorial usage and other basis, must be recognized.'[84] However, no further steps have been taken in consultations between the Sámi Parliament and the Norwegian government to extend further recognition of Sámi rights to marine resources.

The Fjord Fishing Board was established in 2014 with the purpose to strengthen the management of the fjord fisheries, particularly with an emphasis on Sámi use and the importance of this use for Sámi local communities. The area of activity is the counties of Finnmark, Troms and Nordland,[85] but it has been challenged by organisational concerns and inadequate funding to accomplish its mandate. For example, it lacks the resources to be represented in the annual national regulation meeting, which is the most important forum in Norway for establishing fisheries regulation and policy.[86]

However, there has been one positive development in the Sámi fisheries during the last few years. The 'Sámi fishery quota' authorised through section 21 of the Fisheries Participation Act has undoubtedly had a positive impact on the fisheries in the Sámi coastal areas. The quota gives more predictability for small-scale fisheries and the opportunity for a decent income. This has wider repercussions insofar as the necessary fishery-related activities on-shore also become more predictable. As a result, there is increased fishing activity in the traditional Sámi communities, a growing number of vessels and additional landing spots along the Sámi coast. The king crab fishery and the growing resource base of white fish, as well as warmer weather, have also contributed to this growth.

This is how far the protection goes. Beyond the coastal fishery quota, the government has done little to ensure the Sámi right to fisheries. Neither the Ministry of Fisheries and Coastal Affairs nor the Directorate of Fisheries has offered any guidance as to how the protection of the Sámi fishery is to be interpreted or implemented through the annual regulations. This allows interest groups to take different positions, resulting in unpredictability and

[83] ibid 115.

[84] ibid 116.

[85] The mandate is given by the Ministry of Fisheries and Coastal Affairs, *Mandat for Fjordfiskenemnda*, https://www.regjeringen.no/no/aktuelt/dep/nfd/nyheter/2013/fjordfiskenemnda-blir-oppretta/mandat-for-fjordfiskenemnda-/id748027 [1].

[86] Trond Einar Karlsen, 'Fjordfiskenemda er blakk', *Kyst og Fjord*, https://www.kystogfjord.no/nyheter/forsiden/Fjordfiskenemnda-er-blakk.

conflict between the groups regarding their rights and expectations. There are even statements against the Sámi fishery, and the protection of that fishery, of a rather racist character. The first time the Director of Fisheries mentioned section 21 in the preparatory documents for the annual regulation meetings was in 2017, likely as a consequence of incidents at the 2016 meeting. The representative from the Sámi Parliament left the meeting having had enough of the many prejudiced statements in the annual meetings during the discussions about safeguarding the Sámi fisheries.[87]

The protection offered by section 21 is therefore limited in a number of ways. First, the protection is limited to only a few marine species. It does not include king crab, for instance, a new resource that is abundant in parts of the Sámi coastal area and which constitutes 50 per cent of the annual turnover for many small-scale actors. It seems reasonable to assume that other species may become important in the future fishery. In this context, it may be asked whether the Sámi fishery will be sufficiently protected in a changing resource situation in Northern coastal seawaters.

Second, section 21 only includes the right to fish in the so-called 'open group' (a joint quota), as opposed to the 'closed group' (in which each vessel has its own quota). Those in the closed group have a predictable income and find it easier to get financing for both vessels and other livelihood necessities, while those in the open group depend on the annual regulations and therefore must live with more unpredictability. This distinction raises questions as to whether the Sámi fishery should gain the same level of protection as those in the closed group.

## H. The Position of the Sámi Parliament

The Sámi coastal fishery issues continue to be a hot topic on the political agenda of the Sámi Parliament. On 7 December 2017, the Sámi Parliament approved the economic development strategy for coastal Sámi communities in a plenary meeting. The strategy aims to maintain and develop sustainable coastal Sámi communities:

> There is a strong connection between the population trends, employment development, legal rights and economic development. As a basis for sustainable coastal Sámi communities, it will be of essential importance that the wealth creation is happening locally, that measures are taken, and regulations initiated contribute to beneficial activity in the coastal-Sámi communities … The Sámi Parliament request strong and versatile communities, where wealth creation takes place locally, and constitutes the basis for a stable settlement and a living coastal-Sámi culture.[88]

[87] Nils H Måsø, 'Forlot fiskerimøte: – Samehetsen ble for sterk kost', *NRK Sápmi*, 4 November 2016, https://www.nrk.no/sapmi/forlot-fiskerimote_-_-samehetsen-ble-for-sterk-kost-1.13210209.

[88] Sametinget (n 79) 4.

The Sámi Parliament notes that the coastal Sámi communities face substantial demographic challenges. Only the larger towns are growing, while the population of the Sámi districts is continually declining.[89] The number of fishermen decreased by 18 per cent between 2003 and 2014, and the small-scale fleet has dramatically declined.

On the other hand, there is a positive trend in some areas. In the eastern part of Finnmark, the number of fishermen increased by up to 50 per cent between 2008 and 2016.[90] This positive development can partly be explained by the factors mentioned above, ie, the growing resource basis combined with the extra district quota that the Sámi Parliament negotiated in relation to the 2012 amendments, and especially the successful king crab fishery in those areas.[91]

The aquaculture industry is also expanding in the coastal Sámi areas and the government welcomes further growth in that industry. However, there are no reports of an increasing number of employees as result of this industry. Instead, the Sámi Parliament reports that the aquaculture industry is a threat to the fisheries and argues that the enduring employment generated by the fisheries must be prioritised. Thus, as the Parliament states, 'when [there is] conflict between aquaculture industry and the Sámi fishery, the present and the future Sámi fishery must be safeguarded'.[92]

## I. International Criticisms

Both the UN Human Rights Committee and the ILO's Expert Committee have questioned what measures have been taken to safeguard the coastal Sámi right to marine resources.[93] The Human Rights Committee repeated its inquiry in 2016, but it still remains unanswered by the Norwegian government.[94]

Ms Tauli-Corpuz, the UN Special Rapporteur on the Rights of Indigenous Peoples, also brought up some concerns in 2016. She referred to the sea salmon fishing, noting that it is an important part of coastal Sámi culture and income, and arguing that this fishery should be 'protected by special measures to ensure they can be pursued and maintained according to Sámi tradition in a culturally and ecologically sustainable way'.[95] The salmon fishery in salt waters is strictly regulated by the national annual regulations, based on the need to protect and

[89] ibid 21.
[90] ibid 23.
[91] ibid 19.
[92] ibid 23.
[93] Direct Request, Committee of Experts on the Application of Conventions and Recommendations, adopted 2014, published at the 104th ILC Session (2015) and CCPR/C/NOR/Q/6.
[94] List of issues prior to submission of the seventh Periodic Report of Norway. Adopted by the Committee at its 117th session (20 June–15 July 2016).
[95] Human Rights Council (n 22) [78].

reinforce the Atlantic salmon stocks. The regulations allow a traditional salmon fishery only a few days each year. However, non-Sámi anglers fishing in the rivers do not face the same restrictions and this fishery is growing. It may be the case that the strict regulation of sea salmon fishing threatens the Sámi salmon fishery and thus the coastal Sámi culture. The fishermen themselves declare that they will take this case to trial since the government fails to respect their rights.[96]

The Committee on the Elimination of Racial Discrimination (CERD) has also expressed its concerns. In its concluding observation on Norway from 2015, it stated that:

> The 2012 amendments to the fisheries legislation (the Marine Resources Act, the Fisheries Participation Act and the Finnmark Act) did not recognise that the Sámi have established rights to fisheries and other renewable marine resources in the Sámi coastal area, and that the legal frameworks may therefore not be able to withstand future reform.[97]
>
> …
>
> The CERD therefore recommends that the state party review the fisheries legislation and ensure that it fully recognises the Sámi fishing rights, based as they are on immemorial usage and local customs.[98]

In 2017, the National Institution for Human Rights (NIM) published a report on the coastal Sámi rights to a marine fishery. The report criticises the lack of codified legal protection of such rights and refers to several international human rights bodies that express the importance of governmental protection of this group's rights.[99] After concluding that the current governmental protection of coastal Sámi rights is inadequate, the NIM stated that even if the coastal Sámi right to fishery as livelihood exists independent of national codification, codification would give stronger protection of the right. It further claims that:

> This right can only be reduced due to the concern of the sustainable resource management, but in such circumstances the coastal-Sámi fleet must have a preferential-right to the resources over the rest of the fishery-fleet.[100]

The NIM also argues that the Sámi rights to fish as part of their cultural exercise and based on their historic fishing should be enshrined in legislation along with

[96] 'Sjølaksefiskerne varsler rettssak', *Fiskeribladet*, https://fiskeribladet.no/nyheter/?artikkel=52253.

[97] Committee on the Elimination of Racial Discrimination, 'Concluding Observations on the Twenty-First and Twenty-Second Periodic Reports of Norway', CERD/C/NOR/CO/21–22 28 August 2015, [29 (d)].

[98] ibid [30] (f).

[99] Norges nasjonale institusjon for menneskerettigheter (NIM), 'Sjøsamenes rett til sjøfiske', *Temarapport 2016*, https://www.nhri.no/wp-content/uploads/2017/05/Temarapport-2016-Sjøsamenes-rett-til-sjøfiske1.pdf, 4.

[100] ibid 27.

the right to positive discrimination in the allocation of quotas and conservation of the material bases of Sámi culture.[101] In sum, it recommends that:

> The Sámi right to participation in use, management and control over the material livelihood basis must be more properly safeguarded by legislation than the current state, to bring Norway in consistence with international obligations.[102]

The NIM also points to the increasing competition for the use of sea-space, especially from the growing salmon-farming industry, which may exclude the small-scale fiord-fishery. It states that the coastal Sámi co-determination in cases that affect their material livelihood basis must be real and actual, and decisions must be based on an adequate knowledge base.[103]

The UN Human Rights Committee has recently re-affirmed these concerns. In its seventh Periodic Report on measures taken to enforce and safeguard the rights recognised in the ICCPR (2018), it criticised Norway for 'the lack of strong legislative framework ensuring land and resource rights to Sámi people including fishing and reindeer husbandry'.[104]

## IV. FINAL REMARKS

This chapter has demonstrated that the attempt to pass a fishery statute to protect coastal Sámi culture has failed. The amendments to the Marine Resource Act and the Fishery Participation Act only half-heartedly protect coastal Sámi culture. Although the amendments emphasise Norway's international obligations towards the Sámi in the management of marine resources, and thus protection of the coastal Sámi culture,[105] the amendments appear to be a weak echo of the CFC's proposals.

While the current legislation does not prevent governmental regulations that supports Sámi fishing, nor does it acknowledge clear entitlements. Even if the right to participate is now codified in the 2012 amendments, there is no codification of access to resources or protection from competitive large-scale vessels. These rights depend for their protection on annual regulations which can easily be changed under another political regime. The same is more or less the situation when it comes to the participation rights.

As earlier described, the introduction of quotas in the 1990s led to a paradigm shift in the fishery regulations. It has been difficult for younger fishermen in the relevant vessel group to be able to establish themselves as coastal fishermen,

[101] ibid.
[102] ibid 29.
[103] ibid.
[104] Human Rights Committee, Concluding Observations on the Seventh Periodic Report of Norway, 5 April 2018, [36](d).
[105] Prop 70 L (n 20) 123.

the number of fishermen has decreased, and this had a negative impact on the settlement pattern along the coastline. The codification of the right to fishing is intended to remedy this situation.

It is difficult to assess the long-term impact of the amendments, particularly since historical rights to fishing are not recognised and consequently do not provide an independent legal basis for the right to participate. Although the amendments include some statements of principle and although the local fishermen can be granted increased quotas, and the Fjord Fishing Board can have some impact on the regulations, there is no recognition of an enhanced right for the coastal Sámi to participate in the governance of fish resources. The recognition of such rights would have been consistent with both the doctrine of historic rights and international law.

From our point of view, the Sámi Parliament has good reasons to conclude that the 'agreement' of June 2011 did not end the dialogue on the implementation of the proposals of the CFC. Even though the Sámi Parliament gained an increased quota and certain other minor legislative amendments, the solutions laid on the table probably fall below the international law minimum standards because, among other factors, there is no intent to fulfil the commitment of Article 27 of the ICCPR to protect the substantive bases for a minority's culture. Nor is there any intent to identify traditional lands, or more precisely seawaters belonging to the Indigenous Sámi, as required by ILO Convention 169, other than the provision amended in s 29 of the Finnmark Act in 2012, which seven years after it entered into force has yet to be applied.

In effect, the legislators, relying on the Marine Resources Act, which declares that 'the wild living marine resources belongs to the community of the country as a whole',[106] have chosen to protect the general interests of Norwegian society rather than the uncontested fishing traditions, customs and livelihood practices of the local Sámi population that have occurred in the fjords exclusively since time immemorial.

The legal base of this state positivistic position is also buttressed by state policies supporting the ocean fishing fleet, which brings Norway export revenues – as does the aquaculture industry. The doctrine vesting marine resources in the country as a whole was never in conformity with the *opinio juris* among coastal Sámi and other coastal inhabitants in the northern parts of Norway. It mainly developed in the wake of establishing the ocean trawler fleet and industrial fishing in the 1900s, industries which did not accept the historical rights of the coastal people. Summing up, the doctrine contributes to defining rules on rights to marine resources in Norway in such way that a private, independent right to fishing for individuals or local communities beyond the shore slope does not exist beyond an exception for salmon fishing with gear bound to the shore.

[106] Lov 6 Juni 2008 nr 6 (n 75) s 2.

The findings of the CFC say that people living in the fjords and on the coastline of Finnmark, 'on the basis of historical usage and international law of indigenous peoples and minorities, have the right to fish in the sea of the Finnmark'.[107] This means that the government is not quite so free when it comes to allocating quotas, or regulating marine resources in other ways, as the Marine Resources Act suggests. It also means that the legislature has to consider how the coastal populations use seawaters as a basis for livelihood to a larger extent than has been the case in the amendments referred to above.

Despite the CFC's unanimous proposal, Norway is left with a situation where the recognition of the historical rights, which is enshrined in the Constitution, case law and the Finnmark Act, does not reach further than the shore slope, and thus does not cover the full extent of the fishing rights of the coastal Sámi in a comprehensive manner.

Norway elsewhere has a fairly well-developed legal system when it comes to protecting Indigenous rights to land and natural resources. This is currently not the situation in relation to the protection of the vulnerable coastal Sámi culture, which through many generations of assimilation has lost much of its language and visual cultural characteristics, and is now in danger of losing its livelihood.

The absence of adequate recognition of coastal Sámi rights has, as shown above, been addressed by several international human rights bodies. As was also shown, the UN Special Rapporteur on the Rights of Indigenous Peoples has urged Norway to find solutions on regulations related to sea salmon fishing. Despite the recommendation, the Norwegian authorities in the spring of 2018 decided to further restrict the sea Sámi salmon fishery by further shortening the fishing season.[108]

Recently, Carsten Smith, the former Chief Justice of Norway's Supreme Court and head of the CFC, expressed the view that the NIM's report conclusively undermined Norway's official view of the coastal Sámi rights. The NIM's view is a continuation of the CFC's suggestions, and concludes that the 2012 amendments are insufficient to discharge Norway's international law obligations towards the coastal Sámi: 'said in other words, the current legislation is contrary to the state's international obligations'.[109] Smith concluded that Norway must now follow NIM's recommendations and that the Sámi are entitled to quick and generous action through necessary legislation and other measures.

[107] NOU 2008: 5 (n 5) 14.

[108] Forskrift 10 mai 2012 nr 431 om fisketider for fiske etter anadrome laksefisk i sjøen (Regulation on Fishing Periods for Fishing for Anadrome Salmonids in the Sea).

[109] Carsten Smith, 'Sjøsamene vinner til slutt', *Nordlys*, 3 May 2017, http://nordnorskdebatt.no/article/sjosamene-vinner-slutt.

# 10

# *New Zealand/Aotearoa and the Rights of Māori to Natural Resources in Marine Areas*

ANDREW ERUETI

## I. INTRODUCTION

New Zealand (NZ) has one of the largest Exclusive Economic Zones (EEZ) in the world, roughly 20 times the size of its land mass, and full of natural resources and diverse ecosystems. And it has been the site of controversial claims, including claims by NZ's Indigenous peoples, Māori, to fisheries, aquaculture, foreshore and seabed lands, and minerals. These claims have emerged in the context of growing concerns about the health of the marine environment and public access to the coast and fishing, and the demand by business to exploit natural resources with minimal regulatory oversight. In this chapter, I set out the background to the interests claimed by Māori, why and how claims were made and on what basis, and how they have intersected with the demands of business, the general public, and government policy on environmental regulation and privatisation. I explain how government has responded to these claims in the forms of statutory intervention and the incorporation of Māori interests in environmental legislation.

NZ has produced innovative mechanisms to mediate the tension between competing interests in its coastal marine area. Māori have gained considerable economic benefits, especially in relation to commercial fisheries. At the same time, the government response has been inconsistent and there remain significant gaps, especially in relation to rights to the foreshore and seabed, and the mining of the coastal marine area. Yet NZ remains a site of significant innovation and Māori now possess a range of rights and interests in the marine area – all made possible, I suggest, by a persistent Indigenous rights movement and the legal reforms made in response. Probably the most unique reform is the Waitangi Tribunal, a commission of inquiry established to scrutinise Crown acts or omissions for compliance with 'the principles of the Treaty' and to make recommendations to governments on the basis of its inquiries.[1] While the Tribunal can only ever make recommendations, these carry great weight and often lead to Treaty settlements containing monetary compensation, cultural redress and procedural rights (for example, consultation).[2] As we will see, the Tribunal has played an important role in gathering the evidence needed, particularly the evidence of Māori, to support the negotiation of contemporary statutory agreements in the marine area.

Additionally, compared with many other countries, NZ has a robust regulatory process for environmental regulation of natural resources and this includes important protections for Māori interests. The Resource Management Act 1991 (RMA) requires that all decision makers 'take into account the principles of the Treaty of Waitangi'[3] and have 'particular regard' to 'kaitiakitanga' (guardianship by the tangata whenua (Indigenous people))[4] and 'recognise and provide for … the relationship of Māori and their culture and traditions with their ancestral lands, water, sites, waahi tapu [sacred sites], and other taonga [treasures]'.[5] As a result of these provisions, when a local government draws up development plans or grants resource consents to carry out some activity, it must first consider the implications of the plan and consent on the tangata whenua's customary law as it relates to kaitiakitanga, for example.[6] Similar protections for Māori interests in the EEZ are set out in the Exclusive Economic Zone and Continental Shelf Act 2012, which is often described as the RMA of the sea.[7]

## II. ENDURING INDIGENOUS INTERESTS VERSUS THE PUBLIC INTEREST

Māori interests in the NZ marine area are based on the notion of enduring interests, those that have their source in the fact of Māori occupation of NZ

[1] Treaty of Waitangi Act 1975. See also M Palmer, *The Treaty of Waitangi in New Zealand's Law and Constitution* (Victoria University Press, 2008). For the Waitangi Tribunal's comment on the Treaty's intent, see Waitangi Tribunal, *He Whakaputanga me te Tiriti: the Declaration and the Treaty Report* (WAI 1040, 2014).

[2] Excluding orders relating to the return of Crown land transfered to state owned enterprises. For Crown policy on Treaty settlements, see Office of Treaty Settlements, *Ka Tika ā Muri, Ka Tika ā Mua: A Guide to Treaty of Waitangi Claims and Negotiations with the Crown* (March 2015). For comments on the process, see Nicola R Wheen and Janine Hayward (eds), *Treaty of Waitangi Settlements* (Bridget Williams Books, 2012).

[3] Resource Management Act 1991, s 8.

[4] ibid s 7.

[5] ibid s 6.

[6] For comments critiquing the capacity of these provisions to protect Māori interests, see Waitangi Tribunal, *Ko Aotearoa Tenei: A Report into Claims Concerning New Zealand Law and Policy Affecting Māori Culture and Identity* (WAI 262, 2011). Under the RMA, local governments may delegate powers and enter into joint management agreements with tribes. This power has been used, but not extensively. The Tribunal in *Ko Aotearoa Tenei* recommended that the RMA's existing mechanisms for delegation and transfer of powers be amended to remove unnecessary barriers to their use.

[7] Exclusive Economic Zone and Continental Shelf Act 2012.

before the arrival of European settlers. These interests exist in fact – for example, traditional fishing practices – and are regulated according to tikanga Māori (custom and values). Providing evidence of this continuity is a real challenge given the impacts of European settlement. Once established, the interests receive legal recognition through a variety of means. Sometimes these rights are recognised by the courts, under the common law doctrine of Aboriginal title.[8] There is also statutory recognition of enduring Māori interests in the form of agreements made between Māori and the Crown. These resemble the modern treaties of Canada which extinguish Aboriginal title in exchange for statutory rights.[9] I discuss the NZ statutory agreements below relating to sea fisheries,[10] foreshore and seabed lands,[11] aquaculture[12] and efforts to secure an agreement relating to minerals.[13]

This approach to existing rights can be contrasted with government policy on Māori rights on dry land, where there is a greater focus on redress in the form of financial compensation and procedural rights for interests that have been lost by Māori – in particular lands now in the possession of the state or private parties. Almost all tribal land was taken by settler governments soon after the assertion of British sovereignty was made in the Treaty of Waitangi in 1840.[14] Redress is almost always in the form of a statutory settlement negotiated between the state and tribes – often following a Waitangi Tribunal inquiry into the historical basis of the claim.

But the claims to rights in the sea and coastal area (for instance, the foreshore and seabed) have always had a different quality. Legal claims to resources and their resolution have occurred relatively recently within the last few decades. In many cases, customary practices continued 'under the radar', despite the presence of government regulation and the assumption made by the state that natural resources in the marine area were the property of the Crown. For example, the Crown assumed ownership of the foreshore under the royal prerogative as a residual right of the sovereign.[15] Contemporary Māori proprietary claims have

[8] The doctrine of aboriginal title recognises that Indigenous peoples retain interests in their property after the assertion of British sovereignty and that those rights are justiciable, in that the courts may recognise and give effect to them. See PG McHugh, *Aboriginal Title: The Modern Jurisprudence of Tribal Land Rights* (Oxford University Press, 2011).

[9] See, eg, the BC Treaty Commission process, see: www.bctreaty.ca.

[10] Treaty of Waitangi (Fisheries Claims) Settlement Act 1992.

[11] Marine and Coastal Area (Takutai Moana) Act 2011.

[12] Māori Commercial Aquaculture Claims Settlement Act 2004.

[13] See section VI below. For Māori tribal claims to petroleum, see Waitangi Tribunal, *The Petroleum Report* (WAI 796, 2006).

[14] Basil Keane, 'Te Māori i te ohanga – Māori in the Economy – The Alienation of Māori Land', *Te Ara – The Encyclopedia of NZ*, www.TeAra.govt.nz/en/te-maori-i-te-ohanga-maori-in-the-economy/page-4; Richard Boast, *Buying the Land, Selling the Land: Governments and Māori Land in the North Island 1865–1921* (Victoria University Press and Victoria University of Wellington Law Review, 2008).

[15] Richard Boast, 'In Re Ninety Mile Beach Revisited: The Native Land Court and the Foreshore in New Zealand Legal History' (1993) 23 *Victoria University of Wellington Law Review* 145. On the assertion of the royal prerogative in NZ in relation to gold, see David Williams, 'Gold: The Case of Mines (1568) and the Waitangi Tribunal' [2003] *Australian Journal of Legal History* 11.

been a response to commercial and environmental factors, particularly proposals to privatise natural resources or to regulate their exploitation.[16] This, in turn, has attracted public concern, especially where public access and recreational rights are affected as they have been with claims to lakes and rivers, the coastal marine area and the conservation estate. NZ is a small island state with a large coastline and many large rivers and lakes. Public access to and use of water bodies (including fishing) is a quintessential part of NZ's social and cultural life. What makes matters more challenging is that it seems that a significant segment of the NZ public are anxious about the prominent role of Treaty settlements and their perceived potential to entrench ethnic divisions, undermine civil unity and create special rights.

## III. COMMERCIAL AND CUSTOMARY FISHERIES: THE SEALORD DEAL

The 'Sealord Deal' was one of the first of the statutory agreements reached and the first in the marine area.[17] It arose from a proposal by the government to privatise fishing rights in NZ via a Quota Management System (QMS) that allocated fishing quotas to the fishing industry based on their catch history. The QMS was preceded by the dramatic growth of the fishing industry in the 1960s and 1970s, leading to over-fishing and the increased regulation in catch levels.[18] Māori in fact had for more than a century been marginalised from the fishing industry due to the loss of coastal land and the regulation of fisheries from the 1870s.[19] It was simply assumed that Māori has no rights of substance to sea fisheries, that fishing was a public right (subject to regulations) and that the Crown had the right to establish exclusive commercial fishing rights. The shift in the 1980s towards privatisation and regulation of commercial operators had the effect of excluding small-scale Māori fishing operators because their catch fell below statutory thresholds.[20] Many Māori operators living in small coastal communities that were dependent on fishing were effectively shut out of the industry.

[16] As Richard Boast observes: 'It is no accident that those natural resources which have been privatised by statute (fisheries, the radio spectrum) have attracted the greatest amount of litigation from Māori groups. If a resource is unowned, or is nationalised, there is at least some hope of securing interests in it; but it is quite otherwise once privatised.' See Richard Boast, 'Māori Fisheries 1986–1998: A Reflection' (1999) 30 *Victoria University of Wellington Law Review* 111, 134. This is a recurring theme in NZ. A current issue before the Waitangi Tribunal is the Māori claim to ownership of water, prompted by government privatisation proposals. See Waitangi Tribunal, *The Interim Report on the National Freshwater and Geothermal Resources Claim* (WAI 2358, 2012).

[17] Treaty of Waitangi (Fisheries Claims) Settlement Act 1992.

[18] Fisheries Act 1983.

[19] Fish Protection Act 1877. See also Law Commission, *The Treaty of Waitangi and Maori Fisheries; Mataitai: Nga Tikanga Maori me te Tiriti o Waitangi* (NZLC PP9, 1989).

[20] Law Commission Report (n 19) [4.7]–[4.8].

The morality of the exclusion of Māori from their fisheries and subsequent privatisation no doubt led to the search for a more equitable scheme that would recognise their interests. Yet, fundamentally, the Sealord Deal has its basis in the notion of continuity of property interest in a tribal resource, as evidenced by Waitangi Tribunal reports and judicial inquiries. The Deal finds its original source in litigation based, in part, on an aboriginal right to fisheries. The courts found that there was a case for such a proprietary interest[21] – that successive governments were wrong in assuming that the right was merely 'recreational or ceremonial' – and granted an injunction to stop privatisation of fishing rights.[22]

The declaratory judgment was influenced by the wealth of evidence produced by Māori claimants for the Waitangi Tribunal in the *Muriwhenua Fishing Report* (1988)[23] and the *Ngai Tahu Sea Fisheries Report* (1992).[24] Both the Muriwhenua and Ngai Tahu tribes have extensive coastlines, with Ngai Tahu's covering most of the South Island, and fishing was a major part of their tradition. Based on this evidence, Justice Grieg had no doubt that:

> [T]here is a strong case that before 1840 Māori had a highly developed and controlled fishery over the whole coast of New Zealand, at least where they were living. That was divided into zones under the control and authority of the hapu and the tribes of the district. Each of these hapu and tribes had the dominion, perhaps the rangatiratanga, over those fisheries.[25]

The more challenging evidential point was whether tribes had continued to fish substantially and continually, despite the effects of settlement and comprehensive regulation of the resource. Fishing legislation, arguably, had legally extinguished any customary fishing rights. To the extent that there is any conflict between customary rights and statute, the latter always prevails.

However, this question did not need to be resolved by the court as it was an application for injunctive relief, stopping the QMS, until these larger questions could be considered at a later judicial hearing of the substantive issues. Significantly, the relevant statute contained a provision that 'nothing in this Act shall affect any Māori fishing right', which indicated that such rights were not legally extinguished and indeed were expressly preserved by statute.[26]

The government and Māori then negotiated an 'interim settlement' in the form of fishing quota and monetary compensation assuming that the substantive

[21] See *New Zealand Māori Council v Attorney-General* (8 October 1987) unreported, High Court, Wellington (CP 553/87); and *Ngai Tahu Māori Trust Board v Attorney-General* (2 November 1987) unreported, High Court, Wellington (CP 559/87, 610/87, 614/87). See also *Te Weehi v Regional Fisheries Officer* (1986) 1 NZLR 682.

[22] *Ngai Tahu Māori Trust Board v Attorney-General* (n 21) 6.

[23] Waitangi Tribunal, *Muriwhenua Fishing Report* (Wai 22, 1988).

[24] Waitangi Tribunal, *Ngai Tahu Sea Fisheries Report* (Wai 27, 1992).

[25] *Ngai Tahu Māori Trust Board v Attorney-General* (n 21) 6.

[26] Fisheries Act, s 88(2).

issue of rights would be determined by the courts.[27] Soon afterwards, the government agreed to a statutory agreement.[28] In exchange for Māori agreeing to give up their legal claims, the Act provided for the Crown to pay NZ$150 million to fund Māori to purchase Sealord Products Ltd (in a 50-50 joint venture with Brierley Investments), which held 26 per cent of the total fishing quota. Māori were also to receive 20 per cent of all new species of fish brought under the QMS.[29]

The package also included customary fishing regulations and further quotas in exchange for Māori agreeing to stop litigation and give up legal claims. At no point have any of the substantive legal questions been definitively answered. As Richard Boast notes, 'with the injunctions in place, and the substantive proceedings looming, a deal had to be struck, and indeed was. The necessity for a deal and the re-emergence of statutory pragmatism was due to legal uncertainty'.[30]

Under the customary fishing regulations, tangata whenua may establish Mataitai reserves – areas where tangata whenua manage all non-commercial fishing by making by-laws – following consultation with the local community – ie, people who own land in the proximity of the proposed mataitai reserve.[31] Reserves can only be applied for over traditional fishing grounds and must be areas of special significance to the tangata whenua. Tangata whenua may establish bylaws for the reserves, which may restrict or prohibit the taking of a particular species within a mataitai reserve – a significant power of which many New Zealanders are unaware. The process of establishing reserves and the by-laws themselves are heavily scrutinised by the Minister of Fisheries.[32]

There was significant opposition to the Sealord Deal by both Māori and Pakeha (non-Māori). The commercial fishing industry in particular was strongly opposed to the Deal (the Waitangi Tribunal was labelled a 'kangaroo court'), and politicians (for example, John Banks and John Carter) used the issue to stoke up public concerns about the costs of treaty settlements and special treatment.[33] Many tribes were opposed to the Deal too, arguing that they would rather have their claims litigated in the courts than have them settled politically through a statutory agreement. It is interesting to note in this context that the Māori negotiators of the Deal were prepared to accept a

[27] Māori Fisheries Act 1989.

[28] Treaty of Waitangi (Fisheries Claims) Settlement Act 1992.

[29] ibid.

[30] Boast (n 16) 134.

[31] There are two sets of regulations in place, one for the North Island and one for the South Island, although they are similar in most respects. The regulations in the North Island are called the Kaimoana Customary Fishing Regulations 1998 and cover non-commercial customary fishing, which means fishing to provide food for hui (meetings) and tangi (funerals), and which does not involve the exchange of money or other form of payment. See also the Taiapure provisions in ss 174–85 of the Fisheries Act 1996.

[32] Kaimoana Customary Fishing Regulations 1998, reg 11.

[33] B Bargh, *The Struggle for Māori Fishing Rights: Te Ika a Māori* (Huia, 2016).

50 per cent share of fishing interests – a demonstration of goodwill and compromise. Apirana Mahuika on behalf of his tribe, Ngati Porou, appealed to the United Nations (UN) Human Rights Committee claiming the deal violated the tribe's right to culture and self-determination under the International Covenant on Civil and Political Rights (ICCPR).[34] The Committee heard the case long after the Sealord Deal was passed into law and decided that, on balance, it was a sound agreement which was consistent with the ICCPR, and this seems to be the consensus today. Māori now have a significant stake in the country's commercial fishing industry and the right to establish Mataitai reserves for the exercise of customary rights.

However, this would not have occurred without the clear evidence of Māori persistence in fishing, despite the many obstacles presented by government regulation, and the use of the Waitangi Tribunal and courts by Māori advocates, which prompted the political negotiations that culminated in the deal.

## IV. THE FORESHORE AND SEABED

One of the most vexed issues in Māori–state relations in recent times has been the Māori claim to rights to the foreshore (that wetland between high tide and low tide) and the seabed in relation to the Territorial Sea (from low tide seaward for 12 nautical miles), and especially the prospect of Māori acquiring proprietary interests whereby non-Māori could be excluded and the interests sold to third parties.

The *Ngati Apa* (2003) decision of the Court of Appeal recognised that Māori possessed customary rights in the foreshore and seabed, and ruled that legislation had not extinguished any customary title, thus clearing the way for Māori to seek customary rights under both the Māori Land Court's and the High Court's jurisdiction. The Māori Land Court's jurisdiction was the most controversial because it seemed to allow for the granting of freehold titles (this being a right associated with Māori freehold land under the Māori Land Act 1993).[35] This meant that Māori could potentially exclude others from their freehold titles and even sell on the land. The prospect of Māori proprietary interests in the foreshore and seabed, while not clear,[36] unsettled many New Zealanders. Politicians

[34] International Covenant on Civil and Political Rights. See *Mahuika v New Zealand* (2000) 7 HRNZ 629, Comm No 547/1993, CCPR/C/70/D/547/1993 (2000). The UN Human Rights Committee ruled that the Sealord Deal did not violate art 27. The Committee seemed to be influenced by the fact that the deal addressed both their commercial interests and 'the cultural and religious significance of fishing for the Māori'.

[35] See *Ngati Apa v Attorney-General* [2003] 3 NZLR 643 (CA). This was the Māori Land Court's original mandate – that is, to convert lands 'owned by Natives under their customs or usages' into a Crown granted fee simple title. In other words, the Native Land legislation saw Māori customary title translating readily into a right of ownership.

[36] *Ngati Apa* (n 35) [45].

exploited the uncertainty created by the decision raising the spectre of tribes excluding non-Māori from the coast.[37]

Instead of allowing Māori to seek recognition of their rights in the courts, as has been the case in Australia and Canada, the government's response was to enact a statutory regime – the Foreshore and Seabed Act 2004 (FSA) – to manage Māori claims and guarantee public access to the coast. The FSA vested the foreshore and seabed in the Crown.[38] Instead of freehold titles, Māori could apply to either the Māori Land Court or the High Court for 'customary rights orders'[39] and a 'territorial customary rights order' from the High Court.[40] These did not confer proprietary interests, but only the right to engage in particular traditional activities – gathering stones for hangi and launching waka (canoes) were the examples most commonly cited in government publications.[41] The territorial customary rights order could result in a 'foreshore and seabed reserve' in lieu of title, which would recognise the tribe's guardianship of the area, though the land was 'held for the common benefit of the people of New Zealand'.[42] Despite the limited rights conferred by such an order, the FSA imposed onerous requirements of proof before a court order could be made including a requirement of continuing, exclusive occupation.[43]

An appeal to the Waitangi Tribunal by Māori who objected to the proposed FSA led to an urgent tribunal hearing and a report calling for negotiation between tribes and government to resolve the issue.[44] The government refused to follow these recommendations. Two tribes then petitioned the Committee on the Elimination of Racial Discrimination (CERD), which oversees the International Convention on the Elimination of All Forms of Racial Discrimination, seeking an urgent hearing.[45] The CERD heard the claim after the FSA had been enacted, but it was critical of the Act's 'discriminatory elements' and called for more dialogue between Māori and the government.[46] Māori members of the Labour government left the party in protest and formed the Māori Party.[47]

[37] D Brash 'Nationhood' (speech to the Orewa Rotary Club, Orewa, 27 January 2004).

[38] Foreshore and Seabed Act 2004, s 13.

[39] ibid ss 48–51 and ss 73–75.

[40] ibid s 13.

[41] *Recognising Customary Rights under the Marine and Coastal Area (Takutai Moana) Act 2011* (Ministry of Justice, 2015) 3; https://www.justice.govt.nz/assets/Documents/Publications/Blue-Book.pdf.

[42] Foreshore and Seabed Act 2004, s 40.

[43] ibid s 32.

[44] Waitangi Tribunal, *Report on the Crown's Foreshore and Seabed Policy* (Wai 1071, 2004).

[45] International Convention on the Elimination of All Forms of Racial Discrimination, concluded on 21 December 1965, entered into force 4 January 1969, 660 UNTS 195. For comments on the appeal to the CERD Committee, see C Charters and A Erueti, 'Report from the Inside: The CERD Committee's Review of the Foreshore and Seabed Act 2004' (2005) 36(2) *Victoria University of Wellington Law Review* 257.

[46] CERD, Foreshore and Seabed Act 2004 (2005) CERD/C/66/NZL/Dec.1.

[47] Ann Sullivan, 'Tōrangapū – Māori and Political Parties', https://teara.govt.nz/en/torangapu-maori-and-political-parties/print.

At the next election, the National Party formed an alliance with the Māori Party and promised to repeal the FSA. The FSA was repealed and replaced by the Marine and Coastal Area (Takutai Moana) Act 2011 (hereinafter the Takutai Moana Act). To avoid the issue of ownership, the Takutai Moana Act declares that the area, now known as 'the common marine area', cannot be owned by anyone (excepting pre-existing, long-standing private titles).[48] It also preserves existing recreational fishing rights, navigation rights and all other existing uses, including free legal public access in, on or over the common marine and coastal area.[49] As noted in the government's guide on the legislation, 'anyone can continue to walk, swim, sail, kayak, fish or have a picnic in the common marine and coastal area'.[50]

At the same time, the Takutai Moana Act provides for Māori interests that mirror those provided in the FSA – some would say too closely. The Takutai Moana Act continues to draw a distinction between customary rights (now called 'protected customary rights') and title ('customary marine title'). There continue to be difficult evidential standards of continuity and exclusivity for each type of right,[51] and the title does not confer the rights of exclusive occupation and use normally associated with title.[52] However, there are several significant changes. Māori may now pursue redress through two channels in relation to a customary marine title, either through negotiations with the government[53] or through the High Court.[54] If Māori seek an order through the High Court and meet the evidential tests, they obtain a set of procedural rights. If they pursue negotiations with the government, the implication is that there is the possibility of additional or more tailored forms of redress. In either case, Māori need to meet the evidential standards in the Act. Second, the procedural rights for the title holders include permission rights,[55] which grant Māori the right to refuse approval for certain activities in the title area (including withholding permission for a new activity that is carried out under a resource consent)[56] or specified conservation activities (such as declaring or extending marine reserves),[57] although in the latter case there is an exception for any project the Crown considers 'nationally significant'.[58] Title holders may also exclude public access to sites of spiritual significance, known as wahi tapu.[59] The customary

[48] Takutai Moana Act, ss 11 and 21.
[49] ibid ss 26–28.
[50] *Recognising Customary Rights* (n 41), 2.
[51] Takutai Moana Act, s 58.
[52] ibid ss 58 and 60.
[53] ibid ss 94–113.
[54] ibid ss 51–62.
[55] ibid s 62.
[56] ibid ss 66–70.
[57] ibid ss 71–75.
[58] So far, many tribes have applied for customary marine title. There were 145 applications filed before the deadline of 1 April 2017. However, the challenge will be to access those rights, given the very high evidential threshold.
[59] Takutai Moana Act, ss 78 and 79.

title holder also has a right to ownership of minerals, excluding precious minerals like oil and gold.[60]

Customary title will be difficult to obtain, especially for those tribes that have been subjected to intensive settlement and land loss, which is most of NZ's iwi.[61] Due to the scale of land dispossession that followed settlement, many iwi and hapū have not been able to exercise customary rights. At the top of the South Island, for example, tribes were rendered virtually landless because settler governments failed to establish promised reserves and took lands for settler townships and for public works. There are some tribes that have managed to retain significant blocks of land adjacent to the coast. And they will stand to gain customary titles because they are likely to demonstrate the Act's requirements of continuous use. But this leads to the invidious position that those who lost the most are the most disadvantaged. The response may be that this would have been the case under the common law in any event had government not intervened and enacted the Act.[62]

For those able to meet the evidential requirements, there are rights of significance, including the procedural rights granted to holders of customary titles. But they fall short of ownership, which of course was the Act's intention. Free public access, fishing and other recreational activities are allowed to continue in customary title areas. The Takutai Moana Act is an improvement on the FSA. However, when one weighs up what could have been gained if Māori had been allowed to pursue their remedy through the courts following the *Ngati Apa* decision (which is the likelihood of the granting of freehold titles in the foreshore and seabed area) with what has been gained (which is the right to seek rights and title that confer participatory and procedural rights to determine activity within their title area), it is not difficult to see that the legislation remains tipped in favour of the state and the public interest in fishing, navigation and recreational activity, particularly given the evidential barriers to establishing interests in the first place.

## V. MĀORI COMMERCIAL AQUACULTURE CLAIMS

The Māori Commercial Aquaculture Claims Settlement Act 2004 provides for the full and final settlement of contemporary Māori claims to commercial aquaculture space in the coastal marine area. The Settlement Act gives iwi rights to

[60] ibid s 83.

[61] In the recent and first High Court decision of *Re Tipene* [2016] NZHC 3199 under the Takutai Moana Act 2011, Mallon J had no doubt that the applicant for a customary marine title had established exclusive and continuous occupation of the coastal area claim off the Titi Islands, which are adjacent to Stewart Island. However, it is difficult to think of a more remote area of NZ.

[62] The government has said that the remedy for loss of rights is treaty settlements. However, this is a relatively weak substitute for legal rights.

20 per cent of the new aquaculture space created on, or after, 21 September 1992[63] and provides for the allocation and management of aquaculture settlement assets. Any claims relating to aquaculture before September 1992, and/or omissions of the Crown, can be addressed through the Treaty of Waitangi historical claims settlement process. Iwi must apply for a resource consent to establish a new aquaculture space under the RMA.

As a result, Māori will have a significant presence in the NZ aquaculture industry, and this is likely to increase over time as more aquaculture space is allocated under the Settlement Act 2004. The reality is that aquaculture can only be carried out in specific areas suitable for the industry, which means specific tribes stand to gain from it due to their location (ie, Marlborough Sounds and Hauraki Gulf).

This statutory agreement has its genesis in the Māori interests in the coastal marine area as recognised by the Sealord Deal and the *Ngati Apa* decision.[64] There is clear evidence of some customary practices. However, the logic is that if Māori have a strong connection with the marine area and fishing, then any new aquaculture industry should be made available to them. This argument was made by Māori before the Waitangi Tribunal, which recommended a statutory agreement.[65] Indeed, Māori efforts to engage in commercial aquaculture – stymied by local government – led to the *Ngati Apa* decision by local tribes in the Marlborough Sounds. Frustrated tribes saw a claim to the Māori Land Court as a means to bring the government to the negotiation table.

## VI. MINING IN THE MARINE AREA

The extraction of minerals and oil and gas has a long history in NZ dating back to the 1860s gold rush and the discovery of petroleum in Taranaki.[66] All oil and precious minerals (gold, silver and uranium) are vested in the Crown and permits are granted to companies to explore and extract minerals under the Crown Minerals Act 1991 (CMA).[67] In relation to the marine area, another layer of regulation is the Exclusive Economic Zone and Continental Shelf Act 2012, which aims at promoting the sustainable management of the EEZ's natural resources.[68] The general rule is that no person (or company) may undertake any activity, including mining, within the EEZ or continental shelf unless the activity

[63] Māori Commercial Aquaculture Claims Settlement Act 2004.

[64] *Ngati Apa* (n 35).

[65] Waitangi Tribunal, *Ahu Moana: The Aquaculture and Marine Farming Report* (Wai 953, 2002).

[66] R Boast and D Edmunds, 'Maori Claims to Petroleum in New Zealand' [2001] *Australian Mining and Petroleum Association Yearbook* 425.

[67] Crown Minerals Act 1991, s 10: 'all petroleum, gold, silver, and uranium … shall be the property of the Crown'.

[68] Exclusive Economic Zone and Continental Shelf Act 2012.

is authorised by a marine consent.[69] The Environmental Protection Authority (EPA) is responsible for issuing marine consents and ensuring that permit holders comply with the relevant environmental and safety standards.[70]

To date, practically all exploration and extraction of petroleum occurs in the EEZ.[71] Both the CMA and the EEZ have provisions that seek to protect Treaty interests. The Crown Minerals Act, for example, provides that all persons exercising powers and functions under the Act 'must have regard' to the principles of the Treaty.[72] The EEZ provides for a Māori Advisory Committee to advise marine consent authorities 'so that decisions made under this Act may be informed by a Māori perspective'.[73] When applying for a marine consent, companies must submit an Impact Assessment[74] identifying the effects of the proposed activities on the environment and on persons with an 'existing interest', which includes specified Māori interests.[75]

However, the general view is that the two statutes do not adequately protect Māori interests. There are concerns about Māori participation in decision making and the de-prioritisation of Māori concerns about environmental and cultural impacts. Under the CMA, for example, there is no obligation for permit holders to consult with Māori. The EEZ requires that the EPA and marine consent applicant notify (but not consult) iwi authorities, the holders of customary marine title and customary rights (granted under the Takutai Moana Act), and 'others with existing interests who are affected by the application'.[76] Specific types of permit holders are required to provide 'an annual report of the holder's engagement with iwi or hapū whose rohe includes some or all of the permit area', although again there is no requirement that iwi or hapu be involved in the preparation of the reports, nor are reports independently commissioned or reviewed.[77] The Waitangi Tribunal has inquired into the regulation of petroleum and identified the need for tribes' effective direct input into high-level policy making and planning, and their more active involvement in mining activities, including the provision of funding to enable them to engage.[78] Its report, released in 2006, recommended the establishment of an advisory body to the Minister of Energy and new 'district and regional representative bodies for tangata whenua' funded by the government 'for the purpose, among other

[69] Environmental Protection Authority Act 2011.

[70] ibid.

[71] See the amendments to the Crown Minerals Act prohibiting future exploration in the EEZ.

[72] Crown Minerals Act, s 4.

[73] Exclusive Economic Zone and Continental Shelf Act 2012, s 18.

[74] ibid s 38.

[75] The definition of 'existing interest' includes a treaty settlement; the Sealord fisheries settlement; and a protected customary right, or customary marine title recognised under the Marine and Coastal Area (Takutai Moana) Act 2011. See Exclusive Economic Zone and Continental Shelf Act 2012, s 4.

[76] Exclusive Economic Zone and Continental Shelf Act 2012, s 45.

[77] Crown Minerals Act 1991, s 33C.

[78] Waitangi Tribunal, *The Report on the Management of the Petroleum Resource* (Wai 796, 2006).

things, of considering petroleum management issues'.[79] So far, there have been no legislative reforms to give effects to these recommendations.

Māori have sought proprietary rights to petroleum and brought a claim to the Waitangi Tribunal, which found that they had a 'Treaty interest' in petroleum.[80] The recommendation that the Crown engage with tribes to negotiate and agreements on compensation was roundly rejected by the government of the day.[81]

## VII. CONCLUSION

The reforms made over the last three decades relating to treaty settlements, the statutory agreements and the inclusion of Māori interests in environmental legislation have resulted in Māori obtaining a variety of rights and interests in the marine area. Most notable is the Sealord Deal, which makes Māori a major player in the commercial fishing industry. However, for all of these gains, there remain gaps in relation to foreshore and seabed lands, and minerals which due to their value and importance to the public in terms of access and recreational fishing remain off-limits in terms of property rights. For the regulatory codes relating to the environment on the coast, there are repeated concerns by the Waitangi Tribunal and Māori about their ability to facilitate Māori participation in the planning and granting of consents. Yet, what is clear is that the reforms made to date, and in particular the Waitangi Tribunal, will ensure that debates over these unsettled matters will continue as Māori advocates strive for a greater say over the use of the resources (that were once theirs) in their tribal territory.

[79] ibid 185.

[80] Waitangi Tribunal, *The Petroleum Report* (Wai 796, 2003). In relation to Māori claims to gold, see also Waitangi Tribunal, *The Hauraki Report No 2* (Wai 686, 2006).

[81] 'Govt Rejects Iwi Claims on Kupe Royalties' *Daily News* (22 November 2003); 'Clark Rejects Māori Oil Claim' *Dominion Post* (20 May 2003).

# 11

# *Defending Ancestral Waters from the Maritime Incursions of the Modern World* The Tagbanua of the Philippines

JAY L BATONGBACAL

## I. INTRODUCTION

IN THE PHILIPPINES, the enactment of the Indigenous Peoples' Rights Act (IPRA)[1] in 1997 introduced the concept of 'ancestral domain' into the legal system. Though based on a singular Philippine decision on native title during the American colonial period,[2] the term 'ancestral domain' is defined by IPRA comprehensively to include inland waters, coastal areas and bodies of water.[3] This opened the door for Indigenous peoples' claims to marine waters in the Philippines. To date, only one Indigenous peoples' group, the Tagbanua of the Calamianes Islands located on the northern end of the Province of Palawan, has been successful in laying claim and procuring official recognition of ancestral domains that include significant areas of ancestral waters. This success story has been the subject of a number of academic and policy studies focused mainly on the Tagbanua's community-based management of the resources of their island and surrounding maritime space.[4] This chapter provides an overview of

[1] Indigenous Peoples Rights Act 1997 (Republic Act No 8371 of 1997) (IRPA), https://www.ecolex.org/details/legislation/indigenous-peoples-rights-act-1997-republic-act-no-8371-of-1997-lex-faoc013930. See also www.officialgazette.gov.ph/1997/10/29/republic-act-no-8371.

[2] *Cariño v Insular Government* (1909) 212 US 449.

[3] IPRA (n 1) s 3(a).

[4] See, eg, Meaghan E Calcari, 'Indigenous Marine Tenure in a Common Pool Framework: A Philippine Case Study' (Master's Project, Duke University, 2004), https://lawsdocbox.com/Politics/75326167-Indigenous-marine-tenure-in-a-common-pool-framework-a-philippine-

how continuing and unknown incursions of modernity, at least as far as the Tagbanua are concerned, continue to put pressure upon the community and the boundaries of its ancestral domain. Three events are narrated and analysed to highlight the difficulties faced by the Tagbanua community in maintaining and defending their hard-fought ancestral domain from the encroachment of modern projects that, even if they are not located within the domain's boundaries, nevertheless put stress upon the integrity of the Tagbanua's last remaining corner of the world.

## II. INDIGENOUS PEOPLES AND CONTEMPORARY PHILIPPINE LAW

The Philippines is a developing Southeast Asian state, archipelagic in nature and organised under a unitary, presidential form of government originally modelled after that of the US.[5] It has a population of a little over 100 million,[6] scattered amongst 7,641 islands[7] with a combined land area of 300,000 sq km and over 2 million sq km of sea.[8] The fragmented geography has created a great deal of diversity not only in terms of environment, flora and fauna, but also in terms of people and culture. Although most of the population bear the cultural characteristics of a Westernised people on account of prior colonial rule by Spain (1521–1898) and the US (1898–1946), a significant number are classified as Indigenous peoples who have retained much of their pre-colonial cultures and struggle to maintain their Indigenous identity.

The Indigenous peoples of the Philippines face many of the same challenges as Indigenous peoples elsewhere: social and economic marginalisation, loss of ancestral territories, political oppression and racial prejudice. Numbering over 110 distinct ethno-linguistic groups, they have striven against the inroads of Westernisation and globalisation, and today struggle against poverty and marginalisation.[9] In the 1970s, under the repressive regime of martial rule,

case-study-meaghan-e-calcari.html; Robert Charles G Capistrano, 'Indigenous Peoples, Their Livelihoods and Fishery Rights in Canada and the Philippines: Paradoxes, Perspectives and Lessons Learned', www.un.org/depts/los/nippon/unnff_programme_home/fellows_pages/fellows_papers/capistrano_0910_philippines.pdf; Benedeta Mantoan, 'Efficacy of Community-Based Management System to Preserve Access of Small-Scale Fishermen to Coastal Marine Area' (Master's dissertation, Leiden University, 2017), https://openaccess.leidenuniv.nl/handle/1887/52359; Arlene G Sampang, *The Calamian Tagbanwa Ancestral Domain (Coron Is., Palawa, Philippines): Evaluation of Traditional Fishing Practices towards Biodiversity Conservation and Sustainability* (WorldFish Center, 2007), cmsdata.iucn.org/downloads/sampanga_finalreport2007.pdf.

[5] Central Intelligence Agency, 'The Philippines', *CIA World Factbook* (Central Intelligence Agency, 2018), https://www.cia.gov/library/publications/the-world-factbook/geos/rp.html.

[6] Philippine Statistics Authority, 'Philippine Population Surpassed the 100 Million Mark (Results from the 2015 Census of Population)', https://psa.gov.ph/population-and-housing/node/120080.

[7] Gideon Lasco, 'From 7,107 to 7,641' *Philippine Daily Inquirer* (30 March 2017), https://opinion.inquirer.net/102845/from-7107-to-7641.

[8] Central Intelligence Agency (n 5).

[9] Jose Mencio Molintas, 'The Philippine Indigenous Peoples' Struggle for Land and Life: Challenging Legal Texts' (2004) 21 *Arizona Journal of International & Comparative Law*

Indigenous peoples came to the forefront of the struggle against the dictatorship and into the national consciousness due to the Cordillera mountain peoples' dramatic opposition to the World Bank-funded Chico River Dam Project.[10] The dam would have displaced thousands of Igorot tribespeople from their traditional communities and upland agricultural areas had it not been stopped by the determined and creative campaign waged on both cultural and environmental grounds. The campaign crystallised the Philippine environmental movement and linked it closely with the Indigenous peoples' movement in the 1980s.[11]

In the aftermath of the dictatorship, the liberal democratic 1987 Constitution gave voice to Indigenous peoples through specific provisions addressed to their concerns. It ordains that the state 'recognizes and promotes the rights of indigenous cultural communities within the framework of national unity and development'.[12] They are recognised as a marginalised sector entitled to party-list representation in the House of Representatives,[13] and Congress is authorised to create a consultative body to advise the president on policies affecting Indigenous cultural communities.[14]

Section 5 of the 1987 Constitution requires the state to protect the rights of Indigenous cultural communities (ICCs) to ancestral lands:

> The State, subject to the provisions of this Constitution and national development policies and programs, shall protect the rights of indigenous cultural communities to their ancestral lands to ensure their economic, social, and cultural well-being.
>
> The Congress may provide for the applicability of customary laws governing property rights or relations in determining the ownership and extent of ancestral domain.[15]

This duty even extends to protection against agrarian reform, which is a social reform that is also mandated by the 1987 Constitution.[16] More generally,

269, 272–73; see also United Nations Development Programme, 'Fast Facts: Indigenous Peoples in the Philippines', www.ph.undp.org/content/philippines/en/home/library/democratic_governance/FastFacts-IPs.html.

[10] Francisco Magno, 'The Growth of Philippine Environmentalism' (2016) 9 *Kasarinlan* 7, 9.

[11] ibid 9–10.

[12] Constitution of the Republic of the Philippines, 1987 (*Official Gazette of the Republic of the Philippines*), art II, s 22, www.officialgazette.gov.ph/constitutions/1987-constitution.

[13] ibid art VI, s 5(2). Party-list representation was provided by the 1987 Constitution in order to give traditionally unrepresented and marginalised groups such as labour, peasants, urban poor, indigenous peoples, women and youth a means of proportional representation separate from the conventional representation by congressional district.

[14] ibid art XVI, s 12. After ratification of the 1987 Constitution, the President established the Office of Muslim Affairs, the Office of Northern Cultural Communities and the Office of Southern Cultural Communities for this purpose. However, these were all abolished with the creation of the National Commission on Indigenous Peoples under the IPRA (n 1) s 83; Executive Order No 122-A Creating the Office of Muslim Affairs 1987; Executive Order No 122-B Creating the Office for Northern Cultural Communities 1987; Executive Order No 122-C Creating the Office of Southern Cultural Communities 1987.

[15] Constitution (n 12) art XII, s 5.

[16] ibid art XIII, s 6.

section 17 directs the state to protect Indigenous cultures, traditions and communities:

> The State shall recognize, respect, and protect the rights of indigenous cultural communities to preserve and develop their cultures, traditions, and institutions. It shall consider these rights in the formulation of national plans and policies.

The 1987 Constitution provided the basis for further advocacy work in the Indigenous peoples' movement and, 10 years later, a breakthrough was achieved with the enactment of the Indigenous Peoples Rights Act 1997 (IPRA).[17] Indigenous peoples or ICCs are described by the IPRA as people who fall within a number of possible categories. The terms are used to refer to:

> [A] group of people or homogenous societies identified by self-ascription and ascription by others, who have continuously lived as organized community on communally bounded and defined territory, and who have, under claims of ownership since time immemorial, occupied, possessed and utilized such territories, sharing common bonds of language, customs, traditions and other distinctive cultural traits, or who have, through resistance to political, social and cultural inroads of colonization, non-indigenous religions and cultures, became historically differentiated from the majority of Filipinos. ICCs/IPs shall likewise include peoples who are regarded as indigenous on account of their descent from the populations which inhabited the country, at the time of conquest or colonization, or at the time of inroads of non-indigenous religions and cultures, or the establishment of present state boundaries, who retain some or all of their own social, economic, cultural and political institutions, but who may have been displaced from their traditional domains or who may have resettled outside their ancestral domains.[18]

The foregoing definition attempts to encompass all Indigenous peoples' groups across the Philippines in all the various situations in which they find themselves, ranging from oppressed and isolated communities in their remaining ancestral domains to displaced and nomadic groups detached from their original territories. It is quite open-ended, but such an openness is necessary in order to account for more than 110 communities scattered across the archipelago.

The IPRA also expressly recognises the concept of ancestral lands/domains, which is defined to 'include such concepts of territories which cover not only the physical environment but the total environment including the spiritual and cultural bonds to the areas which the ICCs/IPs possess, occupy and use and to which they have claims of ownership'.[19] But the Indigenous concept of ownership is differentiated from that in the general civil law by being described as 'ICCs/IPs private but community property which belongs to all generations and therefore cannot be sold, disposed or destroyed', consistent with the

[17] IPRA (n 1).
[18] ibid s 3(h).
[19] ibid s 4.

view that all ancestral domains and resources 'serve as the material bases of [ICCs/IPs] cultural integrity.'[20] It is expressly described as a communal right not to be construed as co-ownership under the civil law, which makes it *sui generis* in Philippine law.[21]

Ancestral domains and ancestral lands are defined specifically. Ancestral domains comprise:

> [A]ll areas generally belonging to ICCs/IPs comprising lands, inland waters, coastal areas, and natural resources therein, held under a claim of ownership, occupied or possessed by ICCs/IPs, by themselves or through their ancestors, communally or individually since time immemorial, continuously to the present except when interrupted by war, force majeure or displacement by force, deceit, stealth or as a consequence of government projects or any other voluntary dealings entered into by government and private individuals/corporations, and which are necessary to ensure their economic, social and cultural welfare. It shall include ancestral lands, forests, pasture, residential, agricultural, and other lands individually owned whether alienable and disposable or otherwise, hunting grounds, burial grounds, worship areas, bodies of water, mineral and other natural resources, and lands which may no longer be exclusively occupied by ICCs/IPs but from which they traditionally had access to for their subsistence and traditional activities, particularly the home ranges of ICCs/IPs who are still nomadic and/or shifting cultivators.[22]

On the other hand, ancestral lands:

> [R]efer to land occupied, possessed and utilized by individuals, families and clans who are members of the ICCs/IPs since time immemorial, by themselves or through their predecessors-in-interest, under claims of individual or traditional group ownership, continuously, to the present except when interrupted by war, force majeure or displacement by force, deceit, stealth, or as a consequence of government projects and other voluntary dealings entered into by government and private individuals/corporations, including, but not limited to, residential lots, rice terraces or paddies, private forests, swidden farms and tree lots.[23]

Indigenous peoples' rights of ownership and possession of ancestral domains are extensive, and are laid out by the IPRA as well. These encompass the rights of ownership; the right to develop lands and natural resources within the ancestral domain; the right to stay within their territories; the right to re-settlement in case of displacement; the right to regulate the entry of migrants; the right to safe and clean air and water; the right to claim parts of government reservations; the right to resolve land conflicts in accordance with customary laws; the right to possession of ancestral lands; the right to transfer such ancestral land or property to other members of the community; the right to redeem lands transferred to non-members of the ICC within 15 years from the transfer if the

[20] ibid s 5.
[21] ibid s 55.
[22] ibid s 3(a).
[23] ibid s 3(b).

transferor's consent was vitiated and the transfer was made for an unconscionable consideration or price.[24]

Unlike conventional ownership under civil law, ownership of ancestral domains/lands also includes sustainable traditional resource rights,[25] which complement the legal responsibilities of ICCs/IPs to maintain ecological balance within the ancestral domain, and reforest denuded areas.[26] Section 57 of the IPRA further guarantees:

> Natural Resources within Ancestral Domains. – The ICCs/IPs shall have priority rights in the harvesting, extraction, development or exploitation of any natural resources within the ancestral domains. A non-member of the ICCs/IPs concerned may be allowed to take part in the development and utilization of the natural resources for a period of not exceeding twenty-five (25) years renewable for not more than twenty-five (25) years: Provided, That a formal and written agreement is entered into with the ICCs/IPs concerned or that the community, pursuant to its own decision making process, has agreed to allow such operation: Provided, finally, That the NCIP may exercise visitorial powers and take appropriate action to safeguard the rights of the ICCs/IPs under the same contract.

Any use and exploitation of natural resources within ancestral domains must be undertaken only with the free, prior and informed consent (FPIC) of the Indigenous peoples concerned, which is defined as:

> [T]he consensus of all members of the ICCs/IPs to be determined in accordance with their respective customary laws and practices, free from any external manipulation, interference and coercion, and obtained after fully disclosing the intent and scope of the activity, in a language and process understandable to the community.[27]

However, these extensive rights do not necessarily upset the existing distribution of property rights, since the property rights of third parties within ancestral domains that were already existing or vested at the time of the IPRA's enactment were also recognised and respected.[28] Thus, Indigenous peoples' rights are subject to the vested rights of settlers and non-Indigenous persons. It may therefore be necessary to determine the property rights of Indigenous peoples and non-Indigenous parties on a case-by-case basis and in accordance with their specific circumstances.

Rights to ancestral domains/lands are based on native title, described as:

> [P]re-conquest rights to lands and domains which, as far back as memory reaches, have been held under a claim of private ownership by ICCs/IPs, have never been public lands and are thus indisputably presumed to have been held that way since before the Spanish Conquest.[29]

[24] ibid ss 7–8.
[25] ibid s 5.
[26] ibid s 9.
[27] ibid s 3(g).
[28] ibid s 56.
[29] ibid s 3(l).

These are formally recognised by the state through the issuance of a Certificate of Ancestral Domain Title (CADT), a process of delineation,[30] mapping based on proof of customary possession since time immemorial[31] and validation by the National Commission on Indigenous Peoples (NCIP),[32] until actual issuance and registration.[33]

The IPRA has weathered a challenge before the Supreme Court. In *Cruz v Secretary of Environment and Natural Resources*,[34] the validity of the IPRA was directly contested in a taxpayer suit backed by mining companies. The Court divided evenly on the petition, despite being deliberated upon twice, and thus the Act survived the attack.[35] Despite the constitutional and legal mandates in place, the Philippines has not yet ratified International Labour Organization (ILO) Convention No 169, the Indigenous and Tribal Peoples' Convention.[36] This is unfortunate, considering that the Philippines was among the early adopters of the United Nations Declaration on the Rights of Indigenous Peoples (UNDRIP) and even hosted the Asia Workshop for Promotion of the UNDRIP.[37]

## III. THE TAGBANUA AND THEIR QUEST FOR ANCESTRAL DOMAIN

The Tagbanua are an ancient Indigenous people regarded as being among the original inhabitants of the Philippine province of Palawan. Spread across the islands that comprise Palawan, most Tagbanua are lowland shifting cultivators, but one of the three sub-groups referred to as the Calamian Tagbanua inhabit the Calamian Island group (comprised of the islands of Coron, Busuanga and Culion, as well as portions of the Linapacan Islands) located at the northern end of the Palawan mainland.[38] Unlike the other two groups who inhabit the southern portions of the Palawan mainland, the Calamian Tagbanua are semi-nomadic fisherfolk with their own language that is incomprehensible to the other groups.[39] A majority of the Calamian Tagbanua live in the island of Coron,

[30] ibid ss 51, 52(a)–(c).

[31] ibid s 52(d) and (e).

[32] ibid s 52(f)–52(i).

[33] ibid s 52(j)–52(k).

[34] *Cruz v Secretary of Environment and Natural Resources*, GR No 135385, 6 December 2000, http://sc.judiciary.gov.ph/jurisprudence/2000/dec2000/135385.htm.

[35] ibid.

[36] ILO Convention 169, Indigenous and Tribal Peoples Convention, 1989 (No 169), https://www.ilo.org/dyn/normlex/en/f?p=NORMLEXPUB:11300:0::NO::P11300_INSTRUMENT_ID:312314.

[37] Sedfrey M Candelaria, *Comparative Analysis on the ILO Indigenous and Tribal Peoples Convention No 169, Declaration of the Rights of Indigenous Peoples (UNDRIP), and Indigenous Peoples' Rights Act (IPRA) of the Philippines* (International Labour Organization, 2012) 3.

[38] Dante Dalabajan, 'The Healing of a Tagbanua Ancestral Homeland' in Elmer M Ferrer, Lenore P de la Cruz and Gary F Newkirk (eds), *Hope Takes Root: Community-Based Coastal Resources Management Stories from Southeast Asia* (CBCRM Resource Center, 2001) 174.

[39] Dave de Vera and Kail Zingapan, *The Ancestral Lands and Waters of the Indigenous Tagbanwa Communities of Northern Palawan* (Asian NGO Coalition for Agrarian Reform and Rural Development, 2017) 9.

a very small undeveloped and forested island with clear lakes and limestone cliffs from which the name of the larger municipality was drawn. Two tribal *barangay* (villages) inhabit the island, Banuang Daan and Cabugao; a 2005 census recorded 2,242 residents.[40] The rest reside in scattered *sitio* (enclaves) across seven other barangay all around the island. The total population of Calamian Tagbanua was recorded at 10,299 in 1995.[41]

The islanders' lives are based on their interaction with the island's caves (*luyang*), corals (*awuyuk* or *talu*), seawater (*teeb sorobleyen*) and forest (*geba*). They subsist by foraging edible wild tubers and fishing, and eke out a livelihood by trading sea cucumber, seashells and birds' nests with outsiders.[42] Since the late 1990s, the Calamian Tagbanua have also engaged in seaweed farming to derive additional income from the local trade in carrageenan, a seaweed extract widely used by the food industry.[43]

Subsistence fishing and gathering of aquatic foods are still done in the traditional manner by diving, hook-and-line, spears, nets.[44] *Balinsasayaw* birds' nests are gathered by scaling the island's jagged limestone cliffs and descending into dark caves where the birds roost. Historical records indicate that the Tagbanua have been trading birds' nests (used for birds' nest soup) with the Chinese since the thirteenth century.[45]

Despite the incursions of Muslim raiders from the south and the Spanish colonisation of the Philippine Islands in the 1700s–1800s, the Tagbanua were never influenced by other cultures as they tended to retreat into the islands' interior. They enjoyed an autonomous economy and existence due to a low population to resource base ratio, a subsistence economy, and cultural norms that made it a taboo to exploit the forests and waters indiscriminately.[46] Specific limestone caves were held by families and passed on to their heirs, and certain reefs and lake features were held sacred and off-limits to fishing and diving. Things did not begin changing until the mid-1970s, when the local government attempted to take control of the Tagbanua's caves, likely in order for the town mayor to monopolise the birds' nest trade.[47] In the 1980s, the influx of migrants from the Visayas (likewise mostly subsistence fishers) forced the Tagbanua to re-settle and congregate in Coron Island. The imposition of real estate taxes upon the Tagbanua, which penalised failure to pay with confiscation of their lands (including the caves), led the villagers to realise that their survival and homeland were at risk.[48]

[40] Sampang (n 4) 20.

[41] De Vera and Zingapan (n 39) 8. The other barangay are Buenavista, Bulalacao, Decabobo, Lajala, Malawig, Marcilla, Tara and Turda.

[42] Dalabajan (n 38) 174.

[43] De Vera and Zingapan (n 39) 8–9.

[44] Capistrano (n 4) 61.

[45] Dalabajan (n 38) 174.

[46] ibid 175.

[47] ibid.

[48] ibid 176.

In 1985, the Tagbanuas of Coron Island established the Tagbanua Foundation of Coron Island (TFCI) and applied for a Community Forest Stewardship Agreement with the Department of Environment and Natural Resources (DENR). The stewardship agreement was a tenurial instrument by which the government allowed individuals and communities to continue occupying and cultivating areas it considered to be public lands for up to 25 years (renewable for another 25 years) in exchange for protection and re-forestation activities.[49] Encouraged by the success of the TFCI, the other Tagbanua groups scattered across the Calamian formed their own associations in each village[50] and eventually formed a federation of Tagbanua associations called the *Saragpunta*.

By the 1990s, the Tagbanuas were able to leverage the forestry agreements to regain control of the ancestral domain by recovering their caves, which were located inside the defined forest areas.[51] Although fully aware that the instruments were limited to the land, they persisted in their efforts to recover the waters as well. At the time, environmental awareness and advocacy reached new heights with the enactment of the Strategic Environmental Plan for Palawan Law,[52] which established a *sui generis* management regime for the province of Palawan as the country's last ecological frontier, and the National Integrated Protected Areas System Act,[53] which re-organised and enhanced the country's system of national parks and nature reserves, and brought them into line with the country's commitments under the Convention on Biological Diversity. Both laws classified Coron Island as a protected area, but the Tagbanua resisted participating in the various multi-sectoral bodies and management planning activities initiated under them because they viewed them as usurping their community's rights and authority over their ancestral domain.[54]

## IV. THE TAGBANUA ANCESTRAL DOMAIN CLAIM AND TITLE

In 1993, a progressive-minded DENR, which also had jurisdiction over the management and disposition of lands of the public domain, issued an administrative order providing for the recognition and award of Certificates of Ancestral Domain Claims (CADCs).[55] The regulation enabled Indigenous communities to make and document claims to land, resources and rights within defined territories. This was followed by another order providing guidelines for the management of CADC areas and the formulation of Ancestral Domain Management Plans

[49] Capistrano (n 4) 62, citing DENR Administrative Order No 96-29 (1996) issued in accordance with the provisions of the Philippine Forestry Code of 1975.

[50] De Vera and Zingapan (n 39) 10.

[51] Capistrano (n 4) 63.

[52] Rep Act No 7611 (1992).

[53] Rep Act No 7586 (1992).

[54] Dalabajan (n 38) 181–87.

[55] DENR Administrative Order No 92-02 (1992).

for each.[56] The Tagbanua saw these developments as an opportunity to codify their customs, beliefs and practices in the use of their ancestral domains, and to document their claims through mapping and resource assessments with the assistance of non-governmental organisations (NGOs). These were evidence of the Tagbanua's possession and utilisation of their ancestral domain since time immemorial.

The process took much work, beginning with community meetings and informal exchanges among the elders to determine the traditional home ranges of the Tagbanua using oral histories.[57] Traditional knowledge of the sea territories passed on by their ancestors and still in use were used to identify maritime boundaries.[58] The coral reefs, the three largest of which are named *Talung dakulu*, *Talung gesye* and *Nataktakan*,[59] were long known by tradition and considered sacred; these formed the core of the area, while the dive areas for marine species traditionally gathered and used by the Tagbanua were utilised to establish the outer limits of the ancestral waters. These thus came to encompass their ancestral fishing grounds (*panyaan*), fish sanctuaries and reserve areas, diving areas, inter-tidal flats for foraging shells and crustaceans, sandy and muddy shoals, atolls that hosted caves of birds' nests, deep sea areas and other collection areas.[60] Community sketch maps were produced to define boundaries, document place names, and locate camps and resources, as well as geographical features.[61] These also helped to prepare for ground surveys and validation. With the assistance of NGOs, Global Positioning System (GPS) surveys were conducted, and technical survey maps or plans were produced to meet the requirements of the DENR.[62] In all, the Calamian Tagbanua laid claim to seven distinct areas of marine ancestral waters.

The Coron Island claim was the first to be submitted to the DENR, which held the required public hearings at which the claim and evidence, including historical accounts, place names and maps, were not disputed. The municipal council issued and submitted more than 14 resolutions opposing the claim, citing economic interests and incoming project proposals for integrated area protection, but did not dispute the evidence of possession, occupation and utilisation since time immemorial. After assessing the evidence and considering the opposition, the DENR approved the Tagbanua claim and issued the Certificate of Ancestral Domain Claim on 12 June 1998, covering an area of 22,400 hectares of land and waters.[63]

[56] DENR Administrative Order No 92-34 (1992).
[57] De Vera and Zingapan (n 39) 11–12.
[58] ibid.
[59] Sampang (n 4) 21.
[60] De Vera and Zingapan (n 39) 11–12.
[61] ibid.
[62] ibid.
[63] ibid 14.

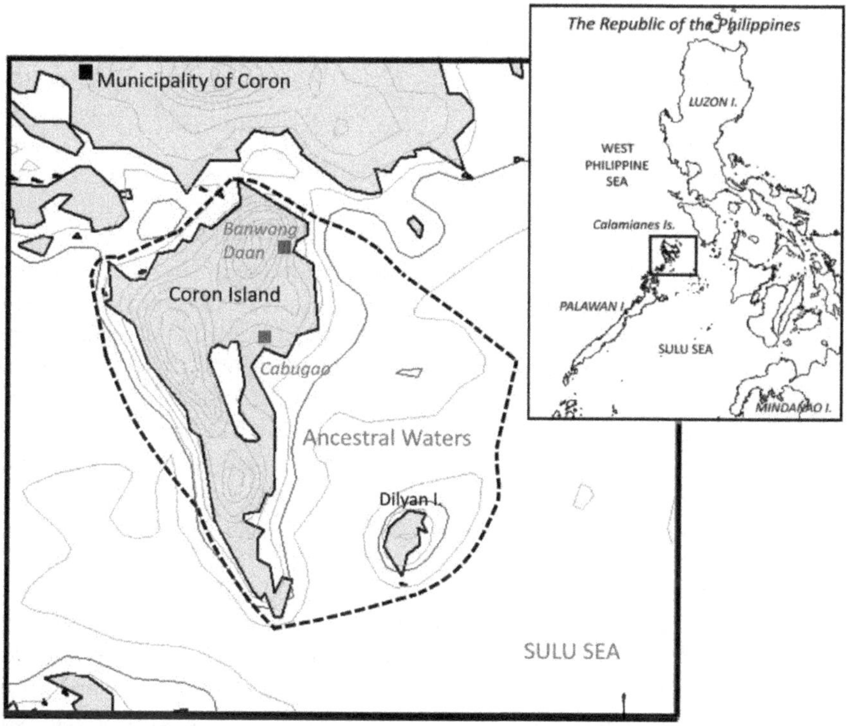


**Figure 11.1** Map of the ancestral domain, including ancestral waters, of the Calamian Tagbanua of Coron Island (enclosed within the dotted line). Based on www.landmarkmap.org

In the meantime, while the Coron Island application was pending, the IPRA was enacted on 29 October 1997. The new law provided for the creation of the National Commission on Indigenous Peoples (NCIP). The NCIP was empowered to accept, process and decide upon applications for recognition of ancestral domains. However, it recognised prior delineation/application processes carried out under DENR regulations and allowed Indigenous peoples to apply for Certificates of Ancestral Domain Title (CADTs).[64]

In 2002, the NCIP converted the Coron Island CADC into a CADT, formally recognising the title and rights of the Tagbanua over their ancestral domains as defined and delineated in accordance with the IPRA. The area was also increased by 2,236 hectares as a result of the NCIP review and validation.[65] The Tagbanua CADT for Coron served as a precedent; in 2010, another CADT was awarded to the Tagbanua, this time over nearby Calauit Island covering 55,539 hectares (of which 93 per cent are ancestral waters). A third CADT application covering

[64] IPRA (n 1) ss 51–53.
[65] De Vera and Zingapan (n 39) 14.

75,639 hectares was reportedly approved in 2010, but has not yet been officially awarded at the time of this writing.

The issuance of the first CADT in favour of the Tagbanua strengthened their hand in the struggle to recover control of their ancestral domain from various levels of government.[66] Since approval of the CADC in 1998, the Tagbanua had formulated an Ancestral Domain Management Plan (ADMP) to serve as the basis for tribal regulation of activities within their lands and waters. It was a compendium of Indigenous practices, enforceable with sanctions in accordance with customary law.[67] The local government of the Municipality of Coron resisted the Tagbanua's efforts by invoking its jurisdiction over municipal waters and tried to limit Tagbanua waters to a mere 50–100 metres from shore.[68] The Province of Palawan posed a threat by including Coron within the Environmentally Critical Areas Network managed by the multi-sectoral Palawan Council for Sustainable Development.[69] The DENR also attempted to take over control of the Tagbanua domain by including it within a protected area under the National Integrated Protected Areas System.[70]

But with the CADT, the Tagbanua were able to successfully defend their exclusive jurisdiction, and the ADMP became more coherent as they set about the task of managing their domain.[71] The ADMP focused on preserving Tagbanua culture, customary rules and resource uses such as fishing.[72] In addition to traditional uses, the Tagbanua incorporated eco-tourism into their economic activities in order to augment their income and benefit from Coron's pre-existing tourism. After the issuance of the CADT, the local government relinquished the management of the popular tourist attractions within the Tagbanua ancestral domain that included Kayangan Lake, two lagoons and the beaches of Coron Island; the Tagbanua were then able to regulate the entry and number of visitors as well as impose small user fees.[73] Funds are deposited into the account

[66] Magnus Torell and Albert M Salamanca, *Institutional Issues and Perspectives in the Management of Fisheries and Coastal Resources in Southeast Asia* (World Fish Center, 2002) 110–13, https://core.ac.uk/download/pdf/7084029.pdf?repositoryId=153.

[67] Dalabajan (n 38) 180–81.

[68] ibid 180. See also Philippine Fisheries Code 1998 (Republic Act No 8550), ss 16–18.

[69] Dalabajan (n 38) 184. The Environmentally Critical Areas Network (ECAN) is essentially a special land and water use plan for the entire Province of Palawan. Inclusion of the Tagbanua ancestral domain in the ECAN would subordinate the area's planning and regulation to that of the province, and thus surrender management to non-Tagbanua 'outsiders'. See also Strategic Environmental Plan for Palawan Act 1992 (Republic Act No 7611).

[70] Dalabajan (n 38) 183–84.

[71] Catherine A Courtney et al, 'Marine Tenure and Small-Scale Fisheries: Learning from the Philippines Experience' (Tetra-tech, 2017) 26, https://land-links.org/wp-content/uploads/2018/02/USAID_Land_Tenure_TGCC_Philippines_Marine_Tenure_Report_Updated.pdf.

[72] See Torell and Salamanca (n 66) 108–11.

[73] Grizelda Mayo-Anda, Loreto L Cagatulla and Antonio GM la Viña, 'Is the Concept of "Free and Prior Informed Consent" Effective as a Legal and Governance Tool to Ensure Equity among Indigenous Peoples?' (Environmental Legal Assistance Center, Inc, 2006) 19, http://dlc.dlib.indiana.edu/dlc/bitstream/handle/10535/2204/Mayo_Anda_Grizelda_Cagatulla_La_Vina.pdf?sequence=1&isAllowed=y.

of the tribe's foundation, which are then re-distributed through community development projects for education, health and cleanliness.[74]

## V. MODERNITY'S CONTINUING INCURSIONS

Despite their initial success in obtaining recognition of their ancestral domains, the Tagbanua remain vulnerable to the inroads of the Westernised majority and are required to constantly defend both their titled and untitled areas from the pressures of development. The enactment of the IPRA in 1997 has not completely and finally addressed the Tagbanua's problems, and they continue to struggle against events and attempts that they perceive to represent a danger to their hold on their ancestral domain. This section examines three such examples.

### A. The Malampaya Deepwater Gas-to-Power Project

In 1992, natural gas in commercial quantities was discovered in the Camago-Malampaya reserve located some 80 km west of Palawan. After due consideration, the national government decided to develop the gas field and established the first petroleum production platform of the country, the Malampaya Deepwater Gas-to-Power Project. It contracted Shell Philippines Exploration, Inc to drill and develop the reserve under Petroleum Service Contract No 38 that would see natural gas production begin in October 2001 to supply natural gas for power generation until at least 2024. The project was a major undertaking (total cost US$4.5 billion) that involved the drilling of submarine wells into the gas reservoir, sub-sea systems, construction and installation of an offshore natural gas production platform, and a 504-km-long natural gas pipeline that connected the production platform with the onshore natural gas processing plant that supplied three power-generating plants in Luzon. Along the way, the pipeline passes through and around the Calamianes Islands.[75]

After initial stakeholder consultations in 1995, the formal environmental impact assessment process began in October 1996 to enable the submission of the Environmental Impact Statement (EIS) in June 1997 and the issuance of the required environmental compliance certificate in December 1997. Six formal stakeholder workshops were held successively between 13 November and

[74] Pia Ranada, 'Talking Ecotourism with the Tagbanua', www.rappler.com//rappler-blogs/pia-ranada/62729-talking-ecotourism-tagbanua-coron.

[75] Jay L Batongbacal, 'EIA as the Start of a Social Bargaining Process: The Malampaya Deepwater Gas-to-Power Project' in Klaus Bosselmann, Ron Engel and Prue Taylor (eds), *Governance for Sustainability: Issues, Challenges, Successes* (IUCN, 2008) 72, https://portals.iucn.org/library/sites/library/files/documents/EPLP-070.pdf.

2 December 1996. In each day-long session, Shell began with a one-hour presentation of the project, its background, technical and scientific aspects, and project national and local benefits; this was followed by participants' break-out group discussions to elaborate upon perceived issues, impacts, problems and concerns as well as suggested alternatives or solutions. A total of 274 people participated in the six workshops, or an average of 45 people each. Shell also conducted a socio-economic survey, and separate focus group discussions with 134 local government officials and personnel.[76]

These complied with the public participation requirements of the EIA process. But the penultimate workshop, held in the Municipality of Coron, turned out to be highly contentious when two distinct groups, a pearl farmers' association and the Tagbanua community, raised objections to the project. While the pearl farmers were concerned over the project's potential impacts on water quality, the Tagbanua were concerned that the project might affect the habitat of the *balinsasayaw* birds whose nests they depended on for their livelihood, as well as their sacred coral reefs. During the time, the Tagbanua were still in the process of documenting and applying for ancestral domain title and they wished to know whether the pipeline would pass through their prospective ancestral waters. They were concerned over the possible impact of a pipeline leak.[77]

A separate consultation meeting was held in Banuang Daan on Coron Island itself, but there is no available public record of this meeting even in the EIA documents submitted. Secondary sources indicate that it took place in October 1997, long after the EIS was submitted, and involved two representatives from Shell meeting with Tagbanua village leaders. The Tagbanua reportedly reiterated their concerns and showed the map of their ancestral domain, stressing the need to compare their domain boundaries with the planned pipeline route and requesting the execution of a formal Memorandum of Agreement assuring access to fishing grounds, providing alternative livelihood activities and specifying the company's environmental accountability in the event of an accident. Despite assurances that the final map of the pipeline route would be provided, the Tagbanua never received further information, and Shell denies that any Memorandum of Agreement was ever discussed. However, Shell asserted that in response to Tagbanua concerns, the pipeline route proposed avoided the coral reef areas in northern Coron and the adjacent Busuanga Islands.[78] Shell

[76] Woodward-Clyde Inc and Shell Pilipinas Exploration BV, 'Malampaya Deepwater Gas-to-Power Project: Environmental Impact Assessment Scoping Report' (Department of Environment and Natural Resources, 1996) 10.

[77] Jay L Batongbacal, 'Developing an Ecological Social Justice Framework for Ocean Energy Technologies: Case Studies from the Philippines' (Doctoral dissertation, Dalhousie University, 2010), 585–87, 590–92, https://dalspace.library.dal.ca/handle/10222/13011?show=full.

[78] ibid 590–91.

even received a Sustainable Development Partnership Award in 2002 for action it had taken.[79]

But while the pipeline passed at least 14 km from the Tagbanua ancestral domain on Coron Island, it is not correct to say that it deliberately avoided the Tagbanua reefs and other domains. As explained by one Tagbanua leader:

> [They] did not say where the pipe passed, and we are not sure either. Before they laid the pipe, they showed us a map of where it would pass. We found out that it passed the center of the ancestral domain in barangay Bulalacao, not Coron Island which was some distance away. Nothing changed in their plans, they just continued it.[80]

The leader refers to the Tagbanua community on separate islands southeast of Culion Island, which is itself located south of Coron. Culion used to be a leper colony and was only recently established as a separate municipality. On the southern tip of Culion Island, the pipeline passes as close as 1.3 km to the shore. A study using geographic information system (GIS) and bathymetric analysis revealed that the pipeline actually deviated from the original proposed route and came even closer to the land. It also crossed shallow coral areas, which are likely fishing grounds claimed by the Tagbanua as part of their ancestral waters. Unfortunately, at the time, the ancestral domain in the Bulalacao Islets off the larger island of Culion had not yet been delineated and the application for the CADC had not been approved. This remains the case today.

The interaction between the Malampaya Project proponents and the Tagbanua is an interesting case study. Shell showcases the Malampaya Project as a demonstration of its adherence to the principles of sustainable development, where a major industrial undertaking in an environmentally critical area is carried out with minimal impact. Shell has been recognised as a classic case study for the attention it paid to stakeholder participation and its response to stakeholder claims,[81] and to a considerable extent this is true; the project's social development and corporate social responsibility programmes have provided tangible benefits to a number of communities along the project's path. But when it comes to the Tagbanua in particular, there is a dissonance in Shell's presentation and reality. Shell's Sustainable Development Award in 2002 was partly based on the prominent claim that it diverted the project pipeline's path to avoid environmentally critical areas, including the Tagbanua's ancestral waters and their sacred reefs.

However, while it was true that the project avoided an environmentally critical area in general, it actually still crossed delineated ancestral domain in areas further south. For the Tagbanua, the major issue was that there were pending

[79] Batongbacal (n 75) 71.

[80] Interview with Tagbanua leader Rodolfo Aguilar, 2006, as cited in Batongbacal (n 77) 619.

[81] Steve Herz, Antonio GM la Viña and Jonathan Sohn, 'Development without Conflict: The Business Case for Community Consent' (World Resources Institute, 2007) 19, http://doc.abhatoo.net.ma/doc/IMG/pdf/development_without_conflict_fpic.pdf.

ancestral domain claims that were not being recognised by the project planners, notwithstanding legislation supporting ownership claims and a process for validating and securing community title thereto. Regardless of its good intentions, Shell was actually unable to respond to the Tagbanua concerns, and possibly aggravated them by laying the pipeline through claimed ancestral waters. Fortunately, the pipeline's environmental impact was minimal and, to date, no untoward incident has taken place. However, the Tagbanua still bear the grievance, as in their eyes, there was an intrusion into their space, undefined though it was.

### B. The RBL Aquaculture Project

Sometime in 2006, private companies secured a permit to establish an aquaculture facility in barangay Buenavista north of the Municipality of Coron. They entered and occupied portions of two Tagbanua enclaves, Sito Makwaw and Sitio Minukbay, forced some tribal members out of their homes and prevented them from cultivating their crops. Workers of the companies also set up their own houses in order for them to tend to the aquaculture facility.[82]

The affected Tagbanua filed a petition with the NCIP against the companies. They invoked their rights as Indigenous peoples, asserting that while they did not yet have a CADT, they had already made a claim for their ancestral domain even prior to the enactment of the IPRA and that the validation of the claim was already pending with the NCIP.[83] They argued that the IPRA did not even require prior issuance of a CADT but already recognised their rights to their ancestral domain.[84] As such, their FPIC was required under the IPRA before any entity, whether public or private, could undertake any activity within their ancestral domain. They also argued that their FPIC had to be certified by the NCIP.[85]

The NCIP took cognisance of the case and assumed jurisdiction. However, this was contested by the private companies, which appealed to the Court of Appeals and then the Supreme Court. The companies attacked the jurisdiction of the NCIP over disputes involving litigants who were not members of the Indigenous peoples, and contested the petitioners' status and identity as Tagbanua Indigenous peoples.

The Supreme Court ruled against the Tagbanua on both counts. On the issue of jurisdiction, the Court held that disputes between parties who are not both members of the Indigenous peoples fall within the general jurisdiction of the regular courts. The NCIP's jurisdiction is limited to disputes between members

[82] *Engr Ben Y Lim et al v Sulpicio G Gamosa et al* [2015] Supreme Court GR No 193964, 25–26.
[83] ibid 25.
[84] ibid; see also IPRA (n 1) ss 3.1, 11.
[85] *Engr Ben Y Lim et al* (n 82) 25. See also IPRA (n 1) s 59.

of Indigenous peoples' groups.[86] While the rationale for this conclusion may be convincing, the ruling on the second point is more questionable.

Focusing on the content of their petition before the NCIP, the Supreme Court noted that the petitioners merely alleged that they were Tagbanua, which it described as a 'conclusion' and 'not an ultimate fact from which [they] can anchor the rights they claim to have been violated'.[87] The Court said that the petition did not mention ultimate facts that led to the conclusion that they were Tagbanuas, that they represented the Tagbanua Indigenous Cultural Community and that they had rights to their ancestral domain, and nor did they mention the acts or omissions of the private companies which constituted a violation of such rights.

The Supreme Court considered the factual demonstration of their identity and authority as 'crucial since intra-IPs' conflicts and contest for representation are not impossible'.[88] Moreover, the Court said that the petitioners 'should have alleged the ultimate facts constitutive of their customs, political structures, institutions, decision-making processes, and such other indicators of indigenous persons' nature distinct and native to them', meaning that they should have asserted their identity 'through a reduction into facts of the definition and description of an indigenous people in IPRA', specifically under section 3(h) of the IPRA. As for the rights to ancestral domain, the Court said that it required historical proof which must also proceed from the allegations of the petition; it further said that the petition should outline and trace the history of the Tagbanua's Indigenous ownership of domain and land.[89] It also thought it significant that the petitioners 'do not identify themselves with the other Tagbanuas who have been awarded a Certificate of Ancestral Domain Claim as of 1998'.[90] As a result, it decided that the NCIP did not have jurisdiction over the Tagbanua's petition 'just by the mere expedient that their petition involves rights of ICCs/IPs'.[91]

This case demonstrates the continuing competition between the IPRA's ideals and the judicial system's ingrained legal bias against Indigenous peoples and systems. Although it is not explicitly described as such, the Supreme Court actually dismissed the action by questioning the Tagbanua's legal standing on the basis of non-compliance with what it interpreted to be jurisdictional requirements based on the IPRA's definitions of Indigenous peoples and the Indigenous concept of ownership. The Court essentially demanded that the Tagbanua allege and prove themselves to be Indigenous peoples as defined by the IPRA, not merely assert that they were such. This stands in stark contrast

[86] *Engr Ben Y Lim et al* (n 82) 31.
[87] ibid 27.
[88] ibid 28.
[89] ibid 31.
[90] ibid.
[91] ibid.

to its requirement for non-Indigenous party litigants, who are able to sustain a court action on the basis of simple allegations of legal capacity (eg, by stating their age, residence and citizenship). Therefore, despite the IPRA, it is still difficult to gain recognition of an Indigenous peoples' identity from the country's judicial system.

### C. The Coral World Park Proposal

In January 2017, Viacom International Media Networks and Nickelodeon, the company behind popular children's cartoons *Spongebob Squarepants* and *Dora the Explorer*, announced that it would be building an underwater resort and theme park in Coron in partnership with Coral World Park Undersea Resorts, Inc (CWP)[92] It was planned to occupy 400–1,000 hectares and open in 2020 to showcase the island's marine life and allow patrons to 'interact with the brand and the iconic characters they love'.[93] Upon hearing the news, reactions from the environmental community and NGOs were swift and sceptical, as the entire Province of Palawan had long been considered to be the Philippines' 'last ecological frontier'.[94] CWP representatives submitted a letter of intent to the Municipal Mayor of Coron on 23 January 2017.[95] As details emerged that the park was planned to be located in the municipality,[96] scepticism turned into outraged opposition.

By July 2017, an informal alliance had quickly emerged among the Tagbanua, civil society groups and environmental organisations. An online petition against the project attracted more than 250,000 signatures.[97] The Tagbanua, through the Tagbanua Tribes of Coron Island Association, Inc (TTCIA), submitted a petition to the DENR, which had announced that it would review the project proposal very carefully once it was submitted.[98] It firmly opposed the project, flatly stating that 'we do not need an underwater theme park in Coron' and warning that: 'The legitimate owners of Coron, if the planned attraction is realized, will lose access to our land, our waters, and will negatively affect our culture

[92] 'Nickelodeon to Build Philippine Underwater Theme Park', https://phys.org/news/2017-01-nickelodeon-philippine-underwater-theme.html.

[93] ibid.

[94] ibid.

[95] 'Developer Submits Letter of Intent for Coron Underwater Theme Park', *ABS-CBN News*, http://news.abs-cbn.com/news/01/26/17/developer-submits-letter-of-intent-for-coron-underwater-theme-park.

[96] 'Alarm as 1,000-Acre Underwater "SpongeBob" Resort Planned for Palawan' *Philippines Lifestyle News*, http://philippineslifestyle.com/alarm-as-1000-acre-underwater-spongebob-resort-planned-for-palawan.

[97] 'VIRAL: Environmentalists Gather Signatures to Protest Nickelodeon Park in Palawan', https://www.rappler.com/science-nature/environment/157947-nickelodeon-water-park-reactions.

[98] 'Cimatu Vows to Carefully Study Nickelodeon Project in Coron' *Manila Bulletin News*, https://news.mb.com.ph/2017/06/14/cimatu-vows-to-carefully-study-nickelodeon-project-in-coron.

and way of life.'[99] The petition was signed by 15 tribal justices, the Tagbanua Council of Elders and members of the tribe.[100] At the press conference for the submission of the petition to the DENR, Amil Abella, representing the TTCIA, declared that: 'The legendary heroes of Coron will unite and defend the last ecological frontier of the country, where we live with freedom and abundance.'[101] They were supported by other groups such as Greenpeace, the Palawan NGO Network, Scubasorero and the Environmental Legal Assistance Center,[102] all very active environmental NGOs with a long track record of achieving positive outcomes in Palawan.

The very strong response took the proponents by surprise. On 22August 2017, mere months after their announcement, Viacom and Nickelodeon issued a press statement withdrawing from the CWP project.[103] This was a major victory for the Tagbanua and environmental advocates, as the withdrawal left CWP without backing for its ambitious plans. CWP insisted that it would not have harmed the marine environment and hinted that the resort would have been located on private property, a former mining site, outside of Coron Island itself.[104] However, it is not clear what area of the Municipality of Coron would have had such characteristics.

In contrast to the previous two events, this incident is a success story in that the Tagbanua, together with other civil society groups, were able to effectively and quickly mount a campaign and prevent a new project from potentially intruding into their domain. The Tagbanua's very firm declaration of opposition was voiced directly to the national government and the public, capturing broad support, and was sufficient to discourage the project's financiers from even continuing their initial association with CWP. Obviously, Viacom and Nickelodeon immediately saw that serious negative consequences and damage to their corporate reputations would result from their association with the project. The timely assertion of rights and declaration of opposition by the Tagbanua persuaded them that persistence would be futile as the host communities were dead-set against the project. In this instance, there was at least a broad recognition of the Tagbanua's interest in protecting their domain and the natural resources within it. Although there was not yet an opportunity to invoke it, the IPRA provided the background threat to the project's viability on account of the requirement for FPIC should the project site turn out to be within ancestral

[99] 'Tagbanua to Nickelodeon: "We Don't Need an Underwater Theme Park in Coron"', www.rappler.com//nation/176949-tagbanua-group-nickelodeon-underwater-theme-park-coron.

[100] ibid.

[101] 'Tagbanuas, NGOs Press Opposition to Nickelodeon' *Palawan News* (27 July 2017), http://palawan-news.com/tagbanuas-ngos-press-opposition-nickelodeon.

[102] ibid.

[103] Jimmy Ravelo, 'Viacom Withdraws from Nickelodeon-Coral World Park Attraction in Coron, Palawan' *Kicker Daily News*, https://kickerdaily.com/posts/2017/08/viacom-withdraws-from-nickelodeon-coral-world-park-attraction-in-coron-palawan.

[104] Jerome Aning, 'No Bikini Bottom for Spongebob in Coron', 25 August 2017, http://newsinfo.inquirer.net/925480/no-bikini-bottom-for-spongebob-in-coron.

waters. Despite CWP's insistence that the prospective site would not be located in Coron Island, the fact that it withdrew so quickly after the Tagbanua and civil society petition and declarations of opposition tends to prove that Coron Island was the intended location.

## VI. CONCLUSION: A CONTINUING STRUGGLE FOR RECOGNITION

The case of the Calamian Tagbanua is a very good example of the continuing struggle of Indigenous peoples for actual recognition of Indigenous community rights in practice, despite the existence of legislation that formally recognises such rights. With respect to ancestral waters, which already present serious challenges due to the absence of the conventional boundary markers such as natural geographical features, the problem of defending the ancestral domain from the intrusions and impacts of modern civilisation is magnified. The boundaries of the ancestral space remain difficult to conceive and perceive in practice; the presence of a map and title still seem not to provide an adequate basis for clear discussion and agreement between Indigenous and non-Indigenous parties over large-scale projects with potential for transboundary impacts. The fact of indigeneity remains open to question, and the law actually seems to make it more difficult to access the judicial system due to the imposition of additional requirements of proof of identity and membership in an Indigenous peoples' group as a prerequisite for pursuing legal remedies against intrusion. But the recognition of interests shared with the rest of civil society concerning the conservation and preservation of the marine environment offers some hope that the acceptance of Indigenous peoples' rights to their ancestral domains is an achievable goal. This is particularly true if it is based on the goal of maintaining and sustaining natural ecosystems and preventing potential harmful and destructive projects (even if they are superficially styled as having environmental and educational aims). In the Philippines, the enactment of the IPRA is but another step in a long and continuing struggle for recognition of Indigenous peoples, their rights and ancestral domains, and their welfare. The story of the Calamian Tagbanua is one of the best cases that manifest the potentials of that struggle, with its own past successes and contemporary and future challenges.

# 12

# *The Rights of Indigenous Peoples in Marine Areas in Russia*

EKATERINA ZMYVALOVA AND RUSLAN GARIPOV

## I. INTRODUCTION

THERE ARE 257,895 people who belong to the officially registered Indigenous small-numbered peoples in the Russian North, Siberia and the Far East. Indigenous peoples comprise less than 0.3 per cent of the total Russian population, but reside in approximately 60 per cent of the country's territory.[1] Their settlements are dispersed in the vast territory of Russia from Murmansk to Chukotka in sparsely inhabited and remote areas with extreme climate conditions.[2] Indigenous territories are strategically important for the state's economy, inter alia because significant biological resources are located in these areas. As a result, the territories of Russia's Indigenous small-numbered peoples have been a target of constant industrial interest for several decades. Thus, both the state and Indigenous peoples are important stakeholders in these territories, resulting in conflicts.

Indigenous peoples are one of the stakeholder groups with respect to access to resources in the marine areas adjacent to territories they have traditionally occupied. In the Russian Federation (RF), the lifestyle of many Indigenous peoples depends upon access to marine areas. Access to marine areas to carry out traditional activities is not only a means of survival, but is also part of the Indigenous culture and way of life. For these Indigenous peoples, any restrictions on access to water-based biological resources can become a 'threat to their traditional way of life, culture, and their existence'.[3] Russian legislation provides

[1] R Garipov, 'Extractive Industries and Indigenous Minority Peoples' Rights in Russia' (2014) 1 *Nordic Environmental Law Journal* 67, 67.

[2] ibid.

[3] R Garipov, 'Resource Extraction from Territories of Indigenous Minority Peoples in the Russian North: International Legal and Domestic Regulation' (2013) 4 *Arctic Review on Law and Politics* 4, 4.

a number of guarantees to Indigenous peoples with respect to marine areas. However, the complexity of the legislation, its frequent changes, the imperfection of the existing norms and other factors often complicate the realisation of the objectives of the legislation.

This chapter describes the relevant Russian legislation as well as the correlation between international norms and domestic legal norms. It also presents Russian legislation dealing with fisheries and marine mammal hunting. Section V presents cases to demonstrate how the legal provisions have been realised. In addition to the description of the current legal regime, the chapter also identifies some problematic aspects of the regime which complicate the realisation of the rights of Indigenous peoples in the marine areas in Russia.

## II. ASPECTS OF THE RUSSIAN LEGAL SYSTEM

This section examines those elements of the Russian legal system necessary to understand the rights of Indigenous peoples of Russia in marine areas.

### A. The Concept of 'Indigenous Peoples' in Russian Legislation

International law uses the term 'Indigenous peoples', while Russian legislation uses the term 'Indigenous small-numbered peoples'. The Federal Law (FL) 'On Guarantees' defines in Article 1(1) Indigenous small-numbered peoples of the RF as 'peoples who live in the territories traditionally inhabited by their ancestors, maintain their traditional way of life and economic activity, number fewer than 50,000 and identify themselves as separate ethnic communities'.[4] Currently there are 257,895 people who belong to the officially registered Indigenous small-numbered peoples in the Russian North, Siberia and the Far East.[5] The law applies a quantitative criterion to the definition of Indigenous peoples in Russia. Zhukov explains that 'initially our national legislation defined indigenous peoples as a subject of the special state support',[6] but that the whole population of Russia was viewed as native. Consequently, the criterion of indigeneity was supplemented by the numerical criterion. As a result, some Indigenous peoples are denied legal support because they consist of more than 50,000 members

[4] FL of 30 April 1999 No 82-FZ 'On Guarantees of the Rights of Indigenous Small-Numbered Peoples of the RF' (hereinafter FL 'On Guarantees') (*Федеральный закон (далее – ФЗ) от 30 апреля 1999 No 82-ФЗ 'О гарантиях прав коренных малочисленных народов Российской Федерации'*).

[5] Динамика численности коренных малочисленных народов Севера ['The Dynamics in the Number of Indigenous Small-Numbered Peoples of the North'], https://narfu.ru/aan/northern_peoples/indigenous_peoples.pdf.

[6] М Жуков, 'Коренность' как содержательное понятие нормативных правовых актов' (2009) 6 Журнал российского права [M Zhukov, '"Indigeneity" as an All-Encompassing Concept of the Legal Acts' (2009) 6 *Journal of Russian Law*] 123, 130.

and thus are not recognised as Indigenous people under Russian legislation. Examples include the Sakha-Yakuts, Komi, Tuvans, Altay, Khakas, Buryats and Karelians. In addition, the application of the quantitative criterion can lead to an absurd situation. For example, if the Nenets, which comprise nearly 50,000 individuals, exceed the 50,000 threshold, they would as a result lose their Indigenous status and thus the state's legal support. In sum, it is difficult to defend the quantitative criterion.

In addition, Russian legislation often uses the term 'Indigenous small-numbered peoples of the North, Siberia and the Far East'. As previously observed by one of the authors of this chapter:

> Whenever the right to traditional fishing is mentioned in other legal acts, the reference is made mostly to the indigenous peoples of the Russian North but not to all other indigenous groups. This is probably due to the fact that most of these indigenous groups inhabit coastal areas and because fishing is one of their most important occupations.[7]

In order to be legally recognised as an Indigenous small-numbered people, an Indigenous community has to be formally registered in the government's Unified List of Indigenous Small-Numbered Peoples of the RF.[8] This list currently contains 47 Indigenous small-numbered peoples, 40 of which inhabit territories of the North, Siberia and the Far East of Russia.

In the context of this chapter, the terms 'Indigenous small-numbered peoples' and 'Indigenous peoples of Russia' are used interchangeably.

## B. Peculiarities of the Russian Legal System

The Russian legal system has been affected by different historical events and developments. Originally, Russia belonged to the civil law tradition typical of Continental Europe, Central America, South America and those parts of Asia that were not part of the British Empire.[9] But both Russia's imperial past as well as the Soviet period affected the legal system's development and resulted in a change of attitude to the nature and significance of law and the way in which it should be enforced.[10] The collapse of the Soviet Union in 1991 contributed substantially to the modification of the civil law tradition in Russia.[11]

[7] E Zmyvalova, 'Indigenous Peoples of the Russian North and Their Right to Traditional Fishing' (2018) 25 *International Journal on Minority and Group Rights* 51, 62.

[8] Regulation of the Government of the RF of 24 March 2000 No 255 'On the Unified List of the Indigenous Small-Numbered Peoples of the RF' (*Постановление Правительства Российской Федерации от 24 марта 2000 No 255 'О Едином Перечне Коренных Малочисленных Народов Российской Федерации'*).

[9] PB Maggs, W Burnham and G Danilenko, *Law and Legal System of the Russian Federation*, 4th edn (Juris Publishing, 2009) 1.

[10] ibid 6.

[11] ibid 7.

According to Marchenko, the legal sources of the Russian legal system can be ranked in hierarchical order as follows:[12]

1. The Constitution of the RF of 1993.
2. International treaties of the RF and universally recognised norms and principles of international law.
3. Federal constitutional laws and federal laws.[13]
4. Legal acts of federal bodies (Acts of the President, the government etc).
5. Legal treaties and laws of the subjects of the RF.
6. Legal acts of bodies of the subjects of the RF.
7. Municipal acts.
8. Judiciary law (or case law).[14]

Russia is a federation. The sub-units of the federation are called subjects of the federation. They have their own bodies of state authority and administration, courts, legislation etc. The federation is bound by the federation treaty and the status of its subjects is recognised as equal in their relations with the federal centre and with each other.[15] However, subjects of the RF have different designations depending on their national-territorial status. They may be referred to as Republics, Krays, Oblasts, Cities of Federal Significance, Autonomous Oblasts or Autonomous Okrugs. Historically, during the existence of the Soviet Union, the Autonomous Okrugs were established to secure the rights of the Indigenous small-numbered peoples in the northern and eastern districts of the country.[16] Gorokhovatsky notes that the National Okrugs were renamed as the Autonomous Okrugs in 1977.[17] At present, it does not seem possible to claim that Indigenous small-numbered peoples mainly inhabit Autonomous Okrugs because in fact they reside in many other subjects of the RF.

There are three different spheres of competence within Russia's federal system: the exclusive competence of the RF (Article 71 of the Constitution), the joint competence of the RF and the subjects of the RF (Article 72 of the Constitution), and the full competence of the subjects of the RF (Article 73 of

[12] See M Marchenko, *Sources of Law* (Prospect, 2008) 115–73.

[13] This group of laws is adopted by the Parliament of the RF. The federal legislation has priority over the legislation of the subjects of the RF and acts of the other federal bodies.

[14] For example, according to art 125 of the Constitution of the RF, the Supreme Court of the RF and the Constitutional Court of the RF have the authority to clarify issues of the Court's practice (in the case of the Supreme Court) and to interpret the Constitution (in the case of Constitutional Court). Thus, according to the Constitution of the RF, the courts are entitled to interpret law. See the Constitution of the RF (1993).

[15] Constitution of the RF, art 5(1) and (4).

[16] С Гороховатский, 'Исторический аспект и перспективы изменения конституционно-правового статуса субъекта Российской Федерации' (2016) 1 Конституционное и муниципальное право [S Gorokhovatsky, 'Historical Aspects and Future Prospects of Changes in the Constitutional and Legal Status of a Constituent Entity of the Russian Federation' (2016) 1 *Constitutional and Municipal Law*] 30, 31.

[17] ibid.

the Constitution). In the event of contradiction between the federal legislation and the legislation of the subjects, the federal legislation prevails. If the issue falls entirely within a subject's competence, the legal acts of the subject prevail.

The issues discussed in this chapter fall within different competences. The RF has exclusive competence regarding the regulation and protection of the rights and freedoms of man and citizen, citizenship in the RF, and regulation and defence of the rights of national minorities.[18] Joint competence covers the following issues:

> b) protection of the rights and freedoms of man and citizen; protection of the rights of national minorities; ensuring the rule of law, legal order and public security; the regime of border zones;
>
> c) issues of possession, use and disposition of land, subsoil, water, and other natural resources;
>
> …
>
> e) nature use; protection of the environment and ensuring ecological safety; especially protected nature territories, protection of monuments of history and culture;
>
> …
>
> l) protection of the natural habitat and traditional way of life of small ethnic communities.[19]

The Russian legal system is based on the separation of powers. The executive power is rather strong in the sphere of the rights of Indigenous peoples in marine areas. Many executive legal acts regulate access by Indigenous peoples to the marine areas and their resources (traditional fishing rules, rules establishing open and closed seasons for fishing, the listing of the territories of traditional habitation of Indigenous peoples etc).

The most important federal legislation dealing with these issues include the FLs 'On Wildlife',[20] 'On Fisheries',[21] 'On Territories of Traditional Nature Use of Indigenous Small-Numbered Peoples of the North, Siberia and the Far East of the RF',[22] 'On Guarantees'[23] and 'Water Code of the RF'.[24] The issues under

[18] Constitution of the RF, art 71(b).

[19] ibid art 72.

[20] FL of 24 April 1995 No 52-FZ 'On Wildlife' (hereinafter FL 'On Wildlife') (*ФЗ от 24 апреля 1995 No 52-ФЗ 'О животном мире'*).

[21] FL of 20 December 2004 No 166-FZ 'On Fisheries and Conservation of Water Biological Resources' (hereinafter FL 'On Fisheries') (*ФЗ от 20 декабря 2004 No 166-ФЗ 'О рыболовстве и сохранении водных биологических ресурсов'*).

[22] FL of 7 May 2001 No 49-FZ 'On Territories of Traditional Nature Use of Indigenous Small-Numbered Peoples of the North, Siberia and the Far East of the RF' (hereinafter FL 'On Territories of Traditional Nature Use') (*ФЗ от 7 мая 2001 No 49-ФЗ 'О территориях традиционного природопользования коренных малочисленных народов Севера, Сибири и Дальнего Востока Российской Федерации'*).

[23] FL 'On Guarantees' (n 4).

[24] FL of 3 June 2006 No 74-FZ 'Water Code of the RF' (*ФЗ от 3 июня 2006 No 74-ФЗ 'Водный кодекс РФ'*).

discussion are largely regulated by the acts of the following executive bodies: the Government of the RF, the Ministry of Natural Resources of the RF (until 2008), the Ministry of Natural Recourses and Environment of the RF (since 2008),[25] the Ministry of Agriculture of the RF (since 2000),[26] the Federal Agency for Fishery, the State Committee for Fishery of the RF (which existed until 2008 and had the authority of the Federal Agency for Fishery)[27] and the Federal Service for Supervision in the Sphere of Nature Use.

## III. INTERNATIONAL LAW ON THE RIGHTS OF INDIGENOUS PEOPLES IN MARINE AREAS IMPLEMENTED IN RUSSIAN LAW

Article 15(4) of the Russian Constitution provides that the universally recognised norms of international law and international treaties and agreements of the RF shall be a component part of its legal system. If an international treaty or agreement of the RF fixes rules other than those envisaged by law, the rules of the international agreement shall be applied. According to Article 69, the RF shall guarantee the rights of the Indigenous small-numbered peoples according to the universally recognised principles and norms of international law and international treaties and agreements of the RF, most of which have been covered in Enyew's chapter in this volume.[28] As he notes, although few instruments specifically reference Indigenous peoples' rights in marine areas,[29] general human rights instruments are relevant.[30]

The most important international legal instruments within the sphere of Indigenous peoples' rights are International Labour Organization (ILO) Convention 169[31] and the United Nations Declaration on the Rights of Indigenous Peoples (UNDRIP).[32] Other potentially relevant instruments include[33] the

[25] The Ministry of Natural Resources of the RF was transformed into the Ministry of Natural Recourses and Environment by the Decree of the President of the RF of 12 May 2008 No 724.

[26] Between 30 September 1992 and 17 May 2000, the Ministry was named the Ministry of Agriculture and Food of the RF.

[27] The State Committee for Fishery of the RF (Госкомрыболовство) was re-created in the system of executive bodies of the RF on 25 September 2007, although similar structures had existed in Russia since 1991. The Committee finished its activity on 12 May 2008 as a result of transformation into the Federal Agency for Fishery.

[28] See Enyew (ch 2 in this volume).

[29] One such instrument of the International Convention on the Regulation of Whaling, discussed in more detail in Fitzmaurice (ch 3 in this volume).

[30] UN Economic and Social Council, Permanent Forum on Indigenous Issues, 'Report on Indigenous Fishing Rights in the Seas with Case Studies from Australia and Norway' (8 January 2010) UN Document E/C.19/2010/2 [4].

[31] International Labour Organization Convention Concerning Indigenous and Tribal Peoples in Independent Countries No 169 (adopted 27 June 1989, entered into force 5 September 1991) 1650 UNTS 383 (hereinafter ILO Convention 169).

[32] United Nations Declaration on the Rights of Indigenous Peoples (adopted 13 September 2007) UNGA Res 61/295 (UNDRIP).

[33] SF Skogvang, 'Local Community Right to Fish: A Sami Perspective' in C Allard and SF Skogvang (eds), *Indigenous Rights in Scandinavia: Autonomous Sami Law* (Ashgate, 2015) 135–39.

International Covenant on Civil and Political Rights (ICCPR),[34] the Universal Declaration of Human Rights (UDHR),[35] Protocol 1 of the European Convention on Human Rights (ECHR),[36] the International Convention on the Elimination of All Forms of Racial Discrimination (ICERD),[37] the Convention on Biological Diversity (CBD)[38] and the International Convention for the Regulation of Whaling (ICRW).[39]

The RF has yet to ratify ILO Convention 169. It argues that the definition of Indigenous peoples and the land ownership rights in the Convention do not meet the requirements of Russian legislation.[40] It also abstained from the adoption of the Declaration and has yet to endorse its contents,[41] since it considers that some of its provisions do not comply with its interests.[42] According to Rogachev, a member of the Russian delegation who participated in the discussion of the Declaration, the UNDRIP 'is not a truly balanced document, in particular regarding land and natural resources or the procedures for compensation and redress'.[43]

The RF has ratified the ICCPR,[44] but the Human Rights Committee (HRC) has voiced its concerns about the improper implementation of the ICCPR in Russia. In its concluding observations on the sixth periodic report of the RF, the HRC drew attention to the point that commercial interests prevail over

[34] International Covenant on Civil and Political Rights (adopted 16 December 1966, entered into force 23 March 1976) 999 UNTS 171 (ICCPR).

[35] Universal Declaration of Human Rights (adopted 10 December 1948) UNGA Res 217 A(III) (UDHR).

[36] Protocol 1 of the Convention for the Protection of Human Rights and Fundamental Freedoms (European Convention on Human Rights, as amended, entered into force 18 May 1954) (ECHR).

[37] International Convention on the Elimination of All Forms of Racial Discrimination (adopted 21 December 1965, entered into force 4 January 1969) 660 UNTS 195 (CERD).

[38] Convention on Biological Diversity (adopted 5 June 1992, entered into force 29 December 1993) 1760 UNTS 79 (CBD).

[39] International Convention for the Regulation of Whaling (adopted 2 December 1946, entered into force 10 November 1948) 161 UNTS 72 (ICRW).

[40] J Rohr, *IWGIA Report 18: Indigenous Peoples in the Russian Federation* (2014) 56, https://www.iwgia.org/images/publications/0695_HumanRights_report_18_Russia.pdf.

[41] Р Гарипов, 'Декларация ООН о правах коренных народов и законодательство Российской Федерации' в В Штыров (под ред.) *Современное состояние и пути развития коренных малочисленных народов Севера, Сибирии, Дальнего Востока Российской Федерации* (Совет Федерации Федерального Собрания Российской Федерации, Москва 2013) [R Garipov, 'The UN Declaration on Indigenous Peoples' Rights and the Legislation of Russian Federation' in V Shtyrov (ed), *Current Status and Ways of Development of Indigenous Small-Numbered Peoples of the North, Siberia and the Far East* (Federal Council of the Federal Assembly of the Russian Federation, 2013)] 319.

[42] General Assembly Press Release, Plenary 107th and 108th Meetings (13 September 2007) GA/10612, https://www.un.org/press/en/2007/ga10612.doc.htm.

[43] ibid.

[44] Decree of the USSR Supreme Council Presidium of 18 September 1973 No 4812-VIII 'On Ratification of the International Covenant on Economic, Social and Cultural Rights and the International Covenant on Civil and Political Rights' (*Указ Президиума Верховного Совета СССР от 18 сентября 1973 No 4812-VIII 'О ратификации Международного пакта об экономических, социальных и культурных правах и Международного пакта о гражданских и политических правах'*).

Indigenous peoples' needs in the RF.[45] In its concluding observations on the RF's seventh periodic report, it expressed concern about the fact 'that insufficient measures are being taken to respect and protect the rights of indigenous peoples and to ensure that members of such peoples are recognized as indigenous'.[46]

The USSR abstained in 1948 when states gathered at the United Nations (UN) to sign the UDHR. Russia ratified the ECHR including Protocol 1 with some reservations in 1998.[47] When it comes to the execution of the rulings of the European Court of Human Rights, Russia has generally complied with obligations to pay small amounts of compensation to victims, but it has rarely followed the recommendations of the Court to introduce changes in legislation.[48] A major change in Russia's attitude to the court's decisions occurred with the YUKOS case in 2017. This decision obliged the RF to pay €1.9 billion in damages to former YUKOS shareholders. It refused to pay on the basis of a ruling of the Constitutional Court of the RF that entitles the Russian Constitutional Court to decide not to implement the ruling of an international human rights court if it contradicts the RF Constitution.[49]

The USSR ratified ICERD in 1969.[50] There have been some challenges in implementing this Convention in Russian legislation. In its concluding observations on the twenty-third and twenty-fourth periodic reports of the RF, the Committee on the Elimination of Racial Discrimination stated its concern that the RF does not provide a comprehensive appraisal of the enjoyment of economic and social rights by Indigenous peoples in Russia.[51] First, the Committee expressed

[45] HRC, Concluding Observations of the Human Rights Committee. Russian Federation, 24 November 2009, CCPR/C/RUS/CO/6 [28].

[46] HRC, Concluding Observations of the Human Rights Committee. Russian Federation, 28 April 2015, CCPR/C/RUS/CO/7.

[47] FL of 30 March 1998 No 54-FZ 'On Ratification of the Convention for the Protection of Human Rights and Fundamental Freedoms and its Protocols' (*ФЗ от 30 марта 1998 No 54-ФЗ 'О ратификации Конвенции о защите прав человека и основных свобод и Протоколов к ней'*).

[48] T Casier, 'A Classic Dilemma: Russia's Threat to Withdraw from the Council of Europe', 2, https://eu.boell.org/sites/default/files/uploads/2018/02/russian_dilemma_0.pdf?fbclid=IwAR0DJKvZ8P4rUh2uQhRJl8Tzke0EZWH4f16Y6yeCqcrfak965K64UR6fu48.

[49] Ruling of the Constitutional Court of the RF of 19 January 2017 No 1-П 'Regarding the Solution of the Question about the Execution of the Rulings of the European Court of Human Rights in Accordance with the Constitution of the RF of 31 July 2014 on the Case of 'Joint Stock Company "OAO 'Neftyanaya kompaniya 'YUKOS' v. Russia" in Connection with Equerry of the Ministry of Justice of the RF' (*Постановление Конституционного Суда РФ от 19 января 2017 No 1-П 'По делу о разрешении вопроса о возможности исполнения в соответствии с Конституцией Российской Федерации постановления Европейского Суда по правам человека от 31 июля 2014 года по делу 'ОАО 'Нефтяная компания 'ЮКОС' против России' в связи с запросом Министерства юстиции Российской Федерации'*).

[50] Decree of the USSR Supreme Council Presidium of 22 January 1969 No 3534-VII 'On Ratification of the International Convention on the Elimination of All Forms of Racial Discrimination' (*Указ Президиума Верховного Совета СССР от 22 января 1969 No 3534-VII 'О ратификации Международнойконвенции о ликвидации всех форм расовой дискриминации'*). See also General Recommendation No 23: Indigenous Peoples, Fifty-First Session, 1997 (A/52/18).

[51] CERD, Concluding Observations on the Twenty-Third and Twenty-Fourth Periodic Reports of the Russian Federation, 20 September 2017, CERD/C/RUS/CO/23-24 [7].

concern with respect to the numerical ceiling of 50,000 individuals, (discussed above), which may prevent a self-identified Indigenous group 'from enjoying legal protection of their lands, resources and livelihoods'.[52] Second, it observed that 'indigenous fisheries face various bureaucratic barriers for obtaining fishing rights in addition to unnecessary restrictions on how to practice fishing, such as the prohibition to use nets, which are not imposed on commercial or recreational fishing (arts. 2, 5 and 6)'.[53] It urgently called on the RF to revise its legislation so as to ensure Indigenous peoples' rights regardless of their numbers so that they 'can enjoy legal and constitutional protection of their cultural, territorial and political rights'.[54] The Committee insists that Russia should ensure systematic consultations with the Indigenous peoples, 'in good faith, in a timely fashion and with the appropriate information being provided'.[55] It also called on the RF to 'remove any discriminatory restrictions on indigenous fisheries and consider ratifying ILO Convention 169 and formally endorse the UNDRIP.[56] Russia ratified the CBD in 1995[57] and the ICRW in 1948.[58] There are also challenges regarding effective implementation of these agreements.[59]

To conclude, despite the fact that Indigenous and small-numbered peoples in Russia have a wide range of declared benefits and rights through Russia's international legal obligations, there is a gap between declared rights and their practical implementation. Kryazhkov writes that 'the Russian legislation concerning indigenous small-numbered peoples could be characterized as unstable, contradictive, often imitational, only initially developed, and not enough adjusted to international law'.[60] Others comment that there is currently no efficient system of legal support and protection for Indigenous small-numbered peoples' interests in Russia and it is necessary to bring the Russian legislation into compliance with international norms.[61] Researchers also observe that there

[52] ibid [23].

[53] ibid [23] (d).

[54] ibid [24] (a).

[55] ibid [24] (c).

[56] ibid [24] (f).

[57] FL of 17 February 1995 No 16-FZ 'On Ratification of the Convention on Biological Diversity' (*ФЗ от 17 февраля 1995 No 16-ФЗ 'О ратификации Конвенции о биологическом разнообразии'*).

[58] Decree of the USSR Supreme Council Presidium of 15 July 1948 'On Ratification of the International Convention for the Regulation of Whaling' (Protocol No 29, para 87) (*Указ Президиума Верховного Совета СССР от 15 июля 1948 'О ратификации Международной Конвенции по регулированию китобойного промысла' (Протокол No 29, п. 87)*).

[59] CBD Fifth National Report – Russian Federation. Executive Summary 8, Successes and Failures of the International Whaling Commission (IWC), http://wwf.panda.org/knowledge_hub/endangered_species/cetaceans/cetaceans/iwc/iwc_successes_failures/?fbclid=IwAR2u687pr3DcncfXDICCL67I_cpOH7TwTnd6Gd6p_nJf-QXQmBjjNUQg_Dk.

[60] В Кряжков, 'Российское законодательство о северных народах и правоприменительная практика: состояние и перспективы', (2012) 5 Государство и право [V Kryazhkov, 'Russian Legislation about Northern Peoples and Law Enforcement Practice: Current Situation and Perspective' (2012) 5 *State and Law Magazine*] 27, 35.

[61] Р Гарипов, 'Законодательство РФ о защите прав коренных малочисленных народов России и его соответствие международным стандартам' (2011) 3 Государство и право [R Garipov, 'Russian Legislation on Indigenous Minorities Rights Protection and its Accordance to International Law' (2011) 3 *State and Law Journal*] 105, 105.

are many different reasons for the problems concerning the implementation of international treaties in general and those concerning Indigenous peoples' rights in particular. The authors of this chapter consider that the existing societal situation in Russia presents the main hindrance to the de facto implementation of these rights. We will return to this issue in section IV below.

The next section examines the Russian legislation that is relevant to the exercise of Indigenous rights in marine areas.

## IV. RUSSIAN LEGISLATION RELEVANT TO THE EXERCISE OF INDIGENOUS RIGHTS IN MARINE AREAS

This section considers the provisions of the Russian legislation establishing the rights of Indigenous peoples of the RF to traditional fisheries and the rights of Indigenous peoples for marine mammal hunting. Article 9(1) of the Russian Constitution declares that land and other natural resources shall be utilised and protected in the RF as the basis for life and activity of the people living in the corresponding territories.[62] This provision is relevant for Indigenous peoples living in the territories of traditional habitation adjacent to marine areas.

### A. Territories of Traditional Habitation

Territories of traditional habitation are areas where the traditional activities of the Indigenous peoples described in this chapter take place. The list of the territories of traditional habitation is approved by the Directive of the Government of the RF of 8 May 2009 No 631-p.[63] The legal regulation of the territories of traditional habitation falls within the joint competence of the RF and its subjects. The RF state authorities decide which territories are recognised as territories of traditional habitation.[64] A legal definition of these territories does not exist in Russian legislation. However, in 2012, a draft law[65] was submitted to the State Duma, including a proposal to introduce this term into legislation.

[62] Constitution of the RF (1993), art 9.

[63] Directive of the Government of the RF of 8 May 2009 No 631-p 'On Approval of the List of the Traditional Habitation Territories, Traditional Livelihood and Traditional Economic Activities of Indigenous Small-Numbered Peoples of the RF' (hereinafter 'On Approval of the List') (*Распоряжение Правительства РФ от 8 мая 2009 No 631-р 'Об утверждении перечня мест традиционного проживания и традиционной хозяйственной деятельности коренных малочисленных народов РФ и перечня видов их традиционной хозяйственной деятельности'*).

[64] Zmyvalova (n 7) 67.

[65] The Draft of FL No 42057-6 'On Amendments to the FL "On Guarantees of the Rights of Indigenous Peoples of the RF" and Certain Legislative Acts of the RF' (*Проект Федерального закона No 42057-6 'О внесении изменений в Федеральный закон "О гарантиях прав коренных малочисленных народов Российской Федерации" и отдельные законодательные акты Российской Федерации'*).

The following definition was proposed: the places of traditional habitation and traditional economic activities of the small-numbered peoples are the territories on which people belonging to small-numbered peoples who have residence registration in these territories reside and carry out traditional economic activities. This draft law was not adopted.

The Paper on the Sustainable Development of the Indigenous and Small-Numbered Peoples of the North, Siberia and the Far East of Russia for the period up to 2025 recognises the preservation of the original habitat and the traditional lifestyle as one of the main tasks necessary to ensure and to develop the traditional way of life of the Indigenous small-numbered peoples of the North.[66] This document provides for priority access for the small-numbered peoples of the North for fishing areas and hunting areas, and biological resources in the territories of their traditional habitation.

Russian legislation establishes a special system for the use of water resources located in the territories of traditional habitation and traditional economic activities of Indigenous small-numbered peoples. This system is regulated by the bodies of executive power of the subjects of the RF according to Article 54(1) of the Water Code. Also, Article 54(2) of the Water Code provides for the right of Indigenous small-numbered peoples to use water resources for traditional nature use.

### B. Fisheries

This section deals with the right to fish for the purpose of ensuring a traditional way of life and traditional economic activities (the right to traditional fishing). It does not deal with the rights that Indigenous peoples of the RF have in common with other citizens with respect to non-professional fishing (sport fishing).

The main economic activity of the Khanty of the Ob and the peoples of the Pre-Amur region (the Negidals, Nanais, Nivkhs and Udeges) is traditional fishing. However, all Indigenous peoples of the North of Russia are engaged in fishing as a subsidiary (secondary) economic activity.[67] According to Article 16(1)[7], traditional fishing of the Indigenous peoples of the Russian North, Siberia and the Far East is one of the types of fishing in Russia.

[66] 'The Paper on the Sustainable Development of the Indigenous Small-Numbered Peoples of the North, Siberia and the Far East of Russia for the Period up to 2025', confirmed by Directive of the Government of the RF of 4 February 2009 No 132-p (*'Концепция устойчивого развития коренных малочисленных народов Севера, Сибири и Дальнего Востока Российской Федерации', утверждена Распоряжением Правительства РФ от 4 февраля 2009 No 132-р*).

[67] Л Соловьева, 'Малые народы Севера и Дальнего Востока' [L Solovyova, 'Small Peoples of the North and the Far East'], http://nacionalsoglasie.kmormp.gov.spb.ru/narody-rossii/malye-narody-severa-i-dalnego-vostoka.

Indigenous peoples have the right to priority access to traditional fishing according to Articles 34 and 49 of the FL 'On Wildlife'. This right includes the first choice of the economic areas for Indigenous people, privileges regarding periods and areas of the catch, gender and age characteristics, the amount of the catch etc. This right can be applied in Russia's internal waters and territorial sea, but not (since 2006) within Russia's exclusive economic zone (EEZ) and continental shelf.[68]

Traditional fishing activities are carried out by both Indigenous peoples and their communities. Indigenous communities carry out their activities under the FL 'On Non-Commercial Organizations'.[69] There are two types of communities: family and territorial-neighbouring communities. There are more of the former than the latter. A family community is a union of relatives. Traditional fishing in the territory of traditional habitation can be carried out by those communities whose main activity is traditional fishing as confirmed by their charters. Traditional fishing can be carried out within or outside the boundaries of a fishing ground. According to paragraph 5 of the relevant Procedure,[70] this water area must be joined to territories of traditional habitation. A fishing ground can be described as a sea area or part thereof, the boundaries of which are defined for the purpose of carrying out different types of fishing, including traditional fishing. Usually, a fishing ground has been traditionally used for fishing. Access to a fishing ground requires approval where there is competition with other Indigenous groups interested in fishing in these water areas. The approval of the lists enumerating fishing grounds is the responsibility of the relevant body of executive power of the corresponding subject of the RF. The approval takes into consideration the interested stakeholders, including Indigenous peoples inhabiting these areas.

Traditional fishing must be carried out by Indigenous peoples by means of traditional methods and tools. There are additional requirements or rules specific

[68] See FL of 31 July 1998 No 155-FZ 'On the Internal Maritime Waters, the Territorial Sea and the Contiguous Zone of the RF' (*ФЗ от 31 июля 1998 No 155-ФЗ 'О внутренних морских водах, территориальном море и прилежащей зоне Российской Федерации'*), art 21(3). For the EEZ and the continental shelf, see FL of 17 December 1998 No 191-FZ 'On the Exclusive Economic Zone of the RF' (hereinafter FL 'On the EEZ') (*ФЗ от 17 декабря 1998 No 191-ФЗ 'Об исключительной экономической зоне РФ'*) and FL of 30 November 1995 No 187-FZ 'On the Continental Shelf of the RF' (*ФЗ от 30 ноября 1995 No 187-ФЗ 'О континентальном шельфе РФ'*), as amended in 2006'.

[69] FL of 12 December 1996 No 7-FZ 'On Non-Commercial Organizations' (*ФЗ от 12 января 1996 No 7-ФЗ 'О некоммерческих организациях'*).

[70] Order of the State Committee for Fishery of the RF of 11 April 2008 No 315, 'On Approval of Procedure for Fishery in Order to Maintain the Traditional Livelihood and Exercise the Traditional Economic Activities of Indigenous Small-Numbered Peoples of the North, Siberia and the Far East of Russia' (*Приказ Госкомрыболовства РФ от 11 апреля 2008 No 315 'Об утверждении Порядка осуществления рыболовства в целях обеспечения традиционного образа жизни и осуществления традиционной хозяйственной деятельности коренных малочисленных народов Севера, Сибири и Дальнего Востока Российской Федерации'*).

to different fishery basins[71] dealing with such matters as the fishing methods and tools that are allowed or forbidden (white lists and black lists, respectively).

In summary, the key elements of the right to traditional fishing of Indigenous peoples in Russia are as follows:[72]

1. The priority status of Indigenous peoples of the Russian North as regards access to traditional fishing.
2. Traditional fishing can be exercised within and outside the limits of fishing grounds provided that such areas are attached to the territories of the traditional habitation of Indigenous peoples.
3. Indigenous peoples of the Russian North have the right to use their traditional tools and methods when fishing traditionally.

### C. Marine Mammal Hunting

Marine mammal hunting is a traditional occupation of the coastal Indigenous peoples in Russia, such as the Nenets, Sámi, Evens, Evenks, Negidals, Nivkhs, Ulchs, Ulta and Oroch peoples in the South of the Far East, and the Chukchis, Koryaks and Siberian Yupik in the North of the Far East. The way of life of the Siberian Yupik, for example, is closely connected to hunting marine mammals, such as whales, walruses and seals,[73] but the only Russian territory where Indigenous peoples still hunt whales is the Chukotka Autonomous Okrug.[74] This Okrug is a unique region because of the ancient and long-standing tradition of the marine hunting culture.[75] Walrus has always been a preferred species to harvest for the people of Chukotka, while the Siberian Yupik used to be known as 'the walrus people' because it was impossible to define any sphere of their life that did not use walrus products.[76]

According to Article 1(1)[1] of the FL 'On Fisheries', biological resources of waters are fishes, water invertebrates, water mammals, seaweed and other water animals and plants in their natural state. According to Article 1(1)[9], fisheries are activities related to the catch of water biological resources, activities related

[71] 'On Fisheries', art 17(1). Fishery basins are geographically defined groups of seas and lakes and pools of rivers flowing into these seas and lakes, and also other water objects which can be used for fishing. The following fishery basins exist in the RF: Azov-Black sea fishery basin; Baikal; Volga-Caspian; West-Siberian; Far Eastern; East Siberian; Western; and Northern.

[72] Zmyvalova (n 7) 82.

[73] J Forsyth, *A History of the Peoples of Siberia Russia's North Asian Colony 1581–1990* (Cambridge University Press, 1998) 70.

[74] Chukotka Aboriginal Whalers to Defend the Whaling Catch Limits, http://xn--80atapud1a.xn--p1ai/press-tsentr/novosti/kitoboi-chukotki-namereny-otstaivat-kvoty-na-dobychu-kita-/?sphrase_id=4789.

[75] I Krupnik and L Bogoslovskaya, 'Climate Change Adaptation: Traditional Knowledge of Indigenous Peoples Inhabiting the Arctic and Far North: Marine Hunters of Chukotka', 6, http://archive.iite.unesco.org/courses/climate_change/en/pdf/MarineHuntersChukotka_en.pdf.

[76] ibid 11.

to acceptance, processing, overload, transhipment, storage and unloading of the water biological resources, and also the manufacture of the products made of fish and water biological resources. Thus, according to the Russian legislation, marine mammal hunting is considered as fisheries and is regulated primarily by the FL 'On Fisheries'. However, the authors of this chapter consider marine mammal hunting in a separate section due to the peculiarities of this subject.

Together with the FL 'On Fisheries', there are also regional laws regulating marine mammal hunting. For example, the Chukotka Autonomous Okrug has a law entitled 'On State Regulation of the Development of the Marine Mammal Hunting in the Chukotka Autonomous Okrug'.[77] This law establishes the main principles of state control and support regarding marine mammal hunting as necessary for the maintenance of the way of life of Indigenous peoples and to ensure the preservation of culture of the Indigenous peoples in Chukotka. The law protects the right to marine mammal hunting using traditional methods, the priority right to choose marine mammal hunting grounds, privileges in timing, areas, quantities of marine mammals, and the exclusive right to whaling for the Indigenous population (Article 2). The law also provides social benefits to hunters and their unions, such as tax deductions, affordable loans, and medical support for hunters and their family members.

## V. CASES

This section examines some examples of the application of the laws examined in the previous sections and illustrates the challenges that confront efforts to realise the rights of Indigenous peoples in the marine areas in Russia. First, the competent bodies often adopt decisions regarding water territories where traditional fishing is carried out without taking into consideration the opinion of the Indigenous peoples. Second, there is a tendency to enhance the priority of industrial interests over interests of Indigenous peoples. Third, many of the existing legal provisions do not correspond to the real life of the Indigenous peoples. Fourth, many legal acts contradict each other. Fifth, the legal norms are not clearly expressed, thus permitting multiple possible interpretations.

To demonstrate the first problem, the authors of this chapter present an example of Sámi traditional fishing in fresh waters. The same problem occurs with traditional fishing in sea waters.[78] This case is a vivid illustration of the challenges the Sámi community experiences with traditional fishing. The example is relevant for all Indigenous peoples in Russia. What makes this

[77] Law of the Chukotka Autonomous Okrug of 9 February 1999 No 09-OZ 'On State Regulation of the Development of the Marine Mammal Hunting in the Chukotka Autonomous Okrug' (*Закон Чукотского автономного округа от 9 февраля 1999 No 09-ОЗ 'О государственном регулировании развития морского зверобойного промысла в Чукотском автономном округе'*).

[78] Zmyvalova (n 7) 77.

case special is that the Sámi managed to quash the Governor's illegal decision regarding their fishing rights.

The Russian Sámi are an Indigenous people living in the Lovozero district of the Murmansk Oblast of the RF.[79] The traditional territories of the Sámi are located on the coasts of the water areas of the Northern Fisheries basin. Traditional fishing in this basin is regulated by the relevant rules for the basin,[80] and permits for fishing in these waters are issued by the Ministry of Fisheries and Agriculture of the Murmansk Oblast. This Ministry has the authority to regulate:

- the fisheries sector, including the powers delegated from the RF in the sphere of preservation and the use of water biological resources;
- the agricultural industrial complex, including agriculture, food and the processing industry; and
- the fishery and agricultural markets, commodity and food products produced by regional producers.[81]

Thus, within the subject of the RF, the Ministry has the same functions as the Federal Agency for Fishery, the State Committee for Fishery of the RF, and is subordinate to it.

In 2017, the Sámi representatives of the tribal community of the Revda urban settlement applied for traditional fishing rights in Lake Umbozero[82] for the following year (2018).[83] The community rented a land plot on the shores of the lake for the purpose of living there and carrying out their traditional way of life. The Ministry refused to grant the Sámi application on the grounds that the lake territory was now related to the municipal entity of the city of Kirovsk and thus the territory was now under its jurisdiction and not the Lovozero district.

The status of the lake had been changed in 2013 by the Law of the Murmansk Oblast.[84] Prior to this, the borderline of the Lovozero district bisected Lake

[79] As recognised by the relevant executive act, the Directive of the Government of the RF 'On Approval of the List' (n 63).

[80] Order of the Ministry of Agriculture of the RF of 30 October 2014 No 414 'On Approval of the Fishery Rules for the Northern Fisheries' (*Приказ Министерство сельского хозяйства Российской Федерации от 30 октября 2014 No 414 'Об утверждении правил рыболовства для Северного рыбохозяйственного бассейна'*).

[81] Regulation of the Government of the Murmansk Oblast of 26 April 2016 No 193-ПП 'On Approval of the Statute (Regulation) on the Ministry of Fisheries and Agriculture of the Murmansk Oblast' (*Постановление Правительства Мурманской области от 26 апреля 2016 No 193-ПП 'Об утверждении Положения о Министерстве рыбного и сельского хозяйства Мурманской области'*).

[82] Саами обратились к президенту России ['The Sámi Appealed to President of the RF'], www.csipn.ru/glavnaya/novosti-regionov/3797#.Wq5nfWrFKUm.

[83] В Селиверстова, 'Было ловозерское, стало наше' [V Seliverstova, 'It Belonged to Lovozero, But Became Ours'], https://www.opentown.ru/novosti/50092.

[84] Law of the Murmansk Oblast 18 June 2013 No 1633-01-ZMO 'On the Abolition of the Settlement of the Murmansk Oblast and on Amendments to Certain Legislative Acts of the Murmansk Oblast' (*Закон Мурманской области от 18 июня 2013 No 1633-01-ЗМО 'Об упразднении населенного*

Umbozero and part of the lake belonged to the Lovozero district.[85] The Charter of the Lovozero district permitted the re-distribution of land plots via a referendum and a poll of local residents, but there had been no such referendum. Nevertheless, as a result of the Oblast Law that changed district territories, the Sámi lost their traditional fishing rights. This occurred even though there had been no prior conflicts with respect to the issue of quotas for the Sámi traditional fishing in the parts of the lake belonging to the Lovozero district.

The Sámi community appealed to the Murmansk Inter-District Nature Preservation Prosecutor's Office,[86] which concluded that the Ministry had acted outside the law.[87] The Sámi appealed to President of the RF to have him resolve this issue and stop the violation of their rights to traditional fishing.[88]

After these appeals and the feedback, the Governor of the Murmansk Oblast signed the Oblast Law of 2 October 2018 changing the legal provisions regarding the water survey of Lake Umbozero.[89] The part which had belonged to Lovozero before the adoption of the law of 2005 was restored to its former legal status. According to the Sámi activist Danilov, Sámi living in Lovozero have applied for quotas for traditional fishing in Lake Umbozero for the next year and are awaiting the decision.[90]

The second problem concerns the priority accorded to industrial interests over the interests of Indigenous peoples by state representatives.[91] As discussed

*пункта Мурманской области и о внесении изменений в отдельные законодательные акты Мурманской области'*).

[85] Law of the Murmansk Oblast of 23 December 2004 No 582-01-ZMO 'On Approval of the Boundaries (Limits) of the Municipalities in the Murmansk Oblast' (*Закон Мурманской области от 23 декабря 2004 No 582-01-ЗМО 'Об утверждении границ муниципальных образований в Мурманской области'*).

[86] Природоохранной прокуратурой выявлены нарушения законодательства о рыболовстве по обращениям представителей коренных малочисленных народов Севера ['The Environmental Prosecutor's Office Found (Disclosed) Violations of the Fisheries Legislation on the Appeals of the Representatives of the Indigenous Small-Numbered Peoples of the North'], http://prok-murmansk.ru/news/9745-prirodoohrannoy-prokuraturoy-vyyavleny-narusheniya-zakonodatelstva-o-rybolovstve-po-obrashcheniyam-predstaviteley-korennyh-malochislennyh-narodov-severa.

[87] Саами Кольского полуострова запретили ловить рыбу в Умбозере ['The Sámi of the Kola Peninsula are Forbidden to Fish in Lake Umbozero'], http://severpost.ru/read/60394. The Prosecutor's office is a supervising body and is not entitled to revoke legal acts. In this case, this legal act can be revoked by the issuing body or the court. However, violations of the law discovered in the Prosecutor's office can become the basis for an appeal to the court by interested citizens (in this case, the representatives of the Sámi community) and the Prosecutor's office itself.

[88] 'The Sámi Appealed to President of the RF' (n 82).

[89] Law of the Murmansk Oblast of 2 October 2018 No 2289-01-ZMO 'On the Amendments in Some Legal Acts of the Murmansk Oblast in the Administrative-Territorial Sphere and the Sphere of Municipal Structure of the Murmansk Oblast' (*Закон Мурманской области от 2 октября 2018 No 2289-01-ЗМО 'О внесении изменений в отдельные законодательные акты Мурманской области в сфере административно-территориального и муниципального устройства Мурманской области'*).

[90] Personal communication (6 November 2018).

[91] This problem has been emphasised by different researchers and representatives of Indigenous peoples. For example, see: Вопрос совершенствования законодательства в области традиционного рыболовства является актуальным, своевременным и требует

in section IV.B above, the lists enumerating fishing grounds must be approved by a relevant executive body and included in an official publication.[92] Stakeholder objections must be considered before publication. Nevertheless, Governors retain considerable discretion and may change the purpose of fishing grounds according to the interests of industrial stakeholders. Two court cases illustrate this second problem.

In the first case, the Itelmen community 'Kavral' appealed against a Directive of the Governor of Kamchatka Kray with respect to fishing grounds.[93] The community argued that it was illegal for the Governor to change the purpose of the traditional fishing ground they had been using since the previous century, especially when the fishing ground was the only accessible fishing area where their traditional fishing methods could be used. Nevertheless, the court supported the Governor's decision.[94] It ruled that the Kavral community could move to other fishing grounds. While there may be some logic to this position, the court effectively disregarded the historically established practice of the community in using this particular fishing area.

The second case is similar. In this case, the Indigenous community of Aleuts 'Kignakh' appealed against the same Directive of the Governor of Kamchatka Kray. The community argued that the Directive violated their traditional fishing rights because the water areas where their traditional fishing had been carried out were re-classified as industrial fishing waters without taking into consideration their opinion and interests. It also claimed that the Governor's decision was illegal due to procedural failings in its adoption. In its judgment, the court agreed that procedures were violated, but concluded that they could be fixed.[95] Accordingly, the Decision was duly re-published in proper form, but again without any recognition of the community's traditional fishing rights.

The third problem concerns the disjuncture between the provisions of the law and the real lives of Indigenous peoples. For example, elements of the

безотлагательного решения ['The Issue of the Improvement of the Legislation in the Field of Traditional Fishing is Topical and Requires an Immediate Solution'], www.csipn.ru/glavnaya/region-news/498-vopros-sovershenstvovaniya-zakonodatelstva-v-oblastitraditsionnogo-rybolovstva-yavlyaetsya-aktualnym-svoevremennym-i-trebuet-bezotlagatelnogo-resheniya#.V6WrN7iLSM8; С Харючи, 'Исторические предпосылки и современные тенденции развития коренных малочисленных народов Севера, Сибири и Дальнего Востока Российской Федерации', в В Штыров (под ред.) *Современное состояние и пути развития коренных малочисленных народов Севера, Сибирии, Дальнего Востока Российской Федерации* (Совет Федерации Федерального Собрания Российской Федерации, Москва 2013) [S Khariuchi, 'Historic Prerequisites and Current Tendencies of Development of Indigenous Peoples in the North, Siberia and the Far East of the Russian Federation' in Shtyrov (n 41)] 37.

[92] Constitution of the RF of 1993, art 15(3).

[93] Appeal to the Fifth Arbitration Appeal Court with respect to the Directive of Governor of Kamchatka Kray of 21 February 2008 No 144-p 'On Approval of the List of the Fishing Grounds' (Directive of Governor of Kamchatka Kray of 21 February 2008).

[94] Judgment of 14 September 2009 No 05АП-384/2009.

[95] Judgment of the Supreme Court of the RF of 28 October 2009 No 60-Г09-4.

market economy included in the fishing laws are alien to Indigenous peoples' lifestyle. These elements of the market economy include fees for the use of the natural resources, auction or other competitive distribution of fishing grounds, and quotas for the use of water biological resources. Similarly, while it used to be possible to submit a handwritten application for a quota for traditional fishing, the Federal Agency for Fishery now requires a typed application.[96] Such a novelty almost destroyed the application process in 2017 in Kamchatka. The Kray Administration had to negotiate with the territorial body of the Federal Agency for Fishery to allow handwritten applications. The negotiated exception applied for 2017. From 20 February 2018, the amendments were introduced. According to these amendments, all columns in applications have to be written without mistakes by hand in block letters or typed.[97]

The fourth problem concerns contradictions between different legal instruments. This may cause the ineffective application of the legal norms regarding traditional fishing. For example, in accordance with the Order of the State Committee for Fishery of the RF of 30 April 2008 No 375,[98] Indigenous peoples could obtain quotas for Pacific Ocean salmon not only in the internal waters and territorial sea, but also in the EEZ of the RF. However, according to another Order of the same institution of 11 April 2008,[99] traditional fishing rights

[96] Supplement No 5 to Administrative Provision of Federal Agency for Fishery Regarding the State-Operated Service on Preparation and Taking Solutions on Granting the Use of Aquatic Biological Resources. Approved by the Order of the Ministry of Agriculture of the RF of 24 December 2015 No 659 'On Approval of Administrative Provision of Federal Agency for Fishery Regarding the State-Operated Service on Preparation and Taking Solutions on Granting the Use of Aquatic Biological Resources' (*Приложение No 5 к Административному регламенту Федерального агентства по рыболовству по предоставлению государственной услуги по подготовке и принятию решения о предоставлении водных биологических ресурсов в пользование. Утверждено приказом Министерства сельского хозяйства Российской Федерации от 24 декабря 2015 No 659 'Об Утверждении Административного Регламента Федерального Агентства по Рыболовству по Предоставлению Государственной Услуги по Подготовке и Принятию Решения о Предоставлении Водных Биологических Ресурсов в Пользование'*).

[97] Проблемы традиционного промысла КМНС обсудили на Камчатке ['The Problems of Traditional Fishing of Indigenous People were Discussed in the Kamchatka'], https://www.kamgov.ru/ko_adm/news/problemy-tradicionnogo-promysla-kmns-obsudili-na-kamcatke-6315.

[98] Order of the State Committee for Fishery of the RF of 30 April 2008 No 375 'On the Confirmation of Distribution of the Generally Permitted Catch of the Pacific Ocean Salmon in Application to the Types of Quotas of the Catch in the Internal Waters of the Russian Federation Including the Internal Sea Waters of the Russian Federation and the Territorial Sea of the Russian Federation and Also the Exclusive Economic Zone of the Russian Federation in Accordance with International Treaties of the Russian Federation Regarding Fisheries and the Conservation of the Water Biological Recourses for the Year 2008' (*Приказ Госкомрыболовства РФ от 30 апреля 2008 No 375 'Об утверждении распределения общих допустимых уловов тихоокеанских лососей применительно к видам квот их добычи (вылова) во внутренних водах Российской Федерации, в том числе во внутренних морских водах Российской Федерации и в территориальном море Российской Федерации, а также в исключительной экономической зоне Российской Федерации в соответствии с международными договорами Российской Федерации в области рыболовства и сохранения водных биоресурсов на 2008 год'*).

[99] FL 'On Approval of Procedure' (n 70).

may only be exercised in the waters adjacent to the territories of traditional habitation of Indigenous peoples.

The fifth problem concerns the vagueness of the formulations of legal norms allowing multiple possible interpretations. This hinders the realisation of Indigenous peoples' rights to traditional fishing. One illustration of this problem is the situation which resulted from the application of an Order of the Ministry of Fisheries and Agriculture of the Murmansk Oblast in 2017 dealing with Sámi fishing rights.[100] This Order and its appendix regulate the list of Indigenous peoples, including Sámi, and their quotas for traditional fishing without defining areas of traditional fishing. Inspectors of the Border Control of the Federal Security Office of the RF in the Western Arctic District challenged Sámi fishing in the EEZ, referring to the provisions of the FL 'On the EEZ', the provisions of which did not directly regulate traditional fishing in the EEZ.[101] The inspectors interpreted the norm to forbid traditional fishing in the EEZ, while the Sámi interpreted the norm to allow their traditional fishing in the absence of clear provision forbidding in the norm. According to Danilov, this led to a situation in which the owners of the vessels who leased them to the Sámi for traditional fishing in EEZ were fined. Now they refuse to provide these vessels again,[102] leading to the result that the Sámi are unable to take their quotas because of the lack of access to vessels and the necessary special equipment (for example, seines).

To conclude, these cases illustrate a number of conflicts between Indigenous peoples and other stakeholders with respect to the exercise of traditional fishing rights. While Indigenous communities have succeeded in some of these cases, overall the cases suggest that Indigenous interests are not accorded the priority they deserve.

## VI. CONCLUDING REMARKS

For many Indigenous communities in Russia, traditional fishing and hunting for marine mammals remain important traditional activities which are essential to

[100] Order of the Ministry of Fisheries and Agriculture of the Murmansk Oblast of 21 March 2017 No 31 'On the Distribution of Quotas on Water Biological Resources for the Purpose of Insuring the Traditional Way of Life and the Realization of Traditional Economic Activity of the Indigenous Peoples of the Murmansk Oblast (Sámi) for the Year 2017' (*Приказ Министерства рыбного и сельского хозяйства Мурманской области от 21 марта 2017 No 31 'О распределении квот добычи (вылова) водных биоресурсов в целях обеспечения традиционного образа жизни и осуществлении традиционной хозяйственной деятельности коренного малочисленного народа Севера (саами) на 2017'*).

[101] Саамские общественники говорят о нарушении прав коренного народа Мурманской области на традиционное рыболовство ['Sámi Activists Speak about Violation of the Rights of Indigenous Peoples of the Murmansk Oblast to Traditional Fishing'], www.csipn.ru/glavnaya/novosti-regionov/3939#.W545lM4zaUk.

[102] Personal communication (6 November 2018).

satisfy their cultural, social, nutritional and economic needs. Despite the fact that most of the international treaties relevant for protecting the rights of Indigenous peoples in marine areas are part of Russian law, in practice it is clear that de jure implementation does not mean that implementation is carried out de facto. In addition, it is necessary to recall that the RF has yet to ratify ILO Convention 169 and join the consensus on the UNDRIP.

The analysis of the national legislation demonstrates that Indigenous and small-numbered peoples have the right to traditional fishing within and outside the limits of fishing grounds attached to the territories of traditional habitation of Indigenous peoples and priority access to traditional fishing. Indigenous peoples of the Russian North have the right to use their traditional tools and methods when fishing traditionally.

Our analysis shows that the realisation of the rights of Indigenous peoples in marine areas is problematic due to various factors. First, the competent bodies often adopt decisions regarding water territories where traditional fishing is carried out without taking into consideration the opinion of the Indigenous peoples. Second, there is a tendency to enhance the priority of industrial interests over the interests of Indigenous peoples. Third, many of the existing legal provisions do not correspond to the real lives of Indigenous peoples. Fourth, many legal acts contradict each other. Fifth, the legal norms are not clearly expressed, thus permitting multiple possible interpretations. In order to resolve the aforementioned problems, a comprehensive approach needs to be applied. In addition to developing the national legislation in Russia and implementing the international standards, it is necessary to strengthen local management capacity and to provide for effective enforcement of the laws designed to protect the rights of Indigenous peoples in marine areas in Russia.

# 13

# *Indigenous Rights in the US Marine Environment*

## The Stevens Treaties and their Effects on Harvests and Habitat

MICHAEL C BLUMM* AND OLIVIER JAMIN

### I. INTRODUCTION

When colonists arrived in what was to become the US in the sixteenth and seventeenth centuries, native Indian tribes occupied most of North America. Settlement was often at the expense of these tribes, sometimes after bloody conflicts, particularly in the eastern and southern parts of the continent. Most tribes were forced to negotiate agreements under some duress, in which they gave up much of their homelands in exchange for smaller reservations. Treaty negotiations were invariably in English, as was the treaty text (usually written in advance of the treaty 'negotiations').

Although over a century ago the Supreme Court characterised Indian treaties as establishing 'government-to-government' relationships,[1] settlers often referred to natives as 'savages' and considered them inferior to white civilisation.[2] This widespread sentiment was at odds with the US government's

* Thanks for comments from Nigel Bankes, Lee Godden, Robert Hamilton, Stephen Langdon, Øyvind Ravna, Evelyn Pinkerton and other participants in the workshop.

[1] See, eg, Nell Jessup Newton et al (eds) *Cohen's Handbook on Federal Indian Law* (LexisNexis, 2005) 26–33.

[2] See generally Brian Dippie, *The Vanishing American* (University Press of Kansas, 1982); Roy Harvey Pearce, *Savagism and Civilization: A Study of the Indian and the American Mind* (University of California Press, 1965). The belief of white superiority was in part grounded in the Manifest Destiny doctrine, a belief that the US had unique moral virtues that justified spreading the American way of life and that the US was divinely ordained to do so. See Robert J Miller, 'American Indians, the Doctrine of Discovery, and Manifest Destiny' (2011) 11 *Wyoming Law Review* 329, 332.

official position, first articulated in the Northwest Ordinance of 1787, which announced that: 'The utmost good faith shall always be observed towards the Indians; their land and property shall never be taken from them without their consent.'[3] The US Constitution, adopted in 1789, granted Congress the exclusive power to 'regulate Commerce with foreign Nations, and among the several States, and with the Indian Tribes'.[4] This Indian commerce clause remains the primary basis of federal authority over tribes to this day.[5]

Against this backdrop, the US Supreme Court, in several decisions by Chief Justice John Marshall (1803–35), established the status of Indian tribes in the US constitutional structure.[6] First, in *Johnson v M'Intosh*,[7] the Court ruled that tribes could not sell their lands to anyone but the federal government.[8] The decision effectively put the federal government in legal (if not practical) control of western development. Virtually all private land titles in the western US trace their origin to the federal or Mexican governments.

Second, in *Cherokee Nation v Georgia*,[9] the Cherokee Nation asked the Supreme Court to enjoin Georgia from enforcing state laws on tribal lands.[10] Although the tribe did not succeed for jurisdictional reasons,[11] Justice Marshall declared that the tribes were 'domestic dependent nations', in a guardian–ward relationship with the federal government.[12] This relationship became the basis for the government's moral and legal responsibility towards the tribes as the tribes' trustee.[13]

Third, in *Worcester v Georgia*,[14] the Supreme Court reinforced the exclusive federal role concerning Indian tribes, ruling that state laws were unenforceable

[3] Northwest Ordinance, ch 8 (a), 1 Stat 50, 52.

[4] United States Constitution, art I § 8 cl 3.

[5] See Geoffrey D Strommer and Stephen D Osborne, 'The History, Status, and Future of Tribal Self-Governance under the Indian Self-Determination and Education Assistance Act' (2014) 39 *American Indian Law Review* 1, 7.

[6] On what is called the 'Marshall Trilogy', see Michael C Blumm, 'Retracing the Discovery Doctrine: Aboriginal Title, Tribal Sovereignty, and Their Significance to Treaty-Making and Modern Natural Resources Policy in Indian Country' (2004) 28 *Vermont Law Review* 713.

[7] *Johnson v M'Intosh* (1823) 21 US 543.

[8] ibid 573–74. Johnson, part of a group of land speculators who purchased first from Indian chiefs, sought to eject M'Intosh, representing settlers who later purchased from the federal government (following a treaty with the Indian tribes). The Supreme Court refused to eject the settlers, opining that under the discovery doctrine, Indian tribes had no right to convey their lands to any entity other than the federal government. Therefore, the conveyance to Johnson was ineffective and the settlers had superior title (ibid 571–72). Under this decision, only the federal government or its sovereign predecessors could obtain clear title Indian tribes and convey that title to a landowner (ibid 593–94).

[9] *Cherokee Nation v Georgia* (1831) 30 US 1.

[10] ibid 16.

[11] ibid 28.

[12] ibid 17.

[13] Cohen (n 1) 419–22.

[14] *Worcester v Georgia* (1832) 31 US 515.

on Indian reservations.[15] The Court declared the Cherokee Nation was a 'distinct, independent political community'.[16]

In the 1840s and 1850s, following Thomas Jefferson's purchase of the Louisiana Territory (stretching to the Rocky Mountains), American settlers began following the Oregon Trail to what is now the Pacific Northwest. The Northwest has been home to numerous Indian tribes for thousands of years who fished abundant salmon in the region's rivers and marine areas for subsistence and for commerce.[17] To avoid conflict and facilitate settlement, territorial governors Isaac Stevens and Joel Palmer negotiated a series of treaties in the mid-1850s.[18] Under these treaties, the tribes conveyed about 64 million acres of land to the federal government in exchange for small land reserves, schools, missionaries and agrarian implements, as well as 'the right of taking fish in common with' white settlers at all native 'usual and accustomed' fishing grounds.[19]

Treaty negotiations made clear that both parties intended that the tribes continue to fish as they always had. Governor Stevens, the chief federal negotiator, well understood the critical importance that the Northwest tribes attached to preserving their fishing rights, writing in a 1854 letter to the commissioner of Indian Affairs: 'It never could have been the intention of Congress that Indians should be excluded from their ancient fisheries.'[20]

Within a couple of decades after the signing of the treaties, non-Indian settlers' fishing increased significantly in response to technological advances in harvesting and marketing salmon.[21] Moreover, after Washington achieved statehood in 1889, the state established 'salmon preserves' where fishing was proscribed, displacing a number of native fishing grounds.[22] Washington courts proved to be quite unsympathetic – even racist – in their interpretation of the treaty fishing right.[23] The tribes consequently turned to federal courts to enforce

[15] ibid 561. The Court overturned the convictions of Samuel Worcester and other missionaries who violated a Georgia law prohibiting non-Indians from residing in Cherokee territory without a state licence (ibid 562–63). The supremacy of federal laws over state laws is assured by the US Constitution's Supremacy Clause: US Constitution, art IV, cl 2.

[16] ibid 659.

[17] Michael C Blumm, *Sacrificing the Salmon: A Legal and Policy History of the Decline of Columbia Basin Salmon* (Vandeplas Publishing, 2013) 57–58.

[18] ibid.

[19] ibid.

[20] ibid 61 (quoting Stevens' letter to the Commissioner of Indian Affairs). While Stevens' hope was to settle the Northwest peacefully, war broke quickly when Stevens opened up Yakima lands for settlement only 12 days after the treaties, in which he had promised the tribes two years to move out of the area were signed. ibid 63.

[21] ibid 61.

[22] Washington Administrative Code 2017, §§ 173-201A0130(98)(a–b).

[23] For example, consider the Washington Supreme Court's statement in *State v Towessnute* (1916) 109 P 478, 481–82 (Wash): 'The premise of Indian sovereignty we reject. The treaty is not to be interpreted in that light. At no time did our ancestors, in getting title to this continent, ever regard the

the treaty promises. The federal courts, including the US Supreme Court, repeatedly confirmed that the treaties of the 1850s reserved to the tribes the 'right of taking fish' that could not be denied by discriminatory state regulations, licence fees or property law concepts.[24] The Stevens Treaties include native harvesting rights in the marine environment, especially in Puget Sound and the Strait of Juan de Fuca; one treaty even includes a right to whale.[25]

This chapter analyses the treaties negotiated between the US and Indigenous tribes as the main source of Indigenous rights in the marine environment. The treaties have not only led to important court decisions recognising rights to harvest and protect fish, they have also proved to be an important factor in encouraging a Pacific Salmon Treaty between the US and Canada, and may become influential in ongoing renegotiations of the Columbia River Treaty between the same two countries. Section II explores treaty fishing rights, focusing on the Lummi Tribe's off-shore harvests and judicial decisions regarding the effect of the treaty rights on state and federal obligations. Section III discusses the Makah tribe's unique treaty right to harvest whales. Section IV discusses the role of treaty rights in US–Canada treaties, especially as a motivating force in negotiations concerning the Pacific Salmon Treaty and amendments to the Columbia River Treaty. Section V assesses how treaty rights have affected proposals for fossil-fuel export terminals towards Asia. The chapter concludes that we may be in the verge of a new era in which democratic branches of governments, and not just the courts, defend treaty rights.

## II. STEVENS TREATY RIGHTS AND HABITAT PROTECTION

When Governor Isaac Ingalls Stevens entered into treaty negotiations with Indian tribes in the Pacific Northwest, he stated: 'I want that you shall not have simply food and drink now but that you may have them forever.'[26] The ensuing Stevens Treaties thus made clear that the tribes and federal representatives intended to protect and preserve the tribes' ability to fish to maintain their way of life.[27] All the treaties contained language recognising the tribes' right to fish at all 'usual and accustomed grounds … in common with' settlers.[28]

During the twentieth century, conflicts between tribal and settler fishermen caused the US Supreme Court to interpret the treaty 'right of taking fish'

aborigines as other than mere occupants, and incompetent occupants, of the soil … The Indian was a child, and a dangerous child, of nature. In his nomadic life style he was to be left alone so long as civilization did not demand his region.'

[24] See section II.

[25] See section III. The whaling rights of Alaskan natives are beyond the scope of this chapter. See the more general discussion of whaling in Fitzmaurice (ch 3 in this volume).

[26] See *United States v Washington* (2016) 827 F 3d 836, 851 (9th Cir) (citing negotiations during the Point Elliot Treaty).

[27] Blumm (n 17) 56–63.

[28] *United States v Washington* (2016) 853 F 3d 946, 861 (9th Cir).

seven times.[29] The states of Washington and Oregon often regulated fishing in a way that discriminated against the tribes and, early on, lower courts were quite complicit in this effort.[30] But under the Supreme Court precedent, courts started striking down state regulations that inhibited tribal salmon harvests. The Supreme Court first interpreted treaty fishing rights to impress an easement on private lands, enabling tribal fishermen to access their reserved fishing grounds.[31] Ensuing decisions construed the treaty right to include insulation from licence fees[32] and protection against discriminatory regulation.[33] In 1979, the Supreme Court affirmed District Judge George Boldt's historic decision holding that the treaty fishing right guaranteed the tribes a supply of fish, not merely an opportunity to fish.[34] Later decisions held that the tribes' share included hatchery fish and that the treaties also protected fish against habitat-damaging activities.[35]

### A. Lummi Off-shore Harvests

The Lummi tribe, inhabiting the area around Bellingham Bay, was one of several Northwest tribes involved in the Stevens Treaties negotiations. The tribe's representatives signed the Treaty of Point Elliott in 1855, guaranteeing the right to fish at their 'usual and accustomed' places,[36] which for the Lummi – whose lives revolved around fishing, especially for salmon – included many locations in the San Juan Islands. Members of the tribe used a unique fishing method called reef-netting, which involved suspending a net between canoes in the path of the

[29] Michael C Blumm, 'Indian Treaty Fishing Rights and the Environment: Affirming the Right to Habitat Protection and Restoration' (2017) 92 *Washington Law Review* 1, 9; Fay G Cohen, *Treaties on Trial: The Continuing Controversy over Northwest Indian Fishing Rights* (University of Washington Press, 1986), discussing, among other cases, *Choctaw Nation v United States* (1886) 119 US 1; *Jones v Meehan* (1899) 175 US 1; *United States v Winans* (1905) 198 US 371; *Seufort Bros Co v United States* (1919) 249 US 194; *Tulee v Washington* (1942) 315 US 681; *Department of Game v Puyallup Tribe* (1973) 414 US 44; *Washington v Commercial Fishing Vessel Association* (1979) 443 US 658.

[30] Blumm (n 29) 10.

[31] *Winans v United States* (1905) 198 US 381, 382. See Michael C Blumm and James Brunberg, '"Not Much Less Necessary than the Atmosphere They Breathed": Salmon, Indian Treaties, and the Supreme Court – a Centennial Remembrance of *United States v Winans* and its Enduring Significance' (2006) 46 *Natural Resources Journal* 489.

[32] *Tulee v Washington* (n 29).

[33] *Department of Game v Puyallup Tribe* (n 29).

[34] *Washington v Commercial Fishing Vessel Association* (n 29) 686.

[35] *United States v Washington* (1982) 694 F 2d 1374, 1379–85 (9th Cir); *United States v Washington* (2016) 853 F 3d 946 (9th Cir), cert denied (2017) 864 F 3d 1017 (9th Cir). Treaty rights also extend to shellfish beds: *United States v Washington* (1998)135 F 3d 618, 634 (9th Cir) (rights include access rights over private lands, where necessary, to beds on private lands, and to 'improved' beds, although not to wholly artificial beds, extend to species not harvested at treaty time, and may be subject to lower court's time, place and manner restrictions). See Mariel Combs, 'The *Boldt* Decision Reincarnated' (1999) 29 *Environmental Law* 683.

[36] Treaty of Point Elliott 1855, 12 Stat 927 (ratified in 1859).

salmon. The 1974 *Boldt* decision declared that: 'Members of the Lummi Tribe are entitled to and shall have, as a matter of right, the opportunity to fish with reef nets in [the Puget Sound].'[37] Judge Boldt added that while non-tribal fishermen licensed by the state may have the privilege of fishing in the same areas in common with the Lummi, only tribal members had a *right* to do so.[38] In late 2017, the Ninth Circuit extended the geographical reach of the Lummi's rights to additional areas.[39]

Despite their victory before Judge Boldt, confirmed by the Supreme Court in 1979, the Lummi have faced challenges on the ground. Over-fishing by non-tribal fishers, and especially the destruction of the salmon's habitat, have contributed to the decline of native salmon species. Lost habitat due to population growth, farming, logging and river pollution damaged the salmon ecosystem.

A recent incident focused debate over off-shore salmon farms and their adverse effects on native species. The state of Washington has the largest marine aquaculture industry in the US, producing about 17 million pounds of Atlantic salmon each year.[40] Farmed salmon poses risks to native species from pollutants, disease and inter-breeding if the farmed salmon are not kept separated from native salmon.[41] In August 2017, a Cypress Island fish farm's net failed and spilled tens of thousands of Atlantic salmon into Puget Sound. The farm contained 305,000 fish; about 160,000 escaped.[42] The spill could have serious adverse consequences, as the older, larger Atlantic salmon may out-compete native chinook salmon and steelhead for food and habitat. The Lummi nation responded to the spill by declaring a state of emergency and proceeded to harvest more than 43,500 farmed salmon to limit consequences on the native fish.[43]

Most, if not all, of the escaped fish ended up captured or dead by November,[44] but the debate over Atlantic salmon farms in the Northwest continues. Cooke Aquaculture – owner of the farm – offered the Lummi $1.3 million to help

[37] *United States v Washington* (1974) 384 F Supp 312, 346 (WD Wash).

[38] ibid.

[39] *United States v Lummi Nation* (2017) 876 F 2d 1004 (9th Cir) (interpreting Judge Boldt's finding of fact 46). Also in 2017, the Ninth Circuit reversed a district court decision and ruled, over the objection of the Makah tribe, that the Quileute and Quinault tribes possessed extensive off-shore rights, including rights to seal and to whale: *Makah Indian Tribe v Quileute Indian Tribe* (2017) 873 F 3d 1157 (9th Cir).

[40] Associated Press, 'Collapse at Salmon Farm Renews Debate about Fish Farming' *ABC News* (24 August 2017), http://abcnews.go.com/amp/US/wireStory/collapse-salmon-farm-renews-debate-fish-farming-49402124.

[41] ibid.

[42] Cary Rosenbaum, 'When Atlantic Salmon Escape in the Pacific, Who Cleans Up?' *High Country News* (22 January 2018), https://www.hcn.org/issues/50.1/tribal-affairs-when-atlantic-salmon-escape-in-the-Pacific-who-cleans-up.

[43] ibid.

[44] Linda V Mapes, 'Escaped Atlantic Salmon Have Disappeared from Puget Sound, But Legal Fight Begins' *Seattle Times* (14 November 2017), https://www.seattletimes.com/seattle-news/environment/suit-filed-over-atlantic-salmon-farm-escape.

recovery efforts, a sum that tribal officials thought under-estimated the long-term costs. The Wild Fish Conservancy filed a citizen suit against Cooke under the Clean Water Act, alleging that the company was negligent in releasing farmed salmon into public waters.[45]

Washington tribes have called for a ban on net-pen aquaculture, the type at issue in the Cypress Island incident, to protect native stocks. Although it appears that the salmon that escaped may not in fact have competed for food – as most of the fish captured had empty stomachs – major worries remain, including whether the escape caused the spread of disease.[46] Pesticide residues and other chemicals have been detected in farmed salmon at greater concentrations than in wild salmon.[47] Accumulation of uneaten food, waste products and drugs beneath net pens has also been linked to localised pollution and the potential contamination of fish and river streams.[48] Canadian studies have found that farmed salmon also harm wild and hatchery salmon through sea lice and viruses.[49] And the prospect of farmed salmon competing for food and habitat or inter-breeding with wild species remains a concern.

Farmed salmon and the risk of escapes could interfere with treaty rights by depriving tribes like the Lummi of their share of salmon, and tribal leaders are concerned about the government's ability to protect the waters they have harvested since time immemorial.[50] Although the Stevens Treaties and the *Boldt* decision give tribes the right to take fish at the usual and accustomed places, how far these rights extend off-shore remain somewhat unclear. If the Lummi file suit against the state to restrict the operation of the farms, the courts will likely have to address this question.

### B. Inter-tribal Conflicts over 'Usual and Accustomed Fishing Places'

The Stevens Treaties promised the right of taking fish at 'usual and accustomed places'. Tribes have spent much time and effort trying to enforce these rights against states, and many cases also involve inter-tribal disputes over fishing sites. Resolving these disputes requires courts to determine what constitutes 'usual and accustomed' fishing places for each tribe.

Judge Boldt, in his landmark decision, found that every fishing location where members of a tribe customarily fished from time to time at and before treaty times, however distant from the usual habitat of the tribe and whether

[45] ibid. The case is scheduled for hearing in 2019.

[46] ibid.

[47] Peter A Bisson, *Assessment of the Risk of Invasion of National Forest Streams in the Pacific Northwest by Farmed Atlantic Salmon* (USDA, 2006) 1–2.

[48] ibid.

[49] ibid.

[50] Rosenbaum (n 42).

other tribes also fished in the same waters, is a usual and accustomed ground or station at which the treaty tribe reserved, and its members presently have, the right to take fish.[51] He proceeded to define the 'usual and accustomed' places for 14 different tribes.[52] Because tribes were accustomed to fishing at numerous locations, and not always to the exclusion of other tribes, reserved treaty fishing sites may be shared with other tribes, which has sometimes resulted in litigation.

In *United States v Lower Elwha Tribe*, for example, the Lower Elwha tribe claimed rights to fish in certain areas initially declared by Judge Boldt to be Makah fishing grounds.[53] The district court decided that the disputed areas were usual and accustomed fishing grounds of both tribes, but found that, at treaty time, the Elwha tribe had excluded Makah fishing in some areas, and thus could exercise the same right today.[54] On the other hand, the Makah controlled fishing in other areas, although this right was subject to joint use and control with the Lower Elwha.[55]

The courts have relied on anthropological and historical evidence to determine whether particular areas were fishing grounds of particular tribes at treaty time.[56] Evidence of a tribe's ability to exclude other tribes from a particular site translates into a present-day right to exclude other tribes; in the absence of such a right, tribes exercise the right to fish in common with other tribes.[57]

### C. The Habitat Issue

When the tribes and the federal government filed suit in 1970 in what would become the *Boldt* decision, they not only sought a declaration of harvest rights but also the inclusion of hatchery fish in that allocation, as well as protection of the environment necessary to maintain the habitat to provide meaningful subsistence and commercial harvests.[58] Judge Boldt agreed with the tribes on the first issue, but deferred on the other two. His successor, Judge William Orrick, ruled in 1980 that hatchery fish were included within the tribes' allocation because the tribes reserved not only a share of treaty-time harvests, but also

[51] *United States v Washington* (1974) (n 37).
[52] ibid 359–83.
[53] *United States v Lower Elwha Tribe* (1981) 642 F 2d 1141 (9th Cir).
[54] *United States v Washington* (1978) 459 F Supp 1020, 1049, 1066–68 (WD Wash).
[55] ibid 1067.
[56] Cohen (n 1) §18.04[2][e][ii].
[57] A lack of demonstrated capability to exclude competitors throughout an Aboriginal claim (as opposed to a treaty-based claim) proved fatal in a 6:5 decision of the *en banc* Ninth Circuit in *Native Village of Eyak v Blank* (2012) 688 F 3d 619, 623 (9th Cir).
[58] *United States v Washington* (1974) 384 F Supp 312 (WD Wash).

a share of future fish runs, a result affirmed on appeal.[59] Yet the habitat issue remained unresolved until the Supreme Court's 2018 decision.[60]

After the Ninth Circuit dismissed the habitat issue on procedural grounds in 1985,[61] the tribes sued the state again in 2001, arguing that road culverts built and maintained by the state blocked salmon migration and their return to spawning grounds. After six years of trial proceedings, Judge Ricardo Martinez concluded that the treaties required the state to refrain from building or operating culverts that hindered fish passage.[62] Years of unsuccessful negotiations among the tribes, the federal government and the state ensued. Consequently, in 2013, Judge Martinez issued an injunction requiring the state to fix some 180 barrier culverts by October 2016 and more by 2030.[63] The state appealed, arguing that the treaties provided no habitat protection injunction and that the remedy provided was over-broad, expensive and would provide little practical gain. But in 2017, the Ninth Circuit unanimously affirmed Judge Martinez's injunction without modification.[64]

The appeals court recognised that during the treaty negotiations, the tribes did not understand that the treaties would enable the government 'to diminish or destroy the fish runs'. Such an interpretation would be wholly inconsistent with Governor Stevens' promise that the treaties would supply food and drink forever.[65] The court also invoked rules of treaty interpretation to conclude that 'even in the absence of an explicit promise, we would infer a promise that the number of fish would always be sufficient to provide a "moderate living" to the Tribes'.[66] In affirming a right to preserve fish habitat, the Ninth Circuit concluded that without such a right, the state could impermissibly 'crowd the Indians out of any meaningful use of their accustomed places to fish', thus violating the purpose of the treaties.[67]

The appeals court relied on tribal and state experts to determine that road culverts: (1) had a significant adverse effect on salmon production; and (2) constituted one of the most recurrent and correctable obstacles to restoring healthy salmon runs.[68] The decision dismissed the state's claim that the injunction was over-broad because the lower court had in fact distinguished between high-priority and low-priority culverts in establishing a tentative

[59] Blumm (n 29) 15.
[60] See n 70 and accompanying text.
[61] The court decided that resolving the habitat issue without concrete facts would be judicially imprudent: *United States v Washington* (1985) 759 F2d 1353 (9th Cir).
[62] *United States v Washington* (2007) No CV 9213RSM, 2007 WL 2437166 [10] (WD Wash).
[63] *United States v Washington* (2013) No CV 70-9213, 2013 WL 1334391 [3] (WD Wash).
[64] *United States v Washington* (n 35).
[65] ibid 964.
[66] ibid 965.
[67] ibid 964.
[68] ibid 972.

schedule for fixing them. Finally, the court rejected the state's argument that the cost of repairs would be considerable and would hurt the state's ability to fund public programmes, finding the state's estimates to be 'dramatically overstated' and observing that federal funding would in fact cover a considerable amount of the cost of correcting the culverts.[69] The Supreme Court accepted review of the case, but deadlocked (4:4) without issuing an opinion, thus affirming the Ninth Circuit's decision.[70]

## III. THE TREATY RIGHT TO WHALE

The Makah tribe, located on Neah Bay on the northwestern tip of the state of Washington, possesses Stevens Treaty rights and exercises them regularly in the off-shore marine environment. The Makah have inhabited the area for thousands of years[71] and are mostly a seafaring people, whose livelihood depended on what the ocean would provide, including whales.[72] The Treaty of Neah Bay, which the Makah signed in 1855, is the only Stevens Treaty that expressly reserves a right to whale.[73]

### A. Treaty Negotiations and the Right to Whale

The US initiated negotiations with the Makah Tribe in January 1855, when Governor Stevens travelled to Neah Bay.[74] Stevens told the Makah that the US wanted to buy some of their land for a fair price. When the Makah refused to pick a head chief, Stevens selected one with whom to negotiate.[75] As was usual in Stevens Treaty negotiations, they were conducted in English and the treaty text was in English, making it difficult for the tribal members to understand the consequences of the negotiations. However, the Makah did make clear that because their land was unfit for agriculture, they were primarily concerned with maintaining a homeland that gave tribal members access to the ocean that would supply "whale and halibut" for their livelihood.[76] At least three Makah 'chiefs' explained that they ought to have the right to harvest fish and take whales where they liked.[77]

[69] ibid 977–78.

[70] *Washington v United States* (2018) 584 US __ (2018).

[71] 'Learn about the Makah', http://makah.com/makah-tribal-info/tribe; Robert J Miller, 'Exercising Cultural Self-Determination: The Makah Indian Tribe Goes Whaling' (2000) 25 *American Indian Law Review* 165, 170–71.

[72] Miller (n 71) 170–71.

[73] Treaty with the Makah 1855, art 4.

[74] Hazard Stevens, *The Life of Isaac Ingalls Stevens* (Houghton, Mifflin & Company, 1901) 474.

[75] ibid 475.

[76] ibid 474, 478.

[77] ibid 474.

The Makah's express desire to maintain fishing and whaling rights has been well documented and understood by reviewing courts.[78] Governor Stevens heard those concerns and specifically promised the tribe that they could keep their whaling culture, and that in fact the US would support tribal members with equipment.[79] Relying on these federal promises, the Makah agreed to cede much of their land. In return, the government included an express right to fish and whale in Article 4 of the treaty:

> The right of taking fish and of whaling or sealing at usual and accustomed grounds and stations is further secured to said Indians in common with all citizens of the United States…[80]

This provision was the only affirmative right to whale recognised in any Indian treaty outside of Alaska.[81] Governor Stevens clearly understood the importance of the 'right of taking fish', reiterating that it 'never could have been the intention of Congress that the Indians could be excluded from their ancient fisheries'.[82] The courts have approved extensive off-shore Makah fishing rights.[83]

### B. Makah Whaling Practices

Whaling had been an essential component of the Makah culture, religion and way of life since time immemorial. Whale oil, blubber and meat were the primary food source for the Makah.[84] Being a successful whaler was the highest social status a Makah could attain.[85] The Makah hunted primarily the California grey whale, usually whaling in the spring when the whales migrated northwards.[86] Tribal members typically employed eight-man crews with specialised canoes, hunting cooperatively, often with several canoes striking together to capture a whale.[87] At treaty time, the Makah harvested four or five whales a year,

[78] *United States v Washington* (1974) 384 F Supp 312, 363 (WD Wash), aff'd (1975) 520 F 2d 676 (9th Cir), cert denied (1976) 423 US 1086 ('Governor Stevens found the Makah not much concerned about their land, apart from village sites, burial sites, and certain other locations, but greatly concerned about their marine hunting and fishing rights').

[79] Treaty with the Makah 1855, art 4.

[80] ibid.

[81] However, in *Makah Indian Tribe v Quileute Indian Tribe* (2017) 873 F3d 1157 (9th Cir), the court approved extensive sealing and whaling rights of the Quileute and Quinault tribes, despite the fact that their treaty did not expressly refer to sealing and whaling, relying on the rule of treaty interpretation based on the tribes' contemporary understanding of their treaty rights.

[82] *Washington v Fishing Vessel Association* (n 29) 666, n 9.

[83] *United States v Washington* (1982) 626 F Supp 1405, 1466–68 (WD Wash) aff'd (1984) 730 1314 (9th Cir) (affirming treaty rights to finfish 40 miles off-shore).

[84] Miller (n 71) 180.

[85] ibid 175.

[86] ibid 176.

[87] James G Swan, 'The Indians of Cape Flattery' (1870) 16 *Smithsonian Contributions to Knowledge* 4, 20–21.

also making use of other whales that washed up on-shore.[88] The tribe consumed almost the entire whale for food, using the rest for crafts like harpoon ropes, tools, and weapons.[89]

Despite their 1,500-year tradition of whaling, the Makah ceased this practice in the 1920s because widespread non-Indian commercial whaling had decimated the population of grey whales.[90] The last Makah whale hunt for roughly 70 years occurred in 1928.[91] But the tribe never stopped recalling the importance this tradition played in their culture.[92] In 1946, the poor condition of whale stocks around the globe led to the signing of the International Convention for the Regulation of Whaling (ICRW), which imposed a ban on whaling for grey whales[93] and eventually led to a moratorium on all commercial whaling worldwide in 1982.[94] The moratorium applied to commercial whaling of all whale species and populations,[95] but also contemplated that nation states could provide evidence to the Commission of the needs of their Indigenous people in order to obtain a quota of whales.[96]

## C. Listing the Grey Whale under the ESA

In 1970, the US listed the grey whale under the Endangered Species Conservation Act (which became the Endangered Species Act in 1973 (ESA)),[97] thus prohibiting the taking of grey whales domestically. With the Whaling Convention Act of 1949[98] that implemented the ICRW, the National Environmental Policy Act (NEPA) of 1969,[99] the Marine Mammal Protection Act (MMPA) of 1972,[100] the ESA was part of a robust framework of domestic legislation regulating the harvest of whales, often at the expense of the Makah's treaty rights. Whether these conservation statutes may limit or terminate treaty harvest rights has never been entirely clear.[101]

[88] James G Swan, *Almost out of the World: Scenes From Washington Territory: The Strait of Juan de Fuca 1859–1861* (William A Katz, 1971) 77 (stating that the tribe used 13 whales in 1859, killing seven and having six wash up on shore).

[89] Miller (n 71) 178.

[90] ibid 250.

[91] ibid 180.

[92] ibid.

[93] International Convention for the Regulation of Whaling, 1946, 161 UNTS 74. The ICRW Schedule of regulations states that 'it is forbidden to take or kill gray whale.'

[94] 'Commercial Whaling Catch Limits', *IWC*, https://iwc.int/catches#com.

[95] ibid.

[96] 'Aboriginal Subsistence Whaling', *IWC*, https://iwc.int/aboriginal. For further discussion see Fitzmaurice (ch 3 in this volume).

[97] 16 USC § 1531 et seq.

[98] 16 USC § 916.

[99] 16 USC § 4321.

[100] 16 USC § 1361.

[101] For example, the Eighth Circuit ruled that members of the Yankton Sioux tribe had a treaty right to hunt bald and golden eagles on the Yankton reservation for non-commercial purposes,

### D. The Makah Tribe's Efforts to Resume Whaling

The recovery of stocks of grey whales led the US to delist the species under the ESA in 1994. Although the Makah had stopped harvesting whales for some 70 years, in the mid-1990s, the tribe approached the federal government to obtain a quota of grey whales allowed by the ICRW.[102] Despite the ESA delisting, the Whaling Convention Act required the permission of the IWC to hunt whales.[103] In 1996, the US informed the IWC that it would present a formal proposal to secure a quota of five grey whales for the Makah.[104]

The National Oceanic and Atmospheric Administration (NOAA) began to work with the tribe to prepare a statement of need for the hunt, but withdrew when it became apparent that it would be unlikely to obtain the three-quarters super-majority of IWC commissioners necessary to approve the quota.[105] Instead, the US pursued a different strategy, and in 1997 submitted a joint proposal with Russia to obtain a quota of grey whales for both the Chukotka people, a tribe of Siberian natives, as well as the Makah.[106] An intense debate ensued at the IWC, and the Commission approved the quota of grey whales for the 1998–2002 period, authorising the harvesting of up to 20 whales for the Makah.[107] The following spring, the NOAA issued regulations approving a Makah harvest of grey whales.[108]

Animal rights groups then sued the federal government, arguing that the NOAA had erred in conducting the required environmental reviews. A federal district court upheld the agency's whaling regulations.[109] In the meantime, the Makah tribe prepared for its first hunt in 70 years, and on the fourth day of its hunt – 17 May 1999 – landed a 30-foot grey whale.[110] The ensuing celebration within the tribe and its supporters stood in sharp contrast to the anger of animal rights activists.[111]

despite the prohibitions on hunting bald or golden eagles in the Eagle Protection Act and the ESA: *United States v Dion* (1985) 752 F 2d 1261 (8th Cir). The Supreme Court reversed this decision, holding that the Eagle Protection Act abrogated the treaty right, but did not decide whether the ESA also abrogated this right: *United States v Dion* (1986) 476 US 734. In another case, the Supreme Court held that the Migratory Bird Treaty Act did not abrogate the Chippewa treaty rights to hunt birds and that Minnesota's accession to the union did not abrogate the Chippewa's usufructuary rights: *Minnesota v Mille Lacs Band of Chippewa Indians* (1999) 526 US 172.

[102] Miller (n 71) 255.

[103] 16 USC § 916(c).

[104] IWC, 'Forty-Sixth Report of the International Whaling Commission' 22.

[105] (1998) 63 Fed Reg 16701, 16703.

[106] *Metcalf v Daley* (2000) 214 F 3d 1135, 1140 (9th Cir).

[107] Miller (n 71) 258.

[108] Aboriginal Subsistence Whaling Quotas, 63 Fed Reg 16,701 (6 April 1998).

[109] *Metcalf v Daley* (1998) No CV-98-05289-FDB (WD Wash).

[110] US Department of Commerce, 'Preliminary Report on Makah Tribe Gray Whale Hunt' (25 May 1999) 1–2; Kit Oldham, 'Makah Whale Hunt Succeeds on May 17, 1999', *History Link.Org*, www.historylink.org/File/5310.

[111] Sam Howe Verhovek, 'Reviving Tradition, Tribe Kills a Whale' *New York Times* (18 May 1999), https://www.nytimes.com/1999/05/18/us/reviving-tradition-tribe-kills-a-whale.html.

## E. Judicial Injunctions and the Makah's Future Whaling Prospects

Animal rights groups unsuccessfully sought an injunction in federal court. They then appealed to the Ninth Circuit,[112] arguing that the process that the NOAA used to authorise Makah whaling was tainted with a pro-whaling bias, as evidenced by the fact that the NOAA issued an environmental assessment (EA) four days *after* it agreed to pursue a quota at the IWC.[113] In a significant setback for the Makah, the Ninth Circuit reversed the lower court's decision and set aside the EA because the government had committed an 'irretrievable commitment of resources' by supporting the tribe's position before evaluating the issue in the EA.[114]

The NOAA produced another EA a year later, deciding that the 'issuance of a quota of five gray whales taken ... will have no significant impact on the eastern North Pacific gray whale population'.[115] The IWC set another quota of 20 whales for the 2003–07 period. But before the Makah could resume hunting, animal rights groups again sued the NOAA.[116] The federal district court rejected the argument that the NOAA had violated the NEPA and the MMPA.[117] But again, the Ninth Circuit reversed this decision on appeal, with much worse consequences for the Makah.[118]

The appeals court ruled that NOAA had to prepare a more detailed environmental impact statement (EIS) instead of an EA, announcing that the IWC quota did not exempt the Makah's whaling from compliance with the MMPA. The tribe relied on an MMPA provision excepting from the statutory ban on the taking of marine mammals, harvests which are 'expressly provided for by an international treaty, convention, or agreement' to which the US is a party.[119] The court rejected this argument because the MMPA exempts only treaty rights pre-dating the statute, which was not the case of the IWC quota, and because the IWC did not 'expressly' provide any whaling quota for the tribe.[120] Instead, the Ninth Circuit ruled that MMPA regulation of treaty rights was necessary to

[112] *Metcalf v Daley* (2000) 214 F3d 1135 (9th Cir).

[113] ibid 1137.

[114] ibid 1145.

[115] US Department of Commerce, 'Environmental Assessment on Issuing a Quota to the Makah Indian Tribe for a Subsistence Hunt on Gray Whales for the Years 2001 and 2002' (2001) 40.

[116] *Anderson v Evans* (2002) 314 F 3d 1006 (9th Cir).

[117] ibid 1015, 1030.

[118] ibid 1030.

[119] Section 1372(a)(2) provides: 'it is unlawful, except as expressly provided for by an international treaty, convention, or agreement to which the United States is a party ... or by any statute implementing such treaty, convention, or agreement, for any person or vessel or other conveyance to take any marine mammals in waters or on lands under the jurisdiction of the United States'.

[120] The court also noted that the IWC defined aboriginal subsistence whaling in terms of 'continuing traditional dependence', which was hard to show, since the Makah had stopped whaling for 70 years. *Anderson* (n 116) 1025.

achieve the statute's conservation purpose.[121] Thus, the Makah hunt required a waiver under the MMPA.[122]

To comply with the court's ruling, in 2005 the Makah filed an application for a waiver under the MMPA, and the NOAA eventually issued a draft EIS on the waiver in May 2008.[123] But the NOAA terminated the EIS in 2012 because of new scientific information suggesting that eastern North Pacific whales and Pacific Coast Feeding Group whales might warrant consideration as separate management units.[124] The NOAA issued a new draft EIS in February 2015, but has yet to produce a final EIS at the time of writing.[125] Consequently, the Makah have held no authorised whale hunts.

This complex and lengthy history illustrates the difficulties that tribes may encounter while trying to exercise Indigenous harvest rights, even when such rights are expressly recognised in a treaty, even when the IWC has approved a quota, and even when there was widespread congressional support for the Makah's right to whale.[126] Years of frustration eventually led five rogue tribal members to go whaling in protest in 2007. This group killed a whale, but were arrested by the US Coast Guard before landing it, generating widespread uproar among the public, the government and the Makah tribe itself.[127] The group's unauthorised action put the Makah in an awkward situation and jeopardised the ongoing administrative process. Makah tribal officials prosecuted the five members under tribal law, but the five men were also convicted under federal law and sentenced to three to five months in jail and 200 hours of community service, a decision that upset tribal rights advocates because it was an even harsher sentence than that requested by the prosecution.[128]

[121] The court applied the 'conservation necessity test', deciding that the MMPA regulated treaty rights because: (1) the US had jurisdiction where the whaling occurred; (2) the MMPA applied in a non-discriminatory manner to treaty and non-treaty persons alike; and (3) regulating treaty rights was necessary to achieve the conservation purpose of the MMPA: *Anderson v Evans* (2004) 371 F 3d 475, 497–98 (9th Cir).

[122] The Ninth Circuit rejected two *en banc* rehearing requests, and the Makah and the federal government decided to comply with the decision rather than appeal and risk an adverse decision of the Supreme Court. See Emily Brand, 'The Struggle to Exercise a Treaty Right: An Analysis of the Makah Tribe's Path to Whale' (2009) 32 *UCD Law Review* 287, 303.

[123] NOAA Marine Fisheries Service, 'Makah Request for MMPA Waiver', www.westcoast.fisheries.noaa.gov/publications/protected_species/marine_mammals/cetaceans/gray_whales/waiver-overview.pdf.

[124] 77 Fed Reg 29967, 29968 (12 May 2012).

[125] NOAA Marine Fisheries Service, 'Draft Environmental Impact Statement on the Makah Tribe Request to Hunt Gray Whales' (February 2015).

[126] In response to the *Anderson* decision, the House Committee on Natural Resources issued a resolution, explaining that: 'Congress disapproves of requiring the Makah Tribe to obtain a waiver and permit under the MMPA and expresses its intent that the Government of the US should uphold the treaty rights of the Makah Tribe.' See HR Con Res 267, 109th Cong (2005).

[127] J Michael Kennedy, 'Tribal Group Kills Whale off Washington' *New York Times* (11 September 2007), www.nytimes.com/2007/09/11/us/11whale.html.

[128] Brand (n 122) 306.

Whether the Makah tribe will one day resume its 1,500-year tradition of whaling, a right explicitly recognised in the Neah Bay Treaty, remains uncertain. If the NOAA issues a final EIS on the MMPA waiver, the EIS will likely face a court challenge by animal groups, which have twice succeeded in the Ninth Circuit. The issue could eventually end up in the Supreme Court, which might finally settle the issue of whether federal wildlife statutes supersede treaty rights.

## IV. THE ROLE OF INDIAN TREATY RIGHTS IN US–CANADA TREATIES

The recognition of treaty rights in fish and habitat over the twentieth century led to the emergence of tribes as a significant political force in the negotiation of treaties with Canada. As tribes witnessed the loss of resources and the degradation of important habitat, they started to assert a right to participate as co-managers in decision making involving public lands and waters affecting their reserved rights.[129] Thus, the effects of the *Boldt* decision were not only on the harvest management policies of the states of Washington and Oregon, but also changed the nature of the negotiations that led to the Pacific Salmon Treaty of 1985 and the renegotiation of the Columbia River Treaty of 1964, ongoing at the time of writing.

### A. The Emergence of Co-management in Decision Making

Following years of legal battles to assert their treaty rights, many tribes and inter-tribal organisations have developed sophisticated natural resources departments based on their unique understanding of species and habitat through centuries of reliance on those resources.[130] Tribes have consequently sought inclusion in land and resource management decision-making as sovereign governments concerned about their people, culture and economic well-being.[131]

The litigation implementing treaty rights to harvest salmon on the Columbia River provides an example of how treaty rights can lead to the co-management of resources. When the states of Oregon and Washington were unable to fairly allocate harvest rights,[132] the federal district court ordered the states and the tribes to agree on the formulation of a plan to manage harvests on an annual basis.[133] The plan spurred the tribes to create an inter-tribal body, the Columbia River Inter-Tribal Fish Commission, to coordinate and

[129] Ed Goodman, 'Protecting Habitat for Off-Reservation Tribal Hunting and Fishing Rights: Tribal Comanagement as a Reserved Right' (2000) 30 *Environmental Law* 279, 282.

[130] ibid 283.

[131] ibid.

[132] Among the more difficult technical and scientific issues that must be resolved several times a year are run-size estimates for several salmon species.

[133] See Penny H Harrison, 'Evolution of a New Comprehensive Plan for Managing Columbia River Anadromous Fish' (1986) 16 *Environmental Law* 705; Howard G Arnett, 'Fisheries Management in

develop scientific, economic and legal information pertinent to successful plan implementation. Judicial oversight of implementation disputes, frequently necessary at the outset, became less necessary over the years, as the states and tribes began to proactively cooperate and to share information, advancing salmon science in the process.

Federal agencies have recognised a role for the tribes in negotiations of treaties involving Pacific salmon and the Columbia River, as discussed in this section, and also concerning decisions involving the siting and construction of fuel export terminals in the Northwest, as discussed in section V. The Columbia Basin Fish Accords, signed in 2008, are another example of co-management practices in the Northwest. The Corps of Engineers and the Bonneville Power Administration signed these agreements with a handful of Northwest tribes, which accepted nearly $1 billion over a decade for salmon restoration projects throughout the Columbia Basin in return for their non-participation in ESA litigation over federal dam operations for 10 years.[134]

## B. The Pacific Salmon Treaty

The treaty rights discussed above granted Stevens Treaty tribes a fair share of the harvest of salmon, 'in common' with settlers. However, American settlers, were not the only ones harvesting salmon in the Northwest. Columbia Basin salmon usually migrate north once they reach the ocean, spending several years in marine waters.[135] Their immense migratory range causes them to move into Canadian waters, and then often into US waters in Alaska before re-tracing their path.[136] This situation engendered friction between the US and Canada over salmon harvest interceptions for most of the twentieth century, eventually leading to the Pacific Salmon Treaty in 1985.

### *i. Treaty Background*

Although the US and Canada agreed that salmon could be harvested only by the countries in whose rivers they spawned,[137] Alaskans harvested salmon which

the Regional and International Contexts: Columbia River Basin (Natural Resource Development in Indian Country Summer Conference, Colorado, 9 June 1988), http://scholar.law.colorado.edu/cgi/viewcontent.cgi?article=1014&context=natural-resource-development-in-indian-country.

[134] 'Columbia Basin Fish Accords', *CRITFC*, www.critfc.org/fish-and-watersheds/fish-and-habitat-restoration/columbia-basin-fish-accords; see also Michael C Blumm, Julianne Fry and Olivier Jamin, 'Still Crying out for a "Major Overhaul" after All These Years – Salmon and Another Failed Biological Opinion on Columbia Basin Hydroelectric Operations' (2017) 47 *Environmental Law* 287, 290–91, 302 (describing BPA's payments of roughly $100 million per year for 10 years). The state of Washington also withdrew from the ESA suit.

[135] Northwest Power and Conservation Council, *Return to the River* (2010) 367–68.

[136] Blumm (n 17) 161.

[137] Thomas C. Jensen, 'The United States-Canada Pacific Salmon Interception Treaty: An Historical and Legal Overview' (1986) 16 *Environmental Law* 363, 369.

spawned both in Canadian rivers and in rivers in the lower 48 states of the US. In response to these Alaskan interceptions, Canada harvested salmon originating from rivers in the lower 48 states, especially from the Columbia River, thus affecting the share of salmon available for the treaty tribes of the Pacific Northwest.[138]

Canada and the US began treaty negotiations in 1971 at a time when salmon supplies were relatively stable and conservation was not an acute concern. However, the 1974 *Boldt* decision – recognising the treaty tribes' right to harvest half of the salmon runs – complicated the process. In an effort to meet its treaty obligations without disrupting existing harvests, the state of Washington responded to *Boldt* by investing in hatchery production. At the same time, Canada doubled sockeye production in the undammed Fraser River by creating new habitat. Both countries were thus interested in ensuring that the other did not harvest the fruits of their investments. But American and Canadian fishers resisted efforts to limit salmon interceptions, as each harvested a significant amount of salmon that had spawned in the other country. Further, a startling decline in West Coast chinook occurred in the early 1980s – in part due to interceptions threatening spawning levels necessary to sustain the salmon runs – prompting the tribes to be active participants in the negotiations.[139]

The tribes had already invoked their treaty rights to restrict ocean harvests in order to ensure that they would receive half of the harvest, relying on the *Boldt* decision and its 1979 affirmance by the Supreme Court. In 1981, the tribes argued in a new lawsuit that Alaskan interceptions were violating their treaty rights to the same extent as the off-shore harvests in Oregon and Washington. The suit helped convince Alaskan representatives not to block treaty negotiations, and eventually persistent lobbying from a coalition of fishing groups, environmentalists and Indian tribes bore fruit. Canada and the US ratified the treaty in 1985, inducing the tribes to drop their suit against Alaska.

### *ii. The 1985 Treaty and its Amendments*

The Pacific Salmon Treaty had two primary goals: salmon conservation and equitable harvest allocation. The treaty requires Canada and the US to manage their fisheries to prevent over-fishing, enhance production and to ensure that each country receives benefits commensurate to the number of salmon spawning.[140] To achieve these goals, the treaty created a new body, the Pacific Salmon Commission, with four members from each country and three bilateral oversight panels to supply technical and regulatory advice to

[138] ibid.

[139] ibid 387–89.

[140] See Treaty between the Government of the United States of America and the Government of Canada Concerning Pacific Salmon (Pacific Salmon Treaty), TIAS #11091, 1985, art III, para 1.

the Commission.[141] The US gave tribal members a seat at the table, as one US member of the Commission was appointed from a list supplied by the tribes, while two representatives of treaty tribes were appointed to a six-member panel responsible for managing Columbia River stocks in treaty waters.[142]

Although the 1985 treaty appeared to solve many problems, it soon became evident that gains in salmon populations during the late 1980s were due to favourable climate conditions, not changes in fisheries management, and consequently populations started declining again in the 1990s.[143] Habitat degradation in Washington and Oregon as well as hatchery practices exacerbated this trend.[144] Moreover, both countries narrowly interpreted the authority of the Commission, thus limiting its ability to manage seasonal harvests. Issues of equity quickly re-surfaced, as Alaskan and Washington fisheries continued to intercept significant numbers of Canadian salmon, while declining populations in Oregon and Washington deprived Canada of the ability to do the same.[145]

In 1993, the Canadian and US governments took over the equity issue from the Commission, but negotiations collapsed when the governments could not reach an agreement on equitably allocating salmon.[146] As a result, both countries reverted to managing their fisheries independently, with no consultation or cooperation.[147] In 1995, however, treaty tribes from Washington, Oregon and Idaho filed suit in federal court to stop Alaskan salmon interceptions.[148] Partly because of Alaska's lack of participation in the Commission's chinook re-building programme, the court banned commercial fishing for chinook in southeast Alaska until 30 September 1995.[149] In the meantime, Canada imposed a transit fee on all US vessels travelling between Washington and Alaska, and increased its over-harvest of salmon, in an attempt to pre-empt Washington fisheries from harvesting in other areas.[150] This so-called 'Pacific Salmon War' led to 100 Canadian fishing vessels blockading the Alaska Marine Highway ferry for three days in the summer of 1997, demanding that the US either curtail catch rates or pay Canada compensation for any excess Canadian salmon its fishers caught.[151]

[141] ibid art II.

[142] Blumm (n 17) 166.

[143] Michal P Shepard and A Argue, *The 1985 Pacific Salmon Treaty: Sharing Conservation Burdens and Benefits* (UBC Press, 2005) 199.

[144] ibid 203.

[145] Daniel Huppert, *Why the Pacific Salmon Treaty Failed to End the Salmon Wars* (School of Marine Affairs, University of Washington, 1995) 11–12.

[146] Austin Williams, 'The Pacific Salmon Treaty: A Historical Analysis and Prescription for the Future' (2007) 22 *Journal of Environmental Law & Litigation* 153, 170.

[147] ibid.

[148] *Confederated Tribes and Bands of Yakama Indian Nation v Baldrige* (1995) 898 F Supp 1477, 1491 (WD Wash) aff'd (1996) 95 F3d 1157 (9th Cir).

[149] ibid 1491.

[150] Williams (n 146) 171.

[151] Paul L Evans, 'Treaty Past, Treaty Present: An Interdisciplinary Analysis of the Pacific Salmon Treaty through Examination of the Values, Culture, and Political Structures that Provide Definition'

The salmon war subsided with the re-authorisation of the Pacific Salmon Treaty in 1999, providing some stability due to three main new reforms. First, the 1999 agreement established long-term fishing arrangements, replacing fixed quotas with 'abundance-based management' methods designed to better promote conservation through in-season monitoring.[152] Second, the amendments required substantial harvest cutbacks from Alaskan fishermen on salmon from transboundary rivers, and Canada agreed to reduce harvests of certain chinook stocks by 36.5 per cent, while the US agreed to reduce harvests by 40 per cent.[153] Third, the amendments established two funds to support investment in scientific approaches to better salmon management and habitat recovery in both countries.

Despite the improvements worked by the 1999 amendments, many problems remain unresolved. Interceptions from both countries remain high, and the alarmingly low survival status of many species exacerbates implementation issues.[154] Tribal treaty rights are among the main casualties of the Pacific Salmon Treaty's failure to curb interceptions, producing declining populations and adversely affecting treaty harvests. However, unlike the Stevens Treaties, neither the US nor Canada has interpreted the Pacific Salmon Treaty as a directive to protect salmon habitat.[155] But the keys to successful salmon management remain in habitat conservation and cooperation in allocating equitable shares of Pacific salmon, while avoiding over-fishing. To a large extent, the ability of Stevens Treaty tribes to enjoy their share of salmon will depend on whether the US and Canada can achieve these goals.

### C. The Columbia River Treaty of 1964

Allocating salmon harvests was at the heart of the Pacific Salmon Treaty, but the Columbia River Treaty was the product of negotiations over the use of the Columbia River for hydropower and flood control. The Columbia River, one of the most highly developed river systems in the world, has a generating capacity of more than 21,000 MW.[156] But because of the adverse effect of dams on aquatic ecosystems and fish migration, salmon protection has become an unresolved issue within the framework of this treaty as well.

(MA thesis, Oregon State University, 2000) 63–64, 66. In 1997, the US Congress then voted to send the US Navy to protect the right of innocent passage through Canadian waters, and the Governor of Alaska threatened to file suit against the Canadian government (ibid 66–67).

152 Williams (n 146) 172.

153 Blumm (n 17) 171.

154 Williams (n 146) 175.

155 Michael C Blumm and F Lorraine Bodi, 'A Shared Resource: The Tragedy of the Commons' in Joseph Cone and Sandy Ridlington (eds), *The Northwest Salmon Crisis* (OSU Press, 1996) 276.

156 NCESD, 'The Columbia River, a River of Power' (2013) 3, www.ncesd.org/wp-content/uploads/2017/03/River-of-Power-Lesson-1-final-2013.pdf.

### *i. Treaty Ratification and its Effect on Natural Resources*

By the 1960s, the US had developed or was constructing almost all of the current large hydroelectric projects on its part of the Columbia River Basin. But the river's flow originated in Canada and remained largely uncontrolled, creating high spring river flows and spills around lower basin dams. These spills did not maximise hydropower production, but they did benefit salmon migration.[157] For years the US sought to convince Canada to dam the upper Columbia to increase the power generating and flood control capability of downstream dams in the US, but Canada refused to do so without obtaining a share of these downstream hydropower and flood control benefits, an approach which was then unprecedented in international law.[158] Not until the US finally agreed to share downstream benefits of upper basin storage on an equal basis was the Columbia River Treaty signed in 1961 and ratified in 1964.[159]

The treaty resulted in the construction of four large storage projects, three in Canada and one in the US, which doubled the basin's storage capacity and dramatically changed the hydrograph of the Columbia River, to the detriment of salmon spawning and migration.[160] Although nothing in the Columbia River Treaty expressly elevated hydropower to the status of dominant use, that hegemony was the practical effect. System operators often cited the treaty as the justification for hydropower's dominance, and the planning processes the treaty instituted to coordinate hydropower production and flood control operations largely ignored the needs of salmon.

Many analysts believe that the treaty has achieved its principal intended purposes of increasing hydroelectric power production and flood control. For example, according to one account, the hydropower from Columbia Basin dams has 'contributed hugely to the reduction of global warming by reducing the use of fossil fuels' and 'provided the Northwest with some of the cheapest electricity in the world'.[161] But a half-century of building large dams has transformed the Columbia River Basin largely into a series of lakes which impose obstacles to salmon spawning and migration, which in turn has adversely affected the tribes' treaty rights.

[157] Blumm (n 17) 99.

[158] ibid.

[159] Treaty between the United States of America and Canada Relating to Cooperative Development of the Water Resources of the Columbia River Basin, 15 UST 1555, TIAS No 5638 (1964). The sharing of downstream benefits on an equal basis was key to Canada's signing the treaty. John Harrison, 'The Columbia River Treaty', *The Oregon Encyclopedia*, https://oregonencyclopedia.org/articles/columbia_river_treaty_1964_ (quoting Nigel Bankes). A dispute between the British Columbian government and the Canadian federal government over how to allocate the construction costs of four dams in Canada delayed the ratification.

[160] Blumm (n 17) 101.

[161] Matthew McKinney et al, 'Managing Transboundary Natural Resources: An Assessment of the Need to Revise and Update the Columbia River Treaty' (2010) 16 *Hastings Environmental Law Journal* 307, 312.

The treaty contains no automatic termination date or renegotiation clause, but after 2014, either party could terminate the power-sharing provisions of the treaty upon giving 10 years' notice.[162] While neither party has given notice to terminate, the potential for termination in 2024 (which coincides with the automatic termination of the assured flood control provisions of the treaty) prompted discussions about modifying the treaty.[163] Changes in the Columbia River Basin should be a main driver of the negotiations, including a change in values concerning how to manage the river, a change in the empowerment of local communities (particularly tribes), a change in the viability of fish populations, and climate change.[164]

*ii. The Future of the Columbia River Treaty: 2024 and beyond*

Canadian and American officials began discussions about renewing the treaty in early 2012. At least in the US, tribes seem determined to have more of a say in these negotiations than in the original negotiations 60 years earlier, as the treaty projects and their operation have caused considerable environmental, economic and cultural losses, including depletion of fish stocks.[165] For the US, protecting tribal rights has become a priority. The US position is that '[a] modernized Treaty should recognize and minimize adverse effects to tribal, First Nations, and other cultural resources in Canada and the United States'.[166] Both countries have identified improved management of the Columbia River's ecosystem as a primary concern, calling for the restoration of fish passage and the re-introduction of anadromous fish to currently blocked areas.[167]

Tribal participation in the treaty renegotiations is a product of a long process of organisation and activism that began with the *Boldt* decision. In 1977, four tribal governments formed the Columbia River Inter-Tribal Fish Commission in 1977 to facilitate tribal participation in fish management.[168] In addition, five upper Columbia tribes whose lands were affected by the Grand Coulee Dam's blockage of salmon migration formed the Upper Columbia United Tribes. In 2005, these tribes entered into a memorandum of understanding with Bonneville Power Administration and the US Army

[162] Columbia River Basin Treaty 1961, art XIX.

[163] Barbara Cosens, 'The Columbia River Treaty: An Opportunity for Modernization of Basin Governance' (2016) 27 *Colorado Natural Resources, Energy & Environmental Law Review* 27, 30.

[164] ibid 33–38; Thomas G Bode, 'A Modern Treaty for the Columbia River' (2017) 47 *Environmental Law* 81.

[165] Brandon Lee, 'Canada: Columbia River Treaty a Boon to the US But Must Benefit All' *The Oregonian* (3 January 2018), www.oregonlive.com/opinion/index.ssf/2018/01/canada_columbia_river_treaty_a.html.

[166] 'US Entity Regional Recommendation for the Future of the Columbia River Treaty after 2024' (13 December 2013) 5.

[167] ibid.

[168] See text following n 133. The four tribes are the Nez Perce, the Yakama Nation, the Confederated Tribes of the Umatilla Indian reservation and the Confederated Tribes of the Warm Springs Reservation.

Corps of Engineers – the principal managers of federal Columbia dams – that recognises the sovereign role of the tribes in the management of fish and water resources.[169]

Both tribal organisations seek to amend the treaty to add to its two primary purposes (hydropower and flood risk management) a third: ecosystem-based function.[170] This addition would account for fish, wildlife, habitat, water quality and health of the river. Actually, 15 Columbia Basin tribes in the US are actively working to re-shape the Columbia River Treaty to protect and benefit tribal culture and resources.[171] These tribes convinced the US treaty negotiators to adopt a 'US Entity Regional Recommendation', which included ecosystem function as a treaty purpose.[172] If a re-negotiated treaty with this purpose aims to improve salmon propagation and migration, this promise could substantially benefit treaty fishing rights.[173]

## V. TREATY FISHING RIGHTS AND FOSSIL-FUEL EXPORT TERMINALS

One of the more surprising developments of recent years has been the extent to which treaty fishing rights have influenced decision makers at the federal, state and local levels to deny required permits for fossil-fuel export projects that could adversely affect salmon and their habitat. These projects include a proposed oil port terminal in Vancouver, Washington, the Gateway Pacific Terminal (GPT) in Cherry Point, Washington, and a rail expansion connected to oil transport in Mosier, Oregon.

### A. The Vancouver Oil Terminal: Treaty Rights Influencing State Decision Makers

In January 2018, the Governor of Washington, Jay Inslee, denied Tesoro Savage's application for a site certification for the Vancouver Energy Distribution

[169] These tribes are the Coeur d'Alene Tribe, the Kalispell Tribe of Indians, the Spokane Tribe, the Kootenai Tribe and the Confederated Tribe of the Colville Reservation. See Upper Columbia United Tribes, 'Member Tribes', https://ucut.org/members-tribes; Upper Columbia United Tribes, 'UCUT and Bonneville Power Administration Partnership', https://ucut.org/fish/ucut-bonneville-power-administration-memorandum-understanding.

[170] See Upper Columbia United Tribes, 'Columbia River Treaty', https://ucut.org/water/columbia-river-treaty; Columbia River Inter-Tribal Fish Commission, 'Adding to Treaty Purposes', www.critfc.org/tribal-treaty-fishing-rights/policy-support/columbia-river-treaty/adding-to-treaty-purposes.

[171] Columbia River Inter-Tribal Fish Commission, 'Columbia River Treaty', www.critfc.org/tribal-treaty-fishing-rights/policy-support/columbia-river-treaty.

[172] 'US Entity Regional Recommendation' (n 166) 2–3. See Bode (n 164) 115–19 (arguing that the treaty should include ecosystem functions).

[173] Duke's Seafood & Chowder, 'Environmental Impact of Salmon Decline: This isn't Just about Fish' *Seattle Times* (26 January 2018), https://www.seattletimes.com/sponsored/environmental-impact-of-salmon-decline-this-isnt-just-about-fish.

Terminal at the Port of Vancouver.[174] The project, first proposed in 2013, would help move an average of 360,000 barrels of crude oil daily from the US interior to West Coast refineries for export to the Asian market.[175] In his decision, Inslee expressed concerns about seismic conditions at the proposed site, the likelihood of an oil spill adversely affecting the Columbia River or the Pacific Ocean, and the potential for fire or explosion at the facility.[176]

Inslee relied on recommendations made by the Washington Energy Facility Site Evaluation Council (EFSEC), an entity that oversees the siting process for major energy facilities. In its report, the EFSEC recognised the rights of the tribes to fish, hunt and gather in their traditional places.[177] The tribes argued that the construction of the terminal would interfere with their treaty rights because of the increased railroad traffic and the risk of an oil spill in the Columbia River. The EFSEC concluded that 'the tribal and economic impacts are great', adding that 'many of these impacts cannot be mitigated', thus creating an 'unacceptable risk' for the tribal people.[178] Given the history of opposition between Washington and the tribes regarding treaty rights, the fact that the state denied the permit application based on treaty rights was a surprising development.[179]

### B. The Gateway Pacific Coal Terminal: Treaty Rights Influencing Federal Decision Makers

Treaty rights also led to the denial of a federal permit for a proposed coal terminal in Cherry Point, Washington. The Lummi tribe opposed the siting on the ground that it would interfere with their treaty fishing rights, as the proposed trestle and associated wharf would occupy 122 acres over water.[180] The US Army Corps of Engineers agreed with the tribe, concluding that a 'tribe's treaty right to fish at its [usual and accustomed] fishing grounds necessarily includes a right of access to those grounds, which is at issue with the GPT project'.[181]

[174] Letter from Governor Jay Inslee to EFSEC (29 January 2018).

[175] Pete Danko, 'Vancouver Oil Terminal Report Details Unavoidable Impacts' *Portland Business Journal* (21 November 2017), https://www.bizjournals.com/portland/news/2017/11/21/vancouver-oil-terminal-report-details-unavoidable.html.

[176] Inslee letter (n 174).

[177] Washington Energy Facility Site Evaluation Council, 'Report to the Governor on Application No. 2013-01' (19 December 2017) 47.

[178] ibid 47–48.

[179] The state of Washington is also facing a lawsuit from Lighthouse Resources Inc after it denied a permit for a new coal terminal in Longview. If the tribes involve themselves in this lawsuit, treaty rights could become a key point of contention in this case. Dylan Brown, 'Trade Groups Back Suit against Wash. for Denying Port' *E&E News* (3 May 2018), https://www.eenews.net/eenewspm/2018/05/03/stories/1060080783.

[180] Samantha Wohlfeil, 'Army Corps Rejects Permit for Coal Terminal at Cherry Point' *Bellingham Herald* (9 May 2016), www.bellinghamherald.com/news/local/article76545117.html.

[181] US Army Corps of Engineers, 'Gateway Pacific Terminal Project and Lummi Nation's Usual and Accustomed Treaty Fishing Rights at Cherry Point, Whatcom County, Memorandum for Record'

The Corps' analysis considered whether the proposal would have a greater than *de minimis* effect on the Lummi's treaty fishing rights. Relying on tribal members' testimonies and on a technical report concluding that members spent one-third of their time fishing the Cherry Point area, the Corps concluded that available information was sufficient to support a greater than *de minimis* effect finding, requiring permit denial.[182] The federal agency rejected the permit applicant's argument that the area was not the most productive in terms of harvest and the effect of the project would be proportionally insignificant compared to aggregate Lummi fishing areas.[183]

### C. The Mosier Track Expansion: Treaty Rights Influencing Local Decision Makers

In late 2016, Wasco County commissioners denied Union Pacific Railroad's plan to expand railroad tracks along the Columbia River Gorge, in a National Scenic Area.[184] This project was particularly controversial, as the proposed siting was in an area where a train wreck had just caused a massive fire, renewing concerns about the safety of oil trains in the region. The Wasco County Planning Commission first approved the project, but the Yakama nation opposed the expansion project, arguing that it would violate treaty rights by increasing train traffic and would interfere with the tribe's ability to access fishing sites along those tracks.[185] The planning commission agreed with the tribe and denied the permit.

Union Pacific appealed the decision to the inter-state Columbia River Gorge Commission. The Commission decided that Wasco County 'properly construed the law of the Columbia River Treaty Tribes' fishing rights by considering whether Union Pacific's application could result in habitat damage in violation of protected treaty rights'.[186] This standard led the Commission to uphold the county's decision, accepting the Yakama nation's evidence that the project would

(9 May 2016) 19. For an assessment of the successful coalition among the Lummi Tribe and various environmental groups that convinced the Corps to deny the project, see Maggie Allen, Stoney Bird, Sara Breslow and Neves Dolsak, 'Stronger Together: Strategies to Protect Local Sovereignty, Ecosystems, and Place-Based Communities from the Global Fossil Fuel Trade' (2017) 80 *Marine Policy* 168.

[182] The '*de minimis* effect' rule was established in *Northwest Sea Farms v US Army Corps of Engineers* (1996) 931 F Supp 1515, 1520 (WD Wash), where the court characterised the role of the Corps in permit decisions affecting Indian treaty rights as a 'fiduciary duty to ensure that the Lummi Nation's treaty rights are not abrogated or impinged upon absent an act of Congress'.

[183] ibid 25–26.

[184] 'Wasco County Rejects Union Pacific Request to Expand' *The Oregonian* (5 November 2016), www.oregonlive.com/pacific-northwest-news/index.ssf/2016/11/wasco_county_rejects_union_pac.html.

[185] ibid.

[186] *Union Pacific Railroad Company v Wasco County Board of Commissioners* (2017) CRGC No COA-16-01, 34.

result in violations of the tribe's treaty rights to hunt, fish and gather traditional foods, and maintain their traditional, religious and cultural practices.[187]

## VI. CONCLUSION

The effect of the Stevens Treaties and their recognition of 'the right of taking fish in common with' settlers took US courts over a century to clarify, and significant questions concerning the treaties' effect on habitat-damaging activities remain even after the Supreme Court's affirmation in the culverts case. But the effect of the treaties is no longer confined to court adjudications. They have also influenced international treaty negotiations and regulatory approvals at the federal, state and local levels. In the wake of the Supreme Court's upholding of the implicit habitat protection promise in the treaties, treaty rights may be undergoing a democratisation process, whereby the rights are not only defended by the tribes and their federal trustee, but also by international agreements and state and local governments. If so, the promises made in the treaties finally may be realised, a century and a quarter after they were made.

[187] ibid 39. Union Pacific has appealed the Gorge Commission's decision to the Oregon Court of Appeals.

# Part IV

# Perspectives on Indigenous Rights in Marine Areas

# 14

# *Marine Protected Areas and Indigenous Rights*

SUE FARRAN

## I. INTRODUCTION

THIS CHAPTER CONSIDERS the rights of Indigenous peoples in the context of measures taken by governments to declare large areas of the world's oceans Marine Protected Areas (MPAs). In particular, it considers the motivation for this form of marine management, the key players involved, and the possible costs and consequences, especially for Indigenous peoples and local communities with long-standing associations with the marine environment.[1] Coastal peoples, notably those living in low-lying areas, on atolls and islands, are vulnerable to a number of factors, including negative consequences caused by climate change. In addition, they may be increasingly vulnerable to what might be described as a race for 'blue planet credentials' among nation-states eager to demonstrate their positive contribution to saving the planet by protecting its oceans. This 'race' has been evidenced in recent years by declarations of ever bigger MPAs, impacting territorial seas and exclusive economic zones (EEZs). In some cases, these MPAs have been declared over the seas of overseas territories, and in other cases by national governments over their own seas. As this chapter will show, while some MPAs may be no more than 'paper parks', the issues raised by their creation are often marginalised compared to the 'blue credentials' which they attract, and there may be potential conflicts of rights and interests which are barely acknowledged.

The use of MPAs to address international and global concerns about the loss of the 'blue commons' are located within the broader international framework

[1] The terms 'marine resources' and 'marine environment' are used broadly in this chapter, recognising the fact that MPAs may include inland waters, lagoons and lakes, estuaries and sea areas, and that those reliant on such resources and waters may be coastal and/or inland dwellers or indeed nomadic.

of the rights of Indigenous peoples (see Enyew's chapter in this volume) and the inclusion within these of rights to marine resources and the marine environment (see Allen's chapter in this volume). Of particular relevance to this chapter is the issue of who are included within the definition of Indigenous peoples, because of the debates surrounding the rights of those whose traditional rights have been impacted by MPAs. However, before considering this issue, I will first set the scene by looking at a recent example of an MPA in order to provide a contextual understanding of the motivation behind establishing an MPA, what is promised through this establishment, who controls the agenda, and who receives the benefits and who bears the burdens. I will then consider the actual and potential conflicts between the rights of peoples who are Indigenous to those parts of the world where livelihoods may be ocean or marine-dependent and where supporters of MPAs are keen that these should be maintained, enlarged or established. In doing this, I will start by considering the challenges of defining the concept of indigeneity. I will then look at what MPAs are, the objectives behind their establishment and the issues that are raised in terms of governance, the equitable distribution of benefits and the sustainability of the protection that is envisaged. The chapter concludes with a critical reflection of current developments in this field of marine rights.

### A. Illustrating the Context in Which a Marine Protected Area May Arise: The Seychelles

In February 2018, a headline caught my attention: 'Debt for Dolphins: Seychelles Creates Huge Marine Parks in World-First Finance Scheme'.[2] The 'scheme' creates two new MPAs around the Aldabra archipelago, which includes the islands of Aldabra, Astove and Assumption (an area of 74,000 square kilometres) where all extractive uses are prohibited, and around the main island of Mahe and Coetivy (which are in the Amirantes Group), where the marine protected area is 134,000 square kilometres and where there is not a total prohibition, but control of activities including fishing. Together these two MPAs cover 15 per cent of the Seychelles Ocean, and the Seychelles government has committed to doubling this by 2021. In other words, 30 per cent of its seas (158,302 square miles)[3] will effectively be taken out of its control and placed in the hands of an American based, non-governmental organisation (NGO): The Nature Conservancy (TNC). The deal is that a US$22 million national debt, owed to the developed countries of the UK, Belgium, France and Italy, has been 'bought' at a discount by The Nature

[2] Damian Carrington, 'Debt for Dolphins: Seychelles Creates Huge Marine Parks in World-First Finance Scheme' *The Guardian* (22 February 2018), https://www.theguardian.com/environment/2018/feb/22/debt-for-dolphins-seychelles-create-huge-new-marine-parks-in-world-first-finance-scheme.

[3] John Liang, 'Seychelles Creates New Marine Protected Areas' *Deeper Blue* (22 February 2018), https://www.deeperblue.com/seychelles-creates-new-marine-protected-areas.

Conservancy[4] and, in future, repayments by the Seychelles will be paid into a trust fund (the Seychelles Conservation and Climate Adaptation Trust) directed at, inter alia, the conservation of the Marine Protected Areas.[5]

Didier Dogley, the Environment Minister for the Seychelles, is reported as stating 'we truly believe these initiatives will create prosperity for our people, conserve critical biodiversity and build resilience against climate change'. These are not the first MPAs in the Seychelles. Prior to this proposal, the Seychelles had a number of MPAs covering an area of around 22 square kilometres: the Sainte Anne Marie National Park, the Baie Trenay Marine National Park, the Curieuse Marine National Parks and the Cousin Island Special Reserve. Although these may have been insufficient to protect the spawning grounds of some of the most sought-after species,[6] it was also evident that even with these much smaller MPAs, there were problems of demarcation and notification regarding restrictions and infrequent enforcement patrols.[7] With an even greater area, it might be asked whether the Seychelles has the resources to address these practical concerns in a sustainable way[8] in order to 'conserve critical biodiversity'.

It is not clear how the proposed MPA will 'create prosperity' for the Seychellois who live on the islands. The main income generators for the Seychelles are tourism and fishing, and from the media coverage, it would appear that some fishers and tour operators are concerned about the controls that will be imposed, both in terms of potential impact on their own business and in terms of realistic enforceability. Others are more optimistic, thinking that it will, in the longer term, lead to better fishing because species will be more abundant. Prosperity may of course come in other forms. There are proposals that the island of Assumption, now in the proposed MPA around the Aldrabra archipelago, is earmarked for a military base for India, and that an agreement has already

[4] This was at a lower interest rate than previously and with some of the debt wiped out by charitable donations of US dollars raised from donors, including celebrities – all good for publicity – such as the Leonardo DiCaprio Foundation, the Nature Conservancy's China Global Conservation Fund, and the Jeremy and Hannelore Grantham Environmental Trust; see ibid.

[5] There is some suggestion that this 'debt-for-climate-change-swap' was made or at least considered in 2016. See Sharon Ernesta, 'Marine Life around Seychelles Aldraba, Amirantes Groups to Be Protected Areas' *Seychelles News Agency* (13 December 2017), www.seychellesnewsagency.com/articles/8272/Marine+life+around+Seychelles%27+Aldabra%2C+Amirantes+groups+to+be+protected+areas.

[6] Hajira Amla, 'Marine Protected Areas in Seychelles Offer Inadequate Protection for Spawning Fish, Says Fish Researcher' *Seychelles News Agency* (7 December 2014), www.seychellesnewsagency.com/articles/1907/Marine+protected+areas+in+Seychelles+offer+inadequate+protection+for+spawning+fish%2C+says+fish+researcher.

[7] This is not a problem that is unique to the Seychelles. Mora et al state that 'the establishment of MPAs is rarely followed by good management and enforcement … which means that the numbers of MPAs and their coverage can be misleading indicators of effective conservation'; Camilo Mora et al, 'Coral Reefs and the Global Network of Marine Protected Areas' (2006) 312 *Science* 1750, 1750.

[8] In 'The Worldwide Costs of Marine Protected Areas' (2004) 101(26) *Proceedings of the National Academy of Sciences of the United States of America* 9694–97, Andrew Balmford, Pippa Gravestock and Callum Roberts have calculated that if the World Parks Congress target of 20–30 per cent of the world's oceans were covered, the cost would be US$19 billion.

been signed.[9] Those familiar with the story of the British Indian Overseas Territory (BIOT) and the US military base at Diego Garcia will see the possibilities of history repeating itself.[10] Vincent Meriton, the Vice-President of the Seychelles, is quoted as saying 'the military base will have to pass environmental assessments and will actually benefit protection, by enabling better surveillance around the isolated archipelago'.[11] The same archipelago has also been identified as having oil-drilling potential and there is already test-drilling going on in the area designated as falling within the MPA.[12] While the new MPAs are apparently part of a government Marine Spatial Plan, the state institution at the heart of the matter is the Ministry of Environment, Energy and Climate Change, which is both the legal watchdog for environmental protection and the ministry responsible for the Marine Spatial Plan. Clearly, there may be tensions within its mandate and with the interests of other public and private corporate bodies involved in the 'prosperity' of the islands.

Building resilience for climate change is of course on the global agenda and is particularly important for those most vulnerable to its adverse consequences. Internationally the Seychelles model is seen as being 'a leader in this field worldwide and may be an example for many other countries'.[13] Plans for a roll-out by Rob Weary, the person behind the TNC plan, include a US$60 million debt swap with Grenada, other islands in the Caribbean and possibly Mauritius. In other words, despite the fact that responsibility for climate change rests with the developed and industrialised nations of the world, not only are many of the effects most keenly felt by coastal and island people in developing countries, but the use of MPAs to build resilience to climate change may also have a disproportionate impact on Indigenous coastal and island communities in terms of location and consequences.

Although the Seychelles is an independent sovereign state (compared to, for example, Pitcairn, New Caledonia or British Indian Ocean Territory (BIOT), which are all overseas territories belonging to metropolitan states and around which large MPAs have been declared),[14] the Seychelles example illustrates not only the vulnerability of islands and the people who live on them to the effects of climate change, over-fishing and marine resource extraction, but also to the

[9] 'Assumption: "Democratise Our Islands" Says Nirmal Shah' *Nature Seychelles* (12 February 2018), www.natureseychelles.org/knowledge-centre/news-and-stories/723-assumption-democratise-our-islands-says-nirmal-shah.

[10] See Stephen Allen, *The Chagos Islanders and International Law* (Hart Publishing, 2014).

[11] Carrington (n 2).

[12] PetroSeychelles is a state-owned company, but the prospective drilling is being undertaken by Wilkes Seamount.

[13] Benoit Bosquet, environment practice manager at the World Bank, quoted in Carrington (n 2).

[14] See Sue Farran, 'Learning from Chagos: Lessons for Pitcairn' in Stephen Allen and Chris Monaghan (eds), *Fifty Years of the British Indian Ocean Territory: Legal Perspectives* (Springer, 2018) 293–317; and see also Dorothée Cambou, Jérémie Gilbert and Marlène Dégremont (ch 8 in this volume).

agendas of other players – here international goals to protect large areas of the world's oceans for the 'common good', particularly when those states are indebted to wealthier and more powerful nations. The Seychelles example also highlights the potential conflicts between the rights of peoples living on these islands and in areas where there is dependency on marine resources or traditional fishing practices, and the protection of those resources through the declaration of MPAs. The question, for the purposes of this volume, might be are the rights of these local people distinct because they are Indigenous, or because they are coastal or marine orientated, or both? In other words, is there a special case to be made for the impact of MPAs on Indigenous peoples' rights? In order to answer this question, it is first necessary to consider who are 'Indigenous peoples' and, second, what are MPAs and how might they affect these rights holders?

## II. WHO ARE INDIGENOUS PEOPLES?

The international legal order which recognises that Indigenous peoples have rights, as well as the nature of those rights is fully canvassed in this volume by Endalew Enyew. Despite the emergence of Indigenous peoples as a class of specific – as well as general – rights holders, there is no consensus about how this class is to be defined or where the lines are to be drawn.[15] Some definitions focus on the colonial suppression of certain people by outsiders, identifying Indigenous peoples primarily as victims of colonialism, while others identify indigeneity with historical claims to territory, or persistent practices of culture and shared language. The United Nations (UN) defines Indigenous communities, peoples and nations as 'those which, having a historical continuity with pre-invasion and pre-colonial societies that developed on their territories, consider themselves distinct from other sectors of the societies now prevailing on those territories, or parts of them'.[16] In the period since the UN was established in 1945, and more particularly the post-1960 era of de-colonisation, this seems to refer primarily to more recent instances of invasion and colonialism, but historically Indigenous people have been subject to war, natural disasters, genocide and other events which have disrupted their associations with place and have given rise to re-location, new identities and changing cultures and languages. Using UN definitions, Cisneros-Montemayor and his team of researchers suggested there are about 370 million people who are considered to be Indigenous (five per cent of the world's population). Of these, about 27 million people in

[15] See John-Andrew McNeish and Robyn Eversole, 'Introduction: Indigenous People and Poverty' in Robert Eversole, John-Andre McNeish and Alberto Cimadamore (eds), *Indigenous Peoples and Poverty* (Zed Books, 2005).

[16] UN Workshop on Data Collection and Disaggregation for Indigenous Peoples: The Concept of Indigenous Peoples, UN Department of Economic and Social Affairs, 2004.

2,000 communities in 27 countries are regarded as being Indigenous coastal people.[17] The focus of their research was dependency on marine resources for food and they used a definition which focused on 'those who are considered to be ethnic minorities, have historical ties to local marine geography and reside within 25 kilometres of the shoreline'.[18]

This type of geographical distinction might be unhelpful in those parts of the world where there is a tradition of exchange and trade in marine resources between coastal peoples and inland peoples, because initiatives that impact on the activities of the former will have consequences for the latter. Similarly, where Indigenous peoples spend only part of the year accessing marine resources – see the example of the Tlingit summer fish camps in Caskey Russell and X̱'unei Lance Twitchell's chapter in this volume, restrictions on fishing or harvesting rights may have wide-ranging consequences. It is also important to recognise the rights of those who do not reside in one place, but travel – by land, ice or sea – from one place to another in a nomadic or semi-nomadic lifestyle.[19]

Although intended to be broad, the above definition is limiting, especially as in the context of this volume, it is pertinent to remember that the oceans and inland waterways have provided pathways to new lands and sustained voyagers and settlers. Traditions of fishing and marine resource harvesting have a long history and for some Indigenous people, stories of origin are closely associated with the sea. However, initiatives such as MPAs may impact on relative newcomers to islands, coastal communities, lake and riverside dwellers, who also have traditional associations with the marine environment. Therefore, some caution should be exercised in arguing that these peoples do not have special rights because they are not Indigenous. Guidance might be taken from an address to the House of Delegates, Palau, in the run-up to the declaration of an MPA around Palau in the Pacific Ocean:

> Surrounded by water, Palauan have developed a life which is inextricably linked with the oceans. We derive food, identity and traditions from our relationship with the ocean. The long standing success of this symbiotic relationship is based on responsibility that each Palauan is taught from childhood that they are caretakers of the sea.[20]

[17] Andres Cisneros-Montemayor, Daniel Pauly, Lauren Weatherdon and Yoshitaka Ota, 'A Global Estimation of Seafood Consumption by Coastal Indigenous People' (2016) 11(12) *PLoS One*, https://www.ncbi.nlm.nih.gov/pmc/articles/PMC5137875.

[18] Yoshitaka Ota and Andres Cisneros-Montemayor, 'For Indigenous Communities, Fish Mean Much More than Food' *The Conversation* (30 January 2017), http://theconversation.com/for-indigenous-communities-fish-mean-much-more-than-food-70129.

[19] For example, the Bajau Laut of Indonesia, Malaysia and the Philippines. See Julian Clifton and Chris Majors, 'Culture, Conservation, and Conflict: Perspectives on Marine Protection among the Bajau of Southeast Asia' (2012) 25(7) *Society and Natural Resources* 716. See also Jérémie Gilbert, *Nomadic Peoples and Human Rights* (Routledge, 2014).

[20] Mr Noah Idechong, Delegate, House of Delegates, Palau, 'Micronesian Sea Traditions – Palau's Marine Protected Areas', www.un.org/depts/los/consultative_process/documents/7abstract_idechong.pdf.

The focus on the relationship of people with the marine environment should also be borne in mind when considering situations where people have been forcefully re-located many generations ago, for example, as slaves or indentured labourers. This point is illustrated by the Chagossians of the BIOT. In the case of the Chagossians, their claim to be Indigenous has been upheld[21] and not only do they self-identify as Indigenous, but also most literature referring to them describes them as such. However, they have been forcefully removed from the land and the marine environment with which they associate. By contrast, the inhabitants of Pitcairn acknowledge that they were not the first people to settle on the islands – Polynesian relics, for instance, have been found – but they clearly identify as a distinctive group with long-standing associations with the sea and its resources. Also, even today, a number of Pitcairners trace their ancestry back to the early settlement of Pitcairn island and the mixed-race descendants of the Bounty mutineers, and distinguish between those who are 'native' to the island and 'outsiders'.[22] Similarly, while the Seychellois may not be regarded by some as an Indigenous people, being historically a mix of African, Indian, Chinese and French immigrants, settlers and slaves, they share a language (Creole), a history of colonial oppression and a distinct culture.

It should also be pointed out that not all peoples make a sharp distinction between marine and terrestrial rights or associations – see, for example, the case studies in this volume – so to categorise some people as coastal and others as not may well be inaccurate and misleading. For example, a report entitled 'Sea Country: An Indigenous Perspective'[23] notes that:

> Indigenous people make no distinction between land and sea. They see themselves as having responsibilities and rights across the land as sea boundaries that have been in place over the last 200 years ... coastal environments are an integrated cultural landscape/seascape that is conceptually very different from the broader Australian view of land and sea.[24]

However, as illustrated by a number of the case studies in this volume, while many Indigenous peoples have fought for and, to varying degrees, secured recognition of their land rights, their claims to rights in marine resources and indeed the sea remain less secure. Capistrano and Charles, for example, point to the fact that governmental and societal recognition of Indigenous rights is often absent and that 'this reality has been particularly apparent with respect to fisheries and other natural resources'.[25] This is a point picked up by Natalie Ban with specific

[21] See Allen (n 10); Jean Claude de L'Estrac, *Next Year in Diego Garcia* (Touria Prayag tr Elp, 2011).

[22] Maria Amoamo, 'Remoteness and Myth Making: Tourism on Pitcairn Island' (2011) 8(1) *Tourism Planning and Development* 1.

[23] 'Sea Country: An Indigenous Perspective', National Oceans Office, Commonwealth of the Government of Australia, 2002.

[24] ibid 2–3.

[25] Robert Charles Capistrano and Anthony Charles, 'Indigenous Rights and Coastal Fisheries: A Framework of Livelihoods, Rights and Equity' (2012) 69 *Ocean and Coastal Management* 200, 200.

relevance to MPAs. She notes that while many countries are establishing MPAs to address the concern of declining marine resources and loss of biodiversity, Indigenous rights and governance are being overlooked.[26] Similarly, in a side event at the Permanent Forum on Indigenous Issues in 2017, the International Union for Conservation of Nature (IUCN) together with other partners hosted an event on 'Marine Protected Areas, Indigenous and Local Communities, and Sustainable Livelihoods'. Speakers highlighted the importance of engaging with Indigenous and local communities, but also the failure to do so effectively.[27]

For the purposes of this chapter and picking up on a phrase used in some of the literature, the concern is with 'Indigenous and local communities'. These terms may or may not be synonymous. The aim is to appreciate that within the broad parameters of human rights, there are various subsidiary rights relevant to marine resources, which may be more significant to some peoples than to others. These include the right to access and use, the right to manage and be involved in decision making and the right to equitable and intergenerational distribution of benefits. These are all issues which have been raised in the context of MPAs, and there are examples across different jurisdictions of differing approaches to the consideration of Indigenous and local rights, the representation, role and participation of Indigenous and local people in determining and managing marine areas, and in determining and distributing any benefits arising from or incidental to such areas.[28] Before considering some of these issues, it is pertinent to ask: what then are MPAs and why are they relevant?

## III. MARINE PROTECTED AREAS

As indicated above, MPAs are integral to a broad, international focus on the environment and natural resources. Of particular relevance is the Convention on Biological Diversity (CBD) 1992, the objectives of which are:

> The conservation of biological diversity, the sustainable use of its components and the fair and equitable sharing of the benefits arising out of the utilization of genetic

[26] Natalie Ban and Alejandro Frid, 'Indigenous Peoples' Rights and Marine Protected Areas' (2018) 87 *Marine Policy* 180.

[27] IUCN at the UN Permanent Forum on Indigenous Issues, 'Marine Protected Areas, Indigenous and Local Communities, and Sustainable Livelihoods', 5 May 2017, https://www.iucn.org/news/global-policy/201705/iucn-un-permanent-forum-indigenous-issues-marine-protected-areas-indigenous-and-local-communities-and-sustainable-livelihoods.

[28] See here the work of S Guénette, R Chuenpagdee and R Jones, 'Marine Protected Areas with an Emphasis on Local Communities and Indigenous Peoples: A Review' (2000) 8(1) *Fisheries Centre Research Reports*, https://open.library.ubc.ca/media/download/pdf/52383/1.0348127/5; and Dermot Smyth, 'Best Practice Recognition and Engagement of Aboriginal Traditional Owners and Other Indigenous People in the Use and Management of Victoria's Marine Protected Areas', Discussion Paper 2012, http://www.veac.vic.gov.au/documents/Best%20practice%20recognition%20and%20engagement%20of%20Aboriginal%20Traditional%20Owners.pdf.

> resources, including by appropriate access to genetic resources and by appropriate transfer of relevant technologies, taking into account all rights over those resources and to technologies and by appropriate funding.

While the initial focus of the CBD is on genetic resources, with respect to the opening words, Article 6 imposes on contracting parties obligations (in accordance with their particular conditions and capabilities) to 'develop national strategies, plans or programmes for the conservation and sustainable use of biological diversity'. The measures that might be appropriate to meet the objectives of the CBD have subsequently been enlarged upon and are constantly under review.

The Strategic Plan for Biodiversity 2011–2020 includes Strategic Goal C, which is 'to improve the status of biodiversity by safeguarding ecosystems, species and genetic diversity'. This has been elaborated upon by what are referred to as the Aichi Biodiversity Targets adopted in 2010 in Nagoya, Japan. There are 20 targets, Target 11 of which states:

> By 2020, at least 17 per cent of terrestrial and inland water areas and 10 per cent of coastal and marine areas, especially areas of particular importance for biodiversity and ecosystems service, are conserved through effectively and equitably managed, ecologically representative and well-connected systems of protected areas and other effective area-based conservation measures, and integrated into the wider landscape and seascape.

This 10 per cent ties in with the Sustainable Development Goals, which aim for the conservation of at least 10 per cent of coastal and marine areas.[29] In 2012, the World Summit on Sustainable Development proposed deadlines for the establishment of MPAs to meet the obligations of states under the CBD.[30] The aim is for the parties to strive to declare 10 per cent of their oceans, encompassed in their EEZs as MPAs, or other area-based mechanisms, by 2020. In 2014, the World Parks Congress increased the recommendation of strict protection to 20–30 per cent of each marine habitat, and to 30 per cent in no-take reserves by 2020.[31] How much of the ocean is protected seems uncertain.[32] Sala and Giakoumi suggest that as of March 2017, 3.5 per cent of the world's oceans were covered by MPAs and of these, 1.6 per cent were strongly protected

[29] UN 2014. See also UN Framework Convention on Climate Change 1992 and the Durban Accord 2005.

[30] The convention opened for signature on 5 June 1992 at the Rio 'Earth Summit' and remained open for signature until 4 June 1993. It entered into force on 29 December 1993.

[31] For progress up to 2012, see Elizabeth de Santo, 'Missing Marine Protected Area (MPA) Targets: How the Push for Quantity over Quality Undermines Sustainability and Social Justice' (2013) 124 *Journal of Environmental Management* 137, 139–40.

[32] Protect Planet suggests there are over 15,000 MPAs, (1,700 of these in the US) protecting 6.9 per cent of the world's oceans. However, the UNEP indicated in December 2016 that more than five per cent of the world's oceans are now protected (3.6 million sq km). See UN News Centre, 14 December 2016, www.un.org/apps/news/story.asp?NewsID=55798#.WFGvurlrLcs.

MPAs.[33] The Atlas of Marine Protection in its SeaStates 2017 Report, presented at a conference in Malta, suggests 3.7 per cent in implemented and actively managed MPAs, with 2.0 per cent being in strongly protected no-take reserves.[34] However, in June 2017, the Executive Secretary of the CBD claimed that the 10 per cent target would be met.[35]

Even if the target of 10 per cent is met, it might be argued that this is a very small area of the world's oceans and, for this reason alone, the impact of MPAs on Indigenous peoples is not of great concern. Yet, it is often in the areas where Indigenous coastal peoples live or around the marine resources that they traditionally use that the biodiversity is greatest and the attraction of declaring an MPA is strongest. While the areas covered by MPAs have in the past been relatively small, in the first two decades of this century, a number of large MPAs (over 100,000 square kilometres) have been declared.

## A. Definition

Aichi Target 11 neither defines the forms of protection or management that might be used, nor does it specifically mention MPAs. Nevertheless, MPAs have been perceived as one of the key (but increasingly not the sole) tools for achieving the target. The UN Food and Agriculture Organization (FAO) suggests that it was the World Summit of Sustainable Development in Johannesburg in 2002 that placed MPAs at the top of the international conservation agenda.[36] However, there is no single meaning of 'MPA' and the term is used loosely by those claiming blue/green credentials in the fight to save the world's oceans. In practice, an MPA is an umbrella term with a wide diversity of meanings. The United States National Ocean Service, for example, suggests that this term can include 'marine sanctuaries, estuarine research reserves, ocean parks, and marine wildlife refuges'.[37] The United Nations Environment Programme (UNEP) simply defines an MPA as: 'A globally applicable, general term to describe any protected area in the marine realm which aims to conserve nature and maintain healthy oceans.'[38] The IUCN defines an MPA as: 'A clearly defined geographical space, recognised, dedicated and managed through legal or other effective means,

[33] Enrich Sala and Sylvaine Giakoumi, 'Food for Thought. No-Take Marine Reserves are the Most Effective Protected Areas in the Ocean' (2018) 75(3) *ICES Journal of Marine Science* 1166.

[34] Atlas of Marine Protections, 'SeaStates 2017 Report Released', www.mpatlas.org.

[35] Secretariat of the Convention on Biological Diversity, 'Global Marine Protected Area Target of 10% to Be achieved by 2020', press release, 5 June 2017, https://www.cbd.int/doc/press/2017/pr-2017-06-05-mpa-pub-en.pdf.

[36] FAO Fisheries and Aquaculture Department, 'About MPAs', www.fao.org/fishery/topic/4400/en.

[37] National Ocean Service (NOAA), 'What is a Marine Protected Area?', https://oceanservice.noaa.gov/facts/mpa.html.

[38] UN Environment, 'Marine Protected Areas (MPA) Definition', *Biodiversity A–Z*, www.biodiversitya-z.org/content/marine-protected-area-mpa.

to achieve the long-term conservation of nature with associated ecosystem services and cultural values'; the World Wide Fund for Nature (WWF) defines it as: 'An area designated and effectively managed to protect marine ecosystems, processes, habitats and species, which can contribute to the restoration and replenishment of resources for social, economic, and cultural enrichment';[39] and the FAO defines it as 'temporally and geographically defined areas that afford natural resources greater protection than is afforded to the rest of an area'.[40] As a consequence, there are a great many MPAs across the world, some on inland and estuarine waters, some on coastal waters and others off-shore.

## B. Purpose

Given the diversity of definitions, it is not surprising to find that the purpose and function of these MPAs also varies. Some MPAs may have primarily ecological objectives, such as preserving and promoting biodiversity, protecting species identified as being at risk, preserving habitats such as coral reefs and/or preventing activities which could have ecologically detrimental effects on the ecology. Others may have human objectives, for example, the protection and preservation of sites of historical or cultural importance, the promotion of tourism, the sustainable management of essential food resources, and the provision of sites for research, monitoring and/or training.[41] Given the broad use of the term, there are, unsurprisingly, MPAs across the globe – some on inland waters such as the great lakes of Canada and some on coastal waters and estuaries. As a result, the extent of MPAs is contested and the areas of effective protection are probably over-estimated.[42]

However, the WWF suggests that it is this diversity of purpose that can make MPAs so valuable, providing the benefits of:

- maintaining biodiversity and providing refuges for endangered and commercial species;
- protecting critical habitats from damage by destructive fishing practices and other human activities and allowing them to recover;
- providing areas where fish are able to reproduce, spawn and grow to their adult size;
- increasing fish catches (both size and quantity) in surrounding fishing grounds;

[39] WWF, 'The Case for MPAs', http://wwf.panda.org/our_work/oceans/solutions/protection/protected_areas.

[40] FAO (n 36).

[41] Protect Planet Ocean, 'What are Marine Protected Areas?', www.protectplanetocean.org/collections/introduction/introboc/mpas/introduction-item.html.

[42] See the Marine Conservation Institute report at the Ocean Conference in Malta in October 2017, www.mpatas.org.

- building resilience to protect against damaging external impacts, such as climate change;
- helping to maintain local cultures, economies and livelihoods which are intricately linked to the marine environment.[43]

Reflection on the above points suggests that it is the no-take or limited-take MPAs that are most likely to satisfy the first three (and possibly the fifth) benefits, and that the fourth is a consequence of and marginal to the creation of a no-take or limited-take MPA. Similarly, the final benefit may be a collateral benefit, although it has been suggested that marine resources in inland, estuarine and coastal waters are more closely tied to livelihoods and local cultures than the distant off-shore marine environment.[44] Indeed, it is difficult to see how, especially in no-take or limited-take MPAs, economies may thrive, particularly if these are dependent on the harvesting and sale of marine resources, and/or revenue generated by commercial fishing licences.

This financial dimension may make some countries dependent on ongoing aid in return for the declaration of an MPA. For example, in 2004, an extensive MPA was declared around Kiribati's Phoenix Islands. This Phoenix Islands Protected Area (PIPA) covers an area of 410,500 square kilometres 'in a nearly uninhabited region of abundant marine and bird life',[45] which encompasses eight small islands and two coral reef systems. This MPA was developed in collaboration with the following non-state organisations: New England Aquarium (NEAq) and Conservation International's (CI) Global Conservation Fund and Pacific Island Program. However, it was recognised at the time that: 'Protecting the Phoenix Islands means restricting commercial fishing in the area, resulting in a loss of revenue that the Kiribati government would normally receive from issuing commercial fishing licences.' To address this, 'NEAq and CI are helping Kiribati design an endowment system that will cover the core recurring management costs of PIPA and compensate the government for the forgone commercial fishing licence revenues'.[46] Whether the financial package that is offered will be sustainable in the long run remains to be seen, and it is also unclear whether any financial compensation will be based on past licence revenue or will factor in possible future licence revenue had the MPA not been declared.

[43] WWF (n 39).

[44] See, eg, Hugh Govan, 'Status and Potential of Locally-Managed Marine Areas in the South Pacific' (SPREP/WWF/WorldFish-Reefbase/CRISP (Coral Reef Initiatives for the Pacific) 2009 Noumea), www.sprep.org/att/publication/000646_LMMA_Report.pdf.

[45] Conservation International, 'World's Largest Marine Protected Areas Created in Pacific Ocean' *Conservation International* (14 February 2008), www.conservation.org/NewsRoom/pressreleases/Pages/PIPA-largest-protected-area-in-pacific.aspx.

[46] Conservation International, 'World's Largest Marine Protected Area Created in Pacific Ocean' (14 February 2008), www.conservation.org/NewsRoom/pressreleases/Pages/PIPA-largest-protected-area-in-pacific.aspx.

The IUCN guidelines on MPAs suggest six categories: 1a – Strict nature reserve; 1b – Wilderness area; II – National park; III – Natural monument or feature; IV – Habitat/species management area; V – Protected landscape or seascape; and VI – Protected areas with sustainable use of natural resources. An MPA will fall into one of the categories where at least 75 per cent of its total area meets the definition. In this chapter, the focus is on those MPAs which fall into the IUCN's categories I and II, because it is these that are likely to be fully or partially no-take, and to have limitations on the extraction of marine resources and therefore the greatest impact on local fishers and communities reliant on marine resources. This is because the IUCN definitions state that a Strict Nature Reserve (Category 1a) is: 'Strictly protected for biodiversity and also possibly geological/geomorphological features, where human visitation, use and impacts are controlled and limited to ensure protection of the conservation values.' A Wilderness area (Category 1b) is: 'Usually large unmodified or slightly modified areas, retaining their natural character and influence, without permanent or significant human habitation, protected and managed to preserve their natural condition'; National Parks (Category II) are: 'Large natural or near-natural areas protecting large-scale ecological processes with characteristic species and ecosystems, which also have environmentally and culturally compatible spiritual, scientific, educational, recreational and visitor opportunities.'[47] The primary objectives for these specific categories are to limit human presence. For example, the primary objective of Category 1a is:

> To conserve regionally, nationally or globally outstanding ecosystems, species (occurrences or aggregations) and/or geodiversity features: these attributes will have been formed mostly or entirely by non-human forces and will be degraded or destroyed when subjected to all but very light human impact.[48]

That of Category 1b refers to long-term protections of natural areas 'that are undisturbed by significant human activity', while Category II, although allowing for more human activity, limits this to visitors (recreation) and education (including possibly research). Scientifically, it has been suggested that no-take reserves are the most effective in restoring and preserving biodiversity and building resilient ecosystems.[49] Therefore, advocates of MPAs are more likely to lobby for these particular forms.

[47] IUCN, 'Guidelines for Applying the IUCN Protected Area Management Categories to Marine Protected Areas', https://www.iucn.org/content/guidelines-applying-iucn-protected-area-management-categories-marine-protected-areas-0.

[48] IUCN, Guidelines for Applying the IUCN Protected Area Management Categories to Marine Protected Areas (supplementary to the 2008 Guidelines) 2011., https://cmsdata.iucn.org/downloads/pa_categories_draft_marine_guidelines_field_testing_version.doc,.

[49] Enric Sala and Sylvaine Giakoumi, 'No-Take Marine Reserves are the Most Effective Protected Areas in the Ocean' (2017) *ICES Journal of Marine Science*, doi:10.1093/icesjms/fsx059.

While the categorisation of MPAs by the IUCN was intended to facilitate accurate data collection, because of the very broad use of the term 'MPA', it is still difficult to ascertain exactly which category all MPAs fall into.[50] Protected Planet suggests that 6.97 per cent of the oceans are protected areas and that there are 15,603 MPAs currently (although a number of these will be estuarine, inshore waters and close coastal waters), with 2.25 per cent being exclusively no-take.[51] Many of the strongly protected marine areas are around those countries which lack sovereignty and are dependencies or overseas territories of other states. These include the Chagos Marine Protected Area (UK), Nazca-Desventuradas Marine Park (Chile), Pitcairn Islands Marine Reserve (UK), the Henderson Islands (UK), Kermandec Ocean Sanctuary and Benthic Protection Area (NZ), and the Pacific Remote Islands National Marine Monument, with fully protected areas around Wake Atoll, Johnston Atoll and Jarvis Island (US). Proposed strongly protected reserves include Trindade e Martin Vaz (Brazil), Ascension Island (UK), Rapa Nui Rahui (Chile), the Clipperton Islands (France) and the Galapagos Islands (Ecuador).

Some of the world's Category 1a MPAs may be uninhabited (for example, the Réserve Naturelle des Terres australes françaises in the Antarctic), but others are not (such as the Papahānaumokuākea Marine National Monument). It is also the case (as illustrated in Table 14.1) that in some developed countries, the percentage of MPAs is greater in their overseas territories' waters than in their national waters.

**Table 14.1** Comparative percentages of national and overseas territories water covered by MPAs

| Country | % of protected national waters | % of protected OT waters |
|---|---|---|
| UK | 27 | 50 |
| US | 42 | 45 |
| France | 31 | 35 |

Even where these percentages do not seem to be so great, as is evident from the list of MPAs above, the larger of these are often declared around more remote islands or over remote areas. It is in these areas that not only is there considerable biodiversity, but there may also be less likelihood of contestation, due in part to low human population size, fewer socio-economic interests, limited resources for advocacy and greater dependency on more affluent/developed nations.[52]

[50] For example, the Ross Sea Region Marine Protected Area, which is the largest in the world, does not have an IUCN designation despite only being created in 2017, nor does the Pitcairn Islands Marine Reserve, which was designated in 2016.

[51] Protected Planet, 'Marine Protected Areas', https://www.protectedplanet.net/marine.

[52] See, eg, the Pitcairn and British Indian Ocean Territory MPAs discussed in Farran (n 14).

## IV. THE CHALLENGES TO RIGHTS IN MARINE PROTECTED AREAS

Ideally, and as claimed for the MPA around Palau,[53] an MPA should align marine conservation, Indigenous rights and cultural revitalisation, especially where the latter is marine-based. Those who advocate MPAs are quick to point to the marine conservation benefits, especially in fully protected areas where there is a policy of no-take and where the MPA has been in existence for some time.[54] In particular, marine scientists point to the impact on the spawning of fish and therefore increased biomass, which, while fishing within in an MPA is prohibited, can spill over into permitted fishing areas for Indigenous inhabitants. Where such inhabitants are dependent on marine resources for their survival (as claimed by the President of Palau), this is clearly significant.[55] However, the scientific evidence is not unanimous. It has been pointed out, for example, that in the case of Palau's extensive no-take MPA, this zone does not encompass most of its coral reefs because it starts 50 nautical miles off-shore. This leaves these reefs vulnerable to exploitation and fails to address problems of over-fishing in waters which are more accessible to local inhabitants within the 50-mile limit.[56] It also fails to address other activities which may have negative impacts on coral reefs – including land-based activities – or to protect those species which use the reefs as breeding grounds.

Besides the preservation of marine biodiversity, the rationales put forward for MPAs are many and varied. For example, in the Seychelles, it was claimed that the creation of these would meet the Seychelles' obligations under the Convention on Biodiversity, support fisheries, tourism and other sectors in the 'Blue Economy',[57] and protect the Seychelles from illegal fishing.[58] Elsewhere – for example, in Pitcairn – arguments supporting an MPA have focused on opportunities for eco-tourism and enhanced employment, although there is no evidence to suggest that this has yet materialised.[59] While MPAs may well be part of wider conservation and environment protection measures, first, an MPA is not the only means of achieving such goals – no-take prohibitions have

[53] In 2015, Palau designated 500,000 square kilometres of its seas (about 80 per cent) as an MPA under the Palau National Marine Sanctuary Act 2015, making this the sixth-largest fully protected MPA in the world.

[54] AM Friedlander, Y Golbuu, E Ballesteros, JE Caselle, M Gouezo, D Olsudong et al, 'Size, Age, and Habitat Determine Effectiveness of Palau's Marine Protected Areas' (2017) 12(3) *PLoS ONE*, http://journals.plos.org/plosone/article?id=10.1371/journal.pone.0174787.

[55] Sarah Gibbens, 'This Small Island Nation Makes a Big Case for Protecting Our Oceans' *National Geographic* (3 April 2017), https://news.nationalgeographic.com/2017/03/palau-marine-protected-area-ocean-fish.

[56] Peter Howson, 'A Huge Marine Reserve in the Pacific Will Protect Rich Tourists Rather than Fish' *The Conversation* (24 October 2017), https://theconversation.com/a-huge-marine-reserve-in-the-pacific-will-protect-rich-tourists-rather-than-fish-85770.

[57] Ernesta (n 5).

[58] Elainia Zachos, 'Ocean Refuge the Size of Great Britain Announced' *National Geographic* (21 February 2018), https://news.nationalgeographic.com/2018/02/seychelles-marine-protected-area-pristine-seas-spd.

[59] See Farran (n 14).

been integral to Indigenous cultures for millennia,[60] and the battle against illegal fishing is long-standing and particularly difficult where a nation's seas are extensive and its resources for patrolling these are limited.[61] Second, while MPAs may contribute to the mitigation of the consequences of climate change, they will not address the complex and multiple causes or consequences of climate change, including terrestrial consequences such as unprecedented rainfall, flooding and landslides which impact on the marine environment. Third, pristine marine environments may well be a tourism draw,[62] but for whom, and will such tourism be compatible with the conservation ethos of MPAs? Moreover, there is the question of who will be the stakeholders and beneficiaries of any resulting tourism. In Palau, for example the Japanese have airport expansion investment interests, and the development of off-shore tourists destinations may be of limited benefit to locals, but of considerable interest to international consortia and wealthy clientele.[63]

Finally, in terms of development, if Indigenous peoples are restricted to non-commercial or limited commercial fishing in those zones designated as domestic fishing zones in which (to quote the Palau example) 'traditional and domestic fishing activities will be allowed to provide fish solely for the domestic market', does this limit the opportunities for economic development for Indigenous and local inhabitants in contexts in which access to and participation in the monetary economy is increasingly a reality and necessity?

## V. INDIGENOUS PEOPLES AND MPAS

In a Technical Rationale document (COP/10/INF/12/Rev.1), it is recommended in implementing measures to achieve the CBD and Aitchi 11 targets that:

> Protected areas should also be established and managed in close collaboration with, and through equitable processes that recognise and respect the rights of indigenous and local communities, and vulnerable populations. These communities should be fully engaged in governing and managing protected areas according to their rights, knowledge, capacities and institutions, and should equitably share in the benefits arising from protected areas and should not bear inequitable costs.[64]

[60] See, eg, the reference to the 'Bul' in the letter of the President of Palau dated 28 October 2018, http://palaugov.pw/wp-content/uploads/2015/10/RPPL-No.-9-49-Palau-National-Marine-Sanctuary-Act.pdf. See also examples from the Manquemap community in Chile and the Nguna-Pele Marine and Land Protected Area Network in Vanuatu, cited by Eva Gurria, 'Celebrating Indigenous Peoples as Nature's Stewards', United Nations Development Programme, 2 May 2017, www.undp.org/content/undp/en/home/blog/2017/5/2/Celebrating-Indigenous-Peoples-as-nature-s-stewards-.html.

[61] An example of alternative means to counter over-fishing can be found in the Pacific in respect of the Nauru Agreement 1982.

[62] See, eg, Palau Visitors Authority, 'Pristine Paradise Palau', https://pristineparadisepalau.com/experiences/nature/national-marine-sanctuary.

[63] Howson (n 56). See similarly the free movement of luxury yachts through the BIOT MPA.

[64] Convention on Biological Diversity, 'TARGET 11 – Technical Rationale Extended (Provided in Document COP/10/INF/12/Rev 1)', https://www.cbd.int/sp/targets/rationale/target-11.

Where this is done successfully, the rights and interests of Indigenous peoples may be appropriately respected and protected. An example can be seen in the case of the Papahānaumokuākea Marine National Monument in Hawaii.[65] Established in 2006 and then expanded in 2016,[66] this MPA covers 582,578 square miles. It is acknowledged in all the publicity surrounding this MPA that the area holds particular cultural significance for Native Hawaiian people, although the archipelago it covers is sparsely inhabited. The name itself means 'a sacred place from which all life springs'.[67] It has been claimed that the expansion of the size of this MPA 'preserves biodiversity and honors cultural traditions' and 'gives a greater voice to Native Hawaiians in managing this resource'.[68] The MPA is managed by the US Fish and Wildlife Service, the National Oceanic and Atmospheric Administration, Hawaii's Department of Land and Natural Resources and the Office of Hawaiian Affairs (OHA) (representing Native Hawaiian interests), which was co-opted in 2017 as a trustee to manage its archaeological and sacred sites.[69] This last move was hailed by the OHA's executive officer as one which:

> [R]ightfully places the Native Hawaiian voice at the highest levels of decision making for this culturally and spiritually significant wahi pana (sacred place) and will help advance our people's understanding of the deep connection of our entire pae'aina (archipelago). We look forward to serving in our new role, in partnership with our co-trustees, to develop and implement a resource management structure that integrates the best of conventional science and traditional practices. We hope that Papahānaumokuākea will demonstrate to the world that integrating science and indigenous knowledge is the best management model to sustain our fragile global environment.[70]

There is considerable support for the management model adopted for this MPA,[71] but its designation has not been without controversy. First, it has been suggested that the Papahānaumokuākea Marine National Monument has been

[65] Kekuewa Kikiloi et al, 'Papahānaumokuākea: Integrating Culture in the Design and Management of One of the World's Largest Marine Protected Areas' (2017) 45(6) *Coastal Management* 436.

[66] The northwestern Hawaiian islands were declared an ecosystem reserve in 2000 and then a national monument in 2006.

[67] PEW Charitable Trusts, 'Papahānaumokuākea Marine National Monument', 24 May 2016, www.pewtrusts.org/en/research-and-analysis/fact-sheets/2016/05/papahanaumokuakea-marine-national-monument.

[68] National Wildlife Refuge Association, 'Papahanaumokuakea Marine National Monument', 19 June 2017. https://www.refugeassociation.org/2017/06/papahanaumokuakea-marine-national-monument.

[69] Governor of Hawaii, 'Governor's Office News Release: OHA Named Co-trustee of Papahānaumokuākea Marine National Monument', 20 January 2017, http://governor.hawaii.gov/newsroom/governors-office-news-release-oha-named-co-trustee-of-papahanaumokuakea-marine-national-monument.

[70] ibid.

[71] See, eg, Heidi Kai Guth, 'Protecting and Perpetuating Papahānaumokuākea: Involvement of Native Hawaiians in Governance of Papahānaumokuākea Marine National Monument' in Jon van Dyke, Sherry Broder, Seokwoo Lee and Jin-Hyun Pail (eds), *Governing Ocean Resources: New Challenges and Emerging Regimes: A Tribute to Judge Choon-Ho Park* (Martinus Nijhoff, 2013) 407.

placed on the United Nations Educational, Scientific and Cultural Organization (UNESCO)'s World Heritage site list without the free, informed and prior consent of Indigenous Hawaiian people. Second, when the area was declared a national monument in 2006, all Indigenous fishing and commercial activity was prohibited.[72] When President Obama expanded this Marine National Monument, there was considerable opposition from industrial and longline fishing companies and Indigenous organisations.[73] Opponents argued that there had been no economic impact assessment and that the expansion would jeopardise the state of Hawaii's duty under its constitution (Article XII, section 7) to 'protect all rights customarily and traditionally exercised for subsistence, cultural and religious purposes for native Hawaiians'.[74] There were also protests from native Hawaiians over what some saw as the continuation of seizure of their lands by federal government.[75] Today, although native Hawaiians are not totally excluded from the MPA, a federal permit is required for 'recreational fishing' and 'removal of resources for traditional Hawaiian cultural purposes'.[76] It is argued that on its expansion, Indigenous peoples were still left out of the consultation, except as general members of the public, despite the fact that the MPA encompasses areas of important cultural and spiritual significance for Indigenous Hawaiians. Third, it has been argued that the very size, cost and remoteness of the MPA presents real challenges for its management.[77] Finally, the way in which the MPA was created, first by an executive order issued by President George W Bush and then by presidential proclamation under the Antiquities Act 1906,[78] by President Obama, has been controversial. This Act allows for discretionary presidential action without the need for lengthy consultation or the safeguard of congressional debate (distinguishing thereby sanctuaries from monuments).[79]

[72] Miliani Trask, 'UNESCO: (Dis)honoring Indigenous Rights', *Cultural Survival*, 2014, https://www.culturalsurvival.org/publications/cultural-survival-quarterly/unesco-dishonoring-indigenous-rights. On longline fishing opposition, see 'Marine Reserve Expansion Shuts out Commercial Fisheries' *Fishermen's News* (1 October 2016), www.fishermensnews.com/story/2016/10/01/features/marine-reserve-expansion-shuts-out-commercial-fisheries/423.html.

[73] Char Miller, 'Obama's Hawaiian Marine Preserve: Massive Potential, Monumental Challenges' *The Conversation* (31 August 2016).

[74] Hawaii Free Press, 'Papahanaumokuakea: OHAs Power Grab Will Harm State's Ability to Continue Trust Responsibility to Native Hawaiians', press release, 27 July 2016, www.hawaiifreepress.com/ArticlesMain/tabid/56/ID/17953/Papahanaumokuakea-OHArsquos-Power-Grab-will-harm-States-ability-to-continue-trust-responsibility-to-Native-Hawaiians.aspx.

[75] Aja Hannah, 'Hawaiian Natives Fight for Their Land' *The Progressive* (1 November 2016), http://progressive.org/magazine/Hawaiian-natives-fight-land.

[76] Juliet Eilperin, 'Obama Creates the Largest Protected Place on the Planet, in Hawaii' *Washington Post* (25 August 2016), https://www.washingtonpost.com/politics/obama-to-create-the-largest-protected-place-on-the-planet-off-hawaii/2016/08/25/54ecb632-6aec-11e6-99bf-f0cf3a6449a6_story.html?noredirect=on&utm_term=.2b74cc107af4.

[77] See Miller (n 73).

[78] For a discussion of the act in respect of MPAs, see Robin Craig, 'Are Marine National Monuments Better than National Marine Sanctuaries? US Ocean Policy, Marine Protected Areas, and the Northwest Hawaiian Islands' (2006) 1(7) *Sustainable Development Law and Policy* 27.

[79] For a critique of Obama's use of the Act, see H Sterling Burnett, 'Obama's Dangerous Use of the National Monument Law' *Forbes Magazine* (12 October 2016), https://www.forbes.com/sites/realspin/2016/10/12/obamas-dangerous-use-of-the-national-monument-law.

It also allows for the President to 'roll back' on such monuments, depending on which lobby is being favoured, a move currently being threatened by President Trump.[80]

It may, of course, be difficult to know the extent to which Indigenous peoples have been consulted or involved in the decision to create an MPA, or the weight given to their views versus, for example, those of specific lobby groups, NGOs, funding agencies and donors. What may be claimed in media reports may not be what actually occurred. An example is the extensive MPA declared around New Caledonia, which is covered in Dorothée Cambou, Jérémie Gilbert and Marlène Dégremont's chapter in this volume.

An extreme example of the exclusion of Indigenous people from the consultation, creation or benefits of an MPA occurred in the case of the MPA declared over 640,000 square kilometres of sea surrounding the BIOT.[81] This was created in 2010, long after the Indigenous inhabitants of the islands had been removed to make way for a US military base on Diego Garcia.[82] Although it has been claimed that '[t]he MPA does not preclude resettlement in the event that Her Majesty's government concludes that it is appropriate to permit and/or support resettlement of the islands',[83] given the no-take nature of the MPA, it is difficult to see how resettled inhabitants of the islands – were that ever to be permitted – could rely on even subsistence fishing, let alone tourism. Although the original no-take designation was successfully challenged by Mauritius in 2015,[84] this was because the declaration of the MPA had not followed the necessary procedures as set out in the Lancaster House Undertakings of 1965 and therefore breached Articles 56(2) and 194(4) of the United Nations Convention on the Law of the Sea (UNCLOS) rather than because a no-take area was declared. This type of international procedural safeguard would be no use to Indigenous inhabitants. The only area which is not designated a no-take area in the BIOT waters is around the military base of Diego Garcia,[85] where over-fishing has been identified as a problem.[86] What has not been challenged is the impact on any potential for developing tourism. Indeed, the establishment of the MPA and

[80] Craig Welch, 'Fishery Managers Seek to Gut Pacific Marine Monuments' *National Geographic* (15 December 2017), https://news.nationalgeographic.com/2017/12/Pacific-marine-monuments-fishing-Trump-environment.

[81] Achieved by way of the British Indian Ocean Territory Proclamation No 1 of 2010, issued by the Commissioner for BIOT on behalf of Her Majesty acting through the Secretary for State.

[82] See Allen (n 10).

[83] Lord Mance quoting the Secretary of State in the case of *R (on the Application of Bancoult (No 2)) (Appellant) v Secretary of State for Foreign and Commonwealth Affairs Respondent)* [2016] UKSC 61A [74].

[84] Chagos Marine Protected Area Arbitration (*Mauritius v United Kingdom*) [2015] Permanent Court of Arbitration.

[85] Peter Sand, 'Fortress Conservation Trumps Human Rights? The "Marine Protected Area" in the Chagos Archipelago' (2012) 21(1) *Journal of Environment and Development* 36.

[86] RP Dunne, Nicholas Polunin and Peter Sand, 'The Creation of the Chagos Marine Protected Area: A Fisheries Perspective' (2014) 29 *Advances in Marine Biology* 79.

the emphasis on the preservation of biodiversity has meant that from the outset, it has been argued that commercial tourism would 'risk ecological damage and disturbance'.[87] In other words, were the Chagossians ever permitted to return in principle to the islands, the MPA could well mean that in practical terms, it would be extremely difficult for them to make a living other than in service roles tied to the MPA.

The experiences of designation of MPAs such as the Parc Naturel de la Mer de Corail in New Caledonia, the Papahānaumokuākea Marine National Monument in Hawaii and the Chagos (or BIOT) MPA suggests that the participation and recognition of Indigenous peoples in the establishment and management of MPAs is variable and uneven.[88] While the role of Indigenous peoples is more obviously being recognised in locally managed coastal marine conservation areas (LMMA)[89] – although even here the experience of Indigenous people may be variable – consideration of Indigenous rights in respect of more distant MPAs is often absent or marginalised.[90] Indeed, those being listened to are far more likely to be conservation lobbyists, marine scientists and politicians hoping to attract green/blue credentials.[91]

## VI. CONCLUSION

The case of *Washington v United States*, discussed by Michael C Blumm and Oliver Jamin in their chapter in this volume, highlights some of the issues touched on in this chapter. One solution proffered in the course of this litigation was the declaration of MPAs. Were that to be the case in this area of the Northwest Pacific, then, first, it might not be the panacea suggested without addressing the land-based activities raised by the litigation and, second, consideration would have to be given to the nature and extent of Indigenous rights to take fish. This second point is important because all too often, where there is acknowledgement of Indigenous fishing rights, it appears to be premised on traditional and limited means of fishing, not commercial fishing.[92] This narrow

[87] Chagos Conservation Trust 'Marine Conservation in the British Indian Ocean Territory (BIOT): Science Issues and Opportunities', report of the workshop held on 5–6 August 2009 at the National Oceanography Centre, Southampton, supported by the NERC Strategic Ocean Funding Initiative (SOFI), Table 3, p 8, chagos-trust.org/sites/default/files/images/southampton-BIOT-workshop.pdf.

[88] For an overview, see Ban and Frid (n 26).

[89] See, eg, Gurria (n 60).

[90] See, eg, the impact on indigenous cultural rights of the designation of the Marianas Trench as a National Monument – Laurie Richmond and Dawn Kotowicz, 'Equity and Access in Marine Protected Areas: The History and Future of "Traditional Indigenous Fishing" in the Marianas Trench Marine National Monument' (2015) 59 *Applied Geography* 117.

[91] See Farran (n 14).

[92] See, eg, the Fish Resources Management Act 1996 of Western Australia, which provides that an Aboriginal person does not require a licence if fish are taken for personal or family use rather than commercial purposes. Proposals to include Aboriginal fishers within the commercial fishing framework appear to present challenges: Ben Fraser, 'Allocation of Fish Resources to Indigenous Western

perspective may overlook well-established practices of fishing for trade (see the chapters by Lee Godden and Nigel Bankes in this volume). It may also be premised on the rather patronising assumption that Indigenous peoples and local fishers have no ambitions to engage in more commercial activities. If Indigenous peoples are to enjoy the same rights to development as other peoples, then native fishing rights need to be allowed to evolve and develop. In practice, however, the approach to Indigenous customary and commercial fishing rights is variable,[93] and the declaration by nation-states of MPAs may be seen as a further example of expanding proprietorial and management claims over those seas which have been historically accessible to Indigenous peoples and local communities. The implementation of MPAs too often sees these rights relegated to privileges or exceptions within a larger controlling framework.[94]

There is also the paternalistic attitude adopted by nation-states and international NGOs that lobby for MPAs, which sees Indigenous peoples congratulated on their commitment to global goals for the protection of the ocean and their self-sacrifice for the greater good. Promises of bright, biodiverse futures, economic advantages or straightforward cash payouts are part of the deal. This has not gone unchallenged. In 2017, a call was made by a group of scientists for a code of conduct for ocean conservation to be adopted in order to ensure that local communities benefit from MPAs and other reserves.[95] Writing in the journal *Marine Policy*,[96] the authors recognised the potential for human rights abuses and damaging social consequences in the context of marine conservation. In particular, they highlighted the problems of lack of consultation and consent, physical displacement, inequitable social impacts, disempowerment of local communities and disruption to traditional resource management.[97] They acknowledged that it is 'difficult to determine the extent to which past marine conservation processes and actions have been inclusive and just in practice'. Therefore, they argued for a code of conduct, a proposal which seems to have been mooted with approval at a Think Tank on the Human Dimensions of Large Scale Marine Protected Areas held in 2016 (University of Washington, Seattle). The draft proposal contains three broad objectives: fair conservation,

Australians' at "Sharing the Fish" Conference, March 2006, www.fishallocation.com/papers/pdf/papers/BenFraser.pdf.

[93] M Durette, 'Indigenous Property Rights in Commercial Fisheries: Canada, New Zealand and Australia Compared', CAEPR Working Paper No 37/2007, www.anu.edu.au/caepr.

[94] Anthony Davis and Svein Jentoft, 'The Challenge and the Promise of Indigenous Peoples' Fishing Rights: From Dependency to Agency' (2001) 25 *Marine Policy* 223.

[95] Diane Toomey, 'A Call for a Hippocratic Oath on Protecting the World's Oceans', *Yale Environment360* (1 June 2017), https://e360.yale.edu/features/a-call-for-a-code-of-conduct-in-the-creation-of-marine-protected-areas.

[96] Nathan Bennett et al, 'An Appeal for a Code of Conduct for Marine Conservation' (2017) 81 *Marine Policy* 411.

[97] ibid 412.

governance and decision making; socially just conservation actions and outcomes; and accountable conservation initiatives and organisations. While this may only be a first step, it takes cognisance of the fact that in the field of the terrestrial conservation of biodiversity, the UN Rapporteur of the Human Rights Council has made public the human rights violations that have occurred, particularly in respect of Indigenous peoples.[98] Addressing the 71st session of the General Assembly, she stated:

> Under international environmental law, all 196 States parties to the Convention on Biological Diversity have agreed that the establishment, management and monitoring of protected areas should take place with the full and effective participation of, and full respect for the rights of, indigenous peoples. They have also set targets which include global expansion of protected area coverage to at least 17 per cent of terrestrial and inland water areas and 10 per cent of coastal and marine areas by 2020. This further underlines the importance that States and conservation organisations implement measures to recognise the rights of indigenous peoples as a matter of priority.

While there are some examples of good practice, predominantly this is not being done, either in respect of terrestrial conservation or marine protection. In the context of MPAs, the developments to date suggest that the rights of Indigenous peoples may be low on the agenda. Indeed, it has been suggested that the designation of MPAs, especially large ones, may be more a matter of geopolitics driven by international competition for 'saving the oceans' status and strategic lobbying by NGOs, charities, research institutions and others that are members of the global environmental network[99] rather than conservation.[100] Were the latter to be the primary concern, it would be a logical first consideration to consult with those who are closest to the sea and its resources, and who over decades and generations have experienced changes in the marine environments in which they live: Indigenous peoples and coastal communities.

[98] Statement of Ms Victoria Tauli-Corpuz, Special Rapporteur on the Rights of Indigenous Peoples, at the 71st Session of the General Assembly, 17 October 2016, https://www.un.org/development/desa/indigenouspeoples/news/2016/10/statement-of-ms-victoria-tauli-corpuz-special-rapporteur-on-the-rights-of-indigenous-peoples-at-the-71st-session-of-the-general-assembly.

[99] For example, the IUCN, the WWF, the PEW Trusts, Conservation International and *National Geographic*. See further on this Yan Giron, 'The Other Side of Large-Scale, No-Take, Marine Protected Areas in the Pacific Ocean' in Simonne Pauwels and Elodie Fache, (eds) *Fisheries in the Pacific* (Pacific-credo Publications, 2016) 77, paras 95–98.

[100] Pierre Leenhardt, Betrand Cazalet, Bernard Salvat, Joachim Claudet and François Feral, 'The Rise of Large-Scale Marine Protected Areas: Conservation or Geopolitics?' (2013) 85 *Ocean and Coastal Management* 1.

# 15

# *Tlingit Use of Marine Space*
# Putting up Fish

CASKEY RUSSELL AND X̱'UNEI LANCE TWITCHELL

[T]hink how good it is that we have good spirits that still bring salmon.

Ḵeixwnéi (Nora Marks Dauenhauer)[1]

## I. SHÓOGUNÁX̱ AAYÍ: THE FIRST THING

THE ABOVE EPIGRAPH comes from a beloved and dearly missed Tlingit elder, scholar, linguist and writer Ḵeixwnéi (Nora Marks Dauenhauer) who walked into the forest, as the Tlingit say when elders pass on, in 2017.[2] It comes from a poem entitled 'How to Make Good Baked Salmon from the River' published in Ḵeixwnéi's first volume of poetry *The Droning Shaman*.[3] The title *Droning Shaman* refers to Ḵeixwnéi's metaphor of the Bering Sea as a continuously chanting, or droning, shaman whose song constantly washes up along the Alaskan coast. It is an apt metaphor to keep in mind as we explore the importance of marine space and its relationship to Tlingit culture and identity. Examining the importance of marine environments to the Tlingit is akin to examining the importance of air to all of humankind. Just as human life is inconceivable without air, so would Tlingit cultural existence be inconceivable without marine environments.

There is a tension in Ḵeixwnéi's 'How to Make Good Baked Salmon from the River' that derives from displacement and colonisation. The speaker compares the 'traditional' preparation of salmon at a dry fish camp along a river in southeast Alaska to the 'contemporary' preparation of salmon in a city, perhaps away

[1] Nora Marks Dauenhauer, *The Droning Shaman* (Black Current, Press, 1988) 11.
[2] For a documentary about the work of Nora, see X̱'unei Lance Twitchell, 'Haa Yoo X̱'atángi Káx̱ Ḵulagaawú: Language Warriors' *YouTube* (17 November 2016), https://www.youtube.com/watch?time_continue=706&v=4J7p0Wd2txU.
[3] Daunenhauer (n 1).

from the Tlingit homeland. The speaker gives cultural and culinary instruction as s/he cooks and, as the poem progresses, walks the line between celebration and warning: celebrating the fact that there are still salmon returning to the streams and rivers, and warning her listeners/readers to pay proper respect (to have 'good spirits') to salmon, and the preparation of salmon, in order to ensure the future return of salmon. The poem is an exhortation to the Tlingit to keep tradition alive even in non-traditional settings. This chapter, at its core, revolves around the concern for cultural survival. We examine what is known as *putting up fish*, which is both a traditional and contemporary cultural practice. We will provide a history of the Tlingit people, outline the importance and process of putting up fish to Tlingit culture, and explore how putting up fish provides the link between traditional and contemporary Tlingit culture.[4]

## II. HAA LINGÍTX̱ SATEEYÍ: WHO ARE THE TLINGIT?

Since time immemorial, it is said by Tlingit storytellers, Tlingit peoples have occupied *Lingít Aaní* in what is now southeast Alaska. The practice of fishing, and subsequently putting up fish, is surely as old as time immemorial as well. Lingít Aaní stretches from southern Tlingit on the border between Alaska and British Columbia up and along the southeast coast, through inland Tlingit territories along the Taku River and Yukon Territory, to the northern Tlingit territories of Glacier Bay and the Yakutat up to Mount St. Elias (see Map 15.1).

The Tlingit are a matrilineal tribe made up of two exogamous moieties whose identities are known and totemised by the *Ch'aak'* (eagle) and the *Yéil* (raven). In some villages, the *Ch'aak'* side is known by the *Gooch* (wolf). Within the two moieties are interwoven levels of identity that harmonise with one another and outline reciprocal relations with other Tlingit peoples. These various levels of Tlingit identity are:

- Yéil/Ch'aak' (moiety).
- Naa (clan).
- Ḵwáan (tribe/village).
- Hít (house).

All these identities, especially at the Naa, Ḵwáan and Hít levels, own inherited tangible and intangible properties, including names, stories, songs, crests, and access to hunting and fishing territory.

[4] A note on the cultural backgrounds of the authors of this chapter: Caskey Russell is a member of the Tlingit Nation through his mother. His Tlingit name is Teew Dachx̱aan, which comes from his grandmother's name. His grandmother was born and raised in Heenya Ḵwáan (Klawock, Alaska), but is from the Naasteidi Kooyu Ḵwáan Kóon Hít (Flicker House) on the eagle/wolf side. Caskey is a member of the large Peratrovich family. Lance Twitchell carries the Tlingit names X̱'unei and Du Aaní Kawdinook, and the Haida name Ḵ'eijáakw. He is from the Tlingit, Haida and Yup'ik native nations, and speaks and studies the Tlingit language.

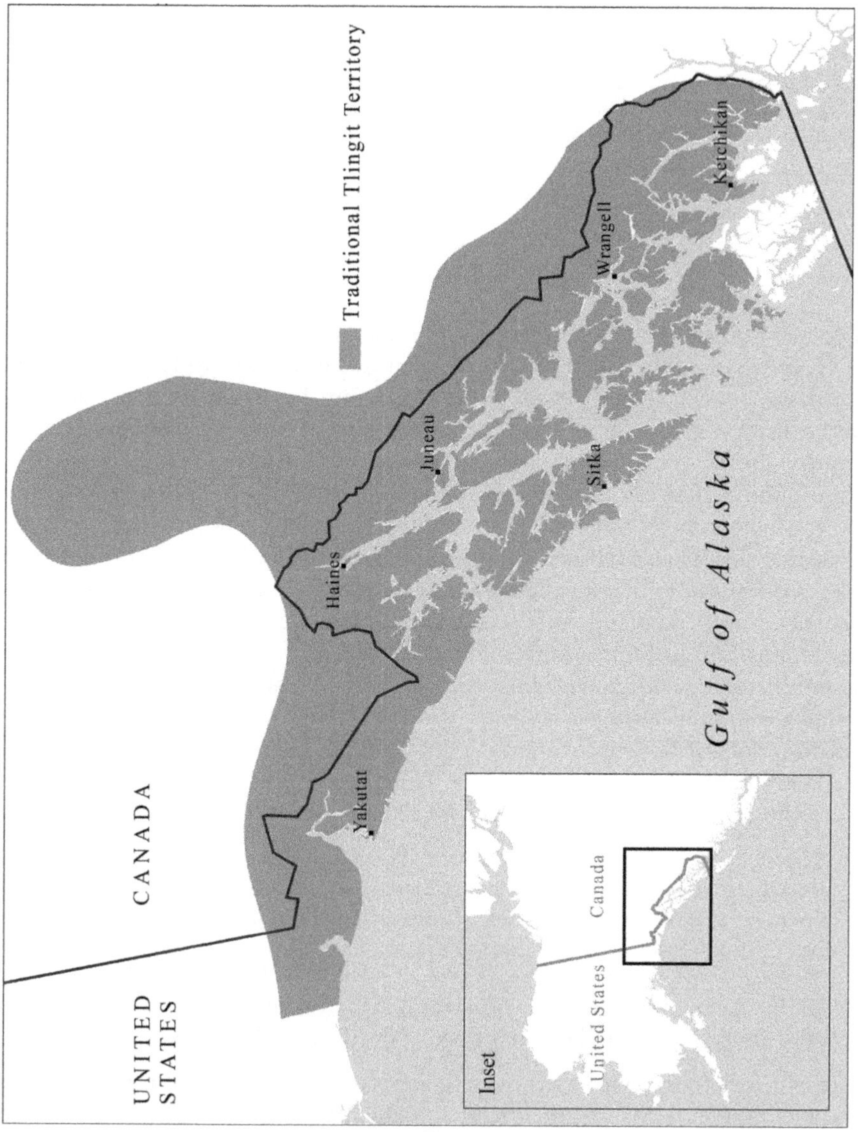


**Map 15.1 Lingít Aaní: traditional Tlingit homeland**

Map produced by Kristen Klaphake.

Boundaries defined based on both linguistic and social criteria.

*Source*: Krauss, Michael E., Gary Holton, Jim Kerr, and Colin T. West. 2011. Indigenous Peoples and Languages of Alaska. Fairbanks and Anchorage: Alaska Native Language Center and Institute of Social and Economic Research.

In conjunction with those identities, some Tlingit peoples also identify with large families that arose in villages across southeast Alaska after contact with Europeans. In more recent times, Tlingit identity, along with that of other Alaskan Natives, has become corporatised with the passage of the Alaskan Native Claims Settlement Act (ANCSA) in 1971,[5] which divided Alaskan Natives into village and regional corporations (for more on this, see below).

## III. CONTACT WITH EUROPEANS: LAND THEFT AND DISEASE

The first known contact Tlingit peoples made with Europeans came on 17 July 1741. A Russian ship called the *St Paul* anchored near present-day Sitka, Alaska, which was known at that time as Sheet'ka Ḵwáan. The *St Paul* stayed over a week in the waters outside Sheet'ka Ḵwáan, during which time the captain, a Russian named Chirikov, ordered two longboats to shore to replenish the *St Paul*'s freshwater supply. Decked out with armed Russian sailors and wooden casks to hold the freshwater, both boats landed ashore at Sheet'ka Ḵwáan. Neither returned. Tlingit and Russian accounts of what became of those longboats differ greatly. These differences illustrate the coming two-and-a-half centuries of conflict between Europeans (and their settler descendants) and the Tlingit. The traditional Russian account assumes that the local Tlingit murdered the Russian sailors. In her well-known work on the Tlingit, anthropologist Frederica de Laguna exemplifies the traditional European version of this episode when she deems it 'a brief hostile encounter'.[6,7]

However, the version recalled in Tlingit oral tradition is quite different. According to the Tlingit elder Mark Jacobs Jr:

> These eight men did not return to their ship. They took this opportunity to escape the cruel and harsh conditions on the Russian ship. As they left the ship, they decided among themselves that they would eventually perish in the hazardous waters of the North Pacific [were they to return to the *St Paul*, which was to sail back to Russia]. Why suffer under such a cruel command until then? The decision to desert was easy … They eventually made contact with some local natives and were accepted and treated with respect, instead of being murdered as the Russian history tells it.[8]

Jacobs further explained that the Russian sailors were aided by the Tlingit in their desertion and were taken to the village of Klawock, where they married with the Klawock Tlingit.

[5] 43 USCA 1601.

[6] To say that De Laguna exemplifies the traditional European perspective on this episode is not meant to diminish her achievements as an anthropologist nor her time spent among the Yakutat Tlingit. It is simply to point out that there are bodies of knowledge that are not available to anthropological inquiry.

[7] Frederica de Laguna, *Under Mt. St. Elias: The History and Culture of the Yakutat Indians* (Smithsonian Institution Press, 1972) 223.

[8] Quoted in Richard A Pierce, *Proceedings of the 2nd International Conference on Russian America, Sitka, Alaska, August 19–22* (Limestone Press, 1990) 5.

During the late eighteenth and early nineteenth centuries, the Russians struggled to get a foothold in Lingít Aaní. The Tlingit resisted, often violently, incursions into their territory, and repeatedly attacked and at times burned Russian forts. By the time of the 1867 Treaty between the US and Russia,[9] Russia's main holding in Tlingit territory was a small stockade at Sheet'ka K̲wáan. The 'sale' of Alaska including Lingít Aaní to America in 1867 has been hotly contested by the Tlingit since the years immediately following the sale.[10] Even within Euro-American jurisprudence, the Tlingit had strong legal footing for their contestation. Article 1 of the Treaty states that:

> His Majesty the Emperor of all Russians agrees to cede to the United States, by this convention, immediately upon the exchange of the ratifications thereof, all the territory and dominion now possessed by his said Majesty on the continent of America and in the adjacent islands.[11]

The 1828 *Webster's Dictionary* defined 'possessed' as *held by lawful title* or *occupied*. Does holding a small stockade constitute occupation of the vast territory – sea and land – of Lingít Aaní? The 1867 treaty with Russia relied upon the 1825 treaty between Great Britain and Russia – in fact, it directly quoted from it – for the demarcation between British territory in Canada and Russian territory to be transferred to America.[12] Russia's control over its claimed territory was even more tenuous in 1825 than it was in 1867. Do boundaries drawn up by two foreign nations without consultation of the Indigenous people who actually own the land constitute 'lawful title'?

Article III of the treaty with Russia purported to grant jurisdiction over Alaskan Natives to America. It states: 'The uncivilized tribes will be subject to such laws and regulations as the United States may, from time to time, adopt in regard to aboriginal tribes of that country.'[13] The US government appropriated for itself the authority to rule over an Indigenous people very few Americans (or Russians for that matter) had met in a territory very few Americans, let alone American leaders, had ever been to.

[9] Treaty Concerning the Cession of the Russian Possessions in North America by His Majesty the Emperor of All the Russias to the United States of America, 30 March 1867, 15 Stat 539.

[10] According to Tlingit scholar and tribal leader Rosita Worl, shortly after the treaty was signed: 'A council of clan leaders convened for several sessions to discuss the sale of Alaska to the United States by the Russians in 1867. Some of the leaders favored war to drive the Americans out, but a prominent leader from Chilkat argued against this action by pointing out the vulnerability of the coastal villages from attacks by the United States war vessels. Instead the Tlingit adopted a diplomatic stance and advised the United States officials that they owned Alaska, that Russians had lived in Alaska only with their permission, and that the United States should give them the money if they wished to purchase Alaska.' Rosita Worl, 'Tlingit At.óow: Tangible and Intangible Property' (PhD dissertation, Harvard University, 1998) 261.

[11] ibid.

[12] Great Britain/Russia: Limits of Their Respective Possessions on the North-West Coast of America and the Navigation of the Pacific Ocean, 16 February 1825, 75 Consolidated Treaty Series 95.

[13] Treaty with Russia (n 9).

We would be remiss, in examining eighteenth and nineteenth-century Tlingit history, if we did not touch on the diseases Europeans brought into Lingít Aaní and the unimaginable devastation those epidemics wrought on Tlingit life and culture. Robert Boyd documents the multitudes of deadly disease outbreaks in the Pacific Northwest and Lingít Aaní. Over the course of only a century (1774–1874) the following epidemics occurred: 1770s smallpox; 1806 smallpox; an unknown epidemic in the mid-1820s (possibly smallpox); 1830s malaria; 1836–37 smallpox; 1838 influenza; 1844 dysentery; 1847–48 measles; 1853 smallpox; and, lastly, 1862–63 smallpox. On top of these epidemics, tuberculosis and syphilis were constant presences infecting Indigenous communities and claiming unknown multitudes of lives. Boyd also notes the presence and deadliness of what was known as 'fever and ague' during this period, which he concludes was most likely malaria. Boyd's text only covers a century. Diseases kept harrowing Indigenous people well into the twentieth century, the Spanish Flu of 1918 being a prime example.[14]

We used the term 'unimaginable' to describe the devastation wreaked on Indigenous peoples by wave after wave of disease. Any discussion of the Tlingit people and Lingít Aaní must necessarily be weighted with the understanding that Lingít Aaní became a graveyard during the century after Europeans arrived. Every Alaskan Native has been affected by the devastation of disease: the stories of clans, houses and lives destroyed in these epidemics still haunt Alaskan Natives.

## IV. TLINGIT RESISTANCE

Throughout the horrors of the nineteenth century, the Tlingit persisted and in the twentieth century took the battle over Lingít Aaní and the rights of Alaskan Natives into courtrooms. They helped create political organisations such as the Alaskan Native Brotherhood (ANB) in 1912 and the Alaskan Native Sisterhood (ANS) in 1915, which fought for land rights, voting rights, civil rights and access to education, among many other causes, on behalf of Alaskan Natives.[15] In 1920, Tlingit William Paul, one of the leaders of the ANB, became the first Alaskan Native admitted to the Alaskan Bar, an astonishing feat at the time. In 1923, Paul

[14] Robert Boyd, *The Coming of the Spirit of Pestilence: Introduced Infectious Diseases and Population Decline among Northwest Coast Indians, 1774–1874* (University of Washington Press, 1999). Though Boyd's text begins with epidemics in the 1770s, he speculates that the period before the 1770s also saw epidemics in the Pacific Northwest. In particular, he hypothesizes (at 14–16) – using the work of Henry Dobyns and Sarah Campbell – that the 1520s smallpox pandemic, which started in 1519 in the West Indies and was brought to Mexico around the time of Cortez's invasion, may have travelled up to the Pacific Northwest Coast.

[15] Of the many good sources for the history of the ANB and the ANS, see Peter Metcalfe, *A Dangerous Idea: The Alaska Native Brotherhood and the Struggle for Indigenous Rights* (University of Alaska Press, 2014).

was elected to the Alaskan Territorial Legislature, becoming the first Alaskan Native legislator.[16] He would be re-elected again in 1925 and in that year would fight against white legislators who had imposed a voter requirement of reading and writing English aimed at disenfranchising Alaskan Natives who had become citizens the previous year due to the Indian Citizenship Act. Paul also brought a lawsuit to the US Court of Claims and, ultimately, to the US Supreme Court (*Tee-Hit-Ton Indians v United States*) in 1955.[17] Paul asserted that the Tee-Hit-Ton, a clan group of the Tlingit, had full ownership of its land and resources. He lost, but the case did establish the key fact that Alaskan Natives had Aboriginal title to the land.[18]

In 1937, the ANB organised the Tlingit and Haida Central Council in order to sue the US government for theft of land and property. The Central Council is the main governing body of the Tlingit and Haida people today. One important twentieth-century example of resistance is the story of the adoption of the 1945 Anti-discrimination Act. Two Tlingit, Roy Peratrovich and his wife Elizabeth, crafted a bill to outlaw racial discrimination in the territory of Alaska. On 8 February 1945, they took it before the Alaskan Territorial Legislature and debated it with the all-white legislators. Elizabeth and Roy Peratrovich were the only natives who spoke on the floor of the senate during the debate. Elizabeth Peratrovich attacked the senators' white supremacy and hypocrisy, and belittled their use of the term 'savagery' to describe Alaskan Natives. Ultimately, the bill passed and was signed into law on 16 February 1945, becoming the first comprehensive anti-discrimination legislation in America.[19]

The last aspect of Tlingit history, identity and culture to touch on is the ANCSA, a federal law passed in 1971.[20] The ANCSA came about after oil was found in Alaska's Prudhoe Bay in 1968 and a pipeline to bring the oil across Alaska from Prudhoe Bay to Valdez was proposed. In order to effect the completion of the pipeline, ongoing Indigenous land claims had to be addressed. Ultimately, the ANSCA retained for Alaskan Natives about one-ninth of Alaskan territory and set aside a payment of nearly US$1 billion. Alaskan Natives were forced to organise themselves into corporations in order to manage corporate resources (primarily timber, mining and fisheries) and finances (ANSCA funds and monies

[16] Metcalfe (ibid) discusses William Paul's work for the rights of Alaskan Natives. See also Fred Paul, *Then Fight for it! The Largest Peaceful Redistribution of Wealth in the History of Mankind and the Creation of the North Slope Borough* (Trafford Publishing, 2003).

[17] *Tee-Hit-Ton Indians v United States* 348 US 272 (1955).

[18] For a detailed discussion of how this case helped establish Aboriginal title, see Metcalfe (n 15) 82–83.

[19] The Central Council of Tlingit and Haida Tribes has published a booklet that documents Roy and Elizabeth's battle for civil rights in Alaska. See CCTHITA, *A Recollection of Civil Rights Leader Elizabeth Peratrovich, 1911–1958* (Central Council of Tlingit and Haida Indian Tribes of Alaska, 1991). See also Caskey Russell, 'Anti-discrimination Act, Alaska Natives, 1945' in D Martinez and J Williams (eds), *50 Events that Shaped American Indian History* (ABC-CLIO, 2016).

[20] ANCSA (n 5) s 1603.

made from corporate interests). The ANSCA created 12 large regional corporations and over 200 smaller village-based corporations. A thirteenth 'regional' corporation was later created for Alaskan Natives living outside Alaska at the time of the ANSCA. Moreover, the ANSCA extinguished all Aboriginal claims to land and marine environments:

> (a) Aboriginal title extinguishment through prior land and water area conveyances All prior conveyances of public land and water areas in Alaska, or any interest therein, pursuant to Federal law, and all tentative approvals pursuant to section 6 (g) of the Alaska Statehood Act, shall be regarded as an extinguishment of the aboriginal title thereto, if any.
>
> (b) Aboriginal title and claim extinguishment where based on use and occupancy; submerged lands underneath inland and offshore water areas and hunting or fishing rights included
>
> All aboriginal titles, if any, and claims of aboriginal title in Alaska based on use and occupancy, including submerged land underneath all water areas, both inland and offshore, and including any aboriginal hunting or fishing rights that may exist, are hereby extinguished.
>
> (c) Aboriginal claim extinguishment where based on right, title, use, or occupancy of land or water areas; domestic statute or treaty relating to use and occupancy; or foreign laws; pending claims
>
> All claims against the United States, the State [of Alaska], and all other persons that are based on claims of aboriginal right, title, use, or occupancy of land or water areas in Alaska, or that are based on any statute or treaty of the United States relating to Native use and occupancy, or that are based on the laws of any other nation, including any such claims that are pending before any Federal or state court or the Indian Claims Commission, are hereby extinguished.[21]

Thus, the ANSCA extinguished any Aboriginal claims to ocean and land territories that were in question at the time, as well as any claims that could potentially come into question in the future. It also ensured that native and Tlingit reality and identity would be intertwined with corporate America. Tlingit scholars and scholars of Tlingit studies have noted the collision of worldviews brought about by the ANSCA: the Tlingit virtues of reciprocity and exchange, the re-distribution of wealth through ceremony, and the demands of protocol and respect for the sea, land and air, and the living systems within them can be read as at odds with the corporate desire to commodify the land and sea – and living things within them – as resources.[22] After the ANSCA, corporate identity became an aspect of Tlingit reality.

[21] ibid s 1603.

[22] See Kirk Dombrowski, *Against Culture: Development, Politics, and Religion in Indian Alaska* (University of Nebraska Press, 2001). See also Caskey Russell, 'Cultures in Collision Cosmology, Jurisprudence, and Religion in Tlingit Territory' (2009) 33 *American Indian Quarterly* 230.

## V. AT X'AAN AANÍ KÁA LINGÍT AT X̱AAYÍ DULYÉX̱ (AT FISH CAMP, TLINGIT FOOD IS MADE)

Throughout Lingít Aaní, there exist extensive fisheries, both ocean and riparian, and the Tlingit have, since time immemorial, nurtured these fisheries as they depended on them not only for sustenance but also for cultural meaning. The Tlingit world revolves around fish. To return to K̲eixwnéi's 'How to Make Good Baked Salmon from a River', one can read in the poem a central Tlingit concept. K̲eixwnéi writes: 'think how good it is / that we have good spirits / that still bring salmon'.[23] The health and sustenance fisheries are bound to the health and well-being of humans. Moreover, the word *still* is important in the context of the poem. As an adverb, 'still' implies up until the present time. Yet, it also contains a hint of foreboding – the notion of *no longer* or *no more*. There may come a time when the salmon do not return, a time when we no longer have good spirits. K̲eixwnéi is exhorting Tlingits to sustain and nurture that healthy symbiosis between human and fish.

Fish form the centre of Tlingit cultural life: gifting and reciprocity, clan designs and totems, and clan ownership of land and sea fisheries all highlight the centrality of fish to Tlingit culture. The practice of harvesting, preparing and preserving fish is known as 'putting up fish'. If we were to closely read the phrase 'putting up fish', it is perhaps the preposition 'up' that strikes us as most curious. It denotes a position relative to the speaker and even offers the image of a person lifting fish up, perhaps in a smoke house or above a fire. Yet, it is what the phrase connotes that is important: putting up fish connotes the preparation and process of catching, cleaning, curing, smoking and storing fish in order to provide fish for a family or clan throughout the year. Putting up fish is the active participation in *Lingít atx̱aayí* or the traditional lifeways of the Tlingit.

It also connotes communal practice: a family or clan working together to ensure survival; the ritual of eating also connotes harmony. According to one Tlingit elder, the ritual and custom of eating together brought peace between two warring Tlingit clans: 'These people had been enemies for a long time. By getting them together, eating together, watching other people laugh – eventually this will let them forget their mountain of problems.'[24]

In pragmatic terms, putting up fish begins with the return of salmon to the rivers. Traditionally, the Tlingit and other Alaskan Natives would move to fish camps in the late spring and summer. Fish camps were structures built along clan-owned rivers. In the camps, one would find shelters, fishing implements,

[23] Dauenhauer (n 1) 14.

[24] Richard G Newton and Madonna L Moss, *Haa Atx̱aayí Haa K̲usteeyíx̱ Sitee, Our Food is Our Tlingit Way of Life: Excerpts from Oral Interviews* (USDA Forest Service Alaska Region R10-MR-50, 2009) 4.

smoke houses, preserving boxes and jars – all the things a clan or house group would need to work together to harvest enough fish to survive the winter. In the camps, the Tlingit eagerly awaited the first signs of salmon coming from the ocean into the river. According to Tlingit elder Lydia George:

> One person was delegated to be responsible for the fish. Every day, he watched the ocean beach for fish jumps and kept track of all movements of the fish. No one was allowed to kill fish before they came up-stream to spawn, they believed if the fish was bothered and disturbed during their migration upstream to spawn, they would turn back and go up another river. Since fish was our main food, we were very careful; the fish were treated well. If a man broke any of our laws, his fishing equipment was taken from him; sometimes his spear was broken up.[25]

With the arrival of the first salmon, the tribes would hold a first salmon ceremony. These differ from tribe to tribe, but they pay honour and respect to the returning salmon, and ensure that the salmon will return again in the future. In an interview given in the 1980s, Tlingit elder Nelson Frank described how observance of traditional law and ceremony helped preserve and nurture fisheries:

> Traditional law … was passed from generation to generation, intact, through the repetition of legends and observance of ceremonials which were largely concerned with the use of land, water, and the resources contained therein. Subsistence living was not only a way of life, but also a life-enriching process. Conservation and the perpetuation of subsistence resources was a part of that way of life, and was mandated by traditional law and custom.[26]

The next weeks in the fish camp would be spent on the communal, if exhausting, labour of putting up fish: harvesting the salmon and bringing it to the preparers to cut, gut and split, and then to the smokers where the salmon would hang for a day or two over a continuous cold smoke, and then to boxes to be stored and preserved or, nowadays, to jars to be fresh packed. Each Tlingit family and clan has its own favourite way of putting up fish and making good dried fish. Anthropologist Madonna Moss interviewed a number of Tlingit elders for their take on how to best put up fish. Tlingit elder Billy James told Moss how his family worked as a team to put up their fish:

> There were a total of ten of us that made a team. The work would continue until the job was finished, which was usually quite late at night, even with all the ten people working. You have to remember that we were working from scratch on 500 fish. The smokehouse is quite large so the fish had to be relayed so they could be hung on poles. There is usually a man standing at the bottom, another above him, and perhaps another person at the very top, when it comes time for hanging the salmon for smoking. An assembly line was organized in relaying the salmon where they would be smoked and dried. There are various methods of preparing fish. Male and female

[25] ibid 5.

[26] As quoted in David F Arnold, *The Fisherman's Frontier: People and Salmon in Southeast Alaska* (University of Washington Press, 2008) 16.

> fish were cut up different ways. On the second day, fish were all taken down and the women took their respective places and the cutting began on the fish.[27]

Tlingit elder Dick Newton discussed how to best prepare salmon – slicing it thin enough to smoke – and also the importance of maintaining the perfect fire so as to smoke but not cook the salmon:

> Slicing and filleting salmon requires skillful hands and very sharp knives. Only a few men have mastered this art, so the women do the intricate slicing while the men bring down the fish and return the finished product so cautiously back on the racks. The time for slicing and filleting should take 2 or 2 1⁄2 days. You cut the fish along the backbone as if filleting. You cut the backbone close to the tail, but leave the tail attached for balance when it is hung on the pole in the smokehouse. The purpose of slicing is to get the salmon thin enough for drying … The amount of heat and smoke is closely controlled to prevent what Tlingit peoples call 'cooking the fish'. If this happens, they either start the process all over again or end up with no salmon at all. If there is not enough heat, the salmon spoils quickly and has to be thrown away. Dry hemlock and green alder are the woods preferred.[28]

Tlingit elder John C Jackson told Moss the importance of letting the first run of salmon pass in order to ensure the survival of the runs (the first salmon ceremony also aided this). Jackson also explained why yellow cedar makes the perfect storage boxes:

> You never smoke and dry the first run in the river and creeks, it is better to wait until they have spawned. If salmon is smoked when it is oily, it turns rancid before winter and spring when it is needed. Color of the flesh on the fish turns light, almost white when it is ready to be harvested and prepared for the smokehouses. This gives the salmon a chance to lay their eggs and run through the cycle for the following years, when the mature fish will return to the creeks. Make boxes out of yellow cedar bark, then pile the salmon neatly in these dry boxes. Cedar bark is known to keep the salmon from getting moldy. Dirt caches were prepared in advance and this is where the salmon was kept until it was needed.[29]

The fish put up in the fish camp were to aid in survival during the long winters and spring, but also for gifting, for feasting, for song and story. The fish camps and the putting up of fish were a time for clan networks and extended families to come together and exchange news, gossip, stories and laughter. By participating in the process of putting up fish, contemporary Tlingit people are performing cultural continuity: working the same fisheries as their ancestors, using the same techniques and at times adapting those techniques when new technology became available – just as their ancestors had. Tlingit technology has always been changing and adapting. Common ways to catch salmon 'traditionally' included spears and gaffs, bone hooks on lines, fish dams (stone tidal traps) and wooden fences,

[27] Newton and Moss (n 24) 7.
[28] ibid 6.
[29] ibid 7.

wooden weirs, barbed harpoons with seal bladder floats, and even reef nets made from cedar bark with floats and sinkers stretched between two canoes. After contact with Europeans, Tlingit peoples imported European fishing technology (especially nets) and around the turn of the twentieth century began to fish commercially in the ocean. As David Arnold has noted, the commercial and subsistence fisheries began to overlap at the turn of the twentieth century.

> When Indians themselves began to participate in the commercial fishery, they often continued to fish near their traditional fishing grounds [fisheries that their clan owned and therefore they had access to]. Tents, drying racks, and smokehouses were erected at makeshift summer fish camps, which served as a base for both commercial and subsistence fishing.[30]

The term 'makeshift' is not perhaps the best adjective as fish camps, though temporary, were located on clan-owned territory and often in the same spot year after year.

As important as the technology used in fishing was the understanding of the *fishing grounds* themselves: in putting up fish, the Tlingit were claiming their clan heritage, which included access to clan-owned fisheries:

> [W]hite fisherman saw the waterways of southeastern Alaska as a vast, common-property resource awaiting their explorations. Native fishermen, on the other hand, saw those same waterways as an intricate map of clan-owned fishing sites, passed down from generation to generation through specific clan lineages … To the Tlingit and Haida people, southeastern Alaska was not a virgin wilderness, but a cultural geography of salmon stream fish camps, Native villages, and canneries.[31]

Putting up fish is not simply catching and preserving fish; it is the active participation in a living tradition – *Lingít atx̱aayí*. Quite literally, putting up fish was and is the custom and practice of participating in one's ancestral heritage.

The attitudes of putting up of salmon, the attitudes of the Tlingit that ensured the return and sustainability of Alaskan fisheries, may gesture towards a revitalised way to treat marine environments. We speak here of the centrality of reciprocity to Tlingit culture: there needs to be a reciprocity revitalisation in Alaska and the Pacific Northwest. The dangerous attitude exposed in the 1867 treaty with Russia that allowed Europeans and Americans to appropriate (and believe they were right in the appropriation) and assert legal authority over Alaskan Natives mirrors their belief that they could do the same with the fisheries of Alaska – that rather than a reciprocal relationship with the salmon, they owned and had authority over the salmon.

To return to Keix̱wnéi's wonderful poem 'How to Make Good Baked Salmon from a River', the message of reciprocity is central: proper respect and treatment are needed to ensure that we will still have good spirits to bring back the salmon. As noted above, the word *still* is important here. There may come a time when the salmon don't return. A time when we no longer have good spirits.

[30] Arnold (n 26) 131.
[31] ibid 130.

# 16

# *Governance of Marine Space*
# Interactions between the Salmon Aquaculture Industry and Indigenous Peoples in Norway and Canada

EINAR EYTHÓRSSON, DOROTHEE SCHREIBER, CAMILLA BRATTLAND AND ELSE GRETE BRODERSTAD*

## I. INTRODUCTION

On the coasts of northern Norway and British Columbia, Canada, the salmon aquaculture industry's growing demands for marine space clash against the rights of Indigenous peoples in coastal areas. Companies receive permits from state authorities who may or may not have considered Indigenous territorial rights. The salmon farming industry approaches space in a generic way, identifying suitable sites based on physical requirements, and paying little heed to Indigenous livelihoods, Indigenous territoriality, Indigenous law or Indigenous relationships to place. Conflicts over Indigenous use of marine space are therefore growing alongside the expansion of this industry.

In this chapter, we focus on the rights and governance landscape in two salmon farming areas where Indigenous peoples have claimed rights to marine space: on the coast of British Columbia and the coast of northern Norway. We examine the differing legal traditions and governance processes used to adjudicate competing rights, interests and jurisdictions in the two countries. We ask how governance outcomes in contested marine areas are shaped not only by the diverse actions and strategies of the actors themselves, but also by institutions,

* The research conducted for this chapter is a part of the projects 'The Arctic Governance Triangle: Government, Indigenous Peoples and Industry in Change' (TriArc), funded by the Norwegian Research Council, and 'Indigenous – Industry Governance Interactions in the Arctic: Environmental Impacts and Knowledge Basis for Management' (IndGov), funded by FRAM – High North Research Centre for Climate and the Environment.

defined here as 'any form of constraint that humans devise to shape human interaction'.[1]

Indigenous rights institutions, such as marine property rights, participation in resource management and consultation requirements, find different expression in Norway and Canada, and we ask what these differences mean for Indigenous jurisdiction over marine space and salmon aquaculture. Our comparative analysis points to the barriers to, and possibilities for, marine governance solutions that reconcile Indigenous rights with the interests of the salmon aquaculture industry.

The production value of farmed salmon has now far surpassed the conventional wild capture fisheries in Norway and British Columbia, and further growth of the industry is a political priority for both the Norwegian[2] and Canadian national governments.[3] In the case of Norway, in less than three decades the structure of the salmon farming industry developed from a large number of small, locally owned production units to large, technically advanced installations owned by multi-national companies. Fish farming is now present along almost the entire Norwegian coastline and is considered as one of the major new industries to replace the oil industry in the future. Salmon farming accounted for approximately 70 per cent of the value of Norway's seafood exports[4] and 12 per cent of the total value of Norwegian exports in 2016.[5]

In the ongoing Norwegian debate about the environmental footprint of salmon farming, the main concerns relate to escaped farmed salmon (followed by genetic interference of escaped farmed salmon with wild salmon stocks) and high abundance of salmon lice[6] (*Lepeophtheirus salmonis*) in salmon pens. Salmon lice are a naturally occurring parasite that reproduces rapidly on fish farms, where the lice have access to high densities of salmon. Salmon lice threaten wild salmon passing through fjords with salmon farms, besides being a huge problem for the industry. Controversies between fish farming and traditional fisheries, both Sámi and non-Sámi, have so far have been moderate. The industry is currently expanding in Sámi fjord areas, and the question of Indigenous rights to marine resources and marine areas has been raised in controversies about the location of salmon farms within traditional resource areas used by Sámi fishing communities.[7]

[1] Douglas North, *Institutions, Institutional Change, and Economic Performance* (Cambridge University Press, 1990).

[2] Nærings-og fiskeridepartementet (Ministry of Fisheries) 2015, 'Forutsigbar og miljømessig bærekraftig vekst i norsk lakse- og ørretoppdrett' (Predictable and Environmentally Sustainable Growth in Norwegian Salmon and Trout Farming) Meld St 16 (2014–15).

[3] *Cohen Commission of Inquiry into the Decline of Sockeye Salmon in the Fraser River* (Canada, Privy Council 2012) vol 3, 11.

[4] Statistics Norway, www.ssb.no/fiskeoppdrett.

[5] Federation of Norwegian Industries, 'Roadmap for the Aquaculture Industry' (2017).

[6] Torbjørn Forseth et al, 'The Major Threats to Atlantic Salmon in Norway' (2017) 74 *ICES Journal of Marine Science* 1496.

[7] Kirsti Strøm Bull, 'Fjordfiske og oppdrettsnæring – en arealkonflikt i saltvann' ('Fjord Fisheries and Fish Farming: A Marine Area Conflict') (2016) 312 *Ottar* 34.

In British Columbia, salmon aquaculture expanded greatly since the industry's infancy in the 1970s and 1980s, when local fish farming companies experimented with various locations, fish stock and rearing methods. Norwegian-owned companies, raising Atlantic salmon, had significant expertise and capital, and soon came to dominate the industry. The province of British Columbia conducted an inquiry into the industry in 1986 and an environmental assessment review in 1995, and followed it up with a seven-year moratorium on new sites.[8] Although these reviews urged caution and highlighted the need for more planning and research amid growing environmental concerns, the industry expanded both the number of sites and the production capacity of individual farms.[9] Three multi-national companies (Cermaq, Marine Harvest and Grieg Seafood) own 90 per cent of the salmon aquaculture site licences in British Columbia. In British Columbia, the farmed salmon harvest has in recent years been nearly four times the harvest of wild salmon.[10] Yet the wild salmon fisheries are the cultural and ecological backbone of British Columbia's coast, nourishing the coastal forest with the carcasses of spawned fish, supporting subsistence and commercial use, and providing the basis for a strong tourist economy and sport fishing industry. First Nations have, for the most part, resisted the growth of the salmon aquaculture industry over the past several decades.[11] The primary concern for First Nations has been the effects of salmon aquaculture on the five species of wild Pacific salmon.

## II. GOVERNANCE OF MARINE SPACE IN INDIGENOUS AREAS

While the technology and organisation of the salmon farming industry may have its similarities in Norway and Canada, the two contexts differ in most other regards. The following describes the most important historical and current interactions between the salmon farming industry, First Nations in Canada and Sámi in Norway, particularly focusing on the governance instruments and conflict alleviation between Indigenous peoples and marine industries in the two contexts.

### A. British Columbia

Salmon farming in coastal British Columbia is concentrated in the sheltered bays and inlets between northeastern Vancouver Island and the mainland, and

[8] The Commission of Inquiry into the Decline of Sockeye Salmon in the Fraser River Canada, 'Aquaculture Regulation in British Columbia' (Department of Fisheries and Oceans, 2011).

[9] ibid.

[10] 'British Columbia Seafood Industry Year in Review' (2016).

[11] Dorothee Schreiber, 'First Nations, Consultation, and the Rule of Law: Salmon Farming and Colonialism in British Columbia' (2006) 30 *American Indian Culture and Research Journal* 19; Nathan Young and Ralph Matthews, *The Aquaculture Controversy in Canada: Activism, Policy, and Contested Science* (UBC Press, 2011).

among the myriad islands off the west coast of Vancouver Island. These are the territories of coastal First Nations, where resource sites were traditionally owned by high-ranking individuals of local kin groups.[12] Resource rights were based on descent from a common ancestor, who originated in a particular place in the group's territory.[13] The chiefs excluded outsiders and regulated access, allowing those with kinship connections to participate in the harvest. When marine space was under Indigenous control prior to colonisation, the institution of the potlatch provided a method of accountability for the resource management activities of the chiefs.[14]

First Nations resisting fish farms are doing so based on the fact that the territories in question were never the subject of treaty or any other agreement. Following the Royal Proclamation of 1763, the co-existence of Indigenous peoples with Canada requires the newcomers to enter into a treaty relationship and, in doing so, to gain permission to move into Indigenous lands. Treaty making, the Royal Proclamation states, is at the discretion of the Indians, 'if at any Time any of the Said Indians should be inclined'.[15]

However, aside from a few pre-Confederation treaties covering small sections of land on southern and eastern Vancouver Island, and Treaty 8 that overlaps into British Columbia from Alberta, no historic treaties were concluded in British Columbia between the Crown and Indigenous peoples.[16] Even after British Columbia joined the Canadian confederation in 1871, colonial officials made no effort to conclude treaties in the province. Instead, a series of reserve commissions travelled through British Columbia beginning in the 1860s and ending with the McKenna-McBride Commission in 1914–16. These commissions were tasked with surveying and marking out reserves, while putting aside or outright denying the existence of Indigenous title to land or water.[17] On the rivers and coast, these reserves were small parcels of land adjacent to important Indigenous fishing grounds that were meant to provide undisturbed access to the fisheries. As Douglas Harris points out:

> [T]o the extent that Native peoples were prepared to accept the reserves allotted by the commission, they did so on grounds that they would retain access to their

[12] Douglas C Harris, *Fish, Law, and Colonialism* (UBC Press, 2001) 19.

[13] Robert Galois, *Kwakwaka'wakw Settlements, 1775–1920: A Geographical Analysis and Gazetteer* (UBC Press, 1994).

[14] Martin Weinstein and Mike Morrell, 'Need is Not a Number: Report of the Kwakiutl Marine Food Fisheries Reconnaissance Survey', prepared for the Kwakiutl Territorial Fisheries Commission (Campbell River, British Columbia, 1994) 37.

[15] The Royal Proclamation of 1763 was issued by King George III to establish a basis of government administration in the North American territories formally ceded by France to Britain in the Treaty of Paris 1763, following the Seven Years' War. The Royal Proclamation is reproduced in the appendix to the Revised Statutes of Canada, 1985 and is available at: https://www.aadnc-aandc.gc.ca/eng/1370355181092/1370355203645#a6.

[16] For further discussion, see Hamilton (ch 1 in this volume) and Bankes (ch 6 in this volume).

[17] Cole Harris, *Making Native Space: Colonialism, Resistance, and Reserves in British Columbia* (UBC Press, 2002).

> fisheries. To the extent that the Dominion and provincial governments could justify these reserves, they did so, in part, on the grounds that Native peoples of the province were fishers and did not need a large agricultural land base.[18]

In Canada, decisions over use of marine areas are not made through planning processes in which First Nations have any significant influence over where fish farming may take place. Canada has a dismal record when it comes to marine spatial planning. Although Canada has undertaken numerous spatial planning exercises for so-called Large Ocean Management Areas, the processes have repeatedly stalled and participants are unable to agree on how the resulting plans should be implemented. In his analysis of marine spatial planning in Canada, Gunnar Sander explains that Canada's unwillingness 'to accept integrated management plans as an overarching framework' adds to problems arising from the consensus-based approach 'in which nobody had the authority to take decisions' and where 'participants concealed disagreements by wordsmithing and [pushing] their solution forward to a next phase of action planning'.[19] A spatial planning process for the Pacific North Coast Integrated Management Area – a marine area that includes the controversial fish farms in the Broughton Archipelago and Discovery Islands – has seen various stops and starts. Although the federal government has recently signed back on to the process, the resulting plan appears to be burdened with the same handicaps identified by Sander. A great number of irreconcilable interests were represented in 'stakeholder' forums, with the 'planning process seek[ing] to develop recommendations through consensus'.[20] As a result, the 2016 plan, which is now in its 'endorsement, implementation, and monitoring' phase, makes no recommendations on the controversy over salmon farming and marine space, simply noting that aquaculture is one of the industries taking place in the planning area.[21]

Its aspirations in marine spatial planning notwithstanding, Canada's decisions on aquaculture are made by the responsible federal and provincial ministries, and these decisions are rarely based on a consensus reached through negotiations with First Nations. Fish farms require a site licence from the province and an aquaculture licence from the federal government. Since 2009, the federal government, through the Department of Fisheries and Oceans (DFO), has held primary responsibility for licensing salmon farms and regulating all environmental aspects of the industry. Fish farm licensing is largely a federal responsibility, but because of its jurisdiction over marine space, British Columbia can refuse to issue site licences and therefore holds the 'trump card' in the governance of salmon aquaculture on the coast.

[18] Harris (n 12) 45.

[19] Gunnar Sander, 'Ecosystem-Based Management in Canada and Norway: 'The Importance of Political Leadership and Effective Decision-Making for Implementation' (2018) 163 *Ocean and Coastal Management* 485, 494.

[20] http://pncima.org/site/plan-development.html.

[21] Pacific North Coast Integrated Management Area (PNCIMA) Initiative, 'Pacific North Coast Integrated Management Area Plan' (2017).

## B. Northern Norway

Marine fisheries along the coast of northern Norway and freshwater fisheries along the large rivers of Fennoscandia have been major pillars of Sámi livelihood since time immemorial. Marine areas in the north have previously not been subject to the same fish farming pressure as areas in west and mid-Norway, but salmon aquaculture is currently expanding its operations in the waters of the northern counties of Troms and Finnmark, which are the traditional settlement areas of the coastal Sámi population. Sámi property and use rights to terrestrial and aquatic natural resources in north Norway, predominantly within the area covered by Finnmark County, have been under assessment for decades.[22] Sámi rights to marine areas, and thereby the right to exclude activities such as fish farming from Sámi sea areas, has not been recognised.[23] However, the first comprehensive assessment of Indigenous fishing rights was carried out as late as 2008[24] by the government-appointed Coastal Fisheries Committee, headed by former Chief Justice Professor Carsten Smith. The Committee concluded that the people of Finnmark, both Sámi and non-Sámi,[25] enjoy an Indigenous and historical right to fish, acquired through centuries of fishing in the waters off the Finnmark coast, and proposed both a new Act to recognise these rights and a resource governance board with equal Sámi and Norwegian participation to govern the Finnmark fishery. The Committee's conclusion was not endorsed by the Norwegian Parliament. However, small-scale fishers' rights in Sámi settlement areas were recognised in an addition to the existing Act of Participation in the fisheries.[26] The Committee did not treat property rights to marine areas as a part of its mandate, but it proposed an addition to the existing Finnmark Act[27] on the issue.

As a follow-up on the conclusion of the Coastal Fisheries Committee, an amendment was made to section 29 of the Finnmark Act in 2012, stating that the Finnmark Commission, whose mandate is to assess use rights and ownership rights to former state land, transferred to the Finnmark Estate in 2006, shall 'also investigate claims on collective or individual rights to fishing grounds in the coastal and fjord areas in Finnmark to the extent that someone with a legal interest in clarification demands it'. To date, few rights claims for marine areas

[22] For further details in relation to this and the following paragraph, see Ravna and Kalak (ch 9 in this volume).

[23] Susann F Skogvang, *Retten til fiske i kystnære farvann* (*The Right to Fish in Coastal Waters*) (Universitetsforlaget, 2012).

[24] Carsten Smith et al, NOU 2008: 5, *Retten til fiske i havet utenfor Finnmark* (*The Right to Fish in the Sea off the Finnmark Coast*).

[25] Finnmark, like the rest of the area constituting the traditional Sámi settlement area, differs from many other indigenous territories, as the indigenous Sámi and non-Sámi peoples have shared the land for centuries.

[26] 'Endringar i deltakerloven, havressurslova og finnmarksloven (kystfiskeutvalet)' ch 11.6.4. Prop 70 L (2011–12).

[27] 'Lov om rettsforhold og forvaltning av grunn og naturressurser i Finnmark fylke' 2005, s 29.

have been filed. The work of the Coastal Fisheries Committee and the scholarly work that has been carried out on the legal history of Sámi and their traditional marine use rights[28] mainly addresses harvesting rights to cod and other marine fish species harvested by the Sámi in fjords and near-shore areas.

Despite the Norwegian government's insistence on centralised management of marine fisheries based on a principle of common, national ownership,[29] local, place-based regulations have been a part of marine governance for a long time. Sámi and Norwegian small-scale fishers filed numerous requests to Norwegian authorities in the nineteenth and twentieth centuries, about spatial fishing regulations in fjord areas for protection of local fish resources vital to their livelihood.[30] These requests, which were not based on claims of pre-existing ownership rights to specific sea areas, were in some cases granted, at least for limited terms. As the salmon farming industry has expanded to the north, the effects of the industry on traditional fjord and coast fisheries in coastal Sámi areas, also referred to as the material foundation for coastal Sámi culture, have entered the discussion.[31] A controversy around a recent decision to withdraw the site allocation for a fish farm in Finnmark (see the Vedbotn case discussed below) following complaints by local Sámi inhabitants illustrates that the existing legal framework does contain protective measures for Indigenous culture, but these depend upon sufficient and early participation of the actors themselves at the right time in the coastal zone planning and governance process.

Until 2010, the Ministry of Fisheries allocated aquaculture sites and collected permission fees for fish farms. However, as a response to critique from the host regions, the authority to allocate sites has been devolved to county councils, while the income from permission fees is distributed to the state, counties and host municipalities. County councils cannot allocate aquaculture sites at their own will; allocation must adhere to municipal plans for coastal areas. Coastal zone plans became a part of Norwegian legislation in 1985 and were originally optional for coastal municipalities.[32] Since then, the relevance of marine and coastal zone spatial planning has increased tremendously, particularly because of the salmon aquaculture industry. These plans are important governance instruments to avoid or minimise conflicts over the allocation of

[28] Kirsti Strøm Bull, *Kystfisket i Finnmark; en rettshistorie.* (*The Coastal Fishery in Finnmark: A Legal History*) (Universitetsforlaget, 2011).

[29] 'Lov om forvaltning av viltlevende marine ressurser (havressurslova)', s 2 (Marine Resource Act 2008).

[30] Einar Eythórsson, *Sjøsamene og kampen om fjordressursene* (*The Coastal Sámi and Their Struggle for the Fjord-Resources*) (Cálliid Lágádus, 2008).

[31] Camilla Brattland and Einar Eythórsson, 'Fiskesløyfa: Spildrafiskernes driftsformer og oppdrettsaktiviteten' ('The Fishing Cycle: The Spildra Fishermen's Adaptations and the Aquaculture Activity') (2016) 312 *Ottar* 23.

[32] Bjørn Hersoug and Jahn Petter Johnsen, *Kampen om plass på kysten. Interesser og utviklingstrekk i kystsoneplanleggingen* (*The Struggle over Space on the Coast: Interests and Development in Coastal Zone Planning*) (Universitetsforlaget, 2012).

marine space to aquaculture and other purposes, through informed decisions, stakeholder participation and transparency.

The Sámi Parliament was established in 1989 as a representative assembly and political institution for the Sámi people. It is recognised as a representative of Sámi interests vis-a-vis the state on affairs relating to marine resource management in regions with a coastal Sámi population. In the context of spatial planning in the coastal zone, Sámi political influence is institutionalised in the Plan and Building Act[33] and the Consultation Agreement between the Sámi Parliament and the Norwegian government.[34] These instruments rest heavily on the International Labour Organization (ILO) Convention 169.[35] Norway was the first country to sign the ILO 169, thus accepting an obligation to consult the Sámi on issues of vital interests to them (Article 6) and recognising their right to participate in the use, management and conservation of resources pertaining to their lands (Article 15).

The adoption of the new Plan and Building Act was a result of successful consultations between the Sámi Parliament and the Ministry of Environment.[36] The Act is an important governance tool in Norway to ensure that planning processes coordinate the state, regional and municipal tasks that have an impact on the use of land and protection of resources. At the time of writing, the government has through consultations achieved consensus with the Sámi Parliament on a proposed bill to amend the Sámi Act.[37] If adopted, the bill will provide a statutory foundation for the state's duty to consult. The bill follows up on the proposals of the Sámi Rights Committee[38] and mainly tracks the current consultation agreement, but will broaden the scope of the duty to consult to include not only state agencies, but also municipalities and county municipalities. If approved by the Storting, municipalities will need to consult with Sámi communities on issues that will affect them, such as aquaculture establishments.

With the 2008 Plan and Building Act, the scope of spatial plans for coastal municipalities was expanded to sea areas within one nautical mile from the shore. Municipal authorities are required to plan in and around these sea areas

[33] 'Lov om planlegging og byggesaksbehandling (plan- og bygningsloven)' 27 June 2008 nr 71. An English translation of this statute is available at: https://lovdata.no/register/loverEngelsk.

[34] 'Avtale om prosedyrer for konsultasjoner mellom statlige myndigheter og Sametinget'. Fastsatt ved kongelig resolusjon 1 July 2006. An English translation is available at: www.regjeringen.no/en/topics/indigenous-peoples-and-minorities/Sami-people/midtspalte/PROCEDURES-FOR-CONSULTATIONS-BETWEEN-STA/id450743.

[35] International Labour Organization (ILO), 'Convention No 169 on Indigenous and Tribal Peoples in Independent Countries', adopted Geneva, 76th ILC Session, 27 June 1989, entered into force 5 September 1991.

[36] Else Grete Broderstad et al, 'Konsultasjoner – prinsipper og gjennomføring' ('Consultations – Principles and Implementation') in Bjørn Bjerkli and Per Selle (eds), *Samepolitikkens utvikling* (Gyldendal, 2012).

[37] 'Endringer i sameloven mv. (konsultasjoner)' Prop 116 L (2017–18).

[38] 'Den nye sameretten' NOU 2007:13.

before any allocation of aquaculture sites can take place. Suitable areas for salmon farming must be specified and mapped in the planning processes, which involve input from several government agencies and stakeholders. Only after a final approval by the County Governor do the plans enter into force. The Plan and Building Act obligates planning authorities to 'secure the natural basis[39] for Sámi culture, industries and society'[40] and grants the Sámi Parliament the authority to file formal objections to new plans about 'issues that are of vital importance for Sámi culture or Sámi industries'.[41] Municipalities are obliged to address such objections, usually by modification of the plan in agreement with the Sámi Parliament. According to the guidelines for coastal zone planning in Norway, coastal zone plans are required to include impact assessments for each proposed aquaculture site, considering objections from government agencies and stakeholders. The impact on the natural basis of Sámi culture is among the issues to be assessed for each proposed location.[42] The Sámi Parliament has adopted its own Planning Guidelines to the Act.[43] Even if these guidelines are not legally binding, they elaborate on the term 'natural basis for Sámi culture' and how it should be operationalised in plans. For instance, traditional fjord and coastal fisheries for cod and other species returning regularly to spawning grounds in the fjords are to be considered as elements of the natural foundation of Sámi culture and, as such, should be given appropriate protection. The Guidelines also underline that cod aquaculture sites must not be established in coastal cod spawning areas (Article 6.1). Relative to Atlantic salmon farming, the extent of cod farming is small and has proven to be challenging for many reasons, including interaction with wild cod.[44]

Riseth and Nygaard note that there is a general lack of knowledge on how to deal with Sámi interests in municipal planning processes, specifically in municipalities outside of the main Sámi regions.[45] In interviews, planners in Troms County note that assessment of impacts on the natural basis of Sámi culture is difficult because of a lack of data and poorly defined criteria on what should

[39] The terms 'natural basis' and 'material basis' are sometimes applied interchangeably.

[40] '[S]ikre naturgrunnlaget for Samisk kultur, næringsutøvelse og samfunnsliv' (Plan and Building Act, s 3-1c).

[41] 'Sametinget kan fremme innsigelse mot slike planer i spørsmål som er av vesentlig betydning for Samisk kultur eller næringsutøvelse' (ibid, s 5-4).

[42] 'Forskrift om konsekvensutredninger' (Klima- og miljødepartementet, Kommunal- og moderniseringdepartementet, 2017); 'Veiledningsnotat – Konsekvensutredninger for planer etter plan- og bygningsloven'. (Kommunal- og moderniseringsdepartementet, 2017).

[43] 'Veileder for sikring av naturgrunnlaget for Samisk kultur, næringsutøvelse og samfunnsliv ved planlegging etter plan- og bygningsloven (plandelen)' (Sametinget, 2010).

[44] Camilla Brattland, 'Proving Fishers Right: Effects of the Integration of Experience-Based Knowledge in Ecosystem-Based Management' (2013) 30 *Acta Borealia* 39.

[45] Jan Åge Riseth and Vigdis Nygaard, 'Samiske hensyn i planleggingen' ('Sámi Concerns in Planning') in Gro Sandkjær Hanssen and Nils Johan Aarsæther (eds), *Plan- og bygningsloven en lov for vår tid?* (*The Plan and Building Act: An Act for Our Time?*) (Universitetsforlaget, 2018).

count as valid elements of this natural basis.[46] The impact assessments for potential aquaculture sites, carried out as a part of the present coastal zone plan for mid- and south Troms, an area known for its substantial Sámi heritage, contain little information about possible impacts on Sámi culture and livelihood. Planners explain that there is a lack of suitable sources of information and a lack of capacity to investigate potential impacts on Sámi interests for each individual site.[47] It seems that such interests are not included unless they are brought into the planning process by local Sámi organisations and/or the Sámi Parliament. The Sámi Parliament's Department for Cultural Heritage, Spatial Plans and Environment[48] has limited capacity to take a proactive stand in planning processes, beyond issues concerning protection of Sámi cultural heritage, as there is no comprehensive database on Sámi marine usage and local Sámi interests that could potentially conflict with salmon farming. But the assessment stage in the planning process is the best window of opportunity for Sámi fishers, communities and associations to influence decisions about the allocation of marine areas for aquaculture. For cases where local Sámi interests have been able to influence the location of aquaculture sites, the usual pattern is that local actors have engaged in the planning process, in alliance with the Sámi Parliament. Once a conflict of interests concerning the natural basis for Sámi culture is raised and documented, the Sámi Parliament can take an advocacy role and raise a formal objection. On the other hand, if the Sámi Parliament is not sufficiently aware of a potential conflict and fails to raise the issue, there are few options available for Sámi communities to contest location of sites. However, local conflicts and protests that materialise after the fact, when aquaculture installations are already in place, may attract media attention and gain attention among environmentalists and Indigenous rights supporters.

## III. CONTROVERSIES OVER AQUACULTURE IN SÁMI AREAS

The Norwegian situation is very different to that of Canada when it comes to the nature of protests and the type of actions carried out by Indigenous and local communities. Coastal zone plans and national salmon protection zones close to river mouths have contributed to a low or moderate conflict level. Under the 'National Salmon Fjord' arrangement,[49] salmon rivers of national

[46] Interviews carried out by authors of this chapter and other participants in the Coreplan research project (www.coreplan.no).

[47] Also, Else Grete Broderstad and Eva Josefsen (Sámi Parliament's report 2016: Samiske interesser i kommunal arealplanlegging. *Perspektiver til fremtidig areal- og miljøpolitikk i Sápmi*) show that challenges of competence and capacity arise for municipalities in the implementation of 'the Sami participation element' of the revised Plan and Building Act.

[48] Avdeling for kulturminner, areal og miljø.

[49] 'Oppfølging av nasjonale laksefjorder' (St prp 32 2006–07).

significance have to a certain extent been protected by a ban on salmon farms along the migration routes, which in some ways can be compared to the recently established 'salmon migration corridor' in British Columbia[50]. However, this arrangement only provides 'soft' protection – salmon migrate all along the Norwegian coast and passing through areas with salmon farms is unavoidable.

There is increasing public concern over the environmental effects of the industry, particularly its impact on wild salmon populations. Growing media coverage of such controversies also contributes to the perception of rising conflict levels in the coastal zone. Besides concerns about genetic interaction between escaped farmed salmon and wild salmon, pollution (including chemicals used for the control of salmon lice) and the impact of the aquaculture industry on fjord habitats and coastal fisheries are debated. A common allegation from fishers, which so far lacks scientific documentation, is that coastal cod tends to avoid spawning grounds in areas with salmon farms. Regular environmental monitoring of fish farms is carried out by the industry itself; the industry does its own reporting to the authorities on the environmental status of their fish farms and the reports are freely available to the public. Independent environmental institutions also check the environmental status of the marine environment around fish farms. Fishers claim that these reporting routines are insufficient and fail to address effects on wild fish and the long-term impacts on the marine ecosystem.

The fjords of Tana and Porsanger, two of the largest coastal Sámi fjord areas, have been mostly free of salmon farms[51] due to concern for salmon stocks in the Tana River, the most important salmon river in Europe, which is currently in a precarious state. In 2017, a salmon farm was established in Vedbotn in the outermost part of the Porsanger fjord, which caused protests, formal complaints to the Directorate of Fisheries and an ongoing campaign from local Sámi to have the farm removed. However, the municipal plan for Nordkapp municipality[52] had already allowed for aquaculture in the area, and the site licence had been granted to Grieg Seafood by the Finnmark county council. The Sámi Parliament had filed an objection regarding Sámi cultural heritage and reindeer herding during the planning process, and had also asked for an impact assessment of the salmon farm site on local Sámi culture, which was not carried out. Some of the local inhabitants in Vedbotn also filed claims of ownership rights to the sea area directed to the Finnmark Commission, arguing that their families and their forefathers at least seven generations back have used the area and its resources, and thus have a right to the land and sea in their traditional areas of habitation.[53] Since the rights claims were filed prior to the establishment of aquaculture in

[50] Andrew Nikiforuk, 'Plan to Close Fish Farms on Salmon Migration Routes a "Step in Right Direction"' The Tyee (16 December 2018), https://thetyee.ca/News/2018/12/16/Salmon-Farms-to-Close.

[51] A small salmon farm at Skjånes in the outer part of Tana fjord closed down in 2007.

[52] 'Kommuneplan for Nordkapp 2015–2026' (Nordkapp commune, 2016).

[53] Finnmarkskommisjonen 2009, www.domstol.no/no/finnmarkskommisjonen.

the area, the presence of new aquaculture sites has fuelled the rights discourse with further arguments that salmon farming interferes with sources of Sámi livelihood and threatens the traditional coastal Sámi culture. The opposition was also related to growing public concerns about the impacts of fish farming on the environment, particularly because the fish farm site in Vedbotn is known as a spawning ground for cod.[54] In January 2019, the Directorate of Fisheries decided to withdraw the site allocation approved by the Finnmark county council based on concern for local Sámi culture and livelihoods.[55] The decision was subsequently revoked by the County Governor of Hordaland and the conflict was still unresolved as of April 2019.

The case of Spildra is a similar case in point. The Fishers' Association in Kvænangen fjord and the Community Association of Spildra island, supported by the Sámi Parliament, managed to prevent a marine area with a regionally important spawning ground for cod from being designated for aquaculture in the coastal zone plan.[56] However, in 2015, soon after the completion of the plan, Marine Harvest applied to the municipality for an exemption from the plan in order to allow the company to establish a fish farm in this area. Despite protests from the two associations, the municipal council voted in favour of an exemption so as to pave the way for the expansion of Marine Harvest's operations in the municipality. Numerous institutions, including the Sámi Parliament, the Directorate of Fisheries, the regional branch of the Fishers' Association[57] and the local associations, filed complaints against the municipality's decision. The leader of the Fishers' Association in Kvænangen indicated to a local newspaper that he was prepared to use civil disobedience or even sabotage against the fish farm if it was established.[58] Unlike in Canada, civil disobedience actions have not occurred in aquaculture conflicts in Norway, but the issue was hotly debated in national and regional newspapers and on social media support groups, as well as at local meetings where the industry, politicians and the public were invited to discuss the issue.

In alliance with the Sámi Parliament, the Kvænangen Fishers' Association and the Community Association of Spildra island filed an appeal to the County Governor, who after consultations with the Sámi Parliament (this is the first

[54] Fishers' knowledge of spawning areas is verified by the Institute of Marine Research and can be found in the Norwegian Directorate of Fisheries' online database Yggdrasil. This spawning area (Strandbukta) was verified as locally important in 2016; see https://kart.fiskeridir.no.

[55] Directorate of Fisheries, Grieg Seafood Finnmark AS – Oppheving av vedtak om tillatelse til akvakultur av matfisk av laks, ørret og regbueørret på lokalitet 10652 Vedbotn i Nordkapp kommune, og anmodning om ny behandling hos Rogaland fylkeskommune (Revocation of the decision on allowing aquaculture of food fish of salmon, trout and rainbow trout on location 10652 Vedbotn in North Cape municipality, and request for new treatment by Rogaland county council), letter of 4 January 2019 to Ingunn Eldbjørg Utsi, Stranda, Repvåg.

[56] 'Kystsoneplan 2013 – 2028' (Kvænangen kommune, 2015).

[57] Fiskarlaget Nord.

[58] Brattland and Eythórsson (n 31).

time an administrative consultation with the County Governor and the Sámi Parliament took place) cancelled the municipality's decision in August 2016. The County Governor is a representative of the national government and, as such, is obliged to accept consultations according to the Consultation Agreement between the Sámi Parliament and the Norwegian government. The Governor's decision clearly stated that the municipality was not free to make exemptions from its own plan, as this would undermine the function of coastal zone plans as a governance tool. In the Vedbotn case discussed above, the municipal council decided to make the site available for aquaculture as a part of a new municipal plan for Nordkapp without responding to the Sámi Parliament's request for an impact assessment of the project on Sámi cultural heritage and the natural basis for Sámi culture in the area. This decision was subsequently endorsed by the county council.

Both cases demonstrate that the Sámi can influence designation of marine areas for salmon farming in planning processes and ensure that existing plans are not undermined. The Sámi Parliament under the current legislation can advocate for Sámi communities and Sámi interests in disputes with local authorities by calling attention to prevailing procedures and Norway's legal obligations to safeguard Sámi culture. This is however no guarantee that Sámi concerns are taken into account in every case as illustrated in the Vedbotn case.

## IV. CANADA: AQUACULTURE CONTROVERSIES IN BRITISH COLUMBIA

In the case of conflicts over salmon farming in British Columbia, public pressure on both the province of British Columbia and the federal government to address siting and environmental concerns has led to a number of public inquiries on salmon farming. The federal Cohen Commission, tasked with investigating the dramatic decline in Fraser River sockeye, delved deep into the question of salmon farming and the federal mandate to protect wild salmon. In its final report, it made a number of recommendations, including that Canada should implement the precautionary principle, revise its salmon farm siting criteria and limit salmon farming along critical sections of wild salmon migration routes.[59] The Commission also expressed concern over the dual mandate of the DFO – on the one hand, to promote the salmon aquaculture industry and, on the other, to protect wild salmon. At the time of writing, almost none of the Cohen Commission recommendations have been implemented.[60]

The courts have repeatedly admonished the DFO for failing to adequately regulate the fish farming industry. In a case that dealt with the transfer of diseased

[59] *Cohen Commission* (n 3) vol 3, Recommendations.

[60] Watershed Watch Salmon Society, 'Cohen Report Card', www.watershed-watch.org/issues/salmon-biodiversity/the-fraser-sockeye-inquiry/cohen-report-tracker.

fish into ocean net pens, the Federal Court in 2015 found that the Minister had 'sheltered behind Marine Harvest's evidence' and made 'unsupported statements of science.'[61] When, in 2018, the Namgis First Nation again asked the court to stop the transfer of diseased farmed fish, the court reiterated its concerns about the DFO's alliance with industry, adding that 'the salmon fishery is of fundamental importance to the asserted Aboriginal rights of the Applicant, yet the Minister has refused to consult with respect to … the potential risk to wild salmon populations and the stewardship of the salmon fishery in the Asserted Territory'.[62]

In the summer of 2017, hereditary chiefs and their supporters from the Namgis First Nation, the Dzawada'enuxw First Nation, the Kwicksutaineuk-Haxwa'mis First Nation and the Mamalilikalla First Nation, occupied two Marine Harvest fish farms and stayed there for several months. In statements to the press given in October 2017, Ernest Alfred, a prominent hereditary chief and one of the leaders of the occupation movement, was unequivocal: 'We have been peaceful occupants and we are not afraid of Marine Harvest or any legal fights they want to get into. They broke the law and occupied our lands without our permission.'[63]

The sustained pressure of the fish farm occupations coincided with the election of a new provincial government, one that had campaigned on the promise to address First Nations' concerns over salmon aquaculture. While the federal government in Canada regulates and licenses salmon aquaculture operations, companies still require a site licence from the provincial government. Without a site licence, a fish farm is not permitted to operate in what are considered provincial waters.

On 11 October 2017, an unprecedented meeting took place between the Premier of British Columbia, his ministers, and 40 hereditary and elected chiefs of the Mamalilikala, Namgis, Tlowitsis, Mamtagila, Dzawada'enuxw and Kwikwasut'inuxw Haxwa'mis First Nations. The meeting was held in the Big House in Alert Bay, on the reserve of the Namgis First Nation. The setting of the Big House was significant. It is the ceremonial space used in proceedings during the potlatch, where Indigenous governance is still practised, and where rights to territory are publicly displayed and acknowledged. In this meeting:

> [T]he leadership and citizens delivered a united message that those Nations are in clear, unequivocal opposition to open-net fish farms in the Broughton Archipelago. The leadership also reiterated that the fish farms in the territories continue to operate without the Nations' free, prior and informed consent.[64]

[61] *Alexandra Morton v Minister of Fisheries and Oceans* 2015 FC 575 [37] and [39].

[62] *Namgis First Nation v Minister of Fisheries and Oceans* 2018 FC 334 [92].

[63] Andrew Nikiforuk, 'Fish Farm Occupations Net High Political Drama' *The Tyee* (26 October 2017).

[64] First Nations Wild Salmon Alliance, 'State of Wild Salmon in Pacific Region', open letter to Dominic LeBlanc, Minister of Fisheries (Canada) and Lana Popham, Minister of Agriculture (British Columbia, 2017) 2.

In June 2018, Lana Popham, British Columbia's Agriculture Minister, announced that three of the Broughton Archipelago's First Nations – the Namgis, Kwikwasut'inuxw Haxwa'mis and Mamalilikulla First Nations – had signed a Letter of Understanding with the province, pledging to reach consensus with the province on decisions to renew fish farm licences. A committee composed of equal numbers of First Nations and provincial representatives was tasked with making recommendations on the future of fish farms in the Broughton Archipelago. The Letter of Understanding outlining the process stated that 'where areas of disagreement persist, the Parties will seek appropriate facilitation, mediation and other methods of conflict resolution in an effort to find common ground'.[65]

In December 2018, the outcome of these negotiations, hailed by British Columbia as a 'ground-breaking government-to-government process', was announced to the public.[66] By the end of 2022, 10 fish farms in the Broughton Archipelago will have ceased operations. Another seven farms in the territory of the Namgis, Kwikwasuit'inuxw Haxwa'mis and Mamalilikulla First Nations will continue operating beyond that date only if the companies involved – Cermaq and Marine Harvest – manage to secure agreements with the three First Nations. An Indigenous monitoring and inspection plan has been put in place for the interim. It will provide First Nations with greater access to information and the authority to monitor fish farms for pathogens, including the right to test hatchery salmon for viruses before the smolts are placed in ocean net cages.[67] The fish farm removals will create a northern, farm-free migration corridor for wild salmon, potentially protecting three key salmon rivers in the area.[68]

On the rest of the coast, the province of British Columbia will no longer renew the licences of fish farming companies after 2022, unless companies have agreements in place with the First Nation in whose territory they propose to operate.[69] First Nations' approval will therefore be a requirement for provincial approval of the site licence. This opens the door to additional private agreements. Some such agreements, such as that between the Ahousaht First Nation and the fish farming company Cermaq (which will be examined in the next section), already exist between the salmon aquaculture industry and some First Nations on the coast.

[65] 'Letter of Understanding regarding a government-to-government process to address finfish aquaculture in the Broughton Area, including recommendations on Provincial Tenure Replacement Decisions', British Columbia and Namgis, Kwikwasut'inuxw Haxwa'mis and Mamalilikulla First Nations, 27 June 2018.

[66] British Columbia, 'Government, First Nations Chart Path for Aquaculture in Broughton Archipelago', press release, 14 December 2018, https://news.gov.bc.ca/releases/2018PREM0151-002412.

[67] ibid.

[68] Nikiforuk (n 50).

[69] British Columbia, 'Factsheet: Salmon Aquaculture in British Columbia, 23 July 2018, https://news.gov.bc.ca/factsheets/salmon-aquaculture-in-british-columbia.

## V. GOVERNANCE WITHOUT GOVERNMENT: IMPACT-BENEFIT AGREEMENTS AND THE FAILURE OF CANADIAN GOVERNANCE IN THE COASTAL ZONE

In the interests of reducing conflict between First Nations and the salmon aquaculture industry, the province of British Columbia in the early 2000s encouraged companies to enter into direct dialogue with First Nations and to negotiate private agreements with affected communities. Agreements between fish farming companies and First Nations are concluded 'after the fact', that is, after fish farming leases have already been assigned by the government, and usually in cases where local First Nations communities have objections to the fish farming operation.

Salmon farming enjoys little popular support in British Columbia, so signing agreements with First Nations is an important business tactic, allowing the industry to boost its legitimacy and break up alliances between First Nations and environmental groups. Industry invests considerable resources in concluding these types of agreements with First Nations. When an initial attempt to sign a business agreement with the Ahousaht First Nation's band council failed, the BC Salmon Farmers Association in 2001 hired an Ahousaht First Nation member to serve as a lobbyist and promote the industry to the community.[70]

The Ahousaht First Nation's Impact-Benefit Agreement (IBA) (also known as the 'protocol agreement') came about in an atmosphere of government inaction and fading political options. The territory of the Ahousaht First Nation is centred in Clayoquot Sound on the west coast of Vancouver Island, which comprises the second-biggest concentration of fish farms, after the Broughton Archipelago. The number of farms and the capacity of individual farms grew steadily during the 1990s. The Ahousaht First Nation was never consulted about the placement of fish farms or how fish farm operations should be regulated. In 1997, a flotilla of vessels, containing more than 200 Ahousaht members, boarded a salmon farm site and demanded its closure.[71] Over the course of the next five years, the community delivered a series of eviction notices to companies and complaints to government regulators about events such as algal blooms, fish escapes and gross violations of the environmental regulations. The provincial government (which at the time had primary responsibility for regulating fish farms) took no concrete action against the fish farming company. Without support from the province for its position, the Ahousaht First Nation turned to negotiations with the company as a last resort. As Deputy Chief Councillor Anne Atleo said at the time: 'It's not an ideal solution … but knowing that the

[70] Donna Harrison, 'Modern Enclosure: Salmon Aquaculture and First Nations Resistance in British Columbia' in Laurie E Adkin (ed), *Environmental Conflict and Democracy in Canada* (UBC Press, 2009).

[71] ibid 61.

government was going to open things up anyway, one of the best things we could have done was to take control and have a positive influence.'[72]

The first 'protocol agreement' between the Ahousaht First Nation and Pacific National Aquaculture (Cermaq) was signed in 2002, and the agreement has been renewed at five-year intervals. In its latest instance, the agreement was negotiated and signed for Ahousaht by a not-for-profit corporate entity known as the Maaqutusiis Hahoulthee Stewardship Society, made up of the hereditary title-holders. The content of the agreement is confidential, but such agreements do not require complete rights assessments, biological/ecological assessments of environmental degradation or economic assessments of actual loss. The agreement commits Cermaq to provide contracting and employment opportunities, fisheries/aquaculture-related scholarships and funds for wild salmon enhancement.[73]

Indigenous leaders in British Columbia respect the decisions that individual First Nations make about whether to enter into business agreements with industry. However, for province-wide Indigenous political organisations, there are shared and urgent concerns over the constitutional recognition of rights and title in salmon aquaculture. As the First Nations Fisheries Council stated in its response to the DFO's consultation plan in 2010: 'First Nations should not have to strike deals after the fact with companies, they should be dealing up front in a decision-making capacity which protects and accommodates their asserted rights and title and allows them a jurisdictional role, not one in which they are fighting for scraps from the industry profits.'[74] 'To be clear', the First Nations Fisheries Council stated:

> B.C. First Nations demand to be involved in all aspects of the creation and implementation of the Regulations and the associated Management Framework, as these will have a significant impact on, and potentially infringe on, asserted rights and Title.[75]

## VI. INTERACTIONS AND MARINE GOVERNANCE INSTITUTIONS IN NORWAY AND BRITISH COLUMBIA

In our description of the two contexts above, interesting differences and similarities between governance interactions arise. In Norway, local and regional governance institutions support a jurisdictional role for Sámi, whereas there is a striking absence of equivalent institutions governing the use of marine space

[72] Dorothee Schreiber and Dianne Newell, 'Negotiating TEK in BC Salmon Farming: Learning from Each Other or Managing Tradition and Eliminating Contention?' (2006) 150 *BC Studies* 79.

[73] Fieldwork by Dorothee Schreiber in Ahousaht, August 2017.

[74] Letter to Minister LeBlanc and Minister Bennett, First Nations Leadership Council (FNLC), 24 January 2017.

[75] Letter to Trevor Swerdfager, Director General, Aquaculture Management, DFO, First Nations Fisheries Council (FNFC), 27 August 2010.

in Canada. While protests pointing at environmental effects of the industry and its consequences for traditional Indigenous livelihoods are similar in content, the strategies are somewhat different. In British Columbia, First Nations use a combination of strategies to extract concessions from salmon farming companies. Direct action, court challenges and negotiation of private agreements with the industry have been used by First Nations, in the face of unwavering government support for the fish farming industry.

In northern Norway, the two cases illustrate that even if the Norwegian planning legislation includes a formal obligation to consider impacts on the natural basis of Sámi culture when sea areas are designated to aquaculture purposes in coastal zone plans, this is unlikely to happen without the mobilisation of local Sámi during the planning process. Better availability of knowledge and strengthened capacity of municipal planning departments, as well as the Sámi Parliament's Department for Cultural Heritage, Spatial Plans and Environment, might enable a more proactive approach to this obligation in the future. However, it seems even more important to build capacity at the local level in order to enable communities and Sámi organisations to engage in the planning process at an early stage.

In British Columbia, First Nations have used the courts to achieve recognition of their claims to marine space, but in practice, their jurisdiction over marine space remains severely limited. British Columbia's courts, as well as numerous federal commissions and audits, have pointed to the failure of the federal government to properly manage the salmon aquaculture industry. When the First Nations of the Broughton Archipelago turned to exercising their Aboriginal title on the ground, their actions coincided with a window of political opportunity, leading to an agreement with the province to phase out fish farming in the territory of three First Nations. However, the Dzawada'enuxw First Nation is seeking a solution that is based on its own jurisdiction, and one that does not depend on the political goodwill of the province. In May 2018, the Dzawada'enuxw First Nation launched an Aboriginal title claim to its traditional territories, including marine territories in the Kingcome Inlet and Broughton Archipelago region that are occupied by Marine Harvest and Cermaq.[76] A month later, it filed an application for an injunction to block the renewal of provincial tenures for open-net pen salmon farms operating in the Broughton Archipelago region.[77]

First Nations have asserted rights to marine space as an extension of their rights to land and as ancestral fishing grounds. The Namgis First Nation, for example, located in the Broughton Archipelago of British Columbia, sought to restrict the fish farming industry by asserting its territorial rights to this watershed and the wild salmon migration route terminating in the river. The Nimpkish River represents the core of the Namgis First Nation's homeland.

[76] Dzawada'enuxw First Nation, 'Claim of Aboriginal Title Filed as a Challenge to Fish Farms', press release, 28 May 2018.

[77] Dzawada'enuxw First Nation, 'Injunction Application Challenges Fish Farm Renewals', press release, 19 June 2018.

Before the watershed suffered extensive habitat destruction and before industrial fishing caused salmon populations to plummet, the Nimpkish River was the fifth most productive sockeye salmon river in British Columbia.[78] In March 2018, the Namgis First Nation, saying that the diminished wild salmon runs could not sustain additional stressors from aquaculture, made a statement of claim that its traditional territory includes the Nimpkish River and Kokish River watersheds and the adjacent marine areas:

> The Applicant asserts Aboriginal rights and title throughout the Asserted Territory, including title to the lands, water, air, marine foreshore and seabed, as well as rights to fishing, hunting, gathering and stewardship. In particular, it asserts that Pacific salmon, including sockeye, chum, pink, chinook and coho, are an integral aspect of their oral history and traditions, way of life, economy, culture, ceremonies, food and trade.[79]

The Nuu-chah-nulth First Nations on the west coast of Vancouver Island, including the Ahousaht First Nation mentioned above, made similar assertions of Aboriginal title in their successful 2009 court case for recognition of Aboriginal rights to fish commercially.[80] In that case, the plaintiffs claimed Aboriginal title to their fishing territories: 'the fishing territories comprise, for each plaintiff, a "test case" river, the foreshore areas and bodies of water below the low water mark and extending 100 nautical miles into the Pacific Ocean'.[81] The Nuu-chah-nulth restricted their title claim to one economic component of the title only – that covered by the fisheries. While the court declined to consider the title claim and expressed doubt about whether a claim to submerged lands was 'legally tenable', it did find an Aboriginal right to fish commercially and was sympathetic to the idea of marine territoriality where Aboriginal rights are concerned.[82] In her 2009 decision, the judge wrote:

> I find that the plaintiffs have proven the necessary site specificity as pleaded … with the exception of the offshore boundary which I would draw at nine miles from shore, that is, from a line drawn from headland to headland within each plaintiff's territory.[83]

First Nations have therefore achieved some limited recognition of marine territorial rights in the courts. Impact-benefit agreements between industry and First Nations are still becoming more common in Canada, where the government withdraws from the scene of conflict and assumes that business agreements fulfil the Crown's obligation to consult and accommodate First Nations on the

[78] Weinstein and Morrell (n 14) 65.

[79] *Namgis v Minister of Fisheries* 2018 FC 334 [5]. For further discussion of these cases, see Bankes (ch 6 in this volume).

[80] *Ahousaht Indian Band v Canada* 2009 BCSC 1494.

[81] ibid [11].

[82] *Ahousaht* (n 80) [502].

[83] ibid [414].

infringement of asserted territorial rights.[84] And while business agreements with industry allow First Nations to exercise at least some degree of influence over the fish farming industry, First Nations political organisations in British Columbia have made it clear in their response to federal aquaculture authorities that industry does not belong at the table when Aboriginal rights and title are being discussed.

The practice of private business agreements between Indigenous communities and industry has so far not been considered relevant in the Norwegian context. Sámi organisations, host communities and municipalities are normally not in a position to bargain directly with companies about benefits, but the industry may make donations to civil society, local culture and even local infrastructure. Unlike the fisheries legislation,[85] the Aquaculture Act[86] does not oblige companies to contribute to society and employment along the coast; aquaculture licences are granted without such requirements. In 2016, however, the Norwegian government established the Aquaculture Fund, an arrangement that distributes funds from the industry to municipalities that facilitate expansion of aquaculture by designating marine space to fish farming. For some coastal municipalities, these payments make a substantial contribution to welfare and infrastructure.[87]

## VII. CONCLUSION

In this chapter we have demonstrated how institutional differences between Norway and Canada, regarding legal foundations of Indigenous rights, planning legislation and government practices, shape governance interactions involving three actors: Indigenous peoples, government and industry. The industrial actors, which are the same aquaculture companies in both cases, engage in governance processes within very different contexts where Indigenous actors play different roles. While municipal planning processes both enable and constrain Sámi influence on the use of marine space in Norway, direct agreements such as IBAs function as the main means of interaction between the industry and Indigenous rights-holders in Canada. In the latter case, this means that the state has taken a back seat in the overall governance of marine space, thus leaving Indigenous communities vulnerable to the power dynamics of the global industry. While tensions from the promise of economic benefits from the

[84] Emilie Cameron and Tyler Levitan, 'Impact and Benefit Agreements and the Neoliberalization of Resource Governance and Indigenous–State Relations in Northern Canada' (2014) 93 *Studies in Political Ecology* 25.

[85] Lov om forvaltning av viltlevende marine ressurser (havressurslova), s 1 (2008).

[86] Lov om akvakultur (akvakulturloven) (2005).

[87] In 2018, payments to coastal municipalities from the Aquaculture Fund totalled €260 million, while payments to regions (county municipalities) came to €44 million; see www.fiskeridir.no/Akvakultur/Tema/Havbruksfondet.

industry to the host communities are similar in both countries, the challenge of economic compensation to host communities is addressed differently: in Canada through IBAs, in Norway and through the government-initiated Aquaculture Fund. Under the current Consultation Agreement between the Sámi Parliament and the Norwegian government, there have been very few opportunities for consultations over the use of marine areas. A broadened right to be consulted, as proposed by a forthcoming bill, might enable Sámi communities to influence the use of marine space through local and regional consultations, and perhaps foster governance interaction between Sámi communities and the industry.

While the concept of Aboriginal title is more clearly articulated in Canadian law than Norwegian law, the involvement of Sámi in the making of legally binding spatial plans opens up avenues for coastal Sámi to participate in high-level decision making over salmon aquaculture – a level of influence that until recently has been impossible for First Nations in British Columbia to achieve. Still, the Sámi influence over coastal zones remains fragile and subject to the political will of the Norwegian state. Indigenous demands for significant decision-making authority over marine areas in British Columbia are underpinned by a system of Indigenous law, in which title-holders have ancestral rights and obligations to specific river mouths, bays and inlets. These rights are less clearly rooted in customary law in the coastal Sámi context in Norway, where the courts are seldom used in cases of conflict over marine space.

The differing constitutional contexts of Norway and Canada limit any direct parallels that can be drawn between the experience of Indigenous peoples in Norway and British Columbia in conflicts over marine space. In the Canadian legal tradition, Aboriginal title is a bundle of rights that includes 'the right to decide how the land will be used … and the right to pro-actively use and manage the land'.[88] And while Aboriginal title is difficult to establish in court, the mere assertion of Aboriginal title, backed by credible research and documentation, requires extensive consultation and accommodation on the part of the Crown. From the perspective of the coastal First Nations in British Columbia, rights to marine territory, including decision-making powers over what may take place in that territory, were never ceded to the Crown. Thus, the context of territorial rights is different from the Sámi case. While section 35 of the Canadian Constitution Act of 1982 recognises and affirms Aboriginal rights, the 1988 Norwegian constitutional amendment maintains the duty of the state to ensure that conditions prevail to enable the Sámi people to maintain and develop its language, culture and way of life. The constitutional recognition of 1988 rests heavily on the prevailing international law at that time, namely Article 27 of the International Covenant on Civil and Political Rights protecting the material

[88] *Tsilhqot'in Nation v British Columbia* 2014 SCC 44.

basis for minority cultures and the individuals belonging to these minorities.[89] The constitutional concept of 'the material basis for culture' blurs the boundary between stakeholder and Indigenous rights-holder, while on the other hand, the Norwegian reading of international law in the late 1980s and later renewed interpretations played a significant role in maintaining the state's duty to actively safeguard the material basis of this culture.

[89] This and the twin Covenant on Economic and Social Rights were incorporated into Norwegian domestic law through the human rights law of 1999; see Ravna and Kalak (ch 9 in this volume).

# 17

# *Indigenising and Co-managing Local Fisheries*

# The Evolution of the Alaska Community Development Quota Programme in the Norton Sound Region

EVELYN PINKERTON AND STEVE J LANGDON

## I. INTRODUCTION: THE WESTERN ALASKA COMMUNITY DEVELOPMENT QUOTA PROGRAMME

NORTON SOUND IS one of six regions in the Bering Sea off the northwest coast of Alaska which benefited from the creation of the Western Alaska Community Development Quota (CDQ) programme. This programme was created when the Alaska pollock fishery was being converted to Individual Fishing Quotas (IFQs) in 1992.[1] This conversion, which mostly privileged the highly-capitalised Seattle-based catcher-processor off-shore trawl fleet, was controversial for two reasons: (1) it privatised a valuable public good by the creation of a form of Individual Transferable Quota[2] through which

[1] Alaska pollock (*Gadus chalcogrammus*) made up 32 per cent of total US landings and 58 per cent of Alaska's landings, giving an average annual ex-vessel value of $400 million in the early 2000s. The stock is generally thought to be managed sustainably and its largest concentrations are in the eastern Bearing Sea: https://en.wikipedia.org/wiki/Alaska_pollock_as_food; K Criddle and J Strong, 'Dysfunction by Design: Consequences of Limitations on Transferability of Catch Shares in the Alaska Pollock Fishery' (2013) 40 *Marine Policy* 91.

[2] An Individual Transferable Quota (called an IFQ in Alaska) is a permit allowing the holder to catch or transfer a fixed share of a total allowable catch (TAC). This transforms the permit into a tradable commodity, although Alaska pollock could only be leased or sold within (not between)

individual firms were thought by many to benefit at the expense of public welfare and equitable distribution;[3] and (2) it threatened to allocate the majority of these benefits in Alaskan marine space to out-of-state parties who provided no benefits to Alaska in terms of either jobs or taxes. Through consideration of divergent opinions on the North Pacific Fisheries Management Council (NPFMC)[4] and especially the political efforts of the Bering Sea Fishermen's Association[5] and the coastal communities which wanted more secure access to raw fish, the resource-dependent and overwhelmingly Indigenous coastal communities of this Bering Sea-Aleutian Islands (BSAI) region demanded some consideration.

These two concerns enabled the NPFMC to create a unique programme designed to assist the coastal communities in the BSAI area which had inadequate infrastructure, low household incomes and high unemployment. Six place-based non-profit organisations (CDQ groups) were formed (see Table 17.2) and were initially allocated 7.5 per cent of the pollock quota. These groups auctioned their pollock quota shares to off-shore trawlers who offered the best mix of opportunities. The lease fees or 'royalties' CDQ groups received were then invested into the kinds of development they sought in pursuing their traditional in-shore fisheries and community infrastructure development. The choices made by the Norton Sound Economic Development Corporation (NSEDC, the northernmost of the six CDQ groups) and the outcomes of its decisions reflect the legislative requirements which were part of this programme, the values of the participating communities, and their own agency in developing and bringing into operation plans to create economic opportunities in the fisheries for village residents. These led to investments in loan programmes to allow not only permit and vessel purchases for the salmon, crab and halibut fisheries, but also to create onshore processing facilities, tendering vessels which bought and transported fish to local processing plants, scholarships for students, and training in fisheries data collection and analysis in partnership with government agencies. Beyond the direct economic benefits of these investment choices are the cultural

the in-shore or off-shore sectors. However, CDQ organisations could lease the quota to any sector (Criddle and Strong (n 1)). Alaska's owner-on-board policy applied to halibut and sablefish IFQs, but was not effective in preventing concentration of quota holdings (M Szymkowiak and A Himes-Cornell, 'Towards Individual-Owned and Owner-Operated Fleets in the Alaska Halibut and Sablefish IFQ Program' (2015) 14 *Maritime Studies* 19).

[3] J Olson, 'Understanding and Contextualizing Social Impacts from the Privatization of Fisheries: An Overview' (2011) 54 *Ocean and Coastal Management* 253; S Macinko and D Bromley, *Who Owns America's Fisheries?* (Island Press, 2002); R Baker, 'Broadening the Benefits from Quota-Based Management in Alaska Commercial Fisheries' (IIFET Portsmouth Proceedings, 2006), https://ir.library.oregonstate.edu/downloads/hh63sw91c.

[4] The North Pacific Fisheries Management Council is the federal body which makes fisheries management recommendations for the exclusive economic zone (EEZ) off Alaska to the National Marine Fisheries Service.

[5] ND Mendenhall, *Rough Waters: Our North Pacific Small Fishermen's Battle; A Fishing Family Perspective* (Far Eastern Press, 2015) 286.

benefits of generating new and enhancing traditional in-shore fisheries, training future leaders and managers of community enterprises, and creating meaningful opportunities for youth to participate in the subsistence lifestyle which is the foundation of these communities.

The CDQ model of resource asset allocation and deployment, one grounded in empowering local populations to collectively utilise resources for the realisation of culturally appropriate ends, provides an alternative to ITQs and holds promise for the development of sustainable patterns of resource utilisation. This chapter explores the de jure and de facto rights and roles being exercised by the communities under this model, and how the benefits flowing from these rights and roles contrast with the benefits assumed to flow from neoliberal models.

## II. WHAT DOES 'DEVELOPMENT' MEAN? THE IMPORTANCE AND IMPLICATIONS OF THE CDQ MODEL

The CDQ programme constitutes a unique promotion of Indigenous access to resources within marine space in a way which supports traditional subsistence lifeways. It is enabled by a federal programme in which CDQ groups are accountable to the government for their use of CDQ revenues which must be 80 per cent dedicated to fishing – and fish processing – related activities and infrastructure. The other 20 per cent can be dedicated to public welfare and community development. However, decisions about how to do all of this are made by a democratically elected board which must represent all the fishing communities in each CDQ group to which it is therefore accountable.[6]

The growth of economic benefits realised from this modest allocation is remarkable. CDQ groups were eventually allocated 10 per cent of all commercial groundfish[7] species in the region. Yet, revenue from the CDQ groups' own fishing and processing has long exceeded lease fee income. In 2013, the aggregated revenue from all CDQ groups was $248.7 million, of which only 23 per cent was derived directly from CDQ lease fees. By 2011, the six CDQ groups held approximately $938 million in assets and had invested more than $176 million in CDQ communities and fisheries activities, including financial services that support small-scale operations targeting salmon, herring, halibut and other near-shore species. CDQ revenue supports permit brokerages and revolving loan programmes for the purchase or retention of limited entry salmon permits within

[6] National Marine Fisheries Service (NMFS), 'The Western Alaska Community Development Quota Program', NOAA Fisheries Alaska Regional Office, Juneau (2017), https://alaskafisheries.noaa.gov/sites/default/files/cdqprogsummary.pdf.

[7] In later years, allocations of halibut and fixed-gear sablefish were made to the CDQ programme as part of the IFQ programme. By 1998, allocations of BSAI non-pollock groundfish (cod, mackerel, flatfish and rockfish), and CDQ crab were established, and CDQ groups were allocated about 10 per cent of each and began participating in all of the major federal groundfish fisheries in the BSAI.

CDQ communities, also providing the financing necessary for resident fishermen to purchase new boats and gear. In 2011, the economic activity generated by the CDQ programme contributed over $4.5 million in Alaska state and regional taxes and fees. In addition, the programme participants made community capital investments of approximately $30 million.[8] These figures demonstrate that the CDQ programme was addressing at least one of the development issues – the concern that benefits from the BSAI fisheries were leaving Alaska.

But how were BSAI coastal communities affected? Social scientists often wonder on whose terms community 'development' happens. In what ways have the CDQ communities been able to develop according to their own values? This chapter documents some of the ways in which the CDQ programme has enabled rural, remote and mostly Indigenous communities to articulate with the mainstream economy in ways which enhance rather than detract from their traditions, identity and values. The programme's whole purpose is to *increase* participation in fisheries for local residents by supporting especially small-scale fishermen in getting boats and permits to fish. This purpose is contrary to the views of neoliberal economists, who regard this as the *last* place a rational actor would invest and instead consider that small boats should be eliminated, as they are presumed to be 'inefficient' (as discussed in Øyvind Ravna and Line Kalak's chapter documenting the elimination of Sámi small boats, a pattern replicated in neoliberalised fisheries in many jurisdictions).[9] This chapter documents and theorises how Indigenous residents articulate with institutions of capitalism and exemplifies the indigenisation of modernity.[10] Table 17.1 summarises major ways in which the CDQ programme functions ideologically and practically in opposition to the neoliberal principles which guide fisheries management in many parts of the world.[11]

[8] NMFS (n 6).

[9] For example, in British Columbia (E Pinkerton and R Davis, 'Neoliberalism and the Politics of Enclosure in North American Small-Scale Fisheries' (2015) 61 *Marine Policy* 303), Iceland (E Eythorsson, 'Coastal Communities and ITQ Management: The Case of Icelandic Fisheries' (1996) 36 *Sociologia Ruralis* 212; N Einarsson, *Culture, Conflict and Crises in the Icelandic Fisheries: An Anthropological Study of People, Policy and Marine Resources in the North Atlantic Arctic* (University of Uppsala Press, 2011)); Tasmania (I van Putten and C Gardner, 'Lease Quota Fishing in a Changing Rock Lobster Industry' (2010) 34 *Marine Policy* 859), New Zealand (J Stewart and P Callagher, 'Quota Concentration in the New Zealand Fishery: Annual Catch Entitlement and the Small Fisher' (2011) 35 *Marine Policy* 631; and Ireland (F McCormack, *Private Oceans: The Enclosure and Marketing of the Seas* (Pluto Press, 2017)).

[10] S Langdon, 'The Integration of Cash and Subsistence in Southwest Alaskan Yup'ik Eskimo Communities' in T Matsuyama and N Peterson (eds), *Cash, Commoditisation and Changing Foragers* (National Museum of Ethnology, Senri Publication No 30, 1991); GR Vizenor, *Manifest Manners: Narratives on Postindian Survivance* (University of Nebraska Press, 1994); National Research Council, *The Community Development Quota Program in Alaska* (National Academy Press, 1999); C Atleo, 'Aboriginal Capitalism: Is Resistance Futile or Fertile?' (2015) 9 *Journal of Aboriginal Economic Development* 41.

[11] Pinkerton and Davis (n 9); E Pinkerton, 'Hegemony and Resistance: Disturbing Patterns and Hopeful Signs in the Impact of Neoliberal Policies on Small-Scale Fisheries around the World' (2017) 80 *Marine Policy* 1.

**Table 17.1** Goals and effects of neoliberal policies in fisheries versus the goals of the CDQ programme

| Neoliberal principles | Effect in fisheries | Goals of the CDQ programme |
|---|---|---|
| Privatize public goods | Benefits go to the individual shareholder or owner of permit or IFQ; many small-scale fishermen forced out of fisheries, sell permits to larger quota holders | Benefits go to community and to optimally increase local access of small-scale fishermen and other locals to job opportunities in processing, research, internships, education |
| Capital accumulation | Skippers, crew and shoreworkers are as few and as poorly paid as possible | Spread benefits as widely as possible; employ as many people as possible |
| Capital accumulation | Leasing-out of ITQs at high prices creates maximum profits for quota owners, but less profitable enterprises for those who lease in ITQs | Lease out community-owned IFQs to local fishermen at no lease cost, thereby allowing their enterprises to be profitable |
| Allocate fixed access privileges which are difficult to change | Lowered capacity and flexibility to take precautionary approach; pressure to maintain the status quo and retain quota despite negative environmental signals | Continual flexibility, learning and adaptation through board meetings of each CDQ group required to have representatives from all communities; meet 6–7 times a year |
| Wellbeing = material wealth | Wellbeing = pursuit of maximum economic yield via efficiency/cost-cutting and tax reduction | Wellbeing = enough cash to pursue a subsistence lifestyle, access all resources of the territory and maintain health despite the high cost of living |
| Deregulation = market rule | ITQs gravitate to wealthier fishermen with the most capital | Permits bought by local residents with NSEDC loans are informally limited to a sustainable number |
| Devolution of responsibility and risk to citizens | Rising costs to the state to support unemployed former fishermen | Reduce unemployment and poverty; provide public benefits; loans to small businesses and fishermen; support subsistence activities; greater citizen connection to resources |

*(continued)*

Table 17.1 *(Continued)*

| Neoliberal principles | Effect in fisheries | Goals of the CDQ programme |
|---|---|---|
| Devolution of responsibility and risk to citizens | Fishing-dependent communities emptied out or become dependent on state funds as traditional livelihoods lost | Communities become more self-sufficient and engaged in addressing community needs |
| Individual greed is positive force in economic growth | Transformation of fishermen's consciousness into solely self-interested *homo economicus* instead of other-directed and community-directed citizens | Increase local beneficiaries' dedication to sustainable management by involvement through research, training, jobs and personal development |
| Financialisation | Use of financial instruments to leverage more capital, eg, private equity firms | Invest in as many fishing vessels, permits and partnerships as possible and also low-risk financials |
| Globalisation | Move activity to cheapest place | Keep fishing and processing local |

The CDQ programme could also be considered a unique form of co-management (defined here as power-sharing) in that government goals and requirements play an important part (eg, the mandate of the programme requires that investments of CDQ income be in fishing-related and other activities which benefit the community and reduce poverty), but the major choices in terms of *how* to achieve those goals are made by the communities. As a co-management system, the CDQ programme operates largely at what political scientist Elinor Ostrom[12] has called the 'collective choice' level, in that CDQ communities are able to exclude outsiders from most benefits, make internal decisions through their own boards about how to allocate funds and opportunities to their members, and choose what fisheries management issues deserve the most immediate attention in their data collection and actions. However, it is unclear to what extent it operates at the highest policy-making level, despite the fact that investments in local fishing permits, processing plants and even part or full ownership of larger trawler vessels increased the stake of BSAI communities in BSAI fisheries. In theory, this should also have increased their voice in relation to how these fisheries are managed. The CDQ representative on the federal North Pacific Fisheries Management Council (NPFMC) has on one occasion had to recuse himself from voting to reduce the allowable bycatch of chinook salmon by

[12] E Ostrom, *Governing the Commons: The Evolution of Institutions for Collective Action* (Cambridge University Press, 1990).

trawler partners. Thus, as discussed below, CDQ community actions at the highest policy-making level are not always consistent with much of community opinion in the NSEDC region. Yet, overall at some levels and in some important ways, the CDQ groups define and exercise considerable control over the form and type of development occurring in their regions, although this control is not uncontested.

## III. MORAL AND POLITICAL FOUNDATIONS OF THE CDQ PROGRAMME

Before discussing the ways in which CDQ groups, as illustrated by Norton Sound, exercise control over development, it is useful to briefly consider the moral and political circumstances which permitted the formation of the programme. The grounds on which the governor of Alaska in the early 1990s urged the federal government to create the CDQ programme were partly moral. Using the rhetoric of the 1992 United Nations Conference on Environment and Development (UNCED) at which he had spoken, Alaska's Governor Wally Hickel emphasised the access rights of adjacent and especially Indigenous communities in a speech, stating that 'Coastal States should support the sustainability and special needs of small-scale artisanal fisheries, local communities and indigenous people, to meet human, nutritional and other development needs'.[13] The UNCED provided important recognition of the importance of food security, adjacency and indigeneity, all of which played important roles in the CDQ programme.[14]

The CDQ programme was also a response to a moment of political opportunity: the need to determine how Bering Sea pollock should be allocated between competing user groups, especially catcher-processors (who ultimately delivered their catch outside Alaska) versus vessels which delivered to in-shore processing plants. When ITQs were about to be introduced in the BSAI pollock fishery in 1992, Dutch Harbor/Unalaska, the largest processing port in the US and a major in-shore processor of pollock, was among the lobbyists for greater allocations to vessels delivering in-shore. In the early 1990s, the in-shore/off-shore allocation issue was advancing through the NPFMC process faster than the introduction of the IFQ programme. Therefore, the structure of the CDQ programme could be seen as a component of the federal BSAI in-shore pollock allocations.[15] In sum, the CDQ programme emerged from a unique combination of moral and political circumstances.

[13] M Treadwell, 'Comments at the 20th Anniversary Celebration of the CDQ Program' Juneau, Alaska (2012).

[14] United Nations Conference on Environment & Development, Agenda 21, Chapter 26, Recognizing and strengthening the role of Indigenous people and their communities (Rio de Janeiro, 1992) 279, https://sustainabledevelopment.un.org/content/documents/Agenda21.pdf.

[15] Although CDQ allocations were not counted as part of the in-shore allocation, they formed part of the discussion of what should be included.

## IV. ABBREVIATED INDIGENOUS HISTORY IN NORTON SOUND

At the time of contact, a mixture of Inupiaq groups in the north and Yup'ik groups in the central and southern areas had occupied the Norton Sound area for thousands of years. Two subsistence patterns characterised the groups: islands-based marine mammal hunters depending on bowhead whale, walrus, bearded and smaller seals, and mainland groups hunting small seals, beluga whales, salmon, crab, tomcod and caribou. When the US assumed jurisdiction from Russia in 1867, the population of the region was approximately 3,500. US whalers entered the region in the mid-1860s, decimating the bowhead whale and walrus populations on which the island populations depended. Starvation and death from a measles epidemic in 1889–90 reduced the population of St Lawrence Island from 1,500 to less than 300.

When the Bureau of Indian Affairs (BIA) assumed jurisdiction over Alaska Natives in 1931, the Solicitor of the Department of Indian Affairs stipulated that 'the natives of Alaska … are entitled to the benefits of and are subject to the general laws and regulations governing the Indians of the United States'.[16] In 1936, the extension of the Indian Reorganization Act to Alaska made it possible for Alaska Natives to organise tribal governments, and some groups in Norton Sound took advantage of this. As a matter of law, they were subject to general federal law concerning their fish and wildlife harvest, but in practice their remoteness and the lack of commercial interest in the species of the region meant that they were able to utilise resources in their customary fashion.

When Alaska became a state in 1959, management of fish and wildlife was transferred from federal to state control; Alaska Natives became subject to state law with no recognition of Indigenous rights to hunt and fish. As the state of Alaska began selecting lands under the terms of the Alaska Statehood Act, Alaska Natives began to understand that neither the federal nor the state governments were attempting to recognise or settle Indigenous rights to land. The Alaska Federation of Natives began to assert Aboriginal rights to land and seek a fair settlement. In 1971, the Alaska Native Claims Settlement Act (ANCSA) was passed, creating a vehicle for the settlement of Alaska Natives rights as recognised under US law. The ANCSA established 13 regional corporations and over 200 local (village community) corporations that were deeded lands and monies to provide for development and subsistence uses.[17] At the same time, the ANCSA extinguished 'aboriginal fishing and hunting rights'. The Bering Straits Native Corporation, encompassing the Norton Sound region,

[16] D Case and D Voluck, *Alaska Natives and American Laws*, 3rd edn (University of Alaska Press, 2014) 384. This statement made clear that Alaska Natives' Indigenous rights to lands and governance were recognised.

[17] Alaska Natives were defined as persons who could demonstrate Alaska Native ancestry in the fourth degree through their genealogical records.

was established under the terms of the ANCSA, but had major financial difficulties and limited funds for investing in local economic ventures; it sought relatively safe investments in order to provide minimal cash dividends to its shareholders. Thus, Alaska Native rights were transformed into shareholders' rights, expressed only through their corporation.

In 1972, the Marine Mammal Protection Act (MMPA) was passed, asserting federal management jurisdiction over marine mammals and including a provision for coastal Alaska Native rights to continue subsistence hunting of marine mammals, subject to conservation. In 1980, in fulfilling the provisions of the ANCSA, Congress passed the Alaska National Interest Lands and Conservation Act (ANILCA) and withdrew large amounts of land for federal governance by various agencies. The ANILCA addressed the outstanding issue of Alaska Natives' subsistence rights by creating a rural preference for Native and non-Native residents when fish and wildlife were scarce (although thereby excluding the approximately 60 per cent of urban-dwelling Alaska Natives). In 1987, the US Supreme Court ruled that the ANILCA does not apply to the exclusive economic zone (EEZ) as its provisions fall only within the territory of Alaska.[18] The federal appeals court further held that the ANCSA did not extend past the geographical boundaries of Alaska and 'thus did not extinguish Aboriginal rights that may exist in the Outer Continental Shelf' (3–200 nautical miles off-shore).[19]

In 1994, the Director of the BIA listed all Alaska Native communities with village corporations as tribes. Through this action, their previously uncertain status as tribes was legally recognised, and tribes began enrolling Alaska Natives as tribal members according to tribal specific criteria.[20]

Alaska Natives of the Norton Sound region thus have a portfolio of rights and eligibilities as members of tribes typically based on residence and Alaska Native corporation shareholders with rights to vote, eligible for services and receipt of dividends, holding marine mammal hunting rights, and rights to some medical services from the regional health corporations. While the foregoing constitute parts of the portfolio of their Indigenous rights, they also have other rights through residency. Under the terms of the ANILCA, Alaska Natives have subsistence priority harvesting rights (in times of scarcity) along with other rural residents on federal lands, but not on state lands or waters, except in rare conditions deriving from their rural residency. Under the CDQ programme, Alaska Natives residing in the region's communities are eligible for the programme by virtue of their membership in Alaska Native Village communities, not on the basis of either their individual Indigenous status or membership in a federally recognised tribe.

[18] Case and Voluck (n 16) 315.
[19] ibid 316.
[20] ibid 327.

## V. WHY WE FOCUS ON THE NORTON SOUND ECONOMIC DEVELOPMENT CORPORATION (NSEDC)

The NSEDC is arguably one of the most successful CDQ groups across a range of features in terms of how it has responded to the conditions in which it finds itself. We explore how it intersects with the people's lifeways, provides benefits, and crafts institutions to achieve its own goals, thereby exemplifying the indigenisation of Western institutions. The NSEDC now has the second-largest population of the CDQ groups, but grew the most moderately between 1990 and 2000 (11 per cent), and between 2000 and 2010 (3 per cent) (see Table 17.2). It contains some 94 per cent of its region's residents, so there are few inland communities who are left out of the programme (the CDQ programme is limited to communities within 50 miles of the coast, so some CDQ groups experience resentment from neighbouring communities just outside their boundaries). It has made good use of liaisons in its responsiveness to local communities. It maintains fish processing operations in three communities, which is especially important to the islands off-shore where one of these operations is located. It is a model of equitable distribution of opportunity, allocating many benefits in equal proportion to the large and small communities. It customises activities at the community level – eg, it doesn't buy halibut in some plants at certain times to ensure that the Savoonga plant on St Lawrence Island in the middle of the Bering Sea gets that opportunity, which is its only real option. It fits the scale of local effort to processing capability and controls capitalisation because fishermen get their loans through the NSEDC – ie, it can control fishing effort through loan provisioning. It has a very high rate of holding local salmon permits in the local area, which has not been true in all CDQ groups. Norton Sound was protected from an urban invasion in permit ownership in earlier years by distance from urban centres, lack of infrastructure, servicing, processing or marketing facilities,[21] and much lower average earnings. In later years, Knapp,[22] building on Langdon,[23] found that access to financing was more important than costs of travel and was thus a key driver of retaining permit ownership, so the NSEDC has played an essential role in keeping permits more local by providing loans for local permits and boats.[24] Because of its remoteness, customary and traditional resource harvesting and use (termed 'subsistence') has remained the foundation of village life for NSEDC communities, especially for those with no commercial fishing opportunities.

[21] Mendenhall (n 5) 288.

[22] G Knapp, 'Local Permit Ownership in Alaska Salmon Fisheries' (2011) 35 *Marine Policy* 658.

[23] S Langdon, 'Transfer Patterns in Alaskan Limited Entry Fisheries', Final Report for the Limited Entry Study Group of the Alaska State Legislature (1980).

[24] Although gear loans were provided from the beginning, the NSEDC took almost a decade before it felt confident enough to supply boat and permit loans, as well as providing tendering services to several communities whose small vessels could not deliver fish without nearby tenders.

**Table 17.2** CDQ groups, communities, population change, percentage of region in CDQ communities

| Region of Alaska | CDQ Group | Number of CDQ communities | 2000 Census population | 2010 Census population | Change in population (%) | % of region living in CDQ communities (2000) | % of region living in CDQ communities (2010) | % change in population in CDQ groups |
|---|---|---|---|---|---|---|---|---|
| Aleutians and Pribilof | APICDA | 6 | 1,143 | 1,295 | 13 | 14 | 15 | 1 |
| Bristol Bay | BBEDC | 17 | 5,932 | 5,417 | −9 | 74 | 72 | −2 |
| Central Bering Sea | CBSFA | 1 | 532 | 479 | −10 | 100 | 100 | 0 |
| Coastal villages | CVRF | 20 | 7,855 | 8,570 | 9 | 47 | 49 | 2 |
| Norton Sound | NSEDC | 15 | 8,488 | 8,731 | 3 | 94 | 98 | 0 |
| Yukon Delta | YDFDA | 6 | 3,123 | 3,210 | 3 | 23 | 26 | 3 |

The history of how the summer red king crab fishery in Norton Sound was transformed illustrates how the NSEDC worked in federal and state regulatory arenas to create policies beneficial to NSEDC residents. Since 1977, the fishery had been prosecuted by distant water catcher-processors. This was very emotionally disturbing to local subsistence fishermen,[25] since their petition to the Alaska Board of Fisheries[26] had initiated the fishery, but they did not end up getting a share.[27] In 1993, a year after the CDQ programme started, this smallest of all the crab fisheries in the BSAI became the only federally managed king crab fishery designated as 'super exclusive' by the NPFMC through a series of events described by Natcher et al. By 1995, 98 per cent of the TAC of

[25] G Powell, R Peterson, L Schwartz, 'The Red King Crab in Norton Sound, Alaska: History of Biological Research and Resource Utilization through 1982' (Alaska Department of Fish and Game 1983) 12.

[26] The Alaska Board of Fisheries is charged with making allocative and regulatory decisions, while the Alaska Department of Fish and Game provides technical, scientific and managerial support.

[27] B Natcher, J Greenburg and M Hermann, 'Impact Analysis of Changes in Fishery Regulation in the Norton Sound Red King Crab Fishery' (1999) 52 *Arctic* 33. This fishery fit poorly with highly capitalised large vessels, which tended to over-fish or under-fish the small quota. However, it was ideal for the multiple small vessels which eventually harvested the quota over a much longer time period, allowing a more exact meeting of quota limits. See S Langdon, 'Foregone Harvests and Neoliberal Policies: Creating Opportunities for Rural, Small-Scale, Community-Based Fisheries in Southern Alaskan Coastal Villages' (2015) 61 *Marine Policy* 347 for a similar situation in the salmon fishery.

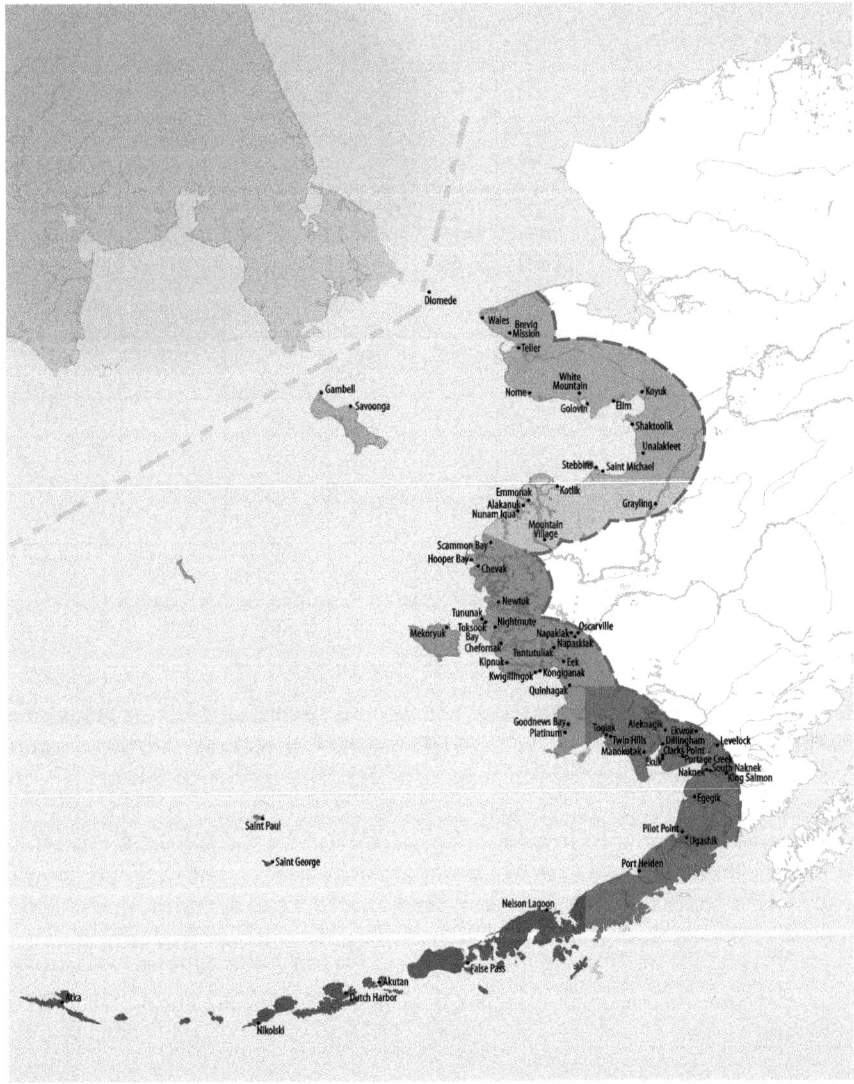


**Figure 17.1** CDQ groups and their communities.

From Western Alaska Community Development Association (WACDA) http://www.wacda.org/pages/cdq-entities.php.

approximately 450,000 lbs was taken by 29 local permit-holders and processed in the NSEDC plant in nearby Nome.[28] This plant buys crabs from local boats only. After 2000, Alaska brought in License Limitation permits for fisheries that were not subject to IFQs, but Norton Sound crab boats under 32 ft were granted

[28] In the initial stages, this fishery was shared with the adjacent Yukon Delta CDQ group.

an exemption.[29] Currently, the NSEDC does not limit the number of residents who can fish for crab (or halibut, which uses the same boats) and supports all who can gear up (currently 36); hence, this fishery is called 'open access'. The fishery is limited instead by the state (the Alaska Department of Fish and Game (ADF&G)) pot limits and by NSEDC caps on loans to fishermen, but, as fishermen re-pay loans, there is room for more loans. As a precautionary measure, the ADF&G transferred eight per cent of the TAC to a winter crab fishery which is conducted through holes in the ice and provides additional employment at a time when other fisheries are not pursued. The NSEDC has invested in research on red king crab populations and has advocated that they be managed cautiously at a conservative exploitation rate. In sum, this story exemplifies how a regional organisation (a CDQ group) can help improve fisheries management in many dimensions, creating a more ecologically and socially sustainable fishery because of more local research and greater knowledge and incentives, less capital expenditure because of proximity and the technology used, and benefits spread more broadly. Table 17.3 below shows the growing benefits distributed by the NSEDC, illustrating the ways in which 'development' is conceptualised and implemented.

**Table 17.3** NSEDC beneficiaries 2003 and 2016 (source: NSEDC annual reports)[30]

| NSEDC beneficiaries | 2003 | 2016 |
|---|---|---|
| Number of residents | 8,493 | 8,700 |
| Fishermen involved in NSEDC fisheries | 119* | 207* |
| Fishermen permit holders | 100 | 172 |
| Employees in seafood processing, buying, tendering (Norton Sound Seafood Products (NSSP)) | 71 | 258 |
| Partner hire: crew on partner vessel | N/A | 20 |
| Fisheries technicians with NSFR &D/ADFG | 15 | 33 |
| Community liaison | 17 | 14 |
| Community employment programme | N/A | 19 |
| Administration (NSEDC and NSSP [processing]) | 24 | 51 |
| Total employment | 302 | 659 |
| Scholarships and vocational training | 177 | 312 |

*(continued)*

[29] North Pacific Fisheries Management Council, 'Norton Sound Red King Crab Fishery' Discussion Paper (2014), 1.

[30] https://www.nsedc.com/publications/annual-reports.

**Table 17.3** *(Continued)*

| NSEDC beneficiaries | 2003 | 2016 |
|---|---|---|
| Internships | 64 | not counted separately |
| Small-vessel loans to fishermen | (8 loans) $89,343 | (26 loans) $334,088 |
| Large-vessel loans to fishermen | (5 loans) $361,056 | (3 loans) $109,327 |
| Small business initiatives | N/A | (6) $160,000 |
| each community** benefit share payment | $35,000 | $150,000 |
| each community special projects | N/A | $60,000 |
| each community large infrastructure | | $1,000,000 |
| each community youth basketball & other school activities | | $12,000 |
| each community alcohol & substance abuse prevention | | $20,000 |
| consolidated bulk fuel purchase to 26 entities | | $4,140,000 |
| community energy fund: Diomede & Teller projects | | $1,018,875 |
| energy subsidy total for all communities | | $1,560,000 |

* In 2016, 143 salmon, 23 CDQ crab, 36 open access summer crab, 22 winter open access crab, 19 CDQ halibut, 23 bait (59 fishermen participated in more than one fishery, but the total number of fishermen was 207). In 2003, 139 salmon, 36 crab, 20 halibut and cod (23 participated in more than one fishery, but the total number of fishermen was 119).

** 'Each community' means that the total must be multiplied by 15 for the total amount paid out.

## VI. WHAT SPECIFIC CO-MANAGEMENT RIGHTS ARE EXERCISED BY THE NSEDC?

Maritime anthropologists have been documenting the sometimes unrecognised exercise of de facto management rights by local and regional organisations since the 1970s. These de facto management rights[31] have functioned to exclude non-local fishermen and to limit and distribute local fishing effort through time and space. Sometimes these rights take the form of legal marine tenure, as in the case of Japanese fishing cooperatives, while at other times they function as informal but effective management instruments because of the power of local organisations to enforce their own rules, as in the case of the lobster 'gangs' of the state of Maine.[32]

[31] We acknowledge that we use the term 'rights' in this section somewhat loosely. We recognise that others would characterise some of these 'rights' as powers, liberties or freedoms. See W Hohfeld, 'Some Fundamental Legal Conceptions as Applied in Legal Reasoning' (1913) 23 *Yale Law Journal* 16.

[32] J Acheson, *The Lobster Gangs of Maine* (University Press of New England, 1988).

The political scientists Schlager and Ostrom[33] have viewed such rules as local institutions informally managing a fishery through the de facto exercise of political power. They usefully distinguished a hierarchy of lower-level (operational) and higher-level (collective choice) rights functioning in different parts of the system, but have viewed rights as mainly extractive and alienable. In addition, Pinkerton and Weinstein[34] viewed these rights from an Indigenous perspective as both rights and *responsibilities for* sustainable management, and included a number of additional activities functioning as de facto rights, not identified by Schlager and Ostrom and not formally identified in the anthropological literature, based on the study of a range of fisheries co-management arrangements. Below we identify an even larger number of rights that the NSEDC is exercising, often de facto rather than de jure. This list serves to recognise the broad range of influence exercised by the NSEDC as to the conduct of many fisheries in Norton Sound and at times the broader BSAI area. Although such influence does not constitute legally recognised power, it should be noted that informal political power, when it proves valuable to the functioning of a political system, is often formalised or institutionalised at a later point.

The NSEDC could be said to exercise three higher-level rights: (1) *identifying problems and issues* which need to be addressed; (2) *visioning a desired future* which deals with these issues; and (3) *contributing to policy making* on these issues. As mentioned above, the NSEDC, through a regular CDQ board member on the NPFMC, can raise policy issues which it believes need to be addressed and also contribute ideas and information about possible solutions. The NSEDC identifies problems and makes its own decisions about what needs to be researched, and also works with ADF&G in data collection on projects it deems important. The NSEDC has also submitted proposals to limit pots, vessel size etc to the Alaska Board of Fisheries, which makes management decisions for state waters. Because the NSEDC takes the initiative in investing in research, it also assists in specifying problems and issues. More controversially for Norton Sound communities, through its partnerships with catcher-processors and other large vessels, the NSEDC is able to exert influence as a player and stakeholder in the BSAI, as discussed below.

The NSEDC could be said to exercise 10 collective choice[35] rights dealing with the internal operations of its fisheries:

(1) *Exclusion rights*: the red king crab fishery illustrates the legal exclusion of non-locals by the federal government, which classified red king crab as

[33] E Schlager and E Ostrom, 'Property Rights Regimes and Coastal Fisheries: An Empirical Analysis' in TL Anderson and RT Simmons (eds), *The Political Economy of Customs and Culture: Informal Solutions to the Commons Problem* (Rowman & Littlefield, 1993).

[34] E Pinkerton and M Weinstein, *Fisheries that Work: Sustainability through Community-Based Management* (David Suzuki Foundation, 1995), http://davidsuzuki.org/publications/reports/1995/fisheries-that-work.

[35] Collective choice rights are rights to make rules about the operation of a fishery: who can be excluded; how the fishery is regulated; how access is allocated etc. See Schlager and Ostrom (n 34).

a super-exclusive fishery in the Norton Sound region. This exclusion is *enforced* by the NSEDC fish processing plant, which will not accept deliveries from non-local fishermen, who therefore would incur significant expense in delivering their catch to a processor outside the region.

(2) The NSEDC indirectly exercises de facto *allocation rights* in its distribution of opportunity to fish, through the provision of financial support in loan and grant allocations. In other words, its capacity to provide loans allows local fishermen to buy permits, boats and gear, which in turn allows fishermen to access local fish.

(3) The NSEDC indirectly exercises de facto *harvest planning/regulation rights* through its control of fishing effort through the number of fishermen to whom it provides loans in open access fisheries. It also controls the timing of the halibut fishery in relation to other fisheries through the timing of when and where its processing plants buy halibut. For example, because of recent low halibut quotas, the NSEDC has supported the small Savoonga plant on an off-shore island which specialises in halibut by not accepting halibut in any of its plants until the king crab fishery is done, and then accepting halibut only at the Savoonga plant.

(4) The NSEDC exercises a certain amount of de facto *monitoring and enforcement of harvest regulations* through monitoring and enforcing delivery to their plants by registered local fishermen only.

(5) The NSEDC exercises de facto *habitat protection rights* through activities such as its advocacy to prevent mining in key salmon habitat, cleaning up marine debris and supporting alternative wind power generation in one community.

(6) Through its presence in the region, the NSEDC engages in *monitoring* the effects of previous mining in key watersheds and to some extent is able to engage in *enforcement of habitat protection* through bringing violations to the attention of the authorities.

(7) The NSEDC's actions in exercising (or not) de facto *conservation rights*[36] have been controversial at the community level in some cases. At one point, it did not support raising the allowable cap on the interception of chinook salmon returning to Norton Sound (and other) streams by the mid-water trawlers which fish pollock (and with which it was partnered in some cases). Federal regulations made by the NPFMC allowed trawlers some interception of 'prohibited species' such as chinook, so any failure to decrease the allowable bycatch is highly controversial in Norton Sound communities. The NSEDC Decennial Review in 2013[37] notes that NSEDC trawler

[36] See R Jones, C Rigg and E Pinkerton, 'Strategies for Assertion of Conservation and Local Management Rights: A Haida Gwaii Herring Story' (2017) 80 *Marine Policy* 154.

[37] Department of Commerce, Community and Economic Development (DCCED), 'CDQ Program Decennial Review Documents', 2013, https://www.commerce.alaska.gov/web/dbs/CDQInformation.aspx.

partner vessels took 40 per cent (rather than the allowable 100 per cent) of the allowable chinook bycatch over the previous five-year period. The trawler bycatch rate on chinook averaged approximately 25 per cent of the allowable bycatch if the very high bycatch year of 2007 is excluded from the average. As discussed below, the high bycatch in 2007 precipitated greater pressure on trawlers to fish cleanly, resulting in more stringent regulation from the NPFMC in subsequent years.

(8) The NSEDC exercised *enhancement rights* when it fertilised lakes to increase the production of sockeye salmon and when it used innovative hatchery techniques such as mist incubation and eye-egg planting to rehabilitate chum, coho and chinook salmon stocks, and even constructed fish habitat.

(9) The NSEDC exercises the *right to secure optimum benefit from the sale of fish* when its processing plants pay fishermen the best price possible that allows processing operations to break even and shoreworkers to be well paid.

(10) A unique right, not previously identified in co-management studies is the *right to community benefits to enhance well-being*. This occurs through the 20 per cent of investments which CDQ communities can make outside the fishery and includes the community benefit share, the consolidated buying of fuel at lower cost, the community energy subsidy, the community energy fund and housing costs for seasonal work in processing plants.

Finally, at the lowest level of power, the NSEDC exercises three operational rights: data collection; data analysis; and access and withdrawal:

(1) The NSEDC is deeply involved in both funding *data collection* and participating in data collection activities with the government and other partners. It contributed approximately $200,000 to research management projects to ADF&G, Kawerak Inc,[38] the Bureau of Land Management and the Native Village of Unalakleet.[39] It is involved in salmon-counting projects using weirs, towers and sonar equipment. It has been a one-third partner in a joint crab tagging study, funded by the North Pacific Research Board.[40] This joint project with the ADF&G seeks to more fully tell the story of where and when Norton Sound red king crab move throughout the year. The NSEDC participates in and supplements the trawl survey which is carried out every three years and is the most important tool used to set harvest guidelines. It has a strong working relationship with ADF&G, and two NSEDC biologists are former ADF&G biologists. ADF&G presents to the NSEDC board

[38] Kawerak, Inc is an Alaska Native regional tribal consortium serving 20 federally recognised tribes of the Bering Strait region through contracts with the state and federal government and additionally sought funding.

[39] NSEDC 2003 Annual Report, https://www.nsedc.com/publications/annual-reports.

[40] The North Pacific Research Board is a federally funded body which must emphasise research designed to address pressing fishery management issues or marine ecosystem information needs.

at least twice a year. The NSEDC funded 2–4 of ADF&G's summer technicians, and ADF&G uses NSEDC data to determine salmon escapement goals. This illustrates the level of trust and cooperation that has developed and adds support to the hypothesis that 'co-management is more likely to develop when fishermen show a willingness to contribute financially (or recruit other sources of support) to the rehabilitation of the resource, and/or contribute to other management functions'.[41]

(2) The NSEDC Fisheries Research and Development (FR&D) programme could be said to exercise *data analysis rights*, in that it promotes scientific research in the Norton Sound region with an emphasis on supporting local fisheries, to explore the potential of under-utilised stocks and, where possible, to enable greater use by local residents. One of its first collaborative efforts was with ADF&G to fund interns working on summer salmon projects, and this collaboration continues today. The FR&D investigated the possibility of a longline fishery for cod and halibut in the northern communities of Teller, Brevig Mission, Wales and Diomede (which are more remote and have fewer adjacent opportunities), unfortunately finding no such possibility. The NSEDC has carried out some of its own research on its vessel *Pacific Star*.[42] It advocated successfully with the Alaska Board of Fisheries for a new exploitation rate based on the new population models. It analyses chum salmon use of estuaries, salmon fecundity, distribution and productive capacity of salmon in several streams, and undertook a crab feasibility study in Little Diomede. It conducts research on red king crab, the most lucrative single-species fishery in Norton Sound, and herring, the largest under-utilised stock in Norton Sound. It identifies deficiencies in the model or raises issues based on its research at Alaska Board of Fisheries meetings.

(3) The third and final operational rights exercised by the NSEDC are *access and withdrawal rights*, ie, the right to access marine space and the right to withdraw fish from that space. The NSEDC or Norton Sound residents hold almost all the local salmon permits, all local permits for red king crab, permits for halibut and herring, and shares of partner vessels which access all other BSAI fisheries. Thus, the NSEDC could be said to hold broad local access and withdrawal rights, even though the quantities are modest. Part of the NSEDC's goal in acquiring shares of partner vessels is to gain broader access to species other than crab and salmon (as a hedge against uncertainties related to climate change etc) and to influence policy in BSAI fisheries. It should be noted that the abundance and diversity of the NSEDC's commercially accessed fish species are relatively low when compared to the population and economic conditions of the Norton

[41] E Pinkerton, 'Attaining Better Fisheries Management through Co-management: Prospects, Problems, and Propositions' in E Pinkerton (ed), *Co-operative Management of Local Fisheries: New Directions in Improved Management and Community Development* (UBC Press, 1989) 3, 27.

[42] NSEDC 2010 Annual Report, https://www.nsedc.com/publications/annual-reports.

Sound region.[43] Thus, there are strong incentives to increase the abundance and sustainable use of local species for both commercial and subsistence purposes.

## VII. DISCUSSION: UNDER WHAT CONDITIONS ARE BROAD CO-MANAGEMENT RIGHTS AND ROLES ACHIEVABLE?

The NSEDC offers a case of reasonably strong although partial (but incomplete) co-management, meaning that there is power-sharing between government agencies and community-based organisations over a wide range of management activities, as described above.[44] These shared powers and rights are sufficient to achieve many of the communities' objectives, which are to maintain viable communities and a subsistence lifestyle which allows the continuance of traditions, identity and self-determination, and the exercise of agency in a number of management areas. In other words, the level of power and rights exercised by the NSEDC has allowed communities of mostly Indigenous people to access fish and marine space on their own terms to a considerable extent. This is what we term 'success' in this context. The discussion below examines the key conditions which made this possible, allowing consideration of how generalisable the case might be. In the case of the NSEDC, there are sufficiently favourable conditions in the nature of the community, the nature of the resource, the nature of the government agency, and external conditions that make the NSEDC institutional arrangement a reasonably successful assertion of co-management rights.[45] There are no absolute rules about the sufficient conditions to produce a desired outcome, but the greater the number of favourable conditions that exist in each category, the greater the possibility of success.

### A. Favourable Conditions in the Co-managing Organisation/Communities

Communities of place which are (a) highly dependent on the fishery and sustainable management of it, (b) where fish are vitally important to the communities economically, socially and culturally, and (c) where communities will mobilise energy to defend fish from habitat-destroying developments have the best chance of exercising co-management rights. Additionally, (d) clear membership rules, relatively small size and shared norms are helpful, as are (e) multi-generational

[43] NSEDC 2006 Annual Report, https://www.nsedc.com/publications/annual-reports.

[44] E Pinkerton, 'Toward Specificity in Complexity: Understanding Co-management from a Social Science Perspective' in DC Wilson, JR Nielsen and P Degnbol (eds), *The Fisheries Co-management Experience: Accomplishments, Challenges and Prospects* (Kluwer, 2003) 61.

[45] A Agrawal, 'Sustainable Governance of Common-Pool Resources: Context, Methods, Politics' (2003) 32 *Annual Review of Anthropology* 243; E Pinkerton and L John, 'Creating Local Management Legitimacy: Building a Local System of Clam Management in a Northwest Coast Community' (2008) 32 *Marine Policy* 680.

knowledge of local fish stocks, habitat and ecosystem links, and (f) strong leadership, clear purpose, political will and the capacity to engage both local communities and outside actors. It is this last condition which is incompletely developed in the NSEDC, in that board members representing villages are not always in a position to question the business decisions made by NSEDC staff, which may sometimes put maximising profits ahead of the values and welfare of village-based in-shore small-scale fisheries. While this situation could be at least partially remedied by board training and investments in excluder devices to minimise bycatch, the CDQ programme has set up a benefit stream from off-shore trawlers which inevitably pits the profits of the latter against community well-being, sometimes creating difficult and contested compromises rather than progress on this issue. Additional conditions which apply to the community and also its external environment[46] are that the community (g) can identify its interests with the public interest and show these interests are not being addressed, (h) has supportive issue networks in academia, non-governmental organisations (NGOs) or government, and (i) has access to logistical and financial resources.

### B. Favourable Conditions in the Resource

Co-management success with a particular fishery is more likely if the fishery (a) has boundary clarity (its migratory range is known), (b) is adjacent (lives enough of its life cycle near the community), (c) is well known and valued by the community (ie, is culturally salient), (d) is fairly dependable in its availability, and (e) is sufficiently abundant to merit management effort. Again, the mid-water and especially the bottom trawl fisheries create both a benefit stream and also dilemmas for community-based management.

### C. Favourable Conditions in the State Agency Which Co-manages

Power-sharing between a community-based organisation and a state agency (the government bureaucracy responsible for managing the fishery) is more likely to happen if: (a) the state agency is not too large to minimise the importance of co-management and small enough to develop personal relationships with the relevant communities/organisations; (b) the scale and scope of its mandate allows it to address power-sharing; (c) it has an open attitude rather than a siege mentality; (d) it has sufficient stature to be a change agent; (e) it understands the importance of local knowledge and the value of combining it with natural science; and (f) it has hands-on experience working with fishermen and local organisations.

[46] A Scott, *Ideology and the New Social Movements* (Unwyn Hyman, 1990).

As was evident from previous sections, all these conditions applied either moderately or strongly in the case of the NSEDC. The conditions provide useful criteria for judging the possibilities for developing such co-management arrangements in other situations.

## VIII. WHAT DOES THIS TELL US ABOUT THE 'DEVELOPMENT' THAT SUBSISTENCE-BASED COMMUNITIES WANT?

Many anthropologists[47] emphasise that traditions shape the direction of economic change in ways often not understood as 'development' by mainstream Western society. For example, people may adopt modern technology, but may use it primarily to make their subsistence activities more effective (but more energy-intensive and expensive). They may seek to earn more money mostly for the purpose of buying this expensive equipment.

In a recent study of Arctic peoples, Poppel[48] provided the following assessment:

> When the relationship to nature, participation in hunting and fishing and consuming traditional foods are regularly emphasised as significant for Inuit [and Inupiaq] in the Arctic, they … indicate … relationships and activities which are important for the quality of life of people. *And, seen in this light, market economic activities as parts of the subsistence way of life 'offer perhaps a sufficient description of the mixed economy in many of the Arctic communities when observed through local eyes.'* (Emphasis in original)

This understanding of economic choices is of course the opposite of the neoliberal view of individuals who maximise income above all other priorities.

Norton Sound Inupiat have higher and healthier levels of physical exercise than other Alaska Natives and US settlers, probably because of their involvement in subsistence activities. Their unemployment rate was 10–12 per cent (of those actively seeking employment) compared to a statewide rate of 7–8 per cent in 2005–09; their median household income was $30,000; and 21 per cent were classified as being below the federal poverty level in 2000. These statistics help explain why the employment that the NSEDC is able to provide is so highly valued, even though it is usually seasonal, because it enables the pursuit of subsistence activities and family life at other times. These data may also shed light on the fact that, even while median household income rose significantly

[47] U Hannerz, *Cultural Complexity: Studies in the Social Organization of Meaning* (Columbia University Press, 1992); M Sahlins, 'What is Anthropological Enlightenment?' (1999) 28 *Annual Review of Anthropology* vi.

[48] B Poppel, 2010 'Are Subsistence Activities in the Arctic a Part of the Market Economy, or is the Market Economy a Part of a Subsistence Based Mixed Economy?' in *Cultural and Social Research in Greenland: Selected Essays 1992–2010* (Ilisimatusarfik/Forlaget/Atuagkat, 2010) 360.

after the CDQ programme started, official poverty rates rose even faster.[49] However, the rate of official poverty may be less important than the fact that death rates due to cancer declined by 41 per cent between 1994–98 and 2004–08, after increasing in the previous decade; now it is almost the same as Natives statewide. Heart disease decreased by 71 per cent from 1984 to 2008 to below the national average, while suicide dropped 20 per cent in the same period. A reasonable hypothesis is that these improvements in positive health indicators are related to increases in employment and community benefits which reduce the cost of living and, perhaps even more importantly, increase a sense of control over the direction and type of development. Chandler and Lalonde[50] found that the lowest suicide rates in British Columbian Indigenous communities were correlated with the highest rates of exertion of agency in self-governance and retention of cultural traditions. Others[51] found that alcoholism in British Columbian Indigenous communities only developed when traditional authority and control over fishing was overwhelmed by industrial development. 'Development' in Norton Sound means people having an increased ability to obtain the valued traditional foods in ways which feel 'modern', what the National Research Council study called 'the indigenization of modernity':[52]

> Also associated are certain valued traits of human character of the kind necessary to undertake an often difficult subsistence existence: a very considerable knowledge of nature and a high degree of technical competence (including competence in dealing with modern technology), highly athletic physical skills, and the sort of mental toughness that combines sagacious prudence with the ability to respond to emergencies and contingencies of famously difficult Arctic conditions.[53]

And:

> Subsistence is indeed much more than subsistence: it is a whole way of life that extends to the people's essential conceptions of themselves and of the objects of their existence.[54]

Some critiques of the CDQ model have claimed that it is accepting and supporting highly capitalised and destructive forms of fishing such as trawling and thus

[49] Western Alaska Community Development Association, Annual Report (WACDA, 2011), www.wacda.org/media/pdf/SMR_2011.pdf.

[50] Norton Sound Regional Health Data Profile, 2010. Alaska Native Epidemiology Center, Anchorage. http://anthctoday.org/epicenter/publications.html. M Chandler and C Lalonde, 'Cultural Continuity as a Moderator of Suicide Risk among Canada's First Nations' in L Kirmayer and G Valaskakis (eds), *Healing Traditions: The Mental Health of Aboriginal Peoples in Canada* (UBC Press, 2009) 221.

[51] E Pinkerton and EN Anderson, *The Kakawis Experience: Report Prepared for Kakawis Family Development Centre* (Tofino, 1986).

[52] National Research Council, *The Community Development Quota Program in Alaska* (National Academy Press, 1999).

[53] M Nelson, 'Bristol Bay Pink, Chum, and Coho Salmon 1968: A Compilation of Catch and Escapement Data', State of Alaska. ADF&G International Leaflet No 28, 1 March 1969, cited in National Research Council (ibid) 39.

[54] J Jorgenson, *Oil Age Eskimos* (University of California Press, 1990) cited in National Research Council (n 52) 39.

buying into rather than indigenising capitalism. We see the situation as one of contested priorities, in which communities struggle to assert their values over the business model to which NSEDC staff sometimes give priority. The indigenisation of modernity is thus not a completed project, but an ongoing struggle. And while the NSEDC could be said to have sided with the trawler fleet at one point in terms of not promoting caps on bycatch, it has also promoted caps at other times. Its annual report for 2003[55] states: 'For reasons of bycatch management and vessel licensing requirements, opportunities to partner with companies and boats have been limited and restricted to a few. Our partnering efforts have focused on boats that use pot gear to harvest sablefish.' Similarly: 'Lack of available CDQ for bycatch and restrictive fishing opportunities outside of the open access fishing periods precluded NSEDC from pursuing and conducting CDQ fisheries for other CDQ flatfish species.' As the NSEDC communities built up their in-shore commercial fisheries through investment of lease fees, they invested especially in partnership with vessels which fished halibut and sablefish. Since 2006, when there was a record level of salmon bycatch,[56] the NSEDC and others have been proposing bycatch limits for salmon in the pollock BSAI fishery, but actions by the NPFMC have been gradual. The National Marine Fisheries Service implemented a programme for the 2011 BSAI pollock fishery to limit bycatch, but this was not considered to be sufficient. Finally in 2016, Amendment 110 was implemented to improve the management of chinook and chum salmon bycatch in the Bering Sea pollock fishery by creating a comprehensive salmon bycatch avoidance programme.[57] Whereas bottom trawling can leave serious incidental damage to the sea bottom in its wake, mid-water trawling has become relatively benign. The Alaska pollock fishery has become one of the cleanest in terms of incidental catch of other species (less than one per cent). When CDQ communities were allocated 10 per cent of species taken by bottom-trawl fisheries, their options for reforming these fisheries were less clear. The NSEDC's CDQ harvest in bottom-trawl fisheries accounted for roughly two per cent of all CDQ royalties in 2006–08. It is possible that CDQ groups began to influence many BSAI policies at a higher level because of an increasing stake in the fisheries. As their assets kept increasing and they were legally required to invest 80 per cent of those assets in fishery-related activities, it became inevitable that the NSEDC would increasingly buy into the mid-water trawling industry. The NSEDC 2012 annual report identifies the challenge of keeping a balance between investment in local activities which support traditional forms of well-being and investment in financial instruments which claim to offer a different kind of security.[58] The complexity of these investment decisions and

[55] www.nsedc.com/wp-content/uploads/NSEDC-2003-Annual-Report.pdf.

[56] Baker (n 3).

[57] https://alaskafisheries.noaa.gov/analyses/search?search_api_views_fulltext=chinook.

[58] Mendenhall (n 5) also reflects along similar lines on the delicate balance the NSEDC attempts to achieve between regional development and maximum profits through profit-making ventures owned by this non-profit (at 369).

the purchasing of IFQs fishing outside of the BSAI show that this is not simple, and some such decisions continue to be contested by NSEDC communities.

Atleo[59] explores the work of three Indigenous scholars who are pessimistic about the ability of Indigenous people to resist 'the borg of capitalism', but expresses optimism about alternatives. Because of its direction by subsistence-based communities focused on the health of local ecosystems for their well-being, the NSEDC offers an example of a regional institution which has used access to capital to further sustainable local management and community health, and demonstrated the capacity of this institution to at least somewhat improve the sustainability of the most highly capitalised distant water fleets.

Finally, critics such as Szymkowiak and Himes-Cornell[60] have failed to grasp what 'development' means when they conclude that the CDQ programme is unable to achieve its objectives because 'in remote and isolated areas, where robust and diversified economies may be unrealistic … long-term subsidisation of these communities is likely necessary'.[61] They use permit ownership data from state fisheries to conclude that: 'Allocations to the Western Alaska CDQ groups have not, with the exception of halibut, resulted in direct fishing opportunities for CDQ residents because of limitations on the availability of local species and the constraints on their participation in offshore fisheries, primarily capital.'[62] Although acknowledging that there are varied circumstances, they imply that local processing plants are not likely to be profitable ventures.

This discussion limits itself to using the NSEDC example to address these claims. Even considering only the state permits, the only ones Szymkowiak and Himes-Cornell measured, there are more overall permits in Norton Sound in 2016 (461) compared to 1992 (431),[63] and a larger portion of them are now locally owned. Furthermore, a sizeable number of permits are federal, and a number of fishermen who do not own permits work on partner boats in the halibut, sablefish and cod fisheries. Still others work as crew and team supervisors on pollock boats. Thus, it is misleading to conclude that the CDQ programme has not created 'direct fishing opportunities' for CDQ residents. In addition, the focus on direct fishing ignores the substantial number of jobs in tendering and processing. Their characterisation of the communities as being subsidised seems to be based on viewing the NSEDC as a mainstream capital-earning venture rather than one based on supplying benefits to the community as a non-profit organisation.[64] The processing plants are not intended to earn money, but to

[59] Atleo (n 10),

[60] M Szymkowiak and A Himes-Cornell, 'Fisheries Allocations for Socioeconomic Development: Lessons Learned from the Western Alaska Community Development Quota (CDQ) Program' (2018) 150 *Ocean and Coastal Management* 40.

[61] ibid.

[62] ibid.

[63] https://www.cfec.state.ak.us/gpbycen/2016/180.htm.

[64] The NSEDC owns for-profit organisations which pay taxes, invest etc, but its core operations support subsistence and small-scale moderate livelihoods.

break even while paying fishermen the maximum possible price and also paying shoreworkers a decent wage. They also do not include as a key part of the analysis the public services provided by the NSEDC. These services are provided not only to the communities in forms which would otherwise be lacking (but sometimes supplied by grants to communities in other parts of the country), but also play many roles often played by the government, thus relieving the government or others from having to supply those services (eg, the 312 scholarships or vocational training supplied in 2016). The 659 jobs created might have been unemployment claims or welfare benefits paid by the government. The taxes paid to state and federal governments, the lower rates of demands on health services because of lower rates of medical needs would not exist without the NSEDC. Perhaps the most important public service provided by the NSEDC is the perspective of local knowledge on what constitutes a healthy fishery and a healthy ecosystem. The local voice which has continually demanded a lowering of salmon interception in the pollock fishery, which is restoring salmon runs to areas damaged by mining and which demands that there not be mines in critical watersheds would not be there if the NSEDC or the CDQ programme in general did not have a place at the NPFMC table and were not able to contribute a local perspective and local knowledge on the issue. It is impossible to replace the value of local people who have co-evolved with local ecosystems and understand what is missing when a new industrial fishery is established which damages components of these ecosystems. Both this local knowledge and funding from the NSEDC has regularly contributed to ADF&G research, and the NSEDC has actively initiated and supported research in areas it has believed to be important.

Nonetheless, it is important to acknowledge the vulnerability of in-shore fisheries as the NSEDC tightens the eligibility standards for loans, as chinook salmon stocks decline, as climate change makes in-shore fishing in small boats more hazardous and as entry into IFQ fisheries becomes more expensive for young people. The NSEDC tightens loan standards both to prevent over-capacity and also because it feels vulnerable to the uncertainty relating to the long-term prospects of fisheries and financial markets.

## IX. CONCLUSIONS

The NSEDC has provided a valuable illustration of the evolution of Alaska's CDQ programme in one region. The opportunities exercised by CDQ community residents derive from their Indigenous status and rights, but do so through a complex of legal decisions and institutions. We have discussed many of the ways in which the programme has enabled the indigenisation of modernity through prioritising traditional subsistence activities and compatible small-scale local commercial fisheries, even while participating in a variety of more highly capitalised fishing ventures which in some instances conflict with the health of these fisheries. It has also created many local jobs in tendering and fish processing, as well as supported training, scholarships and research funding which enables more informed and precautionary management. Sixteen types of co-management rights, including a previously unidentified right, are exercised by the NSEDC at higher and lower levels, and their exercise illustrates both the degree and types of influence a CDQ group can exercise, and also the conditions which enable this to happen. Although the CDQ programme is unique, this examination of supporting conditions advances our understanding of co-management alternatives.

# Index